Advanced Manage
Accounting

An Organisational Emphasis

M. EZZAMEL

Department of Accounting and Management Science,
University of Southampton

H. HART

Formerly of the Department of Accounting and Management Science,
University of Southampton

CASSELL

Cassell Educational Limited
Artillery House
Artillery Row
London SW1P 1RT

British Library Cataloguing in Publication Data

Ezzamel, Mahmoud
   Advanced management accounting : an organisational emphasis.
   1. Managerial accounting
   I. Title   II. Hart, Harold
   658.1'511   HF5635

   ISBN 0-304-31374-2

Phototypeset by Scribe Design, Gillingham, Kent
Printed and bound in Great Britain by Mackays of Chatham Ltd

Last digit is print number: 9 8 7 6 5 4 3 2 1

Contents

Preface

The objective in writing this book has been to overcome some of the shortcomings which its authors have experienced in teaching advanced management accounting over several years. Up to 1980, when the idea of writing the book was conceived, only a very few, pioneering, books were explicitly devoted to the behavioural and organisational aspects of management accounting. Most available management accounting textbooks tended to focus primarily on the technical aspects at the expense of the behavioural and organisational approach. Moreover, even in their coverage of the technical aspects, they tended to emphasise numeracy over concepts.

Today, the picture has changed in part as some excellent new textbooks have become available. Most of these books, however, address either the organisational and behavioural aspects *or* the technical aspects of management accounting. Thus, these two important pillars of the subject remain largely separate in present-day textbooks. This book is a modest contribution towards addressing the problem by explicitly discussing both the organisational and the technical issues within one volume. As suggested in the introduction, some compromise had to be made with regard to the exercise of choice amongst the many possible topics which might be regarded as eligible for inclusion. We hope that the book will be useful, not only to fellow academics involved in teaching and researching management accounting, but also to businessmen and practising accountants.

The book is divided into four parts and seventeen chapters (including the introduction). Co-authorship necessarily entails some editorial work not capable of precise delineation. Subject to this reservation authorship of the individual chapters is indicated in the contents list. It would be impossible to name every person who has offered us support and encouragement during the seven years over which this book was written. Some, however, deserve special mention here.

We owe a great deal to our colleagues at Southampton University. Jeremy Dent, who is now at the London Business School, was extremely helpful and generous with his time and ideas. He has assisted greatly, not only in making important suggestions relating to the organisation of the book but also in reading and commenting extensively on five chapters. Michael Bourn provided insight in his many comments on some chapters. Chris Burke and Ken Hilton have also offered numerous critical comments, but, more importantly, have been a source of invaluable intellectual stimulation.

Several other academic colleagues at different universities have also been extremely helpful. David Cooper patiently read the manuscript and made extensive and important suggestions without which this book would have been greatly impoverished. We also acknowledge the invaluable comments of Kenneth Gee, Trevor Hopper, Anthony Hopwood, Norman Macintosh, and Cyril Tomkins on earlier drafts which were subsequently used as the basis of some of the chapters. All of these colleagues, from both Southampton and other universities, are, of course, in no way responsible for the limitations of this work.

We have been particularly fortunate in dealing with a number of excellent people at Cassell. When the idea of writing this book was initially conceived, we received good support from Tom Perlmutter and Helen Mackay. David Roberts soon took over the responsibility of college editor and he displayed remarkable patience and understanding. Over the last three years it was Simon Lake's turn to experience the frustrations of repeated, but unavoidable, procrastinations on our part. He did an excellent job in providing encouragement and motivation until the manuscript was ultimately completed. Felicity Brown, the house editor, was extremely thorough and helpful in scanning through the manuscript and uncovering a number of errors in both the text and references. Sandra Margolies saw the book through the final stages of galleys and page proofs.

We have also received tremendous secretarial support from Sue Westcott, Lynn Edwards, Barbara Ogley, Cathey Cruickshank, Christina Barry, Dawn Kiell, Lee Ann Ross and Helen Chaisson. These marvellous people have patiently and cheerfully endured all the pressure we inadvertently exerted upon them as they typed and retyped each chapter several times. They have all been extremely understanding, remarkably tolerant and very supportive. We owe them all a great deal.

Last, but not least, we are grateful to our families for the numerous sacrifices they have willingly made over the years, when there was at best only a faint light at the end of the tunnel.

NOVEMBER 1986   MAHMOUD EZZAMEL
                                                                H. HART

For Ann, Gwen, Adam and Nadia

Introduction

Traditional definitions of management accounting are numerous, ranging from statements of what management accounting seeks to achieve in practice to statements emphasising its relationship to other disciplines. However, a common element in most of these definitions has been the emphasis on providing relevant information to decision makers, and in particular to managers involved in the decision-making process. Those who advocate this emphasis can point to several strands of ideas and concepts charting the dynamic and evolutionary processes which have guided managerial accounting towards the fulfilment of this objective. These may be briefly summarised as:

1. The development of a conceptual approach for handling business problems – an approach which implies that the 'right' questions must be asked (e.g. Amey and Egginton, 1973).
2. The adoption of the economic tradition in analysing various management accounting problems in such areas as pricing and resource allocation. In this context, management accounting is typically considered as a sub-set of the 'fundamental discipline' of economics (e.g. Demski, 1973).
3. The emphasis on behavioural, informational, and other aspects concerned with management control and the evaluation of performance.

The nature of the problems encountered in the second and third categories has led various writers to recognise that such problems are likely to involve the use of quantitative techniques other than accounting and will require data not traditionally provided by the accountant (e.g. Anton, Firmin and Grove, 1978). In this context such data would need to be properly specified and this requires a real understanding of the essential nature of the problem.

Further extensions of the boundaries of management accounting have emerged in response to the need created by the growing complexities of the economic and business environment for new accounting concepts and procedures in the planning, control, and decision-making contexts. This response has been, in part, a natural, if somewhat chaotic, process of development; but it can also be seen as a process of outward growth into other traditional fields of study. Also, the roles of management accounting have increasingly come to be perceived as being implicated in the political debates and struggles which take place in arenas such as the organisation and in society as a whole. Accounting information, it has been argued, is a social product and thus has a meaning only in the context and culture in which it is produced (Loft, 1986).

Thus, roles different from the traditional ones have come to be associated with, and to some extent expected from, management accounting. Just as Watts and

Zimmerman (1979) have argued that accounting theories can be developed and sustained for furthering political interests, and that they may be the consequence of ideological debate, so there may equally be a demand for excuses in the context of management accounting (Dent, Ezzamel and Bourn, 1984). Other roles have also been suggested for management accounting, particularly in the context of the broader regulation of organisations and society (Burchell et al., 1980). Taking the position that management accounting has a part to play in organisational and societal contexts, these recent developments aim to explicate its role in creating, defining, and sustaining organisational and social 'realities'. More recently, the roles of management accounting have been expanded to the extent of revealing the intricate and allegedly antagonistic relationships between capital and labour in the organisational arena (Hopper, Storey and Willmott, 1985; Neimark and Tinker, 1986).

In writing a book on advanced management accounting, any of a number of alternative frameworks can be used. The structure of this book falls mainly into an organisational theory framework. As is argued repeatedly throughout succeeding chapters, it is impossible to divorce the study of management accounting from its organisational context. Management accounting is strongly implicated in organisational functioning, both influencing and being influenced by what goes on in the organisation. An orientation to organisation theory should make it easier to gain a better understanding of how management accounting is related to the broad notions of organisational control. It also offers a useful framework which can be used to evaluate much of the management accounting literature. Furthermore, it serves to pin-point directions for future developments in management accounting where traditional techniques and concepts have been shown to be inadequate.

Irrespective of which framework is adopted to provide a perspective on management accounting, it would be instructive to briefly consider the various phases of development which have dominated management accounting thinking. Such an overview is useful in its own right in the sense of highlighting the evolutionary nature of management accounting. It can also be used to explain more fully the rationale behind the organisational theory emphasis adopted in this book.

DEVELOPMENT OF MANAGEMENT ACCOUNTING THINKING

Broadly, the phases of development in management accounting thought may be perceived as proceeding in the following order:
1. the search for 'absolute truth' (a cost accounting focus);
2. the search for 'conditional truth' (a management accounting focus);
3. the recognition of information costs and uncertainty (an 'information-economics' approach);
4. a change in emphasis marked by a trend from a 'normative' to a more 'positive' approach with also, in a different direction, greater emphasis on the control process from both economic and organisational theory perspectives.

These developmental phases, with approximate relevant time periods, are given further consideration below. No attempt has, however, been made to trace the very earliest developments; the historical background has been well documented by Solomons (1968, p.17), who asserts that 'The last three decades of the nineteenth century were marked by what can only be described as a costing renaissance in the English speaking world.' It is, then, the year 1875 that marks the approximate beginning of the first phase indicated below.

The first phase, that is up to approximately 1950,* is marked by a general emphasis on the determination of product costs. Attempts to identify the full cost of producing a unit of output meant that stress was laid on cost allocation and absorption costing, and the control of direct labour, direct materials, and overhead costs. Such attempts, embodying the search for maximum accuracy or precision in the determination of costs, have been referred to by Horngren (1975) as the pursuit of 'absolute truth' or the search for 'true costs'. Demski and Feltham (1976) have, however, preferred the expression 'historical communication approach'. The second phase, spanning the period up to the late 1960s, is marked by an increasing awareness that there is no such thing as a 'true' cost applicable to each and every situation; the cost of a product cannot be viewed as a unique unambiguous figure on which to base managerial decisions relating to such matters as pricing, product profitability, product mix, and management control. Such awareness led to the idea of 'cost relevance', embodying a user-oriented or user decision model approach to cost accounting.

This idea of relevant costs for decisions, with its emphasis on 'different costs for different purposes', owes much to neoclassical economics. The approach not only recognises costs actually incurred, or outlay costs, but also takes cognisance of the opportunity costs associated with alternative transactions not undertaken. It embodies an approach which Horngren (1975) refers to as the 'conditional truth' approach, implying that 'truth' depends on the purpose to which the cost will be applied. Demski and Feltham (1976) use the expression 'user-model' approach to describe the same phase. However, whatever the label, it may be argued that this attitude marks the beginning of management accounting as a separate area of study and practice.

The user-model approach does not in any formal sense incorporate the cost of obtaining information or the benefits that may be generated from alternative courses of action. This defect is remedied by the information-economics approach (the third phase) which is associated with the development spanning the late 1960s and early 1970s. Underlying this approach is the recognition that, not only should one attempt to measure the demand for information in the light of its value, but one should also seek to assess the costs of supplying it, including the costs of accuracy and timeliness.

The introduction of the information-cost factor has prompted the use of the appellation 'costly truth approach' (Horngren, 1975). Kaplan (1982, p.3) has, however, cast doubts on the aptness of such a title on the grounds that, in strictness, 'the concept of "truth" never arises in the information-economics approach'. By this approach the management accounting system is regarded as a special type of information system. In focusing attention on either or both information costs and benefits it is implied that expected decision outcomes must be more desirable than the resources consumed in attaining such outcomes. However, it is important to note that the question of what is desirable is largely subjective. As Demski and Feltham (1976) point out, due consideration must be given to available opportunities and prevailing tastes and beliefs. Desirability is also dependent on the use to which the information will be put and on the cost of producing more accurate measures. Emphasis then is on analysis rather than prescription.

The application of the information-economics approach to accounting involves the mathematical modelling of decisions relating to the selection of accounting systems. The 'information evaluator', in the terminology of Demski and Feltham (1976), is

---

*This date, viz. 1950, is of some significance as it was in that year that considerable interest in management accounting was aroused in the United Kingdom following the visit to the United States of America of the Anglo-American Council on Productivity team on Management Accounting.

confronted with the uncertain costs and benefits of alternative accounting systems and, given all the relevant costs and benefits, the model purports to show how information systems ought to be selected. In this context Sundem (1981) has made the point that the application of information-economics research to management accounting has made an important contribution in encouraging researchers to distinguish between and separately identify 'information system choice' and 'information system design'. It was concentration by earlier researchers on the design aspects which led to a succession, or even proliferation, of new techniques of increasing complexity. Even so, *awareness* of the information system *choice* problem had in some quarters served to stimulate exploration into the cost and/or benefits of applying specific management accounting techniques.

Much of the credit for pioneering the information-economics approach in management accounting thinking must go to Demski and Feltham (1976). The objective of their 'information evaluation approach' was the development of a broader conceptual framework incorporating the two approaches outlined in phases one and two above, i.e. the 'historical communication' approach and the 'user model' approach. Both approaches allegedly suffer from three fundamental defects:
— the lack of a formal integral cost–benefit analysis;
— the doubtful validity of a 'true' cost concept in a world which recognises uncertainty; and
— the illusory and irrelevant nature of the concept of a 'true' cost, whether absolute or conditional, in a multi-person world, where different people will react in different ways to particular measurements.

The information evaluation approach thus extends the analysis into the areas of uncertainty and risk attitudes, as well as that of cost. How well it tackles the problems posed by the multi-person setting of the real world is perhaps a debatable point. Certainly it seeks to draw a distinction between the accountant as information evaluator and the manager as the decision maker who acts on the information supplied to him. The information evaluator has the authority to choose the information system but not to take subsequent action based thereon. Nevertheless, Kaplan (1982, p.13) has suggested that, with the information evaluation approach, the decision maker 'has no useful role other than to be a foil for the information evaluator', and that the optimal policy would therefore be for the information evaluator to select not only the information system but also the action, leaving the manager to *implement* the course of action selected.

Whilst recognising the defects of the user-decision model approach and the corresponding merits of the information-economics approach, difficulties of implementing the latter in a practical framework suggest that the user-decision model cannot be ruled out. Thus, Kaplan (1982) believes it to be a necessary step before the complete information evaluation approach can be used. He advocates the need for an implicit awareness of the fact that any proposed course of action must be subject to a benefit–cost analysis, however informal that may be; the calculations of costs and benefits must however be based on a subjective evaluation.

It has been indicated previously that the information evaluation approach is by no means free from criticism. However, this approach not only provides a useful contribution to management accounting thinking but also serves as a natural transition to the 'principal-agent' approach, which is referred to briefly in the next stage of development.

Developments in management accounting thinking in phase four span the period since the early to mid 1970s to the present time. They have been marked by a spirit of enquiry resulting in a tendency to question what might be called the conventional wisdom of management accounting, and also in a change of emphasis to a 'positive' approach to explain observed practices.

Explicit recognition of uncertainty and information cost led researchers to the view that conventional management accounting wisdom, specifically as related to the 'conditional truth' approach, does not necessarily provide a general basis for the best management accounting practice. This view quite naturally prompted the search for reasons underlying observed practice, thus producing the shift from a normative to a more positive approach, e.g. the enquiry by Zimmerman (1979) into the reasons for the use of 'full' costs. In certain cases the approach has been aimed at attempts to demonstrate 'that conditions exist in which the techniques observed in practice can be shown to be the outcome of rational choice' (Scapens, 1984). Examples of models used in this context are those based on multi-person and agency theory.

The shift in emphasis from normative to positive approach was by no means total; thus, the work of Demski and Feltham (1976), in the information-economics field, reflected primarily an approach which was normative in character in that it was directed to the selection of the information which ought to be reported.

The change in the attitudes of researchers in this period in relation to the role of management accounting practice in theory development is reflected in the view that 'the test of a "good" normative theory includes its ability in explaining existing practice' (Scapens, 1984). Such a test applies equally to behavioural accounting researchers, who in this phase of development were very much influenced by research in the area of organisational behaviour. Of the approaches in this field it was contingency theory which had the greatest impact. Contingency theory, as is the case with most of the approaches derived from organisation theory, primarily regards the management accounting system as a means of attaining control within the organisation – information required for decision-making purposes follows from the specification of the control system. In contrast, the conditional truth and costly truth approaches focus primarily on identifying information, with the control aspect of management accounting being assumed to follow from this decision-making perspective (Scapens, 1984).

The basic assumptions of contingency theory came under severe criticism essentially because of their deterministic nature. Post-contingency models have been proposed to reduce this limitation and their application has been extended, albeit in only a few cases, to the management accounting arena. Emphasis in these models is, again, primarily on the control process but control is perceived as a notion embedded in a nexus of multi-directional relationships between the elements of the control system.

Emphasis on the control process also occupied the attention of management accounting researchers in the quantitative field. Thinking in this direction was reflected particularly in an interest in 'principal-agent' relationships. Attempts to develop *general* multi-person game theory models have not been particularly fruitful; however, some considerable progress has been made with the particular class which is set within the framework of agency theory.

An agency relationship is defined through a set of contractual arrangements, written and unwritten, whereby one party (the principal) hires another party (the agent) to perform some specific function in return for some reward. A classic agency problem is said to exist when the agent can take actions that favour his interests at the expense of those of the principal. The firm can be modelled as a series of principal-agent relationships (Jensen and Meckling, 1976). The agency theory approach recognises that an information and reporting system has an impact on individuals in the sense that the mere act of measuring and reporting the actions of individuals will affect those actions, a phenomenon to which previous writers have drawn attention (e.g. Drucker, 1964). It implies the need to motivate agents (e.g. the manager of a decentralised unit) to act in the best interests of the principal (say, the owner or central management), and stresses the performance evaluation role in the attainment of organisational objectives.

So far as it relates to management accounting thinking, recourse is made to the agency model to identify the combination of employment contract and information system which will serve to maximise the principal's utility function, subject to the behavioural constraints which the agent's self interest might impose. Given a specified set of resources which the agent is employed to manage, the employment contract will stipulate the permissible set of actions and also the performance measure, based on variables observable to both parties (i.e. principal and agent), by which the manager will be evaluated. This measure of performance should be capable of withstanding the maximising actions of the manager; for example, it should not be open to manipulation. The formation of such a model is subject to various technical problems, and in addition a number of limitations have been identified (e.g., Tiessen and Waterhouse, 1983); these are discussed later, in chapters 11 and 12. These problems and limitations restrict the potential value of any results derived from the models.

On the whole, agency theory offers a useful model through which various management accounting topics can be formally analysed. At a more fundamental level, it emphasises the role of management accounting not only as a decision facilitating system but also as a control system for regulating organisational activities (Scapens, 1984). However, as Spicer and Ballew (1983) have argued, the highly structured approach implicit in the agency model is incompatible with present-day organisational complexities. This contrasts with the view that the basis for a theory of management accounting could lie in agency theory (e.g. Baiman, 1982, and Sundem, 1981).

It is quite apparent from the above discussion of phase four that it places strong emphasis on the importance of the interface between modern organisation theories and management accounting. This emphasis is echoed in this book. Without such emphasis it is difficult to evaluate management accounting controls as they are developed in the literature or to make sense of management accounting practice.

In the previous discussion of stages of development in management accounting thinking, reference was made to different levels of truth – namely absolute truth, conditional truth, and costly truth. By contrast, agency theory is not concerned with the pursuit of 'truth' as such; rather, it suggests the search for economic efficiency.

It is not the intention to consider in this introduction the implications of the economics of internal organisation which, it has been suggested, provides an alternative approach (e.g. Scapens, 1984), or a complementary approach (e.g. Ezzamel, 1985) to agency theory. Rather, this will be the subject of a chapter later in this book.

PLAN OF THE BOOK

This book is divided into three main parts and a concluding part. The first part is intended to provide a background for the remaining parts of the book by emphasising the organisational and behavioural context within which management accounting may be studied. The second part addresses various management accounting issues which broadly relate to planning and decision making. In the third part, the roles of various management accounting controls in regulating and monitoring organisational activities and in appraising managerial performance are discussed. Finally, part four provides a brief overview of research in management accounting and hints at potential future research developments in this field.

Part one contains five chapters. Chapter 1 deals with some of the broad issues of organisational design. It reviews a substantial body of literature ranging from classical organisation theory through neoclassical theory to modern organisation theory. Because of the prevalence of the latter theory in much of the contemporary research in management accounting, greater emphasis is accorded to it in that chapter. Various arguments relating to design and behavioural implications are selected for further consideration later in more specific settings, such as the design of management accounting systems and the behavioural implications of accounting controls.

Chapter 2 deals with the notion of organisational goals. It alludes to the problematic nature of goals when related to organisations and considers various definitions and types of goals. It then elaborates on various plausible approaches which aim to describe the dynamic, evolving, and subtle process of goal formation. The chapter closes with a discussion of various expressions of business goals, referring in particular to the profit maximisation hypotheses, managerial models, and finally to satisficing models. The discussion there serves to provide a framework through which much of the management accounting research is later put into context and thus facilitates a more sensible interpretation of it.

Chapter 3 deals with the literature on human motivation and leadership styles. Various theories of motivation are discussed; namely need–hierarchy theory; achievement motivation theory; motivation–hygiene theory; equity theory and expectancy theory. For each theory the main hypotheses are outlined, and the alleged strengths and weaknesses are evaluated. The analysis in that chapter shows that despite some crucial differences the domains of motivation theories overlap, at times quite considerably. The chapter ends with a discussion of various models of leadership styles as they developed, from those seeking to define a universal set of optimal leadership traits, through those suggesting that such traits are dependent on the situational contingencies, to those explicitly acknowledging the role of managerial choice. The point is made there that theories of motivation and models of leadership styles have important implications for the design and use of accounting controls.

Chapter 4 addresses various notions of organisational control as they relate to management accounting. The chapter first reviews some traditional approaches to organisational control, emphasising in particular the various control perspectives advanced by classical and neoclassical organisation theories and by traditional economic theory. This is followed by a discussion of the contribution of the systems-cybernetics approach to organisational control, with particular emphasis on the self-organising properties of open systems to which management accounting control systems are likened. An examination of the literature on the contingency theory of management accounting is undertaken and some of the main deficiencies of that approach are outlined. Finally, a framework for organisational control is presented in which management accounting systems are explicitly related to other organisational control mechanisms in a dynamic, non-deterministic manner.

Chapter 5 deals with issues relating to human information processing. The chapter classifies accounting research relating to human information processing into those using each of the following approaches: the lens model, probabilistic judgement; predecisional behaviour and cognitive style. It highlights various problems to which information processors are prone. It calls attention to some of the implications of different reporting styles from the perspective of information users and it also considers some of the implications of differing cognitive styles of decision makers for the design of management accounting systems.

Part two contains five chapters dealing with various planning and decision-making topics. Chapter 6 contains a discussion of some of the basic notions of utility theory, risk and information economics. Specific reference is made to complete models of information systems choice under conditions of perfect and costless information. The cost of information is subsequently introduced into the analysis and this leads to a discussion of simplified (incomplete) models. In the analysis, a distinction is made between the information evaluator (the information producer) and the decision maker (the information user). An evaluation of the information economics approach is then presented.

Chapter 7 deals with cost concepts, paying particular attention to relevant costs for decision making. Cost relevance is discussed in the context of the 'historical communication approach', the 'user decision model approach', and the 'information evaluation approach'. This is followed by a discussion of opportunity cost and related cost concepts, in particular differential cost. The behaviour and traceability patterns of cost are then analysed, emphasising cost classification in terms of variability, fixity, and semi-variability (-fixity). The concept of attributable cost developed by Shillinglaw is discussed in terms of its relevance to decision making. The chapter ends by considering cost relevance in specific decision contexts, namely profit planning, trade-off decisions, pricing policy, and control.

Chapter 8 discusses cost–volume–profit (C–V–P) analysis under conditions of uncertainty. The chapter opens by outlining the main limitations of deterministic C–V–P models. The introduction of uncertainty into C–V–P analysis is then considered by first referring to the Jaedicke–Robichek model. This is followed by a discussion of models which aim to define the underlying distributions of C–V–P parameters. These are classified broadly into the mathematical–statistical approach and the simulation–model sampling approach. Finally, risk analysis is considered in the context of making optimal break-even decisions. Alternative measures of risk and prices of risk for the purposes of C–V–P utility analysis are discussed. Also, various ways of modelling the relationships between C–V–P parameters, e.g. demand, are analysed.

Chapter 9 covers planning in the short term. It considers planning as a conceptual exercise by examining the essence of planning, and time scales in planning. Some important planning models are also discussed, in particular the Hicksian model, the Modigliani–Cohen model, and the proximate planning model. The chapter further examines the roles of short-term budgets, 'Zero-Based Budgeting' (ZBB), and 'Planning–Programming–Budgeting Systems' (PPBS) in short-term planning. Finally, the chapter contains a discussion of forecasting. Particular attention is paid to an examination of the nature of the forecasting process, the psychological limitations of forecasting, and some of the well-known forecasting methods.

Chapter 10 is concerned with planning in the long term. It provides an analytical framework for formal planning emphasising the role of the administrative system in facilitating strategic decision making. Some of the important limitations of formal planning are pointed out. This is followed by a discussion of how corporate objectives may be incorporated into the strategic plans. Information required for strategy formulations is then considered with emphasis on forecasting, assessing strengths, weaknesses, opportunities, and threats, and the behavioural aspects of information processing. Evaluation of strategic options is discussed by considering strategic portfolio analysis and specific aspects of strategy design. Finally, the chapter contains a brief discussion of financial models in terms of their construction and role in the planning process.

Part three deals with various models of control, but with greater emphasis on accounting controls. Chapter 11 investigates the roles of markets and hierarchies in regulating and monitoring transactions and other functions in organisations. The chapter opens by contrasting the attributes of markets and hierarchies in relation to organisational performance. The economic analysis of centralised (Unitary form, or U-form) structures and divisionalised (Multi-divisional form, or M-form) structures is reviewed. This is followed by a discussion of the contingency theory arguments which are supportive of M-form structures. Empirical research assessing the effects of M-form structures on organisational performance is then described and evaluated. New developments in agency theory relating to the broad notions of organisational control are discussed and an attempt is made to integrate them with the M-form literature. Some of the recent literature on post-contingency theory is discussed and implications for M-form structures are drawn. Finally, hypotheses relating agency theory and post-contingency theory to M-form structures are developed.

Chapter 12 reviews control performance evaluation in divisionalised organisations. A broad perspective on control is adopted in the chapter according to which both structural controls and financial controls are emphasised. Structural controls discussed in the chapter relate to divisional environment, divisional size, divisional interdependence, divisional autonomy and internal audit and reward systems. Financial controls considered are accounting profit, return on investment (ROI), residual income and discounted cash flow (DCF). The conceptual and practical problems with each of these profitability measures are outlined. Some of the implications of risk sharing schemes, in a principal–agent framework, are considered in the context of divisional reward structures.

Chapter 13 deals with transfer pricing in divisionalised organisations. The chapter begins with an analysis of transfer pricing models developed in the traditional economic theory of the firm. The discussion covers various market settings ranging from perfect markets, through imperfect markets, to those situations where no outside markets for intra-company products exist. This is followed by an evaluation of the contributions of mathematical approaches to transfer pricing, specifically addressing the linear programming approach and the decomposition approach. The chapter closes by referring to the behavioural context of transfer pricing and emphasises some of the implications that are relevant to the design of transfer pricing systems.

Chapter 14 is concerned with the conventional management accounting control model. The conventional system is first evaluated in terms of the usefulness of traditional budgets and traditional cost variance analysis for control purposes. This is followed by an examination of cost variance investigation models. These broadly divide into those which are single-period and those which are multi-period. Further, some of these models ignore the costs and benefits of investigation whereas others explicitly take them into account. Finally, the main limitations of conventional variance analysis are discussed and some refinements in this analysis are considered.

Chapter 15 addresses some of the behavioural implications of accounting controls, particularly budgets. The impact of traditional accounting controls on employee behaviour is first considered. Emphasis is laid on the effects of imposed performance targets and on accounting controls-induced pressure. Some of the dysfunctional consequences of such controls are outlined. This is followed by an examination of the arguments made for and against participation in the budgetary process. The extent to which the effects of participation are influenced by personality and environmental factors and the degree to which participation is associated with the creation of budgetary slack are both considered. Finally, the effects of differing patterns of leadership behaviour (leadership styles) and subordinate characteristics on budgetary practices and employee performance are examined.

Part four contains only one chapter, chapter 16. It provides a brief synthesis of past and present research in management accounting. To facilitate the synthesis, a framework is adopted from some of the related disciplines which is then used to provide a classification of management accounting research. The chapter also offers some speculative comments on directions of future research.

REFERENCES

Amey, L.R. and Egginton, D.A. 1973. *Management Accounting – A Conceptual Approach*: Longman.

Anton, H.R., Firmin, P.A. and Grove, H.D. (eds) 1978. *Contemporary Issues in Cost and Managerial Accounting*, 3rd edn.: Houghton & Mifflin.

Argenti, J. 1976. 'Whatever happened to management techniques?' *Management Today*, April pp. 78-9.

Baiman, S. 1982. 'Agency research in management accounting: a survey', *Journal of Accounting Literature*, Spring, pp. 154-213.

Burchell, S., Clubb, C., Hopwood, A.G., Hughes, J. and Nahapiet, J. 1980. 'The roles of accounting in organisations and society', in *Accounting, Organizations and Society*, 5(1) pp.5-27.

Demski, J.S. 1973. 'The nature of management accounting research: a comment', in *Accounting Research, 1960-70: A Critical Evaluation*, Dopuch, N. and L. Revsine (eds): Center for International Education and Research in Accounting, University of Illinois, pp. 69-78.

Demski, J.S. and Feltham, G.A. 1976. *Cost Determination: A Conceptual Approach*: Iowa State University.

Dent, J., Ezzamel, M. and Bourn, M. 1984. 'Reflections on research in management accounting and its relationship to practice: an academic view', in A.G. Hopwood and H. Schreuder (eds), *European Contributions to Accounting Research: The Achievements of the Last Decade*: VU Uitgeverij/Free University Press, Amsterdam, pp. 233-253.

Drucker, P.F., 1964. 'Controls, control, and management' in C.P. Bonini, R.K. Jaedicke and H.M. Wagner (eds), *Management Controls – New Directions in Basic Research*, New York: McGraw-Hill.

Ezzamel, M.A. 1985. 'On the assessment of the performance effects of multidivisional structures', *Accounting and Business Research*, 15 (61), pp.23-34.

Hart, H. 1981. 'A review of some recent major developments in the management accounting field', *Accounting and Business Research*, 11 (42), pp.99-115.

Hopper, T., Storey, J. and Willmott, H. 1985. 'Three perspectives on management accounting', paper presented at the Interdisciplinary Perspectives on Accounting Conference, University of Manchester.

Horngren, C.T. 1975. 'Management accounting: where are we?' in *Management Accounting and Control*: Beyer Symposium, Madison; University of Wisconsin.

Jensen, M.C. and Meckling, W.H. 1976. 'Theory of the firm: managerial behaviour, agency costs and ownership structure', *Journal of Financial Economics*, October, 3, pp. 305-360.

Kaplan, R.S. 1982. *Advanced Management Accounting;* Prentice-Hall.

Loft, A. 1986. 'Towards a critical understanding of accounting: the case of cost accounting in the U.K., 1914–1925', *Accounting, Organizations and Society*, 11(2), pp. 137–169.

Neimark, M. and Tinker, T. 1986. 'The social construction of management control systems', *Accounting, Organizations and Society*, 11 (4/5), pp. 369–395.

Scapens, R.W. 1984. 'Management accounting – a survey paper' in R.W. Scapens, D.T. Otley and R.S. Lister, *Management Accounting, Organisational Theory and Capital Budgeting: 3 Surveys:* Macmillan.

Solomons, D. 1968. 'The Historical Development of Costing' in D. Solomons (ed.): *Studies in Cost Analysis* (2nd edn.) Sweet and Maxwell.

Spicer, B.H. and Ballew, V. 1983. 'Management accounting systems and the economics of internal organization', *Accounting, Organizations and Society*, 8 (1), pp. 73-96.

Sundem, G.L. 1981. 'Future perspectives in management accounting research', a paper presented at the seventh accounting research convocation at the University of Alabama 1981.

Tiessen, P. and Waterhouse, J.H. 1983. 'Towards a descriptive theory of management accounting', *Accounting, Organizations and Society,* **8** (2/3), pp. 251-267.

Watts, R. and Zimmerman, J.L. 1979. 'The demand for and supply of accounting theories: the market for excuses', *Accounting Review,* April, pp. 273-305.

Zimmerman, J.L. 1979. 'The costs and benefits of cost allocations', *Accounting Review,* July, pp. 504-521.

PART ONE
The Organisational and Behavioural Contexts

1

Organisation Design: An Overview

The prevalence of social organisations, in which, of course, must be included the business enterprise, has come to be one of the accepted facts in life: throughout history mankind has been concerned with their various aspects. However, it was not until relatively recently that a systematic body of knowledge about organisations was developed. Within a relatively short period (stretching from the end of the nineteenth century until now) an impressive wealth of literature on organisations has emerged from several disciplines. However, organisation theorists have tended to pursue their analysis from different perspectives. Using somewhat differing, and at times opposing, propositions about the nature of human beings, organisations and their environments, researchers have sought to discover the best ways of structuring organisational activities. Their combined efforts have produced a wide range of ideas.

Organisation design has important implications for the design and use of management accounting systems. Indeed, various models of organisation are built into management accounting systems. For example, the ideas underlying the notion of responsibility accounting can be traced back to classical organisation theory, with its emphasis on accountability through the clear delineation of lines of authority and responsibility. Similarly, the emphasis of neoclassical organisation theory on human motivation has contributed to the more recent tendency towards designing 'humanistic' budgetary systems, which aim to support and develop the human element in the organisation. Also, modern organisation theory, with its systems and contingency orientations, is of immediate relevance to the design of management accounting systems. Thus, the development of various costing mechanisms such as job order costing and process costing can be directly linked to the technological aspects of contingency theory whereby different levels of technological complexity (e.g. unit production versus process production) are purported to have a strong influence on emerging organisational structures. Clearly, then, an understanding of the broader issues of organisation design will contribute to a better understanding of the design requirements of management accounting systems.

The purpose of this chapter is to provide a brief discussion of these organisational ideas. In sections I and II an outline of the antecedents to modern organisation theory is provided, in which classical and neoclassical organisation theories are discussed. In section III systems theory is described and its potential as a framework for integrating both classical and neoclassical theories is considered. In section IV the contribution of contingency theory is discussed. In section V a summary of the chapter is presented.

I. CLASSICAL ORGANISATION THEORY

A typical textbook discussion of classical organisation theory usually provides a classification of a number of schools of thought that are judged to constitute that theory (see for example Kast and Rosenzweig, 1979). Nevertheless, an inspection of the literature suggests that at least three schools of thought form the pillars of classical organisation theory: the bureaucracy school; the scientific management school; and the administrative management school.

The bureaucracy school, as developed by Weber at the beginning of this century, promotes a formal, mechanistic organisational structure with hierarchical control. This is achieved through the use of: (i) functional division of labour, (ii) a well-defined hierarchy of authority, (iii) rules and standard operating procedures and (iv) a specification of exact work duties. Weber described bureaucracy from a formal, technical point of view as an indispensable and efficient form of managing complex organisations.

The scientific management school, as developed by Taylor, advocates a formal, mechanistic form of organising similar to that of the bureaucracy school. However, the emphasis of scientific management is on appropriate specification of tasks. Thus, scientific management contends that there exists 'one best way' of performing every task. It is held that it is management's responsibility to provide specific guidelines for performance, to select employees best suited to the task, and to engage in training them in the most efficient manner. Further, employees are assumed to be motivated solely by economic rewards, which should be linked to performance: by maximising output and efficiency, the employee in turn maximises his reward.

Instead of concentrating on maximum efficiency at the operating level the emphasis of administrative management is on the issues of administration at higher organisational levels. In the late 1920s Fayol developed a comprehensive list of principles of management, which emphasised functional division of labour, clear delineation of the individual's authority and responsibility, order and discipline, centralisation, as well as individual initiative and *esprit de corps*. Following Fayol, the period stretching from the early twenties to the mid sixties witnessed the emergence of various developments which greatly enriched the administrative management school. These included such contributions as the pyramidal organisation structure (Mooney and Reiley, 1931); the emphasis on the need to limit the span of management control (Urwick, 1943); the promotion of the concepts of horizontal communication and employee participation (Follett, 1941) and upward as well as downward delegation of authority to secure subordinates' willingness to accept management authority (Barnard, 1938). Furthermore, Sloan (1964) formalised the concept of coordinated decentralisation, that is decentralisation of operating activities and centralisation of policy decisions, as a more efficient means of managing organisations.

The common features shared by these schools of thought may be summarised as follows:
— Rationality of behaviour is emphasised; it is assumed that it is desirable for the organisation to operate with maximum efficiency.
— The organisation is perceived as a mechanistic system. The formal anatomy of the organisation is prescribed through the division of labour by specialisation; a chain of command; clear delineation of authority and responsibility; limited span of control and a clear distinction between the roles of line and staff personnel. Efficiency is achieved primarily by structuring activities and directing people.
— Human beings are assumed to be motivated primarily by economic rewards. Appropriate incentive schemes are considered sufficient to induce maximal performance from employees.

In summary, the assumptions of classical organisation theory have very strong objectivist and functionalist tones: 'The world of organisation is treated as if it were the world of natural phenomena, characterised by a hard concrete reality which can be systematically investigated in a way which reveals its underlying regularities. Above all else it is a world of cause and effect; the task of the management theorists is seen as the identification of the fundamental laws which characterise its day-to-day operation' (Burrell and Morgan, 1979, pp. 127–128).

To conclude this section, it will be useful to evaluate some of the criticisms raised against classical organisation theory. One such criticism is that its principles are too general to provide specific guidelines for managing organisations. For example, it has been argued that the principle of specialisation does not tell us how tasks should be divided. Note, however, that the way in which tasks should be divided is likely to be influenced by, among other things, the nature of these tasks, managerial choices, and other situational contingencies facing the organisation. Hence, it might be argued, a general theory of organisations need not provide detailed prescriptions for a host of variables which may greatly differ among organisations and over time.

A further criticism is that some of the principles of classical theory are either too rigid or internally contradictory. Thus, it has been argued that, in contrast to Weber's concept of absolute bureaucracy, the extent of bureaucracy may vary from one organisation to another and even within the same organisation. Departments engaged in non-routine tasks may be less bureaucratic than departments engaged in routine tasks (see for example, Hall, 1963). Similarly Burns and Stalker (1961) have argued that organisations facing dynamic environments require flexible, rather than rigid, hierarchies; and Simon (1976) has argued that unity of command is incompatible (internally contradictory) with the principle of specialisation. Moreover, the rigid adherence to bureaucratic rules can lead to displacement of organisational goals (see for example Merton, 1957). Furthermore, empirical evidence suggests that the span of control varies with the type of technology utilised by the organisation (see for example Woodward, 1958).

Many authors have taken issue with the tendency to depersonalise the organisation under classical theory. Thus, it has been argued that in its most undesirable form the classical theory focuses on 'organisations without people' (Bennis, 1966) or on a 'machine model' (March and Simon, 1958). Employees are treated like 'cogs in a well-oiled machine' (Kast and Rosenzweig, 1979). One could argue that this criticism is more than a shade severe. As suggested earlier, some classical theorists showed some awareness of the human element in organisations. Collectively, Taylor, Fayol, Barnard, and in particular Follett, emphasised the importance of employee participation, cooperation between employees and management, 'fair' compensation for the workers, and the importance of stimulating employees' acceptance of management authority. Thus, the human element is not completely ignored in the classical theory. But it is widely accepted that these writers tended to under-emphasise the importance of behavioural issues. For example, it has been argued that the authoritarian nature of the classical theory can lead to employees' alienation, to the detriment of organisational performance (Argyris, 1957). Over-emphasis on job specialisation may narrow the scope of job enlargement and enrichment, with the possible consequence of reducing job involvement (Herzberg, 1966).

Taken as a whole, these criticisms indicate that classical organisation theory is not of universal application. Classical theorists promote mechanistic and deterministic concepts of management, which they reduce to the application of a universal set of rules leaving little scope for managerial discretion. The theory suggests that there is one best way of organising, preordained by a set of scientific principles. As indicated later, this criticism is central even to much of the more recent research. The means for effective design are not unambiguous. Rather, they are influenced by a host of variables, including managerial choice. Nevertheless, the theory emphasises important concepts of formal structure, which form part of the accepted body of knowledge about organisations.

II. NEOCLASSICAL ORGANISATION THEORY

The neoclassical theory developed in response to the need for a theory which explicitly dealt with the human element in organisations. Two related orientations can be identified in this theory: human relations and human resources. The principal contributions of this theory lie in the development and recognition of the concepts of group dynamics, informal organisation, style of supervision, participation management, and self actualisation.

The human relations orientation of neoclassical theory initiated and prompted progress with respect to the first four concepts. Thus, the importance of group dynamics, the way groups function and behave, was emphasised by the findings of the Hawthorne studies. These were inspired by Pareto's notions of social system equilibrium and by Durkheim's analysis of the process of social change as reflected in the dynamics of the relationships between the individual and society, and the relation of the individual personality to social solidarity (Burrell and Morgan, 1979). They represent one of the earliest attempts to use a systems theory approach to analyse organisational situations.

The Hawthorne studies, conducted by Mayo and his colleagues between 1927 and 1932, investigated the relationship between the intensity of illumination and the productivity of workers. The findings suggested, in part, that as illumination was decreased production increased, instead of declining as predicted. The researchers concluded that, as compared with physical conditions, social and psychological variables, such as motivation, and employee supervision, had a much greater effect on production. Thus the Hawthorne studies emphasised the importance of the informal dimensions of the organisation. Researchers observed that the social relationships developed within informal work groups had a stronger effect on production than did group piecework incentives, aptitude and physiological factors. Perhaps the most important contribution of the Hawthorne studies is their use of the systems theory perspective. Thus, Burrell and Morgan (1979, pp. 139–140) point out:

> Society is to be understood in terms of a system tending towards equilibrium; if this equilibrium is disturbed, forces are set in motion to restore it. The equilibrium of modern society has been upset by technological change prompted by the dictates of an economic logic; as a result social forces have been set in motion to restore the balance. This equilibrium model, as applied at the societal level, is transferred in more or less unchanged form to an analysis of the work situation. The individual now becomes an equilibrating system, influenced by the various elements which comprise the situation within and outside work. Behaviour at work is understood in terms of attempts to maintain or restore an equilibrium position. In the work place where the influence of technology and economics are paramount the social organisation acts as one of the principal forces for restoring equilibrium.

The Hawthorne results provided a strong contrast to classical theory with its emphasis on the formal anatomy of organisations. They stimulated a vast body of research stressing the importance of sympathy with subordinates (the consideration dimension of leadership e.g. Halpin and Winer, 1957), group morale (e.g. Lewin, 1958), democratic decision making (e.g. Morse and Reimer, 1956) and management of intergroup conflict (e.g. Likert, 1961). Predominantly, however, these latter developments abandoned the systems theory perspective used in the Hawthorne studies, which represented a limited shift away from objectivism, and merely utilised the *results* of these studies to develop new ideas and hypotheses (Burrell and Morgan, 1979).

In a broader vein, the human resources orientation focused on the consequences of job specification. Emphasising the concept of self-actualisation, this school has argued that jobs should be made intrinsically challenging (e.g. Herzberg, 1968). Thus, for example, McGregor (1960) has argued that employees should be perceived as being active and creative, willing to assume responsibility and potentially capable of exercising self-direction and self-control. Job enrichment and participative management have been advocated as two vehicles for improving employee morale and organisational performance.

The neoclassical theory has made significant contributions to modern organisation thought. One important contribution is its emphasis on both the formal and informal elements of the organisation. The anatomy of the organisation is broadly conceived as encompassing individuals, informal groups and intergroup relationships as well as a formal structure. The importance of the formal organisation is recognised by the neoclassicists but not in quite the same way as by the classicists. Thus, while acknowledging that division of labour by specialisation is important, the neoclassicists point out that specialisation could result in employee alienation, and may promote a feeling of anonymity if tasks are insignificant. Further, the neoclassical theory posits that the span of control should be matched to human and social determinants and, hence, cannot be reduced to a universally applicable ratio. This recognition of the informal anatomy of the organisation is one of the most important attributes of neoclassical theory. The theory perceives the organisation as being a spontaneous association of participants with mutually supportive objectives and needs (both physical and emotional). Hence, factors other than formal specification of tasks affect participants' behaviour (i.e. social and psychological factors). The theory also emphasises the important influence of the informal group on the individual's attitudes and performance (e.g. group pressure).

Scott (1961) identified four determinants underlying the formation of informal organisations: (i) individuals' location and frequency of face-to-face contact, (ii) individuals' occupation, (iii) individuals' interests and (iv) special issues (common causes). He argues that groups formed because of a common cause tend to dissolve once the issue is resolved, whilst groups formed for any of the first three reasons tend to be more permanent. It is through this concept of informal organisation that the neoclassical theory seeks to reconcile the notion that an individual may both comply with performance standards set by management and yet, on occasion, consistently violate these standards. The informal organisation develops norms of conduct for their members which at times conform with, and at other times are at odds with, the values set by the formal organisation.

Another important contribution of neoclassical theory is that it promotes a more comprehensive model of humanity. The theory emphasises the importance of the human element in organisations, and the broader motivational aspects of behaviour. It also emphasises the importance of the need for self-esteem and group belonging, the role of supportive leadership, and the need for self-actualisation. Organisational climate is identified as the strategic organisational variable affecting human motivation. It is held that if the climate is supportive and friendly it promotes productive, creative and cooperative behaviour, whereas if it is autocratic it promotes alienation and hostility.

Notwithstanding these important contributions, neoclassical theory does not provide a comprehensive framework for organisational design. The theory tends to over-emphasise the importance of employee morale at the expense of economic, political, and other environmental variables. Moreover, it advocates decentralised decision making and participative management irrespective of environmental and managerial differences. Further, it aspires to consensus as the organisational ideal, even though in reality organisations appear to be riddled with conflict. In short, it has been argued that neoclassical theory is incomplete, narrowly focused, and has not fully succeeded in integrating the many facets of organisational activities.

III. SYSTEMS THEORY

Several writers have suggested that most of the anomalies of both classical and neoclassical theories can be avoided if a systems approach is adopted in studying organisations. The systems approach, it has been argued, provides a convenient framework within which the concepts from both these theories can be integrated, refined and extended. But an evaluation of this claim requires an understanding of the basic concepts which underlie the systems approach.

Systems theory is not a recent development; it can be traced back to the Aristotelian dictum that 'the whole is more than the sum of its parts'. However, it was not until the 1930s that an integrated systems framework was developed. Many definitions of the term 'system' exist in the literature. One example is the definition provided by Kast and Rosenzweig (1979, p.18) that 'A system is an organised, unitary whole composed of two or more independent parts, components, or subsystems and delineated by identifiable boundaries from its environmental suprasystems.'

This definition implies that the relationships between the system elements create some system properties that are different from those of the separate constituent elements. Yet, the definition also serves to illustrate some of the ambiguity usually encountered in the systems theory literature. For example, it is not clear in this definition how one can unambiguously divide the elements that are relevant in a particular context between those which belong to the system and those which belong to the environment. It is likely, however, that the term 'system' is not amenable to precise description (Hall and Hagen, 1956).

Systems may be classified in different ways. For example, we may distinguish closed systems, which have no interactions with elements not contained within them, from open systems, which exchange energies and information with their environments. Similarly we may distinguish stable systems, whose variables remain within defined limits, from adaptive systems, which respond to their environments to ensure survival (see for example Hall and Hagen, 1956). Bertalanffy (1972) identifies closed systems with the mechanistic approach that is most notable in classical organisation theory. By contrast, the open systems approach may be more representative of the humanistic orientation. General Systems Theory (GST) has been developed to emphasise the dynamic interplay between open systems.

General Systems Theory (GST)

The main contribution of GST is in developing a structure within which various disciplines can be integrated whilst retaining their separate identities. Bertalanffy (1950, 1962), Ashby (1956, 1960), Katz and Kahn (1966), and Beer (1966), amongst others, have used a combination of empirical, intuitive and deductive procedures to derive some key characteristics of GST.

One important characteristic is holism: the properties of a system are not explicable by the summation of the properties of its elements taken in isolation. To explain holism, Angyal (1941) distinguished between relationships and systems. Relationships involve only two members so that they can always be analysed into pairs of relata. The attributes of the relata cause them to enter into a relationship in which they are directly connected. A system, however, may combine an unspecified number of elements that are not analysable into pairs of relata. Elements enter into a system connection through the positional value they have in the system more than through their attributes. Thus, systems cannot be compared with aggregations, because in an aggregation the parts are added whilst in a whole the parts are arranged into a system. In a system all elements are inextricably related to each other. The behaviour of an element in isolation is usually different from its behaviour within the system. Further, as we pointed out above, a system may display properties that are not present in its separate elements. Because of this holistic character of a system, and the interconnectedness of its elements, it may not be sensible, at least in GST terms, to study a system by reference to its parts in isolation (see Bertalanffy, 1962).

As pointed out earlier, systems may be closed or open. Open systems are dynamic and deal with both temporal and spatial patterns. An open system may seek multiple goals, not all of which may be attainable simultaneously, and it will constantly interact with its environment. It imports energy and information from its environment, which it recognises and transforms as they pass through a cycle of events. Then the system exports some product into the environment which, in turn, becomes the input of some other system.

Closed systems are characterised by the phenomenon of positive entropy, 'a universal law of nature in which all forms of organisation move towards disorganisation or death' (Katz and Kahn, 1966). In the long run, closed systems' regeneration is not possible: energy replenishment is not adequately maintained due to lack of exchange with the environment. As the quantity and quality of energy decline, the system experiences increasing entropy. Ultimately, maximum disorder is attained. In contrast, open systems may generate negative entropy. Some irreversible processes in open systems, such as heat transport, always cause positive entropy. But, by importing more energy from its environment than it needs, an open system can achieve negative entropy that more than offsets positive entropy (Bertalanffy, 1950). As Katz and Kahn (1966) pointed out, there is a general trend in open systems to maximise the ratio of imported to expended energy in order to survive and even to live on borrowed time in periods of crisis. This allows open systems to evolve towards higher levels of order, heterogeneity and complexity (Bertalanffy, 1962).

An open system may also be characterised by a steady state, in which the system composition remains constant. Note, however, that a steady state here does not imply a static equilibrium. Rather, it implies a continuous import of energy from the environment and a continuous export of products to the environment, such that the basic character of the system, that is the ratio of the energy exchanges and the relations between elements, is preserved (see Bertalanffy, 1950; Katz and Kahn, 1966). The concept of steady state is usually explained through the use of the term homeostasis. Bertalanffy (1962) defined the term homeostasis as an ensemble of organic regulations which act to maintain the steady state of the organism.

However, the concept of homeostasis should not be applied literally to open systems. What is suggested here is the preservation of the character of the system. The system may exhibit expansion in order to maximise its basic character; it may react to change or anticipate change through growth. But in most cases growth will represent a change in quantity rather than quality. An adjustment in one direction is countered by an adjustment in the opposite direction, in approximate rather than precise movements, so that the character of the system remains the same. These concepts of self-regulation and dynamic equilibrium are central to systems philosophy. They form the basis of the self-maintaining and regenerating characteristics of open systems. The self-regulating mechanism is activated by information feedback, which in turn allows the system to monitor its state and its interchange with its environment. It can also reduce the time lag between input and output, thereby reducing the extent of uncertainty present within the system.

Open systems are also characterised by differentiation. Thus, in order to attain negative entropy, open systems typically move in the direction of increasing differentiation and complexity. Specialised units evolve to tackle the different problems that the system faces, whilst at the same time ensuring its integrity and holism. Open systems also exhibit equifinality. In closed systems, there is a direct cause and effect relationship between the system's initial conditions and its final state. In open systems, however, the final state may be reached from different initial conditions and by different means. This is known as equifinal behaviour.

Structure, or hierarchy, is another important characteristic of open systems. Thus a system is composed of a set of interrelated subsystems each of which is in turn hierarchic until we reach some lowest level of elementary subsystem (Simon, 1962). The partitioning of a system into a set of subsystems is a matter of degree, as is the definition of an elementary subsystem. Interactions take place among, as well as within, subsystems and the chain of events in that context is dynamic.

This may be explained by considering interactions between two subsystems A and B. B produces a stimulus to which A responds, but the response of A elicits the same reaction in B, and the response of B stimulates A to further responses. The chain of events may reach some closure by a return to its point of origin and then the beginning of another cycle of events is triggered (Katz and Kahn, 1966). However the system comprising A and B may intersect in an aggregate way with another system comprising C and D. This results in a hierarchy of interacting subsystems.

Organisations as Systems

Several organisation theorists have argued that most of the characteristics of open systems are readily applicable to organisations. The systems approach has been advocated as an ideal framework within which previous organisation theories could be integrated. Some of the systems theory concepts can even be found in the work of early organisation theorists. The pioneering application of the systems approach to organisational situations by the Hawthorne researchers has already been mentioned in the previous section. Similarly, Barnard (1938) used a systems approach to describe organisations in which he identified system elements (physical, biological, personal and social), their interrelationships, goal-seeking behaviour, and system hierarchy. Selznick (1948) also viewed organisations as cooperative systems, adaptive social structures made up of interacting individuals and groups with formal and informal relationships.

Although several other early examples can be cited, it was not until relatively recently that the adoption of the systems approach as a framework for organisation analysis gathered momentum. Researchers drew various analogies between GST and organisation characteristics. Scott (1961), for example, identified five basic elements of the organisation as a system: the individual and his personality traits; the formal organisation (structure); the informal organisation with all the interactional arrangements which take place between it and the individual; the role patterns generated by formal and informal organisations and the physical setting in which the job is performed. Endorsing the systems view, researchers emphasised the interconnectedness of these elements as well as their combined holistic nature. The organisation has frequently been recognised as a man-made, self-maintaining, goal-seeking structure constantly in a dynamic interplay with its environment.

In the classical and neoclassical analysis the organisation was typically treated as a closed system; organisational issues tended to be investigated within the confines of the organisation, independently of its environment. Although this approach may have some plausibility on the grounds of reducing organisational problems to manageable proportions, it is clearly inappropriate. By contrast, GST conceives the organisation as an open, adaptive system. Katz and Kahn (1966) contrasted the consequences of treating organisations as closed and open systems as follows. Firstly, a closed system approach does not fully recognise the dependence of an organisation on its environment, and such lack of recognition makes much of organisational behaviour inexplicable. In contrast, an open systems approach emphasises the dynamic relationship between an organisation and its environment. Secondly, in a closed system approach more emphasis is placed on rules and procedures which become ends in themselves rather than means of helping the organisation to adapt to its environment. An open systems approach, on the contrary, emphasises the adaptive nature of organisational behaviour. Thirdly, a closed system approach ignores equifinality whilst an open systems approach emphasises it. Fourthly, a closed system approach treats irregularities in organisational performance due to environmental influences as error variances which can safely be ignored. An open systems approach, however, treats environmental influences as forces inseparable from the functioning of the organisation which should be studied and understood. Finally, a closed system approach results in failure to understand and develop environmental feedback. This is a defect that is rectified by open systems.

This contrast between open and closed systems analysis exemplifies the immense contribution of GST to organisation theory. By viewing the organisation as an open system it is possible to draw a more complete picture of its elements and their dynamic and intricate interrelationships. Such a holistic picture of organisational functioning is missing under both classical and neoclassical theories. Thus, although classical theory employs the concept of a man-machine system, it concentrates primarily on establishing standard operating procedures and formal organisation structures. Further, it promotes models of maximising behaviour which are inadequate to explain the dynamic interconnectedness of organisational elements. Although neoclassical theory shifts the emphasis from the formal organisation to the interrelationships among organisation participants, it underrates the effects of environmental variables on organisational behaviour. Thus, under both these theories attention is typically focused on particular functions in specialised areas. The systems approach offers a framework in which the separate elements can be identified and interwoven to form a comprehensive picture of the organisation.

However, several opponents of GST argue that indiscriminate analogies have frequently been drawn between the organisation on the one hand and living organisms on the other, thereby leading to several misleading and ambiguous generalisations about organisations. Scott (1961) warned that for analogies to be valid, they must exhibit inherent structural similarities or implicitly identical operational principles. The extent to which this criterion has been adopted in systems theory may be examined by considering, for example, the common analogy between the social organisation and the human body, with the skeletal and muscular system representing the operating line elements, the circulatory system as staff function, the nervous system as communication system, and the brain as top-level management (e.g. Beer, 1966). The usefulness of such analogy is, perhaps, self-evident. Yet, such analogies cannot be pushed too far. Katz and Kahn (1966) pointed out that because social organisations are contrived by man, rather than being natural phenomena like organisms, they are anchored in the attitudes, perceptions, motivations, habits, and expectations of human beings. Their structures are based on psychological rather than biological matters; hence they do not have to follow an organic life-cycle. Furthermore, GST is mainly concerned with the means by which an organisation adapts to environmental forces. Thus, feedback concepts and the maintenance of the steady state are based on the organisation's adaptation to its environment. However, because the elements of the social organisation can operate through their own volition, unlike the elements of an organism, they can initiate changes and adaptive behaviour from within the organisation. These changes will be difficult to subsume under feedback and steady state concepts (Kast and Rosenzweig, 1972).

Further, some writers tend to dichotomise systems in an absolute way into either closed or open. This is unnecessarily restrictive: the expression 'open systems' connotes openness as well as stable patterns of relationships within boundaries. As Thayer (1972) pointed out, an open system may display many closed system characteristics which conflict with other dynamic characteristics (contrast, for example, stabilisation with adaptation). It is, therefore, more convenient to view the organisation as being 'partially open' and 'partially closed'. Similarly, it may be naive to argue that an open systems approach is always more appropriate than a closed systems approach (e.g. Emery and Trist, 1960). Given some specific circumstances, closed systems analysis may have much to contribute towards attaining greater stability in an uncertain environment (see for example, Beer, 1966).

Consider now the negative entropy property of open systems. In attempting to attain negative entropy the system moves towards growth and expansion. This may appear to be at odds with the attainment of a steady state. Katz and Kahn (1966) pointed out, however, that this contradiction can be resolved once we recognise the subtlety of interaction between sub-systems. Thus, an initial disturbance will result in the mobilisation of resources to restore some balance but recurrent upsets will tend to lead to the development of mechanisms to anticipate future disturbances so that a new more comprehensive and more complex equilibrium will be reached. Organisational stability and growth may therefore be simultaneously attained through the operation of homeostasis. Less defensible, perhaps, is the GST emphasis on growth. If interpreted literally, the systems approach to organisations could be taken to be of little relevance to non-growing (stable or contracting) organisations (Peery, 1972). Even in growth situations, the systems approach could be taken to imply unlimited growth of organisations which is not a realistic phenomenon (Thayer, 1972).

Next, consider hierarchy and goal consensus in the systems framework. As the system achieves negative entropy, hierarchies are developed and so the system tends to move towards structures of higher sophistication. Some writers infer from GST's emphasis on hierarchy a tendency to promote formal and mechanistic concepts of control. For example, Thayer (1972) criticised GST on the grounds that its emphasis on formal hierarchies leads to impersonalisation of human interaction. A related criticism is that the systems approach assumes consensus between organisation participants. Thus, it is argued, the existence of organisational subsystems is purely functional and instrumental; they are assumed to function harmoniously so that the overall goal of the system is achieved. Dahrendorf (1959), however, argued that all authoritarian hierarchies are inherently coercive and breed conflict. Consensus does not provide a satisfactory explanation of goal displacement, nor does it adequately deal with intra-organisational conflict as a source of organisational change (Peery, 1972). In attempting to evaluate these two criticisms it must be recognised that the systems approach is amenable to criticism in so far as it does not explicitly emphasise humanistic concepts of control nor systems conflict. The important point, however, is that systems theory provides a convenient framework within which concepts of power and conflict can be superimposed as appropriate.

There have also been criticisms of GST's emphasis on holism as the basis for analysis. The procedures of 'classical' science use the 'analytical' approach, according to which the analysis of an entity is undertaken by studying its isolated elements. The essence of the systems thesis is that such analytical procedures fail to capture the properties of the whole, since the parts of the system are inextricably related to each other. Some writers have expressed dissatisfaction with this argument. Philips (1972), for example, argued that since the identity of an element is a multi-characteristic phenomenon, a few characteristics can be ignored without the elements being fundamentally altered. For example, the formal structure of the organisation could be studied in isolation, and although its dynamic interactions with other organisation elements would be missed, the formal structure itself would remain the same. Hence, it is argued, a wealth of information can be obtained by investigating parts of a system in isolation.

But this argument sidetracks the basic issues in systems theory. What systems philosophy implies for the social organisation is that interactions between phenomena are just as important, if not more important, than the phenomena themselves, and that such interactions change some of the properties of system elements. Information about separate elements is doubtless precious, but it is incomplete in so far as it does not capture the dynamic and interacting nature of the systems. Such is the systems view, and indeed many of its advocates (e.g. Bertalanffy, 1972) see it as an extension rather than a replacement of classical scientific method.

Some solace is to be found in the argument put forward by Simon (1962). He argued that hierarchic structures in complex systems tend in their dynamics to display the property of 'near decomposability'. In a 'nearly decomposable' system (i) the short-run behaviour of each element is approximately independent of the short-run behaviour of the other elements, and (ii) the long-run behaviour of any element depends in only an aggregate way on the behaviour of other elements. Thus, in such systems, interactions among the elements are weak, but not negligible. And, because sub-parts only interact with one another in an aggregative fashion, the details of their internal interactions can be ignored. The behaviour of the whole can be understood in terms of the interaction among aggregated subsystems. Simon went on to argue that in the dynamics of social systems near decomposability is prominent, particularly in formal organisations where formal authority connects each organisation member with one immediate superior and a small number of subordinates. Even informal communications tend to be largely contained within departmental boundaries. Hence, in the social organisation, he suggests, there are limits on the simultaneous interactions of large numbers of subsystems. The plausibility of this argument must rest on whether the dynamism of even a nearly decomposable system is simple enough to be fully arrested by an investigation process which ignores the detailed interactions between the components of different sub-parts. Yet this approach may provide a working basis for analysis.

The emphasis of GST on the concept of homeostasis and on the notions of self-regulation and dynamic equilibrium has also been questioned on the grounds that such constructs severely constrain the openness of the system. By focusing attention upon the internal relationships within the system and upon the mechanisms that restore the system to a steady state, the notion of equilibrium constrains the system's adaptability to change. As Burrell and Morgan (1979, p. 140) point out, 'the use of such a model carries with it a conservative orientation. The influence of the environment upon the system is constrained by the nature of the assumptions by which it is defined, and explanations of system operation are guided primarily by the assumption that some form of balance will be restored.'

More recent systems researchers have attempted to eliminate, or at least reduce, such inherent conservatism. One such attempt was Buckley's (1967) 'morphogenic systems theory'. Buckley's main concern was with the inadequacy of the equilibrium notion for the study of socio-cultural systems, because their morphogenic properties are distinctly different from those of biological and physical systems. His aim was to develop a systems model which could capture the dynamics of the process of change in society as well as the society's underlying structure. His model links cybernetics, information and communication theory in order to illustrate that the analysis of socio-cultural systems requires a shift of focus from the dynamics of energy transformation (the main concern of traditional GST) to the dynamics of the organisation as triggered by information transmission.

According to Buckley (1967, p. 82), the socio-cultural system is a 'set of elements linked almost entirely by way of intercommunication of information (in the broad sense) rather than being energy – or substance – linked as are physical or organismic systems'. Information is a code of meaning, and society itself is an organisation of meanings which are created through interactions between individuals.

Similarly, Jantsch (1980) advocates a theory of systems dynamics which focuses on the evolution of disequilibrium systems. In this theory the system goals are not taken as well defined or static; they are perceived as being part of the system's evolutionary process. Conflict is seen not as dysfunctional, but rather as a vehicle for change. Disequilibrium forces are seen to lead ultimately to the system's dynamic adaptation, self-organisation and regeneration. These and other notions of cybernetic analysis are discussed further in chapter 4, with particular reference to the concept of organisational control.

In summary, General Systems Theory provides a framework within which different organisation concepts can be meaningfully interpreted. Using GST, the interrelationships among the elements of the organisation and between these elements and the environment are brought to the forefront of the study of organisations. This is an invaluable contribution. Yet, the analysis is overly abstract. Current researchers have sought to provide a more explicit application of the theory. Drawing on a host of empirical findings, a contingency theory of organisation design has evolved. This is discussed in the following section.

IV. CONTINGENCY THEORY

The credibility of the universalistic approaches to organisational design advocated by both classical and neoclassical theories have been challenged by several writers. In particular, contingency theory, a substantial body of empirical 'evidence' which has accumulated over the last three decades, suggests that there is no one best way to organise in all situations. Rather, it is held that the best way to organise is contingent upon the specific circumstances (situational contingencies) that the organisation finds itself in. Thus, contingency theory assumes that in order to be effective the organisation should match its structure with its relevant contingencies.

But what are these situational contingencies (contingency factors)? Initially, researchers attempted to 'discover' the one contingency factor which significantly affects structure. Earlier 'evidence' suggests that in particular this might be the organisation's environment, technology, age, size or power (Mintzberg, 1979). However, more recent evidence suggests that a set of contingency factors taken jointly is likely to be more powerful in explaining variations in organisational structures than is the single contingency factor approach. This literature is briefly reviewed below.

Environment

As indicated earlier, the open systems approach to organisations emphasises the importance of maintaining favourable exchange relationships between the organisation and its environment. In this vein, several researchers attempted to study the association between dimensions of the environment and organisational structure. The main thesis of this research is that environmental contingencies dictate structure: the better the fit between an organisational structure and its environment, the more successful the organisation will be. Mintzberg (1979) identified four basic environmental dimensions: (i) extent of stability (stable *v.* dynamic), (ii) extent of complexity (simple *v.* complex), (iii) extent of market diversity (integrated *v.* diversified) and (iv) extent of hostility (munificent v. hostile).

The dimension of stability has been considered by many writers as the prime source of environmental uncertainty facing organisations. In general, the contingency research here suggests that the more dynamic the environment, the more fluid the structure will be. On the basis of their empirical study, Burns and Stalker (1961) described two forms of structure: mechanistic and organic. They argued that mechanistic structures are appropriate to firms facing a stable environment whereas organic structures are appropriate to firms facing a changing environment. Mechanistic structures are characterised by specialised differentiation of functional tasks, hierarchic structure, clear delineation of authority and responsibility, well-defined rules and procedures, and location of knowledge and coordination exclusively at the top of the hierarchy. Organic structures are characterised by contributive knowledge and experience, continual adjustment of tasks through interaction, ad hoc location of knowledge anywhere within the organisation, lateral rather than vertical communication, and less reliance on rules and procedures.

Lawrence and Lorsch (1967) considered the effects of uncertainty on an organisation's differentiation and integration. They defined differentiation as 'the difference in cognitive and emotional orientation among managers in different functional departments' and integration as 'the quality of the state of collaboration that exists among departments that are required to achieve unity of effort by the demands of the environment' (Lawrence and Lorsch, 1967, p.11). They conducted an in depth empirical study which compared better-performing with worse-performing firms in the same industry as well as the structures of better-performing firms in different industries. They hypothesised that the greater the differences in uncertainty levels faced by an organisation's department, the more differentiated the organisational traits of this department should be. The findings of the study indicated that the better-performing firms achieved a better match between the organisational traits of each department and the demands of its environment. Furthermore, Lawrence and Lorsch reported that the better-performing organisations allocated their resources more effectively to achieve the necessary integration required between the differentiated departments. In general, the better-performing organisations exhibited a high degree of both differentiation and integration.

However, Lawrence and Lorsch also noted that the greater the extent of departmental differentiation, the more difficult it is to achieve departmental integration. How do better-performing organisations succeed in achieving more differentiation and more integration? Their results suggest the following reasons. Firstly, high integration tends to be achieved in highly differentiated organisations by the adoption of more complicated integration mechanisms, e.g. cross-unit teams. Secondly, in better-performing organisations intergroup conflict tends to be resolved through confrontation rather than through force.

The research on environmental complexity suggests that the greater the complexity of the environment the more decentralised the structure will be. As Mintzberg (1979) pointed out, it should not be difficult to distinguish between the stability and the complexity dimensions. For example, a dice roller comprehends his game but cannot predict its outcome and so his environment is simple but dynamic. However, not all researchers clearly distinguish between these two dimensions, perhaps because the environment of many organisations is either complex and dynamic (e.g. the plastics firms of Lawrence and Lorsch) or simple and static (e.g. the container firms of Lawrence and Lorsch). Duncan (1972) distinguished between the two dimensions but indicated that environmental dynamism is a more important contributor to uncertainty than environmental complexity. The results of Hage and Aiken (1967) indicate that participation in decision making is strongly related to the degree of environmental complexity. Pennings (1975) also reported that environmental complexity is significantly correlated to the extent of decentralisation.

The literature on market diversity suggests that increased product diversification leads to divisionalisation. Chandler's (1962) pioneering study indicates that the strategy of diversification adopted by some US organisations caused several of them to divisionalise their structures in order to cope with information overload and to facilitate sub-unit coordination. More recent empirical work (see Mintzberg, 1979) lends support to Chandler's findings. The findings of other studies (e.g. Lorsch and Allen, 1973) also suggest that greater market diversity tends to be associated with greater market differentiation and independence amongst different products. It is held, thus, that market diversity facilitates divisionalisation along product lines. By contrast, it is held that firms with integrated markets will tend to remain non-divisionalised. One reason for this could be that excessive interdependencies may exist amongst activities and products, thereby making them difficult to segregate into semi-autonomous divisions. A second reason could be that the cost associated with duplicated divisional activities, e.g. purchases, may exceed the benefits of divisionalisation.

Finally, the findings of several studies (e.g. Child, 1972a; Lawrence and Lorsch, 1967) suggested that increased environmental hostility (e.g. competition) tends to produce more centralised and tightly controlled structures. Thus, when the organisation operates under conditions of limited competition, substantial slack and greater diffusion of decision making power within the organisation may occur. When competition becomes more severe, the above studies suggest that slack will begin to diminish, and control will generally tend to be much tighter. Further, it is held that, owing to the high cost associated with sub-optimal behaviour in such cases, decision making power tends to be centralised.

To draw together the strands of the research on environment within the contingency theory framework, table 1.1 shows a summary of the findings of that research.

Table 1.1 *The fit between organisational structure and environment.*

Dimension of environment		Appropriate structures
Stability	Stable	Mechanistic (Bureaucratic)
	Dynamic	Organic
Complexity	Simple	Centralised
	Complex	Decentralised
Market diversity	Integrated	Non-divisionalised
	Diversified	Divisionalised
Hostility	Munificent	Decentralised
	Hostile	Centralised

The table shows that these findings suggest that there is an appropriate structure which will give the best fit for the prevailing environmental conditions. Underlying these conditions is a simpler characterisation based on the degree of certainty or uncertainty involved: stable, simple, integrated and munificent dimensions are frequently treated as synonymous with certain environments whilst dynamic, complex, diversified and hostile dimensions are taken to mean uncertain environments. Thus, Thompson (1967) conceived complex organisations as open systems which are indeterminate and faced with uncertainty, but at the same time are rational and seek a degree of determinateness and certainty. Hence, an organisation's main problem in dealing with its environment is how to rationally handle uncertainty. The organisation can remove, or at least reduce, uncertainty by reducing the number of variables operating on it. More specifically, the organisation can cope with uncertainty by 'creating certain parts specifically to deal with it', and 'specialising other parts in operating under conditions of certainty or near certainty', i.e. decentralise its structure. Emery and Trist (1963) have also suggested similar ideas, which prompted Pfeffer (1978, p. 131) to say 'Indeed, the notion of structures contingent on environment with uncertainty being the critical dimension is becoming almost a non-contingent truism in management writing'.

Yet, the notion of environmental contingencies as employed in the literature lacks conceptual clarity. No consensus as yet exists with respect to the definition of the term or with respect to the classification of its dimensions. Moreover, several researchers have argued that technology is a more important contingency factor.

Technology

Both Woodward (1958) and Perrow (1967; 1970) attempted to establish that technological considerations have important implications for the design of effective organisational structures. Woodward developed the concept of 'operations technology', which refers to the equipping and sequencing of activities in an organisation's workflow, and applies primarily to manufacturing organisations. After some initial analysis, Woodward settled on testing the hypothesis that best performing firms are those using organisational structures most appropriate to their technologies. She classified a sample of firms using a scale of increasing technological complexity that progressed from unit production through mass production to process production. The results indicated that the 'best' performing firms in each category tended to exhibit certain common organisational traits, whereas the 'worst' performers were more dispersed. Woodward concluded, therefore, that appropriate organisational structure is contingent upon technology. Because of the importance of this study it is discussed in more detail below.

In unit production, output is not standardised and thus neither tasks nor procedures can be meaningfully standardised. The structures of 'best' performing firms in this category were found to be organic. In these firms coordination was usually achieved by mutual adjustment or by direct supervision. The span of control was narrow for both first-line managers and top managers: the former were directly responsible for production and, hence, tended to work in small groups; the latter were preoccupied with securing orders from customers and could only supervise few people. In contrast, because coordination was largely handled at the lower managerial level, the span of control of middle management was relatively wide. Woodward also reported that there was little differentiation but close and continuous integration between marketing, development and production.

In mass production as opposed to unit production, output is usually standardised. In best performing firms, Woodward's results suggest that tasks were routine and highly formalised by standard operating procedures and clear delineation of authority along the lines suggested by classical organisation theory. Compared with unit production, this resulted in wider spans of control for first-line managers and top managers, but narrower spans of control for middle management. The adopted structures were basically centralised and bureaucratic. The three essential functions of development, production, and marketing were sharply differentiated and communication channels between them were predominantly formal.

Firms in the process production category were reported to be highly automated and their structures were organic in nature. Compared with unit and mass production best performing process production firms relied most on training and indoctrination, and had the highest ratio of clerical and administrative personnel to production personnel. Also, the distinction between line and staff was usually vague. Spans of control were reported to be narrow for both first-line and middle managers but wider for top management. Typically, the structure of these firms consisted of two parts: the technical part with rigid controls and procedures built into the machines, rather than the people, and the social part which was characterised by an organic structure, loose control, and coordination by mutual adjustment.

Perrow (1967; 1970) developed a concept capable of greater generalisation: 'materials technology', which emphasises the characteristics of physical and informational raw materials (people, data, etc.) used. According to Perrow, the organisation is seen as a system of applying technology to raw materials, and hence technology is considered as the defining characteristic of organisations. He identifies two dimensions of technology which he argues are directly relevant to organisational structure. The first is the number of exceptional problems encountered in the work; this varies on a scale from low to high. The second is the nature of the search processes that are undertaken when exceptional problems are encountered: these may be classified into analysable or unanalysable. Analysable search processes can be subjected to logical and systematic search whereas unanalysable search processes require intuition, chance and guesswork. Perrow combined these two dimensions to produce four major categories of technology referred to as routine, technical–professional, craft, and non-routine, as illustrated in table 1.2.

Table 1.2 *Perrow's major categories of technology.*

Search process	Exceptional problems	
	Few	Many
Unanalysable	Craft technology	Non-routine technology
Analysable	Routine technology	Technical–professional technology

Perrow hypothesised that for each type of technology there would be one best set of structural arrangements. To achieve a matching between each category of technology and the appropriate organisational structure he singled out two groups of organisational members: the technical group (upper and middle management), which is concerned with technical control and support of production, and the supervision group (lower management) which is concerned with the direct supervision of people who deal with basic raw materials. Perrow described the interrelationships between these two groups with the aid of four structural characteristics: (i) the discretion each group exercises in performing its function; (ii) the power of each group in mobilising scarce resources; (iii) the means of coordination of the group's activities either through planning or feedback; and (iv) the degree of interdependence between the two groups. Perrow's matchings of technological categories with organisational structures are reported in table 1.3.

Table 1.3 *Task structure. Task-related interactions.*

	Discretion	Power	Coordination within group	Interdependence of groups		Discretion	Power	Coordination within group	Interdependence of groups
Technical	Low	Low	Plan	Low		High	High	Feed	High
supervision	High	High	Feed			High	High	Feed	
		Decentralised					Flexible, Polycentralized		
				1	2				
				4	3				
Technical	Low	High	Plan	Low		High	High	Feed	Low
supervision	Low	Low	Plan			Low	Low	Plan	
		Formal, Centralized					Flexible, Centralized		

Source: C. Perrow 'A framework for the comparative analysis of organisations', *American Sociological Review*, p.199, April 1967. Reproduced with permission.

The work of Woodward and Perrow stimulated a considerable debate in the literature. For example, Starbuck (1965) argued that Woodward's scale of technological complexity reflects smoothness of production; from *ad hoc* irregularity of unit production to regularity of discrete output in mass production to complete smoothness of process production. Later, Reeves and Woodward (1970) described that scale as one of decreasing sophistication of control; as technology becomes more complex so activities become largely unprogrammed and control mechanisms become less standardised, more simple and unsophisticated (the results of Child, 1972b and Khandwalla, 1974 seem to support this argument). Harvey (1968) pointed out that unit production can sometimes be as complex as process production.

Yet, perhaps even more than in the case of environment, the concept of technology is difficult to define. Several researchers emphasised different dimensions of technology (see, for example, Hage and Aiken, 1969; Mohr, 1971). This has prompted Child (1974, p. 14) to point out that the term technology is employed in almost as many different senses as there are writers on the subject. Furthermore, the results of other empirical work have also suggested that other contingency factors such as age and size may play an important role in determining structure.

Age and Size

Various researchers have sought to investigate the extent of association between an organisation's age and size and its structure. Stinchcombe (1965) reported that the structure of an organisation is influenced by the age of the industry in which it operates irrespective of the age of the organisation itself. He rationalises this finding by arguing that industries develop in response to the technical and economic conditions of their time, and as long as these conditions remain the same so structures remain unchanged. Further, traditions and vested interests help in preserving structural configurations (see Mintzberg, 1979). On the other hand, the results of Inkson, Pugh and Hickson (1970) indicated that the older an organisation is, the more formalised its activities are. This may be explained by the suggestion that as organisational learning tends to improve over time, an organisation will usually try to perpetuate the benefits of its learning by formalising it (Starbuck, 1965). The literature on age, however, remains probably the least developed research within the contingency framework.

A more important orientation is the research investigating the effect of size on organisational structure. An outgrowth of Weber's concept of bureaucracy is that large size is more generally associated with bureaucratic structure (Presthus, 1962). Pugh et al. (1969), usually referred to as the Aston Group, studied the association between organisational structure and some 'contextual' variables including size and technology. Their findings suggest that size has a much greater effect on structure than does technology. Larger organisations tend to be more specialised, more standardised and more formalised compared with smaller organisations. They defend these findings by arguing that size causes structuring through its effect on intervening variables such as the frequency of decisions and social control. As the scale of operations increases so the frequency of recurrent activities and repetitive decisions increases and, hence, they are standardised and formalised. The findings of a study by Blau (1970) suggested that increased size causes structural differentiation which, in turn, increases the absolute size of the administrative unit of the organisation.

A number of researchers have sought to investigate the contradictory findings of Woodward as well as Pugh, Hickson and Hinings. Hall (1977) reported that size is a key factor influencing structure given a narrow range of variation in technology. Khandwalla's (1974) results suggest that technology has a selective effect whereas size has a strong effect on structure. These two pieces of evidence can be interpreted to suggest that both size and technology affect organisation structure but in different ways. Thus, organisational size may be modified directly by segmenting a large unit into a number of smaller units (e.g. divisionalisation). Alternatively, the nature of functional activities may be modified through the adoption of different technologies so that a particular administrative system may be adopted (e.g. computerisation of the accounting system). Notice, however, that in a review of the methodologies of some eighty empirical studies on the relationship between size and structure Kimberly (1976) was led to conclude that the term 'size' as used in these studies was too global to permit its relation to organisational structure to be understood adequately.

Power

Some empirical studies have been undertaken to assess the effect of various power dimensions on the design of organisation structure, in particular the presence of outside control of the organisation and the personal power aspirations of organisational participants.

Pugh et al. (1969) reported that dependence of an organisation, which reflects the organisation's relationships with other organisations in its social environment, leads to more centralised authority structures and less decision making autonomy. On the other hand, independent organisations appear to have more autonomy and more decentralised decision making. Furthermore, their results suggest that dependence is strongly related to standardisation of procedures. Reimann (1973) also reported a strong correlation between dependency and formalisation of organisational structure. Thus, it has been argued, external control leads to a concentration of decision making power at the top of the hierarchy and to more reliance on rules and regulations for internal control (see Mintzberg, 1979).

Mintzberg (1979) also observed that the power needs of the members of the organisation, particularly those near the top of the hierarchy, tend to generate structures that are excessively centralised. He pointed out that the evidence for such observation is anecdotal, but plentiful, in the rich history of organisations. Finally, there is some evidence to suggest that fashionable organisational structures have sometimes been adopted with practically no consideration of their appropriateness. This noticeable effect of fashion on organisational structure has been supported by the findings of Woodward (1958) and Stinchcombe (1965). However, the 'evidence' cited above of the effect of power distribution on organisational structure remains largely inconclusive. For example, a study by Aiken and Hage (1968) suggests that organisational dependence leads to decentralised structures with less formalisation and more professionalisation of staff; a finding which is opposed to that reported by Pugh et al. (1969). Pfeffer (1978) attempted to reconcile these two opposing findings by arguing that the critical question for assessing the structural consequences of dependence is where in the organisation the ability to deal with dependence resides. Thus, if the central management can successfully cope with dependence, a more centralised structure will emerge. However, if the management of dependence requires the skills of other organisation members, there is likely to be a greater tendency towards decentralisation.

Evaluation

The above discussion outlines the main contributions, as well as some of the major drawbacks, of contingency theory. Unlike both classical and neoclassical theories, contingency theory discredits the universalistic approach to organising by maintaining that organisational structure is dictated by situational contingencies. In contrast to earlier organisation theories, the contingency research has been, primarily, empirically oriented and consequently has stimulated greater interest in empiricism in organisation theory. Contingency theory identifies several dimensions of situational contingencies and for each dimension a particular organisational structure that is thought to provide the best fit with that dimension is prescribed, so that organisational success can be attained. Many researchers extended the application of contingency theory to different contexts. In particular, several writers used the contingency framework to develop a contingency theory of management accounting (see chapter 4).

However, the quality of empirical research in contingency theory has been strongly challenged by many researchers. Several arguments can be cited to justify this. For example, there has been a frequent tendency among researchers to collapse complex dimensions of any one variable into a single, simple, and possibly misleading characteristic. A prime example here is that of organisational effectiveness. As Pennings (1975) has pointed out, effectiveness is a multidimensional concept with both internal referent (e.g. employee satisfaction), and external referent (e.g. number of new customers). An organisation may be effective with respect to one dimension

but ineffective with respect to others. Yet, almost all contingency studies which incorporate effectiveness concentrate on only one dimension. In fact, the above analysis of the findings of contingency research reveals that there is a confusion of two basic questions.
— What structures do firms adopt in particular circumstances?
— What structures do successful firms adopt in particular circumstances?

Whilst the second question is partially 'tackled' in the research on technology and environment, and to a limited extent on size, the first question is the one mainly discussed in the research on age and power distribution. Another example of the tendency simplistically to reduce complex dimensions is structure, which has frequently been treated as unidimensional. At the very least, this is debatable. Some would argue that organisational structure is a multidimensional concept where, rather than clustering together, structural features constitute separate dimensions of design (see, for example, Hall, 1977). If this is the case, then dichotomising the organisation in clear-cut categories, e.g. mechanistic/organic, can be a misleading oversimplification.

A second point to make is the frequent misspecification of model parameters. To some extent, this is caused by the use of standard statistical techniques. Thus, in many cases only simple bivariate statistics, like correlation coefficients, are used to draw conclusions about complex networks of interrelationships (see Miller, 1981). Further, most statistical techniques adopted in these studies assume independence among explanatory variables whilst frequently there are contingent interrelationships amongst such independent variables (see Pfeffer, 1978). Caves (1980) went even further in asserting that organisation theorists typically handle problems of optimising behaviour by the firm, yet they are less familiar than economists with appropriate means of tackling these problems. As a result, he argued, parameters determined outside the firm are treated as decision variables and vice versa.

Thirdly, as Child (1977) has pointed out, the possibility of the existence of multiple contingencies is not normally accounted for in the contingency literature. Thus, many studies investigated the effect of one contingency factor on organisational structure whilst other factors were ignored. This tended to produce inconsistent findings particularly when in one period, for the same organisation, different contingency factors called for different, and possibly conflicting, structural arrangements.

Fourthly, many of the contingency studies are cross-sectional, and hence they are not likely to fully capture all the dynamic dimensions of the variables they purport to measure. Most organisational changes take time to materialise; this implies that there is usually a time lag between situational change and structural change. The longer the time lag is, the more unlikely it is that the cross-sectional study will successfully capture the relevant correlation.

Fifthly, sampling techniques employed by many researchers may have contributed to the conflicting and confusing findings reported above. In some studies (e.g. that of the Aston Group) no standardisation of sampled companies was adopted: profit seeking and non-profit seeking organisations, or branch plants and independent firms were mixed together in the same sample. Also, in many studies, where concern was primarily with identifying the effect of one contingency factor on structure, samples were not drawn so that other contingency factors were held constant to permit isolating the variations attributable only to that factor (see Miller, 1981).

The overemphasis on empirical investigation at the expense of theoretical development is largely responsible for the lack of conceptual clarity in the contingency framework, which in turn contributed to the confusing and contradictory nature of the empirical results. As indicated earlier, different writers have tended to employ different definitions of the same contingency factor, e.g. technology. Furthermore, some researchers have equated the dimensions of environment with those of technology, for example non-routine technology has frequently been treated as synonymous with dynamic environment. As Pennings (1975) has pointed out, this confusion may be because uncertainty is implied in the dimensions of both technology and environment. For example, dynamic, complex, hostile, and diversified environments and non-routine technologies create uncertainty. However, as suggested earlier, there are subtle differences between these dimensions. Moreover, despite its crucial importance to contingency research, the concept of organisational effectiveness remains largely ambiguous. For example, whilst Etzioni (1964) defines effectiveness as the degree to which an organisation realises its goals, Seashore and Yuchtman (1967) define it as the ability of the organisation to exploit its environment in the acquisition of scarce resources. Although there are some attempts in the literature to reconcile these two approaches (e.g. Hall, 1977) many conceptual issues remain unsettled. It is not clear in the literature, for example, whose perspective should be adopted in measuring effectiveness, e.g. owners *v.* employees, nor is it clear how effectiveness determinant can be distinguished from effectiveness criteria (see, for example, Goodman et al., 1977).

A further, fundamental criticism of the contingency research is its deterministic nature. Thus, it is typically assumed that a particular situational contingency will necessarily dictate a particular structure. This deterministic argument is amenable to criticism on at least two counts. Firstly, it ignores the possibility of more than one organisational structure evolving in response to a given contingency factor. Thus, the important open system characteristic of equifinality is not entertained within the contingency framework. Secondly, this argument underplays the role of managerial choice by assuming that structure is the dictate of situational contingencies.

Child (1972a) pointed out that an organisation may have certain opportunities to select the type of environment in which it will operate (e.g. choice of markets to enter). Further, an organisation may command sufficient power to influence the environment in which it is already operating. Thus, both environmental selection and manipulation are open to many organisations (see for example Cyert and March, 1963 and Thompson, 1967). There is also evidence to suggest that not only do organisations operating in similar environments employ different structures, but they may even be equally successful (Child, 1977). The organisation may also have different perceptions of environmental dimensions (see Weick, 1979) and hence it may not react to observable environmental dimensions as expected. A possible extension of this argument is that perceptions of environmental dimensions might be taken as the consequences, rather than the causes, of organisational designs: 'It is plausible to argue that differentiated structures will perceive a heterogeneous environment, or that decentralised structures will perceive more environmental uncertainty as a consequence of the structural arrangements' (Pfeffer, 1978: p. 132).

Mohr (1971), Child (1972a) and Pfeffer (1978) pointed out that the nature and scale of technology itself is chosen. Thus an organisation typically chooses the domain of its activities (lines of business) which in turn affects the choice of technology. Furthermore, given the tasks and domain of activities, the organisation may still choose the technology it prefers by defining and dividing up tasks so that they match the preferred technology. Furthermore, as Child (1972b) suggested, size may impose constraints upon structural choices but in no way would it completely dictate all choices.

Wood (1979) goes even further in arguing that contingency theory not only underplays the scope for choice but also renders such choice redundant. By treating the organisation as a monolithic entity organised by a homogeneous management, the contingency framework ignores the possibility that different organisational partici-pants may have preferences for different strategies: 'the appropriate change in a particular situation may be very different depending on where one is in the organisation, such that we cannot talk as if there is one choice *for the organisation*. . . . It [contingency theory] still talks as if organisational choice amounts to choice for management, rather than within management, for organisational members, clients, victims and so forth'. (Wood, 1979, pp. 353–354).

Despite these criticisms, there is little doubt that the contingency approach has provided important contributions to our knowledge about organisations and the different patterns of their behaviour. These contributions represent an essential part of modern organisation theory. But the limitations inherent in the hypotheses derived from the contingency approach should be appreciated when evaluating these hypotheses. Furthermore, as the above discussion has shown, the contingency view alone is insufficient as a basis for formulating an integrated body of a modern theory of organisations. For such an integrated theory to be formulated, important concepts contributed by other organisation theories should also be recognised.

V. SUMMARY

This chapter reviewed a vast body of literature on organisation theory. An inspection of that literature suggests that writers subscribe to differing, and at times opposed, views on organisations. Yet, underlying these differing views is, in most cases, one objective: to provide a prescription for the 'best' ways of organising. But if the objective pursued by organisation theorists for decades has been the same, how could their prescribed 'solutions' be so different?

One important reason for this is that the characteristics of the elements of the organisation system are not deterministic. In carrying out their investigations different researchers employed different premises about people, organisation, and situational contingencies. Further, organisation theorists are typically influenced by the ruling ethics and values of their time. As times change, values change, and the approaches adopted by organisation theorists to tackle the same problem change. The evolutionary nature of research has also played an important role in shaping developments in organisation theory. Later researchers, using more sophisticated and rigorous analytical techniques which were not available before, built on the knowledge and experience of earlier researchers. Different conclusions, neither entirely wrong nor entirely correct, were reached.

The nature of the evolutionary process in organisation theory is not dissimilar to that in other disciplines. Scott (1961), for example, noted that the order of scientific evolution of physics and economics took the shape of 'macro-micro-macro' development. Thus, initially each of these disciplines followed a macro point of view. As the discipline developed, attention was directed to the analysis of parts of the system rather than the system as a whole. But as discontent with micro analysis increased, the discipline reverted back to the macro point of view. Scott traces this evolution cycle in organisation theory. Classical organisation theory adopts a macro-organisational point of view; it deals with aspects of the formal organisation that are common to all organisations. Neoclassical theory concentrates on organisational and human behaviour following a 'micro analysis' approach. Contingency theory concentrates on the macro analysis of organisation and human behaviour. Finally, the systems approach focuses on studying the organisation as a whole, albeit using a much broader spectrum than classical organisation theory.

Each of the approaches to organisation theory discussed earlier is an essential part of the body of that theory. Inevitably, as our knowledge of the way people and organisations behave is enhanced, the incompleteness of some of the previously derived concepts becomes evident. But this should not be taken to imply that the approach as a whole is discredited: parts that are relevant should be retained and integrated with the much broader body of modern organisation theory. The paradigm of systems theory offers a broad framework within which a host of rich organisational concepts and philosophies can be integrated. Some of the arguments elucidated here, as well as others, are used in chapter 4 to develop a general framework for the study of the many wide issues of organisational control.

Finally, this chapter has been concerned with several facets of organisational activities and performance without explicitly considering the goals pursued by organisations. A more complete understanding of organisational activities will surely require a careful consideration of the philosophy underlying the concept of organisational goals, the processes which influence the formation of goals, and the variety of ways in which goals can be expressed. These issues are discussed in the following chapter.

REFERENCES

Aiken, M. and Hage, J. 1968. 'Organisational interdependence and intraorganisational structure', *American Sociological Review*, **33,** December, pp. 912-930.

Angyal, A. 1941. *Foundations for a Science of Personality*. New York: Commonwealth Fund.

Argyris, C. 1957. *Personality and Organisation:* Harper.

Ashby, W.R. 1956. *Introduction to Cybernetics:* Chapman and Hall.

Ashby, W.R. 1960. *Design for a Brain:* Chapman and Hall.

Barnard, C.I. 1938. *The Functions of the Executive*. Cambridge Mass: Harvard University Press

Beer, S. 1966. *Decision and Control:* Wiley.

Bennis, W. 1966. *Changing Organisations:* McGraw-Hill.

Bertalanffy, L. Von 1950. 'An outline of general systems theory', pp. 134-165: in *British Journal of Philosophy of Science,* **1.**

Bertalanffy, L. Von 1962. 'General system theory – a critical review' in L. Von Bertalanffy and A. Rappaport (eds) *General Systems: the Yearbook of the Society for General Systems Research*, Vol. VII, pp. 1-20.

Bertalanffy, L. Von 1972. 'The history and status of general systems theory', *Academy of Management Journal,* December, pp. 407-443.

Blau, P.M. 1970. 'A formal theory of differentiation in organisations', *American Sociological Review,* pp. 201-218.

Buckley, W. 1967. *Sociology and Modern Systems Theory:* Prentice-Hall.

Burns, T. and Stalker, G.M. 1961. *The Management of Innovation:* Tavistock.

Burrell, G. and Morgan, G. 1979. *Sociological Paradigms and Organisational Analysis:* Heinemann.

Caves, R.E. 1980. 'Industrial organisation, corporate strategy and structure', *Journal of Economic Literature,* **XVIII,** March, pp. 64-92.

Chandler, A. 1962. *Strategy and Structure:* MIT Press.

Child, J. 1972a 'Organisation structure, environment and performance: the role of strategic choice', *Sociology,* pp. 1-22.

Child, J. 1972b 'Organisation structure and strategies of control: a replication of the Aston study', *Administrative Science Quarterly,* June, pp. 163-176.

Child, J. 1974. 'What determines organisation?', *Organisational Dynamics,* Summer, pp.2-18.

Child, J. 1977. 'Organisational design and performance – contingency theory and beyond', *Organisation and Administrative Sciences*, Summer–Fall, pp. 169-183.

Cyert, R.M. and March, J.G. 1963. *A Behavioural Theory of the Firm:* Prentice-Hall.

Dahrendorf, R.A. 1959. 'The concept of power', *Behavioural Science*, **2**, pp. 201–218.

Duncan, R.B. 1972. 'Characteristics of organisational environent and perceived environmental uncertainty', *Administrative Science Quarterly*, September, pp. 313-327.

Emery, F.E. and Trist, E.L. 1960. 'Socio-technical systems', in C.W. Churchman and M. Verhulst (eds) *Management Sciences: Models and Techniques*, vol. 2. London: Pergamon Press.

Emery, F.E. and Trist, E.L. 1963. 'The causal texture of organisational environments', *Human Relations*, **18**, August, pp. 20-26.

Etzioni, A. 1964. *Modern Organisations:* Prentice-Hall.

Follett, M.P. 1941. 'Constructive conflict', in H. Metcalf and L.F. Ubrick (eds). *Dynamic Administration: The Collected Papers of Mary Parker Follett.* London: Pitman.

Goodman, P.S., Pennings, J.M. and Associates 1977. *New Perspectives on Organisational Effectiveness:* Jossey-Bass.

Hage, J. and Aiken, M. 1967. 'Relationship of centralisation to other structural properties', *Administrative Science Quarterly*, pp. 72-92.

Hage, J. and Aiken, M. 1969. 'Routine technology, social structure, and organisation goals', *Administrative Science Quarterly*, **14**, pp. 360-376.

Hall, R.H. 1963. 'Intraorganisational structural variations: application of the bureaucratic model', *Administrative Science Quarterly*, **7**, 1963, pp.295-308.

Hall, R.H. 1977. *Organisations: Structure and Process:* Prentice-Hall.

Hall, A.D. and Hagen, R.E. 1956. 'Definition of system', in L. Von Bertalanffy and A. Rappaport (eds) *General Systems: the Yearbook of the Society for General Systems Research,* Vol. I.

Halpin, A. and Winer, B. 1957. 'A factorial study of the leader behaviour descriptions', in R. Stodgill and A. Coons (eds) *Leader Behaviour: Its Description and Measurement:* Ohio State University.

Harvey, E. 1968. 'Technology and the structure of organisations', *American Sociological Review*, pp. 247-259.

Herzberg, F. 1966. *Work and the Nature of Man:* Cleveland, Ohio: World.

Herzberg, F. 1968. 'One more time: how do you motivate employees?', *Harvard Business Review*, January–February, pp. 53-62.

Inkson, J.H.K., Pugh, D.S., and Hickson, D.J. 1970. 'Organisation, context and structure: an abbreviated replication', *Administrative Science Quarterly*, pp. 318-329.

Jantsch, E. 1980. *The Self Organizing Universe:* Pergamon.

Kast, F.E. and Rosenzweig, J.E. 1972. 'General systems theory: applications for organisation and management', *Academy of Management Journal*, December, pp. 447-465.

Kast, F.E. and Rosenzweig, J.E. 1979. *Organisation and Management* 3rd edn.: McGraw-Hill.

Katz, D. and Kahn, R.L. 1966. *The Social Psychology of Organisations:* Wiley.

Khandwalla, P.N. 1974 'Mass output orientation of operations technology and organisational structure', *Administrative Science Quarterly*, March, pp. 74-97.

Kimberly, J.R. 1976. 'Organisation size and the structuralist: a review, critique and proposal', *Administrative Science Quarterly*, December **21**, pp. 571-597.

Lawrence, P.R. and Lorsch, J.W. 1967. *Organisation and Environment:* Irwin.

Lewin, K. 1958. 'Group decision and social change', in E.E. Maccoby, Newcomb, and Hartley (eds) *Readings in Social Psychology*. New York: Holt, Rinehart and Winston.

Likert, R. 1961. *New Patterns of Management:* McGraw-Hill.

Lorsch, J.W. and Allen, S.A. III 1973. *Managing Diversity and Interdependence:* Division of Research, Graduate School of Business Administration, Harvard University.

March, J.G. and Simon, H.A. 1958. *Organisations:* Wiley.

McGregor, D. 1960. *The Human Side of Enterprise:* McGraw-Hill.

Merton, R.K. 1957. *Social Theory and Social Structure:* Free Press.

Miller, D. 1981. 'Towards a new contingency approach: the search for organisational gestalts', *Journal of Management Studies*, **18**, (1), pp.1-26.

Mintzberg, H. 1979. *The Structuring of Organisations:* Prentice-Hall.

Mohr, L.B. 1971. 'Organisational technology and organisational structure', *Administrative Science Quarterly*, **16**, December, pp. 444-459.

Mooney, J.D. and Reiley, A.C. 1931. *Onward Industry*. New York: Harper.

Morse, N.C. and Reimer, E. 1956. 'The experimental change of a major organisational variable', *Journal of Abnormal and Social Psychology*, **52**, pp. 120-129.

Peery, N.S. Jr. 1972. 'General systems theory, an inquiry into its social philosophy, *Academy of Management Journal*, December, pp. 495-510.

Pennings, J.M. 1975. 'The relevance of the structural-contingency model for organisational effectiveness', *Administrative Science Quarterly*, September **20**, pp. 393-409.

Perrow, C. 1967. 'A framework for the comparative analysis of organisations', *American Sociological Review*, April, pp. 194-208.

Perrow, C. 1970. *Organisational Analysis: A Sociological Review:* Wadsworth

Pfeffer, J. 1978. *Organisational Design:* Arlington Heights, Ill: AHM Publishing.

Philips, D.C. 1972. 'The methodological basis of systems theory', *Academy of Management Journal*, December, pp. 469-477.

Presthus, R. 1962. *The Organisational Society:* Alfred A. Knopf.

Pugh, D.S., Hickson, D.J., and Hinings, C.R. 1969. 'An empirical taxonomy of structure of work organisations', *Administrative Science Quarterly*, March, pp. 115-126.

Reeves, T.K. and Woodward, J. 1970. 'The study of managerial control', in J. Woodward (ed.) *Industrial Organisation: Behaviour and Control:* Oxford University Press.

Reimann, B.C. 1973. 'On the dimensions of bureaucratic structure: an empirical reappraisal', *Administrative Science Quarterly*, pp. 462-476.

Scott, W.G. 1961. 'Organisation theory: an overview and an appraisal', *Journal of the Academy of Management*, **4**, (1), April, pp. 7-26.

Seashore, S.E. and Yuchtman, E. 1967. 'Factorial analysis of organisational performance', *Administrative Science Quarterly*, **12**, pp. 377-395.

Selznick, P. 1948. 'Foundations of the theory of organisation', *American Sociological Review*, **13**, February, pp. 25-35.

Simon, H.A. 1962 'The architecture of complexity', *Proceedings of the American Philosophical Society*, **106**, (6). December, pp. 467-482.

Simon, H.A. 1976. *Administrative Behaviour* 3rd ed.: Macmillan.

Sloan, A.P. 1964. *My Years with General Motors*, Sidgwick and Jackson.

Starbuck, W.H. 1965. 'Organisational growth and development', in Chapter 11, pp. 451-522, J.G. March (ed) *Handbook of Organisations*, Rand McNally.

Stinchcombe, A.L. 1965. 'Social structure and organisations', Chapter 4 in J.G. March (ed) *Handbook of Organisations:* Rand McNally.

Thayer, F. 1972. 'General system(s) theory: the promise that could not be kept', *Academy of Management Journal*, December, pp. 481-493.

Thompson, J.D. 1967. *Organisations in Action:* McGraw-Hill.

Urwick, L. 1943. *The Elements of Administration*. New York: Harper.

Weick, K.E. 1979. *The Social Psychology of Organising*, 2nd edn.: Addison-Wesley.

Wood, S. 1979. 'A reappraisal of the contingency approach to organisation', *Journal of Management Studies*, October, pp. 334–354.

Woodward, J. 1958. *Industrial Organisation: Theory and Practice:* Oxford University Press.

2

Organisational Goals

In the preceding chapter, organisations were frequently referred to as purposeful goal-seeking entities. Such a view is prevalent in the literature. Organisational activities involve choices among alternative actions. If such choices are to be considered rational, then they must be made with reference to some criteria or goals. Yet, the nature of organisational goals is problematic, to say the least. In what sense do organisations have goals? Can goals really be held by organisations, or are they held by organisational members alone? How do organisational goals evolve? Are they ambiguous? Are they conflicting? Do they inform (affect) action? How do they change over time? Clearly some discussion of organisational goals is warranted at this point.

The study of organisational goals has important applications for the design and use of management accounting systems. The perspective adopted in this book is to view management accounting as being inextricably linked to organisational analysis, which by implication involves dealing with notions such as organisational goals. The goals of an organisation can be seen as part of the situational contingencies in which the organisation operates. In this sense, organisational goals have a strong impact on the precise design of the management accounting system (see chapter 4). Also, identification of these goals facilitates the determination of the overall strategy of the company and the formulation of its short-term and long-term plans, including capital budgeting (see chapters 8, 9 and 10). Further, it facilitates the setting of budgets and standards and the identification of other measures of performance evaluation (see chapters 11 to 15).

Identification of the theories underlying different perceptions of organisational goals and the processes through which goals are formulated is crucial in interpreting the role of accounting in organisations. Thus, if goals are perceived to be well specified and pre-existent, and if action is assumed to be rational and goal-directed, then the role of management accounting can be perceived in terms of helping to align the actions of different organisational members towards the attainment of organisational goals. Alternatively, if goals are not perceived to precede actions, so that actions take place independently of goals, the management accounting system may be called upon to offer post-rationalisation of past actions in order to make them appear legitimate.

This chapter is concerned with organisational goals. Section I contains a discussion of different approaches to defining organisational goals, and of how such goals may be categorised. In section II the goal formation process is described. In section III specific goals that have been discussed in the literature are considered, whilst section IV contains a summary of the chapter.

I. THE CONCEPT OF ORGANISATIONAL GOALS

Definition of Goals

This section explores the notion of organisational goals. It is useful, however, first to refer briefly to some of the different meanings related to the term 'goal'. Ackoff (1970), for example, distinguishes between objectives and goals. Objectives are desired outcomes of behaviour which may be unattainable but must be approachable within a planning period. Goals, on the other hand, are objectives which must be 'attainable within the planning period but need not necessarily be attained'. Thus, a person's objective could be to be wealthy whilst his goal could be to earn a given sum of money in a particular year. According to Ackoff, then, goals are more specific than objectives. Argenti (1974), however, spoke about objectives and aims. Objectives include three dimensions: purpose, ethos and means, whilst aims refer only to the first two dimensions. Thus, the purpose of a middle-line manager in a company could be to become the chairman of the board of directors, his ethos would refer to the way he should behave towards people he interacts with, and his means would be concerned with how to carry out his purpose and ethos. However, for the purposes of this chapter goals and objectives are considered as synonymous (for a similar position see, for example, Drucker, 1969).

One of the important points made in the preceding chapter was that each organisation exists in an environment with which it interacts. In such interactions the organisation will adopt some criteria to guide its activities. In a general sense, one might refer to these criteria as goals. Indeed, most writers perceive organisations as purposeful, goal-seeking institutions. For instance, Etzioni (1961) viewed organisations as 'social units deliberately constructed to seek specific goals'. Similarly, Argenti (1974) suggested that the purpose of the organisation is the reason for which the organisation exists. According to Etzioni (1961, p.6) a goal is 'a desired state of affairs which the organization attempts to realise'. Thus, the term 'goals' may be used to refer not only to the criteria by which an organisation chooses amongst alternatives, but also to the object of choice itself.

Such a definition, however, raises the issue of whether it is feasible for an organisation to have goals. Can we attribute preferences to organisations in the same way as they are attributed to people? Is it sensible to talk of an organisation desiring one state of affairs more than another? Moreover, the selection of an action as the goal of activity implies some commitment of effort and will towards its attainment. Yet will is an attribute of living sentient (feeling) entities. Organisations, in the literal sense, are not sentient. This paradox has given rise to the problem of reifying the organisation – that is, treating the organisation as 'a super individual entity having an existence and behaviour independent of the behaviour of its members' (Simon, 1964).

If reification of the organisation is to be avoided, then it seems that the concept of an organisational goal either has to be rejected, or be defined in a way which reflects the aspirations of people (Hall, 1975; Cyert and March, 1963). However, it is frequently observed that organisations do have goals, at times quite independently of the aspirations of organisational participants. At least in the legal sense, organisations acquire a separate identity. How then can organisational goals be defined?

Classical economic theory treats organisational goals as non-problematic: organisational goals are simply identified with the goals of the owner or entrepreneur. Conformity to such goals is assumed to be achieved by appropriate payments made by the entrepreneur to other organisation members, and a control mechanism which advises staff of entrepreneurial objectives and reports on staff efforts. This approach avoids the reification problem in that it focuses on the goals of a single entrepreneur, yet it is clearly problematic. An organisation, at least in its modern form, is made up of many participants who are likely to have different and conflicting goals. Identification of the goals of the organisation with those of a single person ignores the influence of other members of the organisation. Furthermore, it may not be meaningful to talk of an entrepreneur as if he were an identifiable individual. And, even if one interprets the term broadly enough to encompass many persons, e.g. the top managers in the hierarchy, or the 'dominant coalition', then one implicitly assumes some congruence of preferences among them.

An alternative approach is to recognise the conflicting goals of organisational participants, but nevertheless to argue in favour of some form of consensus prevailing. Goal conflict could be considered to be eliminated through discussion and consideration. The organisation could be modelled as a team-like structure in which participants subscribe to some common or consensual goal (e.g. Marschak and Radner 1972). But here again there is an implied assumption that a consensus will emerge, that we may reasonably talk of shared goals. Clearly, this may be a simplification of the problem.

Cyert and March (1963) argued that both these approaches are deficient. They view the organisation as a coalition and focus on the diversity of participants, including, for example, managers, workers, shareholders, suppliers, customers, lawyers, tax collectors and even regulatory agencies. In their view, conflict is inevitable. Theories of consensus simply fail to recognise this diversity in an organisational coalition:

> Since the existence of unresolved conflict is a conspicuous feature of organizations, it is exceedingly difficult to construct a useful positive theory of organizational decision making if we insist on internal goal consistency.
> (Cyert and March, 1963 p.28).

Moreover, they argued that organisational goals may be ambiguous. Over time, the relative power of different interested groups may change. At any point in time the influence of a group may depend on the nature of the decision being considered. Thus, an organisation may naturally pursue a set of conflicting goals, engaging in apparently inconsistent actions.

Simon (1964) has also emphasised the presence of conflict in organisations. Addressing the complex nature of organisational decision making he argues that the whole mass of decisions made in an organisation constitutes a system in which (i) decision making processes aim at finding feasible courses of action that satisfy a whole set of constraints and (ii) decisions reached in any one part of the organisation become goals or constraints for other decisions under consideration in other parts of the organisation. To be acceptable, actions must satisfy a wide range of conflicting demands (constraints) placed on the organisation. Although sometimes one of these constraints is singled out as the organisational goal, the choice may be largely arbitrary. It may be more meaningful to refer to the whole set of constraints as the goal of the organisation. Goals then may be subtle and ambiguous.

However, in Simon's (1964) analysis, in contrast to that of Cyert and March (1963), a distinction is drawn between personal goals and role-defined goals. The former refer to the personal motives and aspirations of the participants, whilst the latter reflect the aspirations relating to the behaviour appropriate to the role itself. In his role-defined capacities, Simon argues, the individual absorbs the organisational ethos and models his behaviour in compliance with organisational values:

> The ability of an individual to shift from one role to another as a function of the environment in which he finds himself thus helps to explain the extent to which

organizational goals become internalized, that is, are automatically evoked and applied during the performance of the role. By whatever means the individual was originally motivated to adopt the role in the first place, the goals and constraints appropriate to the role become a part of the decision-making program, stored in his memory, that defines his role behaviour.
(Simon, 1964, p.13).

In a sense, then, organisational goals may become self-perpetuating through a process of internalisation. They may acquire an existence independent of the personal motives of participants.

Thompson (1967) distinguished between two types of goals: goals for the organisation and goals of the organisation. Goals for the organisation are 'intended future domains for the organisation'. These refer to the range of products offered, range of customers served, services rendered to the community, etc. They may be held by 'individuals or categories having no affiliation with the organisation', e.g. customers, investors, members of the public, or even members of different departments within the organisation. They are usually multiple and conflicting: each group will try to change the organisation's domains to suit its preferences. On the other hand, goals of the organisation (organisational goals) are the future domains intended for the organisation by the dominant coalition (i.e. the most powerful organisational factions).

Thompson argues that by defining organisational goals in this manner we not only avoid reifying the organisation, but also refrain from viewing its goals as the accumulated goals of all its members. Here, organisational goals are viewed as being determined by the most influential group of organisational members. In this sense, they reflect authority and power:

Organizational goals are established by individuals – but interdependent individuals who collectively have sufficient control of organizational resources to commit them in certain directions and to withhold them from others ...
(Thompson, 1967, p.128).

Most of the previous goal definitions, in particular those of Cyert and March, Simon, and Thompson emphasise the existence of goal conflict. More recent approaches have formalised this notion of conflict by defining the organisation with reference to its contractual relations. Thus, Jensen and Meckling (1976, p.310) defined organisations as '... legal fictions which serve as a nexus for a set of contracting relationships among individuals'. Similarly, Caves (1980) emphasised that the firm rests on contractual relations that unite and coordinate both physical and human assets. An organisation, therefore, can be viewed as the centre of a complex process in which the conflicting aims of participants are managed on the basis of contractual relations. Moreover, contractual relations may be richly defined. Thus they might embrace, for instance, organisational slack and commitments to certain kinds of activities in addition to pecuniary side payments.

These approaches emphasise that conflict need not be intrinsically damaging to the organisation. Indeed, conflict may enrich the dynamic nature of organisational activities. For example, it may stimulate organisations into search behaviour and policy evaluation. On the other hand, conflict may not always be constructive. For example, certain participants may be in a powerful position relative to others, and may unilaterally impose contracts which do not satisfy the demands placed on the organisation. In such a situation conflict may threaten organisational survival.

A possible extension is to question whether goals, in the organisational sense, always precede activities. Lindblom (1959) distinguished between 'rational–

comprehensive' and 'incremental' approaches to problem handling. The 'rational–comprehensive' approach assumes that all obtainable information about all alternative courses of action is considered in decision-making activities. Values and goals are usually assumed to be known clearly before alternatives are considered. Lindblom argued that this approach assumes intellectual capacities and sources of information which are not likely to be possessed by human beings. He pointed out that such approach can only be practised in the case of relatively simple problems. In the case of complex problems, decision makers need to restrict their attention to relatively few values and alternatives. This is what Lindblom called the incremental approach. Here, goals and actions are not distinct from one another but are closely interrelated. In this case 'one chooses among values and among policies at one and the same time. Put a little more elaborately, one simultaneously chooses a policy to attain certain objectives and chooses the objectives themselves ...' (Lindblom, 1959, p. 82).

Moreover, March (1972; 1976) challenged the dogma of pre-existent goals: the notion that decisions flow directly from a set of objectives. Rather he suggests that goals are frequently discovered as a consequence of action:

> Human choice behaviour is at least as much a process for discovering goals as for action on them ... Individuals and organizations need ways of doing things for which they have no good reason. Not always. Not usually. But sometimes. They need to act before they think
>
> (March, 1976, p.72 and 75).

Goals then, whether they belong to an individual, an organisation, or the society, are ambiguous and fluid. They are influenced by human values which, in turn, develop through experience and choice.

The notion that goals are ambiguous and fluid and that they may be decoupled from action has recently been further developed and extended. March and Olsen (1976) have considered various aspects of organisational choice and organisational learning. Cohen, March and Olsen (1972) considered the characteristics of the decision-making process and problem-solving techniques in the presence of goal ambiguity. They extended the concept of the organisation by viewing it not only as a structure for solving well-specified problems and for resolving conflict, but also as a collection of choices. Decisions are viewed as the outcomes of four relatively independent streams: problems, solutions, participants, and choice opportunities. A choice opportunity is modelled as a garbage can into which various problems and solutions are dumped by organisational participants.

In the garbage-can model, goals are decoupled from actions. Choices are made only when problems, solutions, and participants combine in such a way as to make action possible. Goals are likely to be lost or ignored in such contexts and thus actions are not perceived as being goal driven. Three modes of decision making characterise the garbage-can model: oversight, flight, or resolution. Decisions are made by oversight when choice occurs as a result of the problems attached to other choices. Alternatively, problems may leave the choice scene, in which case decisions are made by flight. Finally, problems may be confronted and resolved.

The garbage-can model offers a dynamic and fluid framework for decision making. As Swieringa and Waterhouse (1982, pp. 153–154) point out:

> Problems, solutions and participants move from one choice opportunity to another in such a way that the nature of the choice, the time it takes and the problems it solves all depend on relatively complicated intermeshing of the mix of choices available at any one time, the mix of problems that have access to the organization, the mix of solutions looking for problems and the outside demands on the decision makers.

These developments have clearly enriched interpretations of the concept of organisational goals. Thus, in some cases, goals could be pre-existent, well ordered, non-problematical, and antecedent to action. In these cases emphasis in interpreting actions would be on relating them to goals. In many cases, however, goals may be fluid, vague, ill-defined, and they may indeed be discovered or reformulated as a consequence of action, so that the link between goals and actions is tenuous, ambiguous, or even non-existent. In such cases emphasis is likely to shift from a preoccupation with ensuring that actions are consistent with goals to a concern with the *processes* through which actions are taken, and then possibly legitimised, and goals are formulated and reformulated.

Types of Goals

The above discussion has concentrated mainly on some of the conceptual aspects of organisational goals. As Hall (1977) argued, treating goals as abstract values emphasises that organisational activities are guided by more than the day-to-day whims of individual members. However, abstract goals must be converted into specific guides in order to direct the activities of the organisation. Perrow (1961) pointed out that the lack of adequate distinction between types of goals has fostered the mistaken view that organisational goals are non-problematic. Goals need to be elaborately conceptualised and classified so that their problematic nature is adequately emphasised. Nevertheless, goal classification by type is complex and can be rather tedious; various arbitrary bases for classification can be adopted.

One example of this is Perrow's (1961) classification of 'official' and 'operative' goals. He points out (1961, p.855) that 'official goals are the general purposes of the organisation as put forth in the charter, annual reports, public statements by key executives and other authoritative pronouncements ...'. Official goals are deliberately 'noble', broad in scope and vague. They help to legitimise the existence of the organisation in the eyes of society. The wide scope of official goals covers the possibility that the organisation may pursue some goals in the future which are not seen as important now.

Official goals are not, in themselves, adequate for a full understanding of organisational behaviour. Generally they fail to prescribe adequate criteria for selecting from amongst alternative courses of action. Moreover, they do not give adequate recognition to the unofficial goals pursued by organisational participants. By contrast, operative goals are more specific. They reflect the detailed decision-making criteria employed within the organisation. As Perrow (1961, p.855) pointed out: 'Operative goals designate the ends sought through the actual operating policies of the organisation. They tell us what the organisation actually is trying to do, regardless of what the official goals say are the aims.' Furthermore, operative goals may be inconsistent with official goals; in some cases they may even subvert official goals. Indeed, there is some evidence that the operative goals of an organisation sometimes deviate strikingly from its official goals (see for example Zald, 1963; and Scott 1957).

Perrow (1970) provided another classification of goals in which five goal types are distinguished:
1. *Societal goals,* which represent ends to be achieved for society. One argument concerning the promotion of societal goals by organisations is that of Parsons (1960) who maintains that organisations seek legitimacy in the eyes of society to improve their chances of survival.
2. *Output goals,* which refer to the kind of products the organisation should have. They encompass, amongst other things, not only what business to be in, but also how many businesses to be in, i.e. the extent of product diversification.

3. *Systems goals,* which refer to the operating characteristics and levels of performance of the organisation, e.g. productivity, stability, and profitability.
4. *Product-characteristic goals,* e.g. safety characteristics, and product quality. These goals are, in part, system goals; they may reflect management's preferences as well as the organisation's assessment of its customers' needs.
5. *Derived goals,* which, Perrow argues, are the subsidiary uses to which the organisation puts the resources it generates whilst pursuing its primary goals, e.g. support for some political parties, and provision of staff facilities.

These goals need not be consistent; they represent a set of desired aims the organisation or its participants may have. In the following section the process through which such goals evolve is considered.

II. GOAL FORMATION IN ORGANISATIONS

The preceding analysis concentrated mainly on the issue of whether it is useful, and possible, to consider organisations as having goals and how such goals can be defined. Yet, so far, the process through which goals emerge in organisations has not been explicitly considered. This is one of the most intriguing features of organisations. Several interesting questions could be asked here. For instance, are organisational goals static or do they evolve through time? Do goals emerge as a result of interactions between all organisational members? If so, what is the nature of such interactions? Alternatively, are goals determined by reference to some sub-set of organisational members with ultimate power? If so, with which group or individual does this power reside? Can any group perpetuate its power? If so, how? Is goal conflict typically resolved to the satisfaction of each participant? What means do organisations employ to resolve such conflict?

This sample of questions should suffice to demonstrate that the process which governs the formation of organisational goals should not be taken for granted. The literature in this area is fairly confusing and difficult to assess. Nevertheless, at least three distinct models of goal determination can be traced in that literature: the entrepreneurial model; the Cyert and March bargaining model; and the dominant coalition model.

The Entrepreneurial Model

According to the entrepreneurial model, the ultimate choice of organisational goals resides with the entrepreneur. Given the nature of the exogenous factors facing the organisation, the entrepreneur defines his goals which, in effect, become the goals of the organisation. The agreement of other organisational participants is assumed to be secured at a price, which may involve love, esteem, or prestige, or simply a transfer of money. In essence, what is assumed here is that a principal–agent relationship exists. The principal (the entrepreneur) strikes a contract with the agent (e.g. an employee) according to which the latter consents to commit his efforts towards the attainment of the former's goals. Any conflict that may arise between the agent and the principal is assumed to be resolved through the operation of incentive schemes whereby the agent is rewarded according either to his efforts, his performance or both. The principal, of course, may pursue any goal he pleases. He may for instance go 'empire-building' regardless of its cost. Or he may wish for prestige and acclaim. But to the extent that he is dependent upon the environment for his operations his choices may be constrained. Similarly, to the extent that he is dependent on his agents, so may they constrain his choices.

As indicated earlier, the entrepreneurial model implies the pre-eminence of the interest of one group (the entrepreneurship) all the time. In this sense, power distribution within the organisation assumes a fairly static asymmetrical shape; the ultimate choice of goals for the organisation is only exercised by the entrepreneur. Yet this may not be true of many organisations. Power distribution within the organisation may change dramatically over time: for instance, employees may become as powerful as, or even more powerful than, the entrepreneur. Moreover, under the entrepreneurial model the importance and complexity of goal conflict is under-emphasised. For the most part, descriptions of the model suggest that goal conflict does not really exist. Even when conflict is mentioned, it is usually assumed that it is easily settled. The possible effects of conflict on aspiration levels and on the nature of the organisation's domains are rarely, if ever, made clear. Means of settling conflict do not extend beyond personal rewards: they are hardly ever expressed in the form of commitments to certain kinds of activities.

For similar reasons several writers have challenged the premises on which the entrepreneurial model is based. For example, March and Simon (1958) emphasised the importance of conflict at individual, intra-organisational, and interorganisational levels. They argued that high individual conflict reduces intra-organisational (intergroup) conflict. Such conflict, they argued, is bounded by psychological considerations of individual aspirations on the one hand and structure on the other hand. Underlying structure are the prevailing socio-economic conditions and the organisational decision-making strategy. Krupp (1961) has also criticised the goal consensus (harmony) approach implied by both the entrepreneurial and classical organisation theory models. He argues that the notions of goal conflict and power distribution should be explicitly reflected in any theory which seeks to explain organisational behaviour.

The Bargaining Model

In a similar vein, Cyert and March (1963) stressed the importance of intra-organisational conflict. Their model views the organisation as a more evenly balanced coalition of participants, both internal and external to the organisation. These individuals may be further organised into a number of sub-coalitions. Members of the organisational coalition have different goals, although members of each sub-coalition may have some common interests. Bargaining may take place between internal and/or external sub-coalitions. For example, the organisation may be pressurised into improving product quality by its customers (internal/external bargaining). Alternatively, it may be constrained in its pursuit of efficiency by employee demands (internal bargaining). Both types of bargaining influence organisational goals: goals are the product of multilateral negotiations.

A prominent feature of any coalition model is the use of side payments to manage conflicting claims. Cyert and March (1963), however, promoted an expansive notion of side payments. In their model these embrace not only the familiar pecuniary and non-pecuniary rewards to organisational participants but also commitment on the part of the coalition to certain courses of action. Even organisational policies can be seen as rewards to be negotiated. Moreover, such negotiations may leave many claims unsettled: organisations may operate with unresolved conflict.

Organisational members do not all devote the same attention to the coalition. Some important members (e.g. many shareholders) may frequently be passive. The active group which effectively determines organisational goals is likely to be substantially smaller than the full organisational coalition. The bargaining process is dynamic: changes in the power distribution among organisational members, and changes in environmental constraints may initiate new bargaining scenarios. New negotiations may be started to reflect the new situation. Different sub-coalitions may gain power. They may be able to impose contracts which place other participants at a disadvantage. The relative skill and power of active participants will play an important role in determining outcomes. Moreover, such outcomes need not be internally consistent, or perfectly rationalised.

Such a continuous and dynamic bargaining process would lead to a high degree of instability. Yet in reality, as Cyert and March argued, organisational goals are relatively stable. Such stability is brought about through various internal mechanisms. For example, acceptable and viable past experiences become established precedents which many members will treat as binding. Standard operating procedures become entrenched in the organisational 'memory'. Such precedents make non-negotiable certain issues that might otherwise be debated. Thus they contribute to the stability of organisational goals. Moreover, Cyert and March argued, participants' demands are not all addressed simultaneously. Rather, at any point in time each participant attends to only a small subset of his demands, and this allows the organisation to attend to these demands sequentially.

Cyert and March also pointed out that organisational slack, defined as payments to coalition members in excess of what is required to maintain the organisation, helps in stabilising organisational goals. *Prima facie,* the distribution of slack resources among participants will tend to vary owing to their different powers, skills, and so on. Organisational slack can help in stabilising organisational goals. For example, in bad times, the existence of slack may provide the organisation with opportunities for increasing the total resources available to the coalition.

To sum up, Cyert and March suggested that organisational goals are defined by the organisational coalition. Members of the coalition have different and conflicting goals. Organisational goals emerge from a continuous process of negotiation, which may be stimulated by changes in coalition membership, changes in the organisation's environment, and changes in the relative bargaining strength of participants. Procedures for conflict resolution include accepted past precedents, creation of organisational slack, and limited and sequential attention to goals. Such procedures may not be entirely effective in resolving conflict.

The Cyert and March model provides an appealing framework for the study of goal formation. Negotiation and conflict are important features of organisations. Interdependencies between and within internal and external organisational sub-coalitions are prominent. This is a useful construct which can readily be integrated within the systems theory framework. Thus, the organisation can be viewed as an open system (the total organisational coalition) that comprises a number of sub-systems (sub-coalitions). The sub-systems have reciprocal relationships with each other, with the total system that comprises them and with outside systems. These relationships reflect their mutual interdependence and could be riddled with conflict. The model also emphasises the significance of the differential distribution of power among the sub-systems.

Yet, a number of important issues remain unresolved. For instance, to argue, as Cyert and March did, that the organisation can reduce conflict by sequential attention to goals implies some form of ranking, at least over time. Yet, Cyert and March did not indicate what set of criteria may be used to choose between these goals.

Addressing the relativist position (one that acknowledges differential goals among members but without indicating how they can be ranked) Katz and Kahn (1978, p.240) pointed out that

> It does not explain the complex compromised outcomes of organisational life; it gives no help to those who must choose and wish to choose wisely, nor to those who seek some comprehensive organization theory; it merely imposes the criterion of competing self-interests and awaits the outcome.

Moreover, the Cyert and March model does not explicitly address the process whereby power is created and maintained. For instance, the coalition is modelled as if no particular sub-coalition can sustain its power indefinitely. As Thompson (1967) has pointed out, the organisation is a political arena where different groups seek to promote their interests and one group may clearly dominate the others. Stability in organisational goals may be attained through the self-perpetuation of the strongest group. At times, goals may not so much evolve through negotiation but, rather, may be largely dictated by those in power who may be able to sustain their position over relatively long periods.

The Dominant Coalition Model

Various writers have advanced the notion that the goal-setting process in organisations is controlled by a dominant coalition. However, their conceptions of the formation and stability of the dominant coalition are different. In its extreme form, where the organisation is clearly dominated by its owners, the dominant coalition model reduces to the entrepreneurial model. This may indeed be the case for some organisations, particularly in their early years where considerations of finance and viability are crucial. But as the organisation expands so professional managers become more important. Senior managers may become the dominant group in the organisation. This is the position taken by Gordon (1945), and to a large extent by writers such as Baumol (1958), Marris (1964), Williamson (1964; 1970) and Galbraith (1967).

Further refinements to the notion of the dominant coalition have been introduced by many writers, in particular Perrow (1961), Thompson (1967), Hill (1969) and Pennings and Goodman (1977). Perrow (1961) spoke about an organisational elite who are responsible for setting goals. He argues that its membership will change over time according to a typical sequence: trustee (owner) domination in the early days of the organisation, followed by skill group (e.g. engineers) domination during product or service development and research, followed by management domination as the emphasis shifts to improving long-run market share and pursuing less risky innovations. As environmental forces change, this cycle could be repeated.

In Perrow's analysis, it does not always follow that an elite will emerge to dominate the organisation. In particular, when existing organisational goals are vague with respect to criteria of achievement, or when many task areas (e.g. finance, innovation) are crucial to the organisation, then multiple leadership may emerge. In such cases, there may be no single ultimate power in the organisation. But typically under Perrow's analysis goal formation is approximated by the dominant coalition notions.

Thompson (1967) also considered the role of the dominant coalition in forming organisational goals. Recall that in his discussion of goals he distinguishes between (i) goals for the organisation, which are held by individuals with no affiliation with the organisation and (ii) goals of the organisation (organisational goals), which are determined by the dominant coalition. But, unlike the all embracing concept of organisational membership advanced by Cyert and March, Thompson distinguishes between members and non-members of the organisation; the former are essentially internal participants who have affiliation with the organisation, and the latter are other insiders and outsiders. The dominant coalition includes organisational members, as defined above, but may also incorporate important outsiders. Although in Thompson's analysis the dominant coalition determines organisational goals, non-members may actively attempt to change these goals.

Perceiving organisational control as a process involving the manipulation at each hierarchical level of the decision premises used by lower levels, Thompson argues that the nature and stability of the dominant coalition must depend on its ability to manipulate decision premises. He points out that when the organisation faces greater uncertainty, it will need to rely more frequently on judgemental decision strategies. This, as well as the inevitable increase in power diversity resulting from greater uncertainty, will lead to an increase in the size of the dominant coalition. Similarly a reduction in uncertainty will tend to result in a contraction in the size of the dominant coalition.

But, if the dominant coalition significantly increases in size and in the diversity of the demands of its members, can a powerful individual, or a small group of individuals, emerge to manage the coalition? Thompson argues that in such cases an inner circle emerges, either formally or informally, to conduct the activities of the coalition. The power of the inner circle is likely to be significantly constrained by the goals of members of the dominant coalition who support it. Furthermore, he argues that even in organisations with widely dispersed power there will usually be a central power figure (e.g. chairman of board of directors), quite apart from the inner circle, who can exercise his power so long as he secures the consent of the dominant coalition. The dominant coalition may be viewed as a much smaller subset of Cyert and March's active coalition.

Hill (1969) advocated a goal formation process based on the notion of a dominant coalition which includes only executives; no other internal or external organisational members enter into the dominant coalition. Yet Hill argued that goal formation is achieved as a result of a complex process in which goals are a function of: (i) the organisation's exogenous forces, such as shareholders and customers; (ii) the internal social system, which includes all organisational participants who do not independently possess sufficient power to significantly influence the goal-setting process; (iii) participants who command sufficient power to be able to assert their preferences and (iv) the dominant coalition which is formed through bargaining.

Acting independently or together, the first three forces will define a feasibility polygon within which the management is free to pursue its own motives in establishing organisational goals. Goal choices are thus essentially made by management in cognisance of the requirements of other exogenous and endogenous forces. But the dominant coalition can attain some stability in organisational goals by: (i) negotiating and reassessing the demands of exogenous parties; (ii) engaging in vague settlements with various groups; and (iii) stating goals in broad terms.

The literature on corporate ownership and control offers useful insights in relation to the definition of power groups (elites, or dominant coalitions). Much of that literature would classify a company as being owner controlled (rather than manager controlled) if there is an identifiable interest group which owns a fraction of the company capital, even as low as 5 per cent (e.g. Radice, 1971; Herman, 1982). The implication of such a definition is that it is not necessary for the dominant group in an organisation to be the owner, as traditionally defined through ownership of most of the capital, or the managers, if capital ownership is diffused. An identifiable interest group of shareholders which owns a fraction of the company's capital could muster enough power to define organisational goals and direct managerial actions towards the attainment of those goals.

Subsequent researchers have extended the definition of ownership control further. Nyman and Silberston (1978) offered compelling arguments to suggest that many more companies are owner controlled than is traditionally assumed. In addition to the identifiable-interest-group argument of Radice (1971) they included in their definition of ownership control situations in which companies have interlocking directorates (the managers of some companies being members of the boards of other companies), continuing founder, or non-founder, family interests in terms of stakes held and/or influence on the board of directors, and ownership of some company shares by trustees, a consortium of other companies, or financial institutions. Adopting this broad definition, Nyman and Silberston were able to classify a high percentage of the top 200 UK companies as owner controlled.

Herman (1982), using a more restrictive definition of owner control, classified 17 per cent of the largest 200 non-financial US corporations as being subject to the control of owners. His classification denoted a further 17 per cent of the companies as manager controlled even though strong, active, and numerous outsiders (e.g. owners or outside financial groups) were associated with these companies. The presence of such powerful groups may imply the existence of power sharing, or at the very least latent power which could act as a significant constraint on managerial discretion.

None the less, it must be noted that there has been a major shift in the pattern of corporate control since the turn of the century. The present century has witnessed a significant decline in direct control exercised by majority ownership and financial interest and an increase in direct control by professional management (Berle and Means, 1932; Herman, 1982). But the discretion of such professional managers is usually constrained through other interested groups such as shareholders, creditors, and fellow managers (see chapter 11). These ideas led to the emergence of a substantive body of research addressing the so-called 'separation of management from control' problem, which later became part of the wider agency theory framework.

It has been argued that management-controlled firms pursue goals different from those pursued by owner-controlled firms. Specifically, it has been suggested that owner-controlled firms will pursue profits because this would be in the best interest of the owners. By contrast, it is held, management-controlled firms will pursue growth goals (e.g. Williamson, 1964) and goals which foster the welfare of society (e.g. Watson, 1963). The latter set of goals relate to the 'recent' tendency for corporations to emphasise their responsible social behaviour, a behaviour which is said to emerge from the discretionary power of managers. These issues are discussed further in the following section.

The dominant coalition model provides a useful framework for organisational analysis. The model recognises that substantial conflict could arise between the goals pursued by the organisation and the goals of various exogenous and endogenous factions. Quasi-resolution of conflict may be attained through a bargaining process involving the dominant coalition and other interest groups. Yet it is not assumed that the bargaining process is necessarily as continuous and dynamic as under the Cyert and March model. Consensus in the ranking of different goals can be viewed as a function of the relative power of active sub-coalitions. The relative strength of the dominant coalition, compared with other sub-coalitions, may result in contractual relationships that are not completely acceptable to such groups. The dominant coalition may accept, reject, modify, and aggregate the preferences and expectations of other sub-coalitions (see Pennings and Goodman, 1977). In this sense, the organisation is subject to some form of oligarchic control exercised by the dominant coalition. Alternatively, the dominant coalition may simply operate as an information centre which assembles, encodes and decodes the preferences of different sub-coalitions, so that they may be incorporated into organisational goals. Distribution of power within the dominant coalition itself can be asymmetric. A small group, or even an individual, may acquire enough power, usually through some majority rule, to manage and eventually dominate the dominant coalition. In such a case, that person or small group may be considered as the effective dominant coalition.

Given these expansive notions of the possible power structures within organisations, the dominant coalition model has contributed to knowledge about how organisations operate, how goals may evolve, who may rank these goals and how goals may be stabilised. However, it is not entirely clear how the dominant coalition can be identified at any particular time (especially when some members wield considerable informal power) nor is it clear how affiliation with the dominant coalition changes as the environment and the organisation change. Moreover, the pragmatic importance of the dominant coalition has yet to be established. As Katz and Kahn (1978, p.242) argued: 'Indeed, it remains to be seen whether the dominant coalition exists as a social entity in organizations, or whether it is merely a construct for describing the bargaining process among constituencies.'

So far, the characteristics of the goal formation process in organisations have been considered under the entrepreneurial model, the Cyert and March model, and the dominant coalition model. Collectively, these models suggest that goal formation can be explained in terms of (i) coalition formation, (ii) bargaining, and (iii) conflict resolution. Yet, as indicated above, each of these characteristics is perceived differently by the different models. For example, in the Cyert and March model organisational goals are defined by the organisational coalition, whereas the dominant coalition model emphasises the power of a relatively more stable winning coalition model (e.g. trustees, managers). Also, the Cyert and March model suggests a continuous and dynamic bargaining process whereas both the entrepreneurial model and, to a lesser extent, the dominant coalition model suggest a relatively less continuous bargaining process. Whereas in the entrepreneurial model conflict is assumed to be resolved through the use of side payments which are pecuniary or non-pecuniary, the Cyert and March model advances a more expansive concept of side payments which, in addition, emphasises the importance of policy commitments.

Towards a Synthesis?

Can one then decide which of these models adequately explains the goal formation process in organisations? It is argued here that attempts to single out any one model as the most acceptable in all situations are likely to be inconclusive. Each of these models has an important role to play.

To explain this, consider, for instance, the notion of goal conflict. Etzioni (1961), for example, pointed out that organisations may be classified into three main categories based on the degree of participants' agreement on organisational goals: normative; instrumental; and coercive. A normative organisation is characterised by agreement on and commitment to organisational goals – as in the case of a charitable organisation. In an instrumental organisation goals held by the participants may be neutral in relation to organisational goals, as in the case of business organisations. By contrast, in a coercive organisation organisational goals largely conflict with those of the participants.

In a coercive organisation goals are imposed perhaps by an entrepreneur or by the dominant coalition: the preferences of other organisational participants are largely irrelevant to the goal-formation process. In an instrumental organisation, conflict may be prominent during negotiations although consensus may be eventually attained. In a normative organisation, it is assumed that there exists substantial a priori agreement on organisational goals. As Otley and Berry (1980) pointed out, these three types may exist at different hierarchical levels within the same organisation. Moreover, as indicated earlier, power distribution amongst and within the relevant sub-coalitions may assume different forms: it may be symmetric or it may be asymmetric, and such asymmetry could be static or dynamic.

It may, therefore, be observed that in many small, as well as in some large, stable organisations the goal-formation process is akin to that described by the entrepreneurial model. Also, in organisations with significant dispersion of power, goals may be formed collectively by the active coalition in a manner similar to that described by Cyert and March. As the organisation moves from one stage of transition to another, power over the determination of goals may change hands from one dominant coalition to another. During the period while power is changing hands organisation goals may be blurred, ambiguous and even confused (see for example, Argenti, 1974). Indeed this is likely to be the case whenever there is no clear set of criteria for ordering goals.

Hence, all the three forementioned models form the basis of a comprehensive framework for the study of goal formation in organisations. This line of argument is not inconsistent with that pursued by Thompson and McEwen (1958) in the context of organisational/environmental interactions and their effects on goal formation. Using a continuum ranging from the organisation that is completely dominated by its environment to the one that dominates its environment, they consider the strategies available to the organisations lying in between these two ends for dealing with the environment. Competition with other firms is one strategy which prevents unilateral choice of goals for each of these firms. In the present context, this may be represented by an organisational coalition within which power distribution is finely balanced. A second strategy is bargaining among competing firms in a sense similar to that conveyed by the Cyert and March model. A third strategy is cooption through which the leadership of an organisation absorbs new elements as a means of averting threats to its stability or existence. This could be one of the strategies available to the elite or inner circle in the dominant coalition model. The new elements in the dominant coalition may have their demands met or may be merely pacified through membership. Finally, Thompson and McEwen argue that the organisation can enter a coalition with other organisations which binds all members to a joint action. This strategy may be followed within and between sub-coalitions.

The characterisation of goal formation in terms of the all encompassing framework helps to explain why we may talk about goal dynamism and yet observe goal stability. Further, by implying that at least in some cases goal hierarchy is inevitable, the comprehensive framework makes it easier to interpret the literature on the expression of goals where the pre-eminence of a particular goal is typically assumed. This literature is discussed below.

III. A STATEMENT OF BUSINESS GOALS

One relevant issue that has not yet been considered here is the forms in which the goals of business organisations can be expressed. For instance, are they naturally expressed in the form of profit, or sales revenue, or growth? Moreover, should goals be expressed in terms of maximising an objective function or in another form? The purpose of this section is to provide some discussion of these two areas. A distinction is made between maximising and satisficing models. Under this classification classical entrepreneurial models and managerial models in which something other than profit is assumed to be maximised are considered.

The Profit Maximisation Hypothesis

For many years, profit maximisation has been presumed in economic theory to be the primary goal of business organisations. The traditional economic theory of the firm hypothesises that the rational firm would typically choose a profit-maximising position on the prior assumption that this will be consistent with the maximisation of the owner's wealth. It may be said, therefore, that profit-maximising behaviour reflects rational choice by entrepreneurs. Furthermore, it has been argued that profit maximisation is a prerequisite for firm survival and is validated by the economic natural selection process (Freidman, 1953). Moreover, the proponents of this hypothesis frequently argue that one of its natural properties is that it readily lends itself to equilibrium analysis. Thus, given some initial assumptions about a firm's environment and the supply and demand characteristics of its industry, it is possible to predict the equilibrium position of that firm.

However, the arguments supportive of this hypothesis have been challenged by several writers. It has been suggested that the rationality argument ignores some of the consequences of the separation of ownership from control. For example, Simon (1959) advanced the notion that managers have a vested interest in 'psychic income', i.e. non-monetary perquisites, quite apart from monetary rewards. In attempting to maximise his utility, the manager may balance a loss in profit against an increase in psychic income. In a similar vein, Williamson (1964) argued that managers who control the allocation of resources within the firm can selectively promote their interests at the expense of profits, for instance by building slack into budgets. To the extent that this holds, the normative hypothesis of profit maximisation is at odds with observed business behaviour.

With respect to the survival argument, several writers (e.g. Koopmans, 1957) point out that the conditions under which natural economic selection implies profit maximisation are not ubiquitous. Profit maximisation is most clearly dictated where entry is easiest and where the struggle for survival is keenest. Where competition is weak, goals other than profit maximisation may be more appropriate. Alchian and Kessel (1962) argued that profit maximisation is implied by competition in the capital markets where monopoly rights are allocated to those who can use them most profitably, even if competition in the product markets is not active. Williamson (1964), however, pointed out that the competition in the capital market argument will hold only if there exists a mechanism whereby control over monopoly power can effectively be transferred from managers to shareholders through the capital market. Some of the available empirical evidence indicates the absence of significant control by shareholders over the operations of firms (see, for example, Gordon, 1945). To the extent that this is true, competition in the capital markets may fail to produce the intended effects.

Finally, the equilibrium argument has been criticised on the grounds that the model's assumptions are fairly restrictive. For instance, it can be argued that traditional profit maximisation implies the availability of accurate knowledge of demand and cost functions of the firm and of its competitors. Yet, in the face of uncertainty and imperfect competition, knowledge of competitors' actions and of the firm's optimal actions will be ambiguous, and hence, profit maximisation itself becomes an ambiguous goal (see for example Simon, 1959).

As the above discussion implies, the profit maximisation hypothesis in its traditional form follows naturally from the entrepreneurial goal model under the classic assumptions of perfect competition. Given that in this model the ultimate power for defining organisational goals is assumed to rest with the entrepreneur, important behavioural issues such as managerial discretionary goals and employees' aspirations are not explicitly emphasised. Dissatisfaction with this hypothesis led to the development of two alternative approaches to the expression of business goals. Firstly, various writers held on to the maximisation hypothesis but replaced profit maximisation with the maximisation of something else subject to a given set of constraints (managerial models). Secondly, other writers advanced the notion that firms tend to satisfice rather than maximise their objective function (satisficing models).

Managerial Models

Williamson (1967, p. 12) defined managerial models as those which are 'concerned with the behaviour of the management of large firms in circumstances where the management has access to or has secured for itself a considerable degree of latitude in directing the affairs of the corporation.' He pointed out that managerial theories are only applicable if two conditions are satisfied: (i) competition is attenuated so that survival is not a pressing concern for the firm; and (ii) capital markets are imperfect so that management can apply discretion.

One version of managerial models is the sales revenue maximisation model suggested by Baumol (1958) and Galbraith (1967). In this model, the firm is assumed to maximise its sales revenue or sales growth subject to a profit level adequate to ensure its survival. Another version is the model suggested by Marris (1964) in which managers are assumed to maximise the growth rate subject to a security restraint. A third version is Williamson's (1964) model of managerial discretion. In this model it is assumed that the management operates the firm so as to maximise a multidimensional utility function which contains hierarchical staff emoluments and discretionary profits subject to a minimum profit constraint.

Proponents of managerial models argue that these models are based on more realistic behavioural assumptions than is the profit maximisation hypothesis. For example, in rationalising his model, Baumol (1958) contended that instead of seeking to maximise profits, oligopolistic businessmen seek in reality to maximise sales revenue. Once his profits exceed some 'vaguely defined minimum level' the businessman will be prepared to sacrifice further increases in profits in favour of larger sales revenues, presumably to enjoy the non-pecuniary benefits usually associated with the latter. Other writers have extended this model and demonstrated how the minimum level of profit can be defined formally (e.g. Needham, 1969). Galbraith (1967) argued that maximisation of sales growth is the overwhelming choice of the technostructure for at least two reasons. Firstly, unlike profit maximisation, sales growth maximisation is consistent with the personal and pecuniary interests of the technostructure: sales expansion means output expansion which, in turn, means expansion of the technostructure. Secondly, sales expansion is the best protection against contraction (with sales contraction implying the possibility of some of the technostructure losing their pecuniary emoluments or even their jobs!). Williamson

(1964) provided some 'evidence' from field studies which indicates that firm behaviour appears to be consistent with the predictions of his managerial discretion model. Notice, however, that the evidence cited above is not necessarily wholly conclusive: results drawn from personal observations and case studies (e.g. Baumol; Williamson) may not be amenable to generalisation.

Several other researchers have engaged in more extensive testing of the hypothesis that owner-controlled firms pursue goals different from those of manager-controlled firms. However, the evidence remains inconclusive. For example, supportive evidence (i.e. greater profits in owner-controlled firms and higher growth in manager-controlled firms) has been offered by Florence (1961), Nyman and Silberston (1978), and Cubbin and Leech (1983) but *not* by Fatemi, Ang and Chua (1983).

The effects of the prevailing type of corporate control on organisational goals remain ambiguous. Indeed, some have argued that *both* manager-controlled and owner-controlled companies pursue profitable growth as a broad goal (Herman, 1982). Non-owner managers, Herman argues, may have the interest to seek goals other than profits and to be 'image conscious' in terms of social responsibility. However, they rarely have the freedom for independent action. As suggested earlier, managerial actions are shaped and constrained by the latent power of owners and creditors, which may be manifested in stock market pricing, credit terms, owner inquiries, takeover threats, and so on. Moreover, managerial discretion is restricted through collective decision making, monitoring by peers and subordinates (see chapter 11), rules of behaviour, and overall corporate ethos.

Managerial models therefore substitute managerial goals for entrepreneurial goals in the firm's objective function whilst entrepreneurial goals are treated as part of the constraints. Because of the separation of ownership from control in many companies, it is assumed that managers are in a position to exert considerable influence on the rankings and levels of organisational goals; but see the discussion in the previous section. Yet, managerial models are essentially maximisation models. All profit and non-profit maximisation models seem to be rather rigid. For instance, whilst recognising that in interacting with environmental forces the firm may change the level of its goals, the domain of the objective function is assumed to be invariant over time (e.g. maximising sales revenue). Furthermore, the nature of goal conflict and the techniques for managing such conflict are not explicitly addressed under maximisation models. The impact of changes in employees' aspiration levels on the levels of organisational goals is not made clear. In summary, managerial models are only slightly less restrictive than the profit maximisation model; they concentrate on single, focal organisations with a single central goal, and they frequently postulate limited environmental settings.

Satisficing Models

Several writers have argued that it is more useful to address the levels of organisational goals in terms of satisficing rather than maximising. In particular, Simon (1959) has asserted that the way firms operate closely approximates to satisficing behaviour.

One justification for satisficing behaviour could be that cognitive limitations in the face of environmental uncertainty impose considerable constraints on the firm's ability to maximise its objective function. Notice, however, that much of the contemporary economic analysis deals with constrained maximisation models in which the firm is assumed to optimise its objective function subject to a set of constraints reflecting, among other things, uncertainty and the cost of information (see, for example, Marschak and Radner, 1972). In this sense, satisficing behaviour may be considered as some form of constrained maximisation. The second justification for satisficing behaviour has its roots in the theory of motivation; it is usually assumed that drive is a stimulus for action. Once the drive is satisfied action terminates. Furthermore, the conditions for satisficing a drive are not necessarily fixed, but can change according to changes in an individual's aspiration levels, which in turn change with personal experience. Simon (1959) argued that if business behaviour is to be explained in terms of this theory firms must be expected to satisfice rather than maximise. Cyert and March (1963) also argued that changes in the aspiration levels of participants can change their demands on the organisational coalition which may lead to changes in the levels of organisational goals. Given that the organisational coalition comprises individuals with different aspiration levels and with conflicting goals, they argued that organisational goals would typically be expressed in satisficing terms.

Yet it may be argued that the distinction between satisficing behaviour and maximising behaviour is not important. As aspiration levels tend to adjust to attainable levels of performance, in the long run the former will tend to be very close to the maximum attainable level. This argument, however, is not straightforward. It is generally recognised that given the rate of increase or decrease in performance, the aspiration level may exhibit short-run lags behind performance or alternatively may exceed performance. Simon (1959) argued that when performance falls below the level of aspiration two effects are triggered: firstly, search behaviour is introduced, and secondly, the aspiration level adjusts downwards until goals reach levels that are practically attainable. Practically attainable goal levels may, of course, be below the maximum attainable level. The downward adjustment of aspiration level need not imply inefficiency. Margolis (1958) identified two necessary conditions for the aspiration level to imply efficiency: (i) it must be high enough to ensure the firm's long-run survival and (ii) the aspiration level for future periods must be at least equal to the aspiration level associated with current normal profits.

If satisficing behaviour is expressed in terms other than constrained maximisation, it will be difficult to conceive a single optimal position for the firm. For instance, Eilon (1972) pointed out that under satisficing behaviour if the manager cannot specify adequate trade-offs to reconcile goal conflict, 'then the way in which he proceeds is to determine not the best solution to a problem, but a solution that is "good enough"'. But a 'good enough' solution may mean different things to different people.

One important point that emerges from the preceding discussion is that it is not likely that any one goal expression will adequately and fully explain the behaviour of all firms at any one time, or of any one firm all the time. Rather, the behaviour of the firm at any particular time may approximate any of these goal expressions. This is compatible with the view of organisation as a dynamic system, and with the nature of the goal-formation process discussed earlier. During the course of its lifetime, the firm may adopt different expressions for its objective function: in one period it may act as a profit maximiser, in another period it may seek the attainment of some 'satisfactory' level of performance, and in yet another period it may seek to maximise managerial non-pecuniary rewards.

Clearly, the nature and form of the firm's objective function and set of constraints in a given period will be influenced by the state of its environment, the nature of its coalition, and the characteristics of its side payments. For instance, consider the case of a firm whose survival is clearly threatened. In such a case it is possible that the different factions within the organisational coalition may closely identify themselves with the firm's interests even if they have conflicting personal interests. The firm may adopt drastic measures, e.g. cost reduction and sales expansion, some of which may not be acceptable in more prosperous periods. In this case, such behaviour may be difficult to distinguish from that of a firm which acts as a profit maximiser. Yet, if in another period the firm's survival is not at stake and if its managerial elite has managed to dominate the organisational coalition, then the behaviour of the firm may be more closely aligned with some version of the managerial models (see Phillips, 1967; but also see the above discussion under 'Managerial Models').

It is not the intention here to imply that goals are dictated by a deterministic contingency framework in which a unidimensional relationship exists between some exogenous and endogenous contingencies and the resulting goals. Indeed, in many cases, organisational behaviour may not correspond to some predetermined notion of rationality; it may be at odds with common sense, it may even be suicidal. However, even in the absence of supporting empirical evidence, it is plausible to argue that for many reasons organisational goals are likely to assume expressions that may vary across firms and over time. Below, some empirical evidence on the kinds of goals business firms appear to have is presented.

Empirical Evidence

Empirical evidence on alternative expressions of business goals is rather sparse. Furthermore, the data on which such evidence is based is typically obtained using either mailed questionnaires or interviews with senior company managers. Hence, reported organisational goals are likely to reflect official rather than operative goals. Moreover, the familiar limitations of such data collection techniques could undermine the validity of the empirical evidence. Below, two empirically based studies are reviewed.

The first study is the one undertaken by Dent (1959) in which the top executives of 145 US business establishments were interviewed with respect to the goals which their businesses pursue. The study provides some interesting findings. Firstly, he reported that the goals most frequently expressed by management were profits, public service in the form of good products and employee welfare. Also, other goals were considered important, in particular, growth, efficiency, meeting competition and operating the organisation. In 75 per cent of the cases the management indicated that their company pursued more than one goal (multiple objectives). Secondly, profit was the most frequent objective mentioned; over one half included it among the first three objectives. Dent pointed out that concern for profit might have been more in reality than was directly apparent from the findings of the study. Thus, management might subsume profit under other objectives, e.g. employee welfare. Thirdly, the results of the study indicate that goal orientations of managers were influenced by, amongst other things, three organisational characteristics: company size, extent of its unionisation and the nature of its labour force. Thus, as company size increased, more managers mentioned good products as a goal. Furthermore, over the entire range of size the number of managers who subscribed to employee welfare as a goal increased in unionised companies compared with non-union companies. Finally, the higher the proportion of staff to shop-floor employees in the company, the less was the emphasis on profit and the greater was the emphasis on growth.

The second study is that by Bhaskar and McNamee (1983) which attempted to investigate company goals in the United Kingdom when companies evaluate capital investment proposals. The study covered 118 large UK companies and the results were obtained using a mailed questionnaire.

On the whole, the findings of this study were in agreement with some of the findings of the Dent study. Thus, 96 per cent of the respondents reported that their companies have more than one goal, with over 80 per cent stating that they have more than four goals. The most frequently expressed goals were profitability, growth, liquidity, and risk. Profitability was overwhelmingly considered by respondents (77 per cent) to be the primary goal of the company. Finally, the evidence indicates that, at least for the sample studied, there exists a primary goal and surrogate goals acting as proxies for that primary goal. The primary goal may comprise profitability, growth of profitability and the recognition of an acceptable level of risk. The surrogates may include turnover ratios, depth of skills, age of assets, and liquidity.

It is not intended to evaluate here the methodologies employed in the above two empirical studies, although their limitations should be acknowledged, for instance, focusing on the perceptions of top managers and excluding lower-level subordinates. More important in the context of this chapter is to relate their findings to the literature on organisational goals. Several useful observations emerge from these findings. Firstly, most business organisations seem to consider profit as their (or one of their) major goal(s). This lends support to the profit maximisation hypothesis, in so far as it emphasises the importance of profit, and to managerial and satisficing models which include profit as a constraint in the firm's objective function. Secondly, most organisations seem to pursue multiple goals. Thirdly, goal orientation seems to be influenced by organisational characteristics. In so far as organisational characteristics differ across companies, differences in goal orientation may be observed. Recall, however, that the findings of the above empirical studies probably relate more to official goals than to operative goals. Caution must be exercised in interpreting such findings.

IV. SUMMARY

Business organisations have typically been viewed as purposeful, goal-seeking institutions. Almost exclusively, the literature on organisations is modelled on the presumption that organisational goals precede and guide organisational action. Thus, it is generally held that in seeking rational behaviour the organisation selects those alternatives that come closest to the attainment of its goals. The discussion contained in this chapter has led to the emergence of some fairly fundamental conclusions.

Firstly, to avoid reifying the organisation by asserting that it has the human qualities of motivation and desire, organisational goals may have to be identified with those of its participants. Alternatively, organisational goals may be defined by reference to organisational domains (Thompson), or roles and ethos (Simon). In this sense, goals may be attributed to the domains and roles of the organisation (organisational goals) by the most dominant group of participants in contrast to those held by other internal and external participants (participants' goals).

Secondly, there appears to be a wide spectrum of viable goal formation strategies open to organisations. The goal formation process of any particular organisation for any specific point in time may reflect any of these strategies. Goals are likely to evolve as a result of the interactions among members of the total organisational coalition, or between members of the sub-coalition that happens to dominate the organisation at the time. Alternatively, in some instances goals may reflect the preferences of only one person (the central power figure), given a particular power distribution within the organisation.

Thirdly, given the divergent preferences of organisational participants and the uncertainty facing organisations, goals will tend to be multiple, conflicting, and inconsistent. Dynamic bargaining within and between sub-coalitions will take place, and side payments involving pecuniary and non-pecuniary rewards as well as policy commitments may be used to resolve part of the existing goal conflict. Conflict may not be necessarily manifest in all business organisations nor at all hierarchical levels. When it exists it may not always be intrinsically damaging to the organisation. Indeed, many organisations seem to survive despite the existence of some considerable conflict (Cyert and March, 1963).

Fourthly, the presumption that organisational goals precede organisational action does not always hold. Goals are dynamic, fluid, and ambiguous. Organisational choice may be considered as much a process for discovering goals as for acting on them (March, 1976). Moreover, goals may be fairly ambiguous. This is so in particular when the organisation is in a state of transition while power is changing hands from one group to another or when power distribution within the organisational coalition is finely balanced. Even when there is a clear set of criteria for ordering goals they may deliberately be made vague so that participants may feel that such goals are not inconsistent with their diverse demands.

Fifthly, organisational goals seem to assume a wide range of expressions in the literature. Both the notions of maximising and satisficing have been advanced in that literature. Moreover, the notion of maximisation may relate to profit maximisation, or alternatively to some version of managerial models (e.g. maximisation of sales or some managerial non-pecuniary function). The limited empirical evidence reviewed earlier relates to official, rather than operative, goals pursued by companies. Such evidence indicates that, although it can be generally assumed that profit is the most important single goal business organisations seem to pursue, it is crucial to recognise the importance of other goals, e.g. growth and employee welfare. Moreover, this evidence suggests that organisational goals are influenced by various organisational characteristics, e.g. size, which in turn are influenced by the type and extent of interaction between the organisation and its environment. In so far as organisational characteristics differ between companies, different companies may have different goal orientations.

REFERENCES

Ackoff, R. L., 1970. *A Concept of Corporate Planning*: Wiley.

Alchian, A. A. and Kessel, R. A., 1962. 'Competition, monopoly, and the pursuit of pecuniary gain', in *Aspects of Labour Economics*: National Bureau of Economic Research.

Argenti, J., 1974. *Systematic Corporate Planning*: Nelson.

Baumol, W. J., 1958. On the theory of oligopoly, *Economica*, **25**, pp. 187–198.

Berle, A.A. and Means, G.C., 1932. *The Modern Corporation and Private Property*, Macmillan.

Bhaskar, K. and McNamee, P., 1983. Multiple objectives in accounting and finance, *Journal of Business Finance & Accounting*, **10**(4) Winter pp. 595–621.

Caves, R. E., 1980. Industrial organization, corporate strategy and structure, *Journal of Economic Literature*, **XVIII**, March pp. 64–92.

Cohen, M. D., March, J. G., and Olsen, J. P., 1972. A garbage can model of organizational choice, *Administrative Science Quarterly*, **17**, pp. 1–25.

Cubbin, J. and Leech, D., 1983, 'The effects of shareholding dispersion on the degree of control in British companies: theory and measurement', *Economic Journal*, June, pp. 351–369.

Cyert, R. M. and March, J. G., 1963. *A Behavioural Theory of the Firm*: Prentice-Hall.

Dent, J. K., 1959. Organizational correlates of the goals of business management, *Personnel Psychology*, **12**, Autumn, pp. 365–393.

Drucker, P. F., 1969. *The Practice of Management*: Pan Books.
Eilon, S., 1972. Goals and constraints in decision-making, *Operational Research Quarterly*, March, pp. 2–15.
Etzioni, A., 1961. *A Comparative Analysis of Complex Organizations*: Free Press.
Fatemi, A.T., Ang, J.S. and Chua, J.A., 1983. 'Evidence supporting shareholders wealth maximisation in management controlled firms', *Applied Economics*, February, pp. 49–60.
Florence, P.S., 1961. *Ownership, Control and Success of Large Companies*, Sweet and Maxwell.
Freidman, M., 1953. *Essays in Positive Economics*: University of Chicago Press.
Galbraith, J., 1967. *The New Industrial State*: Houghton Mifflin.
Gordon, R. A., 1945. *Business Leadership in the Large Corporation*, Brookings Institution.
Hall, F. S., 1975. Organization goals: the status of theory and research, pp. 9–32 in J. L. Livingstone (ed.), *Managerial Accounting: The Behavioural Foundations*: Grid.
Hall, R. H., 1977. *Organizations: Structure and Process*: Prentice-Hall.
Herman, E.S., 1982. *Corporate Control, Corporate Power*, Cambridge University Press.
Hill, W., 1969. The goal formation process in complex organizations, *Journal of Management Studies*, 6(2), pp. 198–208.
Jensen, M. C. and Meckling, W. H., 1976. Theory of the firm: managerial behaviour, agency costs and ownership structure, *Journal of Financial Economics*, 3, October, pp. 305–360.
Katz, D. and Kahn, R. L., 1978. *The Social Psychology of Organizations*, 2nd edn: Wiley.
Koopmans, T. C., 1957. *Three Essays on the State of Economic Science*: McGraw-Hill.
Krupp, S., 1961. *Patterns in Organizational Analysis: A Critical Examination*: Chiltern Co. Book Division.
Lindblom, C. E., 1959. The science of 'muddling through', *Public Administration Review*, 19, Spring, pp. 79–88.
March, J. G., 1972. Model bias in social action. *Review of Educational Research*, 42(4), pp. 413–429.
March, J. G., 1976. 'The technology of foolishness', in J. G. March and J. P. Olsen (eds), *Ambiguity and Choice in Organizations*: Universitetsforlaget, pp. 69–81.
March, J. G. and Olsen, J. P., 1976. *Ambiguity and Choice in Organizations*: Universitetsforlaget.
March, J. G and Simon, H. A., 1958. *Organizations*: Wiley.
Margolis, J., 1958. The analysis of the firm: rationalism, conventionalism, and behaviourism, *The Journal of Business*, 31, pp. 187–199
Marris, R., 1964. *The Economic Theory of 'Managerial' Capitalism*: The Free Press of Glencoe.
Marschak, J. and Radner, R., 1972. *Economic Theory of Teams*: Yale University Press.
Needham, D., 1969. *Economic Analysis and Industrial Structure*: Holt, Rinehart and Winston.
Nyman, S. and Silberston, A., 1978. 'The ownership and control of industry', *Oxford Economic Papers*, pp. 74–101.
Otley, D. T. and Berry, A. J., 1980. Control, organisation and accounting, *Accounting, Organizations and Society*, 5(2), pp. 231–244.
Parsons, T., 1960. *Structure and Process in Modern Societies*: Free Press.
Pennings, J. M. and Goodman, P. S., 1977. 'Toward a workable framework', pp. 146–184 in P. S. Goodman and J. M. Pennings (eds), *New Perspectives on Organizational Effectiveness*: Jossey-Bass.
Perrow, C., 1961. The analysis of goals in complex organizations, *American Sociological Review*, 26, pp. 854–866.
Perrow, C., 1970. *Organizational Analysis: A Sociological View*: Belmont.
Phillips, A., 1967. 'An attempt to synthesise some theories of the firm', pp. 32–44 in A. Phillips and O. E. Williamson (eds), *Prices: Issues in Theory, Practice, and Public Policy*: University of Pennsylvania Press.
Radice, H.K., 1971. 'Control type, profitability and growth in large firms: an empirical study', *Economic Journal*, September, pp. 547–562.
Scott, J. C., 1957. Membership and participation in voluntary associations, *American Sociological Review*, 22, pp. 315–326.

Simon, H. A., 1959. Theories of decision making in economics and behavioural science, *American Economic Review*, **49**, June, pp. 253-283.

Simon, H., 1964. On the concept of organization goal, *Administrative Science Quarterly*, **9**, pp. 1–22.

Swieringa, R.J. and Waterhouse, J.H., 1982. 'Organizational views of transfer pricing', *Accounting, Organizations and Society,* **7**(2), pp. 149–165.

Thompson, J. D., 1967. *Organizations in Action*: McGraw-Hill.

Thompson, J. D. and McEwen, W. J., 1958. Organizational goals and environment: goal setting as an interaction process, *American Sociological Review*, **23**, February, pp. 23–31.

Watson, T., Jr., 1963. *A Business and Its Beliefs*, McGraw-Hill.

Williamson, O. E., 1964. *The Economics of Discretionary Behaviour: Managerial Objectives in a Theory of the Firm*: Prentice-Hall.

Williamson, O. E., 1967. 'A dynamic stochastic theory of managerial behaviour', pp. 11–31 in A. Phillips and O. E. Williamson (eds), *Prices: Issues in Theory, Practice, and Public Policy*: University of Pennsylvania Press.

Williamson, O.E., 1970. *Corporate Control and Business Behaviour*, Prentice-Hall.

Zald, M. N., 1963. Comparative analysis and measurement of organizational goals: the case of correctional institutions for delinquents, *The Sociological Quarterly*, **4**(2), pp. 206–230.

3

Human Motivation and Leadership Styles

Research into work motivation and human behaviour has become one of the central topics in organisational analysis. From an organisational theory perspective such research is crucial for at least two reasons. Firstly, if work motivation and human behaviour can be sensibly modelled, management may be able to manipulate appropriately the relevant variables in such a manner that particular levels of motivation are attained. Secondly, understanding the nature of human motivation facilitates a better understanding of human behaviour and thus makes it possible to explain why a particular individual behaves in a particular manner.

In the context of management accounting, research on work motivation and human behaviour is also important. Accounting controls represent part of the work setting (e.g. work rules, environment) of an individual. They also reflect management philosophy towards coordinating, guiding, and evaluating performance. Viewed in this context, accounting controls are likely to impact, both directly and indirectly, on motivation and consequently on behaviour. A clear identification of the nature of the variables which affect performance and the ways in which they interact is important in making sensible evaluations of the effectiveness and desirability of alternative accounting controls. These implications for management accounting lay some emphasis on the juxtaposition of accounting and behavioural studies.

This chapter deals with motivation, human behaviour and leadership styles. Section I contains a discussion of some important theories of human motivation. These are need-hierarchy theory, achievement motivation theory, motivation-hygiene theory and equity theory. In section II expectancy theory is first discussed and then extensions of the theory in the context of management accounting are considered. Section III is devoted to a discussion of various theories of leadership styles. Finally, section IV contains a summary of the chapter.

I. SOME THEORIES OF HUMAN MOTIVATION

Numerous theories of human motivation have been developed in the literature. Each of these theories tends to be based on a set of assumptions about motivation and human behaviour, some of which are common to most theories whilst others are theory specific. Moreover, although the theories have different emphases and orientations, their domains overlap in many parts.

This section considers four theories of motivation. These are need-hierarchy theory, achievement motivation theory, motivation-hygiene theory, and equity theory. These are typically known as 'content theories'. Of the main theories of motivation, this listing leaves out expectancy theory, which is usually classified as part of 'process theories'. For convenience of presentation, expectancy theory is discussed in the following section, along with some extensions of the theory in the context of management accounting.

Need-Hierarchy Theory

The need-hierarchy theory, developed by Maslow (1943; 1954), is one of the earliest and most important theories of motivation. The theory posits the existence within an individual of a number of needs which instinctively influence his behaviour. These needs are genetic and they include, in an ascending order, physiological needs (e.g. food), security (e.g. safety), love needs (e.g. group membership), esteem needs (e.g. desire for strength or prestige), and self-actualisation needs (i.e. to realise one's potential). In addition to these five basic needs Maslow identified three more needs which were not always mentioned in his analysis or explicitly recognised as characteristic of all people. These include the desire to know and understand (cognitive needs), aesthetic needs (desire for beauty in one's surroundings), and deficiency, deprivation and growth needs (e.g. avoiding pathological states).

In Maslow's analysis, the five basic needs are arranged into what he calls 'a hierarchy of prepotency'. Physiological needs are deemed the most prepotent and hence are lowest in the hierarchy, and the process continues in that manner. Once a need is satisfied it ceases to be a motivating force and attention is shifted to the need immediately above it.

Maslow (1954) pointed out that, on average, the specified hierarchy of needs is expected to hold, but will not necessarily hold for every single individual. Thus, a certain class of individuals may never aspire to higher needs when lower needs are satisfied, as for example some of those who permanently live on the poverty line. He also referred to some cases where the five basic needs could be accorded rankings different from those specified in his theory.

The need-hierarchy theory has had a significant impact on the organisation theory literature. The theory offers one approach to management. The implications of that approach may be summarised as follows.

— Firstly, by controlling work conditions so that various important individual needs are satisfied the management may be able to motivate individuals to behave in some desired manner. Clarke (1960) pointed out that once one moves beyond safety needs, it is desirable to manipulate work conditions to activate the highest possible need level.
— Secondly, the theory implies that human behaviour is a function of work conditions. When work conditions are poor employees focus on aspects of the work itself in relation to lower needs. As conditions improve they shift their focus to the supervisor's behaviour, and as these conditions further improve their focus reverts back to the work itself, but in this case directed to self-actualisation (Campbell, 1971).
— Thirdly, the theory implies that employees' motivation is influenced by their positions in the organisational hierarchy. As employees move up that hierarchy they will be motivated by higher need levels.

An important feature of the need-hierarchy theory, it has been argued, is that it is not concerned with the motivational aspects of the individual per se but rather with groups of individuals. As Miner (1980) pointed out, it is particularly relevant to the use of managerial policies in handling issues relating to human resources.

The usefulness of the need-hierarchy theory is not limited to linking needs to individual motivation and performance. The use of the theory was extended by Tuzzolino and Armandi (1981), who linked the need hierarchy to organisational performance and social responsibility. They perceived the organisation as having lower-level needs (physiological and safety), which are represented by healthy profitability, sound dividend policy, competitive position, and so on. A purposeful organisation is expected to satisfy these needs first before seeking to fulfil affiliative needs (e.g. trade association), esteem needs (e.g. product leadership), and self-actualisation needs (e.g. community relations, job enrichment). Viewing the organisation in these terms may offer more insights into assessing its effectiveness and understanding its relationships with other organisations and with society.

Notwithstanding the perceived advantages outlined in the above discussion, criticisms of the need-hierarchy theory abound. These may be classified into those relating to the degree of its logical consistency; those related to definition and measurement difficulties and those related to the degree of empirical support for that theory. It has been frequently argued that the theory is inherently inconsistent and that it confuses needs (what is good for a person) and values (what is perceived by the individual as good), like aesthetic needs and beauty as a value (e.g. Locke, 1976a). Similarly, various criticisms have been levelled against the theory in relation to the definition and measurement of variables. Thus, the theory contains various *ad hoc* definitions, as in the case of self-actualisation, and these at times tend to be tautological (Miner, 1980). Self-actualisation can vary among individuals and without identifying the individual it is difficult to know how and when it is activated. Moreover, the theory does not provide operational definitions for most variables. Although several attempts have been made to develop appropriate measures for these variables (e.g. Porter, 1964) they have some inherent bias and are thus inadequate to use in a conclusive test of the theory.

Several researchers attempted to empirically test some aspects of the need-hierarchy theory. Wahba and Bridwell (1976) reviewed the findings of most of these studies. They identified three areas in which the theory has been tested, but with little support in each area:
1. The hypothesis that the correlation coefficients between items measuring the same need would be higher than between items measuring different needs.
2. The hypothesis that people's rankings of the five basic needs would correspond with the way they are ranked in the theory.
3. The hypothesis that the most important need stimulating behaviour at the time is the one in which deprivation is felt to be greatest and that the most gratified need is the least activator.

Whether such lack of support for the theory is a reflection of the inadequacy of the theory itself or of the proxy measures of variables used is difficult to ascertain. Most writers, however, discredit the theory itself (e.g. Korman, 1977), but few have attempted to refine its basic statements. Alderfer (1972) rearranged Maslow's five basic needs into three needs: existence (physiological needs, and material safety needs); relatedness (interpersonal safety, esteem needs and love needs) and growth (self-confirmed esteem needs, and self-actualisation needs). He then proceeded to derive a number of propositions which turned out to be consistent with those of Maslow's except in two cases which were the reverse of Maslow's: (i) the less that relatedness needs are satisfied, the more that existence needs will be desired and (ii) the less growth needs are satisfied, the more relatedness needs will be desired. He further derived, tested and revised a number of propositions relating to the impacts of desires on satisfaction. Many of these propositions, however, were empirically derived from the same data set used to test them and, hence, there is an element of inherent bias in them. The refined theory is therefore a set of empirical generalisations with a lower level of abstraction than Maslow's formulations (Miner, 1980).

Achievement Motivation Theory

Despite these, and other, refinements to the need-hierarchy theory most researchers remain discontented with that theory. Attempts were made to develop alternative theories, one of which is achievement motivation theory, which was mainly developed by McClelland (1961; 1962; 1975). The theory identifies three motives which impact upon behaviour: achievement, power and affiliation. These motives are arranged into a hierarchy which, unlike that in Maslow's analysis, varies across individuals as each of them assigns positive and negative feelings about relevant phenomena that occur. Moreover, through increased learning, the individual may change the nature and magnitude of his feelings towards the same phenomenon.

Achievement motivation is particularly activated in the case of individuals with a strong need for achievement. But for achievement itself to be so strongly desired, work situations must be endowed with some specific characteristics. These situations must make it possible for an individual to assume responsibility and to obtain credit, even if only in the form of intrinsic satisfaction, for outcome. Moreover, achievement situations are those with intermediate levels of difficulty, since easy tasks and too difficult tasks tend to be demotivating. Finally, these situations are characterised by clear feedback on the success of individual effort.

In McClelland's analysis, power motivation is represented by a hierarchy of four stages. Initially, power is derived through association with powerful people. Next, the source of personal power becomes oneself. As that increases so the individual moves to the third stage in which power motivation involves exercise of power over other people in a competitive manner. Finally, emphasis shifts from oneself to some good common goal and thus power derives from influencing people to attain such goal. McClelland also distinguished between two forms of power – personalised and socialised. Personalised power relates to personal dominance and a will to win. Socialised power combines both motivation and inhibition where the main concern is with group goals and motivation.

McClelland then related these different types of power motivation to managerial performance. In his analysis the effective manager emerges late in the third stage as socialised power is acquired (this implies the addition of inhibitory tendencies). Nevertheless, individuals at earlier stages can function effectively in some managerial capacity.

The implications of affiliation motivation have also been explicitly considered in this theory. Strong affiliation is held by McClelland to induce negative consequences on managerial performance, since it could lead a manager to make exceptions for inefficient performance by subordinates.

Further refinements in the achievement motivation theory were introduced by subsequent researchers, in particular Atkinson (1977) and Weiner (1972). Atkinson's contributions include several useful notions which make the theory more general. He modelled achievement motivation as a function of the individual's own drive, his expectations of the success of a given task, and how attractive to him such success is. Performance is viewed as a means to a future end rather than an end in itself. He also described the dynamism of motivational change as a given motive gradually weakens through satisfaction and ultimately gives way to a new motive.

Weiner's main contribution is the development of 'attribution theory' according to which an individual attributes credit to the outcome of his own efforts rather than to chance. Success and failure may be attributed to an individual's own ability, his effort level, the difficulty of the task, and luck. Individuals can vary considerably in the ways in which they attribute their own failure or success to each of these factors. Thus, it is held that individuals with high need for achievement are likely to attribute their failure not to inability but to not trying hard enough, whereas those with low need for achievement will attribute failure to their inherent inability.

The theory stimulated a large number of empirical studies. The results of these studies are generally supportive of the achievement motivation and affiliation motivation notions (e.g. Steiner and Miner, 1977), but somewhat mixed in the case of power motivation (e.g. Cumin, 1967; McClelland, 1961). Empirical studies have also been generally supportive of the extensions introduced by Atkinson and Weiner. This supportive evidence must be viewed with some caution, however, because a large number of the related empirical studies were conducted in laboratory settings and may thus not be adequately representative of real-life settings. Although this theory is by no means a complete theory of human motivation, it provides some useful insights into explaining observed human behaviour. By identifying for an individual the level of achievement motivation, the stage of power motivation, and the extent of affiliation motivation, so we may be able to predict and understand his behaviour. The theory is particularly useful in inferring and understanding the behaviour of managers at different organisational levels.

Motivation-Hygiene Theory

One of the variables which was not adequately addressed in the literature reviewed so far is job satisfaction in terms of its sources and its potential effect on motivation. Herzberg (1966; 1976) developed the motivation-hygiene theory in order to specifically address these issues. The theory postulates that (i) factors causing positive job attitudes are different from those causing negative attitudes, and (ii) factors and personal effects associated with sequences of job events differ according to whether such events are long-term or short-term. Herzberg identifies a number of factors which are expected to lead to job satisfaction. These are achievement, recognition, the challenging nature of the task itself, responsibility, and advancement (promotion). Satisfaction of these factors leads to positive feelings and better performance. Job dissatisfaction, however, results from different (hygiene) factors which are categorised as company policies and practices, interpersonal relations, physical working conditions, job security, benefits, and salary. Good hygiene improves performance up to a point beyond which motivation (e.g. intrinsic job aspects) is needed.

Herzberg suggests that organisations ought to organise their industrial relations departments into a sub-unit which deals with hygiene matters and another which deals with motivation. This, he argues, would help them to emphasise motivators and build them into jobs. Job enrichment is particularly emphasised as a crucial motivating force. This theory has also been empirically tested by many researchers, and the results are fairly supportive of the hypotheses inherent in the theory. Support, however, is not straightforward in the sense that several factors emerged as satisfiers and dissatisfiers, e.g. salary, status. Moreover, job satisfaction often appeared to lead to favourable performance, whereas job dissatisfaction appeared to be less often associated with unfavourable performance (Schwab, DeVitt and Cummings, 1971).

Various other deficiencies reflected in the design of empirical research supportive of the theory cast doubt on the overall validity of that research (e.g. Miner, 1980).

Equity Theory

An outgrowth of motivation-hygiene theory is that job dissatisfaction was frequently reported to be the result of feelings of unfairness. This notion was articulated by Adams (1963) in the context of social exchange relationships between individuals. In an exchange, an individual gives something (input) in return for something (outcome). If input is not recognised as relevant or not 'appropriately' valued by the other party in the exchange then inequity is likely to occur. In exchange relationships a reference, e.g. a co-worker, is usually used in evaluating the equity of an exchange relationship. Thus, inequity occurs when, for a given individual, the ratio of outcomes to inputs significantly differs (i.e. is smaller or greater) from the ratio perceived for the reference source. But the motivational force of unfavourable inequity is likely to be activated at a lower disparity level compared with favourable inequity.

Perceived inequity breeds dissatisfaction, as manifested in the feeling of anger (unfavourable inequality) or guilt (favourable inequality). As a result of inequity, tension emerges as a motivating force which aims to reduce and ultimately remove inequity; the amount of tension created being proportional to the extent of inequity. Methods of reducing inequity include altering or distorting inputs and outcomes, changing the reference source and, at the extreme, job transfers, absenteeism or even resignation.

Various propositions derived from equity theory have been empirically tested and the results are mostly supportive of the theory (e.g. Leventhal et al., 1969). The theory has important implications for human performance in organisations. Thus, by appropriately changing work circumstances, improvements in performance can be achieved. Moreover, equity theory can help in explaining human behaviour following intentional or unintentional inequity.

The theory, however, has a number of limitations. Thus, in several situations it is not possible to derive precise inferences about human behaviour. For example, when multiple reference sources exist, it is not entirely clear which source will be selected. Similarly, it is not clear which of the available equity-attaining strategies will be selected by a particular individual, nor is the order in which they will be pursued specified. Further, it has been suggested that empirical research on equity theory is static in the sense that it ignores the time dimension of inequity (Vecchio, 1982). In response to this criticism, Cosier and Dalton (1983) extended equity theory by explicitly incorporating a time parameter in the mathematical specification of the theory. This allows for studying the effects of trends, time lags, and prior inequities in a particular organisational setting.

The theories reviewed thus far have progressed in their hypotheses about motivation and human behaviour from an initial universalist stance in which behaviour is assumed instinctive (need-hierarchy theory) to an almost individual-specific behaviour reflecting objective and subjective differences across individuals (later theories). The theories also emphasise either group behaviour (need-hierarchy theory), individual behaviour (achievement motivation theory), or both (equity theory and motivation-hygiene theory). None of these theories, however, explicitly modelled an individual's behaviour as a function of his perceptions of forces that operate on him and the expected rewards that he may attain for his efforts. Expectancy theory goes a long way towards addressing this notion.

II. EXPECTANCY THEORY AND MOTIVATION

A basic tenet in expectancy theory is that an individual's behaviour is influenced by his subjective perceptions of the internal and external forces which impact upon him (Lewin, 1951). Some of these forces drive the individual towards a particular goal whereas others constrain his progress towards that goal. Following this basic notion, several writers developed various formulations of expectancy theory. The most important developments so far are those by Georgopoulos, Mahoney and Jones (1957), Vroom (1964), Galbraith and Cummings (1967), Porter and Lawler (1968), and Graen (1969). These developments essentially assume that an individual chooses his behaviour on the basis of two variables. Firstly, his expectations that his behaviour will lead to a specific outcome. Secondly, the strength of the individual's performance or personal utility, for a given outcome, from his effort (the sum of the valences).

Georgopoulos et al. (1957) attempted to identify factors associated with different levels of employee productivity. In their analysis they considered (i) individual needs as reflected in the goals pursued, (ii) individual perceptions of the relevance of behaviour in attaining goals and (iii) the extent of freedom from restraining forces the individual has in following the desired path. They hypothesised that if an individual perceives high productivity as a path leading to the attainment of his goal(s), he will tend to be a high producer and vice versa; but the extent to which this relationship may be observed depends on the extent of the individual's freedom to act. If such freedom is severely restricted, the hypothesised relationship may not hold.

Vroom (1964) further extended the work of Georgopoulos et al. He assumed that, in preferring one outcome out of many alternative outcomes, people anticipate experiencing feelings of satisfaction (valence) which would arise if the preferred outcome should occur. Valences may be positive or negative. The individual may arrange his behaviour in such a manner that outcomes with positive valence are maximised and those with negative valence are minimised. An outcome may have valence in its own right or (outcome–outcome link) with anticipated sources of satisfaction and dissatisfaction.

In his analysis Vroom also emphasised the role of expectancy, that is the probability that the choice of a particular alternative action will lead to a desired outcome (action–outcome link). Together, expectancies and total valence produce a force which motivates an individual towards a particular action. Vroom applied these formulations to various situations, in particular, occupational choice, job satisfaction, and job performance.

Galbraith and Cummings (1967) suggested that valences divide into two types: intrinsic and extrinsic. Intrinsic valences relate to goal-directed behaviour, such as feelings of competence. Intrinsically valent behaviour is intrinsically motivational because it leads to satisfaction. Extrinsic valences are those associated with the consequences of behaviour, such as reward which is contingent on work-goal accomplishment.

Porter and Lawler (1968) extended Vroom's concept of motivational force by incorporating a larger number of variables into the model and by introducing various feedback loops which make the model more dynamic over time. The variables included in their model are value of reward (valence), effort–reward probability which divides into effort–performance (expectancy) and performance–reward (instrumentality), effort (force), role perceptions, rewards, perceived equitable rewards and satisfaction. Several multiplicative functions were then defined for combinations of these variables, for example multiplying value of reward by effort–reward probability yields effort. The feedback loops operated in two ways.

Firstly, to the extent that performance leads to reward, the perceived effort–reward probability is increased. Secondly, as satisfaction occurs after receiving a reward, it influences the future value of that reward.

Graen (1969) further developed the role perception variable contained in the Porter and Lawler model. In his model, he introduced the notion of work role which refers to the behaviour expected by the organisation of an incumbent of a given position, for example incumbent of a particular job. Outcomes accrue to an individual from the attainment of such work roles.

All these various versions of expectancy theory have been empirically tested by the original contributors as well as others. On the whole, the results are supportive of the theory with the extent of support being strong in the cases of Vroom, Porter and Lawler, and to some degree Graen, but weak in the cases of Georgopoulos et al. and Galbraith and Cummings.

Expectancy theory has become popular mainly because it combines some of the important features of earlier motivation theories, for example equity theory, and because it has significantly extended the domain of research into human motivation. Moreover, many of the expectancy models have various similarities with expected utility theory and some argue that expectancy theory is a special case of decision theory (Mitchell, 1977; see also chapter 6). To the extent that expected utility theory is perceived as useful in the context of organisational analysis so may expectancy theory be similarly viewed.

In the context of the management accounting literature, Ronen and Livingstone (1975) developed an expectancy theory model based on an earlier model suggested by House (1971). Formally, the model is expressed as follows:

(1)

$$M = IV_b + P_1(IV_a + \sum_{i=1}^{n} P_{2i} EV_i)$$

where
M = motivation to work;
IV_a = intrinsic valence associated with successful performance of the tasks;
IV_b = intrinsic valence associated with goal-directed behaviour;
EV_i = extrinsic valences associated with the ith extrinsic reward contingent on work-goal accomplishment, $i = 1, 2, \ldots n$;
P_1 = the expectancy that goal-directed behaviour will accomplish the work-goal (a given level of specified performance); the measure's range is $(-1, +1)$;
P_{2i} = the expectancy that work-goal accomplishment will lead to the ith extrinsic reward; the measure's range is $(-1, +1)$.

In the model expressed in (1) above, the individual's motivation to work depends upon his subjectively determined values of intrinsic and extrinsic valences and on relevant expectancies. Specifically, these include (i) expected intrinsic valence associated with goal-directed behaviour, independent of actual achievement and (ii) expected intrinsic and extrinsic valences associated with work-goal attainment.

Changes in the parameters of the above model are likely to lead to changes in the expected values of intrinsic and extrinsic valences, which, in turn, are likely to influence an individual's motivation to work. Supervisors may therefore manipulate some of these parameters in order to induce some specific changes in an individual's motivation and hence in his behaviour. For example, the superior can change the level and nature of extrinsic rewards related to work-goal achievement (e.g. bonuses, promotions). Likewise, by manipulating the role of the subordinate in goal setting and the extent of control over his task-directed effort the superior can influence the intrinsic valences associated with goal achievement. The superior can also influence the intrinsic valences related to goal-directed behaviour by changing working conditions, offering support in periods of stress, and being considerate of his subordinate's needs. Not only can the superior influence the valences, but he can also influence the expectations. By supporting the subordinate's efforts, he can increase the expectancy that the effort will lead to work-goal achievement, P_1. Similarly, through interaction, the superior can increase the subordinate's expectancy that work-goal achievement will lead to extrinsic reward, P_{2i} (see Ronen and Livingstone, 1975).

Following House, Ronen and Livingstone hypothesised that three classes of situational variables determine which behavioural attributes of the superior are instrumental in increasing work motivation. These are the needs of the subordinates, environmental demands and the task demands of subordinates. The superior's behaviour is perceived as legitimate by the subordinate to the extent that it leads to the latter's immediate or future satisfaction. Such perception is thus influenced by the subordinate's characteristics (e.g. need for achievement). Again, work environment may lead to actions by the superior which could influence the extent of the subordinate's satisfaction. For example, the more unsatisfactory the task the more likely that the subordinate will resent pressure from the superior to improve productivity. Finally, to the extent that the superior's behaviour is supportive of the subordinate in dealing with the demands imposed by his task, for example frustration or threat, the subordinate's satisfaction and perceived expectations of rewards will increase.

The expectancy model advanced earlier is useful in illuminating the various factors which impact upon an individual's level of motivation. It also illustrates alternative ways that a superior may pursue to influence the behaviour of his subordinates in a particular direction. Moreover, it offers a framework in which much of the accounting budgeting-related research can be meaningfully integrated, an aspect which will be discussed in chapter 15.

Ronen and Livingstone (1975) pointed out a number of ways in which the budgeting process influences the parameters of the expectancy model. These mainly emanate from the role of the budget as a communication tool. Firstly, given that the budget represents management's expectation of successful performance, it implicitly indicates the extent of expected extrinsic rewards contingent upon budget attainment by the subordinate (EV_i). In this sense the budget process, and the set of extrinsic rewards contingent on successful performance, together define to the subordinate the set of external valences associated with work-goal achievement. Secondly, the perceived difficulty of the budget influences the subordinate's expectancy that his effort will lead to budget achievement (P_1). Revisions of expectancy will be based on deviations of previous levels of performance from previous budgets. Thirdly, the subordinate may revise his estimates of the expectancy that work-goal achievement will lead to a particular extrinsic reward (P_{2i}) in the light of the extent of the superior's consistency in rewarding successful performance. Furthermore, the extent to which past achievements are recognised by superiors is likely to influence the subordinate's expectation of the level of future extrinsic valences associated with work-goal achievement (EV_i). Fourthly, the budget may influence the intrinsic valence associated with goal-directed behaviour (IV_b) by increasing the subordinate's satisfaction through reducing task ambiguity and facilitating coordination of activities.

However, the model as expressed in (1) above is restrictive. In particular, it implies that, associated with any work-goal, there is but one outcome perceived by the individual. Yet, in most cases, for a given work-goal there are a number of potential outcomes, which may be equal to, below, or above that work-goal, and the individual may seek any of these outcomes (Rockness, 1977). With each of these alternative outcomes there will be an associated level of effort to be exerted by the individual and associated intrinsic and extrinsic rewards.

Allowing for these possibilities, Rockness (1977) extended the basic expectancy model in (1) into the following multiple-goal multiple-outcome expectancy model:
(2)
$$F_i = \sum_{j=1}^{n} IV\ effort_j + P_1(\sum_{k=1}^{n} IV\ outcome_k + \sum_{l=1}^{n} P_{2l}\ EV_l)$$

where

F_i	= force toward a particular work outcome i,
$IV\ effort_j$	= the intrinsic rewards directly associated with effort to achieve a particular outcome,
$IV\ outcome_k$	= the intrinsic rewards directly related to achieving a particular performance outcome,
EV_l	= the extrinsic rewards which are dependent on a particular performance outcome,
P_1	= the expectancy that effort will lead to a particular performance outcome,
$\bar{P}_{2l}$	= the expectancy that achieving a particular performance outcome will lead to extrinsic rewards EV_l.

According to the model expressed in (2), increases in the expected rewards lead to greater force towards performance which in turn leads to higher levels of performance. Alternatively, it could be argued that the individual engages in performing at a specified level for which the force is strongest. The rewards take cognisance of the cost of effort required to achieve a given level of performance.

Rockness maintained that his model was consistent with expected utility theory and with behaviour in organisations. Given the trade-off between expected rewards and the cost of effort, the individual is assumed to direct his maximum effort toward the performance level which will lead to the maximum *net* expected rewards. Thus, in a budgeting context, with other variables remaining the same, higher performance can be attained by increasing rewards offered across the budget continuum. Moreover, the model offers an explanation of why an individual may be motivated to attain a given budget level but lacks motivation to achieve another budget level. Thus, for a given reward structure, increase in the budget level may lead to increase in performance until a point is reached where expected rewards do not justify the difficulties associated with budget attainment. In essence, as the budget difficulty increases, the cost of effort increases, the net expected rewards decrease, and satisfaction decreases. Finally, the effects of feedback on budget performance depend on the effect of the specific feedback on model parameters. Feedback may indicate the need to revise budgets upwards or downwards thereby leading to changes in performance. Rockness tested a number of hypotheses derived from his model in a laboratory setting. His results lend support to the hypotheses and, hence, to the model.

The refinements offered by Rockness (1977) clearly enhance the usefulness of the basic expectancy model. However, the expectancy approach to analysing human motivation remains restrictive both in scope and in orientation. Most of the currently available expectancy models exclude environmental variables such as the extent of subordinate participation in target setting, leadership style, and the effects of work group membership. Furthermore, the models so far developed do not adequately explain the link between motivation and performance. By manipulating the parameters which impact upon motivation, it is held that desired changes in performance could be attained. But it is not made entirely clear how changes in performance can be predicted nor what else besides motivation will influence performance.

Even more fundamental criticisms have been raised against expectancy theory. For example, Locke (1976b) pointed out that the concept of hedonism, as implied in the expected satisfaction of valences, is untenable; in many cases human behaviour may be self-punitive. He also questioned whether individuals can ever engage in the extremely complex cognitive processes implied by expectancy theory, for example, the assumed multiplicative functional form of many variables. Further, the theory does not account for impulsive behaviour or unconscious motives; behaviour is assumed to be calculated and rational. Moreover, the theory assumes that motivation is geared towards maximising behaviour. To the extent that non-maximising behaviour is sought by individuals, the theory does not fully explain human motivation.

III. LEADERSHIP STYLES

As indicated earlier, expectancy theory emphasises the importance of the role that a manager can play in influencing the intrinsic and extrinsic valences of his subordinates. It is, therefore, important to consider different styles of managerial leadership and the influence each has on subordinate motivation. The literature on leadership styles seems to have followed a pattern of development not dissimilar to that of the much broader literature on organisation theory. Thus, initially, researchers' efforts centred around prescribing or describing what can be held as a universal set of leadership traits which hold irrespective of prevailing situational contingencies. This line of research was followed by a contingency leadership school which posits that leadership traits are contingent upon situations facing the leader. Finally, a post-contingency school recently emerged which emphasises the importance of managerial choice. These views are briefly considered below.

Universal Leadership Traits

The search for that set of leadership traits with universal applicability has occupied the attention of several researchers belonging to differing organisation theory schools. Thus, the view held by classical organisation theorists is that human beings are just one of the factors of production employed by the organisation. In assuming responsibility for the management of these human beings, the organisation leadership is entrusted with the tasks of directing people's efforts, motivating them, and modifying and controlling their actions to comply with organisational interests. Without such deliberate intervention by the leadership, it is held, people are likely to be passive and resistant to organisational needs. Such is the essence of 'theory X' as identified by McGregor (1960). The leadership style promoted by this theory is premised on authoritarian notions of control where reward and punishment are seen as the basic vehicles for securing subordinate cooperation. The leadership elite are expected to display greater orientations towards tasks and develop a military-style human hierarchy which emphasises depersonalisation of superior–subordinate relationships.

This authoritarian leadership style has been challenged by neoclassical organisation theorists. These writers reported several empirical results which indicate that authoritarian leadership styles are likely to result in subordinates' resistance to power, their alienation and frustration. It is held that these effects will eventually lead to dysfunctional behaviour and adverse consequences on performance (e.g. McGregor, 1960). Accordingly, they advocate a more democratic leadership style whereby management should provide more humane work conditions and more friendly and less formal human relations. Subordinates are assumed to be responsible, ambitious, and responsive to monetary, non-monetary, and sentient rewards. The leader is assumed to think highly of his subordinates and, on the whole, be employee-centred rather than task-centred. This leadership style has been referred to by McGregor (1960) as 'theory Y'.

The results of several empirical studies have been cited in support of theory Y. In general, these results seem to indicate that theory Y leadership style leads subordinates to internalise managers' high regards for them and thus motivate them towards higher performance. More specifically, the results suggest that higher performance is achieved as a result of superiors focusing their primary attention on:
— the human aspects of their subordinates' problems;
— establishing effective work groups with high performance goals;
— ensuring that, in general, subordinates are subject to low work pressure rather than close supervision;
— being helpful and non-punitive when observing poor subordinate performance;
— on the whole being primarily employee-centred rather than task-centred (see for example, Kahn, 1956; Katz and Kahn, 1951, 1952; Likert, 1961; Tannenbaum, 1962 and 1966; Tannenbaum and Kahn, 1958, and Levine, 1973).

Yet, despite this wealth of empirical work, the results remain, at best, inconclusive. For instance, it is quite difficult, if not impossible, to ascertain from these studies whether it is really the theory Y leadership style that is conducive to better performance or that better performance influences the quality of leadership. Greene (1975) reported that the nature of influence between superiors and subordinates is reciprocal rather than one-sided. Moreover, these results do not successfully reconcile the high performance that, at least in some cases, seems to be associated with theory X leadership style.

Ghiselli (1963, 1971) studied the effects of a number of trait characteristics on leadership effectiveness. Eight personality traits and five motivational traits were selected. Personality traits consisted of intelligence, initiative, supervisory ability, self-assurance, affinity for the working class, decisiveness, masculinity–femininity, and maturity. Motivational traits consisted of the need for occupational achievement, self-actualisation, power over others, high financial reward, and job security. On a scale ranging from zero to 100, Ghiselli (1971) assessed the relevance of each of these traits for managerial success. The results are shown in table 3.1.

Ghiselli's results lend more support to theory Y compared with theory X (contrast the score for working-class affinity with the score for the need for power over others). More fundamental, perhaps, is the fact that his results emphasise the importance of cognitive and motivational characteristics for leadership success compared with theory X type characteristics. The results of several other studies lend support to Ghiselli's work (e.g. Dunnette, 1967; Nash, 1965).

All the above leadership models assume the existence of some trait characteristics that are universally associated with 'better' leadership style, and hence with higher subordinate performance. Several leadership theorists, however, criticise such universalist approaches on the grounds that they ignore the effects of situational

Table 3.1 *Ghiselli's personality and motivational traits*

Very important for managerial talent	100	Supervisory ability
	76	Occupational achievement
	64	Intelligence
		Self-actualisation
	61	Self-assurance
		Decisiveness
	54	Lack of need for security
	47	Working-class affinity
	34	Initiative
	20	Lack of need for high financial reward
	10	Need for power over others
	5	Maturity
Plays no part in managerial talent	0	Masculinity–femininity

contingencies on leadership style. More specifically these writers argue that rather than assume that there exists a dominant leadership style that is appropriate to all situations, the effective leadership style depends upon the prevailing contingencies.

Contingency Leadership Models

The models

Several versions of the contingency approach to leadership style have been suggested in the literature. Fiedler (1964, 1967) developed a contingency model the essence of which is that group or organisational effectiveness depends upon two interacting factors: (i) the personality of the leader (leadership style) and (ii) the degree to which the situation gives the leader control and influence. Leadership style could be employee-centred (relationship-motivated) or task-centred as indicated earlier. Fiedler measured leadership style using the Least Preferred Co-worker (LPC) scale according to which the leader is asked to describe the one person with whom he or she has been able to work least well. A task-centred leader is assumed to describe the least preferred co-worker in negative, rejecting terms and is characterised by failure to differentiate between a subordinate's achievements at work and his attributes in non-work related capacities. An employee-centred leader is assumed to be capable of differentiating between such different capacities.

The degree of the leader's situation control was measured using three sub-scales that indicate the degree to which (i) the leader is, or feels, supported by group members (leader–member relations), (ii) the task is clear-cut and structured (task structure) and (iii) the leader is able to obtain compliance through organisational sanctions (position power). The higher each of these is, the greater the situational control is assumed to be.

Fiedler's results indicate that desirable leadership characteristics depend upon the extent of situational control. Briefly speaking, the results suggest that task-centred leaders perform best when situational control is either high or low. On the other hand, employee-centred leaders seem to perform best when situational control is moderate. Fiedler rationalises these findings as follows. When situational control is high, the leader will be assured that his goals will be attained. Hence, an employee-centred leader will be concerned less with interpersonal relations with the group and more with securing esteem from his superiors by adopting task-oriented behaviour. On the other hand, a task-centred leader, being assured that the task will be accomplished, will devote more time to improving interpersonal relations with his subordinates.

When situational control is low there will be greater doubt that the leader's goals will be attained. Task-centred leaders will concentrate on task accomplishment whilst employee-centred leaders will focus on improving interpersonal relations with the group. Thus, Fiedler (1978a, p. 115) argued 'we cannot really talk about a "good" leader or a "poor" leader. Rather, leaders may be good in situations which match their leadership style and poor in situations in which leadership style and situational control are mismatched.'

Subsequently several refinements to the basic Fiedler model have been introduced by Fiedler (1971, 1972a, 1972b, 1973a, 1973b, 1978a, 1978b), Fiedler and Chemers (1974), Fiedler, Bons and Hastings (1975), Fiedler, Chemers and Mahar (1976), Mitchell et al. (1970), Bons and Fiedler (1976), and Csoka and Fiedler (1972). These studies introduced refinements in the leader–member relations classification, the Least Preferred Co-worker (LPC)–performance relations, and extended the domain of the original model from interacting task groups to coacting task groups. Moreover, these studies extended the basic contingency model to the domain of leadership dynamics by considering the effects of training and experience on performance. The findings here suggest that neither variable has any favourable effect on performance. For instance, it is held that leader training increases his influence and control through improved leader–member relations, task structuring, and position power. But, it is argued, such changes are equally likely to shift an individual into a good LPC situation match or out of it. Hence, an improvement in one person will be cancelled out by a decreased effectiveness of another. Overall, Fiedler's work stimulated a large body of research that was aimed at validating his results. Subsequent empirical research, however, suggests that Fiedler's results are inconclusive (Graen, 1969).

Vroom and Yetton (1973) have also developed two contingency models of leadership style: normative and descriptive. In their normative model they distinguish five management styles and seven situational variables. Management styles range on a continuum from autocratic, through consultative, to group democratic decision-making. Situational variables include characteristics such as the degree of problem structure, and the levels of goal congruence and conflict among subordinates. Vroom and Yetton argued that a profile of a particular decision-making problem on such situational characteristics should determine the appropriate leadership style. They cited the results of a limited number of empirical investigations which lend some support to the validity of their normative model (see also Yetton and Vroom, 1978).

In their descriptive version of the leadership model, Vroom and Yetton attempted to find out whether managers use all five leadership styles prescribed in their normative model, and which factors in the situation influence their choice of a decision process. The evidence that Vroom and Yetton cited lends support to the argument that problem characteristics are determinants of leadership style. Thus, managers seem to change their style as a function of the relevant situational characteristics:

> Whereas once there were only participative or autocratic managers, we now find that it makes as much sense to talk about participative and autocratic problems. Furthermore, there is likely to be interaction between individual and situational factors. Certainly, the studies have established the importance of situational factors as determinants of the level of subordinates' participation in decision making.
> (Yetton and Vroom, 1978, p. 146).

The premise on which the Vroom and Yetton model is based is that the more the decision situation requires the skills and the cooperation of the subordinates, the more will democratic leadership be appropriate in order to foster these skills and secure the requisite cooperation. The converse is assumed to hold for situations requiring modest skills and little cooperation.

In another contingency theory approach to leadership style attention has been focused on identifying the smallest number of dimensions that would adequately describe leader behaviour, and investigating how each dimension influences effectiveness in different situations. Using 'evidence' from studies of subordinates' perception of a leader's characteristic behaviour and leader self-description, two leadership dimensions were identified: 'initiating structure' and 'consideration' (e.g. Halpin and Winer, 1957).

'Initiating structure' reflects the extent to which an individual is likely to define and structure his role and those of his subordinates towards attaining organisational goals. A high score on this dimension indicates that the leader plays an active role in directing his subordinates' activities through, for example, planning and communications. 'Consideration', on the other hand, reflects the extent to which the leader is likely to display, in his work relationships with subordinates, mutual trust and respect for their feelings.

The results of various empirical investigations show some considerable consistency with respect to identifying both the initiating structure and the consideration dimensions of leadership. Furthermore, high correlations between consideration and job satisfaction have been reported (e.g. Fleishman, 1973; Badin, 1974). However, as Korman (1966) pointed out, only low correlations with performance have been reported for both initiating structure and consideration.

House (1971) developed a path–goal model of leadership in which he hypothesised that task complexity influences the relationships between leadership style and performance and satisfaction. He argued that with high task complexity individuals are likely to derive satisfaction and motivation from performing the task itself. Thus, it is held, the consideration dimension of leadership will be unrelated to effectiveness; indeed, in this situation it is redundant. On the other hand, the initiating structure dimension will facilitate the attainment of the path–goals and, thus, will be directly related to satisfaction and performance. When the tasks are routine and structured, House argued, considerate leadership will help reduce task frustration and will improve satisfaction and performance, whilst initiating structure will be viewed as excessive control and will be uncorrelated with performance and negatively correlated with satisfaction.

The findings of a subsequent study by House and Dessler (1974) provide supportive 'evidence' for House's model. However, the results of other studies contradict those reported above. For example, Downey, Sheridan and Slocum (1975) reported that considerate leadership was most related to job satisfaction, whilst initiating structure was not related to perceptions of performance, irrespective of task structure. Further, Stinson and Johnson (1975) reported that initiating structure and satisfaction were more positively correlated when tasks were more highly structured and repetitive than when they were not. Moreover, Katz (1978) has reported that the strength of the relationships between the dimensions of leadership style and the criteria of performance and satisfaction seem to be contingent upon the type of intragroup conflict experienced by subordinates. The results of his field study and laboratory experiment indicate that a positive relationship between performance and the structuring dimension exists, and that this relationship was intensified when high affective conflict was present. This is in contrast to what one might expect: subordinates experiencing intragroup conflict and stress may be expected to desire less structuring and more considerate leadership.

An evaluation

Several propositions concerning the initiating structure and consideration dimensions on the one hand, and job satisfaction, subordinate's morale, and performance on the other hand have been formulated by several writers (see, for example, Fleishman 1973; Badin 1974; Kerr et al. 1974). However, because of the nature of the empirical 'evidence' provided by the relevant studies, most of these propositions are fairly weak. Just as the contingency theory of organisational design stimulated a substantial body of research so did the contingency theory of leadership style. Several researchers sought to test the validity of the propositions derived by the various contingency models of leadership. As indicated earlier, the findings of many studies do not seem to point in the same direction and in some cases are contradictory. A detailed consideration of this literature is beyond the scope of this chapter but an example will suffice to illustrate the point.

Consider for instance Fiedler's leadership model. Although support for the basic Fiedler model has been reported by some researchers, only in a few cases has the model been comprehensively supported (see in particular Chemers and Skrzypek, 1972). The majority of other 'supportive' studies report only partial support (e.g. Hovey, 1974; Csoka, 1975; Schneier, 1978). The findings of many other studies do not support, and at times contradict, Fiedler's model. Thus, in a study by Vecchio (1977), an analysis of the correlations between Least Preferred Co-worker (LPC) and group task performance provides no support for the model. Further, a study by Utechet and Heier (1976) indicates that the behaviour of leaders did not correspond to the behaviour predicted by the model for leaders' (LPC) scores.

Similarly, several studies, as Fiedler (1972a) conceded, have raised considerable doubt regarding the view that low LPC leaders are task-centred whilst high LPC leaders are employee-centred. This has led Fiedler to revise his position by arguing that leadership behaviour is a consequence of the individual's primary and secondary motive systems in interaction with the unfavourableness inherent in the situation. For example, Fiedler contends, low LPC leaders would be principally task-centred in unfavourable situations but as the latter become more favourable so they would tend to exhibit more consideration towards their employees. This is known as the motivational hierarchy interpretation. Yet, the findings of subsequent research (e.g. Larson and Rowland, 1973; Rice and Chemers, 1975; Green and Nebeker, 1977; Schneier, 1978) indicate that the motivational hierarchy interpretation has much more support in the case of leaders with high LPC scores compared with those with low LPC scores; the latter do not appear to vary their behaviour according to the degree of situational favourability.

Several more examples can be cited to illustrate the conflicting nature of the 'evidence' in respect of any of the contingency leadership models discussed earlier. Suffice it to say that the only safe conclusion that can be made is that the propositions of the contingency theory of leadership are, at best, inconclusive. Indeed, the main criticisms that have been raised against the contingency theory of leadership are virtually the same as those raised against the contingency theory of organisational design.

One basic criticism is related to the methodologies employed in the empirical studies. In particular, references to measurement limitations have frequently been made. This can be exemplified by further considering Fiedler's model. Several studies employed different measurement and classification systems of leader–member relations, task structure, and position power (see, for example, McMahon, 1972). Similarly, the basic Fiedler model postulates reliable and stable measures of LPC.

Yet, several subsequent studies (e.g. Stinson and Tracy, 1974; Fox, 1976; Rice, 1978) have indicated that LPC measures are not stable over time. Various *ad hoc* classifications and inconsistent measures have also been used in different studies thereby making their results difficult to generalise. Furthermore, the propositions of the contingency models of leadership are typically drawn from cross-sectional studies (and this is true of all contingency leadership models) when what is really needed is longitudinal evidence. Short-run data could be misleading in the sense that adverse implications of, say, authoritarian leadership on employee morale and productivity may only become noticeable in the long-run.

A second limitation commonly shared by the contingency models of leadership is the ambiguity of much of their terminology. Thus, although the primary goal of these models is to prescribe/describe the most effective leadership styles, leadership effectiveness is rarely defined. When effective leadership is defined, it is normally defined by reference to the attainment of organisational goals (see, for example, the models developed by Fiedler, and Vroom and Yetton). To the extent that organisational goals are narrowly defined to encompass only the goals of the dominant coalition, the derived propositions may cover only relatively few dimensions of effective leadership. Other important concepts are characterised by similar ambiguity. For instance, it is not clear what the meaning of LPC is; an investigation of Fiedler's work reveals that several different interpretations of LPC have been used. Likewise, Vroom and Yetton faced similar problems in defining and classifying situational contingencies.

Thirdly, doubts have been expressed about the usefulness of contingency models of leadership for managerial guidance. The proponents of these models argue that they would be useful in guiding management in matters such as leaders' transfer, rotation, selection, training and so on. Yet, in order to put these models to practical use, one needs to know in advance the values of contingency variables for which different leadership styles are required. Without such knowledge, leadership style and situational contingencies may be mismatched. Moreover, some rather 'odd' implications may be deduced from these propositions. Thus, Fiedler's work indicates that the leader should be placed in a situation appropriate to his LPC score. But it is held that it is easier to change the aspects of the situation than to change the attributes of the leader as measured by his LPC score. The leader is expected, therefore, to modify his leadership situation in order to attain a greater degree of situational favourableness. But this type of reasoning could have some undesirable implications:

> Make no mistake about what Fiedler and his associates are suggesting here. Despite the ever-present possibility of leader change through illness or transfer, they are seriously recommending that in some circumstances good leader–member relations should intentionally be harmed, or goal clarity impaired, or other element of situational favourableness altered so as to establish congruence with a leader's LPC score, even though the chance of a substantial shift in LPC by even the same leader, after only a few weeks time, is quite likely.
> (Schriesheim and Kerr, 1977, p. 54).

Fourthly, just as in the case of the contingency theory of organisational design, the contingency models of leadership are mechanistic and deterministic. The dynamic multi-directional interactions between situational contingencies and leader characteristics are typically ignored. Thus, in the context of, for example, the Fiedler model, the leader is perceived to have choices with respect to his style and the manipulation of situational variables. Yet clearly these choices must be partly constrained by the existing organisational structure. Doubts have also been expressed about the adequacy of authoritarian leadership in any organisational setting, given people's natural reaction against this type of leadership (e.g. Yankelovich, 1974). Moreover, the simple characterisation of leadership along the authoritarian-democratic dimension or consideration-initiating structure dimension with only one mode being effective for a given set of situations is rather restrictive. Leadership characteristics are much more complex than this. Acknowledging this point, several researchers have attempted to consider a more complex set of leadership characteristics.

Yukl (1971) demonstrated that initiating structure and consideration are independent of the authoritarian-democratic continuum: a leader can initiate in an authoritarian or a democratic manner. Similarly, an authoritarian leader can be considerate to his subordinates whilst a democratic leader can be harsh. Given this reasoning, Yukl advanced a multiple-linkage model which covers all four dimensions in determining leadership effectiveness. He thus argued that consideration by the leader motivates subordinates to work better and, hence, improves performance. Yukl also maintained that the higher the leader's initiating structure (concern for performance), the greater the effect of consideration on performance. Again, he contended that democratic leadership increases subordinate motivation and this is particularly the case when groups identify with management goals, support the leader, and acquire the requisite skills. Further, Yukl suggested that initiating structure improves performance because leaders in this case can improve subordinates' skills and the structuring of the task-role organisation. Finally, he argued that democratic leadership will influence task-role organisation as long as subordinates are skilled and motivated.

Mintzberg (1973) advocated using 10 dimensions to categorise leadership behaviour. These dimensions represent a set of roles for the leader as figurehead, leader, liaison officer, monitor, disseminator, spokesman, entrepreneur, disturbance-handler, resource-allocator, and negotiator. The dimensions, it is held, are comprehensive enough to explain adequately the nature of managerial work. Similarly, Korman, Noon, and Ryan (cited in Korman, 1977) identified in their empirical work five leadership behaviour dimensions: (i) intellectual, planning, and analytic skills, (ii) respect for subordinate competence, (iii) concern and responsibility, (iv) dysfunctional self-presentation and (v) planning and adequacy of perspective.

Butler (1978, p. 152) suggested a model in which leadership is seen as 'a process in which the leader has certain choices to make concerning his style and manipulation of situational variables, but these choices are, in fact, partly constrained by structure'. He defined leadership power as a two dimensional concept combining both formal and informal power. He cites 'evidence' which suggests that if the leader succeeds in making tasks more specific and more routine, he will inevitably increase his power over his subordinates. But the extent of manoeuvre available to the leader to increase his power depends upon the organisational structure. Organisational structure affects the leader's situation and, thus, provides both opportunities and constraints for the leader. For example, Butler reports that workflow rigidity is negatively correlated with informal power; in a situation of low workflow rigidity it is easier for the leader to develop and increase his informal power (e.g. by having time for informal conversation with subordinates).

Similar analogies linking leadership styles and other dimensions of organisational structure can be drawn. Thus, Pugh et al. (1968) classified organisational structure into three dimensions: structuring of activities; concentration of authority; and line control of workflow. To sum up, Butler (1978, p. 160) concluded his study by arguing that leaders are overwhelmingly made by the organisation within which they have to operate. The organisation, in turn, is greatly influenced by the context within which it operates ... But the leader does have some choice. In order to increase his power he must assess his situation in relation to the organisation structure within which he operates.

Clearly, none of the above studies provides an exhaustive list of leadership dimensions. They are merely cited as examples to illustrate the inadequacy of the simple notions of leadership dimensions advocated by the contingency models of leadership.

IV. SUMMARY

Discussion in this chapter has focused primarily on aspects of human motivation and leadership styles. This involved consideration of various theories of human motivation, some specific reference to the use of expectancy theory in management accounting, and finally a discussion of some important models of leadership styles.

In considering theories of human motivation, several interesting points emerge. Firstly, hypotheses concerning human motivation were initially universalist, in the sense of positing instinctive behaviour, but gradually became individual-specific. Secondly, the theories differ in terms of whether their unit of analysis is the individual, the group, or both. For example, it could be argued that the need-hierarchy theory emphasises group behaviour, the achievement motivation theory emphasises individual behaviour, and equity theory focuses on both individual and group behaviour. Thirdly, the set of variables identified by each theory as being particularly prominent in the context of human motivation varies across theories. As more theories were developed new motivational variables were included in the analysis, sometimes at the expense of previously specified variables which were later perceived as being less important.

Notwithstanding these differences the domains of motivation theories overlap, at times quite considerably (contrast, for example, equity theory and expectancy theory). Each theory has had its fair share of empirical support but in the main most of these empirical tests are fraught with considerable measurement problems.

Models of leadership style appear to have followed an evolutionary path not dissimilar to the one followed by organisation theory itself. Initially, the models attempted to define a universal set of leadership traits appropriate to all situations. This was followed by contingency formulations in which leadership traits were assumed to be dependent on the prevailing situational contingencies. Finally, a post-contingency approach emerged in which the role of managerial choice is acknowledged.

Irrespective of the inherent limitations of each of the theories of motivation and the models of leadership styles, they all have important implications for the design and use of accounting controls. Some indication of this importance has already been alluded to in this chapter in considering the extensions of expectancy models to the management accounting context. Other illustrations of the relevance of much of the above literature to management accounting literature are offered throughout this book, but in particular in chapters 14 and 15.

REFERENCES

Adams, J. S. 1963. Towards an understanding of inequity, *Journal of Abnormal and Social Psychology*, **67**, pp. 422–436.

Alderfer, C. P. 1972. *Existence, Relatedness, and Growth: Human Needs in Organisational Settings*: Free Press.

Atkinson, J.W. 1977. Motivation for achievement, in T. Blass (ed.) *Personality Variables in Social Behaviour*. Hillsdale, NJ: Erlbaum Associates pp. 25–108.

Badin, I. J. 1974. Some moderator influences on relationships between consideration, initiating structure and organizational criteria, *Journal of Applied Psychology*, **59**, pp. 380–382.

Bons, P. M. & Fiedler, F. E. 1976. Changes in organizational leadership and the behaviour of relationship and task-motivated leaders, *Administrative Science Quarterly*, **21**, pp. 453–473.

Butler, R. J. 1978. Towards an organisational control and power theory of leadership, in B. King, S. Streufert and F. E. Fiedler (eds) *Managerial Control and Organisational Democracy*: V. H. Winston and Sons, pp. 151–162.

Campbell, D. B. 1971. Relative influence of job and supervision on shared work attitudes, *Journal of Applied Psychology*, **55**, pp. 521–525.

Chemers, M. M. and Skrzypek, G. J. 1972. Experimental test of the contingency model of leadership effectiveness, *Journal of Personality and Social Psychology*, **24**, pp. 172–177.

Clarke, J. V. 1960. Motivation in work groups: a tentative view, *Human Organization*, **13**, pp. 199–208.

Cosier, R. A. and Dalton, D. R. 1983. Equity theory and time: a reformulation, *Academy of Management Review*, **8**(2), pp. 311–319.

Csoka, L. S. 1975. Relationship between organizational climate and the situational favourableness dimension of Fiedler's contingency model, *Journal of Applied Psychology*, **60**, pp. 273–277.

Csoka, L. S. & Fiedler, F. E. 1972. The effect of a military leadership training: a test of the contingency model, *Organizational Behaviour and Human Performance*, **8**, pp. 395–407.

Cumin, P. C. 1967. TAT correlates of executive performance, *Journal of Applied Psychology*, **51**, pp. 78–81.

Downey, H., Sheridan, J., and Slocum, J. 1975. Analysis of relationships among leader behaviour, subordinate job performance and satisfaction: a path-goal approach, *Academy of Management Journal*, **18**, pp. 253–262.

Dunnette, M. 1967. Predictors of executive success, pp. 7–48 in F. R. Wickert and D. E. McFarland (eds), *Measuring Executive Effectiveness*. New York: Appleton-Century-Crofts.

Fiedler, F. E. 1964. A contingency model of leadership effectiveness, pp. 149–190 in L. Berkowitz (ed.) *Advances in Experimental Social Psychology*, vol. 1. New York: Academic Press.

Fiedler, F. E. 1967. *A Theory of Leadership Effectiveness*. New York: McGraw-Hill.

Fiedler, F. E. 1971. Validation and extension of the contingency model of leadership effectiveness: a review of empirical findings, *Psychological Bulletin*, **76**, pp. 128–148.

Fiedler, F. E. 1972a. Personality, motivational systems, and behaviour of high and low LPC persons, *Human Relations*, **25**, pp. 391–412.

Fiedler, F. E. 1972b. The effects of leadership training and experience: a contingency model interpretation, *Administrative Science Quarterly*, **17**, pp. 453–470.

Fiedler, F. E. 1973a. Personality and situational determinants of leader behaviour, pp. 41–61 in E. A. Fleishman and J. G. Hunt (eds) *Current Developments in the Study of Leadership*. Carbondale, IL: Southern Illinois University Press.

Fiedler, F. E. 1973b. Predicting the effects of leadership training and experience from the contingency model: a clarification, *Journal of Applied Psychology* **57** pp. 110–113.

Fiedler, F. E. 1978a. Situational control and a dynamic theory of leadership, pp. 107–131 in B. King, S. Streufert, and F. E. Fiedler (eds) *Managerial Control and Organizational Democracy*. New York: Wiley.

Fiedler, F. E. 1978b. The contingency model and the dynamics of the leadership process, pp. 59–112 in L. Berkowitz (ed.), *Advances in Experimental Social Psychology*, vol. 11. New York: Academic Press.

Fiedler, F. E. and Chemers, M. M. 1974. *Leadership and Effective Management*. Glenview, IL: Scot, Foresman and Co.

Fiedler, F. E., Bons, P. M. and Hastings, L. L. 1975. New strategies for leadership utilization, pp. 233–244 in W. T. Singleton and P. Spurgeon (eds) *Measurement of Human Resources*. New York: Halsted Press.

Fiedler, F. E., Chemers, M. M., and Mahar, L. 1976. *Improving Leadership Effectiveness: The Leader Match Concept*. New York: Wiley.

Fleishman, E. A. 1973. Twenty years of consideration and structure, in E. A. Fleishman and J. G. Hunt (eds) *Current Developments in the Study of Leadership*. Carbondale IL: Southern Illinois University Press.

Fox, W. M. 1976. Reliabilities, means, and standard deviations for LPC scales: instrument refinement, *Academy of Management Journal* **19** pp. 450–461.

Galbraith, J. and Cummings, L. L. 1967. An empirical investigation of the motivational determinants of past performance: incentive effects between instrumentality, valence, motivations and ability, *Organizational Behaviour and Human Performance* **8** pp. 237–257.

Georgopoulos, B. S., Mahoney, G. M., and Jones, N. W. 1957. A path-goal approach to productivity, *Journal of Applied Psychology* **41** pp. 345–353.

Ghiselli, E. 1963. The validity of management traits related to occupational level, *Personnel Psychology* **16**, pp. 109–113.

Ghiselli, E. 1971. *Explorations in Management Talent*. Pacific Palisades, Calif: Goodyear Publishing.

Graen, G. B. 1969. Instrumentality theory of work motivation: some experimental results and suggested modifications, *Journal of Applied Psychology Monographs* **53** part 2.

Green, S. G. and Nebeker, D. M. 1977. The effects of situational factors and leadership style on leader behaviour, *Organizational Behaviour and Human Performance* **19** pp. 368–377.

Greene, C. N. 1975. The reciprocal nature of influence between leader and subordinate, *Journal of Applied Psychology* **60** pp. 187–193.

Halpin, A. and Winer, B. 1957. A factorial study of the leader behaviour descriptions in R. Stogdill and A. Coons (eds) *Leader Behaviour: Its Description and Measurement*. Ohio State University.

Herzberg, F. 1966. *Work and the Nature of Man*. Cleveland: World.

Herzberg, F. 1976. *The Managerial Choice: To Be Efficient and To Be Human*. Homewood, IL: Dow-Jones-Irwin.

House, R. 1971. A path-goal theory of leader effectiveness, *Administrative Science Quarterly* **16** pp. 321–338.

House, R. and Dessler, G. 1974. The path-goal theory of leadership, in J. G. Hunt and L. L. Larson (eds) *Contingency Approaches to Leadership*. Carbondale, IL: Southern Illinois University Press.

Hovey, D. E. 1974. The low-powered leader confronts a messy problem; a test of Fiedler's Theory, *Academy of Management Journal* **17** pp. 358–362.

Kahn, R. L. 1956. The prediction of productivity, *Journal of Sociological Issues* **12**(2), pp. 41–49.

Katz, D. and Kahn, R. L. 1951. Human organisation and worker motivation, pp. 146–171 in L. Reed Tripp (ed.), *Industrial Productivity*. Madison, Wis: Industrial Relations Research Association.

Katz, D. and Kahn, R. L. 1952. Some recent findings in human relations research, pp. 650–665 in E. Swanson, T. Newcomb, and E. Hartley (eds) *Readings in Social Psychology*. New York: Holt, Rinehart and Winston.

Katz, R. 1978. Towards a theory of the leadership process, in B. King, S. Streufert, and F. E. Fiedler (eds) *Management Control and Organizational Democracy*. Washington, D. C.: V. H. Winston & Sons.

Kerr, S. A., Schriesheim, C. A., Murphy, C. J. and Stogdill, R. M. 1974. Towards a contingency theory of leadership based upon the consideration and initiating structure literature, *Organizational Behaviour and Human Performance* **12**, pp. 62–82.

Korman, A. 1966. Consideration, initiating structure and organizational criteria – a review, *Personnel Psychology*, **19**, winter, pp. 349–362.

Korman, A. 1977. *Organizational Behaviour*. Englewood Cliffs, N. J: Prentice-Hall.

Larson, L. L. and Rowland, K. M. 1973. Leadership style, stress, and behaviour in task performance, *Organizational Behaviour and Human Performance* **9** pp. 407–420.

Leventhal, G. S., Weiss, T. and Long, G. 1969. Equity, reciprocity, and reallocating rewards in the dyad, *Journal of Personality and Social Psychology* **13** pp. 300–305.

Levine, E. L. 1973. Patterns of organizational control in microcosm: group performance and group member satisfaction as a function of differences in control structure, *Journal of Applied Psychology* **58**, pp. 186–196.

Lewin, K. 1951. *Field Theory and Social Science*: Harper.

Likert, R. 1961. An emerging theory of organization, leadership and management, in L. Petrullo and B. M. Bass (eds) *Leadership and Interpersonal Behaviour*. New York: Holt, Rinehart and Winston.

Locke, E. A. 1976a. The nature and causes of job satisfaction, pp. 1297–1349 in M. D. Dunnette (ed.), *Handbook of Industrial and Organizational Psychology*: Rand McNally.

Locke, E. A. 1976b. Personnel attitudes and motivation, *Annual Review of Psychology* **26** pp. 457–480.

Maslow, A. H. 1943. A theory of human motivation. *Psychological Review* **50** pp. 370–396.

Maslow, A. H. 1954. *Motivation and Personality*. New York: Harper and Row.

McClelland, D. C. 1961. *The Achieving Society*. Princeton, NJ: Van Nostrand.

McClelland, D. C. 1962. Toward a theory of motive acquisitions, *Harvard Business Review* **40**(4) pp. 99–112.

McClelland, D. C. 1975. *Power: The Inner Experience*. New York: Irvington.

McGregor, D. 1960. *The Human Side of Enterprise*. New York: McGraw-Hill.

McMahon, J. T. 1972. The contingency theory: logic and method revisited, *Personnel Psychology* **25** pp. 697–710.

Miner, J. B. 1980. *Theories of Organizational Behaviour*: The Dryden Press.

Mintzberg, H. 1973. *The Nature of Managerial Work*. New York: Harper and Row.

Mitchell, T. R. 1977. Expectancy and expected value: decision models for organizations, *Organization and Administrative Sciences* **8** pp. 97–115.

Mitchell, T. R., Biglan, A., Oncken, G. R. and Fiedler, F. E. 1970. The contingency model: criticism and suggestions, *Academy of Management Journal* **13** pp. 253–267.

Nash, A. 1965. Vocational interests of effective managers: a review of the literature, *Personnel Psychology* **18**, pp. 21–38.

Porter, L. W. 1964. *Organizational Patterns of Managerial Job Attitudes*: American Foundation for Management Research.

Porter, L. W. and Lawler, E. E. 1968. *Managerial Attitudes and Performance*. Homewood, Ill: Irwin.

Pugh, D. S., Hickson, D. J., Hinings, C. R., and Turner, C. 1968. Dimensions of organization structure, *Administrative Science Quarterly* **13** pp. 65–105.

Rice, R. W. 1978. Psychometric properties of the esteem for least preferred coworker (LPC) scale, *Academy of Management Review* **3** pp. 106–117.

Rice, R. W. and Chemers, M. M. 1975. Personality and situational determinants of leader behaviour, *Journal of Applied Psychology* **60** pp. 20–27.

Rockness, H. O. 1977. Expectancy theory in a budgetary setting: an experimental examination, *Accounting Review*, October, pp. 893–904.

Ronen, J. and Livingstone, J. L. 1975. An expectancy theory approach to the motivational impacts of budgets, *Accounting Review*, October, pp. 671–685.

Schneier, C. E. 1978. The contingency model of leadership: an extension to emergent leadership and leader's sex, *Organizational Behaviour and Human Performance* **21** pp. 220–239.

Schriesheim, C. A. and Kerr, S. 1977. Theories and measures of leadership: a critical appraisal of current and future directions, pp. 9–45, 51–56 in J. G. Hunt and L. L. Larson (eds) *Leadership: The Cutting Edge*. Carbondale, Ill: Southern Illinois University Press.

Schwab, D. P., DeVitt, H. W., and Cummings, L. L. 1971. A test of the adequacy of the two-factor theory as a predictor of self-report performance effects, *Personnel Psychology* **24** pp. 293–303.

Steiner, G. A. and Miner, J. B. 1977. *Management Policy and Strategy*. New York: Macmillan.

Stinson, J. and Johnson, T. 1975. The path-goal theory of leadership: a partial test and suggested refinement, *Academy of Management Journal* **18** pp. 242–252.

Stinson, J. E. and Tracy, L. 1974. Some disturbing characteristics of LPC score, *Personnel Psychology* **27**, pp. 477–485.

Tannenbaum, A. S. 1962. Control in organizations: individual adjustment and organizational performance, *Administrative Science Quarterly* **7**, pp. 236–257.

Tannenbaum, A. S. 1966. *Social Psychology of the Work Organization*. Belmont, Calif: Wadsworth Publishing.

Tannenbaum, A. S. and Kahn, R. L. 1958. *Participation in Union Locals*. Evanston, Ill: Row, Peterson and Co.

Tuzzolino, F. and Armandi, B. R. 1981. 'A need-hierarchy framework for assessing corporate social responsibility', *Academy of Management Review,* **6**(1), pp. 21–28.

Utechet, R. E. and Heier, W. D. 1976. The contingency model and successful military leadership, *Academy of Management Journal* **19** pp. 606–618.

Vecchio, R. P. 1977. An examination of the validity of Fiedler's model of leadership effectiveness, *Organizational Behaviour and Human Performance* **19** pp. 180–206.

Vecchio, P. 1982. 'Predicting worker performance in inequitable settings', *Academy of Management Review,* **7**, pp. 103–110.

Vroom, V. H. 1964. *Work and Motivation*: Wiley.

Vroom, V. H. and Yetton, P. W. 1973. *Leadership and Decision Making*. Pittsburgh: University of Pittsburgh Press.

Wahba, M. A. and Bridwell, L. G. 1976. Maslow reconsidered: a review of research on the need hierarchy theory, *Organizational Behaviour and Human Performance* **15** pp. 212–240.

Weiner, B. 1972. *Theories of Motivation: From Mechanism to Cognition*. Chicago: Markham.

Yankelovich, D. 1974. Turbulence in the working world: angry workers, happy grads, *Psychology Today* pp. 80–89.

Yetton, P. W. and Vroom, V. H. 1978. The Vroom-Yetton model of leadership: an overview, pp. 133–149 in B. King, S. Streufert, and F.E. Fiedler (eds) *Managerial Control and Organizational Democracy*: V. H. Winston & Sons.

Yukl, G. A. 1971. Toward a behavioural theory of leadership, *Organizational Behaviour and Human Performance* **6**, pp. 414–440.

4

Organisational Control and Management Accounting

by Jeremy Dent and Mahmoud Ezzamel

The notion of organisational control is susceptible to many different interpretations. Different researchers approach the topic from their own particular backgrounds and stress different aspects of the totality of the organisational control process. For the purposes of this chapter, however, it seems sensible to adopt a broad definition of organisational control, which will then be used to consider the contribution of management accounting.

The need for a mechanism for the internal control of an organisation is self evident. It arises from the fundamental nature of organisations. The organisation embodies a coalition of participants. Each participant may have his own, possibly divergent, demands and some discretion in his choice of actions. Organisational control may be interpreted as the problem of ensuring some consistency in organisational activities. But demands change over time. The operating characteristics of the organisation evolve. Information is unevenly distributed. Participants may engage in strategic manoeuvering. Organisational control is thus complex and multifaceted.

In this chapter it is argued that the study of organisational control has been only partial. Researchers tend to concentrate on different elements of the control process and often ignore the complexities of the organisational context. Yet it is precisely the complex interaction between different controls which gives organisations their coherence in a dynamic evolving world.

Section I of this chapter contains a description of some traditional approaches to the problems of organisational control, and their influence on accounting research. Section II contains a discussion of a somewhat modified systems approach to characterise the interconnectedness of organisational functioning in an explicit way. Section III considers the ambiguous role of information in organisational control, and section IV presents a framework for analysis. In section V conclusions are drawn, and implications for future research are discussed.

I. SOME TRADITIONAL APPROACHES TO ORGANISATIONAL CONTROL

Consider, for a moment, a moderately-sized manufacturing organisation operating in a relatively stable environment. The organisation may be subject to a range of conflicting demands. It may market a number of products. It may have a complex technology with production centred at several different locations. It may have a critical flow of resources between production centres. Information about the environment and the operating characteristics of the organisation may be concentrated at localised points. Such data as is transmitted to other members may be biased or randomly inaccurate, and subject to processing delay. The task of coordinating the separate activities of such an organisation is likely to be formidable. Moreover, recognition of environmental/technological change and instability adds a further dimension to the control process. Effective control implies some sensitiy to changing patterns of demand, technology, and economic and social expectations.

The Classical Approach to Control

Not unnaturally writers from different disciplines respond to the complexitiy of the problem in different ways. For example, in what Arrow (1964) has termed the 'classical businessman's view' emphasis is placed on the need for decentralised coordination. In this approach the problem of control is tackled through the establishment of one integrated plan of action for the organisation as a whole. The plan is devolved into a series of specific coordinated tasks for each segment or participant in the organisation. Formal rules and procedures limit the discretion required at lower levels in the organisation. Emphasis is placed on vertical control through the line of authority. Centralised coordination is seen as essential in the face of the sheer complexity of organisational operations.

Such is the essence of the classical approach to management. The central planners are considered to have superior knowledge of the interrelationship and operating characteristics of the organisation. Moreover they are presumed to be better able to take a corporate view of the organisation and its interrelationship with the environment. Tasks are unambiguously defined. Minimal flexibility is permitted to subordinates. Power, in the sense of the formal authority conferred by the organisational hierarchy, is relied upon. Compliance is engineered through the use of sanctions and rewards.

In contrast, other theorists have tended to argue that the centralised approach to organisational control is potentially sub-optimal (e.g. Williamson, 1975). For one thing it is likely to be inefficient. As the size and complexity of the firm increases the centralised approach may impose a considerable load on the planning authorities. Extra communication channels will be required to transmit organisational and environmental data to the planning officials, and detailed plans to lower organisational levels. Moreover, centralisation may not be particularly effective. Data typically does not flow noiselessly within an information system. Random errors occur, filtering effects take place and biases are introduced. Thus plans may not reflect the underlying circumstances of the firm. Nor is the centralised approach instantaneous. Data communication is subject to delay, plans take time to be prepared. In a dynamic environment adaptation may be impaired.

These researchers have considered the possibility of developing a decentralised alternative to the problem of organisational control (see chapters 11, 12, and 13). If, it is argued, the firm can be treated as a number of semi-autonomous subunits, and decision making devolved to those levels in the organisation where information is available at first hand, so it may be possible to increase the efficiency and the effectiveness of control procedures. Data is likely to be more accurate. The load on communication channels is reduced as operating decisions are taken by local managers. Subordinates are also encouraged to adapt to prevailing circumstances.

Of course, there are likely to be problems in coordinating the actions of individual decision makers. Far-reaching interdependencies may exist between subunits, for example, in the form of resource transfers between units, or in the form of external effects imposed by some units upon others. The full extent of these interdependencies may not be immediately apparent to decision makers at the operating level, neither may there be any incentive for local managers to take them into account. Certain units may be in a position of power relative to others and there may be a temptation to engage in 'unfair practices' detrimental to the organisation as a whole. Various structural and financial controls have been designed to address these problems (see chapters 12 and 13).

Such a liberal approach to organisational control may be appealing. Nevertheless, on closer inspection one is inclined to focus on potential difficulties in implementation. The problem posed by intraorganisation externalities, for instance, is quite significant. The control of externalities through the price mechanism is known to be feasible (e.g. Collard, 1973), but it will generally necessitate some measure of centralised planning (Davis and Whinston, 1962). The recognition of uncertainty further complicates the issue. Each subunit manager will face a choice under uncertainty, and his choices will depend partly on his attitude towards risk. In the absence of insurance against uncertain consequences or specific reward structures such as those discussed in the theory of agency (e.g. Holmstrom, 1979) only by chance will local managers take appropriate decisions.

Neoclassical Approaches to Control

The efficiency and effectiveness of decentralised control is, therefore, debatable: the optimal strategy in any particular situation is not clear cut. A priori, no particular procedure can be unambiguously defended. To an extent, however, the issues of control are only partially addressed by such mechanistic considerations. Cyert and March (1963) for example, focus on the divergent goals of individual participants, and on the conflict and bargaining that takes place within the organisation (see chapter 2). In their analysis, organisations are perceived to exist and thrive with considerable latent conflict of goals. The formal and informal bargaining procedures that are developed are fundamental elements of the organisational control process; hence the attention given to organisational equilibrium (inducements–contribution theory, March and Simon, 1958), and side payments (Cyert and March, 1963). Control, in this sense, is not predominantly a problem of formal structure, but a behavioural or social problem.

This issue is touched upon in the structural analysis. The classical view, for example, is characterised by the assertion that man is naturally lazy and wasteful, and that appropriate behaviour can be bought by an exchange of money. The formal reward structure is an essential element of the classical 'control package'. This presumption forms the basis of the economic analysis of agency theory (see chapter 11). On the other hand, much of the economic literature on decentralisation takes conflict as non-problematic (e.g. Marschak and Radner, 1972). The immense diversity of individual needs and aspirations is a distinguishing feature of organisations, and should be recognised in the analysis of organisational control.

This focus on the richer social and psychological aspects of organisations has been the hallmark of neoclassical organisational researchers. Principles of specialisation, hierarchy and impersonality are held to frustrate individual needs for autonomy, responsibility and self-actualisation (e.g. McGregor, 1960; Likert, 1961). Effective performance, these writers have argued, is only obtained when tasks are made intrinsically stimulating and rewarding. Job enlargement and job enrichment programmes are advocated to increase the size, scope and variety of work (e.g. Herzberg, 1966). Participation schemes and management-by-objectives are advocated to encourage ego-identification with corporate goals (e.g. Bennis, 1966). The emphasis on job involvement and self control is central to the human resources analysis of organisational control.

In a slightly different vein, the human relations school, including such writers as Lewin (1947) and Likert (1961), have stressed the role of groups and the informal organisation in influencing organisational activities. Groups, particularly cohesive groups, it is argued, exert a powerful influence on behaviour. Individuals have affiliative needs which can be satisfied by a group, such as a sense of belonging, support, reinforcement, security, encouragement and so on. Membership of a group involves mutual commitment and shared ideals. From these develop attitudinal norms and behavioural expectations. Discipline is enforced through a system of informal sanctions and rewards. Group support may be withdrawn. Members may be ridiculed or ostracised (e.g. Tannenbaum, 1966).

Group pressure is thus a potentially significant source of control which should be harnessed towards organisational effectiveness. According to Likert (1961) intergroup conflict should be handled by explicit incorporation of 'linking pins' in organisational design. Change should be managed through consensus and group acceptance. The creation of a supportive work environment is considered to be central to high morale and efficiency. Thus, it is argued, the 'consideration' and 'initiating' dimensions of leadership are crucial elements in organisational control (e.g. Halpin and Winer, 1957).

The human orientation of neoclassical organisation theory stands in some contrast to the structural and economic orientation. The emphasis on individual aspirations and group cohesiveness adds another dimension to the control process. On the other hand, the position of these researchers is almost ideological. Conflict is treated as evil, symptomatic of poor management, and something to be eliminated. Harmony and consensus are seen as indicative of good health (Baritz, 1960). Yet this proposition is equivocal at best. Unresolved conflict may be good or bad; it may generate functional and dysfunctional consequences (Pondy, 1967). Consensus may breed complacency and an unquestioning acceptance of the status quo. Organisations may need a measure of conflict to stimulate change and innovation.

Implications for Accounting

These approaches do illustrate different conceptions of control, and they have each had their impact on accounting thought. The authoritarian approach to organisational control has been the basis for much of the traditional practice of management accounting. Budgetary procedures serve to facilitate control through centralisation. Targets are specified for each functional area of the firm. Variance analysis procedures serve to reinforce the threat of sanctions and rewards. As the firm's environment becomes increasingly hostile or dynamic, or its operations increasingly complex and interdependent, so a greater emphasis is placed on the need for budgetary control. Budgets become tighter; standards become more rigorously enforced and formal authority becomes more in evidence (e.g. Argyris, 1952; Caplan, 1968).

The human orientation of neoclassical theory has led to an impressive volume of accounting research into the motivational impact of budgets (e.g. Hofstede, 1967; Stedry, 1960; Tosi, 1975), covering such issues as the impact of budgets on dysfunctional managerial behaviour (e.g. Schiff and Lewin, 1970; Hopwood, 1972; Otley, 1978), the effects of budgetary participation (e.g. Becker and Green, 1962; Searfoss and Monczka, 1973; Kenis, 1979), the accounting implications of group dynamics (e.g. Flamholtz, 1975) and human resource accounting (e.g. Flamholtz, 1972).

Similarly the research on decentralisation has led to the development of measures for assessing the financial performance of decentralised units (e.g. Solomons, 1963) and evaluations of transfer pricing mechanisms (e.g. Abdel-khalik and Lusk, 1974).

But, underlying this research are implicit assumptions about the nature of organisational control and the role of accounting in organisational functioning. Control is perceived as a homogeneous goal-oriented process. Objectives for accounting are taken as unambiguous. In reality, however, organisations are complex and multi-faceted. Goals may be loosely articulated (March, 1979). Controls may exhibit a measure of inconsistency (Westerlund and Sjostrand, 1979). Accounting may serve in a multiplicity of roles (Burchell et al., 1980). Guided, or perhaps confused, by the conflicting pressures of many interacting forces, organisations sustain a chaotic existence.

Thus there is a need to focus explicitly on accounting in its subtle organisational context to draw out its role in organisational control (Hopwood, 1978; Burchell et al., 1980). A valid model of organisations must at least attempt to integrate the various processes of organisational control in order to portray one organic interacting whole. It must explicitly focus on the richness and diversity of the organisation, its participants and its procedures, both formal and informal. Only such an aggregate view is likely to present a coherent picture of the organisational control process. Such a view seems to be lacking in the accounting literature.

To develop this theme the next section describes first the cybernetic approach to organisational control and then some recent developments in systems thinking. This approach, it is claimed, provides an integrated framework for organisational analysis. The third section examines more specifically the role of accounting in organisational control.

II. A SYSTEMS–CYBERNETICS APPROACH TO ORGANISATIONAL CONTROL

The holistic emphasis is the hallmark of a systems approach to organisational analysis. Within a general systems theory (GST) framework no system is isolated from the universe of systems. The universe is characterised as an indivisible and interacting whole. But it is precisely this highly complex interaction which endows systems with control, which drives them towards a dynamic coherence. Systems rely quite fundamentally on interaction for their viability (see chapter 1).

Of course, there may be operational problems in analysing interactions within the universal system. Conceptually it may be difficult to define boundaries between sub-systems. But, in general, sub-systems consisting of less than the whole can be recognised. At any particular level in the hierarchy of systems, boundaries can be drawn round some sets of phenomena and sub-systems and their interactions with their immediate environments can be identified. With an appropriate degree of resolution (Lowe and McInnes, 1971) some arbitrary level of elementary systems (a convenient unit of analysis) can be focused upon. By successively addressing the communication patterns between elementary systems and between systems and their immediate environments, an understanding of the interconnectedness of the whole can be attained. This is the approach of cybernetics. It is claimed to provide a vehicle for reconciling the holistic approach of GST with the practical problems of designing systems for control. By explicitly facing the complexity of the world this philosophy is designed to achieve effective control.

The analysis of Ashby (1956, 1960) identified self-regulation and self-veto as the essential elements for a cybernetic design. A necessary condition for self-regulation is the characteristic error-controlled negative feedback loop: a mechanism capable of continuously monitoring the state of a process and automatically feeding back appropriate corrective signals. This presupposes that the control mechanism exhibits the requisite degree of variety (Ashby, 1956), and has sufficient information carrying capacity (Shannon and Weaver, 1949). The variety of potential control signals must be at least sufficient to control the variety of possible states: 'Only variety can absorb variety.' Now consider two finely-balanced, interacting, self-regulating systems, and let the first system be subjected to some disturbance. If its balance is upset, the self-regulatory mechanism will act to restore its internal equilibrium. But this change in the state of the first system may have some consequential effect on the balance of the second system, whereupon the self-regulatory mechanism of the second system acts to restore its internal equilibrium. But this change in the state of the second system may in turn destroy the balance of the first system, and so the cycle repeats itself.

Loosely speaking, Ashby (1960) has argued that this self-vetoing facility, coupled with requisite variety, is sufficient to ensure ultimate coordination and stability. For, in the absence of intermediate disturbance, the self-vetoing process must inevitably lead to the attainment of a mutually compatible combination of states, even as a consequence of random mutation. This is the operation of the 'homeostat'.

The world, however, is characterised by change, and casual observation suggests that the rate of change tends to increase over time. How then is stability to be engineered? If on average the interval between successive disturbances approaches the time taken for the system to stabilise, then there will be a tendency to oscillate interminably. Indeed, Beer (1966, ch. 16) has argued that Ashby's trial and error hypothesis is simply insufficient to explain the apparent order of the universe. This view is widely accepted by modern systems theorists (e.g. Jantsch, 1980). Certainly, random mutations are an essential prerequisite for adaptation, for it is mainly through experimentation that knowledge is acquired; but some more purposive explanation is required.

In Beer's (1966) analysis this is accomplished through the concept of memory. If the system is endowed with memory, in the sense of some sequential learning device capable of absorbing the past history of the system, then bias is introduced into the random mutations of the self-vetoing process. More specifically, if positive reinforcement is introduced through an approximation to the Bayesian probability revision procedures of statistical decision theory, then, so it is argued, the dynamics of the system can be structured so as to ensure progressive convergence towards a global consistency. As Beer (1966, p. 368) commented:

> Nature does not lead an exact or even closely predictable process here: nor does the cybernetician. It is enough that the mutations of an adapting system should not be entirely hazardous, but should be biased, for positive feedback can be relied upon to steer the progressive bias towards viable behaviour – once the bias exists.

The cybernetic design offers some insight into the problems of organisational control. These essentially simple concepts serve to structure effective stabilisation schemes even for highly complex interacting systems. Layer upon layer of self-regulating mechanisms are tightly knit together in the intricate homeostatic designs created by cyberneticians. Integrated information linkages serve to draw sub-systems into a coherent functional whole.

Cybernetic concepts form the basis for many of the more traditional management controls, for example, the principle of management by exception, or in a more specific context, budgetary control and variance analysis. But the cybernetic model is much richer in its implications than this. Control in the early cybernetic view was not perceived as authoritarian or coercive, rather it was based on principles of self-control and mutual adjustment (Ashby, 1960). Although this basis might appear to have been subverted in the work of later cybernetic theorists, principles of autonomy and flexibility are still claimed to lie at the heart of their designs (Beer, 1972). As systems exhibit a greater degree of variety so they become more difficult to control from without. The cybernetic design emphasises the importance of structuring for control from within.

This emphasis on self control is evident in the organisational literature. For example, it is frequently observed that as an organisation's environment becomes more dynamic or as its technology becomes more complex, so there will be a greater need to decentralise decision making (e.g. Burns and Stalker, 1961). As the degree of decentralisation increases, so there will be a greater need for lateral communications to coordinate interdependent activities (e.g. Lawrence and Lorsch, 1969). In a heavily centralised system, the variety encountered by the organisation will be transmitted hierarchically. Escalating through the system, it will tend to be amplified by interaction. Ultimately such a system might simply collapse from chronic overload. The cybernetic principle of self control, in contrast, absorbs variety 'like a sponge'. Variety is matched with variety.

One response to increasing variety is to increase the capacity of the information system to transmit data (Galbraith 1972, 1977). In situations of low variety this may be feasible. On the other hand, as variety increases beyond some limit, it may become impossible to make sense of the sheer volume of data in the system. At that point the controller becomes over-loaded (Beer, 1966; Kerr *et al*, 1975). Organisations in fact respond in many ways in the face of variety. For example, they may establish buffer inventories to absorb environmental fluctuations (Thompson, 1967), or they may form cartels to suppress the variety in their environments. These examples are of organisations seeking to absorb variety at source. They are illustrations of structuring for self control.

In the accounting literature there has been some limited discussion of the principle of self control. The long-standing centralisation *v.* decentralisation debate may be interpreted as an attempt to introduce more flexibility at lower levels in the organisational structure. The discussion of responsibility centres – profit centres, investment centres and so on – is perhaps evidence of this development.

Similarly, certain behavioural studies can be considered in a cybernetic light. The interest in motivation is essentially oriented towards obtaining a higher degree of goal congruence between the individual and the organisation. In other words it is an attempt to internalise self control at the atomistic level. Expectancy models, for example, formalise a hypothetical relationship between work goal achievement and organisational reward structures (e.g. Vroom, 1964; Porter and Lawler, 1968; and in an accounting context, Ronen and Livingstone, 1975). The usefulness of this research in a cybernetic sense is to conceptualise the feedback loop at the lowest level. A similar analysis could be applied to some of the group dynamics research including some participation literature (e.g. Vroom, 1964; Becker and Green, 1962).

Nevertheless, despite this limited recognition of the importance of self control it is widely acknowledged that accounting controls in practice are basically coercive and authoritarian. They tend to emphasise control by imposition rather than control by mutual adjustment. For example, Caplan (1966) has argued that budgeting procedures are heavily centralised and rigidly structured. Some empirical evidence supports this observation (e.g. Argyris, 1952, Caplan, 1968). Moreover the hierarchical orientation of accounting information flows may simply be inadequate to cope with the degree of lateral communications necessary for the coordination and integration of decentralised organisational sub-systems (Lawrence and Lorsch, 1969; Galbraith, 1977).

The above discussion might be taken to imply an unqualified endorsement of the cybernetic model, but this is not the view intended here. The cybernetic model is very mechanistic in its conception, and imposes an unduly rationalistic framework for the analysis of organisational control. It posits the existence of a well-defined meta-systemic goal, and at least some degree of goal consensus amongst participants (Lilienfeld, 1978). But, as indicated in chapter 2, organisational goals may be ambiguous, conflicting, ill-defined and fluid (e.g. Hedberg and Jonsson, 1978). Moreover they may not even pre-exist organisational activities. It may be that goals serve only to rationalise past choices (Weick, 1979); or they may be the product of those choices (Lindblom, 1959; March, 1972, 1979). In addition, the cybernetic notion of adaptation is very narrowly conceived. As Ashby's (1960) concept of 'ultra-stability' suggests, the cybernetic design is predominantly concerned with stabilisation. It is dynamic only in the sense that the system is seen to be continually adapting to variety – its overriding emphasis is on the attainment of a predetermined set of goals within a given structure. In this view attention is centred on the equilibrium of the present. But in a dynamic sense the present is nothing more than the product of evolution. The environment not only exhibits variety, but is itself evolving. Adaptation is much more richly endowed. Goals evolve and continue to evolve, structures evolve and continue to evolve. The present is merely transient. Viable systems exhibit self-organising properties to carry them through tomorrow.

Self-Organising Properties

The cybernetic analysis has certainly furthered our understanding of the stabilisation of given structures within predetermined limits. But the motion of equilibrium which is frequently implied in the cybernetic analysis is restrictive. As the discussion in chapter 1 suggests, equilibrium primarily focuses on the internal relationships in the system. External factors are acknowledged only in so far as they induce disequilibrium (Burrell and Morgan, 1979). The notion of equilibrium is inadequate for the study of socio-cultural systems whose morphogenic properties are distinctly different from those of biological and physical systems (Buckley, 1967). Thus, the dynamics of coherent systems, systems whose structure and form evolve themselves in a coherent way, have been only partially addressed.

The new evolving theory of systems dynamics, in contrast, centres attention on the natural and continuing evolution of disequilibrium systems (Jantsch, 1980) and on the dynamics of the process of change in the system and in its underlying structure (Buckley, 1967). The learning patterns foreseen by Beer (1966) are formalised into a macroscopic theory of evolution. Conflict is seen to reinforce change. Goals themselves become part of the wider evolutionary process. This theory addresses natural, self-organising adaptive capabilities. No longer is interest centred on the solid structure of the present. Equilibrium serves only to define the limiting form of today. The centre of interest is the dynamics of disequilibrium. The only stability observed is the extraordinary coherence induced by disequilibrium forces collectively driving the system towards self renewal and regeneration.

This richer notion of adaptation, with its emphasis on self organisation, is prominent in some of the more recent organisational literature. For example, Hedberg et al (1976) discuss the paradoxical prescription for a self-designing organisation. Similarly Argyris and Schön (1978) emphasise the importance of designing organisational structures which facilitate learning and adaptation. Structure is no longer taken as an immutable given state. Rather it is seen as fluid and evolving.

Yet adaptation is almost antipathetic to the practice of management accounting. Controls, primarily, are centred on the internal order of the present. They emphasise a static state in the internal operations of the organisation. They take the state of the environment as given. They discourage innovation and experimentation. In the analysis of Katz and Kahn (1978) they serve as 'maintaining systems' – they operate to perpetuate the status quo. Their message is resistance and entrenchment. Relatively little attention is directed at change, at forces in the environment, at the evaluation of trends, towards the stimulation of adaptive behaviour.

There is no intention to imply that organisations have no need for maintaining systems. Organisational coherence emerges from the complex interplay of the many conflicting forces shaping organisational behaviour (Katz and Kahn, 1978; Hedberg et al, 1976). There is a need in most organisations, most of the time, both for maintaining systems to soak up variety and preserve some stability, and for adaptive systems to stimulate innovation and experimentation. But this latter role seems to have been almost neglected in accounting practice, and to a great extent in the accounting literature. Not that innovation and experimentation are easy to stimulate; on the contrary, it is not immediately obvious how that may be achieved. Analysis, however, suggests that systems are triggered into adaptive responses; that unexpected outcomes reach some threshold beyond which systems are stimulated into search behaviour (March and Simon, 1958; Jantsch, 1980). There is also some consensus that standard operating procedures tend to filter away environmental inconsistencies and encourage a complacency towards environmental change (Cyert and March, 1963; Hedberg and Jonsson, 1978).

Accordingly, it may be appropriate to counteract this tendency by deliberately introducing ambiguity into accounting controls, for instance, by reporting a more diverse set of quantitative and non-quantitative data. Focusing on environmental inconsistencies in a non-reductionist approach might bring sub-systems into closer contact with their environments. Such 'semi-confusing' information would serve to destabilise the status quo, to trigger search behaviour at a lower threshold of environmental change. In a sense this would be an attempt to shift emphasis from problem solution, the traditional concern of management accounting, to problem identification. As Hedberg and Jonsson (1978) observe,

> there are information systems which offer less discretion to decision makers than others, and which lead to organisational rigidity; and there are information systems which stimulate organisations to experiment and innovate, and which foster organisational flexibility.

This destabilising role is far removed from the received philosophy of management accounting. The significance attached to flexibility, ambiguity and experimentation is in stark contrast to the rigidity and precision of traditional control procedures.

III. INFORMATION AND CONTROL

A central theme of the preceding analysis has been the significance attached to information flows. Indeed in the systems-cybernetics approach, effective control relies critically on appropriate information flows. As organisations encounter variety, so information flows support coordination and adaptation. This emphasis is not unique to cybernetic analysis, but recurs in a wide range of management literature. For instance, as indicated in chapter 1, Lawrence and Lorsch (1969) observed that as organisations encounter increasing variety, for example, as a result of the unpredictability of their environments, so differentiation occurs. As organisations become increasingly differentiated so there is a greater need for integration. Integration in this sense, it might be argued, is primarily an informational phenomenon. Overlaid on the hierarchical structure can be various possible degrees of lateral linkages ranging from temporarily constituted task forces through to fully institutionalised matrix designs. These are considered to increase the lateral flow of information between interconnected sub-systems and so establish (homeostatic) coordinating mechanisms.

Galbraith (1972, 1977), in his information processing characterisation of the firm, has argued that improvement in lateral relations is merely one alternative to investment in the more familiar vertical information system. Faced with variety and interconnectedness firms may seek to encourage control through mutual adjustment by improving lateral information flows; alternatively they may seek to improve the effectiveness of hierarchical control systems. Investment in vertical information systems, for instance, reducing transmission delay and increasing data accuracy, would facilitate more timely revision of corporate plans, thus expediting coordination without the need for on-the-job consultation between interdependent subunits.

In addition, Galbraith notes, organisations can take steps to reduce their need for information. Creating slack, for example, by establishing buffer inventories or relaxing technical specifications, can have the effect of reducing the degree of connectedness between interdependent subunits and hence their requirement for communication. Alternatively, organisations may seek to structure self-contained tasks to facilitate resolution of problems without reference to bodies external to the subunit. The creation of separate design, manufacturing and marketing departments for each product or product group, and their organisation on a product basis is a common approach to divisionalisation (Ezzamel and Hilton, 1980). Organisations therefore face alternatives, both in terms of strategies for increasing the flow of information, and in terms of strategies for reducing their need for information.

Galbraith's analysis is useful in so far as it highlights some of the interdependencies between organisation structure and information system design. Clearly such interdependencies have important implications for accounting. Yet these are only partially addressed. A more recent development in accounting research has been the attempt to develop a formal contingency framework for the design of management accounting systems. This is discussed below.

The Contingency Theory of Management Accounting

The contingency theory of management accounting is a relatively recent development in accounting research. Drawing on the organisational literature (e.g. Woodward, 1965; Lawrence and Lorsch, 1969) this line of research has sought to isolate those variables with implications for design of a firm's information system. Through a combination of a priori reasoning and empirical validation, propositions are developed formalising the relationship between the situational contingencies of a firm and the appropriate nature of its information system. Organisational effectiveness, it is argued, will be improved by attaining an appropriate fit between the characteristics of the organisation's situation (the situational contingencies) and the characteristics of its Management Information Systems (MIS).

MIS are not identical to management accounting systems, the latter being the main concern of this book. Management information systems are typically concerned with the development, design, and implementation of computer-based information systems. Because of their joint concern with information design and flow, the distinction between MIS and management accounting systems is frequently blurred (Macintosh, 1985). Some of the studies reviewed below focus on MIS and others focus on management accounting systems. For convenience of presentation the following discussion focuses on MIS, but it is assumed that the implications for management accounting systems are the same.

The contingency theory of organisational structure identifies four main variables with important implications for organisation design: technology; environment; age and size; and power distribution, both internal and external (see chapter 1). The literature on the contingency theory of management accounting, however, has primarily focused on the implications of only technology and environment for the design of MIS. Thus, the implications of age and size have been largely neglected (but see Merchant, 1984). Furthermore, only recently have researchers attempted to investigate the political implications of power on the design of MIS (e.g. Cooper, 1980).

In considering the effects of technology on the design of MIS, researchers have tended to distinguish between (i) certain contingencies, where environment is highly certain and technology is fairly routine, and (ii) uncertain contingencies, where environment is highly uncertain and/or technology is non-routine, with a distinction in each case between independent or interdependent tasks. Dent and Ezzamel (1986) used this classification to summarise and evaluate the contingency research in management accounting. The following discussion draws heavily on their work.

1. The Certain Contingencies Cases

Consider first the case of a firm with independent, routine tasks operating in an environment characterised by low uncertainty. With independent tasks, differentiation and integration requirements are expected to be low. This case may be characterised by crystallised standards of desirability (performance) and complete knowledge of cause–effect relationships (Thompson, 1967). This appears to provide a convenient setting for efficient centralisation facilitated by the possible development and use of unambiguous standard procedures (Mechanic, 1962; Thompson, 1967; Lawrence and Lorsch, 1969; Waterhouse and Tiessen, 1978). The nature of information most relevant in this case is likely to be precise and unambiguous, with a clear focus on single rather than multiple solutions to encourage quick and decisive action (e.g. Macintosh, 1981).

Given the above position, Ginzberg (1980) suggested that the relevant MIS design may be labelled 'procedural independent'. This design has two important characteristics. Firstly, it enhances control over tasks by reducing the discretion of task performance and/or making greater use of standard procedures. Secondly, it attempts to reduce the need for information processing, thus achieving a satisfactory match between information processing needs and information processing capacity.

Therefore, with routine, independent tasks and a certain environment, the role of the MIS as seen by the contingency theory is primarily one of exerting hierarchical control, and its nature is precise and unambiguous. Although the small number of unusual operating conditions encountered with routine tasks is systematically analysable (Perrow, 1967), a 'seat of the pants' approach to decision making may be preferred to the analytical approach on the basis of economic efficiency (Gordon and Miller, 1976).

Turning now to the case of routine but interdependent tasks in an environment with low uncertainty, the findings of Lawrence and Lorsch (1969) suggest that the greater the measure of differentiation between organisational subunits, the greater the need for integrating devices to improve consistency and to minimise intraorganisational conflict. The potential of the MIS as a powerful integrating mechanism has been recognised by many writers, for example, Gordon and Miller (1976); Ginzberg (1980). Thus, given the above setting Ginzberg (1980) argued that the relevant MIS is one of the type 'procedural interdependent'. This system should enhance control and coordination of interdependent tasks by facilitating lateral information flow and information sharing. Thus, since greater task interdependence is likely to call for greater subunit integration, the MIS should foster this integration by providing data relevant to subunit interdependencies (Watson, 1975).

2. The Uncertain Contingencies Cases

Consider now the case of a firm with non-routine technology operating in an uncertain environment. Non-routine tasks are usually characterised by many exceptions, with less systematically analysable search processes (Perrow, 1967). The literature suggests that organisational uncertainties, i.e. task non-routineness and environmental uncertainty, have demonstrable effects on the structure and distribution of authority within the organisation. Thus, one of the sources of influence within the organisation is the ability of the individual, or subunit, to successfully cope with uncertainty; see for example Burns and Stalker (1961); Thompson (1967); Hickson et al (1971). This depends, at least in part, on the uniqueness of knowledge and skills of the individual, and on the availability of information relevant to the prevailing uncertainties. Thus, for example, Waterhouse and Tiessen (1978), and Mintzberg (1979) point out that technological and environmental uncertainties lead to greater decentralisation. Furthermore, organisation structures which evolve in response to greater uncertainty in contingency factors are typically organic (Burns and Stalker, 1961). Here, a procedural emphasis to the MIS is likely to be inadequate. Such systems emphasise hierarchical control and minimal diffusion of authority (e.g. Pfeffer, 1978). Moreover, they fail to address the diversity of conditions encountered by the organisation.

Various writers have investigated some of the implications of organisational uncertainties for the design of MIS. Amongst them, Khandwalla's (1972) results suggest that the extent of sophistication of the control system of an organisation is highly correlated with the intensity of competition in product markets and the complexity of economic conditions. In such circumstances MIS are called upon to help not only in the problem-solving area but also in integrating and coordinating organizational activities and in assessing performance. Such associations, however, were not observed in the case of marketing and price competition. Similarly, Bruns and Waterhouse (1975) argued that as organisations face uncertain contingencies, so they tend to decentralise decision making. Managers in more decentralised organisations tend to perceive themselves as having more influence and participating more in the budget process than managers in more authoritative and centralised organisations. Furthermore, the findings reported by Daft and Macintosh (1978) suggest that significantly high correlations exist between the extent of technological uncertainty and the style of MIS. Amigoni (1978) observed that environmental discontinuity has a more drastic effect on the design of MIS than does structural complexity. Thus, in the face of increased structural complexity, he argued, organisations can successfully cope by merely adding new accounting tools to those currently in use, whilst increasing environmental discontinuity often necessitates the replacement of obsolete tools by new ones. This point therefore highlights the potential impact of different situational contingencies. Thus, in the face of different contingencies, organisations may require significantly different information and control systems.

In this setting, much of the information required is likely to be less precise, and frequently ill-defined with multiple focuses. Gordon and Narayanan (1984) reported that as decision makers perceive greater environmental uncertainty they tend to seek external, non-financial, and *ex-ante* information in addition to other types of information. Similarly, Chenhall and Morris (1986) observed a significant association between environmental uncertainty and broad scope and timely information; the greater the uncertainty, the more managers sought broad scope and timely information. Daft and Macintosh (1981) noted that, in general, greater task variety was associated with greater reported amounts of information-processing activity. Greater task analysability was found to be associated with the reported processing of equivocal information. In the context of a firm with independent tasks and non-routine technology in an uncertain environment, Ginzberg (1980) advocated an MIS design called 'decisional independent'. Instead of attempting to increase hierarchical control, this system emphasises the use of decentralised decision making, the institutionalisation of more effective decision models, and the localisation of information required for performance to minimise the need for subunit interaction.

Turning now to the complementary case in which the environment is uncertain and tasks are non-routine but interdependent, the presence of task interdependencies calls for greater use of integrating measures, as indicated earlier. The study by Chenhall and Morris (1986) suggests that broad-scope information, aggregated information, and integrated information were perceived as useful by managers of subunits with interdependent activities. Macintosh and Daft (1987) reported that departmental interdependence is related to the emphasis placed on three elements in a package of management controls. Standard operating procedures were an important control device when interdependence was low. The budget and statistical reports were used more extensively when interdependence was moderate. When departmental interdependence was high, the role of all three control systems diminished. In this case, Ginzberg (1980) argued that the use of a 'decisional interdependent' MIS facilitates the development and maintenance of decentralised structures by emphasising shared decision models, shared information, and the coordination necessary for decentralised decision making by interdependent subunits. Thus Ginzberg argued that a 'decisional interdependent' MIS is important for coordinating the activities of highly differentiated subunits with high integration requirements.

An Evaluation of Contingency Theory

The above outline shows how the contingency theory of management accounting might be seen to provide a coherent conceptual approach towards the design of management information systems. However, such a view might be premature, and there are significant reservations about this literature. As this theory draws heavily on the contingency theory of organisational structure, it seems appropriate first to provide a perspective by referring to some anomalies of the organisational research.

In chapter 1 some of the more technical limitations of the contingency approach to organisation design were identified. These may be summarised as: (i) lack of precision in defining contingency factors; (ii) misspecification of model parameters and use of perceptual measures as proxies for organisational characteristics; (iii) use of cross-sectional approaches to measure dimensions of variables that can only be meaningfully measured by employing longitudinal approaches; (iv) lack of consideration of the effects of multiple (and possibly conflicting) contingencies on structural configurations; (v) lack of consideration of the implications of intraorganisational heterogeneity, e.g., where the firm deals in different sorts of markets, or has different technologies and (vi) frequent use of defective sampling techniques.

Although several organisation theorists have long been aware of these limitations, e.g. Child (1972a); Pennings (1975); Wood (1979), until very recently there has been little awareness of these issues in the accounting research. It is therefore hardly surprising that these limitations are prominent in the literature on the contingency theory of management accounting. When contingency factors are discussed they are either taken for granted (e.g. Gordon and Miller, 1976) or interpreted differently by different researchers. Further, the MIS literature typically considers only the effects of single contingency factors one at a time (e.g. Gordon and Miller, 1976) or of several contingency factors which are perceived to have a similar impact (e.g. Waterhouse and Tiessen, 1978). Thus, the effects of different contingency factors, or of combinations of contingencies with differing and conflicting implications for MIS design, are seldom considered; nor is the possibility that a firm's contingencies may be difficult to classify due to intraorganisational differences.

The techniques used to derive propositions concerning the design implications for MIS also raise considerable doubt about their credibility. Thus, in several cases (e.g. Gordon and Miller, 1976) assertive propositions are derived with neither conclusive empirical evidence nor sound theoretical foundations. In most cases the contingency formulation is taken for granted as the ultimate framework for MIS design. It is implicitly assumed that by achieving an appropriate fit between the MIS and the relevant contingency factors, other things being the same, organisational effectiveness will improve. Yet organisational effectiveness is rarely included as a dependent variable in experimental designs. The empirical evidence suggests little more than the fact that different information systems exist. A link between situational contingencies, MIS design configurations and organisational effectiveness has yet to be established (Otley, 1980).

Organisational effectiveness is a rather elusive concept. In chapter 1, some of the difficulties experienced in the wider organisational literature in measuring effectiveness were discussed. These include:

1 a lack of clarity in the concept of effectiveness;
2 the tendency to describe effectiveness along a single dimension, suppressing its multidimensional and possibly conflicting characteristics; and
3 separate problems of research design which have not as yet been resolved, including (i) the need for longitudinal studies to reflect changes in effectiveness over time; (ii) the bias in the perception of effectiveness resulting from the individual researcher/respondent frame of reference; and (iii) the possible need for developing different effectiveness criteria for different organisations.

Daunting conceptual and empirical problems need to be satisfactorily resolved before sensible conclusions about organisational effectiveness can be drawn. Indeed, the existence of these problems has prompted Child (1977) to conclude, in the context of the organisational research, that there is no conclusive evidence that matching organisation structure to contingency factors has an important influence on performance.

The above discussion will have elucidated some of the limitations of the MIS research. But more fundamentally, the contingency framework understates the role of choice in formulating strategies for organisational control (see chapter 1). Decisions with regard to organisational structure and MIS design are presumed to be dictated by the need to adapt to contingency requirements; organisations are not permitted to have preferences for outcomes other than those implied by contingency factors. Yet in dealing with uncertainty, organisations may only seek to reduce its extent to manageable levels and in so doing often follow different strategies (Weick, 1979; Miller, 1981). The design implications of contingency theory promote a deterministic view in asserting that under a given set of contingencies there is only one best way to manage. Wood (1979) went even further in arguing that contingency theory not only underplays the scope for choice but also renders such choice redundant. By treating the organisation as a monolithic entity organised by a homogeneous management, the contingency framework ignores the possibility that different organisational participants may have preferences for different strategies.

Thus contingency theory is premised on existing authoritarian concepts of control. Metaphors like Simon's (1977) 'rational man' metaphor and Weick's (1979) 'military' metaphor dominate the contingency framework. The MIS is considered only in its procedural or decision support mode (Gorry and Scott-Morton, 1971). The much wider psychological orientations of organisational control and intraorganisational power considerations are hardly addressed (Cooper, 1980). Information systems are not neutral in their impact on behaviour (Drucker, 1964). All sorts of effects, both functional and dysfunctional, may be stimulated by particular information system characteristics (e.g. Argyris, 1952; Lawler and Rhode, 1976). Certain characteristics may render an information system more susceptible to strategic manipulation (Schiff and Lewin, 1970) and information may be used to further power and influence within the organisation (Bariff and Galbraith, 1978). March and Simon (1958), for example, refer to the concept of 'uncertainty absorption' whereby subjective inferences are drawn from a body of evidence and fed into an information system, becoming legitimised organisational 'facts'. These 'facts' in turn shape organisational choices. Managers may manipulate information passing to their colleagues to create confusion and ambiguity as a cover for the expansion of their particular empires (Dalton, 1959). Superiors may falsify information passing to subordinates to create dissent and competition (Pondy, 1967). Subordinates may alter and suppress information passing to their superiors in a way compatible with their ends (Thornton, 1974). At all organisational levels participants play a role, whether consciously or unconsciously, in determining the shape, quantity and quality of information flows.

To an extent organisations may instigate formal and informal controls to counteract this phenomenon. But in many cases there may be neither the time nor the knowledge to eliminate, or even reduce, it. Equally important is the possibility that managers may willingly allow information to be suppressed and manipulated by subordinates to reduce ambiguity and overload (Westerlund and Sjostrand, 1979). To the extent that such manipulation facilitates managerial decision making, it may not be entirely undesirable. However, organisational adaptation is likely to be impaired, and it may be appropriate to design information systems which offer less scope for manipulation and suppression, for example, by establishing direct information linkages, and avoiding to some extent standard aggregation procedures. Moreover, multiple channels of communication, providing horizontal as well as vertical linkages, may focus managerial attention on crucial inconsistencies which might otherwise go unobserved.

All in all, the role of accounting in organisation control is little understood (Burchell et al, 1980). How it interacts with other control processes has only been partially addressed in the literature. There is a need for further analysis within a global organisational framework. One such attempt is discussed below.

IV. A FRAMEWORK FOR ORGANISATIONAL CONTROL

In this section, the framework developed by Dent and Ezzamel (1986) for the analysis of organisational control is discussed. The framework draws on previous research, much of which has already been discussed in this chapter. In order to facilitate the presentation of the Dent and Ezzamel framework, a brief summary of the relevant points made so far is presented first.

In the first section of the chapter the nature of the organisational control process was characterised. Several different schools of organisational analysis were identified, each providing insight into the control of organisational activities. Some dimensions of structure were considered briefly, relating to the efficiency and effectiveness of alternative planning procedures. The rationale of the classic prescription for centralisation was discussed. Difficulties associated with such authoritarian procedures were outlined, including the dispersion of essential knowledge, and the noise and filtering effects that occur in the transmission of information. Drawing on the economic literature, it was argued that centralisation was likely to be particularly costly not only in terms of the necessary staff and the information technology, but also in terms of the speed of adjustment to environmental change. On the other hand, difficulties associated with decentralised procedures were noted including those of internalising interdependencies and external effects, and of risk sharing. It was argued that the structural analysis was overly mechanistic. Organisations exist through the efforts of people, and people have divergent goals and aspirations. Conflict and the constant negotiation that takes place within organisations are essential elements of the control process. Recognition of group pressure, and the power of the informal organisation, is crucial to an understanding of organisational functioning. Moreover, issues of structural design are more richly endowed. People look to organisations for satisfaction of a variety of needs. Job characteristics and leadership style may have a significant impact on the quality of individual performance. These social and psychological insights into organisational functioning have provided a different focus for organisational researchers. Their analysis, however, constitutes a complementary view of the organisational control process. Only through integration of the ideas of different management theorists can a coherent and comprehensive framework of organisational control be developed.

To formalise this eclectic approach the discussion was extended to include principles of cybernetic analysis. It was indicated that the homeostatic concept placed emphasis on control through mutual adjustment, conflict being thoroughly embedded in the model, and that organisations constantly evolve in response to internal and external stimuli. The significant contributions of the cybernetic analysis include the recognition of the interconnectedness of the whole; the emphasis on self control; and the nature of organisational adaptation. The organisation was characterised as being subject to continual disequilibrium forces driving it inexorably onwards through time.

Over time, it was argued, an organisation may change its activities, its structure, its personnel and so on. Thus a completely new and expansive concept of organisational control was acquired. Attention was drawn, however, to some of the mechanistic ideas and rationalistic orientations of the cybernetic model.

Drawing on the implicit orientation of the cybernetic analysis, the important role played by information in organisational control was emphasised. Whether the MIS is viewed as a vehicle for enhancing the information processing capacity of the organisation (e.g. Galbraith, 1972), or as a political vehicle for exerting control (e.g. Pfeffer, 1978), or as a decision-support system (e.g. Burchell et al, 1980), information processing is recognised as a key organisational activity. Thus, as organisations encounter increasing variety and interconnectedness, so information plays a crucial role in supporting effective coordination and adaptation. Moreover, both the structure of communication channels and the nature of the data are relevant to MIS design. As the need for organisational adaptation increases, so there may be a need for a more diverse and destabilising set of information.

To formalise this intuitive analysis, the contingency theory of management accounting was considered. It was pointed out that researchers have sought to associate characteristics of the firm's information system with its technology and environment. By achieving a fit, so it is argued, between the contingency factors and the information system, organisational effectiveness will be improved. However, the existing research is incomplete in so far as contingency factors are under-specified. Moreover, organisations face alternatives for coping with internal and external variety. The means of effective organisational control are not necessarily dictated by situational contingencies.

The preceding discussion will have demonstrated that organisational control is a total process. As Westerlund and Sjostrand (1979) point out, it is common in organisations that many controls operate simultaneously. To this extent it is almost impossible to isolate the separate effects of a particular means of control. Only by considering the process as a whole can the significance of one element *per se* be appreciated. The process of organisational control is not susceptible to tidy and precise analysis. Any formal approach will inevitably be incomplete. Nevertheless, drawing on the above ideas, Dent and Ezzamel (1986) identify five elements which can be sensibly incorporated in the framework. These are:

1. *Contingency factors.* Traditionally, this set is said to contain an organisation's environment, its technology, its age and size, its internal and external power distribution, and ownership characteristics. Other factors can be added to this list: for example, organisational goals (Dermer, 1977) and the type of personnel employed by the organisation (Child, 1977).

2. *Information system characteristics.* Here two sets of characteristics can be distinguished: (i) structural characteristics such as the orientation of the information system (internal/external), the sources of data (internal/external), the structure of information linkages (lateral/vertical), the scope of the information system (global/localised); (ii) other characteristics referring to the nature of information, for example, the diversity and ambiguity of information, the extent of predictive data, and the timeliness and frequency of the data.

3. *Structural configuration.* Under this heading three related sets of characteristics can be identified. At the individual level there are such attributes as the degree of job specification and task variety, the definition of individual responsibilities, the organisation of tasks and the degree of differentiation. Organisational attributes would include lines of formal authority (functional/product/matrix orientations), flexibility of formal structure, organisational reward structures, the informal

organisation, and the extent of integrating mechanisms. There is also a third category of decision making and leadership characteristics, for example, the extent of formal and informal decentralisation, leadership style and managerial consideration.

4. *Managerial choices*. This set relates to managerial input into the control process. Managerial choices encompass three broad types of decision: strategic choices, structural choices (including information system choices) and tactical choices. These represent the means whereby managers may attempt to influence an organisation's functioning.

5. *Organisational activity*. Given the organisational infrastructure established by the preceding elements of the framework, the term activity is used here to refer to the actual workings of the organisation. Thus it embraces such attributes as the cohesiveness and morale of informal groups, levels of conflict and anxiety within the organisation, and dimensions of organisational effectiveness. Also included are measures of economic efficiency, for example, levels of task performance, productivity, profitability, and stock market performance, as well as socio-economic indicators, for example employee earnings, satisfaction, and societal benevolence. In addition, it might be appropriate to consider here organisational flexibility and adaptation.

To an extent these elements may be difficult to distinguish precisely. Although important in an empirical context, such precision is not crucial to the present exposition, and might only serve to confuse. In any event, in consistency with the preceding analysis, it is not the elements in isolation that are emphasised here, but rather their interactions. Figure 4.1 offers a diagrammatic representation of the five elements in the framework.

In a contingency approach, the nature of the contingencies facing the organisation would be presumed to dictate the appropriate choice of structural configuration and MIS design. This would be represented by arrows running from the contingency factors to managerial choices, and from managerial choices to structure and information system. Arrows running from these two elements to organisational activity could be used to show the impact on organisational effectiveness of an appropriate fit between these two elements and the contingencies. Such a characterisation would, however, be incomplete and potentially misleading. As indicated earlier, a more realistic representation would reveal a great deal more interaction amongst the elements.

Interactions Between the Five Elements

Consider first the relationship between the organisation and its contingency factors. Traditionally, contingency theorists have tended to perceive the organisation as a *passive* adaptor to its situation. The behaviour of the organisation is seen by them as being fully dictated by the nature of its contingencies. However, it has been argued that managers face alternatives in coping with their contingencies. Moreover, the interaction between the organisation and its contingencies is not one-sided, but rather each exerts a measure of influence over the other.

Take, for example, the influence of the environment. Many authors have commented on the role of the organisation in *managing* its environment (see chapter 1). Thus Cyert and March (1963) advanced the concept of a 'negotiated environment'. In their view, organisations negotiate with their competitors, suppliers, customers and so on to control the uncertainty in their environments. Similarly Thompson (1967)

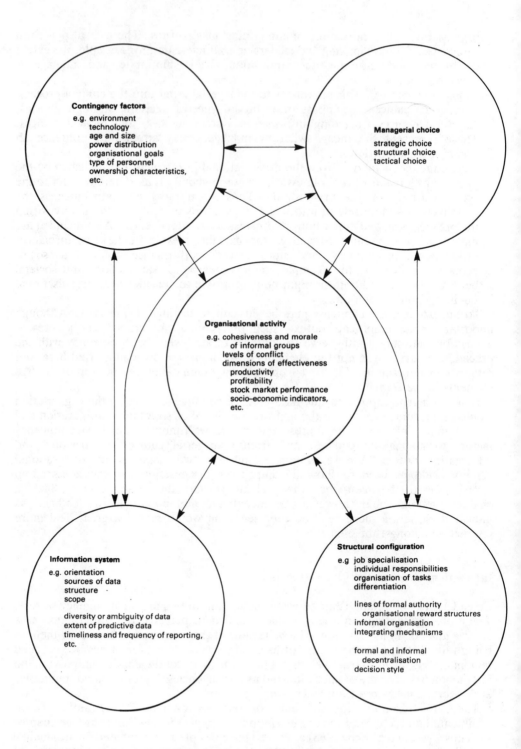

Figure 4.1 *A framework of organisational control (Source: J.F. Dent and M.A. Ezzamel (1986), Organisational control and management accounting: a contingency critique.)*

spoke of smoothing policies (e.g. advertising, off peak pricing), and observed that organisations attempt to place their boundaries around activities which would otherwise be crucial contingencies. Stronger propositions have been advanced by Weick (1979) who seemed to suggest that through a process of enactment, organisations literally create the environments they observe. Indeed Ackoff (1979) went so far as to suggest that the dominant 'predict and prepare' philosophy is symptomatic of a mechanistic age, and proposed a proactive philosophy of 'redesigning the future'.Thus, to some extent at least, organisations play a role in shaping the environments in which they operate.

Similar propositions could be made with respect to the other contingency factors. Thus the nature of the firm's technology is in part controlled by managerial choices, and the size of organisational units will be influenced by policies of vertical and horizontal integration, growth and divisionalisation. Moreover, both information system characteristics and structural configuration may have a direct impact on the nature of the firm's contingencies. Thus, for example, the information released by the organisation will influence its public image and its financial prestige; and the extent of vertical and horizontal integration will affect the degree of environmental variety. Similarly, the nature of organisational activities will also impinge directly on the situational contingencies. Thus situational contingencies are not exogenous 'given' factors in the control process. Rather the organisation may exert a significant measure of control over these factors, and proactive management may be at least as important as skilful adaptation (Ackoff, 1979).

No intention is made here to imply that situational contingencies are without significance to the organisation. Contingency factors, however defined, exert at least a constraining influence on managerial choices. For example, contingency factors may constrain top management's choice of, say, one particular strategy from a set of potentially available strategies. Alternatively, the long-term plans of the organisation may have to be modified to accommodate the requirements of some specific contingencies. Similarly, situational contingencies may exert a constraining influence on managerial choice of information system characteristics, structural configuration and organisational activities.

Moreover, contingencies may have a direct impact on the other elements of the framework. Thus, as an organisation's technology becomes more complex, for example, so individuals may become more specialised and increasingly feel the need for different types of information. Hence there may be a direct information system effect. Further, owing to the inevitable increase in specialisation in the above setting, subordinates are likely to find it easier to manipulate information passing to their superiors. This will have important implications for the formal and informal power distribution within the organisation, and in particular it may lead to an increasing extent of formal and informal decentralisation: hence a direct structural effect may be observed. Furthermore, an increase in uncertainties caused by situational contingencies may directly constrain the scope of organisational activities and the indices of its effectiveness.

Consider, next, managerial choices over structural configuration and information system. Traditionally, it has been assumed that managerial choices with respect to these two elements are homogeneous and congruent. This assumed unilateral planning by top managers of choices under their control reflects the traditionally dominant view of imposed control. However, management's ability to exert control within the organisation is likely to be conditioned by many factors. These may include the extent to which the organisation is internally or externally constrained, past and present organisational activities, existing organisational structures, the information made available to managers, managerial competence and the extent of control exercised by subordinates over their managers. Notice also that the framework shows patterns of bi-directional influence between structural configuration and information system. Thus, one would expect that the nature of the firm's information flow may constrain the choice of organisational structure, whilst the existing organisational structure could have specific design implications for the information system.

Finally, consider the interactions involving organisational activity. The figure shows contingency factors, managerial choices, structural configuration and the MIS all influencing organisational activities. Notice, however, that in view of the resultant organisational activities top managers may introduce changes into organisational strategies, structure and information system. Moreover, organisational activities may have a direct impact on structural configuration and MIS characteristics as well as on the situational contingencies.

Even though figure 4.1 is a simplified abstraction from reality, it still exemplifies the difficulties of understanding organisational control processes. Organisations are extremely complex. The diagram conceals a mass of detailed interaction as well as the dynamic nature of organisational processes. For obvious reasons it was not possible to show the passage of time along a third dimension. Yet organisational processes are dynamic. They change over time, and over time they induce changes in organisational activities. Driven by conflicting forces through time organisations follow different paths, and they adopt different strategies for control. The framework is also fairly general. It depicts a number of interactions, and deliberately refrains from ranking them in any order of importance. Nevertheless, organisations do differ, both amongst themselves and over time, and it may not be unreasonable to expect to observe differences in their control strategies. For some organisations managerial choices may be crucially important, whereas for others, structure or information system characteristics may be paramount. Moreover, some organisations may place more emphasis on strategic management, seeking to manipulate and pre-empt their environments, whereas others may seek to consolidate their position by concentrating on existing activities and improving their efficiency (Gordon and Miller, 1976; Miles and Snow, 1978).

Some accounting implications of this perspective have been explored in the literature. For example, Hedberg and Jonsson (1978) have discussed self-annihilating information packages. They suggested that information should be coded with an expiry date to shake organisations out of their complacency. Decision makers should be required to test, periodically, the validity of their premises and beliefs. More specifically Earl and Hopwood (1980) have discussed how differences in the consensus of beliefs might influence information use. Drawing on Thompson and Tuden's (1959) classification they distinguished differences in the certainty of cause and effect relationships from differences in the certainty of objectives. Given high uncertainty of objectives and cause and effect relationships, they argued, organisations need 'idea machines' to promote creative experimentation. On the other hand, given a consensus on objectives and cause and effect relationships organisations are considered to need 'answer machines' to promote informed and rational decision making. In the intermediate case of consensus on objectives but the uncertainty of cause and effect, they advocated 'learning machines' to assist in the process of discovery and judgement. Finally, in the case of agreement on cause and effect but minimal consensus on objectives, they advocated 'dialogue machines' to promote informed compromise.

In practice, however, the MIS may be used in different roles. Given high uncertainty on both dimensions, for example, the MIS may serve principally to rationalise decisions. Or given low uncertainty of cause and effect relationships but high uncertainty of objectives, the MIS may be used as 'an ammunition machine'. Such behaviours do occur and may not be difficult to rationalise. But rather than dismissing them as manifestations of dysfunctional behaviour, we should seek to understand the part such behaviours play in shaping organisational activities and their evolution over time. As yet there is no framework in which such phenomena may be functionally interpreted.

V. CONCLUSIONS AND IMPLICATIONS FOR RESEARCH

This chapter attempted to describe the process of organisational control, and some of the ambiguous roles which accounting may play. The subtle interplay of the various mechanisms which shape organisational activities and stimulate their evolution over time has been emphasised. It has been argued that this process is not susceptible to tidy and precise analysis. Organisational control is immensely more complex than is generally recognised. Simplistic characteristics are potentially misleading. Briefly, the above arguments may be summarised as follows.

Firstly, organisations are not merely passive adaptors to their situation: they influence and are influenced by that situation. This implies that the management of contingencies may assume at least as much significance in organisational control as the management of the internal functioning of the organisation. Secondly, organisational control is a broad concept. Thus, the presence of intra-organisational conflict and power, and the phenomenon of information manipulation need to be explicitly recognised. Such an approach is consistent with the view expressed by Westerlund and Sjostrand (1979, p. 109) when they pointed out that 'all action taken in an organisation can be regarded as means of control as long as it influences members' activities'. Thirdly, organisational control is a much more liberal concept than is traditionally believed. Thus, self control and mutual adjustment are at least as important as control through dominance. Fourthly, the various elements of the organisational control process are linked in a complex set of interrelationships. Although some useful insights can be gleaned from studying each subsystem in isolation, it is important to adopt a global approach to organisational analysis if a fuller understanding of organisations is sought. Fifthly, organisational activities are not static but dynamic and stochastic and are also characterised by renewal and regeneration. This has obvious implications for the interpretation of effectiveness. Sixthly, notions of rationality and consensus are not always useful in interpreting organisational processes. Such processes are often inconsistent, and functionally so. Conflict may stimulate organisations into innovative behaviour. Seventhly, organisational means for control are in themselves equivocal: different organisations facing similar contingencies can, and do, successfully promote dissimilar strategies and structures. Finally, in formalising the framework, variables were deliberately not classified into sets of dependent and independent variables, nor was a greater weight attached to the effects flowing from any one particular element. Instead, lines of multiple causality were depicted. The pre-eminence of any one particular element in the control process can only exist with reference to a focal organisation at a particular point in time.

It seems that at least two sets of questions need to be asked.
1. How does accounting fit in the totality of organisational activities? How do observed abuses of accounting interact with other organisational mechanisms?

2. What forces shape the accounting function in organisations? Why do accounting practices take the form they do? How do accounting practices evolve over time? Such questions should, perhaps, be addressed before deriving normative accounting propositions.

These conclusions may be familiar. Nevertheless they do not seem to have been widely recognised in accounting research. Notions of causality, rationality and separability pervade the literature. Interactions are suppressed: consensus is perceived as intrinsically desirable, organisational objectives are presumed. Prescriptions typically fail to address the dynamic evolving nature of organisational activities. The wisdom of such approaches has been questioned here. A false sense of order and coherence is created. In reality the role of accounting in organisational control is little understood. How do we proceed from here?

One possibility would be to concede the impossibility of modelling organisational functioning, and to argue that the process of organisational control is a gigantic mess that is not susceptible to any form of structuring or analysis. But research along the notions of ambiguous goals, evolving life cycles, and dynamic interacting systems may require a revolution in methodology. To argue along these lines, however, would be to accept that partial knowledge is as good as may be hoped for, or, at the extreme, that research into organisational control is a fruitless endeavour. This is not an appealing argument.

Another possibility would be, in the first instance, to raise the level of resolution of existing research: that is to say, to lift the focus of our attention from the minutiae of accounting to the interaction of accounting in aggregate with other aggregates of organisational processes. As noted in chapter 1, this approach has been advanced by Simon (1962). He argued that complex systems may tend in their dynamics to display the property of 'near decomposability'. In a nearly decomposable system: (i) the short-run behaviour of each element is approximately independent of the short-run behaviour of the other elements, and, (ii) the long-run behaviour of any element depends in only an aggregate way on the behaviour of other elements. Because elements only interact with one another in an aggregate fashion, the details of their internal interactions can be largely ignored in macro research: the behaviour of the whole can be understood in terms of the interactions amongst aggregate sub-systems.

Clearly, the plausibility of this argument will depend upon whether the interactions within even a nearly decomposable system are simple enough to be captured by an investigation process which ignores the detailed functioning of the elements. Not all the researchers would endorse this view. Yet it does simplify the task, in that we may be able to further our understanding of the role of accounting in organisational control by aggregating organisational processes into several large bundles and initially focusing only on the interactions between the bundles. In this manner it may be possible to make some sense of the problem, gradually lowering the level of resolution until a useful picture emerges.

Such a 'top–down' strategy may be criticised for being similar to what Lindblom (1959) has, in a different context, described as a root (comprehensive) approach, with all the problems thereby entailed. It is argued here, however, that the proposal is more in line with the 'soft-systems' approach advocated *inter alia* by Checkland (1981). At least in the analysis of human systems, it may be necessary in the first instance to adopt a higher level of resolution to obtain some perspective of the totality of the problem. As Checkland (1981, p. 165) commented:

> it has been found most useful to make the initial expression of a building up of the *richest possible picture* of the situation being studied. Such a picture then enables selection to be made of a viewpoint (or viewpoints) from which to study further the problem situation.

Certainly, the extant incremental (branch) approach has contributed significantly to our knowledge of accounting, and we are moving gradually towards a better understanding of the whole. On the other hand, the phenomena to be studied are so immensely complex that the overall picture may never emerge, or may tend to be obscured by the detail. The soft-systems approach, in contrast, places the overall picture in its ambit in the first instance, and keeps it there.

The discussion above suggests that if meaningful insights are to be obtained, then systems dynamics must be explicitly captured in research design. The control process described earlier is inextricably linked with notions of disequilibrium, change, and evolution. This suggests the limited usefulness of cross-sectional analysis *per se*. Yet the methods of longitudinal research are comparatively underdeveloped. For example, is historical time an adequate substitute for real time? How can we control for the vagaries of chance? How can comparative case studies be designed? These questions are yet to be adequately addressed in the literature.

In conclusion, accounting research needs to be reoriented away from the tradition of partial analysis towards the totality of its organisational context, and away from the tradition of statics towards the dynamics of organisational functioning. There is a desperate need to improve our understanding of the way in which organisational activities evolve over time and how organisational processes interact to shape these activities. Only such a total approach will explain why and how accounting is intertwined with organisational functioning.

REFERENCES

Abdel-khalik, A. R. and Lusk, E. J., 1974. Transfer pricing – a synthesis, *Accounting Review*, January, pp. 8–23.

Ackoff, R. L., 1979. The future of operational research is past, *Journal of the Operational Research Society*, **30** (2) February, pp. 93–104.

Amigoni, F., 1978. Management planning and control systems, *Journal of Business Finance and Accounting*, Autumn, pp. 279–291

Argyris, C., 1952. *The Impact of Budgets on People*: Controllership Foundation.

Argyris, C. and Schön, D. A., 1978. *Organizational Learning: A Theory of Action Perspective*: Addison-Wesley.

Arrow, K. J., 1964. Control in large organizations, *Management Science*, April, pp. 397–408.

Ashby, W. R., 1956. *Introduction to Cybernetics*: Chapman & Hall.

Ashby, W.R., 1960. *Design for a Brain*, 2nd Edn: Chapman & Hall.

Bariff, M. L. and Galbraith, J. R., 1978. Intraorganisational power considerations for designing information systems, *Accounting, Organizations and Society*, pp. 15–27.

Baritz, L., 1960. *The Servants of Power*: Wesleyan University Press.

Becker, S. and Green, D., 1962. Budgeting and Employee Behaviour, *Journal of Business*, October, pp. 392–402.

Beer, S., 1966. *Decision & Control*: John Wiley.

Beer, S., 1972. *Brain of the Firm*, 2nd Edn: Allen Lane, The Penguin Press.

Bennis, W., 1966. *Changing Organizations*: McGraw-Hill.

Bruns, W. J. and Waterhouse, J. H., 1975. Budgetary control and organizational structure, *Journal of Accounting Research*, Autumn, pp. 177–203.

Buckley, W., 1967. *Sociology and Modern Systems Theory*: Prentice-Hall.

Burchell, S., Clubb, C., Hopwood, A. G., Hughes, T. and Nahapiet, J., 1980. The roles of accounting in organisations and society, *Accounting, Organizations and Society*, **5** (1) 1980, pp. 5–27.

Burns, T. and Stalker, G. M., 1961. *The Management of Innovation*. London: Tavistock.

Burrell, G. and Morgan, G., 1979. *Sociological Paradigms and Organisational Analysis*: Heinemann.

Caplan, E. H., 1966. Behavioural assumptions of management accounting, *Accounting Review*, July, pp. 496–509.

Caplan, E. H., 1968. Behavioural assumptions of management accounting – report of a field study, *Accounting Review*, April, pp. 342–362.

Checkland, P. B., 1981. *Systems Thinking, Systems Practice*: Wiley.

Chenhall, R. H. and Morris, D., 1986. The impact of structure, environment and interdependence on the perceived usefulness of management accounting systems, *Accounting Review*, January, pp. 16–35.

Child, J., 1972a. Organizational structure, environment and performance: the role of strategic choice, *Sociology*, pp. 2–22.

Child, J., 1972b. Organization structure and strategies of control: a republication of the Aston study, *Administrative Science Quarterly*, June, pp. 163–176.

Child, J., 1977. *Organisations: A Guide to Problems and Practices*. London: Harper and Row.

Collard, D. A., 1973. 'External effects', in L. R. Amey (ed.) *Readings in Management Decision*: Longman.

Cooper, D. J., 1980. 'A social and organisational view of management accounting', in M. Bromwich and A. G. Hopwood, (eds) *Essays on British Accounting Research*: Pitman.

Cyert, R. M. and March, J. G., 1963. *A Behavioural Theory of the Firm*: Prentice-Hall.

Daft, R. L. and Macintosh, N. B., 1978. A new approach to design and use of management information, *California Management Review*, pp. 82–92.

Daft, R. L. and Macintosh, N. B., 1981. A tentative exploration into the amount and equivocality of information processing in organizational work units, *Administrative Science Quarterly*, 26, pp. 207–224.

Dalton, M., 1959. *Men Who Manage*: Wiley.

Davis, O. and Whinston, A., 1962. Externalities, welfare and the theory of games, *Journal of Political Economy*, June, pp. 241–262.

Dent, J. F. and Ezzamel, M. A., 1986. 'Organisational control and management accounting: a contingency critique', forthcoming.

Dermer, J., 1977. *Management Planning and Control Systems*: Irwin, 1977.

Drucker, P. F., 1964. Controls, control and management, in C. P. Bonini, R. K. Jaedicke, and H. M. Wagner (eds) *Management Controls, New Directions in Basic Research*: McGraw-Hill.

Earl, M. J. and Hopwood, A. G., 1980. From management information to information management, in H. C. Lucas Jnr. *et al* (eds) *The Information Systems Environment*: North Holland.

Ezzamel, M. A. and Hilton, K., 1980. Divisionalisation in British industry: a preliminary study, *Accounting and Business Research*, Spring, pp. 197–214.

Feldman, M. S. and March J. G., 1981. Information in organizations as signal and symbol, *Administrative Science Quarterly*, 26, June, pp. 171–186.

Flamholtz, E. G., 1972. Towards a theory of human resource value in formal organizations, *Accounting Review*, October, pp. 666–678.

Flamholtz, E., 1975. Small group interaction and task performance: its implications for managerial accounting, in J. L. Livingstone (ed.) *Managerial Accounting: The Behavioural Foundations*: Grid.

Galbraith, J. R., 1972. Organisation design: an information processing view, in J. W. Lorsch, and P. R. Lawrence, (eds), *Organisation Planning: Concepts and Cases*: Irwin.

Galbraith, J. R., 1977. *Organisation Design*: Addison Wesley.

Ginzberg, J., 1980. An organizational contingencies view of accounting and information systems implementation, *Accounting, Organizations and Society*, pp. 369–382.

Gordon, L. A. and Miller, D., 1976. A contingency framework for the design of accounting information systems, *Accounting, Organizations and Society*, pp. 59–70.

Gordon, L.A. and Narayanan, V.K., 1984. Management accounting systems, perceived environmental uncertainty and organization structure: an empirical investigation, *Accounting, Organizations and Society*, 9(1), pp. 33–47.

Gorry, G. A. and Scott-Morton, M. S., 1971. A framework for management information systems, *Sloan Management Review*, pp. 55–70.

Halpin, A. and Winer, B., 1957. 'A factorial study of the leader behaviour descriptions', in R. Stogdill, and A. Coons, (eds) *Leader Behaviour: Its Description and Measurement*: Ohio State University.

Hedberg, B. and Jonsson, S., 1978. 'Designing semi-confusing information systems for organisations in changing environments', *Accounting, Organizations and Society*, pp. 47–64.

Hedberg, B., Nystrom, P. C. and Starbuck, W. H., 1976. Camping on seesaws: prescriptions for a self-designing organization, *Administrative Science Quarterly*, **21**, March, pp. 41–65.

Herzberg, F., 1966. *Work and the Nature of Man*. Cleveland, OH: World.

Hickson, D. J., Hinnings, C. R., Lee, C. A., Schneck, R. E., and Pennings, J. M., 1971. A strategic contingencies' theory of intraorganisational power, *Administrative Science Quarterly*, June, pp. 216–229.

Hofstede, G. H., 1967. *The Game of Budget Control*: Van Gorcum.

Holmstrom, B., 1979. Moral hazard and observability, *Bell Journal of Economics*, Spring, pp. 74–91.

Hopwood, A. G., 1972. An empirical study of the role of accounting data in performance evaluation, empirical research in accounting: selected studies, Supplement to *Journal of Accounting Research*, **10**, pp. 156–182.

Hopwood, A. G., 1978. Towards an organizational perspective for the study of accounting and information systems, *Accounting, Organizations and Society*, pp. 3–14.

Hunt, J. W., 1972. *The Restless Organization*: Wiley International.

Jantsch, E., 1980. *The Self-Organizing Universe*: Pergamon.

Katz, D. and Kahn, R. L., 1978. *The Social Psychology of Organisations*, 2nd Edn: John Wiley.

Kenis, I., 1979. Effects of budgetary goal characteristics on managerial attitudes and performance. *Accounting Review*, October, pp. 707–721.

Kerr, S., Klinoski, R. J., Tolliver, J., and Von Gunov, M. A., 1975. 'Human information processing', in J. L. Livingstone, (ed.) *Managerial Accounting: The Behavioural Foundations*: Grid.

Khandwalla, P., 1972. The effect of different types of competition on the use of management controls, *Journal of Accounting Research*, Autumn, pp. 276–285.

Kimberly, J. R. and Miles, R. H., 1980. *The Organizational Life Cycle*: Jossey-Bass.

Lawler, E. E. and Rhode, J. G., 1976. *Information and Control in Organizations*: Goodyear.

Lawrence, P. R., and Lorsch, J. W., 1969. *Organization and Environment*: Irwin, first published 1967.

Lewin, K., 1947.'Group decision and social change', in T. M. Newcomb, and E. L. Hartley, (eds.) *Readings in Social Psychology*: Holt.

Likert, R., 1961. *New Problems of Management*: McGraw-Hill.

Lilienfeld, R., 1978. *The Rise of Systems Theory: An Ideological Analysis*: Wiley.

Lindblom, C. E., 1959. The science of muddling through, *Public Administration Review*, Spring, pp. 79–88.

Lowe, E. A., and McInnes, J. M., 1971. Control in socio-economic organisations: a rationale for the design of management control systems, *Journal of Management Studies*, May, pp. 213–227.

McGregor, D., 1960. *The Human Side of Enterprise*: McGraw-Hill.

Macintosh, N. B., 1981. A contextual model of information systems, *Accounting, Organizations and Society*, pp. 39–53.

Macintosh, N. B., 1985. *The Social Software of Accounting and Information Systems*: Wiley.

Macintosh, N. B. and Daft, R. L., 1987. Management control systems and departmental interdependencies: an empirical study, *Accounting, Organizations and Society*, **12**(1), pp. 49–61.

March, J. G., 1972. Model bias in social action, *Review of Educational Research*, pp. 413–429.

March, J. G., 1979. 'The Technology of Foolishness', in J. G. March, and J. P. Olsen, *Ambiguity and Choice in Organizations*, 2nd Edn: Universitetforlaget.

March, J. G., and Simon, H. A., 1958. *Organizations*: John Wiley.

Marschak, J. and Radner, R., 1972. *Economic Theory of Teams*: Yale University Press.

Mechanic, D., 1962. Source of power of lower participants in complex organisations, *Administrative Science Quarterly*, December, pp. 349–364.

Merchant, K. A., 1984, Influences on departmental budgeting: an empirical examination of a contingency model, *Accounting, Organizations and Society,* **9** (3/4) pp. 291–307.

Miles, R. E. and Snow, C. C., 1978. *Organizational Strategy, Structure and Process*: McGraw-Hill.

Miller, D., (1981) Towards a new contingency approach: the search for organizational Gestalts, *Journal of Management Studies*, pp. 1–26.

Mintzberg, H., 1979. *The Structuring of Organizations*: Prentice-Hall.

Otley, D. T., 1978. Budget use and managerial performance, *Journal of Accounting Research*, Spring pp. 122–149.

Otley, D. T., 1980. The contingency theory of management accounting: achievement and prognosis, *Accounting, Organizations and Society*, pp. 413–428.

Pennings, J. M., 1975. The relevance of the structural–contingency model for organizational effectiveness, *Administrative Science Quarterly*, September, pp. 393–409.

Perrow, C., 1967. A framework for the comparative analysis of organisations, *American Sociological Review*, pp. 194–208.

Pfeffer, J., 1978. *Organizational Design*. Arlington Heights, IL: AHM Publishing.

Pondy, L. R., 1967. Organizational conflict: concepts and models, *Administrative Science Quarterly*, September, pp. 296–320.

Porter, L. W. and Lawler, E. E., 1968. *Managerial Attitudes and Performance*: Irwin.

Ronen, J. and Livingstone, J. L., 1975. An expectancy theory approach to the motivational impacts of budgets. *Accounting Review*, October, pp. 671–685.

Schiff, M. and Lewin, A. Y., 1970. The impact of people on budgets, *Accounting Review*, April, pp. 259–268.

Searfoss, D. G., and Monczka, R. M., 1973. Perceived participation in the budget process and motivation to achieve the budget, *Academy of Management Journal*, pp. 541–554.

Shannon, C. and Weaver, W., 1949. *The Mathematical Theory of Communication*: University of Illinois Press.

Simon, H. A., 1962. The architecture of complexity, *Proceedings of the American Philosophical Society*, vol. 106, no. 6, December, pp. 467–482.

Simon, H. A., 1977. *The New Science of Management Decision*, Prentice-Hall.

Solomons, D., 1963. *Divisional Performance: Measurement and Control*: Irwin.

Sorter, G. H., and Becker, S. W., (with the assistance of Archibald, T. R. and Beaver, W. H.), 1964. Corporate personality as reflected in accounting decisions: some preliminary findings, *Journal of Accounting Research*, Autumn, pp. 183–192.

Stedry, A., 1960. *Budget Control and Cost Behaviour*: Prentice-Hall

Tannenbaum, A., 1966. *Social Psychology of the Work Organization*: Wadsworth.

Thompson, J., 1967. *Organizations in Action*: McGraw-Hill.

Thompson, J. D. and Tuden, A., 1959. 'Strategies, structures and processes of organizational decision', in J. D. Thompson et al. (eds), *Comparative Studies in Administration*: University of Pittsburgh Press.

Thornton, R., 1974. Controlling the technician: the adversary approach, *MSU Business Topics*, Summer.

Tosi, H., 1975. 'The human effects of managerial budgeting', in J. L. Livingstone (ed.), *Managerial Accounting: The Behavioural Foundations*: Grid.

Vroom, V. H., 1964. *Work and Motivation*: Wiley and Sons.

Waterhouse, J. H. and Tiessen, P., 1978. A contingency framework for management accounting systems research, *Accounting, Organisations and Society*, pp. 65–76.

Watson, D. J. H., 1975. 'Contingency formulations of organisational structure: implications for managerial accounting', in J. L. Livingstone (ed.), *Managerial Accounting: The Behavioural Foundations*: Grid.

Weick, K. E., 1979. *The Social Psychology of Organising*, 2nd Edn: Addison-Wesley.

Westerlund, G. and Sjostrand, S. E., 1979. *Organizational Myths*: Harper and Row.

Williamson, O., 1975. *Markets and Hierarchies: Analysis and Antitrust Implications*: Free Press.

Wood, S. 1979. A reappraisal of the contingency approach to organisation, *Journal of Management Studies*, October, pp. 334–354

Woodward, J., 1965. *Industrial Organisation: Theory and Practice*. London: Oxford University Press.

5

Human Information Processing

by Philip L. Powell

This chapter looks at some of the problems people experience in using information. The major thrust of management accounting has been the provision of information and the development of control mechanisms based on that information. Implicit in this idea is the view that people are able to acquire and use information effectively. Much work has been done in fields other than accounting, such as psychology, organisational behaviour and sociology, relating to the heuristics and biases people exhibit in their information usage. Whereas the motivational effects of management accounting control mechanisms are now well documented (see chapter 15), the accounting field has been slow to absorb many of the ideas on human information processing (HIP). Since 1967 a growing number of HIP studies have been undertaken in the auditing field, yet the management accounting area has been relatively neglected. This is perhaps because, by comparison with management accounting, the auditing field is better understood and its purposes and decisions well defined. Defined, that is, in the sense that its procedures are more amenable to programming. The interest of large auditing firms in auditing research has obviously had an effect. Conversely management accounting coverage is far broader and what constitutes goals or good decisions is harder to determine. The 'American Accounting Association Report on Courses in Management Accounting' (1972) recognised the need to integrate, amongst other things, behavioural science material into management accounting teaching but this seems to refer largely to motivation and control rather than HIP. Indeed, as early as 1966 Caplan raised objections to the behavioural foundations of management accounting. He saw management accounting as being very much based on Theory X assumptions – an assumption that the employees' approach to organisational goals is a negative or passive one. He also questioned the organisational goals that were stated. There appeared to be a need to bring psychological and behavioural elements into the rationale of management accounting systems.

The development of the literature on human information processing will be surveyed with particular regard to its impact on management accounting. Hence, in reviewing the literature the approach will be to concentrate on the broad techniques used, and the results found, rather than to look in detail at specific studies. Otley (1983) pointed out that most psychological findings regarding human information processing have been replicated in accounting contexts. Libby and Lewis (1977; 1982) have produced two excellent literature reviews in this field, as has Ashton (1982) and the reader is directed to these as a starting point for further study.

In looking at the literature, the nature of the subjects and the conditions under which the empirical testing was carried out should be borne in mind. Frequently, especially in North America, MBA students have been used as subjects and reservations have been expressed on the use of students and others as surrogates for accountants and financial analysts (Abdel-khalik 1974; Ashton and Kramer 1980). It should also be noted that subjects' laboratory behaviour may diverge considerably from real-world actions.

The accountant exists in a world of decision making. His role, as traditionally perceived, is to acquire information, filter it and pass it on to others in a meaningful form. Both the recipients of the information and the accountant make decisions based on the accountant's interpretation of the data. Unfortunately for him information is difficult to acquire and its relationship to the event it describes is often tenuous. Once he has the information the accountant is expected to process it accurately. Here also he exhibits problems – in attaching the proper weightings to items and in aggregating the data adequately.

It could be argued that these are growing problems. Organisations are becoming more complex, a function not only of their size and their increased ability to generate information but also of a greater sophistication in the level of analysis undertaken. For example, explicit recognition of uncertainty requires a method of quantifying and analysing it. This in turn requires a realistic view of the forces that cause the uncertainty and the ways in which these forces interact. Neoclassical organisation theory recognises that behavioural factors affect management (see chapter 1). Indeed, Scott (1961) identifies personality as one of five basic elements of the organisation when viewed as a system. HIP problems could also be viewed as introducing unintentional information asymmetry into the organisation.

Whilst one can talk of heuristics and biases which people commonly exhibit, the fact that human beings display individual differences must not be overlooked. This means that people have characteristic tendencies in their cognitive processes which influence their decision-making behaviour. Neither can the influences of stress, crisis and conflict on man's behaviour be ignored. Each of these factors will influence his decision making. A brief look at the literature on the nature of expert versus novice decision processes will also be undertaken. Finally there exists the organisational framework in which the decision making is carried out. This may impose upon the information user certain constraints and methodologies of action.

In this chapter all these items will be considered further in order to gauge their likely impact on management accounting.

Libby and Lewis (1977 and 1982) classified information processing variables into three areas. These relate to the input, which is concerned with the information set; the process, which looks at the decision maker and the output, which is the decision. At each of these stages variables which affect the decision process are identified. They also identified four types of study. Firstly the lens model approach based on the work of Brunswik (1952); secondly studies of probabilistic judgement; thirdly work on predecisional behaviour; and lastly cognitive style. Ashton (1982) took a broader approach, dividing the field into lens model studies and subjective expected utility research. The Libby and Lewis approach will be broadly followed here. The chapter is divided into four sections, addressing each of these areas. The techniques used in accounting research into HIP are borrowed heavily from their earlier psychological counterparts (Kahneman et al. 1982 is an excellent review example).

Underlying human information processing research is the basic model of man as an information processor. Hogarth (1980) identified four major concerns regarding man's limited information processing ability – perception of the information, the nature of processing, processing capacity, and memory. Perception of information is selective not comprehensive. Because man's sensors (eyes, ears etc.) are constantly assailed by numerous stimuli, he must be selective in order to cope. The nature of man's cognitive make-up dictates that he is largely sequential in his processing of information. Thus the order in which information is acquired may influence how it is used. Limited mental processing capacity requires people to indulge in strain-reducing activities when analysing and combining data. These strain-reducing activities take the form of heuristics or rules of thumb. Obviously, the use of heuristics means that optimal calculations are precluded and hence the resultant actions may be sub-optimal. Lastly, people have limited memory capacity. Miller (1956) assessed human short-term memory as being capable of holding seven (plus or minus two) pieces of information simultaneously. Whilst long-term memory has much greater capacity it suffers from distortion – especially in recall. Recognition is more accurate than recall. People will recognise facts presented to them whilst being unable to recall them. Recall is based on cues – uncued recall is difficult. Wrong or irrelevant cues may trigger inaccurate responses. In this context cues can be thought of as prompts or stimuli. It is also worth noting that people can usually remember actions, given conditions; but rarely conditions, given actions.

The consequence of limited information processing ability is 'bounded rationality'. Bounded rationality is a concept identified by Simon in 1961 and further examined in Newell and Simon (1972). They defined the problem as it exists as the task environment, whilst the problem solver's representation of the task is termed the problem space. Due to limited processing ability the problem space is a simplified model of the task environment. The behaviour with respect to the problem space may be rational but that with respect to the real situation may not be. Hence rationality is bounded by the simplified perception of the situation.

I. LENS MODEL STUDIES

The lens model was developed in 1952 by the psychologist Egon Brunswik (1952). It was first used in an accounting context in 1972. The lens model describes the decision situation with reference to the interaction between the environment, the cues that the judge (or decision maker) receives and the response. The decision maker is viewed as receiving a number of overlapping cues. The relationship of these cues to the actual event (and to the judge) is not explicit, hence he is regarded as viewing the event through a 'lens' of cues. The judge gets a distorted view of the situation, yet the nature and extent of this distortion is unknown.

Synthesising Brunswik's original work, Libby and Lewis (1982) identified three 'basic tenets' of the lens model framework. These are (i) behaviour is primarily a function of the nature of the environment; (ii) the numerous cues evident to the individual are usually imperfect and redundant predictors of the environment and (iii) in response to this unpredictability and redundancy, individuals develop a range of substitutable processes for task achievement. This may have implications for expectancy theory models (see chapter 3). Expectancy theory postulates that the individual's motivation is a function of his subjective perceptions of his environment. If the cues the individual uses are poorly related to the actual task then he may be motivated towards achieving a spurious goal.

Research using the lens model is performed using a regression model or analysis of variance (ANOVA) models to measure the importance of cues and hence to measure the accuracy of the subject's judgement. Simple linear models have been found to perform as well as more complex non-linear models (for instance Wiggins and

Hoffman 1968). It is worth noting that these studies are usually highly structured, being performed in laboratory conditions, where a limited, known task and set of cues are provided. This may limit their real-world value.

The use of this technique is now widespread. In the main it has been used in auditing research to investigate such items as internal control and the determination of materiality. Elsewhere it has been used with regard to the prediction of bankruptcy and stock market prices. This should not be taken to imply that there are no implications for management accounting in these studies. In such research, the role of individuals as processors of information is paramount. The setting of the research may be auditing, but the tasks, and hence the findings, should be readily applicable in a management accounting context.

Lens studies can be classified into three types. These are identified by Libby (1981) as (i) clinical versus statistical judgement; (ii) multiple cue probability learning; and (iii) policy capturing.

Clinical Versus Statistical Prediction

Early work in this area focused on the ability of clinical diagnosticians to make unaided judgement on various medical tasks. Their conclusions were compared to those made by simple statistical models. The result could be interpreted as a measure of the accuracy of the judgement of the human decision makers. Originally it was assumed that the decision maker would outperform a regression model. The results, however, indicated otherwise. In all cases the models were found to outperform the humans. This phenomenon has been termed 'bootstrapping'. Two factors appear to cause this result. Firstly, models are consistent over time; people for a variety of reasons are not. Secondly, the model should weight cues in an optimal way. Human decision makers were found to misweight cues, which resulted in errors.

The accounting research in this area is slightly at odds with its psychological counterparts. Accounting studies have shown a higher level of human achievement than had been found with the analysis of clinical diagnosticians. Indeed, Libby (1976) found that some bank loan officers outperformed their models.

A financial area in which several studies have been undertaken is bankruptcy or failure prediction. These usually rely on the work done by Beaver (1966) and others on the use of accounting ratios as predictors of business failure. In these studies, the ability of human judges is matched against a simple environmental model. Libby (1975) reported that bank loan officers were quite accurate in their failure predictions (although not matching the model) and high consensus was displayed among judges. Consistency over time was high as was the predictability of the subjects' responses.

Earlier comments indicated that the structured nature of much of this research cast some doubt on its usefulness. Frequently subjects were presented with cues and their response was based on this predetermined cue set. In reality, decision makers can specify the information cues that they want in order to make a judgement. Abdel-khalik and El-Sheshai (1980) attempted to allow their subjects to choose their information cues. The task of predicting business failure was presented to 28 bank lending officers. Judgement was based on pieces of information requested by the subjects up to a maximum of four items from a set of 18. Each of the information items had an associated cost.

Commenting on the results the authors state that 'human predictions of default fell short of the predictive ability of the mathematical models...mainly because of the less than optimal choice of information cues' (pp. 337). They further add that it is information choice not weighting that is important.

A management accounting study was undertaken by A. H. Ashton (1982). It focused on the predictive ability of magazine executives in determining quantity of advertising in a 14-year period in *Time* magazine. The results were consistent with previous studies in that an environmental model outperformed the individuals. A systematic under-prediction bias was exhibited by the subjects.

Trotman, Yetton and Zimmer (1983) pointed out that auditing judgements are not usually the concern of one individual. Auditing is frequently a team activity, so it is not surprising that single auditors underperform judgemental models. Groups may perform better than individuals. Hence the group processes involved in these decisions should be considered. Problems might arise due to the hierarchical nature of auditing teams. In studying this sort of problem it would be necessary to weight accurately the contributions of team members. A further observation was made by Bamber (1983), to the effect that auditors usually make judgements based on the work of other auditors. They therefore need to assess the reliability of their subordinates in making their final decision.

Multiple Cue Probability Learning

Decision makers are required to make predictions on the basis of a number of cues which may be probabilistically related. Multiple cue probability learning looks at the factors in the environment that inhibit or promote learning in such situations.

There are three major areas of interest to the management accountant in the multiple cue research. These are the role of feedback; the use of reporting formats; and the effects of changes in accounting rules.

The first area involves the role of feedback in decision making. If control mechanisms based on accounting data are going to be used, then feedback on performance needs to be provided to the individuals involved. 'Good' feedback should lead to improved performance in the future, whilst poor feedback is likely to have the opposite effect.

R. H. Ashton (1982) in a review of human information processing in accounting found only two lens model studies which were management accounting based. In one of these, Harrell (1977) used Anthony's (1965) management planning and control framework to investigate the role of feedback. Using 75 USAF officers based at the Air Training Command, Harrell investigated two of Anthony's assumptions. These were that middle managers' control decisions were influenced strongly by the organisational goals emphasised by more senior managers, and that these control decisions accurately incorporated the specific importance of the organisational goals. The staff of the Air Training Command were responsible for monitoring the performance of the base's pilot training wings. The experiment attempted to highlight how the subjects' control decisions were influenced by the relative importance of goals emphasised by their seniors. The training wings were considered to have five primary goals, with the aim to find the relevance of each goal to the decision maker. Each of the training wings were rated as satisfactory or unsatisfactory on each of the goals. The subjects were required to rate the wings overall on an eight point scale.

The 75 subjects were divided into five groups of which one was given no policy statement (group 1) and four were given an 'official' policy statement on the importance of various goals. Of these four groups, one received no feedback on their decisions (group 2), one was told that senior management had reached decisions which agreed with the policy statement (group 3), another that senior management had ignored the policy statement (group 4) and the final group (group 5) was fed random feedback. Analysis of the results showed that group 2 had made significantly different decisions from group 1 indicating that policy statements had an effect. The results from groups 2 and 3 were similar. The fourth group made different decisions from groups 2 and 3 indicating that contradictory feedback had an influence. Group 5, which received random feedback, made decisions not significantly different from group 2 (the no feedback group).

Harrell's conclusion was that managers' control decisions are influenced by the organisational goals that are emphasised by their seniors. However, the decision makers were unable to accurately weight the importance of specific goals. Harrell suggests that it is an inability to process accurately the information received that causes managers to make decisions inconsistent with organisational goals. Feedback is seen to be a successful way to mitigate this problem. This does seem to assume that managers are only interested in their seniors' goals. Organisational and agency theory work postulates, however, that different groups within the organisation will seek to attain different goals.

The second area of interest to management accounting is that of report formats. The management accountant has a reporting function, both to those from whom he receives the data, in the form of feedback, and to others who will base their decisions on his information. Accounting numbers are usually reported as just that, often being a tabulation of year end results or departmental variances. Yet it has long been accepted that information can be more easily assimilated through graphical or pictorial presentation. There has been a recent trend, especially in supplemental reporting to employees, of using graphs and other pictorial devices to portray information. The underlying assumption seems to be that the less sophisticated the user group, the more use there needs to be of non-numerical representations of the data.

Moriarity (1979) has tried to address one of the major drawbacks of graphs, that is that they can only represent a few variables with clarity. By using as a basis Chernoff's schematic human faces, Moriarity represented 13 variables in a form that his subjects could easily understand. Each feature of the face represented a financial aspect of the company concerned. For example, the size and shape of the face were determined by four ratios relating to sales and working capital. Relatively financially naive subjects were able to classify firms as failed or non-failed on the basis of these faces far more easily than by using accounting data. An interesting second result was that subjects using multidimensional graphics significantly outperformed a statistical model. The faces presumably made the weighting of factors easier and allowed inconsistencies to be more easily observed.

A later study by Stock and Watson (1984) found that subjects using schematic faces outperformed those using conventional, tabulated accounting data in making judgements. Since the order of presentation of the tabulated data was randomly constructed, hopefully control was allowed for data presentation problems. Data presentation has an effect on peoples' perception of results. For instance, primacy and recency effects mean that more attention is paid to the ends of a series than the middle. Thus, the subjects may have reacted to poorly presented data rather than making poor judgements. Primacy entails paying undue attention to the first elements in a series and is a form of anchoring. Conversely, recency involves concentrating on the final few elements and may be thought of as a use of the availability heuristic when a final conclusion is arrived at (both anchoring and availability are discussed further in section III). A further factor, but one that has not been highlighted in the literature, is mentioned in Guilfoyle (1986). She related how stock dealers, when confronted with columns of figures, only used the right-hand set in their decision-making process.

Indeed, the decision makers were doing this despite having stated that the left-hand column contained the more valuable data. In the Stock and Watson work the performance of the group using schematic faces was also not significantly different from a decision model, which contrasts with Moriarity's earlier finding.

Perhaps it can be deduced that models are better than humans at handling solely numerical data, yet there is no need to require humans to make decisions based only on this type of data. Whilst not expecting practising management accountants to present financial results to their superiors in the form of cartoon faces, this line of study does indicate the scope for alternative presentation methods.

The third area of interest to the management accountant investigates the effect of changes in accounting rules on the use of cues to which the rules gave rise. This is a study of functional fixation. Functional fixation refers to the inability of individuals to change their use of (accounting) numbers when the methods underlying the numbers alter. R. H. Ashton (1982) reported four pieces of functional fixation research. The basic technique used is to present the subject with a problem to solve and then change the accounting basis of the data. The subjects' judgements should be altered by the change in the accounting basis. If no change is apparent then functional fixation is present. For instance, Ashton (1976) gave his subjects a product pricing decision to make. They were then told that an accounting change had occurred and received new data. Ashton claimed that a sizeable proportion of the subjects used 'old' decision rules where new rules were called for. Thus the subjects exhibited functional fixation.

Swieringa, Dyckman and Hoskin (1979) criticised Ashton's methodology. Their results, using the same type of study, showed that decisions did alter in the light of new information. It is not clear in either of these studies to what extent the subjects were functionally fixated rather than merely exhibiting the use of the anchoring and adjustment heuristic (see section III). Anchoring and adjustment would involve insufficient adjustment of decisions in the light of new information rather than the application of an irrelevant decision rule. Other researchers have suggested that functional fixation has been present in their subjects. For example, Abdel-khalik and Keller (1979) reported functional fixation in bank officers in relation to an accounting change from FIFO to LIFO.

Policy Capturing

Policy capturing is concerned with the judgemental policies of individuals. In many situations there is interest in the agreement (consensus) between individuals on existing or proposed matters or in the importance of individual cues in the decision process. The amount of self-awareness that judges possess in their own decision processes is also scrutinised. Policy capturing attempts, by using the lens model paradigm, to investigate these areas. Consensus is of interest for two reasons. Firstly, consensus is needed in order to reach an acceptable and easily implemented conclusion. Secondly, insights gained from observing the decision process should enable the process by which consensus is reached to be better understood.

Research studies generally use ANOVA techniques or multidimensional scaling. Work in this area has tended to focus on auditing. The majority of studies investigate internal control and materiality, though once again the management accountant does carry out tasks similar to these, so the relevance to the management accounting should not be underplayed.

R. H. Ashton (1982) identified 11 studies of internal control evaluation. Few studies of note seem to have been undertaken since then, most being replications. By and large these studies involve the rating of various internal control systems by the judges. The majority of these studies derive from Ashton's 1976 work. In his research 63 auditors were presented with 32 payroll cases. Each case contained six internal control questions pre-answered 'yes' or 'no' to indicate a strength or weakness. The auditors were asked, using a six-point scale, to evaluate the overall strength of the system.

The stability of judgement over time was also examined by repeating the study with the same subjects at a later date. Libby and Lewis (1982) summed up the results of this research thus;

> Auditors' evaluations exhibited a high degree of between judge consensus and consistency over time in their evaluations. They relied most heavily on the separation of duties in forming their judgements and were quite aware of their judgemental processes (p. 235).

Ashton and Kramer (1980) compared the judgements of auditors and students in performing the same internal control task. The results showed that, as might be expected, the students were less predictable and had less self-insight than the auditors. These differences may have been attributable to the students' age, lack of experience or wealth.

Brown (1983) used the same methodology to investigate the degree of reliance external auditors felt they could place on internal auditors' findings. The results of consensus amongst the subjects were in line with Ashton's results. Stability over time was found to be high. Interestingly, less experienced auditors were found to have more insight into their own judgement processes than their more experienced counterparts. The tentative explanation for this was that the experienced auditors related the judgement task to familiar audit settings. This runs counter to the work on expert versus novice performance which would suggest that the auditors with greater experience would have more scripts or prototypes to call upon and hence would be expected to outperform their colleagues.

The materiality research is exemplified by that of Moriarity and Barron (1976). Their aim was to investigate the 'black box' of judgement of materiality and hence shed light on why auditors faced with the same evidence reach different conclusions. The subjects were required to estimate pre-audit materiality. Results indicate that the decision makers were consistent in their judgements, yet there was low inter-person consensus.

Joyce (1976) studied expert judgement in the audit planning process. The individuals were observed to exhibit significant differences in self-insight and a low degree of consensus. The author comments that this lack of self-insight could have important implications for training. On the job auditing training often involves the communication of professional expertise from senior to junior members of staff. If these senior staff members are unaware of their decision processes then they could be communicating poor decision rules to their juniors.

Biggs and Mock (1983) investigated the causes of the low degree of consensus between auditors. They point out that most studies have sought to establish the existence, or lack, of consensus, yet few have looked at the reasons why this should be the case. Using verbal protocol analysis – analysing a transcript of the decision maker verbalising his decision processes – they sought to establish the problem space of each of their subjects. It was hypothesised that individuals' different problem spaces will lead to different decisions. Biggs and Mock identified four factors which seemed to account for a substantial amount of the decision variance. These were, firstly the information search strategy employed by the subject; secondly the variation in the reliance placed on internal control results; thirdly the number of alternatives considered; and lastly the decision heuristics employed by the individual. These can only be tentative results given the very small sample size yet they give a valuable insight into possible reasons for the lack of consensus between experienced auditors. In contrast, bond raters were found to display high levels of confidence in their judgement in a study by Danos, Holt and Imhoff (1984). They also exhibited a high degree of inter-person consensus.

Broadly, the implications for management accounting of lens model studies can be summarised as follows. The superiority of simple mathematical models over human decision makers in certain situations should not be regarded as a threat. Rather, this finding should be exploited. Decision aids can be designed for models used in structured decision situations thereby allowing decision makers sufficient time to concentrate on unstructured problems. For example, operational research models should be used in deterministic situations as an alternative to managerial judgement. There is also a strong suggestion from the literature that the form of presentation of reports needs to be carefully considered if the recipients are to derive maximum use from them. Alternatives to numerical data seem to offer most in this area. Feedback, too, is important. The management accountant needs to have a reporting back as well as a reporting function. Financial reporting often has a public relations aspect. Activities such as income smoothing and the changing of reporting bases are designed to offer signals to the market. Internal reporting needs have none of this gloss, although in the principal/agent dichotomy of agency theory this may not be the case. Changes in accounting methods should be highlighted so that the decision maker can adjust his decision rules accordingly. Training would also seem to have an important role in promoting consensus. Care should, however, be taken to avoid structured training which may result in decision makers becoming functionally fixated by their training rules.

II. PROBABILISTIC JUDGEMENT

Probabilistic judgement considers the decision maker's use of subjective probabilities. It is perhaps useful at this point to consider what is meant by subjective probabilities and how people use probabilities.

Work, such as that by Jaedicke and Robichek (1964) in the area of cost–volume–profit analysis, focuses on the need to take uncertainty into account when looking at particular problems. Uncertainty is expressed via the use of probability distributions to describe the model parameters. For instance a probability function will be attached to next year's sales and hence to next year's profit. The world is seen as probabilistic, yet, as Hogarth (1980) pointed out, this is merely because one is unable to appreciate or quantify the factors that underlie occurrences. There are a multitude of factors which affect next year's sales. If one were able accurately to assess these forces then one could put a value on future turnover. However this cannot be done, so one assumes that happenings are probabilistic.

To appreciate probabilities there needs to be an awareness of randomness. Most of the processes that a management accountant deals with have a random element. Any control process or variance analysis is bound to be affected by non-controllable factors. In investigating variances, one should only investigate those which are deemed 'significant'. However, people tend to underestimate the degree of randomness that an in-control process can generate. There is an expectation that processes will produce 'normal' results. Hogarth (1980) stated that any process will generate fluctuations in its performance around its mean level. This is not only true of machinery. Human performance is also likely to fluctuate. Hogarth suggested that this may have an implication for 'management by exception'. Poor performance is likely to be followed by better performance. If the process has a random element, this increase in achievement will occur regardless of any intervention from an outside authority. The reverse of this is also likely to be true. Hence, intervention in such a process is unnecessary unless the 'bounds of significance' are crossed.

Coupled with the problem of randomness is that of independence. Many of the events that the management accountant deals with are statistically independent. That is, the probability of one event is not in any way affected by another event. Despite awareness of independence people still exhibit tendencies such as those exemplified by the 'gambler's fallacy'. This is the ability to delude oneself that a process with a known, fixed probability does however change.

The human, then, is not very good at using probabilistic information. The accountant's job, however, requires him to use probabilities. Whilst some of these probabilities can be considered as a simplifying device (as in next year's sales forecast), other probabilities are real. That is, they come from statistical estimation.

In most cases the accountant will have some prior knowledge of the situation under consideration. For instance in an auditing case the auditor will have an assessment of the company's internal control system and probably prior years' audit papers. Therefore, he has a prior probability distribution regarding the situation. According to probability theory, he should use Bayesian techniques to update his probability estimate in the light of new information. It is further assumed that he aims to maximise his expected utility for any given action. In order to maximise one's utility it is necessary to consider all alternatives.

Often when performing expected value calculations the choice result is very sensitive to the probabilities used in estimating the payoffs. Hence confidence in the probability inputs is needed if the results are to be relied upon.

Bayesian results are usually seen as the benchmark by which human use of probabilistic information is judged. Yet, in the real world all the requirements of Bayes' theorem are seldom present. Collingridge (1982) identified five factors that must be satisfied for proper use of Bayesian techniques. These are (i) all states are identified; (ii) all options are identified; (iii) all payoffs are known; (iv) all relevant data has been gathered; and (v) all interpretations of the data are known. Hence the use of Bayes' theorem should be treated with care if the above requirements are not all satisfied. That is not to say that use of Bayes' theorem in the real world is to be avoided. Holt and Cooper (1983) pointed out that, despite the above, using Bayesian techniques can ensure that what is known is treated in a logical and consistent manner.

The literature on probabilistic judgement seeks to evaluate the decision maker's capabilities at each of the decision stages. As Libby and Lewis (1982) suggest, often only the final choice can be observed, not the components which lead to it. In order to disaggregate this problem, researchers have tended to study separate, constituent parts, of the decision process.

Just as the review of research on lens model studies was divided into separate areas along the lines of Libby and Lewis (1982), so the same subdivisions will be followed here too. R. H. Ashton (1982) referred to this body of work as the subjective expected utility (SEU) model.

Probabilistic judgement literature focuses on three different areas. Firstly, the elicitation of subjective probabilities. Secondly, the common heuristics and biases people employ in using information, together with tests on the subject's ability to evaluate information. Finally, there are studies which examine expert judgement using the framework of a normative decision theory. Again, the methods employed in accounting research are methodologically based on psychological research. The research results from the two fields are not dissimilar.

Subjective Probability Elicitation

Despite being a relatively new field, accounting actually predates, at any sophisticated academic level, the study of probability. Hacking (1975) pointed out that the modern concepts of probability are less than 300 years old. Taking up this theme Nisbett et al. (in Kahneman, Slovic and Tversky, 1982) alluded to a concept of probability handling becoming more 'natural' for people as their exposure to it increases. They pointed to the growing use of probabilistic information in such everyday situations as weather forecasts and sports reports.

Subjective probabilities reflect the individual's degree of belief, or confidence, that a particular outcome or event will occur (Savage, 1954). Eliciting these probabilities involves finding methods for drawing out of the individual these, sometimes subconscious, probability assessments.

It should not be assumed that subjective probabilities are an 'optional' device in management accounting. That is, subjective probabilities should be viewed as an internal part of management accounting analysis, not as a sophisticated addendum. Business forecasting, for instance, is only a means for assessing the probabilities assignable to future events (see chapter 8). Chesley (1975), in a review article on subjective probability elicitation, points out that in a number of accounting fields subjective probabilities are needed. He cited their use in control theory, capital budgeting, depreciation accounting, human resource accounting and for confidence intervals for financial statements. Clearly a number of these areas are relevant to management accounting.

Two research approaches are identified; one involves the study of the quality of peoples' estimates of probabilities, whilst the second goes back a stage to examine the processes which determine how the estimates arise.

One of the major problems encountered is the lack of a positive theory for subjective probability elicitation. Results from Chesley's own work are echoed by later writers who agree that the major determinant of a subject's performance regarding probabilities is the elicitation technique used. Crosby (1981), for instance, found this to be the case in an auditing context. Results mirror findings from other fields in that the ordering of questions put to subjects was important. Also, some of the heuristics discussed later were evident (chiefly anchoring). Libby and Lewis (1982) summed up the research findings as being the following: '(1) that most decision makers are overconfident, (2) that training seems to improve performance and (3) experts sometimes perform very well' (p. 251).

These results are perhaps ambivalent for the accountant. The notion of prudence is not helped by the over-confidence decision makers display. However, the effect of training might mitigate this. Accounting research has primarily focused on auditing in this area, yet there is no evidence that other accounting fields would display different results. Given the emphasis on training in the auditing profession, one might argue that auditors would be likely to out-perform others in probabilistic tasks.

Wallsten and Budescu (1983) examined the literature on the reliability and validity of experts' probability assessments. Experts have been shown to be highly reliable in probability encoding and their assessments tend to be very valid (reliability here being synonymous with consistency, and validity meaning that the subjects' views are accurately expressed). Few studies were found to have used experts as subjects, most using only novices. As a final note the recent interest in the use of Bayesian techniques in auditing for the assessment of internal control will need to take account of the pitfalls of subjective probability assessment highlighted in the literature.

Heuristics and Biases

Just as man exhibits bounded rationality because a situation is too complex for him to fully comprehend, so he may use strain-reducing activities in his information processing. These strain-reducing activities are in the form of heuristics and biases. Heuristics can be defined as rules of thumb or simplifying processes which result in an acceptable end product but this outcome will seldom be optimal. Just what defines an acceptable decision is hard to determine. It is perhaps best if the decision maker is made aware of his probable use of heuristics and can then judge for himself the likely impact that they will have had on his judgement.

There is no shortage of psychological literature on the impact of heuristics and biases (e.g. Tversky and Kahneman 1974). Perhaps as a result of the volume of psychological work appearing in this area, it was one of the first to catch the attention of accounting researchers.

Commonly, three heuristics are discussed, although Sage (1981) has identified 27 biases. The boundaries of what constitutes a particular heuristic are blurred, hence broader categories are more useful for management accounting purposes. This section will concentrate on the three most common, namely: representativeness, availability, and anchoring and adjustment.

Representativeness involves assessing the probability that process B generated event A, by the degree to which A resembles B. If A is seen to be highly representative of B then the probability that B gave rise to A is considered high. Thus, this heuristic can be thought of as a type of stereotyping of the observed event. It could be argued that stereotyping is an efficient short cut since presumably stereotypes only arise after considerable reinforcement of some idea or experience. Nevertheless, use of the representativeness heuristic will lead to certain systematic biases in the individual's estimation of probabilities. Tversky and Kahneman (1974) have identified five major biases. These can be summarised as (i) an insensitivity to prior probabilities; (ii) disregard of the impact of sample size on the variance of the sampling distribution; (iii) misconceptions of the likelihood of different sequences resulting from a random process; (iv) insensitivity to the predictability of data resulting in unwarranted overconfidence in judgements; and finally (v) an illusion of validity, that is people are overconfident in their judgements.

R. H. Ashton (1982) reported that most accounting studies of heuristics have concentrated on representativeness. Swieringa et al. (1976) investigated a number of the results that Tversky and Kahneman had reported. Their tests, which were not all accounting based, failed to substantiate all the earlier premises. The authors' conclusion is that heuristics are not radical departures from a normative Bayesian approach but a simplification of that approach.

The availability heuristic concerns the ease with which occurrences of a particular event can be brought to mind. People will assess the likelihood of event A occurring by the number of instances of A that can be remembered. In a business context the probability that a firm will fail could be judged by the number of similar firms which failed that can be recalled. The work on availability is again based on Tversky and Kahneman (1974). They describe four biases which may be exhibited if this heuristic is used. These are categorised as follows: (i) biases due to the retrievability of instances – the more easily retrieved (from memory) the instance, due to familiarity or saliency, the more likely the event is seen as being; (ii) biases due to the effectiveness of the search set. The context in which the search is performed may determine the ease with which an event is recalled; (iii) biases of imaginability – these occur when instances are not stored in memory but constructed when required; the ease with which one can construct the situations is viewed as a measure of the frequency of the actual event; and lastly (iv) illusory correlation – where people perceive a correlation which may not exist. Tversky and Kahneman state that availability explains illusory correlation. The frequency with which two events co-occur is judged on the strength of the associative bond between them. A strong bond leads one to conclude that the events are frequently paired.

Availability seems to have largely escaped the attention of accounting researchers. Neither Libby and Lewis (1982) nor R. H. Ashton (1982) reported any accounting studies specifically related to availability. However, in the light of the similarity between results in accounting and other fields, it is likely that accountants exhibit tendencies to use the availability heuristic to the same extent as subjects in other professions. The work by Libby (1985) seems to be the first investigation of availability in an accounting context. He used a group of experienced auditors as subjects. The subjects were required to highlight significant financial statement errors via an analytical review. This review was undertaken prior to any (hypothetical) further audit investigation. Of interest to Libby was the perceptions of error frequency exhibited by the auditors. The results indicated that the availability heuristic was employed when identifying errors.

The third heuristic considered is anchoring and adjustment. One of the reasons zero base budgeting (Pyhrr 1970) (see also chapter 9) has gained a following, albeit somewhat limited in a practical context, is that budget setters in normal environments tend to use anchoring and adjustment. That is, the present year's budget is some function of the previous year's budget. This will tend to perpetuate the current situation and not allow expanding budgetary groups to expand fast enough whilst cushioning underperforming areas from justifiable cuts. The anchoring and adjustment heuristic involves picking a starting point (the anchor) and insufficiently adjusting it in the light of new information. The weight attached to further information is less than that for the initial information set. Different starting points will yield different end points and hence different final decisions.

Three potential factors account for anchoring and adjustment according to Tversky and Kahneman (1974). These involve firstly insufficient adjustment, secondly biases in the evaluation of conjunctive and disjunctive events, and thirdly anchoring in the assessment of subjective probability distributions. The second factor acknowledges that people overestimate probabilities that are conjunctive whilst underestimating disjunctive ones. This is illustrated by gamblers who prefer to bet on conjunctive situations rather than simple situations and who also prefer simple situations to disjunctive ones. The third area refers to the fact that people will give confidence intervals that are too narrow (i.e. they are overconfident) when estimating quantities.

Psychological research has identified the use of anchoring and adjustment in a number of situations. Libby and Lewis (1982) commented that in the accounting field results have, however, been inconclusive. They report that Joyce and Biddle (1981), in a study of auditors, found little evidence of anchoring. The conservative nature of the audit approach and the trained nature of the subjects might have accounted for this. It is worth noting that most of the psychological studies used statistically naive undergraduate students as subjects, whereas accounting students and subjects have usually had some prior statistical training.

Magee and Dickhaut (1978), in an investigation of cost control, studied subjects' choice of problem-solving strategies in an uncertain environment. Different heuristics were used by individuals when the problem environment was altered. The subjects were able to choose their own heuristic solution and, the authors hypothesise, would choose the optimal heuristic for the situation. Whilst not explicitly mentioning anchoring, the authors do allude to various heuristics being employed by their subjects.

Kinney and Uecker (1982) reported the use of anchoring and adjustment by auditors in an experimental setting. They also claim that the anchoring hypothesis is incomplete. They conclude that 'the hypothesised anchoring effect did not always occur and the magnitude of the effect was affected by other factors'.

It is also worth looking at one further heuristic – hindsight bias. Ashton (1982) described the research findings thus:

> it was found that the knowledge that an outcome had occurred increased its perceived prior probability of occurrence, whilst the knowledge that an outcome had not occurred decreased its perceived prior probability of occurrence.
> (pp. 107).

Fischhoff (1982) commented that people consistently exaggerate what they think that they could have predicted. This leads to overconfidence in their own perceived foresight ability. It is likely that the management accountant will experience his own hindsight bias, or that of others, in the course of his work. The failure to predict cost overruns or the inability to foresee a rise in the price of oil, for example, are seen as incompetence by people who, after the event, are supremely confident in their own ability to predict the actual outcome. The short-term planning model described in chapter 9 discusses the intertemporal dependencies in planning. If such dependencies exist, then a planning process which does not use explicit past data and predictions may suffer from the effects of hindsight bias.

Normative Framework Research

The normative framework research detailed in Libby and Lewis (1982) uses a framework in which to describe the decision making behaviour of individuals. Newton (1977) studied accountants' decision processes when resolving materiality issues. Her hypothesis was that the judgement made in each case 'is influenced by the degree of uncertainty about the final resolution of the issue and the [individuals'] willingness to accept the risk of an incorrect decision'. She found her subjects did in some sense take the probability of an event occurring into account in their decision process. A further interesting point is that the results showed that 55.3 per cent of the subjects were risk averters whilst, surprisingly, 34.2 per cent were risk seekers.

Ward (1976) reported that the general concept of materiality was shared by most professional accountants. There was also general agreement and consensus concerning the relative importance of factors that should be taken into account when assessing materiality. This is slightly at odds with the work on consensus amongst auditors which has generally shown great differences in self-insight and a low degree of consensus.

Drawing together the issues in the probabilistic judgement literature, the overriding need is for an awareness, by the management accountant, of the processes highlighted. An awareness may aid decision making in such instances as the investigate/do not investigate dichotomy, the assigning of probabilities to model parameters in cost–volume–profit analysis, and capital budgeting problems. Caution needs to be used whenever probabilities are employed. Not only are these probabilities likely to be poorly derived but also poorly used. The research on eliciting subjective probabilities is inconclusive. Tentatively, it is possible to say that training is helpful. Producers and users of accounting data seem to exhibit heuristic use in their activities, yet any measurement of this tendency is suspect with the tools currently available.

III. PREDECISIONAL BEHAVIOUR

Decision making is not a static, one-input, process. Rather it is dynamic, often using many inputs which are not readily available but have to be searched for. A simple decision analysis framework, such as that described by Hogarth (1980), involves seven steps. These include structuring the problem, assessing uncertainties and consequences, gathering information, evaluating alternatives, sensitivity analysis for the consequences and uncertainties, and finally, choice. To this could be added monitoring and feedback. Whilst not suggesting that all problem solvers follow such a rational, sequential path, it can be assumed that some element of all these steps is carried out. Sometimes the decision maker will be aware of the process he is following, although often some elements may be vague or carried out subconsciously.

Predecisional behaviour research investigates the processes prior to the final choice. It differs from the work that has been discussed up to now in that the decision process is no longer regarded as a 'black box'. With few exceptions, lens model studies and probabilistic judgement studies primarily focus on inputs and final outputs. Predecisional behaviour research considers the decision process in detail.

Einhorn (1976) neatly summed up decision-making tasks in the real world. He stressed that the task is not clearly defined and the information desired needs to be searched for. The information that is acquired is not necessarily reliable and the extent of its accuracy is unknown. Finally, hypothesis formation occurs within a broad range of possibilities. This strongly contrasts with the structured nature of laboratory research used in much of the lens model and probabilistic judgement research discussed in sections I and II.

At the beginning of this chapter reference was made to the Newell and Simon work on bounded rationality in human information processing. Predecisional behaviour research is related to this work and draws on the same techniques of analysis.

Studying a decision being made is not a simple task. The mere fact that a researcher is trying to observe the process will often affect the way it is carried out. Numerous problems are likely to be encountered. Firstly the decision maker may be unable to communicate his ideas. This may be due to inarticulacy or because he has no awareness of his decision processes. Decision makers also tend, if asked, to give 'textbook fiction' methods of problem solving. That is, they claim to use the rigorous models of decision analysis they have been taught should be applied in such cases. They are loath to admit that the actual processes they use are much simpler. Examples exist (see, for instance, the literature on knowledge acquisition for expert systems) of experts being ashamed of their decision processes because they feel that to reveal simple decision rules makes them appear 'less expert'. Lastly the decision maker may suffer from memory problems when asked to explain his actions.

The above problems are most apparent if the decision maker is asked to verbalise his judgement process. Such a verbalising technique is often used in predecisional behaviour analysis. Verbal protocol analysis is then used on the transcripts of the decision sessions in order to highlight the important aspects of the process.

Perhaps a better method of analysing decision making is for the observer to be as unobtrusive as possible. A technique that utilised this is the study of eye movements. It is hypothesised that one can identify the important elements that a person uses to reach a decision by recording their eye movements and length of eye fixation. The amount of use of particular pieces of information can be judged from the eye contact the decision maker has with it. The sequence of information search can also be judged from the individual's eye movement progression. It is then possible to build up a picture of how the individual searches for information, the order in which the information is used and the amount of time each information item holds his attention.

The third major technique used is explicit information search. Here each piece of information is separated and the subject is required to ask for the data item that he requires. A record of the sequence of information items used, together with a note of the time spent with each piece, gives a guide to the relative importance of various items. Payne, Braunstein and Carroll (1978) discussed these three methods in greater detail.

Libby (1981) discussed three of the major areas of research. These are (i) the structure of expert memory; (ii) the role of hypothesis in directing information search and (iii) the selection of alternative decision rules.

Problem solving by experts relies heavily on their use of memory. As discussed in the introduction, human short-term memory is very limited whereas long-term memory has virtually infinite capacity. Newell and Simon (1972) likened human memory to that of a computer. Indeed, they went further and pointed out the analogy between computer and human information processing systems. Both the human and the machine have three types of memory; short-term, long-term (both internal) and external. For the human, external memory is anything he cares to record in any form. The nature of expert memory has been widely investigated with some of the most interesting work being done in the field of artificial intelligence. In order to construct a computer system to perform some of the tasks of human experts it is necessary to comprehend how human experts use strain-reducing heuristics to limit the information processing involved in decision taking. For instance, expert chess players outperform novice ones. This is not achieved merely by evaluating all the possible moves within a game. Clearly, with approximately 10^{120} feasible moves in an average game, enumerating them is not realistic. Libby (1981) reported Chase and Simon's 1973 work based on DeGroot (1965). Expert chess players were able to recognise meaningful patterns of chess pieces very rapidly. The experts could store these patterns in short-term memory whilst the novices, with less experience to call upon, could not.

Eggleton (1976) suggested that individuals form abstracted prototypes of processes. These prototypes form the basis for future predictions. Any distortions in the generation process, using heuristics for instance, will cause prediction errors in future estimates using the prototypes. Cautious empirical support was offered for the hypothesis, although the task involved was tangential to accounting. Commenting on the results Cohen (1976) cast some doubt on the methodology of the experimental design. Mock (1976) questioned the relevance of Eggleton's work for accounting although he went on to concede that there may be accounting implications in this type of study.

It is possible to see a place for Eggleton's work in the study of the role of hypothesis in information search. Just as early lens model work was clinically based, so studies of hypothesis generation have frequently been performed in medical settings. The results suggest that clinical experts have a large number of hypotheses stored in long-term memory. From these they retrieve a small number of hypotheses relevant to the current situation. Libby (1981) commented that these hypotheses are representative. That is, the clinicians use the representativeness heuristic as a strain-reducing device in their selection of potential solutions. If this is the case, and the subjects do make expert decisions whilst using limiting biases, then perhaps heuristics should be viewed as a beneficial rather than harmful method of solution selection. Additional data is then gathered by the expert in an attempt to confirm one of the initial set of hypotheses. It would seem that clinicians are using a backward-chaining search strategy. That is, they start from a conclusion and try to confirm or disconfirm it. This seems plausible since the alternative, forward chaining (or data driven), entails gathering all the data available before trying to reach a conclusion. In a medical setting gathering all the data prior to hypothesis generation would be too time consuming. It would also entail excessive use of short-term memory.

Libby (1981) pointed to the possibility of anchoring in evidence screening and also availability in hypothesis generation from memory. One of the most significant findings was that the majority of errors in the final diagnosis were accounted for by errors in initial hypothesis generation. If this is a globally applicable finding then it has implications for training. The aspiring expert needs to be equipped with a full range of hypotheses in order to retrieve a relevant set when confronted with a new problem.

The selection of alternative decision rules (Libby 1981) is consistent with a bounded rationality view of the world. That is, since the complexity of many tasks is beyond the capabilities of the individual, he tends to use simplifying processes. This has been shown to occur in the mathematics of decision making. For instance, non-compensatory models will be used as a substitute for compensatory ones.

It is possible to see management accounting implications in each of Libby's three areas of predecisional behaviour researching. Accounting experts acquire their expertise via a long process of 'osmosis'. That is, the process of learning involves gradual absorption of the techniques needed. If it was possible to distil the essence of accounting expertise from existing experts then the system could be short-circuited by the use of appropriate training. This could involve the teaching of heuristic problem-solving methods as well as a set of rigorous techniques for solution derivation. There is, however, a suggestion that expertise is based on pattern recognition. Pattern recognition is largely derived from experience, possibly limiting the potential for taught elements.

The design of decision aids to assist the information search and to help in the selection of alternative decision rules might prove a fruitful area. Decision aid design will be discussed further below.

IV. COGNITIVE STYLE

Cognitive style is concerned with the characteristic methods of functioning that individuals exhibit. Macintosh (1985) pointed out that cognitive style should not be confused with personality. Cognitive style is a subset of personality. Others (for instance Holt and Cooper 1983) stated that both cognitive style and personality are component parts of individual differences and that these two, together with demographic and other factors (such as aptitude and motivation) combine to account for differences in human functioning.

The majority of cognitive style research in the accounting field has focused on the design of information systems and more specifically on how to tune the information system to the needs of the user. The management accountant is likely to be involved in designing management information systems. He should, therefore, be aware of the differing styles of users and attempt to incorporate this in his design.

There is, however, no reason why differing cognitive styles should not be a contingent factor in organisational design. Just as behavioural factors are given a place in organisational theory, so too should cognitive factors. For instance, it is likely that the management of a start-up computer software house will have different cognitive styles from those of an established multinational corporation.

Cognitive style or personality will also impact on many other management accounting elements, such as participation in processes, motivation theory, attribution theory (see chapter 3), leadership style and even cost concepts. Expanding this last area as an example, as outlined in chapter 7, Demski and Feltham (1976) see cost as an arbitrary concept, whereas Buchanan (1969) postulates that cost is subjective. These writers acknowledge that cost is related to (amongst other factors) the individual's attitude to risk and uncertainty. Different psychological types may, then, view cost differently.

Whereas the factors that were considered earlier in this chapter pointed to consistent modes of action of subjects in general, the work on cognitive style looks at functioning at the individual level. Hence the cognitive style findings should always be borne in mind when analysing other studies since they could affect the results. Unless individual differences are accounted for the results may only reflect the specific subject's responses and may not be applicable in a general context. Thus, when constructing a judgemental experiment one should be aware that the findings will not only reflect the ability of the subjects but also the nature of the task, individual differences and such factors as stress and conflict.

There is no doubt that individual differences exist although the exact nature of these is unclear. Macintosh's (1985, p. 105) conclusion from this work is that 'individuals with different cognitive structures should prefer, and work better with, different types of accounting and information systems'. Further, he adds that matching cognitive style characteristics with system characteristics should ensure more effective use of the systems. This matching should be undertaken both on the basis of the cognitive style of the user and his personality. The cognitive style elements are detailed below. For Macintosh the personality traits of relevance are basically divisions along Jungian lines (for instance introversion v. extroversion).

Sage (1981) reported on the work of Mason and Mitroff (1973) who have identified five essential variables in information system design. They argued that the human element is an integral part of the management information system. The first of the five elements seen as important is the psychological-type variable. Here the authors distinguish between sensing and intuitive types in information gathering, and feeling versus thinking individuals in information evaluation. Secondly, the problem variable determines the degree of structure inherent in the problem. Thirdly, the organisational context variable is concerned with the control structures evident. Fourthly, the method-of-evidence-generation variable relates to the inquiry system available (for instance, databased, model-based, etc.). Lastly, the mode of presentation variable is concerned with the report style. Sage commented that only the first of these is specifically related to cognitive style.

Macintosh (1985) discussed two of the most important cognitive style variables. First is the classification of individuals into high and low analytics on the basis of their ability to differentiate objects from their contexts. High analytics can distinguish discrete elements of a problem, low analytics cannot. If managers are low analytics then they will tend to reject highly structured information systems. Research by Doktor and Hamilton (1973) did not, however, support this.

Benbasat and Dexter (1979, p.747) reported that 'structured/aggregate reports are preferable for high analytic decision makers, and database inquiry systems ("events" approach) are preferable for low analytics'. A replicated and extended study by the same authors (Benbasat and Dexter, 1982) confirmed the earlier findings. Decision aids enabled low analytics to perform at the same level as high analytics. Benbasat and

Taylor (1982) have also been rather scathing about cognitive style research. They have argued that the underlying theory is inadequately developed, that the assessment tools may be lacking and that research design is often faulty.

Macintosh (1985) also distinguished between analytics and heuristics. Heuristics, as the name implies, use very *ad hoc* procedures to process information and are not aware of their processes. By contrast, analytics process information in a very structured, formal, explicit manner. It is unlikely that an individual will exhibit all the tendencies of one type of decision maker. Rather, one methodology will tend to dominate although aspects of both approaches may be apparent.

Mock, Estrin and Vasarhelyi (1972) stated that the heuristic decision approach 'is characterized by trial and error, ad hoc sensitivity analysis, muddling-through, and satisficing behaviour. In contrast, an analytic approach emphasizes model building, mathematical analysis, and optimization' (p. 132). The authors' conclusions were that the subjects' decision approach was a significant factor affecting payoffs and decision times. However, decision approach was not found to affect learning patterns.

Two aspects of interest in the study of cognitive style were addressed by Weber (1978). He attempted to investigate, amongst other things, the usefulness of decision aids to auditors in determining overall reliability of an accounting system. He also looked at the impact of psychological and demographic variables on his subjects' decision making. Psychological and demographic factors were not found to play a significant part in auditors' decision processes. Weber suggested two reasons for this. Firstly, professional auditor training may mitigate these factors. Secondly, constructs developed in psychology may not be appropriate to an auditing setting. Subjects using decision aids were found to perform better than those without decision aids. Weber, however, questions the methodology used to investigate decision aid use.

Vasarhelyi (1977) added a note of caution to the debate on designing person-specific decision support systems. Whilst he finds some support for relating system design to managers' decision styles, he points out that the costs of doing this may outweigh the benefits.

Traditional control theory assumes a consistent response from a given stimulus for all individuals. In reality there will be an interaction between the individual, his cognitive make up and the stimulus he receives. This is termed differential peaking. Lusk (1979) stated that little evidence of differential peaking has come to light. His own work bears this out. In a study of report usage he found little evidence of differential peaking. This would tend to support a very traditional view of information system design which does not overly emphasise individual differences.

The Effects of Conflict, Stress and Crisis

Working in an organisation can be stressful. At times the organisation may undergo crisis or the individual be in conflict with others. The amount of stress will depend, for instance, on the nature of the job and the position held. The reaction of people to stress, conflict and crisis will vary from individual to individual. However, people under stress do exhibit certain common tendencies.

Shapiro and Gilbert (1975) studied the effects of stress on high-level decision makers in political positions. Their findings indicate that, when under stress, decision makers tend to reduce their search for information and consider fewer alternatives. There was the opposite effect to the normal anchoring and adjustment heuristic in that the subjects tended to overreact to individual, isolated pieces of information rather than adjust insufficiently as the anchoring and adjustment heuristic would suggest. This behaviour results in the selection of alternatives in a suboptimal fashion.

Janis and Mann (1977) reported five functional relationships between psychological stress and decision conflict. Firstly, the degree of stress was found to be a function of those relationships which the decision maker expects to remain unsatisfied after implementing a decision. Secondly, it was a function of the degree of commitment of the individual to adhere to the present course of action in the light of new opportunities or threats. Thirdly, the failure to identify a better decision than the current least objectionable one will lead to defensive avoidance. Fourthly, stress was related to the anticipated insufficiency of time to perform the task that the decision maker thinks he will have. Lastly, Janis and Mann found that a moderate degree of stress is beneficial in that it induces a vigilant effort to scrutinise all alternative courses of action.

There would seem to be additional need for decision aids to assist decision makers in times of stress, conflict or crisis. An interesting example of organisational response to crisis is given by Bourn and Ezzamel (1985). They observed a power shift towards the accounting department as a result of the increasing need of the organisation to rely on the accounting information system. The authors document the changing role of the accounting information system from that of passive answer provider to that of an ideas generator during the crisis life-cycle. The conclusion seems to be that a good accounting information system needs to be proactive rather than reactive. It is worth noting that organisational politics plays as big a part as cognitive style in determining the validity of the information system.

V. SUMMARY

This chapter has attempted to draw together the disparate strands of literature on human information processing. The review has highlighted a number of problems to which information processors are prone.

It is easy to come away with a very poor view of man's ability to use information. This view may be unnecessarily pessimistic (Holt and Cooper, 1983). It should be remembered that, in spite of the common failings identified, people do cope with unstructured situations and do make intelligent decisions under difficult circumstances. The human possesses a flexibility in approach that a model cannot hope to emulate.

From a management accounting perspective, there needs to be an awareness of the problems that both information receivers and contributors display. Thus when eliciting or reporting information, the management accountant should try to be as explicit as possible in communicating his ideas. Whilst this may seem facile, it should be stressed that one should not overestimate the user's information-handling capability.

Lens model studies would suggest that there are occasions when simple models of the decision process will perform better than human decision makers. These situations should be identified and appropriate models used. Providing relevant feedback should become an integral part of the accountant's work.

The method of reporting should be that which is most easily understood by the recipient. Consideration needs to be given to alternative forms of reporting. In some cases the same information might be presented in a number of formats, allowing the user the choice. This is becoming a realistic possibility with widespread use of microcomputers and software which allows rapid representation of data in various forms.

Training appears to be a vital aspect in mitigating some information processing biases. Consensus can be improved by adequate education as can such areas as the appropriate use of probabilities. The area of probability use is a major stumbling block for decision makers. Training and the use of decision aids in this field would seem to be very beneficial.

Heuristics and biases commonly used have been identified. An awareness of typical cognitive biases should help reduce their effects. The use of some of the debiasing techniques discussed in Sage (1981) might be helpful.

Finally the decision maker needs to be viewed as an integral part of the decision process. His abilities, perceptions and failings should be borne in mind when designing an information system. However, in doing this the costs and the benefits derived from better decisions should be uppermost in the decision maker's mind.

REFERENCES

Abdel-khalik, A. R., 1974. On the efficiency of subject surrogation in accounting research, *Accounting Review*, October, pp. 743–50.

Abdel-khalik, A. R. and El-Sheshai, K., 1980. Information choice and utilization in an experiment on default prediction, *Journal of Accounting Research*, Autumn, pp. 325–342.

Abdel-khalik, A. R. and Keller, T. F., 1979. *Earnings or Cash Flows: An Experiment on Functional Fixation and the Valuation of the Firm:* American Accounting Association.

American Accounting Association, 1972. Report of the committee on courses in managerial accounting, supplement to the *Accounting Review*, pp. 1–13.

Anthony, R. H., 1965. *Planning and Control Systems:* Harvard University Press.

Ashton, A. H., 1982. An empirical study of budget-related predictions of corporate executives, *Journal of Accounting Research*, pp. 440–449.

Ashton, R. H., 1976. Cognitive changes induced by accounting changes: experimental evidence on the functional fixation hypothesis, studies on human information processing in accounting, supplement to *Journal of Accounting Research*, pp. 1–17.

Ashton, R. H., 1982. Human information processing in accounting, *Studies in Accounting Research:* American Accounting Association.

Ashton, R. H. and Kramer, S. S., 1980. Students as surrogates in behavioural research: some evidence, *Journal of Accounting Research*, Spring, pp. 269–277.

Bamber, E. M., 1983. Expert judgement in the audit team: a source reliability approach, *Journal of Accounting Research*, Autumn, pp. 396–412.

Beaver, W. H., 1966. Financial ratios as predictors of failure, in Empirical Research in Accounting: Selected Studies. Supplement to *Journal of Accounting Research*, pp. 71–111.

Benbasat, I. and Dexter, A. S., 1979. Value and events approaches to accounting: an experimental evaluation, *Accounting Review*, October, pp. 735–750.

Benbasat, I. and Dexter, A. S., 1982. Individual differences in the use of decision support aids, *Journal of Accounting Research*, pp. 1–11.

Benbasat, I. and Taylor, R. N., 1982. Behavioural aspects of information processing for the design of management information systems, *IEEE Transactions on Systems, Management, and Cybernetics*, **SMC-12**, (4), July/August.

Biggs, S. F. and Mock, T. J., 1983. An investigation of auditor decision processes in the evaluation of internal controls and audit scope decisions, *Journal of Accounting Research*, Spring, pp. 234–255.

Bourn, A. M. and Ezzamel, M., 1985. The accounting department, the accounting information system, and the accounting language in an organisation experiencing financial crisis, University of Southampton Working Paper.

Brown, P. R., 1983. Independent auditor judgment in the evaluation of internal audit functions, *Journal of Accounting Research*, pp. 444–455.

Brunswik, E., 1952. *The Conceptual Framework of Psychology:* University of Chicago Press.

Buchanan, J. M., 1969. *Cost and Choice: An Inquiry in Economic Theory:* Markham.

Caplan, E. H., 1966. The behavioural assumptions of management accounting, *Accounting Review*, July, pp. 496–509.

Chesley, G. R., 1975. Elicitation of subjective probabilities: a review, *Accounting Review*, April, pp. 325–37.

Cohen, J. L., 1976. Discussion of patterns, prototypes, and predictions: an exploratory study, studies on human information processing in accounting. Supplement to the *Journal of Accounting Research*, pp. 132–8.

Collingridge, D., 1982. *Criteria Decision Making: A New Theory of Social Choice*: Francis Pinter.

Crosby, M. A., 1981. Bayesian statistics in auditing: a comparison of probability elicitation techniques, *Accounting Review*, April, pp. 355–365.

Danos, P., Holt, D. L. and Imhoff, E. A., 1984. Bond raters' use of management financial forecasts: experiment in expert judgment, *Accounting Review*, October, pp. 547–573.

DeGroot, A. D., 1965. *Thought and Choice in Chess*: Mouton.

Demski, J. S. and Feltham, J. B., 1976. *Cost Determination: A Conceptual Approach:* Iowa State University Press.

Doktor, R. H. and Hamilton, W. F., 1973. Cognitive styles and the acceptance of management science recommendations, *Management Science* **19** (9), pp. 884–894.

Eggleton, I. R. C., 1976. Patterns, prototypes, and predictions: an exploratory study. Supplement to the *Journal of Accounting Research*, pp. 68–131.

Einhorn, H. J., 1976. Synthesis: accounting and behavioural science. Supplement to *Journal of Accounting Research*, pp. 196–206.

Fischhoff, B., 1982. 'For those condemned to study the past: heuristics and biases in hindsight' pp. 335–355 in Kahneman, Slovic and Tversky, *Judgment Under Uncertainty: Heuristics and Biases*: Cambridge University Press.

Guilfoyle, C., 1986. Big bang will bring AI explosion to city, *Expert System User*, March.

Hacking, I., 1975. *The Emergence of Probability*: Cambridge University Press.

Harrell, A. M., 1977. The decision-making behavior of Air Force officers and the management control process, *Accounting Review*, October, pp. 833–841.

Hogarth, R., 1980. *Judgment and Choice*: Wiley.

Holt, J. and Cooper, D. F., 1983. 'Information and decision-making in tactical command and control', discussion paper, University of Southampton.

Jaedicke, R. K. and Robichek, A. A., 1964. Cost–volume–profit analysis under conditions of uncertainty, *Accounting Review*, October, pp. 917–926.

Janis, I. L. and Mann, L., 1977. *Decision Making*: Free Press.

Joyce, E. J., 1976. Expert judgment in audit program planning, studies in human information processing in accounting. Supplement to the *Journal of Accounting Research*, pp. 29–60.

Joyce, E. J. and Biddle, G. C., 1981. Anchoring and adjustment in probabilistic inference in auditing, *Journal of Accounting Research* Spring, pp. 120–145.

Kahneman, D., Slovic, P. and Tversky, A., (eds), 1982. *Judgment Under Uncertainty: Heuristics and Biases*: Cambridge University Press.

Kinney, W. R. and Uecker, W., 1982. Mitigating the consequences of anchoring in auditor judgments, *Accounting Review*, January, pp. 55–69.

Libby, R., 1975. Accounting ratios and prediction of failure: some behavioural evidence, *Journal of Accounting Research*, Spring, pp. 150–161.

Libby, R., 1976. Man versus models of man: the need for a non-linear model, *Organisational Behaviour and Human Performance*, June, pp. 23–26.

Libby, R., 1981. *Accounting and Human Information Processing: Theory and Applications*: Prentice-Hall.

Libby, R., 1985. Availability and the generation of hypotheses in analytical review, *Journal of Accounting Research*, pp. 648–667.

Libby, R. and Lewis, B. L., 1977. Human information processing research in accounting: the state of the art, *Accounting, Organizations and Society*, **2** (3), pp. 245–268.

Libby, R. and Lewis, B. L., 1982. Human information processing in accounting: the state of the art in 1982, *Accounting, Organizations and Society*, **7** (3), pp. 221–285.

Lusk, E. J., 1979. A test of differential performance peaking for a disembedded task, *Journal of Accounting Research*, pp. 286–294.

Macintosh, N. B., 1985. *The Social Software of Accounting and Information Systems*: Wiley.

Magee, R. P. and Dickhaut, J. W., 1978. Effect of compensation plans on heuristics in cost variance investigations, *Journal of Accounting Research* Autumn, pp. 294–314.

Mason, R. O. and Mitroff, I. I., 1973. A program for research on management information systems, *Management Science*, **19** (5), pp. 475–485.

Miller, G. A., 1956. The magical number seven, plus or minus two: some limits on our capability for processing information, *The Psychological Review*, March, pp. 81–97.

Mock, T., 1976. Discussion of patterns, prototypes, and predictions: an exploratory study, studies on human information processing in accounting. Supplement to the *Journal of Accounting Research*, pp. 139–144.

Mock, T. J., Estrin, T. L. and Vasarhelyi, M. A., 1972. Learning patterns, decision approach and value of information, *Journal of Accounting Research*, pp. 129–153.

Moriarity, S., 1979. Communicating financial information through multi-dimensional graphics, *Journal of Accounting Research*, Spring, pp. 205–223.

Moriarity, S. and Barron, F. H., 1976. Modelling the materiality judgments of audit partners, *Journal of Accounting Research*, Autumn, pp. 320–341.

Newell, A. and Simon, H. A., 1972. *Human Problem Solving*: Prentice-Hall.

Newton, L. K., 1977. The risk factor in materiality decisions, *Accounting Review*, January, pp. 97–108.

Otley, D. T., 1983. 'Behavioural and organisational research in management accounting', pp. 136–158, in Cooper, D. and Scapens, R. (eds) *Management Accounting Research and Practice*: Institute of Cost and Management Accountants.

Payne, J. W., Braunstein, M. L. and Carroll, J. S., 1978. Exploring predecisional behavior: an alternative approach to decision research, *Organisational Behavior and Human Performance*, February, pp. 17–44.

Pyhrr, P. A., 1970. Zero-base budgeting, *Harvard Business Review*, November-December, pp. 111–120.

Sage, A. P., 1981. Behavioural and organisational considerations in the design of information systems and processes for planning and decision support, *IEEE Transactions on Systems, Man, and Cybernetics* **11**, (9), September.

Savage, L. J., 1954. *The Foundations of Statistics*: Wiley.

Scott, W. G., 1961. Organisation theory: an overview and an appraisal, *Journal of the Academy of Management*, **4**(1), April, pp. 7–26.

Shapiro, H. and Gilbert, M., 1975. *Crisis Management: Psychological and Sociological Factors in Decision Making*. McLear VA: Human Sciences Research Inc.

Stock, D. and Watson, C. J., 1984. Human judgment accuracy, multidimensional graphics, and humans versus models, *Journal of Accounting Research* Spring, pp. 192–206.

Swieringa, R. J., Dyckman, T. R. and Hoskin, R. E., 1979. Empirical evidence about the effects of an accounting change on information processing, in Burns T. H. (ed.), *Behavioural Experiments in Accounting III*: Ohio State University, pp. 225–259.

Swieringa, R. J., Gibbins, M., Larsson, L. and Sweeney, J. L., 1976. Experiments in the heuristics of human information processing, studies on human information processing in accounting. Supplement to the *Journal of Accounting Research*, pp. 159–187.

Trotman, K. T., Yetton, P. W. and Zimmer, I. R., 1983. Individual and group judgments of internal control systems, *Journal of Accounting Research*, Spring, pp. 286–292.

Tversky, A. and Kahneman, D., 1974. In D. Kahneman, P. Slovic and A. Tversky (eds), *Judgement Under Uncertainty: Heuristics and Biases*: Cambridge University Press (1982).

Vasarhelyi, M., 1977. Man-machine planning systems: a cognitive style examination of interactive decision making, *Journal of Accounting Research*, Spring, pp. 138–153.

Wallsten, T. S. and Budescu, D. V., 1983. Encoding subjective probabilities: a psychological and psychometric review, *Management Science* **29**, (2), February, pp. 151–173.

Ward, B. H., 1976. An investigation of the materiality construct in auditing, *Journal of Accounting Research* Spring, pp. 138–152.

Weber, R., 1978. Auditor decision making on overall system reliability: accuracy, consensus and the usefulness of a simulation decision aid, *Journal of Accounting Research*, Autumn, pp. 368–388.

Wiggins, N. and Hoffman, P. J., 1968. Three models of clinical judgment, *Journal of Abnormal Psychology*, February, pp. 70–77.

PART TWO
Planning and Decision Making

6

Decision Theory and Information Economics

Most of the conventional management accounting literature is based on neoclassical economic theory, which invokes models of rational choice and expected utility. Rational choice is particularly problematic under conditions of uncertainty. In such cases, knowledge relating to measures of risk and the prices at which risk can be borne by decision makers is crucial. As many management accounting models explicitly deal with issues of uncertainty, an understanding of these models requires a good grasp of axioms of rational choice, utility functions and risk. One of the aims of this chapter is to provide a brief coverage of the topic.

The main aim of the chapter, however, is to introduce the information economics approach. The development of this approach offers a real potential for making significant advances in the management accounting area. The approach has its origins in the economics literature but has subsequently been developed further in the management accounting literature over the last 20 years.

The information economics approach is based on axioms of rational choice and utility theory. Its main focus is on developing a formal model to facilitate the choice of optimal information systems. The model is normative and invokes a number of abstract assumptions about the relevant parameters and the behaviour of decision makers. The model also seeks to explicate the role of information in situations involving choice amongst information systems, such as management accounting systems. It also explicitly accounts for the costs and the benefits of information.

In order to provide a coverage of these two topics this chapter has been organised into six sections. Section I deals with expected utility theory and develops definitions of the meaning and the price of risk. Section II introduces the notion of information economics and develops some measures of the cost and value of information. Section III considers the possibilities of developing more simplified models of choice by relaxing some of the assumptions made in section II. Section IV outlines the implications of distinguishing those who develop information from those who use it. Section V provides an evaluation of the information economics approach. Finally, section VI contains a summary of the chapter.

This chapter offers a natural background for part two of this book. Part two essentially deals with some of the conventional topics of management accounting. This part stands in some contrast to parts one and three with their strong organisational emphasis.

I. EXPECTED UTILITY THEORY AND RISK

The discussion that follows in the remaining sections of this chapter, and indeed in many chapters in this book, draws on the theory of rational choice, which is based on the expected utility model. The theory of rational choice attempts to identify and explain the objects of choice and the method of choice under conditions of uncertainty. The theory may act both as a *guide* to individual decision making and as a *description* of decisions taken by various individuals. The theory is therefore relevant to the main topic of this chapter – which relates to the choice of optimal information systems. This section deals with the axioms of rational choice and utility functions, attitudes towards risk and measures and prices of risk.

Axioms of Rational Choice and Utility Functions

The theory of rational choice under uncertainty is based on five main axioms (assumptions) relating to an individual's behaviour. These axioms are (see Von Neumann and Morgenstern, 1947; Fama and Miller, 1972):

1. *Completeness*. For the entire set of uncertain alternatives, s, and individual either prefers alternative x to alternative y, y to x, or is indifferent between the two.
2. *Transitivity*. Individuals are consistent in their preferences such that if x is preferred to y, and y is preferred to z, then it follows that x is preferred to z. If an individual is indifferent between x and y and is also indifferent between y and z then he must be indifferent between x and z.
3. *Substitution* (independence). If an individual is indifferent between x and y, and if z is any other alternative, then he will be indifferent between two gambles A and B, where A offers a probability p of receiving x and a probability (1-p) of receiving z, and B offers a probability p of receiving y and a probability (1-p) of receiving z. This implies that preferences with respect to outcomes of risky alternatives are independent of the risky alternative itself.
4. *Measurability* (certainty equivalent). If alternative x is preferred to alternative y, and alternative y is preferred to alternative z, then there exists a unique probability p such that the individual will be indifferent between attaining y for certain or attaining x with probability p and z with probability (1-p).
5. *Ranking*. If alternatives y and w lie somewhere between x and z, and the individual is indifferent between y and a gamble between x (with probability p_1) and z, whilst also indifferent between w and a second gamble between x (with probability p_2) and z, then if $p_1 > p_2$, y is preferred to w.

These are the basic axioms of the cardinal utility model. They imply that individual decision makers are completely rational, just as is typically assumed in the conventional economic and accounting literature. The empirical validity of some of these axioms has been strongly challenged by several researchers (e.g., Luce and Raiffa, 1957; Markowitz, 1959; Masse, 1962; Raiffa, 1968). For example, under the substitution (independence) axiom, when equally desirable alternatives are used to generate a third alternative with the same expected return but with lower risk compared with each of the original alternatives, all three alternatives will be considered independent of each other, and individual preferences will be assumed to be independent of risk. Yet, some individuals may prefer an alternative that promises the same return as another alternative, but that carries less risk. Similarly, the behaviour of individuals does not always conform to the axioms of transitivity and certainty equivalent because of people's differing attitudes towards risk. Despite these limitations, expected utility theory provides the main theoretical underpinning of rational choice by individuals in economic theory and finance. It is also widely used in conventional management accounting analysis dealing with issues such as value of information, stochastic cost–volume–profit analysis, variance investigation models and so on.

The axioms of choice given above are typically used to derive utility functions for individuals, with each function representing an individual's preferences towards expected decision outcomes. In this analysis, the individual is assumed to aim to maximise utility that may be expected. The derived expected utility function has two properties:

1. It is order preserving in the sense that if the utility of x is greater than the utility of y then x will be preferred to y.
2. It can be used to rank combinations of risky alternatives.

Formally, the expected utility of outcomes associated with a particular risky alternative can be expressed as follows:

1.

$$E[U(\tilde{Y})] = \sum_{i=1}^{n} p(\tilde{Y}_i)U(\tilde{Y}_i)$$

where
$E[U(\tilde{Y})]$ = expected utility of outcome associated with alternative $\tilde{Y}$,
$p(\tilde{Y}_i)$ = probability of random outcome $\tilde{Y}_i$ occurring, and
$U(\tilde{Y}_i)$ = utility associated with random outcome $\tilde{Y}_i$.

Attitudes Towards Risk

The finance literature typically distinguishes between three types of decision makers in terms of their attitude towards risk: risk lovers, risk neutrals and risk averters (see, for example, Copeland and Weston, 1979). Each of the three types of decision makers will prefer more wealth to less wealth, i.e. the marginal utility of wealth is positive. Figure 6.1 depicts the three types of utility functions.

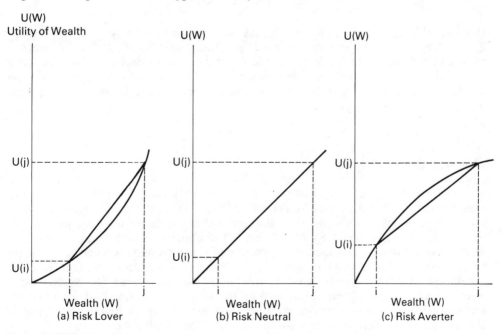

Figure 6.1 *Utility functions.*

It is clear from this figure that the marginal utility of wealth is positive (i.e., $U' > 0$, where U is utility), but that incremental wealth gradually adds less marginal utility than before the risk averters (i.e. $U'' < 0$) whereas it has greater marginal utility than before the risk seekers (i.e. $U'' > 0$). The finance literature and most of the conventional management accounting literature assume that decision makers are risk averse (see figure 6.1c). Each of these decision makers would:

— Have a strictly concave utility function.
— Always prefer more wealth to less wealth ($U' > 0$).
— Have a decreasing marginal utility of wealth as wealth increases ($U'' < 0$).

The utility function of a risk-averse decision maker can be represented by the following quadratic expression:

2.

$$U(Y) = a + bY + cY^2$$

where a, b and c are the parameters of the utility function. The expected value of the utility function in **2** is:

3.

$$E[U(\tilde{Y})] = a + bE(\tilde{Y}) + cE(\tilde{Y}^2)$$

where $\sim$ denotes random variables. The expected value of a random variable squared is equal to the variance of the distribution plus the mean squared:

4.

$$E(\tilde{Y}^2) = \sigma_Y^2 + \bar{Y}^2$$

Substituting **4** into **3**, we obtain:

5.

$$E[U(\tilde{Y})] = a + b\bar{Y} + c(\sigma_Y^2 + \bar{Y}^2)$$

that is, the expected utility in **5** has two characteristics of the probability distribution: the mean and the variance (see Haley and Schall, 1979). The term c assumes different values for decision makers with differing attitudes to risk. Thus, c = 0 for a risk neutral, $c > 0$ for a risk seeker, and $c < 0$ for a risk averter. For a risk averter, the higher the variance (which is a surrogate for risk), the lower the expected utility of a particular expected return.

Measures and Prices of Risk

Various proxies for risk based on measures of dispersion of distributions have been suggested in the literature (see Markowitz, 1959). The most popular measure of risk used in traditional portfolio theory is the standard deviation (or the variance) around the mean of the distribution of returns. Traditional portfolio analysis assumes, amongst other things, that the utility function of the decision makers is quadratic (as in expression **2** above) and that expected decision outcomes (for example, returns on securities) are normally distributed. In this latter case, the probability distribution of outcomes can be completely specified once the mean and the standard deviation are known. Under either assumption, however, decision makers will be interested only in the mean and standard deviation (or variance) of the distribution.

If the decision situation involves a single asset, the variance of the returns is calculated in a straighforward manner. If the decision situation involves a combination of assets (a portfolio), then the variance is given by:

6.

$$\sigma_P^2 = \sum_{i=1}^{n} \sum_{j=1}^{n} w_i w_j r_{ij} \sigma_i \sigma_j$$

where
σ_P^2 = the variance of the returns of a portfolio,
w_i = the proportion of money invested in asset i,
r_{ij} = the correlation coefficient between the returns of the two assets i and j,
σ = the standard deviation.
Expression **6** can be rewritten as:

6a

$$\sigma_P^2 = \underbrace{\sum_{i=1}^{n} w_i^2 \sigma_i^2}_{\substack{\text{variances} \\ \text{of assets}}} + \underbrace{2 \sum_{i=1}^{n} \sum_{\substack{j=1 \\ i \neq j}}^{n} w_i w_j r_{ij} \sigma_i \sigma_j}_{\text{covariances of assets.}}$$

Using traditional portfolio analysis, the risk-averse decision maker will seek to maximise expected return for a given level of risk, or minimise risk for a given level of expected return. Although there is a quantifiable, unambiguous measure of risk as reflected in the variance or standard deviation of returns, there is *no unique* price of risk that is accepted by all decision makers. Rather, individual decision makers trade off risk and return guided by their own utility functions, and thus the price of risk is likely to vary from one decision maker to another.

The extension of traditional portfolio theory into what is now known as capital market theory has resulted in the development of a new measure of risk for individual assets *and* of a *unique* price of risk that is assumed to be accepted by all risk-averse decision makers under conditions of market equilibrium. The model developed is known as the Capital Asset Pricing Model (CAPM). The main difference between the CAPM and traditional portfolio theory is that under the former lending and borrowing are allowed at a risk-free rate of return. According to the CAPM, the equilibrium return on asset i is given by (see Sharpe, 1964):

7.

$$E(R_i) = R_f + [E(R_m) - R_f]\frac{\sigma_{im}}{\sigma^2 m}$$

7a

$$= R_f + \beta_{i,m}[E(R_m) - R_f] \; ; \beta_{im} = \frac{\sigma_{im}}{\sigma^2 m}$$

where
$E(R_i)$ = the expected return on risky asset i,
$E(R_m)$ = the expected return on the market portfolio, for example, the *Financial Times* all-share index,
R_f = the return on a risk-free asset, for example, well-supported government bonds,
$\sigma^2 m$ = the variance of the returns of the market portfolio, and
σ_{im} = the covariance of the returns of asset i with the market returns, where σ_{im}
= $r_{im}\sigma_1\sigma_m$.

The implications of the CAPM in **7** and **7a** for decision making in the face of uncertainty are twofold. Firstly, the appropriate measure of risk for an individual asset (or project) is *not* its variance but rather its covariance with the market return. Total risk of an asset as reflected in its variance is composed of the covariance term and an element of risk that is specific to that asset. Specific risk can be diversified away by holding several assets and thus the decision maker cannot be compensated, in terms of obtaining greater returns, for bearing that risk. The covariance term (or the beta term) is not diversifiable (systematic risk) because it is linked to the general movements in the economy and thus decision makers are compensated for bearing it: the greater the covariance the greater would be the expected return.

The second implication relates to the price of risk. Under the CAPM the price of risk is the excess of the expected return on the market portfolio over the return from a riskless asset. This price is assumed to be determined through the capital market mechanism when the market is in equilibrium. It is therefore assumed to be invariant amongst decision makers.

The discussion in this section has been concerned with choice under uncertainty. It has been suggested that, in order to understand this topic, it is necessary to consider the axioms of rational choice, attitudes of decision makers towards risk and measures and prices of risk. This formal analysis is relied upon, in part, in developing the discussion of information economics in the following sections of this chapter. Much of this formal analysis also underlies some of the subsequent chapters in this book, particularly those chapters that deal with conventional management accounting models (see chapters 8, 10, 12 and 14).

II. INFORMATION ECONOMICS

Management accounting systems are an important source of information. The conventional view of management accounting systems is that they are concerned with the collection, processing, evaluation and communication of information to decision makers. Even the more recent views of management accounting, which emphasise its political and symbolic roles, still consider management accounting systems as the information centre in the organisation (see chapter 4).

In general, the collection, processing, evaluation and communication of information are not costless. Indeed, accounting information can simply be viewed as a commodity that can be obtained (that is, produced or purchased) at a price and that is expected to generate some benefits in the context of specific decisions. Early decision models in the management accounting literature ignored information costs and often failed to quantify information benefits. Many of these early models typically invoked the conditions of certainty. Under these conditions, it is assumed that the decision maker has all the necessary information at no cost. Even when the models were extended to account for uncertainty, information costs were not considered. Examples include stochastic cost–volume–profit analysis models (see chapter 8) and some variance investigation models (see chapter 14).

Subsequent researchers have sought to address this problem by explicitly considering the value and cost of information. The result has been that information is ultimately treated as a costly commodity, and thus the orientation of management accounting is moved away from the 'conditional truth' approach, i.e., different costs for different purposes, towards the 'costly truth' approach (see Scapens, 1984; also the Introduction to this book). An important implication of this latter approach is that it is no longer possible to analyse and evaluate decision models independently of the costs and value of information; both have to be considered in conjunction with it.

The information economics approach was developed from the mid 1960s onwards with much of the pioneering work being contributed by Marschak and Radner (1972). Accounting researchers used the Marschak and Radner work as the corner-stone in their modelling of information economics (e.g., Feltham, 1968; Crandall, 1969; Feltham and Demski, 1970; Demski, 1970, 1972a, 1972b, 1980; and Demski and Feltham, 1972). Many of these researchers have been concerned with using mathematical modelling to approach the problem of the selection of accounting systems on the basis of their uncertain costs and benefits. The problem is then one of choice under uncertainty. The analysis initially proceeds by assuming that information can be obtained at no cost. This assumption is subsequently relaxed and the costs of information are explicitly incorporated into the model.

A Formal Specification of the Choice Problem*

In the context of this analysis, the decision maker is assumed to face a problem of selecting a specific act, a, from a complete set of available acts, A, such that $a \in A$ (i.e. a is an element of A). The outcome of each act (or decision) is contingent upon the relevant set of states of the world, S, that are mutually exclusive so that only one state, s, will occur and $s \in S$. The probability of each state occurring is expressed by the probability function $\phi(s)$. Different acts (or decisions) are assessed in terms of their expected utilities, with the utility of the cash flow of a particular outcome being expressed as U (s, a) for all $s \in S$ and $a \in A$.

Assuming that the decision maker is an expected utility maximiser, he would evaluate the expected utility of each decision and select the one with the highest expected utility. The expected utility of decision $a \in A$, $E(U|a)$ is:

8.

$$E(U|a) = \sum_{s \in S} U(s,a)\phi(s).$$

The optimal act, i.e. the one with the highest expected value, $a^* \in A$ is:

9.

$$E(U|a^*) = \max_{a \in A} E(U|a)$$

$$= \max_{a \in A} \sum_{s \in S} U(s,a)\phi(s).$$

The formal presentation given above indicates that the choice problem facing the decision maker can be described through the specification of four parameters.
1. A, the set of acts available to the decision maker.
2. S, the set of possible states of the world.
3. ϕ, the probability function relevant to the states of the world.
4. U, the decision maker's utility function.
These parameters are specified on the basis of the decision maker's existing level of experience. For example, S would not contain all states of the world that may exist. Rather, it would contain only those states of the world that the decision maker considers, on the basis of his or her existing knowledge and experience, to be relevant.

The model is assumed to be complete if all four parameters are 'correctly' specified; that is, all alternatives of all parameters perceived by the decision maker to be

---

*The formal analysis presented here draws on Demski (1980). The notations used are kept as close as possible to those used by Demski to facilitate cross referencing.

necessary at the time of model specification are included in the model. However, errors are permissible in complete models, for example, the decision maker may ignore a significant alternative in the belief that it is irrelevant. The exact specification of the model is thus dependent upon the level of the experience of the decision maker; as the latter changes, so may model specification. The assumption of model completeness implies that the role of information is *ex ante* and it relates specifically to revising prior probabilities.

Complete Choice Models and the Role of Information

In information economics, accounting information is viewed as a message, or a signal, to the decision maker about future states of the world. The signal may change the experience of the decision maker and may result in him reviewing his expectations. The signal could contain perfect or imperfect information.

Perfect Information

Perfect information is information that is error free, and thus the state of the world signalled by the information will obtain with certainty. The typical choice situation considered in information economics is one in which the signal is received after the model has been formulated but *before* the choice has been made. Armed with perfect information, the decision maker will clearly select the act, in conjunction with the revealed state, that will maximise his expected utility. Specifically, the choice of the decision maker will be a function of the perfect information he receives, that is, he will choose the act that maximises the expected utility for the state of the world revealed by the information.

In probabilistic terms the availability of perfect information reduces the choice problem to one under complete certainty. Upon receiving the signal the decision maker will revise the probability function $\phi(s)$ into $\phi(s_i|$ revelation of $s_i)=1$, where s_i is the state of nature revealed by perfect information. In this analysis, information is assumed to be costless. The expected value of perfect information is measured by the difference between the maximum utility of the optimal act, given the availability of information, and the maximum utility of the optimal act before obtaining the information. The expected utility given perfect information is expressed as:

10.
$$E(U|\text{perfect information}) = \max_{\alpha(s)} \sum_{s\in S} U(s,\alpha(S))\phi(s)$$
$$= \sum_{s\in S} \phi(s)\{\max_{a\in A} U(s,a)\}$$

where $\alpha(s)$ is any rule that assigns only one act $a \in A$ to each state $s \in S$. The expected value of perfect information is the difference between equations **10** and **9**.

Imperfect Information

Given the prevalence of uncertainty, one would expect that information would be imperfect in the sense that it would not reveal with certainty which state of nature will occur. Assume that the decision maker has received information signal y from the information system η. If this signal changes the experience of the decision maker then he or she will revise his or her prior probabilities $\phi(s)$ into posterior or conditional probabilities $\phi(s|y, \eta)$ in a manner consistent with Bayes' Theorem.

Each information system η_i could generate various signals y_i's related to a particular state of the world. To make the analysis tractable, however, it is usually assumed that each information system η_i is noiseless in the sense that it provides only *one* signal about each state. The information system could range from one that offers no information, i.e., one with exactly the same signal for all states, to one that is perfect in the sense of offering different signals with each signal being appropiate and specific to a particular state.

In general, imperfect information does not allow the decision maker to distinguish each state from all other permissible states. For example, information system η_3 would be imperfect if it provides the same signal y_2 for both states s_1 and s_2; in this case the decision maker cannot distinguish s_1 from s_2. This is clearly different from the case of perfect information where the decision maker is assumed to have all the rules that relate states to acts.

Using Bayes' Theorem, the decision maker will utilise the imperfect information (signal y) to change his prior probabilities into conditional probabilities as follows:

11.

$$\phi(s|y,n) = \begin{cases} \dfrac{\phi(s)}{\phi(y|\eta)} & \text{if } y = \eta \ (s) \\ 0 & \text{otherwise} \end{cases}$$

The decision maker will calculate the expected utility of each act, for example, act a_1 as follows:

12.

$$E(U|a,y,\eta) = \sum_{s \in S} U(s,a,\eta)\phi(s,y,\eta).$$

The decision maker's objective would be to maximise the conditional expected utility:

13.

$$E(U|y,\eta) = \max_{a \in A} E(U|a,y,\eta).$$

The specification of equations **12** and **13** has two important implications:
1. Revised probabilities, ϕ $(s|y,\eta)$, are used instead of prior probabilities, $\phi(s)$.
2. The information system is explicitly incorporated as a parameter in order to indicate that its use is *not* cost free.

Cost and Value of Information

The expected utility of the optimal act, $E(U|$ y, $\eta)$, is given in equation **13** above. Once this has been calculated, the expected utility of an information system, $E(U|\eta)$, can be determined as below:

14.

$$E(U|\eta) = \sum_{y \in Y} \phi(y|\eta)E(U|y,\eta)$$

Equation **14** has two important characteristics:
1. The expected utilities are summed across all permissible signals, $y \in Y$.
2. The probability function $\phi(y,\eta)$ reflects the probability of each signal produced by the information system.

By calculating $E(U|\eta)$ for each information system it is possible to evaluate different systems. Thus, information system i will be considered at least as good as information system j, if and only if:

15.

$$E(U|\eta_i) \geq E(U|\eta_j),$$

which implies that the expected utility of the decision situation with information system i is at least as high as the expected utility of the decision situation with information system j.

However, even though the information system is included in expressions **14** and **15**, neither expression explicitly accounts for the cost and value of the information system. The problem, now, is how to rewrite expression **14** so that it does account for the cost and value of the information system.

If we were concerned with decision makers with linear utility functions (i.e. risk neutrals), then it would have been easy to expand expression **14** to account for the cost and value of the information system. The reason is that, with a linear utility function, incremental utility can be evaluated in monetary terms independently of the absolute amount of utility, i.e. maximising monetary reward is consistent with maximising expected utility.

As indicated in the previous section, utility functions are typically non-linear (most frequently concave, indicating risk aversion). With a non-linear utility function, incremental utility cannot be evaluated independently of the relevant absolute amounts of utility. Specific utility increments will reflect different amounts of monetary values at different points on the utility function (notice that for a risk averter the marginal utility of money decreases as wealth increases).

One possible approach to dealing with this problem would be to determine the *selling price* $\hat{k}$, that is the minimum amount of money (certainty equivalent) that the decision maker would accept in return for selling the decision opportunity, or the choice problem, including the information system η. This could be expressed as:

16.

$$U(\hat{k}_i) = E(U|\eta_i)$$

where $\hat{k}_i > \hat{k}_j$ if and only if $E(U|\eta_i) > E(U|\eta_j)$. The value of information will be the difference between $\hat{k}_i$ and the minimum amount the decision maker would accept in order to sell the decision opportunity *without* the information, k_0:

17.

$$\text{Value of information} = \hat{k}_i - k_0$$

The above analysis has been based on the central notion that information is a commodity, or an important factor in the decision process, that can be used to improve the quality of decisions. The desirability of an information system is measured in terms of alternative systems, expectations, tastes and so on. Alternative information systems are evaluated using expression **14**. The preferred system will be the one with the maximum expected utility:

18.

$$E(U|\eta^*) = \max_{\eta \in H} E(U|\eta)$$

where H represents the set of permissible information systems.

The model developed so far contains two types of uncertainty. Firstly, there is the uncertainty related to the future states of the world; this is handled by identifying the most preferred act given a particular signal from a particular information system.

Secondly, there is the uncertainty concerning the signals from the information systems given that these signals contain imperfect information. The probability of each signal is specified and the information system that is selected is the one that maximises expected utility across all possible signals.

III. SIMPLIFIED MODELS OF CHOICE

So far, the analysis has focused on an elaborate and a complete model, that is, a model in which the set of signals include 'no signal' and the set of information systems include 'no system'. If information systems are costless, one would assume that the most elaborate and complete model will be selected by the decision maker. Information systems, however, are costly and this may lead the decision maker to select a simplified model. Moreover, the decision maker may be unable to completely identify desirable alternatives or to completely specify his preferences to the extent required under complete analysis. When simplified analysis is invoked, the decision maker will tend to separate the utility evaluation into benefits and costs.

· Simplified models represent partial analyses of the choice situation that will not guarantee that the most desirable act will be identified (Eilon, 1974; Holloway, 1979). The potential of sub-optimal behaviour under simplified models indicates the possibility of incurring a cost; in this case the cost represents the difference between the expected utility associated with the optimal act (the one generated by complete analysis) and the expected utility of the act selected under simplified analysis. However, simplified analysis uses less information than is usually required under complete analysis and thus, if such savings in information costs are significant, simplified analysis may be economically worth while (see Demski and Feltham, 1976).

The process of model simplification is evolutionary and heuristic in nature. Using 'rules of thumb' based on experience rather than formal analysis, the decision maker decides on

— The extent of model complexity.
— The amount of search required to identify relevant alternatives.

Demski (1980) illustrates how the simplified model is derived through an iterative process involving two major steps of specification and testing. Thus, the decision maker uses his current experience to construct an initial model. The model would be based on a number of assumptions that greatly simplify relationships between relevant parameters. Indeed, in complex situations some such parameter relationships (e.g., future period effects) may be ignored altogether in model specification. The model is then tested in order to establish whether or not it approximates well the choice situation. On the basis of these tests, the decision maker decides whether to accept the model as it is or refine it further. Ideally, he would be attempting to balance the expected benefits of improved decision making against the expected costs of introducing greater complexity into the model.

Model Simplification

In what ways can the decision maker engage in model simplification? Clearly, there are many possibilities, an exhaustive list of which is beyond the scope of this chapter. Demski (1980) provides a useful framework through which model simplification can be attained. This includes the simplification of each of the main parameters of the model specified earlier:

— Relying on less-detailed, instead of complete, representation of the act, which is denoted as d. In this specification some classes of acts are completely ignored; for example, possible changes in fixed facilities when considering short-run decisions.
— Using less-detailed specification of the states of nature, $\theta \epsilon \Theta$ instead of $s \epsilon S$. This can be achieved by ignoring multi-period effects of decisions, or by ignoring some states altogether (such as the effect of natural disasters on delivery schedules).
— Using a simplified probability function that will now be concerned with estimating the probability of occurrence of $\theta \epsilon \Theta$, $\phi(\theta)$, instead of $s \epsilon S, \phi(s)$.
— Using a simplified utility assessment. Complete utility assessment relies on the outcomes that in turn depend upon the choice of acts and the occurrence of a particular state. Thus, the simplification of acts and states of nature and of their relationships should be reflected in simpler utility assessments. Moreover, the utility assessment itself can be made more simple by using approximate notions such as the mean-variance measure of risk (see section I of this chapter). The simplified utility function, or objective function, is denoted $R(\theta,d)$.
— Using a constrained set of decision variables. Thus some decision variables may be excluded because they are impracticable, whereas others may be ignored because they are not desirable. In this case the decision variables are assumed to be members of the set of available alternatives and these depend on the parameters and their predicted values, $D(\theta,\phi)$.

The simplified decision model may now be expressed as:

19.
$$E(R|d^*) = \max_d \sum_{\theta \in \Theta} R(\theta,d)\phi(\theta)$$
$$\text{subject to } d \epsilon D(\theta,\phi).$$

One good example of simplified models is linear programming (see Scapens, 1985). Linear programming models contain numerous simplifications. Firstly, the functional forms are assumed to be linear, e.g., unit prices and unit variable costs are assumed to be constant, and fixed costs are assumed to be the same within the relevant range. Secondly, the choice situation facing the decision maker is restricted, for example, it may involve the production and sale of a given number of products. The constraints (e.g., floor space; machine hours) are well defined and the model does not account for possibilities of increasing them. Thirdly, traditional linear programming assumes certainty, and thus only one state of the world is considered. Clearly the model can be made more complex, for example, by including non-linear functions, changes in constraint and production sets and uncertainty (see chapters 8 and 14). The expected benefits of these refinements, however, will have to be carefully assessed against their expected costs.

The simplified model represented by expression **19** differs from the complete model represented by expression **9** in section II in some crucial respects. Firstly, as suggested above, the model parameters are incompletely specified: this is true of acts, states, probabilities, utilities and decision variables. Secondly, the best act associated with the simplified model, d^*, is not strictly the decision maker's preferred choice. Specifically, d^* is *one*, but not the only, determinant of the ultimate choice by the decision maker. The decision maker would thus view d^* as information. Thirdly, the incomplete specification of the simplified model may lead to *ex ante* information having an impact beyond the probability assessments. Indeed, the effects of *ex ante* information may occur outside the domain of the simplified model.

This latter point is particularly important, for it indicates a change in the role of information as we move from a complete model to a simplified model. It will be recalled that in a complete model probability revisions occur only *after* receiving a signal from an information system. Before receiving that signal, the complete model is assumed to reflect the decision maker's existing knowledge at the time of model specification. By contrast, in formulating a simplified model the decision maker would deliberately suppress part of the range of some parameters, some of the relationships between parameters and, at the extreme, some decision variables. Such changes could be based on *ex ante* information.

Demski (1980) developed this argument further to demonstrate the role of information in facilitating the planning and control functions in simplified models. Planning refers to the process through which the decision maker determines an optimal decision based on his initial predictions and the 'best' simplified decision model. Following the initial implementation of selected plans, new information (feedback information) becomes available to the decision maker and this provides him with the basis to exercise control. Control in this sense is twofold; it embraces:

1. Adaptation of implementation of parts of the plans that have not yet been implemented.
2. Changes in the simplified model itself.

Thus, control involves changing current plans, because of revised predictions, as well as evolving the model itself. Because in a simplified model many decision variables are deliberately left out as exogenous (environmental) variables, such a model offers an incomplete account of how the decision maker uses an information signal.

This altered role of information in the simplified model can be expressed as:

20.
$$E(R|d^*,y,\eta) = \max_{d} \sum_{\theta\in\Theta} R(\theta,d,|y,\eta)\phi(\theta|y,\eta)$$
$$\text{subject to } d\in D(\theta,\phi|y,\eta).$$

In the complete model, change is restricted to Bayesian probability revisions from $\phi(s)$ to $\phi(s|y,\eta)$. By contrast, in **20** revisions could be based on Bayes' theorem, or could be completely subjective. In summary then, simplified models offer the decision maker *information* rather than reliable measures of preference. The information offers the decision maker a basis for changing present plans as well as changing the model itself. The benefits of revisions in plans and in the system have to be carefully balanced against the costs of introducing these revisions. Although it may not be possible to quantify the loss that may be caused by model simplification, it may be possible to estimate the expected benefits of model revisions (Scapens, 1985).

IV. SEPARATION OF ROLES OF INFORMATION PRODUCER AND INFORMATION USER

Thus far, the analysis has assumed that information is selected and used by one and the same decision maker. Subsequent literature emphasised task specialisation by separating those who produce information from those who use it. The person who selects the information system is denoted the *information evaluator*, whereas the person who uses the information is called the *decision maker* (see, for example, Demski, 1972b, 1980; Demski and Feltham, 1976; also Introduction to this book).

The distinction between the information evaluator and the decision maker is of practical significance. In most organisations the two roles are separated. Thus, the chief accountant or the controller would typically select the accounting system with the data flowing from that system to be used by separate decision makers. Even when the two tasks are located within the same person, the distinction between the two tasks is relevant when considering simpler choice models like those discussed in the previous section. In this case 'cost-effective simplifications vary with the decision problem' (Demski, 1980, p.64) and thus it is important to structurally separate the choice of information system from the use of information.

The information evaluator selects the information system that produces the signals but does not act on the signals themselves. Using previous symbols, if $\eta \in H$ is a particular information system and $y \in Y$ is a particular signal produced by the system, then H is the set of available information systems perceived by the evaluator and Y is the set of signals that may be produced. In this analysis, it is assumed that the decision maker and the evaluator have identical specifications of the possible states of the world. Further, it is assumed that the evaluator's utility is dependent on the act selected by the decision maker and on the state that occurs. The information system selected by the evaluator, $\eta \in H$, is costly and will thus affect the evaluator's utility assessment. The evaluator's utility assessment is represented by $\tilde{U}(s,a,\eta)$ and it indicates the utility that will occur if information system $\eta \in H$ is selected and state $s \in S$ occurs in conjunction with the decision maker taking act $a \in A$.

The evaluator would need to specify the probabilities relating to states of the world, the signal produced by the system, and the act that the decision maker will take based on the signal. If ϕ (s) is the probability that state $s \in S$ will occur, and if each information system classifies the state in S using $y = \eta(s)$, then the signal probabilities will be:

21.

$$\phi(y|\eta) = \sum_{s \in S} \phi(s)$$

$$\text{such that } y = \eta(s)$$

and the conditional probabilities will be:

22.

$$\phi(s|y,\eta) = \begin{cases} \dfrac{\phi(s)}{\phi(y|\eta)} & \text{if } y = \eta(s) \\ 0 & \text{otherwise.} \end{cases}$$

The evaluator will also need to specify the probability that the decision maker will select act $a \in A$ given the signal $y \in Y$ from the system $\eta \in H$. The evaluator's perception of the decision maker's choice is expressed as ϕ (a|y,η).

The evaluator's objective would then be to identify the system that maximises expected utility. With these changes, expressions **12**, **14**, and **18** can now be rewritten respectively as:

23.

$$E(\tilde{U}|,a,y,\eta) = \sum_{s \in S} \tilde{U}(s,a,\eta)\phi(s|y,\eta)$$

24.

$$E(\tilde{U}|\eta) = \sum_{y \in Y} \phi(y|\eta) \sum_{a \in A} \phi(a|y,\eta)E(\tilde{U}|a,y,\eta)$$

and

25.

$$E(\tilde{U}|\eta^*) = \max_{\eta \in H} E(\tilde{U}|\eta)$$

The information evaluation process is depicted in figure 6.2 below. The process involves:
— Specification of the information system, $\eta \in H$.
— Generation of signal, $y \in Y$.

— Choice by the decision maker of act, a ∈ A.
— Probability of occurrence of state of the world, s ∈ S.
— Utility function, Ū(s,a,η).
   The evaluator's utility assessment is influenced by:
— His or her perceptions of the act that will be selected by the decision maker.
— The expected cost of the information system.
— The probability that a particular state of nature will occur.
The evaluator will need to predict the signal generation process, φ(y|η); the decision maker's act, φ(a|y,η); and the probability of the occurrence of the state of the world, φ(s|y,η).

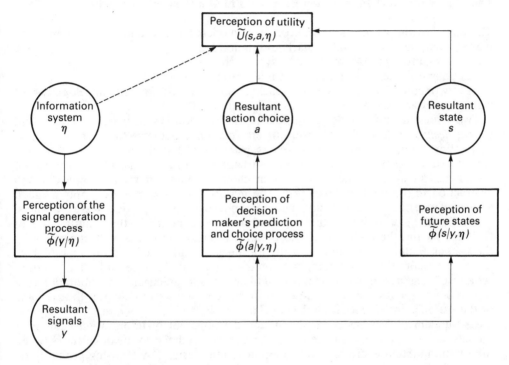

Figure 6.2 *Information evaluation process. Adapted from J. S. Demski*, Information Analysis *(Reading, MA: Addison-Wesley), 2nd Ed., 1980, p. 69. Reprinted with permission.*

   The distinction between the evaluator and the decision maker has been extended using the agency theory framework (see for example, Baiman, 1975; Demski and Feltham, 1978; Demski, 1980). The decision maker is modelled as an 'agent' being hired by the evaluator or 'principal' to select and implement act a ∈ A. The decision maker receives a fee for his services and the evaluator obtains the outcome less the decision maker's fee. The problem for the evaluator is to motivate the decision maker to provide the effort and deliver the outcomes desired by the evaluator.
   In this analysis, the information is perceived as providing an evaluation that is used in structuring and monitoring the contractual arrangements between the evaluator and the decision maker. This information helps in revising the probability function so that φ(a|y,η) is treated not as an input to the analysis, but rather as an outcome of it. The ultimate value of information is dependent upon the risk attitudes of both the principal and the agent. This topic is discussed more explicitly in chapter 11 and 12.

V. AN EVALUATION OF THE INFORMATION ECONOMICS APPROACH

Now that the various aspects of the information economics approach have been identified in the previous sections, an important question is 'what implications does this approach have for management accounting?' This section offers an evaluation of information economics models from the perspective of management accounting. The discussion initially concentrates on the main contributions of the models. Subsequently, some of the limitations of these models are pointed out.

The Contributions of Information Economics to Management Accounting

The development of information economics models has had an immense impact on management accounting, particularly in relation to:
1. Focusing attention on information system choice.
2. Emphasising the important role of information.
These two contributions have far-reaching implications for the development of management accounting research, as indicated below.

Two issues are important in considering information systems: *system choice* and *system design*. Before the extension of information economics to the management accounting area, accounting researchers primarily focused on the system design considerations to the exclusion of system choice considerations. Overemphasis on system design at the expense of system choice resulted in great complexity and abstraction in the models developed. The majority of these models simply avoided explicit reference to information benefits and costs. New models were advanced primarily on the basis of their technical and academic superiority; the quantification of the benefits and the costs was left to the practitioners concerned with implementing the system. Failure to account explicitly for the costs and benefits of information has, however, resulted in an overemphasis on mathematical elegance and sophistication. As a result, the new models did not lend themselves to practical implementation (see in particular stochastic cost–volume–profit models discussed in chapter 8, and some of the variance investigation models in chapter 14).

As Sundem (1981) has pointed out, the development of information economics models encouraged management accounting researchers to distinguish between information system choice and information system design. By focusing primarily on system choice, information economics has redressed the previous imbalance in favour of focusing on system design; both system aspects are clearly important.

Emphasis on information system choice has contributed to a clearer understanding of the role of the management accounting researcher with respect to offering advice to the evaluator (Scapens, 1984). Demski (1973) suggested that the accounting researcher can advise the evaluator in relation to information systems in three ways. Firstly, by analysing specific choice problems which would imply extending the choice models developed previously. Secondly, by developing new system alternatives e.g., introducing behavioural considerations, so that the evaluator could generate a more complete specification of possible information systems. Thirdly, by analytically or empirically testing system alternatives and providing information to the evaluator about the problems of implementing alternative systems.

The second major contribution of information economics to management accounting relates to emphasising the important role of information. In the complete analysis, information is assumed to be costless and its expected value cannot be negative because the evaluator can always choose to ignore it. Thus, complete analysis implies a complete specification of the information relating to all admissible decision parameters. The role of information in this context is restricted to the systematic revision of expectations about future states. With complete information the complete model should guarantee the identification of the most preferred action. Hence, the act choice can be delegated to the complete model.

The recognition that information is costly leads to a change from complete to incomplete (simplified) models and to a shift in the role of information. The problem facing the evaluator in this case is how to balance the benefits of obtaining more information against the costs of increasing model complexity. With a simplified model, it is no longer possible to delegate the act choice to the model, since there is no guarantee that the model will identify the evaluator's most preferred act. Instead, the optimal act determined by the simplified model is viewed as information. Moreover, information may have an impact that goes beyond the systematic revision of probabilities. For example, information can be used to alter existing plans and even to change and evolve the model itself.

This emphasis on the role of information is insightful. It explicitly highlights the central role of information in management accounting information systems. It indicates that information is ubiquitous in organisations. Further extensions of information economics models using the agency theory framework offer further support for this notion. Such analysis shows that information can play a vital role in structuring contractual arrangements in organisations, and in monitoring such arrangements over time. The analysis also shows that information can be used to evaluate past performance *as well as* to guide future decisions (see Demski, 1980). This evaluation of the role of information is consistent, in emphasis if not in orientation, with the organisational views of information discussed in part one of this book. This point is further discussed below.

Some Limitations of the Information Economics Approach

Despite the important contributions of information economics models to management accounting, these models have some serious limitations. These limitations are divided here into technical and behavioural. The technical limitations do not challenge the basic premises on which the models are based. Rather, they take these premises as given and focus primarily on the properties of the models. By contrast, the behavioural limitations challenge the very bases on which the models are constructed.

Consider first the technical limitations. One of the basic technical limitations is that the information economics model focuses on the *evaluator's* preferences. Although the evaluator's outcome is assumed to be dependent upon the decision maker's choice, the decision maker is perceived to react mechanically to the information system. Also, as Demski and Feltham (1976) pointed out, the dependence of the evaluator's outcome on the decision maker's choice creates a real possibility for gaming, or opportunistic behaviour.

The second technical limitation relates to the lack of generalised prescriptions concerning the definition of the 'most optimal' types of information or information systems. The main conclusion of the information economics approach in this respect is that information and information systems are situation specific. This is what is known as the 'costly truth' approach; that is, truth is attainable in the sense that a most desired information system exists, but such systems vary from one situation to another. This is similar to the typical contingency theory views, according to which the optimal design of accounting information systems is contingent upon the prevailing situational contingencies (see chapters 1 and 4). Clearly, many researchers would argue that the lack of general prescriptions is not a limitation, but rather a recognition of the practical difficulties that render generalisation impossible.

The third technical limitation relates to the normative orientation of the information economics approach. The approach addresses the problem of how information systems '*ought*' to be selected. The approach may not be completely helpful in explaining the process through which information systems are selected in reality, even though the analysis of simplified models helps to explain why such models exist and persist in practice.

This normative orientation is probably responsible for another technical limitation of these models. Like many normative models, the information economics model uses too many variables and is thus quite complex. This may render it impracticable to implement. Indeed, some writers have dismissed the approach altogether (e.g. Anthony, 1973). Whilst we do not wish to subscribe to such a drastic view, it is none the less important to appreciate that some of these limitations are quite significant.

Consider now the behavioural limitations of the information economics approach. It should be recalled that the whole approach is based on the axioms of rational choice discussed in section I of this chapter. This implies that the information evaluator is assumed to be a rational, utility-maximising individual. This also invokes the traditional goal model in which it is assumed that goals precede action, and that they are unambiguously defined and well ordered. The discussion in chapter 2 indicates that although such a goal model may exist in reality, it is by no means the only or even the most prevalent model. Thus, the Cyert and March (1963) bargaining model, and the garbage can model (Cohen, March and Olsen, 1972) are at least as defensible as the rationalistic goal model. Goals may be fluid, conflicting and not susceptible to clear ordering. Moreover, goals may be discovered, or at least reformulated, through action. Action is not necessarily goal driven; it may be decoupled from goals.

By emphasising rationality and orderly choice, the information economics approach may thus fail to fully explain the choice of information systems. Similarly, such emphasis imparts a purely functional role to information. Information is viewed as a commodity, and the decision of whether or not to acquire it is an economic decision based on the quantification of its benefits (in terms of uncertainty reduction and improved decisions) and costs. From an organisational theory perspective, this is a restrictive role for information. As indicated in part one of this book, information plays a multitude of roles in organisations. It can play a rationalistic role similar to that espoused by the information economics approach. Information can also act as symbols and signals conveying particular meanings in particular circumstances (Feldman and March, 1981). Information can also play an important role in shifting the focus of power in organisations. Therefore, the decision to acquire or not to acquire information is not always based on economic arguments.

VI. SUMMARY

This chapter has been concerned mainly with an exposition of the theory of rational choice and some aspects of the information economics approach. The theory of rational choice underlies most of the conventional management accounting literature and an understanding of this is therefore quite important if one is to appreciate the rationale and orientation of such literature. Information economics, a relatively recent development in the management accounting literature, can be traced back to the late 1960s. Despite its recent introduction to the accounting arena, the information economics approach soon gained ascendency as an important and highly topical issue in the leading accounting journals. This approach has had a profound impact on management accounting research.

Section I dealt with expected utility theory and risk. Various axioms that underlie rational choice were identified. Different utility functions were defined in terms of decision makers' attitudes towards risk (i.e. risk seeker, risk neutral and risk averter). Two measures of risk were identified: the variance around the mean of the distribution and the covariance of an asset's returns with the returns of the market portfolio. Moreover, two prices of risk were defined: the first is decision maker-specific, depending on the trade off he or she makes between risk and return as reflected in his or her utility function. The second price of risk is an equilibrium price for all decision makers and was defined as the excess of the market return over the return of a riskless asset.

The remaining sections of the chapter dealt with the information economics approach. The value and costs of information concepts were introduced in section II. It was shown that the choice problem facing the decision maker requires the specification of four parameters: acts, states of nature, probability function and the decision maker's utility function. In the complete model these parameters are defined by the decision maker on the basis of his experience at the time of model specification. Perfect information is assumed to be costless and its role is simply restricted to the reduction of uncertainty through a systematic revision of prior probabilities. The analysis was then developed further to show how the costs and benefits of imperfect information (i.e., information that does not allow the decision maker clearly to distinguish each state from all other permissible states) can be calculated. Moreover, a criterion was developed that permits the decision maker to evaluate different information systems.

Recognition that information is costly implies that only incomplete (or simplified) models can be used. Section III dealt with the choice of simplified models. With a simplified model, there is no guarantee that the act most desired by the decision maker will be identified. Therefore, the choice problem cannot be delegated to the simplified model, which is simply viewed as information. The role of information in simplified models may go well beyond the revision of prior probabilities. Information can lead to changes in existing plans and also to changes in the model itself. But, most importantly, simplified models are not necessarily sub-optimal. If the decision maker carefully balances the costs and the benefits of additional information (and thus of a more complex system) the simplified model may turn out to be optimal.

The analysis then proceeded in section IV to distinguish between the information evaluator (information producer) and the decision maker (information user). The evaluator's utility was assumed to be dependent upon the act selected by the decision maker, the state of nature that occurs, the signal that will be produced by the system, and the cost of the information system. Once the evaluator identifies the probabilities of each of these variables, his objective would be to identify the information system that maximises his expected utility. The analysis was extended further using the agency theory framework. Depicting the evaluator as the principal and the decision maker as the agent, it was suggested that information can be used to structure and monitor contractual relationships.

Section V offered an evaluation of information economics models. It was suggested that the information economics approach presents two major contributions to management accounting. Firstly, it distinguishes between information system choice and information system design, and focuses attention on the former. This is particularly useful given the predominant emphasis of conventional management accounting research on system design. Secondly, it emphasises the important role of information as a mechanism of uncertainty reduction, and as a means by which current plans and information systems themselves can be changed.

However, the information economics approach has several limitations, which have been classified into technical and behavioural. The technical limitations are:
— The approach creates a real potential for opportunistic behaviour by the decision maker.
— The approach may not be strictly helpful to practitioners, given that the optimal information system is situation-specific.
— The model is normative, and thus may not completely explain systems choice in reality.
— The model is too complex.

The behavioural limitations relate to the model's emphasis on rationalistic, goal-oriented action and the restrictive view of the role of information. Goals may be unambiguous or ambiguous, and may precede action or be created through action. Indeed, goals and actions may be decoupled. Moreover, although information may be acquired on the basis of cost-benefit analysis, it can also be acquired to act as symbols and signals of particular messages and to effect changes in power relationships within organisations.

However, these limitations should not detract from the real and immense contributions of the information economics approach to management accounting. Some of these contributions will be indirectly traced out later in this book, particularly in chapters 8 and 14.

References

Anthony, R., 1973. 'Some fruitful directions for research in management accounting', in N. Dopuch and L. Revsine (eds), *Accounting Research 1960–70: A Critical Evaluation*. Centre for International Education and Research in Accounting, pp. 37–68.

Baiman, S., 1975. The evaluation and choice of internal information systems within a multi-person world, *Journal of Accounting Research*, pp. 1–15. Spring.

Cohen, M.D., March, J.G. and Olsen, J.P., 1972. A garbage can model of organizational choice, *Administrative Science Quarterly*, **17** (1), pp. 1–25.

Copeland, T.E. and Weston, J.F., 1979. *Financial Theory and Corporate Policy*: Addison-Wesley.

Crandall, R.H., 1969. Information economics and its implications for the development of accounting theory, *Accounting Review*, pp. 457–466, July.

Cyert, R.M. and March, J.G., 1963. *A Behavioral Theory of the Firm*: Prentice-Hall.

Demski, J.S., 1970. Some decomposition results for information evaluation, *Journal of Accounting Research*, pp. 178–198, Autumn.

Demski, J.S., 1972a. Information improvement bounds, *Journal of Accounting Research*, pp. 58–76, Spring.

Demski, J.S., 1972b. Optimal performance measurement, *Journal of Accounting Research*, pp. 243–258, Autumn.

Demski, J.S., 1973. 'The nature of management accounting research: a comment', in N. Dopuch and L. Revsine (eds), *Accounting Research 1960–70: A Critical Evaluation*. Centre for International Education and Research in Accounting, pp. 69–78.

Demski, J.S., 1980. *Information Analysis* 2nd edn. Addison-Wesley.

Demski, J.S. and Feltham, G.A., 1972. Forecast evaluation, *Accounting Review*, pp. 533–548, July.

Demski, J.S. and Feltham, G.A., 1976. *Cost Determination: A Conceptual Approach*: Iowa State University Press.

Demski, J.S. and Feltham, G.A., 1978. Economic incentives in budgetary control systems, *Accounting Review*, pp. 336–359, April.

Eilon, S., 1974. Mathematical modelling for management, *Interfaces*, **4**(2), pp. 32–38, February.

Fama, E.F. and Miller, M.H., 1972. *The Theory of Finance:* Holt, Rinehart and Winston.

Feldman, M.S. and March, J.G., 1981. Information in organizations as signal and symbol, *Administrative Science Quarterly*, pp. 171–186, June.

Feltham, G.A., 1968. The value of information, *Accounting Review*, pp. 684–696, October.

Feltham, G.A. and Demski, J.S., 1970. The uses of models in information evaluation, *Accounting Review*, pp. 623–640, October.

Haley, C.W. and Schall, L.D., 1979. *The Theory of Financial Decisions*, 2nd edn. McGraw-Hill.

Holloway, C.A., 1979. *Decision Making under Uncertainty:* Prentice-Hall.

Luce, R.D. and Raiffa, H., 1957. *Games and Decisions*: Wiley.

Markowitz, H., 1959. *Portfolio Selection*: Wiley.

Marschak, J. and Radner, R., 1972. *Economic Theory of Teams:* Yale University Press.

Masse, P., 1962. *Optimal Investment Decisions*: Prentice-Hall.

Raiffa, H., 1968. *Decision Analysis:* Addison-Wesley.

Scapens, R.W., 1984. 'Management accounting: a survey paper', in R.W. Scapens, D.T. Otley and R.S. Lister, *Management Accounting, Organisational Theory and Capital Budgeting, 3 Surveys:* Macmillan.

Scapens, R.W., 1985. *Management Accounting: A Review of Recent Developments:* Macmillan.

Sharpe, W.F., 1964. Capital asset prices: a theory of market equilibrium under conditions of risk, *Journal of Finance*, **19**, pp. 425–442, September.

Sundem, G.L., 1981. 'Future perspectives in management accounting research. Paper presented at the Seventh Accounting Research Convocation at the University of Alabama.

Von Neumann, J. and Morgenstern, O., 1947. *Theory of Games and Economic Behavior:* Princetown University Press.

7

Relevant Costs for Decision Making

In this chapter an attempt is made to explore cost relevance in various decision areas. Initially the point is made that there is no 'true' or 'unique' cost which is universally applicable and that any simplistic view of cost relevance in other than quite general terms is fraught with difficulties. Consideration is then given to the influence on 'cost relevance' of operating in an uncertain world and to the criticism put forward by Dillon and Nash (1978) that, despite the generalisation that relevant costs for managerial decisions should fall into the dual categories of 'incremental' and 'future' costs, the incremental approach may not in every case be appropriate.

Various conceptual issues are examined, particularly the idea of sacrifice and the opportunity cost concept, the related concept of differential cost, and the arguments for the use of opportunity cost in preference to differential cost. Various applications of the opportunity cost approach are considered, and situations are identified to illustrate the possible derivation of opportunity cost from the 'dual prices' in the linear programming optimal solution.

Comparison of the behavioural and traceability characteristics of cost leads to an exploration of the meaning of 'fixed cost' and the distinctions between fixed and variable cost; 'variability' and 'directness' are contrasted and the concept of 'attributable cost' is examined; 'relevant costs' are then considered in the context of certain specific decision-making areas.

After some discussion of the relevance of 'full' cost, possible reasons are given for the tendency in management accounting literature to 'play down' the conceptual relevance of such cost. This leads to some discussion of the grounds for retaining conventional absorption costing schemes in a practical context. One plausible explanation for such retention links cost allocation with managerial behaviour, an explanation supported by Zimmerman (1979) by drawing on specific cost allocation situations. The chapter concludes with the opinion that 'full' cost does have a part to play in the determination of relevant costs for certain purposes and in certain situations but that, generally speaking, it lacks the flexibility which may be required for managerial decision-making purposes. The suggestion that overhead allocations serve as a proxy variable for opportunity costs may provide some conceptual justification for the use of 'full' cost, but this is most unlikely to be the reason why it is employed in practice.

The chapter is divided into six sections. Section I contains a discussion of cost relevance. Section II deals with opportunity cost and related cost concepts. The behavioural and traceability characteristics of cost are considered in section III. Section IV deals with specific relevant costs for decision making whereas section V

160

contains a discussion of the relevance of full cost. Finally, a brief summary of the chapter is contained in section VI.

I. COST RELEVANCE

By definition the term 'relevant cost' must necessarily signify the cost which arises from a particular managerial decision and thus, in the circumstances envisaged, serves to influence the choice of the decision maker. This simplistic view is, however, fraught with considerable difficulty when the issue of implementation arises. Thus, as is generally well recognised, there can be no such thing as a 'true' or 'unique' cost which is universally applicable to all situations in all circumstances, or indeed to similar situations in similar circumstances. This view is exemplified by the argument of Demski and Feltham (1976) who maintain that cost is essentially an arbitrary concept allied to the decision-maker's approach to his problem, including of course his attitude to risk. Buchanan (1969) has likewise stressed the subjectiveness of cost as something personal to the decision maker. As far back as 1938 Coase, referring to the difficulties associated with attempts to classify costs rigidly, made the point that in the decision-making field the best procedure would appear to be 'to try to discover what costs would be avoidable if a particular course of action were taken. . . . This linking of cost analysis to particular decisions makes any mechanical classification of costs almost impossible. The costs whose variations are of significance for one decision will be of no significance for others. There are innumerable decisions and each one may require a different classification' (page 130). Implicit in all these views is the need to take cognisance of the decision maker's attitudes to risk and uncertainty.

Demski and Feltham have argued that the question of what cost to assign to various products, processes, divisions or actions is essentially one of information choice. Their analysis, from which is developed their 'information evaluation approach', is based on developments in decision theory with explicit recognition of the separate specialist roles of the accountant as information decision maker, and the manager as the decision maker who will select the course of action to be pursued. As a preliminary step in their analysis they examine two other general approaches, both of which have had substantial influence on developments in accounting thought.

The first of these, which they designate the 'historical communication approach', occupied a prominent position in accounting literature up to approximately twenty years ago but is still not without its advocates. It is based on the idea of a general-purpose information source, whilst not rejecting the existence of diverse purposes which costs may be required to serve. The essence of this approach is that 'the best way to serve the user is to formulate clear rules for measuring costs' (Demski and Feltham, 1976, p. 3), so reducing to a minimum any ambiguity about the meaning of cost. The user is left to make his own adjustments for any shortcomings of the data provided. The user therefore adapts to the information rather than the reverse.

The idea of 'absolute truth', implicit in the approach described above, gives way to one of 'conditional truth' in the second general approach which Demski and Feltham refer to as the 'user decision model approach'. In this, explicit recognition is given to the possibility that different data may be generated by different decision models. The richness of the 'user decision model approach' is conceded by Demski and Feltham, who nevertheless maintain that both this and the 'historical communication approach' suffer from three fundamental defects. These are (i) that cost benefit analysis is not explicitly integrated in either approach; (ii) that the concept of a true cost implies certainty and this renders both models invalid under uncertainty and (iii) since different people may react differently to particular measurements, the concept of a true cost is irrelevant in a multiperson world.

Recognition of these defects has prompted Demski and Feltham to pursue their 'information evaluation approach' which is based on an explicit resource allocation perspective. In their approach, any specific form of measurement will be considered desirable to the extent that it produces an outcome of greater utility than the resources consumed. However, what is desirable is obviously a subjective issue in that due consideration must be given to available opportunities and prevailing tastes and beliefs. Furthermore it is dependent on the use which will be made of the data and the cost of producing more accurate measures. In this approach no attempt is made to specify categorically which type of measurement is preferred, and emphasis is therefore laid on analysis and not prescription.

The influence on cost relevance of operating in an uncertain world was given further emphasis by Dillon and Nash (1978). Their argument is based on the view that the decision maker's attitude to risk taking is reflected in his utility function. When conditions of uncertainty prevail, costs (or revenues) considered irrelevant in the context of conventional incremental analysis may become relevant with the introduction of utility analysis as the decision maker moves along his preference function. Two other conditions are necessary for this 'distortion' to arise, namely: non-linearity of decision maker's utility function and the involvement of relatively substantial monetary amounts.

Dillon and Nash make the point that the shape of the utility function is generally non-linear. Hence, in the conditions stipulated, the conventional incremental approach to decision making needs to be used with caution, and incremental analysis is not a universally applicable tool.

It will be apparent from much of the foregoing discussion that there is considerable difficulty in attempting to define relevant costs other than in quite general terms. Thus, conventionally, it is generally considered that, in a decision-making context, the costs which the accountant should supply to the decision maker should fall into the dual categories of 'incremental' and 'future' costs. Yet, as indicated above, the incremental approach may not in every case be appropriate (Dillon and Nash, 1978). Again, although it is usually suggested that joint costs are irrelevant in a decision-making context, given certain conditions it will be rational to allocate joint costs for the purpose of profit maximisation (Walters, 1960; Hart, 1973). Joint costs are, of course, those common costs which arise in a situation where two or more products are unavoidably produced together by virtue of the essentially indivisible nature of the factors of production, not only plant and organisational facilities, but also materials and labour costs. More recently, it has been suggested that overhead cost allocations may have a beneficial role by acting, firstly, as a 'lump sum tax' to control a manager's consumption of perquisites, secondly as proxies for 'costly to observe' non-zero opportunity costs associated with the sharing of 'fixed' resources (Zimmerman, 1979) and thirdly as a means of uncertainty absorption (Ezzamel and Bourn, 1987). The original contribution of Baxter and Oxenfeldt (1961) should also be mentioned as a forerunner to Zimmerman in suggesting that 'the traditional costing margin – overhead plus profit – may serve as a rough guide to opportunity cost' (p.303).

The difficulties exemplified above would not appear to obviate the need to discuss some specific cost concepts and to examine, albeit in a purely illustrative way, their possible applicability in certain situations. Such applications, however, are not intended to be prescriptive, the analysis offers guidelines only, not rigid rules. Indeed, in conditions of uncertainty it becomes particularly apparent that the decision maker's choice is paramount and the various points noted above should be borne in mind. Thus, in particular, one should consider available opportunities and prevailing tastes and beliefs.

As a framework for discussion some important conceptual issues are examined below, starting with the essence of cost and the opportunity cost concept.

II. OPPORTUNITY COST AND RELATED COST CONCEPTS

It is generally considered that incurrence of a cost necessarily involves some form of sacrifice. Thus, an economic cost reflects the sacrifice of economic value or exchange value. This raises the implication that other possible courses of action (alternatives) exist, an assumption which leads directly to the concept of opportunity cost. The essence of opportunity cost relates to resource scarcity. It lies in the necessity to forgo alternatives: a necessity imposed when any decision is made and one which was recognised by Wicksteed (1910), who defined relevant cost 'in the sense of alternatives still open which must now be relinquished in order to produce this specific article' (p.380).

The Opportunity Cost Concept

Arnold and Scapens (1980) have surveyed the historical background to the development of the concept of opportunity cost. They draw attention to three main areas in which conventional accounting in this context may be regarded as defective, namely its emphasis on historical costs, its concern with the allotment of fixed overhead and its failure to take explicit cognisance of forgone alternatives. As indicated previously, explicit recognition of the last point is the essence of opportunity cost.

As regards the first area, emphasis on historical costs, there can indeed be few decision makers who will base their decision on past costs, except insofar as such costs are an acceptable guide to the future; even then, the historical costs would require some adjustment to reflect the impact of inflation and other changes in circumstances. The superiority of the opportunity-cost concept in this context is obvious since it requires that consideration be given to those alternative resource uses which are currently available at the time of the decision.

Again, opportunity cost, by its emphasis on the cost of change and the consequent irrelevance of fixed costs, overcomes the second criticism levelled at conventional accounting – its concern with the allotment of fixed overheads. However, it should be noted that this particular point of criticism would also be met by the application of the incremental approach to decision making.*

It will be clear from the foregoing discussion that the idea of sacrifice as the essence of cost is reflected in the notion of opportunity cost, concerned as it is not so much with actual monetary outlays but rather with the benefits forfeited by employing resources in the particular way chosen in preference to the best alternative use. Amey (1968, p. 451) does, however, take the view adopted here that in an operational context a meaningful interpretation of opportunity cost should stress '*net* revenues

---

*Dillon and Nash (1978) refer to the 'conventional incremental approach to decision making'. Presumably they mean the incremental approach as conventionally applied and are not intending to imply that the incremental approach is itself conventional.

'forfeited', i.e. gross receipts forgone less the costs avoided by not adopting the best alternative.

This viewpoint is placed in perspective in the following illustration depicting a deterministic situation where a particular market condition ('state') is assumed and the cash inflows and outflows for three distinct possible new products ('alternatives') are as given.

Opportunity costs: alternative approaches

	Product		
	A	*B*	*C*
Cash inflows (£'000)	30	20	25
Cash outflows (£'000)	10	5	7
Net cash inflows (£'000) (i.e. profit or possibly contribution)	20	15	18
Net advantage or surplus/(disadvantage or deficit)	2	(5)	(2)
Opportunity cost using the preferred approach indicated above	18	20	20
Alternative calculation of opportunity cost using the 'incremental profit' approach (see, for example, Bierman and Dyckman, 1971)	0	5	2

It can be argued that in substance these are merely alternative methods of presentation, since the decision criterion in both cases is for management to select the 'alternative' which shows the lower opportunity cost figure. Likewise, it has been argued that it is not generally *necessary* to impute opportunity cost, although there may be circumstances in which to do so will be more convenient (Amey 1968). Thus, by simple taxonomic approach, i.e. a listing and comparison of alternatives, the same decision would be reached by selecting the 'alternative' which offers the highest-valued, positive differential net revenues. This serves to rank the possibilities in order of profitability, i.e. in the above example: A 20; C 18; B 15. To attempt to derive opportunity costs from these figures merely serves to set lower limits to the most profitable opportunities.

It should be noted that the ranking of 'alternatives' by comparing their respective opportunity costs has been criticised on the grounds that the opportunity cost of one 'alternative' cannot be determined until the opportunity cost of other 'alternatives' is known (see Gould, 1974; 1977). This could be the position where all 'alternatives' lie inside the business (Amey, 1968). This serves to emphasise that the main importance of the opportunity-cost concept is that it forces the decision maker to *consider all* 'alternatives'.

The deterministic assumption inherent in the foregoing discussion tends to obscure the difficulties associated with attempts to measure opportunity cost in conditions of uncertainty. Thus, in the simple illustration given above, only one market condition ('state') was introduced into the problem. Realism would, however, suggest that consideration be given to various possible states and that probabilities be assigned to each. Assuming this to be possible, an expected value figure can then be derived from the data.

Up to this point opportunity cost, as a concept, has been considered in isolation. There are, however, certain related concepts which invite discussion and these are examined below.

Opportunity Cost and Related Concepts

The point has already been made that imputation of opportunity cost in a decision calculation is not essential and that a correct choice between alternatives can be made by the simple process of listing and comparing the revenues/costs which would vary with the decision taken. This latter process may be referred to as the 'differential cost approach'.

The terms 'differential cost', i.e. the difference between the costs of alternative actions, in a decision-making context is synonymous with incremental or avoidable cost. In a narrower sense however the term 'incremental cost' may be reserved for the increase in recorded costs associated with increases in production which, in a short-run situation, may be equated with 'marginal' or 'variable' cost.

Avoidable (or escapable) costs are often viewed as synonymous with incremental costs (see e.g. Amey and Egginton, 1973). From a narrower viewpoint 'avoidability' or 'escapability' has been associated primarily with retrenchment, whereas incremental costs have been linked with some form of increase in activity (see e.g. Dean, 1951). This narrow distinction is, however, seldom observed in either a theoretical or operational context, and in seeking to draw comparisons with the opportunity cost concept it is convenient in this discussion to use the expression 'differential cost' to embrace both 'incremental cost' and 'avoidable cost'.

The idea of differential cost is inherent in the 'taxonomic approach' referred to previously. The differential and opportunity cost concepts both have their roots in the same fundamental idea in that they both focus attention on the costs of change, and both are defined only in relation to the particular course of action contemplated and at the time envisaged. They do, however, depict different approaches to a problem, but both will produce the same numerical answer provided that opportunity cost is viewed in terms of *net* revenues forgone and the resulting figure is compared with *net* differential revenues, i.e. differential (incremental) revenues less differential (incremental) costs.

The use of opportunity cost as distinct from differential cost seems to be generally defended on the grounds of convenience, expediency and to some extent economy. Amey (1968) offers no general rule for the identification of cases in which it might be more convenient to impute opportunity cost than to use the taxonomic approach. However, he suggested that

> they will often be cases which do not call for simultaneous solution of the value of
> alternative plans and opportunity cost *and* in which the opportunity cost is represented by
> an alternative outside the firm which takes the form of financial investment ('lending') or
> not borrowing.
> Amey, 1968, p. 451.

Horngren (1977) views the situation in terms of expediency and, presumably, economy. He argues that both the taxonomic approach and the opportunity cost approach lead to the same results, but that the use of opportunity cost is justified on the grounds that many alternatives will be rejected outright without a formal analysis. Similarly, Shillinglaw (1977) defends the use of the opportunity cost concept on much the same grounds.

Clearly, some courses of action can be dismissed as unacceptable without recourse to detailed consideration and analysis. However, it could be argued that these are not required to be incorporated into the formal analysis if the differential cost approach is adopted, in which case the argument for the preferred use of opportunity cost on the grounds of expediency and economy is of doubtful validity. In conducting a formal evaluation of alternative uses of inputs it will be the *best single excluded alternative* which will be selected for comparison in adopting the opportunity cost approach. This is not necessarily clearly identifiable and an opportunity cost may then have to be imputed. An obvious example would be the notional interest that could be earned on a capital sum which it is proposed to employ in a certain course of action.

One need not elaborate on the obvious point that elimination of a cash inflow is equivalent to the generation of a cash outflow, yet this would imply a forgone opportunity if resources which are currently employed optimally are diverted to a less profitable use. The inherent dangers of such a switching of resources are 'highlighted' by the opportunity cost approach.

McRae (1970), pointing out that in the standard text books opportunity cost is or is not a synonym for incremental cost, and that the question may or may not be important, seeks to reduce confusion by formulating the definitions in systems terms. Thus, opportunity costs may be associated with the various *inputs* to the system and also with the various *uses* of the system itself. The systems approach envisaged requires a distinction to be drawn between inputs and outputs, a distinction which provides the basis for the respective definitions which McRae offers.

He invokes two assumptions: (i) that the alternative outputs from a production system use the identical inputs in identical proportions, and (ii) that the alternative uses of the inputs are independent of one another. Opportunity cost (an output measure of cost) is then defined as 'the revenue sacrificed by not using the *system* in its most profitable alternative use'. Incremental cost (an input measure of cost) is defined as 'the sum of the revenue sacrificed by not using *each of the inputs* to the system independently of one another in their most profitable alternative use' (McRae 1970, p. 320). In the light of these definitions McRae concludes that incremental cost provides a floor to opportunity cost, and that the task of measuring opportunity cost is synonymous with the task of maximising the profit from the use of the resources under a firm's control. Presumably what is meant by this last statement is that a true figure of opportunity cost can only be determined if the optimal profit situation is known, but the act of measurement should not of course be confused with performance itself.

The value of McRae's contribution would seem to lie in his critical examination of the various definitions found in the literature and in the degree of precision which he seeks to import by attempting to give a distinct and unambiguous meaning to the terms 'opportunity cost' and 'incremental cost'. It is doubtful if anything is gained in an operational context by this particular approach, but the analysis attempted should serve to focus the mind on these distinctions. For this reason McRae's suggestions are incorporated in this discussion.

Applications of the Opportunity Cost Concept

Amey (1968) examined the applicability of opportunity cost to a number of cases which he classified broadly as single-period/multi-period decision problems and internal/external alternatives. For convenience the problem areas considered may be listed under the headings: constrained maximisation; alternative uses of existing resources; internal transfers; trade-off decisions; inventory investment; and budgeting. Asset valuation, which was also discussed by Amey in the context of opportunity cost, is not included in the foregoing list as this problem area is not directly concerned with resource allocation issues.

In some of the cases noted above, e.g. maximisation of the firm's objectives subject to constraints, transfer pricing in divisionalised organisations, and developing operating budgets, the linear programming approach may be appropriate. In such cases opportunity cost can be derived from the 'dual' prices in the optimal solution.

Dual prices as opportunity costs have also been suggested for: (i) evaluation of the effects of small deviations from the optimal plan (Carsberg 1969); (ii) evaluation of budget variances (Samuels 1965a; Demski 1967). A specific application of (i) is that suggested by Arnold (1973) in the context of interim pricing. This suggestion would involve the possible use of dual prices as a screening device to set minimum prices for new products, the minimum price being that which will just cover opportunity costs. The applications suggested by Samuels (1965a) and Demski (1967) are discussed in chapter 14; the topic of transfer pricing is considered in chapter 13.

In addition to the foregoing, attempts have been made by various writers to indicate other possible practical applications or implications, and/or assess in controlled conditions the probable extent of the usage of opportunity cost information assuming its availability. Some of these attempts are referred to below.

It is well recognised that in the managerial decision-making field the costs which are relevant to a decision must satisfy two criteria, namely that of futurity and that of attributability (or relevance) to the decision. The requirement of futurity is obviously crucial to any decision which will result in the incurrence of costs, or indeed the earning of revenues, at some date or dates in the future. This requirement must lead to problems of uncertainty.

Associated with the aforementioned criteria is the frequently cited view that past or sunk costs are irrelevant in the context envisaged. Despite the validity of this view in appropriate circumstances, there is an inherent danger in the tendency to treat as costless any unused capacity which could be absorbed by a new capital investment project, as this attitude could conceivably lead to sub-optimal investment decisions. Blum and Brooks (1976) have pointed out that such unused capacity has an opportunity cost in that it could possibly be used for a more profitable alternative *future* project. This is a point which should be borne in mind in making investment decisions, and is one which highlights the inherent complexity of the nature of 'relevant' costs.

Attention was focused on the opportunity cost concept in different circumstances in various reported experiments designed to ascertain the extent of the usage of opportunity cost information as opposed to information on outlay costs. In the first of these experiments (Becker et al., 1974), a series of choices were required to be made between two projects, one of which included some opportunity cost information and one of which did not. The analysis of the results showed that a statistically significant number of participants made decisions which indicated either that they ignored the opportunity cost information or that they treated opportunity costs as inferior to outlay costs. The implication that this might be attributed to the conventional accounting format is apparent in the conclusion that 'People intuitively take opportunity costs into account except when the decision alternatives are presented in formalised accounting style.' (Becker et al., 1974, p. 327).

In the second experimental study (Neumann and Friedman, 1978), explicit opportunity cost information was presented for both projects. It was found that such costs were in fact used in a statistically significant majority of the choice situations, with the possibility of some small degree of discounting of the available data on *opportunity costs*.

Apart from seeking the answers to certain specific questions, the aim of the third study (Friedman and Neumann, 1980) was to attempt to reconcile the findings of the earlier experiments. The results suggested that, if decision makers are aware of the fact that some opportunity costs *are* relevant in a particular situation, they will request and use such information. They will however only *use* it if the quantum is known; they will make no attempt to impute figures for opportunity cost where information regarding its magnitude is not available.

The findings reported above were based on laboratory studies, with the consequent limitations which these imply. There would appear to be little empirical data available to indicate the extent to which the opportunity cost approach is used in practice (Arnold and Scapens, 1980). Intuitively, however, business men, whether or not they are familiar with the concept as an abstraction, may in cases of a simple choice between alternatives make use of the underlying idea of opportunity cost. In support of this view Parker (1980) draws attention to two early records, dated respectively 1617 and 1805–7, which indicated an intuitive awareness of the basic ideas of avoidable cost and opportunity cost and the fact that costs which remain the same under all alternatives are irrelevant. Interestingly however, as he points out, the examples were drawn from practice and not from the literature of the time. The ideas inherent in the examples did not appear in the literature of economics until the last three decades of the 19th century and were not the subject of recorded discussion by academic accountants until the 1930s.

It has been argued so far that opportunity cost, by its emphasis on sacrifice, is central to the meaning of cost. An adequate discussion of cost relevance does, however, also require consideration of certain behavioural and traceability characteristics of cost. These are reviewed below.

III. BEHAVIOURAL AND TRACEABILITY CHARACTERISTICS OF COST

Behavioural Characteristics

Analysis of cost behaviour patterns lays emphasis on the distinction between fixed and variable costs. Cost classification by reference to the criterion of cost responsiveness to volume changes thus follows this fixed/variable dichotomy.

On the question of variability, accountants have tended to follow economic analysis in emphasising cost as a function of output to the exclusion, in general, of other independent variables. Hence, by definition, total variable costs tend to vary proportionately with output volume, whereas total fixed costs tend to be unaffected by such variations, at least over a 'relevant range' of output.

Clearly, volume of production is by no means the only independent variable of which cost is a function. Volume is common to all manufacturing operations and is likely to be the one which is subject to the most frequent and greatest degree of change. Even so, output itself depends on both volume and rate of production, and both these aspects of production seem relevant. Despite the existence of other short-run influences on cost, for example factor prices, production lot size, degree of utilisation of plant, and variety of output, the general assumption in cost analysis studies based on the fixed/variable dichotomy is that independent variables other than output are kept constant during the production period.

In a recent survey relating to identification of fixed and variable costs, Coates et al. (1980) apparently found some polarisation of attitudes, ranging from the view that 'in these days all costs except the bought out variables are fixed' to 'cost behaviour is not simply a matter of fixed and variable, it is much more complex than this, and one cannot afford the resources to carry out detailed cost behaviour studies'.

Apart from the complexities associated with the introduction of additional independent variables into the cost function, the distinction between fixed costs and variable costs is by no means clear-cut and is often determined arbitrarily; it is valid only in relation to a given period of time and over a given range of activity. Furthermore, it is often possible to reduce variable costs at the expense of fixed costs, e.g. reducing labour costs by the introduction of labour-saving equipment. The attitude of management itself may even determine whether a cost is classified as fixed or variable, or the particular accounting method adopted may be the deciding factor. This anomaly has been recognised in the case of depreciation where accounting method does not necessarily reflect the economic relationships. Thus, depreciation calculated on the straight-line basis results in a fixed charge per annum, but this reflects the true position only if the diminution in value of the asset is a function of time as opposed to wear and tear caused through usage. On the other hand, accounting method places depreciation in the variable cost category if it is calculated on a production unit or production hour basis irrespective of the true behaviour pattern. To reflect economic reality one should therefore consider the nature of the asset and seek to determine whether loss in value is a function of use or time; in the former case it would be a variable cost, in the latter case a fixed cost. Applying these criteria, assets in the same department might then be dealt with in different ways, as indeed might different parts of the same asset such as the engine and the chassis of a motor vehicle, thus placing depreciation of the whole asset in the semi-variable category.

Another anomaly arises in the case of labour costs which may in many cases assume the characteristics of a fixed cost. The 'ratchet effect' may also operate in respect of direct wages insofar as, in the very short run, decreases in output may not necessarily be accompanied by reductions in variable costs, whereas for increases in output the wages costs would tend to increase.

The point has already been made that accounting estimates of cost behaviour patterns are generally considered valid only in relation to a given range of activity. It is only over such a relatively narrow range that an assumption of linearity in the cost function can be defended. As is already known, over the whole range of output the total variable cost pattern as depicted in economic theory would be curvilinear. This is based on the contention that initially, i.e. at the lower output ranges, marginal cost will begin to fall as the output process becomes more efficient; there will then be a tendency for such costs to be constant over a given range and, ultimately, as a result of production constraints and possible increases in input factor costs there will be an increase in marginal costs at higher levels of activity.

The validity of the conventional accounting cost behaviour model is confined not only to a given relevant range of activity but should also be viewed in the context of the particular time period under consideration. Thus, in short-run cost analysis, cost is related to output changes within the limits of a time span during which the size of the plant is regarded as fixed, whereas, in the very long run, the concern is not circumscribed by its present policies and commitments. Between the very long run and the very short run there will be innumerable intermediate time periods in which the firm can make partial adjustments to its production factors. Even so, in such intermediate periods the firm will not be entirely free of its previous commitments.

The whole question of cost relevance is thus related to the length of the period under consideration. However, it should not be overlooked that decisions which are apparently of a short-run nature may have 'knock-on' effects into subsequent periods.

The inference generally drawn from any discussion of cost in relation to time periods is that in the very short run all costs will be fixed, whereas in the very long run all costs will be variable. Attempts to justify this conclusion might well follow the line that, since the facilities required to maintain production capacity will need to be replaced and their size is likely to respond to long-run changes in volume, then in the long run all costs will be variable. Such arguments, although defensible, do not fit strictly into the framework of the narrow definitions of 'fixity' and 'variability'. The level at which productive capacity is replaced will be influenced by expected future demand for the firm's output, but once the replacement decision has been implemented the firm is committed to a whole range of fixed costs arising from the replacement decision. In effect, the firm will have changed its cost structure by substituting a new 'tier' of fixed costs. This does not, however, mean that the fixed costs in the original cost structure have changed in proportion to output volume, but rather that the anticipated future activity may have determined the level of fixed costs in the overall revised cost structure. Such costs, i.e. 'sunk' or 'committed' costs, are fixed by virtue of their connection with those items of plant and equipment and with the basic organisational structure.

Possibly some would suggest that all fixed costs fall into this category of 'sunk' or 'committed' costs. However, it is not entirely satisfactory merely to state that certain costs are fixed over a relevant activity range without posing the question 'why are they fixed?'. The further analysis prompted by this line of enquiry indicates the inadequacy of the single 'fixed cost' classification and reveals the fact that costs acquire 'fixity' for different reasons. Thus, apart from the category of 'sunk' or 'committed' costs already referred to, some costs are fixed as a result of a budget appropriation decision at the beginning of the period whereas others might possibly fall into a residual category.

Costs fixed by budget appropriation decisions are of the type generally referred to as 'discretionary fixed costs', 'managed costs', or 'programmed costs' which, typically, would include such items as advertising, and research and development expenditure. The nature of such costs has prompted the suggestion that if the budget is set as a function of volume the costs behave as variable costs. This should, of course, be viewed with some caution in view of the dangers of distorting normal cause and effect relationships. Thus, one would reasonably expect sales and production orders to result from advertising expenditure and not to be the cause of such outlays. Furthermore, if the research and development budget is specified as a percentage of sales revenue, the apparent linearity of the relationship is unreal, as the amount to be spent is still 'fixed' by management.

Since some fixed costs do not readily fall into either of the categories previously discussed, it would seem that a third (or residual) category should be recognised. This would include such items as general staff welfare costs, which are fixed in the sense of being unavoidable and, although discretionary as regards actual amount, are nevertheless fixed for an indeterminate period of time extending beyond the budgetary period.

'Discretionary fixed costs' are, of course, 'controllable' by nature, but 'committed costs' do not respond to short-term decisions. This serves to emphasise the need in appropriate circumstances, such as the evaluation of the performance of respective segments of the business, for a distinction to be drawn between different types of fixed costs.

Any discussion of cost behaviour would not be complete without some consideration of those costs which are neither wholly fixed nor wholly variable (i.e. 'semi-variable' or 'semi-fixed') and those costs whose behaviour follows a 'stepped' pattern. Generally the terms 'semi-variable' and 'semi-fixed' are regarded as synonymous, describing those costs which include both a fixed and a variable cost element. The common identity of the two expressions is, however, not universally accepted. Thus, Bierman (1963) regards a semi-variable cost as one which is 'basically variable, but not a continuous function of activity', whereas he would take the view that a semi-fixed cost is 'essentially fixed but may have to be increased if production is increased'. An example of the former would be an overtime or shift premium payable if working hours exceed a basic minimum; the implication of the latter is that the fixed cost will move by a vertical step to a higher plateau when production exceeds a certain level.

Some costs which are basically variable will display a 'stepped' cost pattern arising from their indivisible nature and because the services which stem from them cannot be stored for future use. As a practical measure the size of the steps in relation to the normal range of operations is relevant to the cost classification process in this context. Thus, relatively small steps will usually suggest that the stepped costs be treated as variable (step-variable costs), whereas if a cost plateau extends substantially over the whole 'relevant range' of activity such cost may be regarded as fixed.

Cost Traceability

Too much emphasis cannot be laid on the fact that variability is not the same as directness; variability is concerned with cost behaviour, whereas directness relates to traceability. Directness is a relative term in the sense that a cost which is traceable to a cost centre or production centre may or may not be traceable to the ultimate product unit. In a broader context it can be argued that all 'relevant' costs must be traceable in the sense that they are identifiable with the particular decision or course of action, a point which emerges in the subsequent discussion of the 'attributable cost' concept.

Various reasons may be put forward to account for the apparent tendency on some occasions to associate variability with directness and, conversely, to confuse fixity with non-traceability. Firstly, direct product costs are variable by nature. Secondly, costs are, in practice, typically analysed or projected on the basis of their functional and hence traceable characteristics. Thirdly, differences exist in the accountants' and economists' terminology concerned with overhead. As regards the latter point, to the economist overhead is a fixed cost of production, whereas in accounting terminology it is equated with 'indirect costs' (i.e. the indirect elements of materials, labour, and expense), the distinguishing characteristic of which is their non-traceability to specific cost centres or cost units. Since such non-traceable costs may well have a variable content, 'non-traceability' cannot be equated with 'fixity'.

The two distinct cost dichotomies previously discussed, i.e. the one based on behavioural characteristics and the other based on traceability, have not been accepted universally as mutually exclusive (e.g. Marple, 1963; and Shillinglaw, 1963). Operating statements designed to depict various types of performance margin attributable to different segments of the business (e.g. divisions, products, etc.) will require cost classification on the basis of both behavioural and traceability characteristics. Thus, determination of segment contribution is dependent on the establishment of cost behaviour patterns, but traceability of costs to business segments is of obvious importance in determining 'short-run performance margins' and 'segment margins' (e.g. Horngren, 1977; and Hart, 1973). It should be emphasised, however, that the determination of profit by the marginal costing approach does not in itself involve classification by reference to the direct/indirect dichotomy: it is the further aspect of segment performance evaluation which requires this additional analysis.

The concept of attributable cost, developed by Shillinglaw (1963), is another instance where the clear-cut dichotomies previously referred to are not upheld. This concept is discussed below.

The Concept of Attributable Cost

Recognising that the decision-making process will not necessarily be served wholly by costs which fall neatly into either the short-run or the long-run pattern, Shillinglaw put forward the 'attributable cost concept' as an attempt to make the long-run marginal cost concept more operational. The type of decision to which the application of the concept was envisaged was given the label 'quantitative policy decision', embracing those decisions which are likely to remain in force for a period of time and are expected to provide a continuing answer to a recurring question. Examples given by Shillinglaw include establishment of delivery policies, quantity discounts and customer selection. The fact that the decision is not confined to a unique situation serves to distinguish the 'quantitative policy' decision from both the 'investment type' decision and the 'tactical or current operating' decision. It is further distinguished from the investment type decision in that it does not involve negative differential cash flows in one or more time periods in order to achieve positive differential cash flows in future time periods, and from the tactical, or current operating decision, in regard to the duration for which it is expected to remain in force.

'Attributable cost' includes the short-run variable costs and also those fixed costs that are significantly divisible, i.e. those fixed costs which rise in steps but only in response to substantial changes in output. It includes, therefore, short-run variable costs, divisible fixed costs, and indivisible traceable costs.

It should be noted that the variable cost classification shown above includes for this purpose all variable costs, both manufacturing and non-manufacturing. Indivisible fixed costs do not, of course, vary with changes in the volume of activity, whereas divisible fixed costs do so vary if the volume changes are significant, a characteristic which, as Shillinglaw points out, would comply reasonably well with the definition of short-run variable costs if the word 'significant' were deleted.

Conceptually, attributable cost is nothing more than a particular application of a relevant cost to certain types of decision which extend beyond the short term. It represented an attempt to bridge the gap between the short and long run periods. Clearly, there are practical difficulties associated with the actual identification and measurement of the 'relevant' costs applicable to the particular decision-making area envisaged, but its conceptual appeal as such is not thereby diminished.

As yet no attempt has been made in this chapter to apply the concepts discussed in this and earlier sections. However, the question of practical applicability is one which cannot be ignored and some specific decision-making areas are therefore considered below, together with indications of cost concepts which may be relevant in each case. It is emphasised that these are merely intended to be illustrative.

IV. SPECIFIC RELEVANT COSTS FOR DECISION-MAKING

As was indicated earlier, in a managerial decision-making context the relevant costs are those which can be associated with the particular course of action. Such costs must have the characteristics of a future cost and also a differential cost, or indeed opportunity cost if this can be viewed as the counterpart of differential cost. Emphasis here is therefore on ex-ante costs which change with the decision.*

In the next two sections this approach will be applied to profit-planning and 'trade-off' decisions respectively. Pricing policy, a managerial decision-making area involving rather unique issues, is reserved for subsequent discussion. This is followed by some consideration of cost relevance in relation to certain aspects of control.

Cost Relevance and Profit-Planning

Planning as a separate issue is dealt with in some detail in chapters 9 and 10. This section essentially deals with costs in relation to profit planning in rather general terms.

There are obvious dangers in the use of 'full cost' (i.e. cost derived on an absorption cost basis) in the profit-planning field. Thus, absorption of total costs into products tends to obscure the essential behavioural distinctions between fixed costs and variable costs and has the effect of 'averaging' fixed costs on a unit basis over a given volume of production. The result is that unit costs and unit profits calculated at that given level of production and product mix may be valid only in respect of that specific situation.

This line of reasoning applies not only to manufacturing costs but equally, if not more so, to non-manufacturing costs where there is an added danger which may arise from attempts to treat certain non-manufacturing costs as variable with sales revenue. Thus, it is tempting to suggest that sales revenue varies directly with the numbers of sales representatives employed within the firm, or that costs attributable to a salesman should vary directly with the sales revenue produced by him. However, even if it can be shown that relationships of this kind do apply in some particular case, their validity depends on the process of averaging and is applicable only in an overall sense.

Applying the criteria of 'futurity' and 'attributability to the decision' it is then the variable costs which will be the relevant costs in a profit-planning situation in the short term. In the longer term, assuming the necessity to add to the existing fixed cost structure, the relevant 'differential' or 'incremental' costs will include some appropriate element of fixed cost. Indeed, if all the constituent elements are identifiable and quantifiable it may be that Shillinglaw's concept of 'attributable cost' is relevant in this situation.

Cost Relevance and Trade-Off Decisions

It may be argued that all decisions involve a 'trade-off' in some sense. However, in a business decision-making context, the term is generally associated with the type of decision discussed below. In such cases, from a purely economic view-point, the decision-maker is concerned with the incremental net revenues arising from the decision. This may involve simply a consideration of incremental/avoidable costs, or it may involve also, according to the nature of the decision, a consideration of incremental revenues. In any event the costs which are relevant to the decision will be the 'differential' costs, bearing in mind that the opportunity cost approach to the analysis may be more convenient.

*The implications of Demski and Feltham's information evaluation approach should also be borne in mind. See chapter 6.

The category of decisions referred to here as 'trade-off' decisions would include:
— Accept/reject a special order at a price below normal selling price.
— Which of two or more mutually exclusive orders to accept.
— Sell a product in its existing state or subject it to further processing.
— Make/buy.
— Continue/discontinue a particular product or segment of the business.
— Buy/sell internally or outside the organisation.

In all these cases policy considerations other than purely economic issues are likely to have some bearing on the decision itself. These will usually be specific to the decision-maker and thus it is not appropriate to speculate on them in the present context.

The first case referred to above, viz. accept/reject decisions, is a classical example of 'marginal cost pricing' in a situation where manufacturing capacity is not fully utilised. The relevant costs are the incremental (differential) costs which, in view of the existence of spare factory capacity and the short-term nature of the problem, will be variable costs. Apart from the policy issues referred to above, acceptance of an order at a price below normal selling price is based on certain assumptions such as:
— The price offered makes a contribution to fixed costs.
— The price is the best obtainable in the circumstances.
— Spare capacity exists.
— Normal selling price will not be depressed as a result of accepting the offer.
— Customer goodwill will not be affected adversely.

'Product-mix' decisions, the second case referred to above, vary considerably in complexity but may all be treated as optimisation problems. The cost accountants' simple marginal costing approach, which advocates the concentration of production on those opportunities which maximise the contribution per unit of the 'key factor' or 'limiting factor' of production, is valid only in circumstances where there is only one limiting factor. The existence of more than one such factor introduces difficulties which will normally require a mathematical programming approach. The reason is that maximisation of contribution per unit of limiting factor assumes advance knowledge that such factor(s) will be used up completely in maximising profits, a fact which can usually only be determined by the cost accountants' simple 'marginal costing' method if a *single* scarce factor exists (Samuels, 1965b; Amey, 1965).

The mathematical programming approach may indeed be regarded by the accountant as the natural extension of the principle of marginal costing or 'as simply a means for extending the advantages of using marginal costing (direct costing) as the basis for short-run decisions on price and output' (Samuels, 1965a, p. 183).

References above to the 'marginal costing' technique suggest that 'marginal costs' are the costs which are relevant to the type of optimisation situation envisaged. This is the case if marginal cost is construed as the cost associated with changes in production level within the existing fixed cost structure; in other words the costs which are relevant are the variable costs, since it is these costs which, when deducted from sales revenue, yield the contribution i.e. the expression that it is sought to maximise.

The third case, 'sell or process further', is often used as an example to illustrate the equivalence in quantitative terms of differential cost and opportunity cost (Amey and Egginton, 1973; Hart, 1973), either of which will therefore be relevant depending on the viewpoint adopted. In this case, however, it is highly improbable that the differential cost will be identical with the variable costs incurred unless it is a question of utilising what would otherwise be spare capacity. The decision to embark on further processing operations will not normally be a 'one-off' or short-term decision and is likely to involve some additions to the fixed cost structure. In such a case the incremental costs of further processing (for comparison with incremental revenues) will be the variable costs of the processing plus the increment in fixed costs arising from the decision.

In make or buy decisions the situation may be such that there are no gross incremental revenues associated with the decision. This would be the case if, following a decision to buy, say, the component from an outside source, the assumed spare capacity would remain idle. In this event the decision simply rests on the question of incremental or avoidable costs, which in view of the existence of spare capacity would, subject to the caveat below, be derived from a comparison of the outside supplier's delivery price with the variable costs of producing the component internally. If, however, there exists the possibility of renting out the spare capacity, the decision-maker must then also consider the incremental revenues (i.e. rental income) accruing from the decision to buy outside, which may alternatively be viewed as the opportunity cost of utilising the spare capacity to make the component with the firm's own resources.

The caveat referred to above is associated with the idea of 'creep' (Dixon, 1953) which identifies the natural tendency for fixed costs associated with added fringe activities to 'creep into the operating costs structure'. As applied to the present context the danger is that the process of utilisation of available spare capacity to manufacture component parts may assume greater dimensions than those originally contemplated, with the possibilities of encroachment on normal manufacturing capacity and increase in fixed costs. This should not arise if the activity in question is of a purely short-term nature, but it does suggest the need for serious cost studies before the decision is taken.

Product-line decisions are dependent on changes in costs/revenues expected to arise if a product, service, or department is discontinued. The obvious requirement is therefore to determine which costs are avoided by the decision, bearing in mind the essential element of unavoidability associated with joint costs. The essential criterion of cost relevance is then that of 'segment traceability'; all costs directly traceable to the segment in question will be avoided by the decision to abandon that segment. Fixed costs which are apportioned to business segments are relevant to the decision only if, and to the extent that, the decision to discontinue results in a change in the scale of such costs.

One important aspect of product-line decisions is the interdependencies which will often exist among products; the dropping of one product may have serious repercussions on the sale of other products in the company's range. Again, since the product/department concerned may be assumed to make some contribution to common fixed costs it is essential for the decision maker to examine carefully the areas of possible deployment of the resources currently utilised in the segment under consideration. If there are no opportunities of utilising the resources more profitably the segment should be retained provided that it makes a contribution to common fixed overheads.

Decisions relating to transfer-pricing have some common features with both make/buy decisions and accept/reject decisions. The subject of transfer pricing is discussed in chapter 13. The concern of this section in the context of transfer pricing is with the costs which might be relevant to the decision. The treatment here is somewhat simplified by the deliberate omission of issues such as externalities.

If no constraints are imposed on the receiving (distribution) division's freedom of action to meet its purchasing requirements from the manufacturing division or from an outside source of supply (assuming this to exist), the situation from the corporate viewpoint would have the characteristics of a make or buy decision. The net advantage to be derived by adopting the optimal course of action would be determined by a comparison of the respective avoidable costs, i.e. the outside supplier's delivery price on the one hand and, assuming no changes in fixed costs, the variable costs of the manufacturing division on the other hand. The distribution division will merely seek to minimise its cost. This means that in the decision rule 'transfer price' will be substituted for variable costs of the manufacturing division.

The decision of the manufacturing division, faced with a request to lower the price charged to the distribution division, will be of the nature of an accept/reject decision, with the emphasis which such decisions place on the need for the agreed price to make an appropriate contribution to fixed costs.

Reverting to the make or buy decision analogy referred to above it might also be necessary to consider the separate issue of opportunity cost when determining which costs are relevant to the decision. Assume that the company currently manufactures two products, say P and Q, the latter being the one which is also available on the outside market. Assume further that the manufacturing division could operate at full capacity by switching all its resources to Product P. From a corporate viewpoint the relevant costs would include the revenue forgone by utilising some of the limited capacity in the production of Q. Relevant costs would thus include an avoidable cost element *and* an opportunity cost element.

In concluding this section on trade-off decisions it should be noted that the contribution approach is of some considerable significance in the context of special decisions involving a choice between alternative courses of action. It is also worth noting, that in all the cases discussed, with the possible exception of make or buy decisions, the ultimate decision hinges on a comparison of differential costs incurred as a result of the decision and differential revenues flowing from the decision. Make or buy decisions will frequently involve a comparison of differential costs only.

Cost Relevance and Pricing Policy

Despite the conflict of opinion regarding the precise role of costs in pricing, there would be few who would subscribe to the view that costs are totally irrelevant. The strongly supported belief that optimal price depends on both costs and demand relationships is derived from the neoclassical view propounded by Marshall (1920) that price was governed neither by cost of production alone nor by marginal utility alone, but by the interaction of these forces as expressed in demand and supply. The influence of Marshall is still evident in the underlying assumption of pricing theory that optimal behaviour of an economic unit will be determined by the relationship between marginal cost and marginal revenue. Thus, assuming an objective of profit maximisation and appropriately shaped cost curves, optimal output is the production volume at which the firm's marginal revenue is equal to its marginal costs. Assuming that the firm's demand curve can be estimated, the optimal selling price can then be determined.

The optimisation aim of marginal analysis, with its general implication of profit maximisation, suggests that the demand function is probably of greater importance than cost. It is, indeed, a weakness of the conventional cost-plus pricing formula, if strictly applied, that demand is ignored. However, the price which customers are willing to pay for a product may have little or no relationship to its cost of manufacture. Thus Cyriax (1965) suggested that

> the most advanced thinkers, especially in the consumer goods industries, are inclined to
> think first of the price that a product can fetch in its various markets, and to work back
> from there to the calculations of the profit and costs.

Elaborating the same point Spencer and Siegelman (1964, p. 388) remarked:

> To achieve this goal (the largest expected net profit) requires a knowledge of product inter-relationships, particularly from the demand standpoint, since it is the demand elasticities rather than cost considerations alone that are usually more relevant for pricing purposes.

Following this line of argument it may well be that total profit is maximised by increasing the price (or reducing the production cost) of a 'profitable' line as opposed to applying the same procedure to a 'non-profitable' line. A logical approach to profit planning should in fact treat cost and price as two independent variables, each to be separately controlled if optimal overall profit is to be attained.

One of the practical difficulties is that pricing policy is inextricably bound up with product policy, with profit depending on both of them. Cost is obviously of relevance to product and promotional policies, but the relevant cost is unlikely to be 'full cost'. If the problem is whether to drop or continue an existing product line then, as indicated previously, avoidable cost will be the relevant cost; whereas, if the problem is to determine which of two competing products should be marketed, the relevant costs will be the differential costs of the alternative products.

A fairly typical attitude among businessmen seems to be that there should exist a fair or equitable relationship between price and cost, the ideal price being one which will cover all costs plus a target return on capital employed in the business. A cost-plus formula approach of this nature, whilst ignoring demand if rigidly applied, may indirectly allow for the forces of demand through a conscious adjustment by the decision maker of the required mark-up on total cost, the actual price then being an adjusted cost-plus price. Nevertheless, the approach itself does assume price to be a function of cost. As against this, it may be argued that, where price is a market-determined going rate, or is even possibly related to the costs of competitors, then costs are dependent on price or in other words are 'tailor-made' to a predetermined price.

The use of marginal (incremental) cost as an aid to price determination is well recognised in the context of marginal business (or special situations) or as a trade depression pricing policy. However, there appears to be a general reluctance to employ it as a pricing instrument in its own right in preference to a full cost approach. The marginal cost approach to pricing does allow directly for the forces of demand but, apart from the latent suspicion with which it is regarded by business men, its application is constrained by the difficulties associated with the forecasting of price–demand relationships. On this point Savage and Small (1967, p. 201) made the very apt comment:

> Generally a business would do better to consider first whether better estimates of incremental cost and demand could not be obtained without great expense before applying a prescription for pricing policy which gives inadequate consideration to demand and may attribute false precision to existing cost estimates.

To conclude, it may be said that costs are not without relevance to pricing decisions. Indeed in situations involving 'cost-plus' contracts or competitive bidding by tender the relationship is a direct one based normally on full-cost considerations, but no doubt affected in the case of tenders by conjecture regarding the level of competitors' costs or possible bids. In general, however, the role of product costs in pricing strategies is rather imprecise. The minimum acceptable price will not normally be affected by external demand conditions, but will be cost-related. The relevant cost for this purpose will be variable cost or, more precisely, the external opportunity costs of the resources involved in the manufacture of the product. Any price in excess of this cost will serve to contribute to fixed costs and profit. Determination of an *optimal* price depends on the availability of knowledge of the demand schedule for the firm's products.

Cost Relevance in Relation to Control

In a managerial accounting context it is a generally accepted view that financial control of a firm's activities can be exercised through budgets. As control devices, however, budgets merely serve to monitor expenditure; they do not in themselves measure the efficiency with which resources have been utilised. Effective monitoring of expenditure presupposes the setting up of some standard of comparison. This introduces the concept of a standard cost, a pre-determined cost or an assessment of what the cost ought to be under prescribed conditions of performing a particular process or operation, or of producing a commodity or rendering a service. The deviation of actual cost, when subsequently determined, from the standard cost set up in advance of events, provides a measure of the extent by which the target is missed. A standard which is reasonably representative of a future cost may be used for planning purposes, but the main advantage of standard costing lies in the area of cost control. Thus, by analysing a 'variance', i.e. deviation from standard, the cause of the deviation can be pin-pointed and appropriate corrective action taken.

As is already known, standard costing can be used in conjunction with either 'absorption costing' or 'marginal costing'. In the latter case fixed costs are deducted in total from the net contribution (i.e. standard contribution as adjusted by appropriate variances) irrespective of the scale of production, thereby removing a possible source of misunderstanding regarding the apparent profits created in the short term by a build-up of stocks. The 'volume variance' would also be removed by this approach, but the control features of standard costing in conjunction with flexible budgets would be retained. This is discussed further in chapter 14.

The use of linear programming in the context of standard costing has also been suggested. Samuels (1965a) suggests the use of the dual variables as the basis of an opportunity costing system for production planning and control. Moreover, Demski (1967) criticises the conventional standard cost system for its failure to act as an opportunity cost system by disregarding changes in planned results, except as signalled by implication or use of an adjusted budget. These suggestions are given further consideration in a later chapter (chapter 14) in which the conventional management accounting control model is reviewed.

V. THE RELEVANCE OF FULL COST

In the various illustrations of possible applications of cost concepts it might well appear that there has been a tendency to discount the applicability of 'full cost' except perhaps in certain areas of pricing. This tendency to play down the relevance of full (or 'absorption') cost is indeed generally apparent in modern management accounting literature. The main reason seems to be the arbitrary nature of overhead (and joint cost) allocations which render suspect the resulting figures for decision-making purposes. For example, a decision to close down a department which is deemed a 'loss-maker' on a 'full cost' basis might well be ill-conceived – the decision maker must look at the contribution made by that department and the alternative opportunities for the investment of resources made available if closure were effected.

Summarising what can be taken as a fairly general view among academic accountants, Zimmerman (1979, p. 505) makes the point that

> Except for inventory valuation for financial and tax reporting, government contracting, rate-setting, cost documentation for possible anti-trust suits (e.g. the Robinson–Patman Act, 1936)* or cost-plus pricing, the accounting literature generally recommends avoiding cost allocations.

The reason is that a conventional absorption costing scheme tends to obscure the kind of cost information that is really necessary for decision making.† Nevertheless such conventional schemes are still in use, and one very plausible explanation for this links cost allocations with managerial behaviour (Horngren, 1977; Kaplan, 1977). In support of this explanation Zimmerman (1979) draws on two distinct cost allocation situations concerned respectively with: (i) control over a manager's discretionary spending on (i.e. consumption of) perquisites in the form of non-pecuniary items which enter into his utility function and (ii) control over (rationing of) the use by departments of internally-provided services.

Following the reasoning of Williamson (1964), Zimmerman makes the point that overhead cost allocations can serve as a lump-sum tax which when imputed to an 'agent' may, under certain assumptions, reduce his spending on perquisites.

Moreover, the sharing of a 'fixed' resource involves possible 'costly-to-observe' non-zero opportunity costs (or externalities) in the form of delay costs, deterioration in the service provided and eventual costs arising from the need to expand the service. Zimmerman has shown that overhead allocations (not necessarily *full* absorption) can serve as proxy variables for such opportunity costs. This implies 'internalising' externalities, which can enhance the value of the decentralised firm by forcing each manager to take cognisance of all the costs which he generates in these ways when, by his chosen mix of inputs, he increases his consumption of the 'fixed' resource. If top management had access to perfect and complete knowledge of all cost functions, and could thus estimate 'true' shadow prices, there would be no need to use overhead allocations as proxies.

The apparent linkage exhibited in these two situations between overhead allocations, managerial behaviour, and organisational structure, leads Zimmerman (1979, p. 505) to infer that 'in practice cost allocations are used, at least in part, to solve certain organizational control problems'. Owing to the lack of sufficient evidence (see Ezzamel and Bourn, 1987) it is difficult to empirically assess Zimmerman's arguments. Nevertheless his carefully reasoned arguments represent a praiseworthy attempt to rationalise overhead allotment procedures. Conceding the evident attraction of the suggestion of adapting the 'traditional' costing approach to an opportunity cost-based scheme in this way, Coates (1980, p. 177) makes the point that not only is it 'apparently untried and untested in an empirical situation' but that 'it also has something of the "if you can't beat them, join them" element about it'. In other words, it seeks to rationalise an approach which is known to exist fairly extensively. The explanation could be much simpler than Zimmerman suggests, reflecting a feeling in business that it is essential, particularly in the context of pricing policy, to have a figure which purports to be a 'true' full cost figure, despite the fact that this cost can only be determined through arbitrary overhead allotment procedures (see Ezzamel and Bourn, 1987).

---

*This is of course in the context of the USA background; as regards the UK one could substitute here: 'cost documentation submitted as evidence to support a merger or to refute allegations of "monopoly-price" setting'.

†Note however the cautionary observations of Dillon and Nash (1978) referred to earlier in this chapter.

It seems that the conclusion to be drawn is that full cost does have a part to play in the determination of relevant costs in some specific situations (see Dillon and Nash, 1978). Thus, apart from its possible application to income reporting and inventory valuation, it may well be relevant to certain areas of price determination. However, cost information based solely on such costs lacks the flexibility which is generally required for managerial decision-making purposes. The suggestion that overhead allocations serve as a proxy variable for opportunity costs may provide some conceptual justification for such a procedure, but this is most unlikely to be the reason why full cost is used in practice.

Further research in this area would seem to be indicated if more acceptable explanations are to be obtained. However, the long-established practice of making overhead allocations might restrict the analysis, hence the resulting explanations may have to be treated with some degree of caution.

In concluding this section it is appropriate to refer to some cautionary comments by Hamlen, Hamlen and Tschirhart (1977) which could be of some relevance in the context of Zimmerman's analysis. Their concern is with the danger of possible sub-optimal decisions when a charge to a divisional unit through a joint cost allocation scheme exceeds that which the division would incur by contracting out independently for services currently provided within the organisation. Sub-optimal decisions should, therefore, be rendered unprofitable through the mechanism of the joint cost allocation scheme. The criterion of unprofitability is, they argue, equivalent to the concept of the 'core' used in game theory.

VI. SUMMARY

In this chapter the idea of cost relevance has been developed through an enquiry into the nature of cost and the characteristics of various cost concepts. With the proviso that references to possible applications were meant to be purely illustrative and not prescriptive, the cost concepts were then considered in the context of specific situations to determine which of the several concepts might be relevant thereto.

Throughout the chapter the intention has been to emphasise that cost measurement must necessarily be the result of subjective experience; it must, for decision-making purposes, be based on a forward-looking cost concept, and hence it is inevitably fraught with uncertainty.

There is little evidence available to indicate the extent to which opportunity cost is applied in practical situations. Many possible applications have been suggested, but probably one of its most important possible roles is in the context of evaluating performance in the light of opportunities which have emerged subsequent to the preparation of the original plan.

Full cost may be relevant in certain situations, but sophisticated attempts to explain the reason for the adoption of full cost in practice have not really been proven. The reason may in some cases be far less subtle than attempts at rationalisation sometimes suggest, and may indeed be connected with adherence to tradition and the view that knowledge of 'full' cost is essential to the maintenance of a satisfactory pricing structure.

REFERENCES

Amey, L. R., 1965. Mathematical programming in accounting – a comment, *The Accountant*, 5th June, pp. 765–767.

Amey, L. R., 1968. On opportunity costs and decision making, *Accountancy*, July, pp. 442–451.

Amey, L. R. and Egginton, D. A., 1973. *Management Accounting – a Conceptual Approach*: Longman.

Arnold, J. A., 1973. On the problem of interim pricing decisions, *Accounting and Business Research*, Spring.

Arnold, J. A. and Scapens, R., 1980. 'The British contribution to opportunity cost theory', pp. 155–173 in M. Bromwich and A. Hopwood (eds) *Essays in British Accounting Research*: Pitman.

Baxter, W.T. and Oxenfeldt, A.R., 1961. Costing and pricing: the cost accountant versus the economist. *Business Horizons*, Winter, reprinted in D. Solomons (ed.), *Studies in Cost Analysis*, 2nd edn, 1968. The Law Book Company, Sydney, Australia.

Becker, S. W. et al., 1974. Opportunity costs – an experimental approach, *Journal of Accounting Research*, Autumn, pp. 317–329.

Bierman, H. Jr., 1963. *Topics in Cost Accounting and Decisions*: McGraw-Hill.

Bierman, H. Jr. and Dyckman, T. R., 1971. *Managerial Cost Accounting*. New York: Macmillan.

Blum, J. D. and Brooks, Le Roy D., 1976. Capital budgeting under conditions of unused capacity, *Cost and Management* (Canada), May/June.

Buchanan, J. M., 1969. *Cost and Choice: An Inquiry in Economic Theory*: Markham.

Carsberg, B. V., 1969. *An Introduction to Mathematical Programming for Accountants*: George Allen and Unwin.

Coase, R. H., 1938. Business organisation and the accountant. *The Accountant*, reprinted in D. Solomons (ed.), *Studies in Cost Analysis*, 2nd edn, 1968. The Law Book Company, Sydney, Australia.

Coates, J. B., 1980. Commentary on 'The British contribution to opportunity cost theory', pp. 174–177 in M. Bromwich and A. Hopwood (eds), *Essays in British Accounting Research*: Pitman.

Coates, J. B., Smith, J. E. and Stacey, R. J., 1980. 'Report on a survey of the operation of management accounting in practice', University of Aston 1980.

Cyriax, J. R., 1965. Pricing policies and costs, *Management Accounting* (UK) December. London: ICMA.

Dean, J., 1951. *Managerial Economics*. Englewood Cliffs, NJ: Prentice-Hall.

Demski, J. S., 1967. An accounting system structured on a linear programming model, *The Accounting Review*, October, pp. 701–712.

Demski, J. S., 1968. Variance analysis using a constrained linear model, pp. 526–540 in D. Solomons (ed.) *Studies in Cost Analysis*, 2nd edn. The Law Book Company, Sydney, Australia.

Demski, J. S. and Feltham, J. B., 1976. *Cost Determination: A Conceptual Approach*: Iowa State University Press.

Dillon, R. D. and Nash, J. F., 1978. The true relevance of relevant costs, *Accounting Review*, January, pp. 11–17.

Dixon, R. L., 1953. Creep, *Journal of Accountancy*, July.

Ezzamel, M. and Bourn, M., 1987. 'Why do firms allocate costs?' in J. Arnold, D. J. Cooper and R. W. Scapens (eds), *Case Study Research in Management Accounting*: ICMA.

Friedman, L. A. and Neumann, B. R., 1980. The effect of opportunity costs on project investment decisions: a replication and extension, *Journal of Accounting Research*, Autumn, pp. 407–419.

Gould, J. R., 1977. 'The economist's cost concept and business problems', in W. T. Baxter and S. Davidson, *Studies in Accounting Theory*: Sweet and Maxwell.

Hamlen, S. S., Hamlen, W. A. and Tschirhart, J. T., 1977. The use of core theory in evaluating joint cost allocation schemes, *Accounting Review*, July, pp. 616–627.

Hart, H., 1973. *Overhead Costs – Analysis and Control*: William Heinemann.

Horngren, C. T., 1977. *Cost Accounting – A Managerial Emphasis*. Englewood Cliffs, NJ: Prentice-Hall. See also 1973 edition.

ICMA, 1974. *Terminology of Management and Financial Accountancy*. London ICMA.

Jensen, M. C. and Meckling, W. H., 1976. Theory of the firm: managerial behaviour, agency costs and ownership structure, *Journal of Financial Economics*, October, pp. 305–360.

Kaplan, R., 1977. Application of quantitative models in managerial accounting: a state of the art survey, pp. 50–71 in *Management Accounting – State of the Art*: University of Wisconsin Press.

Marple, R. P., 1963. 'The relative contribution approach to management reporting'. Republished in 1965, p. 412, in R. P. Marple (ed) *N.A.A. on Direct Costing; Selected Papers*: Ronald Press.

Marshall, A., 1920. *Principles of Economics*, 8th edn: Macmillan.

McRae, T. W., 1970. Opportunity cost and incremental cost – an attempt to define in systems terms, *Accounting Review*, April, pp.315–321.

Neumann, B. R. and Friedman, L. A., 1978. Opportunity costs: further evidence through an experimental replication, *Journal of Accounting Research*, Autumn, pp. 400–410.

Parker, R. H., 1980. 'History of accounting for decisions', pp. 262–276 in Arnold, J., Carsberg, B. and Scapens, R. (eds), *Topics in Management Accounting*: Philip Allan Publishers.

Samuels, J. M., 1965a. Opportunity costing: an application of mathematical programming, *Journal of Accounting Research*, Autumn, pp. 182–191.

Samuels, J. M., 1965b. 'Mathematical programming in accounting', *The Accountant*, 27 February, pp. 264–8.

Savage, C. I. and Small, J. R., 1967. *An Introduction to Managerial Economics*: Hutchinson University Library.

Shillinglaw, G., 1963. The concept of attributable cost, *Journal of Accounting Research*, Spring, pp. 73–85.

Shillinglaw, G., 1977. *Managerial Cost Accounting*, 4th edn: Irwin.

Spencer, M. H. and Siegelman, L., 1964. *Managerial Economics*: Irwin.

Walters, A. A., 1960. The allocation of joint costs with demands as probability distributions, *American Economics Review*, June, pp. 419–432.

Wicksteed, P. H., 1910. *The Common Sense of Political Economy*: Macmillan.

Williamson, O. E., 1964. *The Economics of Discretionary Behaviour: Managerial Objectives in a Theory of the Firm*: Prentice-Hall.

Zimmerman, J. L., 1979. The costs and benefits of cost allocations, *Accountng Review*, July, pp. 504–521.

8

Stochastic Cost–Volume–Profit Analysis

For many years cost–volume–profit (C–V–P) analysis has frequently been employed by management in the context of making choices among alternative profit planning decisions. Examples of these decisions include consideration of the sales volumes required for different levels of profit and the effects of changes in the levels of sales volume (sensitivity analysis). The usefulness of this analysis, however, is very limited because it has some inherent drawbacks. The most serious of these limitations is the failure of traditional C–V–P models to treat risk explicitly.

To illustrate this particular deficiency, consider a firm which is faced with alternatives A and B; both having the same unit variable cost and selling price. Under traditional C–V–P analysis, both alternatives are equally desirable. But, as Jaedicke and Robichek (1964) have pointed out, in a realistic situation this analysis does not distinguish the relative desirability of the two alternatives because it ignores both the level of expected sales and the degree of uncertainty associated with sales. Thus, if the expected sales of A are greater than those of B, other things remaining the same, then A would be preferred to B. Even if the expected sales of A and B were the same, one alternative may be preferred to the other because of its relative risk position. Risk, therefore, needs to be explicitly considered in the context of C–V–P analysis.

This chapter is devoted to reviewing the literature which extends traditional C–V–P analysis through the explicit treatment of risk. In general this literature has focused on two main issues. Firstly, attempting to define the underlying probability distribution of model parameters either through mathematical–statistical analysis or through simulation techniques. Secondly, deriving optimal definitions of risk and price of risk to guide risk-return trade-offs so that optimal profit planning decisions may be made. Throughout the analysis, however, it is evident that the pioneering model proposed by Jaedicke and Robichek (1964) is frequently used as a point of departure. One section of this chapter is devoted to a discussion of this model, and another section to a discussion of the limitations of the traditional C–V–P model.

In summary, section I of this chapter contains a discussion of some of the limitations of deterministic C–V–P models. Section II describes and evaluates the Jaedicke–Robichek model. Section III provides an overview of the literature on defining the underlying probability distribution of the parameters of C–V–P models. In section IV a discussion of risk analysis and optimal break-even decisions is given. Finally, section V provides a summary of the chapter.

I. LIMITATIONS OF DETERMINISTIC C–V–P MODELS

For many years C–V–P analysis has been a popular research topic in academic and professional journals and textbooks. However, not until Jaedicke and Robichek's work (1964) has C–V–P been treated in the context of uncertainty. In this section an overview of traditional deterministic C–V–P analysis is provided with the intention of illuminating its usefulness and limitations.

Consider first a simple traditional C–V–P model. In this model the profit equation is expressed as

(1)

$$Z = Q(P - V) - F$$

where Z = profit; Q = sales volume; P = unit price; V = unit variable cost; and F = fixed cost. The break-even volume is derived by setting Z = zero and solving for Q in **(1)**. The break-even volume derived from **(1)** provides a summary statistic of price and cost (variable and fixed). It gives an indication of the profitability associated with different levels of activity. It is also potentially useful in the context of profit planning in the sense of indicating the level of activity required to achieve a given profit target.

By and large these intended benefits are not fulfilled because of the limiting nature of the basic assumptions underlying the simple model expressed in **(1)** above. These assumptions are:

1. The profit function is assumed to be linear; the unit selling price, unit variable cost and fixed cost are all assumed constant at different production levels. In reality, such parameters may be non-linear.
2. Both product mix and factors of production mix are assumed to be constant over time.
3. The traditional model is overly simplistic in the sense that it basically deals with single products and single time periods. In reality, firms produce multiproducts under multiple production constraints. Moreover, most profit planning decisions are of a multi-period nature.
4. The traditional simple model is deterministic; unit sales, unit selling price, unit variable cost and fixed cost are all assumed to be certain rather than stochastic (uncertain) parameters.

During the 1960s and the 1970s, several researchers extended the simple traditional C–V–P model so that it could be employed in less restrictive business settings. The remaining part of this section contains a brief review of those extensions relating to the first three assumptions. The literature dealing with the fourth assumption is reviewed more extensively in the remaining sections of this chapter.

The Linearity Assumption

One attraction of the linearity assumption in the context of C–V–P decisions is that it makes the analysis straightforward. However, it also renders the results far less useful by abstracting away from reality. Vickers (1960) argued that traditional C–V–P models should be brought into closer conformity to economic theory. By invoking the economist's concepts relating to the behaviour of revenue and cost functions (i.e. curvi-linear), Vickers demonstrated not only that there will be *two* break-even points for the firm in any one period but also that there is an *equilibrium* condition. The equilibrium condition shows the position within the profit area at which profit is maximised, in contrast to the untenable linear analysis under which profit is assumed to keep on increasing as activity level expands.

Following Vickers, several writers sought to explicitly incorporate non-linear functions in formal C–V–P models. Goggans (1965), Givens (1966), and Morrison and Kaczka (1969) used differential calculus for the solution of break-even points with curvi-linear parameters. It can be seen in that analysis that the linear C–V–P model is only appropriate for a midrange of activities for which the break-even parameters are approximately linear. Once the activity level is outside this midrange, the linear model becomes clearly inadequate.

It is worth noting, however, that even the above curvi-linear specification of the C–V–P parameters is fairly static. As Vickers (1960) notes, it implies *stable* output rates and smooth, continuous and reversible movements between alternative activity levels. Thus, it is not always possible to regulate additional fixed costs that were incurred with a greater activity level when the firm engages again in lower activity levels. The shapes of the cost and revenue curves are not assumed to alter in a manner that would reflect the incidence or degree of change that may occur in market structures and production technology.

The Constant Mix Assumptions

As indicated earlier, simple traditional C–V–P analysis assumes a constant mix both for products and factors of production. This implies that the firm operates within the strict confines of a given configuration of market structures and technology. Yet, in reality, such configurations frequently change therefore precipitating cultural, structural and policy changes in many organisations. Moreover, innovative (prospective) organisations at times actively precipitate market and technological changes. To be more useful, C–V–P models need to be dynamic by explicitly allowing for such changes. It may be that, as Kaplan (1982) argues, changes in technology are better handled through formal capital budgeting analysis rather than through formal C–V–P models. It is suggested here, however, that the utility of C–V–P analysis can be greatly enhanced if sensitivity analyses of potential changes in markets and technologies can be performed.

The Single Period, Single Product Assumptions

To handle the more realistic business settings involving multiple products under conditions of multiple constraints researchers have integrated more complex mathematical models, particularly mathematical programming, with traditional C–V–P analysis. Jaedicke (1961) used linear programming to perform break-even analysis in the multi-product case. Charnes et al. (1963) used linear programming and goal programming to deal with break-even analysis for multiple products with multiple production constraints. They also considered the effects of variations in product mix on the 'optimal' solution, and integrated spread sheet analyses with the C–V–P model. They pointed out that the evaluation of alternatives would be more informed if it was based upon the shadow prices (opportunity cost) generated by mathematical programming. Manes (1966) incorporated break-even analysis into a multi-period capital budgeting model in determining the amount of periodic sales required in order for the investment to break even. He also integrated C–V–P analysis with economic theory by including the effects of different costs of capital on the investment decision.

The main contributions of the introduction of multi-product, multi-constraint and multi-period situations into the basic traditional C–V–P model may be summarised as follows. Firstly, in a multi-product situation there will be an infinite number of product mixes which will lead to break-even. Secondly, when multi-products share common resources the optimal solution is attained by producing and selling those products with the highest contribution margin per unit of *constraining resource* rather than simply producing those products with the highest contribution margin per product unit. Thirdly, if some or all of the fixed costs related to a particular product are avoidable at zero production, the optimal product mix can be determined in a multi-constraint situation by using mixed-integer programming (Kaplan, 1982). Fourthly, in multi-period investment decisions, periodic break-even sales should not only cover periodic fixed costs but also the investment's cost of capital.

The developments reviewed above have led to considerable refinements in the simple traditional C–V–P model. The model has now become much more complex, perhaps much too complex, but it remains overly deterministic. The literature which specifically addressed this problem is reviewed in the following sections. Much of this literature has been stimulated by the pioneering work of Jaedicke and Robichek (1964). In the following section the Jaedicke–Robichek model is discussed in some detail. The remaining sections deal with the subsequent literature.

II. STOCHASTIC C–V–P ANALYSIS: THE JAEDICKE–ROBICHEK MODEL

The Jaedicke–Robichek (hereafter J–R) model takes issue with the traditional C–V–P model for its failure to account for uncertainty, which is associated with each of the parameters expressed in (1). The profit equation under the J–R model involves the rewriting of (1) into:

(2)
$$E(Z) = E(Q)[E(P) - E(V)] - E(F)$$

where E denotes expected value.

However, as a first approximation the J–R model initially assumes that price, unit variable cost and fixed cost are all certain. In this case, the uncertainty in profits will be only caused by uncertainty in sales volume. The probability distribution of sales volume is assumed to be constructed from relevant historical demand data or from

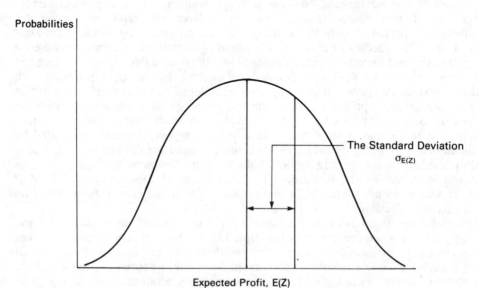

Figure 8.1 *The normal probability distribution of profits*

subjective estimates. The J–R model invokes the normality assumption with respect to the probability distribution of sales volume. It is well known that a normal probability distribution can be completely determined if its mean and standard deviation (first and second moments) are known (see figure 8.1).

By superimposing the probability distribution of sales volume on the traditional profit graph the J–R model can be used to inform decision makers about the risk associated with the break-even volume (see figure 8.2). Using the properties of the normal distribution, several probabilities can now be computed, for example, (i) the probability of at least breaking even, (ii) the probability of profits being greater than a given amount and (iii) the probability of incurring a loss of a given amount. A basic assumption of the J–R model is that since the probability distribution of sales volume is normal, the probability distribution of profits will also be normal. It turns out that this is only true under some special conditions as is shown later.

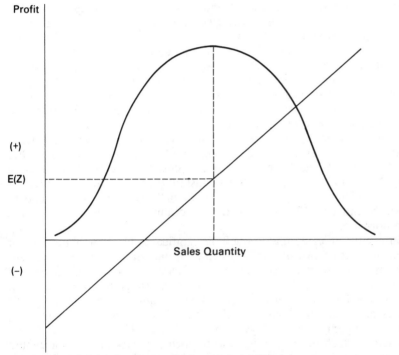

Figure 8.2 *Probability distribution of sales and the profit curve*

Subsequently, the assumptions that price, unit variable cost and fixed costs are constants were relaxed and these three parameters were treated as stochastic but with known probability distributions. Using an example in which the above random variables were assumed to be independent, Jaedicke and Robichek showed that the risk of profitability, as measured by its standard deviation, increased as a result of the variability in each of these three parameters. The model also indicated that once C–V–P is considered in the context of uncertainty the best alternative cannot be determined without knowledge of the firm's attitude toward risk.

The J–R model is undoubtedly an important contribution to the literature on C–V–P analysis. It has shown how uncertainty can be explicitly incorporated into such analysis. This has led to a major shift in our conceptualisation of C–V–P models by formulating them in a stochastic rather than a deterministic framework. However, many academics have taken issue with the basic assumptions underlying the J–R model. The objections against the model that have so far been raised in the literature may be classified as empirical, technical, and conceptual.

The empirical objections relate to the assumption of normalcy of sales volume. Ferrara, Hayya and Nachman (1972) cite evidence from Holt et al. (1960) which indicates that the frequency distribution of sales is affected by the average rate of sales. It also indicates that the normal distribution is seldom an adequate approximation of the frequency distribution of sales. Only when the raw sales data are transformed using the lognormal or gamma distributions will approximation to normality obtain.

The technical criticism centres on the inaccuracy of the Jaedicke and Robichek claim that if all the components of profit are normally distributed and independent of each other the resulting profit is also normally distributed. Ferrara et al. (1972) have pointed out that this implies that Jaedicke and Robichek are assuming that the multiplication of two normal variables yields a normal variable. Ferrara et al. have argued that this is only approximately true under certain conditions. To define these conditions they relied both on statistical reasoning and simulation results. The statistical argument (based on Craig, 1936) is that if $X = Q$ and $Y = P - V$ are two normally distributed variables, then the distribution of their product, XY, is a function of the correlation coefficient of X and Y, r_{xy}, and the reciprocals of their coefficients of variations (the mean of a variable divided by its standard deviation). As the reciprocals of the coefficients of variations approach infinity (or as the coefficients of variations become very small), the probability density function of XY approaches the normal distribution. In terms of the coefficient of variation (C.V.), if either C.V.$(X) \to 0$ or C.V.$(Y) \to 0$ then the variable in question may be considered a constant and thus XY would be the product of a constant times a normal which results in a normal variable. Therefore, if C.V.$(X) = 0$ then there would be no need to impose an upper bound on C.V.(Y) in order to obtain a density function that approximates to normalcy.

The simulation results indicated that at the 0.05 significance level the hypothesis of normalcy for the product of two normally distributed and statistically independent random variables is accepted if the sum of the coefficients of variation of the two variables is less than or equal to 12 per cent. Ferrara et al. suggested, however, that this limitation may not be significant in most business problems because the profit equation variables analogous to X and Y will have relatively small coefficients of variation. In a subsequent paper, Hayya and Ferrara (1972) suggested a less conservative guideline which recommends that the normalcy hypothesis be accepted at the 0.05 significance level if $\rho_1 \rho_2 \geqslant 100$, where $\rho_1 = 1/\text{C.V.}(X)$ and $\rho_2 = 1/\text{C.V.}(Y)$.

Kottas and Lau (1978a) suggested that the conclusions of Ferrara et al. (1972) were not valid for two reasons. Firstly, they extended the chi-square goodness-of-fit test, which has been designed for the purposes of theoretical distributions, to apply to approximations. Secondly, they used too small a sample size in their simulation ($n = 500$). In conclusion, Kottas and Lau argued that the results of Ferrara et al. are sample size dependent with the guideline becoming more stringent as sample size increases. In response to these criticisms Hayya, Ferrara and Saniga (1978) drew a distinction between 'statistical significance' and 'practical significance'. The former, they pointed out, is based on a standard method of determining the probability of making a Type I error (α) whereas the latter is subjective in the sense of being based upon arbitrary criteria used to evaluate a specific problem. Their concern was with practical significance rather than statistical significance. They also tested the robustness of the

Ferrara et al. results by considering different ways of determining sample size in the context of simulation. Their analysis indicated that the sample size used by Ferrara et al. yielded a percentage error of 4 to 5 per cent which, they argue is fairly acceptable for an estimation.

So far, two main criticisms of the J–R model have been considered: empirical and technical. A third criticism is of a conceptual nature. More specifically, it questions the adequacy of using the standard deviation of a density function as a proxy for risk. For convenience of presentation the discussion of this point is given in section IV below. For now, it would suffice to point out that with the development of the Capital Asset Pricing Model, other proxies for risk, like the covariance of returns of an asset with the market portfolio, are more appropriate than the standard deviation at least in the context of some decisions. But before this is discussed in more detail some of the more recent developments in stochastic C–V–P models, which address the problem of defining the underlying distributions of model parameters, are considered first.

III. DEFINING THE UNDERLYING DISTRIBUTIONS

The J–R model is essentially based on a mathematical–statistical approach in which the properties of a particular theoretical distribution (the normal) are invoked. In attempting to generate the underlying distributions of the parameters of C–V–P analysis subsequent, and more elaborate, stochastic C–V–P models either followed the mathematical–statistical approach or a simulation approach. Both approaches are discussed below.

The Mathematical–Statistical Approach

Recent developments in stochastic C–V–P analysis using the mathematical–statistical approach advocate the use of either Tchebycheff's theorem or the lognormal method. Both methods are concerned with handling distributions which either do not approximate normality or which cannot be identified, be they normal or non-normal.

The use of Tchebycheff's theorem in the context of stochastic C–V–P analysis has been advocated by Buzby (1974). He points out that most probabilistic models require that the analyst be able to identify the distributional form of the data. However, in many cases this may not be possible. The analyst may not have access to data records or sufficient resources to allow him to empirically identify the distribution. Even if the distributional form can be identified, the complexity of the model used may preclude the identification of the distribution of the resultant variable.

To deal with this problem, Buzby suggests using Tchebycheff's theorem. This, he points out, will be feasible as long as the mean and the standard deviation of the distribution can be calculated. In such cases, probability statements about the mean can be made without needing to know the distributional form, the reason being that in a distribution with a finite mean and variance the size of deviations from the mean and probabilities are closely connected. In univariate analysis the standard form of Tchebycheff's inequality is:

(3)

$$P_r(|X - E(X)| \geq b) \leq \frac{\sigma^2}{b^2}$$

where X is a random variable; $E(X)$ is its expected value; σ^2 is the variance of X; and b is an arbitrary constant. Expression **(3)** means that the probability that a random variable X will differ from its mean by b or more units (b > 0) is always less than or equal to σ^2/b^2. Setting b = kσ expression **(3)** can be manipulated to obtain:

(4)

$$P_r\left(|X - E(X)| \geqslant k\sigma\right) \leqslant \frac{1}{k^2}$$

If E(X) = £10,000, σ_X = £5,000, and the range of interest is ± $2\sigma_X$ around E(X) then,

$$P_r\left(|X - E(X)| \geqslant 2(£5000)\right) \leqslant \frac{1}{(2)^2}$$

$$P_r\left(|X - E(X)| \geqslant £10,000\right) \leqslant \tfrac{1}{4}$$

Thus, regardless of the distributional form of profits, deviation from the mean of X by two or more standard deviations is no more probable than 0.25 (viz. ¼).

Expression **(4)** represents Tchebycheff's inequality in its weakest form because all that it requires is that the variable has a finite variance which would imply that it also has a finite mean. There exists a family of Tchebycheff's inequalities, each of which applies to specific situations as more information about the distribution becomes available. With more information, more precise probability statements can be made.

Johnson and Simik (1974) proposed using the distribution-free Uspensky's and Hoeffding's probabilistic inequalities in stochastic C–V–P analysis. They prefer these inequalities to Tchebycheff type inequalities because they result in better probabilistic bounds. But as in Tchebycheff's inequalities the distribution form of profit and its constituent variables need not be derived. Moreover, the bounds obtained by such inequalities hold for any distribution function.

A stochastic C–V–P model based on a univariate (but not multivariate) Tchebycheff inequality, like expressions **(3)** and **(4)**, has the advantage of being relatively simple and possibly more acceptable to businessmen (Johnson and Simik, 1974; Buzby, 1975). It does, however, have some important limitations. Firstly, Hayya, Ferrara and Saniga (1975) argue that Tchebycheff's theorem is extremely conservative because of its excessive emphasis on minimising Type I errors at the expense of Type II errors even though the latter are more important in many cases. For example, in the context of quality control, it would allow a higher proportion of defective units to go through inspection even though the resulting cost (Type II error) would be greater than the cost of increasing the inspection sample (Type I error). Secondly, for some inequalities a complete distribution cannot be developed. For example, when the distributional form is unknown, probabilities can only be calculated for deviations beyond the 1σ range. This is because the solution becomes meaningless for a k ≤ 1 in expression **(4)** in the sense that the probability would be greater than or equal to one. Thirdly, compared with some other statistical techniques, e.g. the Kolmogorov–Smirnov test, the Tchebycheff inequalities produce less accurate probabilities (Buzby, 1974; Hayya et al., 1975). Fourthly, probability inequalities yield only lower and upper bounds to the actual probability (i.e. maximums and minimums) with equality occurring very infrequently. The extent to which such bounds approximate the true probability cannot be determined *ex ante* (e.g. Johnson and Simik, 1974). Finally, the method does not typically allow for the calculation of probabilities within one standard deviation from the mean.

These limitations led some researchers (e.g. Hayya et al., 1975) to suggest using more powerful tests like the Kolmogorov–Smirnov test instead of Tchebycheff's inequalities. The Kolmogorov–Smirnov goodness-of-fit test is a distribution-free test (i.e. it does not require that the data used should have a specific distributional form). It can be used to handle differing distributions such as the exponential, the gamma, the normal, and the lognormal. It is quite powerful for very small samples, say 15–20 observations. However, like the Tchebycheff inequalities it does require knowledge of the population mean and standard deviation.

Prompted by some of the limiting assumptions of the J–R model, particularly the assumptions of normality and independence of model parameters, Hilliard and Leitch (1975) proposed using a lognormal approach to stochastic C–V–P analysis. Specifically, they point out that: (i) the J–R model is justifiable only for small coefficients of variation (no greater than 12 per cent as indicated by Ferrara et al., 1972) and when the price, P, and the unit variable cost, V, are deterministic; (ii) the assumption of parameter independence is unrealistic since sales volume, price and variable cost are often correlated and (iii) in a normal distribution the lower bound is ∞ and this could impart negative values on sales, prices, variable costs and fixed costs.

The lognormal model proposed by Hilliard and Leitch is based on two assumptions: (i) sales volume, Q, and contribution margin, P–V, are lognormally distributed and (ii) fixed costs, F, are deterministic. If Q is lognormal, the density of Q would be

(5)

$$f_q(X) = (1/X\sqrt{2\pi\sigma'}) \cdot \exp\left(-0.5[\log(X) - \mu']^2/\sigma'^2\right)$$

$$0 < X < \infty$$

where σ' and μ' are the standard deviation and the mean of log Q respectively. It is clear from **(5)** that Q is non-negative. When the coefficient of variation is large, the lognormal distribution is significantly skewed to the right. Figures 8.3 and 8.4 compare normal and lognormal distributions with a large and small coefficient of variation respectively.

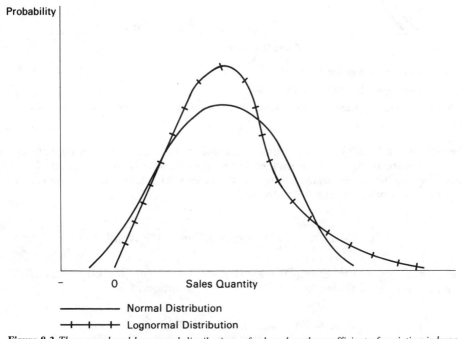

Figure 8.3 *The normal and lognormal distributions of sales when the coefficient of variation is large*

In figure 8.3, the lognormal distribution is significantly skewed to the right in contrast with the normal distribution because of the high coefficient of variation. The figure also shows the distinct possibility of negative values occurring in a normal distribution. In figure 8.4 the two distributions are very similar due to the coefficient of variation being very small. Hilliard and Leitch argue that the lognormal assumption is intuitive in the context of C–V–P analysis regardless of the value of the coefficient of variation because it does not allow sales and contribution to have negative values and because normality of C–V–P parameters is not warranted. Moreover, their model also allows for possibilities of interdependence between parameters.

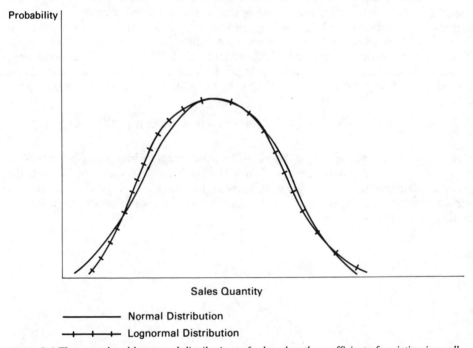

Figure 8.4 *The normal and lognormal distributions of sales when the coefficient of variation is small*

The Hilliard and Leitch model assumes that sales volume, Q, and unit contribution $(C = P - V)$ are bivariate lognormal which implies that profit is lognormal. This is because the product of bivariate lognormal variables is also lognormal. As in (5), the distribution of profit, Z^*, can be expressed as:

(6)

$$f_z^*(X) = (1/X\sqrt{2\pi}\sigma^*) \cdot \exp(-0.5|\log(X) - \mu^*|/\sigma^{*2})$$

$$0 < X < \infty$$

where $\mu^* = E(\log Z^*) = E(\log(Q) + \log(C))$ and $\sigma^{*2} = \text{var}(\log(Q) + \log(C))$. A change of variable technique leads to the exact distribution of Z:

(7)

$$P_r(Z \leq X) = F_z(X) = P_r(Z^* \leq X + \mu_f)$$
$$= F_z^*(X + \mu_f)$$

where μ_f is fixed cost. By taking differentials of (7) we have

(8)

$$f_z(X) = \frac{dF_z(X)}{dX} = F_z^*(X - \mu_f)$$

Using (6) and (8) the distribution of profit is given by

(9)

$$f_z(X) = (1/|X + \mu_f|\sqrt{2\pi\sigma^*}) \cdot \exp\{-0.5|\log(X + \mu_f) - \mu^*|^2/\sigma^{*2}\}$$
$$-\mu_f < X < \infty$$

Probabilistic statements about various profitability levels can then be made.

The lognormal model presented above has several attractive properties as discussed earlier. Lau and Lau (1976), however, take issue with the model. Their criticisms centre on two points. Firstly, they argue that by grouping price and variable cost as one variable (P − V) and by treating fixed cost as a deterministic variable, the richness of the Hilliard and Leitch model is reduced considerably. Hilliard and Leitch (1976) argue in response that this is a small sacrifice when contrasted with the increase in model flexibility arising from the treatment of dependent variables, large coefficients of variation, and the rigorous identification of the profit distribution. Secondly, Lau and Lau question the desirability and intuitiveness of the lognormal assumptions. They point out that once the mean and standard deviation are defined, the lognormal distribution takes on a certain degree of positive skewness determined by the values of the mean and standard deviation. Thus, the degree of uncertainty of the stochastic process determines the skewness of the distribution: the higher the extent of uncertainty the more positively skewed the distribution becomes. Moreover, if the skewness and standard deviation are defined for a lognormal distribution, its mean is fixed automatically. This, they argue, is devoid of any empirical content. Finally, they also correctly point out that not all random variables have positive skewness. They provide an example in which (P − V) = C is negatively skewed. There is also a problem with the distributional form implied by the Hilliard and Leitch model. If P and V are lognormally distributed, then it is not possible for (C = P − V) to be lognormally distributed. Hilliard and Leitch attempted to avoid this problem by assuming that (C = P − V) is lognormally distributed. If this is the case, it is not clear what distributional forms P and V take. Kottas et al. (1978) show that for (C = P − V) to be lognormally distributed, V may have to be *negatively* skewed. This clearly contradicts the universality of positive skewness implied by Hilliard and Leitch.

Other mathematical–statistical models have been developed to deal with C–V–P analysis under uncertainty. These include the probability tree approach, and the optimistic, pessimistic, most likely method. The first approach assumes independence between these variables. The utility of both methods is, however, limited because they both provide little information concerning the distribution of the model variables (see Driscoll et al., 1984).

The Simulation-Model Sampling Approach

The problems associated with attempts to handle the underlying distributions of C–V–P parameters using the mathematical–statistical approach have prompted some researchers to advocate the use of simulation techniques. One of the earliest studies in this area is that by Ferrara et al.(1972) who used simulation to develop a 'normalcy approximation criterion' that was then applied to the J–R model as explained earlier. More notable contributions to the use of the simulation approach in the context of C–V–P analysis have been made by Liao (1975) and Kottas and Lau (1978b). These studies are reviewed below.

Liao (1975) used a technique known as model sampling, or distribution sampling, and a curve-fitting technique in order to obtain estimates of the profit probability distribution and the moments of the distribution. It is held that, through multiple trials, model sampling can be used to determine the nature of a probability distribution that would be difficult, or impossible, to determine by standard statistical procedures. Under model sampling, the C–V–P parameters are treated as random variables. Employing a random number generator, model sampling is used to calculate one profit value from each set of random parameters. By repeating the sampling process, certain characteristics of the profit distribution can be obtained. The model determines the sample profit points, but it *does not* identify the distributional form.

Specifically, the use of Liao's model sampling technique involves the following steps:

1. An initial sampling of a small number of profit values (say 60) is used to estimate the standard deviation of sample mean profit.
2. This estimate is used to determine the sample size required to confine the profit mean within a given confidence limit (say 95 per cent).
3. A large sample simulation is performed using the sample size derived from (2), say 900 numbers, and an estimate of the first four moments of the profit distribution (the mean, the standard deviation, the skewness, and the Kurtosis) is undertaken based on the simulation results.
4. The estimated four moments are used to fit a Pearson's curve to the profit numbers. This curve-fitting technique estimates the theoretical probability distribution underlying a given frequency distribution.
5. Probabilities of attaining given profit levels are obtained by numerically integrating the fitted Pearson's curve.

Liao (1975) has shown that his model sampling approach can handle not only the J–R type independent and normally distributed parameters but also the more realistic dependent and non-normally distributed parameters. He argues that using model sampling yields more precise probabilistic statements compared with mathematical–statistical models, like Tchebycheff's theorem, or probabilities derived directly from frequency distributions.

Kottas and Lau (1978b) analysed stochastic C–V–P situations using a direct simulation approach which, they contend, is superior to model sampling and to mathematical–statistical models. Many of the limitations of the mathematical–statistical models have already been discussed. Below, the merits of direct simulation are contrasted against those of other simulation techniques and in particular model sampling. In comparing the two approaches, Kottas and Lau (1978b) invoke four criteria: (i) power of accurate modelling; (ii) technique simplicity; (iii) implementation cost and (iv) solution accuracy.

With respect to power of accurate modelling, they point out that both direct simulation and model sampling are 'powerful' enough to handle diverse probability distributions and dependency forms which cannot be handled by mathematical–statistical models. Thus, even under the lognormal approach, where dependency can be allowed for, no allowance is made for the possibility that some of the C–V–P parameters may assume a distributional form that is not lognormal. Kottas and Lau also argue that, compared with model sampling, direct simulation requires little computer based analysis and is thus without sacrificing technical robustness a simpler technique. With regard to implementation cost they contend that although large sample simulation can be very costly, direct simulation needed for stochastic C–V–P analysis is inexpensive particularly if compared with model sampling. The most significant difference between the two approaches appears to relate to the extent of solution accuracy.

Typically, two main questions are pertinent in stochastic C–V–P analysis: (i) the calculation of the probability of attaining a particular profit level and (ii) the calculation of the level of profit that can be obtained with a given degree of uncertainty. Kottas and Lau evaluated the solution accuracy of direct simulation and model sampling with respect to both questions. Their results indicate that direct simulation outperforms model sampling in both cases. They attribute the inferior solution accuracy of model sampling to two sources of errors: (i) sampling errors in the moment statistics of profit used in curve fitting as they are simulated, rather than true, population moments and (ii) even if sampling errors do not occur, the Pearson's fitted curve may not correspond to the theoretical distribution of profit and thereby distorted probabilities result. This last error arises because an infinite number of density functions can be fitted to a given set of four central moments. Kottas and Lau report that in 95 per cent of the time the last error alone is more than twice as large as the total error associated with direct simulation.

Whichever simulation technique is used, it is obvious that the simulation approach as a whole offers a useful means of handling the distributional form of profits. The simulation approach stands in some contrast with the mathematical–statistical approach. Not only do both approaches differ in methodology but they also differ in focus. Thus, whereas the mathematical–statistical approach addresses the question of distributional form of model parameters from a theoretical point of view, the simulation approach tackles the same issue by repeated trials of sampling. Moreover, whereas the mathematical–statistical approach explicitly focuses on the distribution form, not only of profits but also of quantity, price, variable cost, and fixed cost, the simulation approach only explicitly focuses on profits.

Neither approach is without limitations. Earlier, some of the limitations associated with the mathematical–statistical approach have been discussed. These can be summarised under mathematical inconsistency and excessive and unrealistic assumptions (see Kottas, Lau and Lau, 1978). The former relates to the problems of attempting to identify the distributional form of the product of two random variables under the normalcy assumption, and of the difference between two random variables under the lognormal assumption. The latter refers to the imposition of the same distributional form (be it normal or non-normal) on *all* the C–V–P variables. It is quite possible that, in a particular situation, different variables could assume different distributional forms.

The simulation approach has also been frequently criticised. Most of the criticisms centre on the following. Firstly, sampling errors in the estimation of profits can be excessive (e.g. Ferrara et al., 1972). Secondly, the required computer resources tend to be fairly excessive (e.g. Liao, 1975, but see Kottas and Lau, 1978b). Thirdly, companies in practice may lack the necessary expertise to engage in simulation (e.g. Buzby, 1974; 1975). Fourthly, although simulation results produce a probability distribution of profits, they do not provide a clear insight into the effects of each of the C–V–P parameters (e.g. price, sales, volume) on profit (Kottas and Lau, 1982). Fifthly, in some cases, like investment appraisal, higher-order central moments of the distribution of profits are needed. Simulation is typically inefficient in estimating higher-order moments because the latter tend to have large standard errors (Kottas and Lau, 1982).

Clearly then, both approaches have their advantages and disadvantages; most of the advantages can be retained if both are treated as complementary. Simulation is a versatile and more realistic approach, whereas the mathematical–statistical approach is more analytical. Starr and Tapiero (1975) made a similar suggestion by arguing that only in situations when mathematical models fail should simulation techniques be used to generate the required distributions. In their analysis of stochastic linear C–V–P they examined the probability distributions of break-even points as well as the probability moments of profits (i.e. the mean, the variance, and higher moments) using Tchebycheff's inequality.

Two more recent extensions of the Starr and Tapiero analysis followed. Ekern (1979) considered the distribution of stochastic break-even points. He suggested that when the probability of a negative unit contribution is non-negligible break-even analysis becomes obscure. Specifically, unless the probability of a negative unit contribution is zero, it cannot be known in advance whether a given quantity exceeding the break-even volume is desirable. He then proposed the use of an approximation procedure (the Geary–Hinkley transformation) to generate the probability distributions of break-even points in those cases where the probability of negative unit contribution is small. He argued that the Geary–Hinkley procedure is powerful, yet simple and is more practical than simulation.

Kottas and Lau (1978c; 1982) proposed a practical approach to investigating the probability distribution of profits based on its first four moments. Their analysis covers not only situations where C–V–P parameters are independent of each other, but also incorporates cases where these parameters are correlated. The profit moments are computed from the component variables, price (P), unit variable cost (V), sales volume (Q), and fixed cost (F) by taking these components one at a time and constructing in turn the moments of $C = (P - V)$; $t = CQ$; and $Z = t - F$. Kottas and Lau pointed out that their procedure uses simple formulae and is more practical than simulation.

IV. RISK ANALYSIS AND OPTIMAL BREAK-EVEN DECISIONS

The main focus in this section is on the ways in which risk and utility analysis can be incorporated into C–V–P models, and on alternative methods of modelling the relationships between the appropriate parameters so that optimal decisions can be made. Risk analysis involves not only choosing the 'appropriate' measure of risk (be it the variance, semivariance, covariance, and so on) but also determining the optimal price of risk, that is the increase in return required by a decision maker in order to take on one extra unit of risk. Modelling the appropriate parameters involves making specific statements which link such parameters on causal rather than *ad hoc* bases. This may include modelling the relationship between demand and price, and the effects of demand and production on sales volume. Such considerations of risk and utility analysis need to be explicitly considered in the context of C–V–P analysis if optimal production decisions are to be taken.

Risk and Utility Analysis in C–V–P Models

It will be recalled that incorporated in the J–R model is a measure of total risk in terms of the standard deviation of profits. However, one of the main problems with that model, as well as with traditional C–V–P models, is the emphasis on single product firms. Most firms, in reality, are multi-product and it would be more instructive to conceptualise risk in this more realistic setting. An implicit assumption in the J–R model and the traditional C–V–P models is that from the analysis of the single product case it is easy to generalise about the multi-product case. This is a sensible argument when demand for the firm's various products is independent. However, in reality, demand interdependence is very frequent and this merits careful consideration in the design of stochastic C–V–P models. Johnson and Simik (1971) addressed this problem. They assumed that sales volume, Q, is a random variable whilst the contribution margin per unit $(C = P - V)$ is constant over the relevant volume range. Their analysis proceeded as follows: assume a company sells n products in quantities q_1, $q_2 \ldots q_n$ with means μ_1, $\mu_2 \ldots \mu_n$. The variance–covariance matrix for the n demanded products is:

(10)
$$\begin{bmatrix} \sigma_1^2 & \rho_{12}\sigma_1\sigma_2 & \cdots\cdots & \rho_{1n}\sigma_1\sigma_n \\ \rho_{21}\sigma_2\sigma_1 & \sigma_2^2 & & \\ \cdot & & & \cdot \\ \cdot & \cdot & & \\ \cdot & \cdot & & \cdot \\ \rho_{n1}\sigma_n\sigma_1 & \rho_{n2}\sigma_n\sigma_2 & \cdots\cdots & \sigma_n^2 \end{bmatrix} = \begin{bmatrix} \sigma_{11} & \sigma_{12} & & \sigma_{1n} \\ \sigma_{21} & \sigma_{22} & & \sigma_{2n} \\ \cdot & & & \cdot \\ \cdot & \cdot & & \\ \cdot & \cdot & & \cdot \\ \sigma_{n1} & \sigma_{n2} & & \sigma_{nn} \end{bmatrix}$$

where $\sigma_{ij} = \sigma_i^2$ (i.e. the variance of q_i) if $i = j$
$\quad\quad = \rho_{ij}\sigma_i\sigma_j$ (i.e. the covariance of q_i and q_j) if $i \neq j$, since ρ_{ij} is the correlation coefficient between q_i and q_j.

Since each q_i is assumed to be normally distributed, q_1, $q_2 \ldots q_n$ are jointly normally distributed. Let p_i and v_i be the unit price and variable cost for product i, then the unit contribution margin will be $(c_i = p_i - v_i)$. Also, let f_i be the fixed cost for product i. Total profits, Z, will equal:

(11)
$$Z = \sum_{i=1}^{n} c_i q_i - \sum_{i=1}^{n} f_i$$

In (11) above, Z will have a univariate normal distribution where:

(12)
$$E(Z) = \sum_{i=1}^{n} c_i \mu_i - \sum_{i=1}^{n} f_i, \text{ and}$$

(13)
$$\sigma^2(Z) = |c_1, c_2 \ldots c_n| \begin{bmatrix} \sigma_{11} & \sigma_{12} & \cdots & \sigma_{1n} \\ \sigma_{21} & \sigma_{22} & \cdots & \sigma_{2n} \\ \cdot & & & \cdot \\ \sigma_{n1} & \sigma_{n2} & \cdots & \sigma_{nn} \end{bmatrix} \begin{bmatrix} c_1 \\ c_2 \\ \cdot \\ c_n \end{bmatrix} = \sum_{i=1}^{n}\sum_{j=1}^{n} \sigma_{ij} c_i c_j$$

Johnson and Simik showed that the total profit variance, $\sigma^2(Z)$, is dependent on the covariance between the profits of different product lines. Thus, the smaller the covariance terms, the smaller is $\sigma^2(Z)$, the greater is the probability of achieving target profit levels and the smaller is the probability of incurring losses.

Dickinson (1974) extended the Johnson–Simik model by examining the reliability of estimating the means and variances of the past distributions of sales volume for each product, q_i. He considered the historic values of monthly sales volume in the immediate past (the most recent 12 months) assuming that each is normally, or near normally, distributed but independent of each other. The reliability of the model was tested by comparing the estimated and true values of the parameters.

In the previous two models, as well as the J–R model, two basic assumptions about risk and attitude towards risk are made. Firstly, the variance of profit is the appropriate measure of risk for firm decisions. This is implied in the Johnson–Simik model even though they incorporated the covariance of a product's sales with sales of the firm's other products. Secondly, managers make decisions based on the trade-off between expected profit and risk for the firm, without explicitly considering the risk attitudes of shareholders. The finance literature, particularly that related to the Capital Asset Pricing Model (CAPM), has demonstrated that the appropriate measure of risk for the firm is *not* the variance of its profits, but instead the covariance of profits with the return on the market portfolio (e.g. Haley and Schall, 1979, ch. 7). Moreover, the analysis of financial decisions in the literature is typically based on the notion of maximising shareholders' wealth.

Magee (1975) addressed these two issues by deriving a model based on capital market equilibrium and an explicit assumption that the manager's goal is to maximise shareholders' wealth. He invoked the conditions under which shareholders would be unanimous in approving management decisions: (i) all investors would be concerned with the mean and variance of returns; (ii) the return (profit) of a firm is a function of managerial decisions and (iii) investors have homogeneous expectations with respect to the distribution of security prices. Using CAPM, Magee derived the following expression:

(14)

$$\left\{ \frac{\delta}{\delta y_j} E[\check{Z}_j(y_j)] - \lambda \cdot \frac{\sigma}{\sigma y_j} \text{Cov}\left[\check{Z}_j(y_j), \tilde{r}_m\right] \right\} > 0$$

where: y_j denotes management decision variable, λ is the market price of risk, Cov is the covariance coefficient and $\tilde{r}_m$ is the market return with $\tilde{\ }$ denoting random parameters.

As long as **(14)** held, shareholders would unanimously agree with management decisions if they maximised the decision variable y_j. This means that **(14)** can be written as:

(15)

$$\text{Maximise } \left\{ E[\check{Z}_j(y_j)] - \lambda \text{ Cov}\left[\check{Z}_j(y_j), \tilde{r}_m\right] \right\}$$

Expressions **(14)** and **(15)** show that it is the expected value of profit and the covariance of profit with the market portfolio (rather than the variance of profit) that are the important parameters in the decision model. The trade-off between risk and return is not dependent on the manager's risk preferences but rather reflects the *market's* equilibrium trade-off relationship as measured by $\lambda = |E(\tilde{r}_m) - R_f|/\sigma^2 r_m$ with R_f denoting the risk-free return. By way of contrast, the expression to be maximised as implied by the J–R and the Johnson–Simik models would be of the form:

(16)

$$\text{Maximise } \left\{ E(\check{Z}_j) - \phi_j(\sigma_{z_j}) \right\}$$

where ϕ_j is a measure of the firm's risk-return trade-off as reflected in the manager's risk preferences.

By comparing **(15)** and **(16)**, it becomes evident that they may lead to different decisions for at least two reasons. Firstly, because of differences in the measures of risk – (15) uses the covariance term whereas (16) uses the standard deviation of profit. Secondly, because of differences in the prices of risk – (15) uses the market price, λ, whereas (16) uses the manager's risk price, ϕ_j. Notice also that the covariance term in (15) is between the product's sales and the market return, which can be viewed as shareholders' alternative investment opportunities. It should be noted, however, that the postulated shareholders' unanimity with respect to (15) can only hold as long as the three conditions stipulated by Magee hold. Magee cited empirical evidence which lends some support to conditions (i) and (ii), but condition (iii), relating to homogeneous expectations by shareholders, has not yet been references rather than shareholders' preferences, and used the standard deviation (total risk) instead of the covariance of profits with the market portfolio (systematic risk) as a measure of risk. empirically substantiated.

Adar, Barnea and Lev (1977) developed a stochastic C–V–P model which combined the probability characteristics of environmental variables with the risk preferences of decision makers. The firm's decision makers were assumed to be risk averters who would aim at maximising the utility of profits. They would engage in ranking alternative pairs of expected profit, $E(Z_i)$, and standard deviation of profit, such that alternative i is preferred to alternative j as long as $E(Z_i) > E(Z_j)$; $\sigma_{Zi} \leqslant \sigma_{Zj}$ or $E(Z_i) \geqslant E(Z_j)$ and $\sigma_{Zi} < \sigma_{Zj}$. Their model showed that optimal production decisions depend on the risk attitudes of decision makers, fixed cost, F, and the price of risk which they set equal to $\bar{C}/\sigma_u$; that is expected unit contribution margin, $\bar{C}$, per unit of standard deviation of price, σ_u, where $P = \bar{P} + u$. The model can then be used to examine the consequences of alternative courses of action on the level of utility through their effects on price, marginal cost, fixed cost and so on.

One particularly interesting feature of the model developed by Adar et al. was the sensitivity of its results to changes in fixed costs. Thus, changes in fixed costs were traditionally assumed irrelevant to short-run production decisions because they do not affect marginal costs. However, in the context of the above model, changes in fixed costs lead to changes in the wealth of the firm. Such wealth changes affect decision makers' attitudes towards risk and, thus the firm's production decision. Consider, for example, a firm whose attitude to risk is one of decreasing absolute risk aversion. As the firm's profits (wealth) increase, its marginal risk premium decreases. A fixed cost increase would result in a decrease in the firm's wealth thereby leading to a higher risk premium being required on risky projects. Ultimately, this would cause the firm to reduce production, as some projects that were previously acceptable came to be deemed non-optimal. Notice, however, that unlike the Magee model, the Adar et al. model emphasised management preferences rather than shareholders' preferences, and used the standard deviation (total risk) instead of the covariance of profits with the market portfolio (systematic risk) as a measure of risk.

Optimal Decisions and the Relationship between Model Parameters

Several studies have focused on refining the basic C–V–P model to help management attain optimal production levels. Jarrett (1973) used Bayesian decision theory in investigating the question of whether management should choose a given alternative based on its own estimates of decision parameters or postpone the decision until additional information becomes available. The approach involves determining the costs and benefits of additional information on profit levels and standard deviation. Thus, if V_m is the expected value of profits should a predictor of future events be available and V_o is the expected profit of the optimal alternative without the benefits of future predictors, then:

(17)

$$V_m = V_o + V_u$$

where V_u is the expected cost of uncertainty, or the expected value of perfect information. It represents the maximum amount that management would be prepared to pay to hire a predictor of future events.

The value of V_u can be reduced by obtaining additional information via sample information which is used to provide revised estimates of the mean and standard deviation of profits. These should bring V_o closer to V_m and hence reduce V_u. The costs of sample information must be compared against its benefits or expected value, V_s which is given by $V_s = V_u - V_u^*$, with V_u^* denoting the revised expected cost of uncertainty given sample information. The benefit of additional sample information is in reducing uncertainty regarding the prediction of future events.

The relationships between demand, prices and production

One basic issue that has not been adequately considered in the literature reviewed so far is the relationship between demand and price. In some C–V–P models (e.g. Jaedicke and Robichek, 1964) price and sales quantity were assumed statistically independent. In other models (e.g. Hilliard and Leitch, 1975) interrelationships between price and sales quantity were specified but on a statistical, *ad hoc*, rather than causal, basis. In economic analysis, however, demand is treated as a function of price. A number of researchers have sought to explicitly incorporate the demand function in stochastic C–V–P models.

Morrison and Kaczka (1969) treated demand as a linear function (a tangent to the demand curve at a predetermined point). They then proceeded to calculate the volume at which maximum profit would obtain given the above information. Ijiri and Itami (1973) introduced a causal demand function in a quadratic cost–volume relationship to investigate the effect of delay in demand information on total production costs and ultimately on profits. Their analysis showed that delay in demand information is subject to the law of increasing marginal loss: the loss increases more than proportionately as the delay increases. Kottas and Lau (1979) used linear and non-linear demand and cost functions in C–V–P analysis. Demand was treated as a function of price whilst cost was treated as a function of variable and fixed costs. In this sense, price was considered the decision variable, which can be manipulated to effect desired expected changes in demand. They incorporated the mean and standard deviation of profits into a utility function and demonstrated how optimal decisions concerning production levels could be made. Constantinides, Ijiri and Leitch (1981) incorporated a linear demand function in their stochastic C–V–P model to express the causal relationship between sales quantity and price. Their model assumed that the parameters of the demand and cost functions are multivariate normal. They demonstrated the ability of their model to handle different managerial objectives such as profit maximisation, profits or sales exceeding a target level and the maximisation of the discounted cash flow value of a project.

An interesting aspect of the C–V–P models so far discussed, whether they incorporated demand on an *ad hoc* or causal basis, relates to their implicit assumptions about the type of market in which the firm operates. Models that treated demand on an *ad hoc* basis assumed the firm to be a price taker operating in a perfectly competitive market whereas those that incorporated demand and price as causally related assumed that the firm would operate in a monopolistic market. Both types of markets are extremes: in reality most firms operate somewhere between the two extremes. Karnani (1983) addressed this problem by extending C–V–P analysis to the case of competitive oligopoly. In his model the firm is assumed to aim for maximising a utility function using the mean–variance framework. His analysis shows that the firm's competitive strength depends on the level of its costs, its risk-return trade-off, and quality of information about uncertain demand and costs.

The explicit incorporation of the demand function in C–V–P analysis has imparted greater realism, as well as complexity, to C–V–P models. Thus, rather than simply hypothesising *ad hoc* statistical dependence between price and quantity a causal relationship, based on economic analysis, is used. Moreover, the assumption of linearity in the demand function makes it easier to determine the probability distribution of profits since the distribution becomes a linear combination of random variables (Constantinides et al., 1981). Whilst non-linear demand functions, like those used by Kottas and Lau (1979), are likely to be more realistic than linear functions they tend to be less mathematically tractable.

Two further developments in stochastic C–V–P models merit consideration here: incorporation of the effects of demand and production on sales volume, and estimation of the random parameters of the model. First, consider the former development. The C–V–P models discussed thus far take into account only that portion of variable costs relating to sold units whilst ignoring those attributable to unsold units. This may result in overestimating profits in cases when production exceeds demand and units which have been inventoried cannot be sold because, for example, they are perishable or become obsolete. Previous C–V–P models would be appropriate only when demand is known with certainty or when demand is unlimited so that any unsold units will eventually be sold. In both cases sales quantity, Q, and demand, D, will be the same, at least eventually. Shih (1979) argued that when demand is uncertain and no future demand for unsold units exists variable costs associated with unsold units should be taken into consideration before arriving at expected profits. He developed a model in which the quantity of sales, Q, is determined in relation to production volume, X, and demand D, as follows:

(18)

$$X, \text{ if } D \geqslant X$$
$$D, \text{ if } D < X$$

Combining **(18)** and **(1)** we obtain

(19)

$$X(P - V) - F, \text{ if } D \geqslant X$$
$$PD - VX - F, \text{ if } D < X$$

Notice that in **(19)** the total variable cost of production, VX, is included in both cases in order to reflect the consequences of over-production. When demand is known in advance, then $X = D = Q$ and thus equation **(19)** reduces to **(1)**. Likewise, if demand were unlimited or unsold units could eventually be sold the second part of **(19)** would drop out and **(19)** would reduce to **(1)**. Shih demonstrates that in **(19)**, the probability distribution of profit depends on both the distributional form of demand and planned production volume rather than on sales volume alone.

The second development is the estimation of the random parameters of the C–V–P model. One of the most popular parameter estimation methods is the use of regression analysis to predict future values from a sample of historical data. The predicted parameter values, however, are not likely to be the same as the actual (true) values and are thus subject to chance variations (standard error of estimate). Liao (1976) illustrated how chance variations of estimated revenue and cost functions in C–V–P models can be determined and how they affect break-even analysis. He showed that when chance variations are not considered the estimated break-even points become deterministic (i.e. each has a single value). By contrast, with chance variations incorporated in the analysis, break-even points would be expressed as a range which tends to be broader with a higher confidence limit and vice versa. The estimates derived by Liao, however, are not totally adequate because his model parameters were not treated as random variables. Moreover, the internal estimates derived by Liao are only useful for single-period but not multi-period analysis. To overcome these problems, Cantrell and Ramsay (1984) proposed using maximum likelihood point estimators which are suitable for both single-period and multi-period break-even analysis. Their model incorporates a semi-variable cost function (in addition to wholly fixed and wholly variable costs) and a constant price demand function.

V. SUMMARY

As a starting point in this chapter, some of the obvious limitations of deterministic C–V–P models have been identified. These included the linearity assumption of cost, revenue, and profit functions; constant product mix and factors of production mix; concentration on single-product, single-period analysis; and, most importantly, the assumption that model parameters are certain rather than stochastic. The first section of the chapter reviewed some of the extensions to the basic traditional model. These extensions related only to the first three limitations and thus the model parameters were still treated as if they were known with certainty. The extensions included allowing for non-linear functions, changes in product mix and factors of production mix, and incorporating multi-product, multi-constraint and multi-period analysis.

Despite these refinements to the basic C–V–P model, it remained essentially deterministic because it did not explicitly handle uncertainty. The first attempt to incorporate uncertainty in C–V–P analysis was made by Jaedicke and Robichek (1964). Their pioneering model, however, contained some restrictive assumptions. In particular, model parameters were assumed independent and normally distributed. Moreover, total risk (the variance/standard deviation) was used as the relevant measure of risk and the price of risk was assumed to be based on the decision maker's (the manager's) own preferences for risk-return trade-off without consideration of shareholders' preferences.

Subsequent developments in the literature thus sought to address two basic questions. Firstly, how could the underlying probability distribution of profits and other C–V–P parameters be generated? Secondly, how could risk be appropriately defined and priced so that optimal break-even decisions could be made?

Attempts to identify the underlying distributions classify into two basic approaches: the use of the mathematical–statistical approach and the simulation technique. Under the mathematical–statistical approach either specific distributional forms were invoked (for example, the normal distribution or the lognormal distribution) or suggestions were made to use distribution-free models (like Tchebycheff's inequality). The analysis in such cases was typically based on formal models which at times involved the use of some complex formulae. Simulation has been advanced as a more practical and economical alternative, particularly if relatively small sample sizes are adequate to approximate the underlying distribution. Given that neither approach is conclusively superior, more recent literature advocates two alternative strategies. Firstly, using a particular approach when the situation is appropriate for that approach to be used; secondly, using simpler, and more practical statistical methods (for example, the four moments approach) as an alternative to simulation, particularly when many simulation runs are required to estimate the distribution.

The literature dealing with the questions of risk definition and the price of risk has also made major advances. Instead of total risk (profit variance) the covariance of the firm's profit with the market portfolio has been advocated as the appropriate measure of risk. The equilibrium price of risk has also been derived from the Capital Asset Pricing Model and this price, in equilibrium, has been found to be invariant among different investors. Further developments have concentrated on the relationships between model parameters. Thus, instead of assuming that C–V–P parameters are independent of each other, or imposing some *ad hoc* statistical relationship amongst them, the relationships have been investigated on causal bases. Demand has thus been treated as a linear or non-linear function of price under different market situations. Moreover, the effects of demand and production on sales volume, particularly when unsold units are perishable or become obsolete, have been considered.

In summary, compared with the traditional C–V–P model more recent models have been invested with much greater realism. Unfortunately, they have also become either much more mathematically complex or more technically sophisticated (e.g. simulation).

REFERENCES

Adar, Z., Barnea, A. and Lev, B., 1977. A comprehensive cost–volume–profit analysis under uncertainty, *Accounting Review*, January, pp. 137–149.

Buzby, S. L., 1974. Extending the applicability of probabilistic management planning and control models, *Accounting Review*, January, pp. 42–49.

Buzby, S. L., 1975. Extending the applicability of probabilistic management planning and control models: a reply, *Accounting Review*, October, pp. 832–834.

Cantrell, R. S. and Ramsay, L. P., 1984. Some statistical issues in the estimation of a simple cost–volume–profit model, *Decision Sciences*, **15** (4), Fall, pp. 507–521.

Charnes, A., Cooper, W. W. and Ijiri, Y., 1963. Breakeven budgeting and programming to goals, *Journal of Accounting Research*, **1** (1), Spring, pp. 16–43.

Constantinides, G. M., Ijiri, Y. and Leitch, R. A., 1981. Stochastic cost–volume–profit analysis with a linear demand function, *Decision Sciences*, **12** (3), July, pp. 417–427.

Craig, C. C., 1936. On the frequency function of XY, *The Annals of Mathematical Statistics*, 1936, pp. 1–5.

Dickinson, J. P., 1974. Cost–volume–profit analysis under uncertainty, *Journal of Accounting Research*, Spring, pp. 182–187.

Driscoll, D. A., Lin, W. T. and Watkins, P. R., 1984. Cost–volume–profit analysis under uncertainty: a synthesis and framework for evaluation, *Journal of Accounting Literature*, **3**, pp. 85–115.

Ekern, S., 1979. Stochastic breakeven points, *Journal of the Operational Research Society*, **30** (3), pp. 271–275.

Ferrara, W. L., Hayya, J. C. and Nachman, D. A., 1972. Normalcy of profit in the Jaedicke–Robichek model, *Accounting Review*, April, pp. 299–307.

Givens, H. R., 1966. An application of curvilinear breakeven analysis, *Accounting Review*, January, pp. 141–143.

Goggans, T. P., 1965. Breakeven analysis with curvilinear functions, *Accounting Review*, October, pp. 867–871.

Haley, C. W. and Schall, L. D., 1979. *The Theory of Financial Decisions*: McGraw-Hill.

Hayya, J. C. and Ferrara, W. L., 1972. On normal approximations of the frequency functions of standard forms when the main variables are normally distributed, *Management Science*, **19** (2), October, pp. 173–186.

Hayya, J., Ferrara, W. and Saniga, E., 1975. Extending the applicability of probabilistic management planning and control models: a comment, *Accounting Review*, October, pp. 826–831.

Hayya, J. C., Ferrara, W. L. and Saniga, E. M., 1978. On the appropriate size of samples in 2 tests: a reply to Kottas and Lau, *Accounting Review*, January, pp. 252–259.

Hilliard, J. E. and Leitch, R. A., 1975. Cost–volume–profit analysis under uncertainty: a log normal approach, *Accounting Review*, January, pp. 69–80.

Hilliard, J. E. and Leitch, R. A., 1976. C–V–P analysis under uncertainty: a log normal approach – a reply, *Accounting Review*, January, pp. 168–171.

Holt, C. C., Modigliani, F., Mutch, J. F. and Simon, H. A., 1960. *Planning Production Inventories and Work Force*: Prentice-Hall.

Ijiri, Y. and Itami, H., 1973. Quadratic cost–volume relationships and timing of demand information, *Accounting Review*, October, pp. 724–737.

Jaedicke, R. K., 1961. Improving breakeven analysis by L. P. technique, *NAA Bulletin*, March, pp. 5–12.

Jaedicke, R. K. and Robichek, A. A., 1964. Cost–volume–profit analysis under conditions of uncertainty, *Accounting Review*, October, pp. 917–926.

Jarrett, J. E., 1973. An approach to cost–volume–profit analysis under uncertainty, *Decision Sciences*, **4** (3), July, pp. 405–420.

Johnson, G. L. and Simik II, S. S., 1971. Multiproduct C–V–P analysis under uncertainty, *Journal of Accounting Research*, Autumn, pp. 278–286.

Johnson, G. L. and Simik, II, S. S., 1974. The use of probability inequalities in multiproduct C–V–P analysis under uncertainty, *Journal of Accounting Research*, Spring, pp. 67–79.

Kaplan, R. S., 1982. *Advanced Management Accounting*: Prentice-Hall.

Karnani, A., 1983. Stochastic cost–volume–profit analysis in competitive oligopoly, *Decision Sciences*, **14**, pp. 187–193.

Kottas, J. F., Lau, A. H. L. and Lau, H. S., 1978. A general approach to stochastic management planning models: an overview, *Accounting Review*, April, pp. 389–401.

Kottas, J. F. and Lau, H. S., 1978a. On the accuracy of normalcy approximation in stochastic C–V–P analysis: a comment, *Accounting Review*, January, pp. 247–251.

Kottas, J. F. and Lau, H. S., 1978b. Direct simulation in stochastic C–V–P analysis, *Accounting Review*, July, pp. 698–707.

Kottas, J. F. and Lau, H. S., 1978c. Stochastic breakeven analysis, *Journal of the Operational Research Society*, **29** (3), pp. 251–257.

Kottas, J. F. and Lau, H. S., 1979. A decision model with stochastic cost and demand curves, *Omega*, **7**, pp. 80–81.

Kottas, J. F. and Lau, H. S., 1982. A four moment alternative to simulation for a class of stochastic management models, *Management Science*, **28** (7), July, pp. 749–758.

Lau, A. H. L. and Lau, H. S., (1976). C–V–P analysis under uncertainty – a log normal approach: a comment, *Accounting Review*, January, pp. 163–167.

Liao, M., 1975. Model sampling: a stochastic cost–volume–profit analysis, *Accounting Review*, October, pp. 780–790.

Liao, M., 1976. The effect of chance variation on revenue and cost estimations for breakeven analysis, *Accounting Review*, October, pp. 922–926.

Magee, R. P., 1975. Cost–volume–profit analysis, uncertainty and capital market equilibrium, *Journal of Accounting Research*, Autumn, pp. 257–266.

Manes, R., 1966. A new dimension to breakeven analysis, *Journal of Accounting Research*, **4** (1), Spring, pp. 87–100.

Morrison, T. A. and Kaczka, E., 1969. A new application of calculus and risk analysis to cost–volume–profit changes, *Accounting Review*, April, pp. 330–343.

Shih, W., 1979. A general decision model for cost–volume–profit analysis under uncertainty, *Accounting Review*, October, pp. 687–706.

Starr, M. K. and Tapiero, C. S., 1975. Linear breakeven analysis under risk, *Operational Research Quarterly*, **26** (4), pp. 847–856.

Vickers, D., 1960. On the economics of breakeven, *Accounting Review*, July, pp. 405–412.

9

Planning in the Short Term

This chapter opens with an enquiry into the essential nature of planning and its role within the decision-making process. Forecasting, as an adjunct to planning and as an attempt to identify areas of uncertainty, is then briefly reviewed and reference is made to the various principal types of plans discussed in the literature. In considering the difficulties associated with the determination of timescales in planning, emphasis is laid on the dangers of attempting to view short-term planning or budgetary periods in isolation and the concomitant need to take cognisance of inter-temporal dependencies. Attempts to satisfy this latter requirement are considered in the subsequent discussion of certain specific planning models.

The planning techniques embodied in short-term budgets are then considered together with the basic concepts underlying 'Zero-base Budgeting' (ZBB) and 'Planning–Programming–Budgeting Systems' (PPBS). The approach is critical rather than descriptive, with some emphasis laid on the interdependency of sectional budgets and on the reasons advanced for the apparent lack of enthusiasm with which ZBB has been received in practice notwithstanding its conceptual appeal.

The remainder of the chapter is devoted to the nature and limitations of the forecasting process. Starting from the premise that some element of forecasting is essential to all planning exercises, the point is made that, although rather simple mechanistic methods may often produce accurate *short-term* forecasts, the complexity of the decision-making process in a modern business context, coupled with the need to minimise the effects of uncertainty, must inevitably call for more formal explicit forecasting procedures. The danger of under-estimating the full extent of environmental uncertainty and the resulting misplaced confidence which may thereby be instilled in the forecaster constitute a serious limitation on the effectiveness of the forecasting process. The adequacy of business forecasting may also be called into question if based solely on economic and technological factors without due regard to social and political implications.

Citing the view that serious errors in human decision making can be attributed to 'superficial information search and processing biases', reference is then made to the main sources of bias at successive information processing levels; examples of specific sources of bias are noted; and various ways of seeking to minimise errors associated with bias are discussed. There then follows an examination of some suggestions that were put forward by Hogarth and Makridakis (1981) with the object of achieving a greater degree of realism in forecasting and planning.

The chapter closes with a discussion of various forecasting methods and an examination of the efficacy of planning, both short-term and long-term, in this age of uncertainty.

I. PLANNING AS A CONCEPTUAL EXERCISE

The Essence of Planning and the Nature of Plans

It appears that there is no universally recognised definition of planning; however, most writers would agree that planning 'involves attempts at purposeful, future oriented decision making' (Hogarth and Makridakis, 1981). If conceived of as a set of formal procedures, planning would involve the need to search for and analyse threats and opportunities, to exercise choice by selecting the most appropriate opportunities, to arrange for their implementation and to monitor performance through feedback (Ansoff and Brandenburg, 1967). In simple terms a plan is then a statement of the actions which it is intended should be pursued over a given time period, the outcome being dependent on the state of the environment that prevails.

Planning is often referred to as a branch of decision making; an activity which becomes necessary only if alternatives exist. However, unless a plan is subsequently activated it is not necessarily a decision. Both plans and decisions, though, do involve the need to exercise a choice amongst alternative actions. In general such choices will be of a continuous and sequential nature, subject to revision in the light of information that subsequently becomes available. However, if the planner adopts a contingency-type approach ('responsiveness planning') it is *expected* that plans will be revised to reflect subsequently available information about 'state variables' (i.e. the environment), production possibilities, and so on. In systems theory terms, there is greater need for emphasis on *continuous* adaptation to environmental change, in contrast to the notion of *periodic* planning, so entrenched in accounting practice (see chapter 4).

The approach inherent in 'responsiveness planning', i.e. the development of procedures for modifying plans, is implicit in, and of particular importance to, the type of planning model designated as 'partially constrained' (Starr, 1971). In such a model environmental configurations are considered as dynamic forecasts or alternative predictions. Moreover, some network paths are considered stochastic so that from a given junction point either one or another path – but not both – can be followed. As opposed to this the 'fully constrained planning model' is characterised by the predictability of the environmental configuration. In the same terminology the 'threshold-constrained model' is a special class of partially constrained system in that the possible pay-offs include some that are catastrophic and which, if followed, would lead to ruin.

Decision making under uncertainty, as epitomised by the partially constrained planning model, is then essentially concerned with the selection of the most appropriate course of action given one's expectations concerning the likelihood of the occurrence of the state variables. Endogenous variables, such as production estimates, are thus defined by such chosen course of action. Expectations regarding future states are the outcome of the *forecasting* process; planning models are preceded by forecasts which, whilst not eliminating uncertainty about the future, do, nevertheless, constitute attempts to define it in probabilistic terms. Business forecasting can never do more than provide a means of assessing the probabilities assignable to future events; it cannot offer an accurate view of the future and the degree of accuracy must decrease with the extension of the length of the time span. The aim of forecasting should thus be to identify areas of uncertainty so that planning can proceed by developing policies which take cognisance of the sources of uncertainty in the environment. It should be emphasised at this point that in the present context forecasting is viewed as being concerned substantially with the modelling of trends in the state variables. In a more complete analysis one might be concerned with evaluating the pay-off function, i.e. the functional relationship between actions and their consequences, by forecasting the effects of different decisions. An example would be to assess the impact on demand of different types and levels of advertising expenditure.

All businesses make plans in some sense of the word albeit, as is the case with forecasting, with varying degrees of rigour and sophistication. Thus, the plan may, for instance, merely constitute a broad canvas of management's expectations for the future position of the business or, at the other extreme, it may be a highly dynamic, detailed, and all-embracing corporate plan. Even so, empirical studies have indicated that formal plans are not found so extensively as the classical theory of expectations might suggest (e.g., Cyert and March, 1963), one explanation for this being the existence of uncertainty.

Discussion in the literature of the various types of plans has generally followed classification bases which are substantially conceptual, dimensional, or temporal, rather than the purely functional concerning such areas as production, marketing, distribution, finance and investment. Most of the classification criteria adopted include, as a bare minimum, the categories of strategic plans and tactical (or operating) plans which may be distinguished, on the lines suggested by Ackoff (1970), as summarised in table 9.1.

Table 9.1 *Strategic and tactical planning*

	Strategic	Tactical
Duration	Concerned with decisions that have enduring effects that are difficult to reverse	Of shorter range
Scope	Broader – the more factors affected by a plan the more strategic it is	Narrower
Goals/means	Concerned with formulating goals and selection of 'means'	Concerned with selecting means to pursue specific goals

The terms 'strategic' and 'tactical' are thus only relative. If this terminology is employed the concern of the present chapter is essentially with tactical planning, with greater emphasis on those aspects which are more closely associated with managerial accounting.

Operational planning has the same connotation as tactical planning since it embraces plans for the various operating areas over the short and medium term. With this analogy in mind it is not difficult to reconcile Ackoff's rather abstract classification with the more concrete one suggested by Ansoff (1965) who classifies plans into the three separate categories of 'operating plans', 'administrative plans', and 'strategic plans'. Strategic planning is concerned with determination of overall objectives and formulation of policy. Operating, or tactical, planning is concerned with the allocation of resources in the short and medium term to achieve the firm's objectives. Finally, administrative planning embraces those tactical plans concerned with organisational structure and the optimal use of resources within the framework of the strategic objectives. This broadly parallels the analysis adopted in chapter 4 in which managerial choice was viewed as encompassing strategic choice, structural choice and tactical choice, as representative of the means whereby managers attempt to control an organisation's functioning.

'Strategic planning' is often regarded as synonymous with 'corporate planning', although some writers would take the view that decisions taken in the corporate planning framework do not necessarily have to be of a long-term nature. Corporate planning is, however, usually regarded as a process extending beyond the short and medium term, and it is discussed in the context of planning in the longer term in chapter 10. What is important to emphasise at this stage is that the activity, or series of activities, described as 'corporate planning' should embrace the whole of the activities of the organisation, which is thus viewed in the corporate sense as an entity. Operational or tactical planning at a functional level, embracing, for example, the activities of production, marketing, distribution, finance and manpower planning, must in a formal planning system be undertaken within the framework of the overall strategic plan.

In a practical context it seems that in most planning areas there will be both strategic and operational elements. Thus, in the sense that production is planned to match demand in the long term, production planning is strategic by nature. However, production plans are needed at various stages, covering short, medium, and long term. As Higgins (1976, p.87) points out

> The annual manufacturing plan lies in the medium-term range and is the most important example of *aggregate planning*...the basic format of the annual manufacturing plan is relatively simple, listing total output planned by product by factory in relation to opening and closing inventory levels and subdivided into equivalent monthly figures.

In so far as production scheduling is viewed as an activity distinct from production planning it is, in essence, shorter term but may, in some concerns, be regarded as a medium-term activity.

Product planning is an important element in the annual marketing plan but has obvious longer-term applications in such areas as the development of new products. Likewise, marketing planning is generally conceived within the framework of the annual marketing plan, but undoubtedly this also has strategic elements. Distribution planning embraces many operational activities, such as inventory management and transport planning and scheduling. Where it involves such aspects as investment in distribution depots or provision of the company's own delivery system, it is essentially strategic by nature. Manpower planning has an important part to play in the context of the corporate plan but, again, it has obvious applications at the operational level. Finally, financial planning, often viewed as a distinct planning area linked with both operational planning and corporate planning, clearly involves strategic issues (e.g. financing and capital investment policies) and operational issues, as reflected, for instance, in short-term budgets.

The foregoing discussion has been focused on the planning activity as such. Some consideration is now given to the question of timescales in the planning process.

Timescales in Planning

In chapter 7 reference was made to the short term and long term in economic analysis. In that discussion it was apparent that the distinction depended fundamentally on the question of adaptation and did, therefore, tend to be relative. Hence, although in a practical planning context the firm's objectives will be difficult to translate into specific actions unless related to a specific planning horizon, it is not easy to make generalisations regarding the specific length of planning periods.

Whilst conceding that the terms 'long range' or 'short range' as applied to planning in a business context generally imply a given time span, Drucker (1959, p. 245) nevertheless maintains that, strictly speaking, 'short range' and 'long range' describe *stages* in a decision and not actual time spans. Following this line of reasoning 'short range' would describe 'the stage before the decision has become fully effective, the stage during which it is only "costs" and not yet "results"...' whereas the 'long range' would apply to 'the period of expected performance needed to make the decision a successful one'. To ascribe these shades of meaning to designations related to timescales is valid in the case of decisions to embark on certain specific projects such as afforestation; such validity is, however, less obvious in the more general business context. Thus, it could be argued that the operational or tactical plan, although in most instances one of short-term duration, is developed within the framework of the overall long-term strategy and is therefore a stage in the attainment of overall objectives. Even so, the decisions based on operational plans are likely to become fully effective in the actual time span envisaged. To this extent the time span only represents a *stage* in a decision when viewed as a 'milestone' by which progress is measured towards the attainment of longer-term performance goals.

The actual duration of the planning period is determined by the nature of both the business and the decision and is to a large extent linked with the question of uncertainty. Unless one can assume completely stable conditions, some element of uncertainty must inevitably be present at least as a result of technological development and environmental changes. It is reasonable to expect that the impact of such changes will be much less noticeable in short-term planning, and that the horizon up to which the formulation of plans is useful tends to be shortened considerably by the presence of uncertainty (Modigliani and Cohen, 1961). Relevant to this is the suggestion (e.g. Starr, 1971) that uncertainty can be reduced by breaking down a long planning horizon into a number of smaller ones, which, however, merely seems to imply the adoption of a shorter time span because of the inherent difficulties associated with longer-term plans. Starr (1971) further suggests that the gap between planning horizon alternatives can to some extent be bridged by developing a planning process that can provide a sequence of dependent decisions.

There are obvious dangers in failing to give due recognition to the continuous nature of business operations by attempting to view short-term planning or budgetary periods in isolation. Thus, a non-optimal situation may arise whereby planned (budgeted) results are achieved in one period only at the expense of future performance. The need to take cognisance of inter-temporal dependencies has wide implications for accounting in general and is accentuated by the accounting period concept, which may, of course, be applied to the budgetary period. This recognises the need for reporting accounting data by reference to arbitrary periods of time within the whole lifespan of the business; a requirement dictated by expediency and one which, in financial reporting, introduces numerous valuation problems. Not the least of such problems is that of inventory valuation. It should also be noted that the decision to hold inventories may be cited as an example of a 'sequential decision' with consequences extending well beyond the current period and possibly over the economic life-span of the business. Such a decision has, then, obvious inter-temporal implications which, ideally, should be recognised explicitly in the budget plan.

It will be appreciated that recognition of inter-temporal dependencies is just as important as the recognition of the inter-dependencies of different activities and different business segments in the same planning period. Thus, a dynamic approach to planning would require information on those constraints applicable in future periods which might nevertheless be affected by decisions this period. The point is well made by Amey (1979, pp. 27–28):

> Both the past and the future may interact with the present. The past is relevant because the consequences of plans implemented in one period become initial conditions affecting the plans to be made in the next. The future may be relevant because certain parts of the

current period's plan may affect, directly or indirectly, some future constraints and hence the firm's opportunity sets in later periods. The optimal plan for the current period may then depend on the form and (if they are parameterized) the parameters of the future constraints. Furthermore, optimality of the first period's plan, consistent with optimizing over the firm's planning horizon, may depend on the optimal values of certain elements of plans for future periods.

This approach obviously requires a decision to be made on the duration of the period to be covered by the plan (viz. the planning horizon).

The position which obtains, in practice, on this particular issue of recognising inter-temporal dependencies is not one that can be fully substantiated. Amey (1979) suggests that, in the preparation of operating budgets, the businessman typically makes little systematic use of information which relates to periods extending beyond the budget period, although this does not exclude the possibility of some degree of implicit dynamic planning by setting bounds on certain end-of-period balances such as current assets and current liabilities. It should be noted, however, that the optimal decision rule may in the particular circumstances, and even after full analysis, turn out to be one based on rule of thumb.

The desirability that budget plans should give explicit recognition to inter-temporal dependencies calls for the discussion of those planning models in which attempts have been made to satisfy this requirement.

The Hicksian Model; the Modigliani–Cohen Model; and 'Proximate Planning'

The general features of dynamic planning models, as considered above, serve to distinguish them from static models, which would imply planning for a *series* of *discrete* periods on the basis of the information available to the firm at the beginning of each specific period. The attempt to depict an essentially dynamic process by means of a static model is indeed one of the weaknesses of conventional budget plans.

The Hicksian (1946) model and the Modigliani–Cohen (1961) (M–C hereafter) model are examples of dynamic production models. They have the common feature that both take the view that for each period the firm plans up to the horizon but, as viewed from t=0, acts only on the plan of the first period. Also held in common is the assumption that the plan of that period is not subject to revision.

There are, however, some significant differences between the two models. Thus, in the Hicksian model it is assumed that the firm plans *all* its important operational activities for *each* and *every* period up to the horizon, which is assumed to extend over the economic life of the firm. The optimal course of action selected as at t=0 does, therefore, extend up to t=n, i.e. up to the end of the firm's effective life. The fact that planning horizons may, and do, vary for different activities and will never in normal circumstances extend over the firm's entire operational life is ignored. By way of contrast, the view inherent in the M–C model is that at any planning stage one need only select the optimal set of decisions for the first period, 'optimal' being construed as that component, attributable to the first period, of the optimal set of plans over the planning horizon. Hence, although optimality is viewed by reference to the whole planning horizon, there is no comprehensive future plan as such and aspects of future periods are taken into consideration only to the extent that they affect the optimal course of action of the current period, thus providing guidance to the decision maker in choosing his first move.

In the M–C model future conditions that are considered relevant to present decisions are referred to as 'relevant anticipations', but a distinction is drawn between 'formal' relevance/irrelevance and 'practical' relevance/irrelevance. Thus, certain future conditions which, at a particular time, are formally relevant may, in fact, subsequently turn out to be practically irrelevant on the grounds of difficulty or cost–benefit considerations. Determination of which aspects are practically relevant is not entirely possible without the introduction of considerations of uncertainty into the model.

It would appear that the M–C model accords more with reality than does the Hicksian model. What is particularly important in the consideration of dynamic planning models is the extent of their practical feasibility, even allowing for the reduction of complexity arising from the exclusion at each planning stage of those aspects of the future which are considered irrelevant. On this issue Amey (1979) concludes that except in small and simple businesses the dynamic budget planning problem would not be computationally possible, even if analytically manageable, except at a relatively trivial level. The planner may therefore be compelled to apply static analysis to problems which have obvious dynamic characteristics. This need not however imply a total abandonment of a dynamic approach to planning. Thus, Amey (1979), recognising the generally insurmountable difficulties associated with full dynamic planning, has, by way of compromise, suggested an approach which he refers to as 'proximate planning'. In essence the effect of this would be to substitute for the full dynamic problem a series of one-period *proximate* problems with the same main characteristics as those of the original problem. In addition to the initial conditions, the main dynamic characteristics to be retained would be the relevant components of future plans and the relevant future constraints when formulating the current planning problem, so modifying the objective function to reflect the interaction of present and future dependencies. The degree of error introduced by proximate planning is related not only to the competence of the planner but also to the firm's ability to learn from experience.

From the earlier discussion of the essence of planning it is apparent that there exists an obvious relationship between planning and control models. Thus, 'responsiveness planning', 'dynamic planning', and indeed any rectification of original plans, assume the existence of adequate control procedures. This relationship does not, however, imply that a single model can serve the dual purposes of planning and control; indeed it has been argued with some force (e.g. Amey, 1979) that, to be effective, the models should be separate and distinct. The rationale underlying this contention will be examined in chapter 14.

Before proceeding to a discussion of planning techniques some further reference to the question of planning within a contingency framework seems desirable. The contingency approach to organisational design has already been described and evaluated in chapters 1 and 4. A contingency approach to planning generally implies some form of 'responsiveness planning' model which may provide for alternative predictions about the state of the environment, as in the 'partially constrained' planning model. Planning in a contingency framework does, therefore, negate any idea of a single planning path. It is implicit in the scenario approach which recognises the need to consider a wide range of possible developments and to describe a number of possible futures for the organisation.

In this section planning has been viewed from a conceptual perspective and various planning models have been examined. The following section contains a discussion of the planning techniques embodied in short-term budgets and the basic ideas inherent in 'Zero-base Budgeting' (ZBB) and 'Planning–Programming–Budgeting Systems' (PPBS).

II. SHORT-TERM BUDGETS, ZBB, AND PPBS

Short-Term Budgets

It is probably the case that, in a practical business framework, the most widely accepted view of a budget is that it depicts an explicit and systematic representation of a plan in quantitative terms. It has been argued that budgets can be regarded as the principal element in business planning (Amey, 1979). Even stronger is the claim by Argenti (1978) who, referring to budgetary control in the short term, describes it as 'the number one management tool'.

The budget may be a 'fixed' (or 'static') budget, useful for planning but of dubious value in evaluating performance in that it makes no allowance for the impact on costs and/or revenues of various alternative production and/or sales volumes. On the other hand a 'flexible' budget depicts the intentions and expectations of management for a number of situations, with appropriate adjustment of variable and semi-variable costs for various levels of activity.

Budgeting in the business context is a well-established activity. Indeed, Solomons (1952) has referred to its 'respectable antiquity', crediting de Cazaux (1825) with the quality of foresight reflected in the chapter devoted to budgeting in his book *Eléments d'économie privée et publique'*. Solomons also mentions the work of Bunnell (1911) who described a system of incorporating budgets into cost records. In a less structured and more cost-orientated sense, Sowell (1973) traced various applications of the cost estimate as far back as the early guild and domestic systems of British industrial development.

The idea that the budget is an *ex ante* financial or quantitative interpretation of a policy to be pursued over a defined period of time (ICMA, 1974) gives rise to the concept of the master budget, in which all the various subsidiary budgets are co-ordinated. The extent to which this master budget is decomposed, and the nature and composition of the sectional budgets, are matters which depend on such factors as the size, industrial grouping and organizational structure of the firm. It is doubtful if any of the sectional budgets can be viewed in complete isolation, although the degree of interdependency is more obvious with some of the budgets than with others. Thus, the sales budget will determine the level of the production budget in physical, monetary and component terms, having in mind the planned inventory situation. It will also affect the selling and distribution budget. Again, the production budget will interact with the plant utilisation budget, the purchasing budget, the personnel budget and production cost budget. The capital expenditure and R & D budgets are in essence longer term, but have obvious links with the planned sales situation in the longer term. The cash budget, which is related to all other sectional budgets, exemplifies the provisional nature of the sectional budgets when initially prepared. The aggregate demands on cash resources reflected in the master budget may, for example, indicate the need for curtailment of planned expenditure in certain areas or possibly, as in the case of the capital expenditure budget, the postponement of certain capital projects.

Not only is there considerable doubt regarding the practicability of viewing sectional budgets as wholly separable, but it is also highly questionable whether the sequential approach generally suggested in management accounting textbooks is entirely appropriate. Admittedly one must begin by establishing an agreed overall target such as the planned rate of return on capital employed, and this might then suggest that in the case of, say, a manufacturing concern the appropriate starting point would be the sales forecast and subsequent sales budget, followed by the production budget, and so on. If however one allows for the aforementioned interrelationships and the constraint usually referred to by practitioners as the 'principal budget factor' or 'governing factor'*, it may be inappropriate to advocate any generalised sequential budgeting process.

In very general terms one may summarise the essentials underlying the preparation of the master budget as: forecasting, planning and coordination. In a budgetary control system there must also be added the control aspect or monitoring requirement, involving frequent comparisons between actual and budgeted results and the taking of appropriate action on the principle of 'management by exception'. This control aspect is discussed later in chapter 14.

One important criticism that is worthy of note is directed at the planners who have adapted what is essentially a short-term planning tool (the one-year budget) to longer periods of time, for example a five-year period which Argenti (1978) suggests is applicable to virtually every large company. There are three essential differences between short-range and long-range planning that militate against the use of the same procedures for both planning horizons. Firstly, long-term planning requires multiple forecasts compared with the single forecast generally found in practice in the one-year plan. Secondly, it is more difficult to allow for inflation in the longer term. Thirdly, there are differences in orientation regarding resource utilisation. Thus, the short-term budget sets out the company's intentions concerning the exploitation of its *existing* resources. In contrast, planning for the longer term suggests consideration of wider strategic issues regarding the whole shape and character of the company in the future.

The lack of dynamism in budgetary planning in conventional budgeting has already been pointed out. A further defect relates to the unsatisfactory specification of the system to which the planning process is to be applied. This criticism is applicable not only to budgetary practice but also to accounting literature which has rarely provided a definition of the system which is being planned or controlled (Amey, 1979).

From a non-statistical viewpoint complete specification of the system would require an explicit statement of the planning objectives, forcing management to identify the feasible alternatives and constraints. Amey argues that constraints relating to technology, resource availability, demand and institutional factors are seldom reported explicitly, and some of them are possibly not considered at all. Because budget planning is concerned with economic resource allocation, it should be guided by economic principles. Thus, Amey argues, all the variables should be measured in economic, not accounting terms.

Taking into account statistical considerations, a primary requirement of the formulation of any model in mathematical terms is the careful selection of the variables to be included. However, on the grounds of choice and classification of variables, and explanation of the jointly dependent variables by an equal number of structural equations, Amey (1979, p.17) concludes that:

> in accounting and business practice the system is underdefined. It is underdetermined (the included endogenous variables are not fully explained explicitly); a number of exogenous variables which significantly affect the behaviour of the system are probably omitted; and the dynamic aspects of operations are largely ignored.

As one example of an omitted exogenous variable one could cite, *inter alia*, the behaviour of competitors, a consideration of which could lead to substantial benefits of more permanent duration than those resulting from, say, a more obvious policy of cost reduction.

*The 'principal budget factor' is generally defined as 'the factor, the extent of whose influence must first be assessed in order to ensure that the functional budgets are reasonably capable of fulfilment'.

ZBB and PPBS

The concept of the 'zero-base' is not new, and indeed zero-base budgeting apparently goes back as far as 1964, when it was introduced into the US Department of Agriculture. As a formalised procedure it was, however, first described by Pyhrr (1970; 1973).

The approach is that each manager must justify his entire budget request and must prepare in respect of each activity or operation a 'decision package' in which he analyses cost, purpose, alternative courses of action, measures of performance, consequences of not performing the activity and benefits. He must also identify a minimum spending level and indicate the expected costs–benefits associated with additional expenditure levels on that activity. In brief, then, the basic philosophy of zero-base budgeting is that total, as opposed to incremental, expenditure is reviewed and each budget request must be justified in its entirety as a complete programme in competition with other programmes as users of scarce resources. It is therefore distinguished from traditional budgeting by the reference base adopted, which in the conventional incremental-type budget will be the previous level of appropriation, thus serving to legitimise this level and failing to question explicitly the intrinsic value or efficiency of past activities (Eilon, 1981).

The conceptual appeal of ZBB has prompted a number of publications in the USA in recent years. Of some particular interest is the work of Stonich (1977) based on experiences in designing and implementing zero-base budgeting systems in more than seventy-five organisations. In the light of its conceptual appeal, and its promising features as a practical planning and control instrument, it seems quite remarkable that this challenging technique has apparently not been received with enthusiasm at a practical level. Sherlekar and Dean (1980) investigated the performance of ZBB in its first year of operation in the Federal Government of the USA. The investigation itself was based on a study initiated by the US Office of Management and Budget (1977) in 16 departments and agencies in the US Federal Government. Eleven criteria were selected by Sherlekar and Dean as a basis for evaluating the strengths and weaknesses of ZBB and these were ranked in terms of an 'effectiveness index'.

Eilon (1981) commented on the inherent difficulties associated with such an evaluation exercise, for example, the degree of objectivity, reliability, and consistency of the responses. On the question of objectivity Sherlekar and Dean made the point that federal agencies could be politically motivated to offer favourable evaluations of ZBB as a planning and budgeting tool in order to appear cooperative. At the same time, they may underrate it as a tangible cost-saving tool in order to avoid paying a possible price in terms of budget costs. The rather remarkable fact that the agencies did not regard ZBB as an effective tool for cost-saving, which was given the lowest ranking of the eleven criteria, coupled with the respondents' statement that budget justification was enhanced by ZBB, prompted Eilon's (1981) comment that it 'highlights the respondents' bias and the human reaction of individuals who tend to manipulate such a tool for their own purposes'. An important result of ZBB highlighted by the study is the substantial benefits of a largely non-quantifiable nature which allegedly accrued from the introduction of ZBB, namely: improved communication, understanding and participation. The conclusion is, then, that, despite some success, the failure of ZBB to match up to the original expectations of its promoters lies in its dependency on the cooperation of those charged with its implementation and thus encountering the natural defensive human instincts of self-preservation and self-interest.

A question prompted by the foregoing conclusion is whether ZBB is likely to be more suitable in certain types of industry. It has been suggested (Wetherbe, 1976; Lin, 1979) that it is more appropriate for service-oriented units than for output-oriented units. Subject to certain caveats regarding methodology and small sample size, this proposition received strong support from the results of a field study by Wetherbe and Montanari (1981). They particularly emphasised the need to give explicit recognition to ZBB as an integral part of the planning process, concluding that, without such an organisational framework, the initiation of a ZBB programme could result in failure.

Turning to PPBS, one should reiterate at this point that PPB is not a short-term planning instrument; it may be described as multi-period but not dynamic in the sense used earlier in this chapter. Despite this, the unique features that distinguish it from the conventional business budget serve to justify its inclusion here, albeit by way of a brief reference.

PPBS has been distinguished from traditional systems of budgeting (see, for example, Amey and Egginton, 1973) mainly on the grounds that the latter are heavily oriented towards emphasising input, detailed financial control and existing organisational units (e.g. divisions, departments). As against this PPB emphasises objectives and output and seeks rational resource allocation. A highly important feature of PPB is its construction by reference to functional groupings of activities which have a common objective (i.e. programmes) and not the conventional organisational subdivisions. The result is that budgets prepared on this basis are more directly related to plans and total system objectives; the programme structure is dictated by the objectives of the entity and, within that structure, the lower levels of the organisation compete for resources.

In terms of practical applications PPB has been encountered most frequently in government and government agencies, particularly in North America. Its principles are, however, applicable to the private sector, and Dougharty (1972) has illustrated its application to the development of corporate strategy in a 'typical business corporation'.

To conclude, perhaps the main advantages of PPB lie in the type of thinking which it imposes on the analyst and also in the evaluation of various alternatives within the framework of the objectives of the firm.

III. FORECASTING: NATURE AND LIMITATIONS/DIFFICULTIES

The Nature of the Forecasting Process

Earlier it was suggested that both planning and forecasting may be undertaken with varying degrees of rigour and sophistication. Thus, they may both be substantially of the nature of intuitive processes; on the other hand the plan may be based on data provided by sophisticated forecasting methods. What can be stated categorically is that some element of forecasting is essential to all planning exercises even if the forecasts constitute in a rather general way informed estimates of the probable course of events or are based on extrapolation of past experience. Indeed, if no attempt is explicitly made to forecast, all decision makers, even at a purely individual level, must make some basic assumptions about the future, for example, as regards available alternatives and future states of the environment. In the context of modern business it is, however, apparent that the complexity of the decision-making process and the need to minimise uncertainty must inevitably call for the exercise of explicit and more formal forecasting procedures. Extrapolation, for example, may in many cases fail to reflect satisfactorily the changing alternatives, constraints and inter-temporal dependencies of the situation (Amey, 1979).

The required degree of precision associated with forecasts depends not only on the nature, size, and complexity of the business, but also on the time span. Thus, production scheduling will require precise sales forecasts in the short run, but it is the trend and range of sales which assume greater importance in the long term. In any event, as indicated earlier, the degree of precision obtainable must necessarily decrease with the extension of the forecasting horizon. Hogarth and Makridakis (1981) pointed to the existence of considerable inertia in most economic phenomena which enhance the predictive value for the short term (three months or less) of the present states of many variables. They observed that short-term forecasting and planning is the only form 'for which forecasts can be reasonably accurate and where real gains can be made consistently'. Moreover, simple mechanistic forecasting methods can often generate accurate short-term forecasts and may even outperform more sophisticated approaches (e.g. Armstrong, 1978; Makridakis and Hibon, 1979).

It is apparent that in any serious attempt at forecasting the forecaster is faced with many difficulties and the process itself is not without its limitations. Thus, apart from the element of instability which is almost inevitably present in all but the shortest of time periods, there are other limitations and difficulties many of which are related to forecasting bias; some of these are briefly referred to later in this section. At this point, however, attention should be drawn to one important but perhaps intuitively obvious factor which limits the effectiveness of the forecasting process. This relates to the apparent tendency on the part of some forecasters and planners to fail to estimate the full extent of environmental uncertainty (see, for example, Hogarth 1975; Robinson 1972). Underestimation of such uncertainty may have the undesirable effect of attributing to the forecaster mistaken confidence in his own judgement (Lichtenstein, Fischhoff and Phillips 1977) as well as the consequent danger that forecasts are overtaken by unforeseen events. There is also the danger which arises from the spurious impression of certainty that may be conveyed by 'single-figure' forecasts, the usefulness of which is obviously very limited. Selective presentation of forecasts in terms of probabilities would go some way to remove this danger.

In recent years questions have been raised regarding the adequacy of business forecasting based solely on economic and technological factors (see, for example, Wilson, 1977). The suggestion is that new dimensions to planning and forecasting should be introduced to take in social and political factors. This aspect is more appropriately dealt with in the context of long-term planning (see chapter 10); at this point suffice to say that implementation of the suggestion will introduce into the forecasting model a greater degree of realism. At the same time, however, it will introduce additional areas of uncertainty, so adding to the difficulties associated with the forecasting process.

In the light of increasing complexity and instability in the general economic, technological, political and social environment, Argenti (1976) has questioned the value of seeking what might only be marginal improvements in forecasting accuracy through the introduction of a few more variables into the forecasting equation. This is only one part of his general criticism levelled at the proliferation of techniques, their complexity and the questionable value of some of them in a present-day practical business context. His advocacy of the more 'simple' techniques is well argued and understandable, but recognition of the inevitability of the inaccuracy of forecasts in an age of increasing uncertainty is not a sufficient justification for the exclusion of social and political factors from the forecasting model.

Psychological Limitations/Difficulties in Forecasting

There is available a substantial body of evidence supporting the view that serious errors in human decision making can be attributed to 'superficial information search and processing biases' (e.g. Hogarth, 1975; Janis and Mann, 1977; Slovic, Fischhoff and Lichtenstein, 1977). This evidence has been related to forecasting and planning by Hogarth and Makridakis (1981), who have summarised the main sources of bias at successive information processing levels, namely: information acquisition, processing, output, and feedback. It seems inappropriate here to recite in full such sources of bias but, by way of illustration, one or two areas of general application are referred to below.

In regard to information acquisition one may cite as examples of sources of bias selective perception and bias connected with data presentation. Misperception of 'chance fluctuations' (for example, the gambler's fallacy) is a typical source of bias in connection with feedback. The law of small numbers and regression bias exemplify sources of bias connected with information processing.

In various ways one can seek to minimise errors associated with bias. Thus, in the context of information acquisition, the sampling base could be extended as widely as is practicable, hasty acceptance of forecasts should be avoided, and information search should not be confined to a purely confirmatory role. Mechanical procedures could be employed to minimise aggregation errors. Methods of dealing with judgemental biases have been suggested by Kahneman and Tversky (1979) and Spetzler and Stael von Holstein (1975). The main concern of the former was with intuitive prediction; they did however stress that, even in the case of forecasts based on simulation or mathematical models, intuition and opinions play an important role. This indicates the dual need to analyse those factors which impair the accuracy of expert judgements and to develop procedures to improve their quality. The debiasing strategy which they advocated represents an attempt 'to elicit from the expert relevant information that he would normally neglect, and to help him integrate this information with his intuitive impressions in a manner that respects basic principles of statistical prediction'. Application of this approach to the prediction of uncertain quantities and the assessment of probability distributions reveals two common biases, nonregressiveness of predictions and overconfidence in the precision of estimates.

In pursuing their argument for realism in forecasting and planning, Hogarth and Makridakis (1981) put forward certain suggestions for some 'reconceptualising' in this field. Basically their argument rested on the need for an adaptive approach to environmental change. Such an approach would, they maintained, involve consideration of four distinct issues, namely:
1. Human limitations, particularly in regard to the need to develop the right sort of attitudes to the inevitable uncertainty surrounding future conditions.
2. The functions that the process of forecasting and planning can perform, not only the obvious functions but also those in the nature of side-effects, such as the motivational and control aspects of planning. These ancillary functions should be specified and the reality of their alleged benefits examined in the light of other more direct ways in which they can be achieved.
3. The degree of precision with which goals and forecasts are specified and the need to link this with the planning timescale. This is of more relevance in the long- and medium-term planning contexts and, on this point, Hogarth and Makridakis commented on the inherent deficiencies of the 'action–outcome–feedback loops' associated with long- and medium-term plans. They accept the need for objectives that define direction but argue that 'the precision with which such direction is specified should...be an inverse function of the length of the planning horizon' (Hogarth and Makridakis, 1981, p. 128).
4. A cost–benefit analysis of the goals (possibly conflicting) which the process of forecasting and planning is designed to achieve. This is also of great relevance to the medium and long term.

In the context of the costs–benefits associated with the forecasting and planning system, a distinction is drawn between the cash gains and losses resulting from the degree of accuracy of the forecasting and planning procedures in themselves and the effects of such procedures on the organisation in terms of such matters as motivation and commitment. Hogarth and Makridakis argued that the 'operational decision-theoretic concepts' that are relevant to these issues are:

— Sensitivity analysis to test the relative robustness of alternative strategies to forecasting errors.

— Information evaluation, i.e. assessment of costs–benefits associated with the possibility of enhanced accuracy in forecasts.

— Multi-attribute utility analysis to assist both planning and organisational design. This involves recognition and specification of both the obvious functions and the side-effects of forecasting and planning (F & P), as mentioned previously in this section, and also the recognition of forecasting and planning goals, the extent of their compatibility and/or the extent to which trade-offs are acceptable. The point is made that, by using the framework of multi-attribute utility analysis as a conceptual tool, 'different F & P systems and plans can be considered as decision alternatives where the dimensions of evaluation (i.e., attributes) are both organizational consequences (e.g., flexibility, motivation, control) and the more traditional F & P measures (e.g., relative expected performance in dollar consequences)' (Hogarth and Makridakis, 1981, p. 131).

There are obvious difficulties associated with the formulation of the forecasting and planning problem within the framework of a multi-attribute model. Hogarth and Makridakis, however, supported their advocacy of this approach by pointing to its success in providing insights into complex problems in a wide range of applications (e.g., Edwards, Guttentag and Snapper, 1975; Keeney and Raiffa, 1976). They concluded by reaffirming their view that an approach within the decision-theoretic framework which they discussed is one way to secure greater realism in forecasting and planning.

In the foregoing discussion certain limitations generally applicable to the forecasting process have been considered. Below, the nature and effectiveness of certain forecasting methods, particularly as applicable to the short term, are reviewed briefly.

Forecasting Methods

Forecasting methods may be classified in various ways; one approach suggested by Higgins (1976) is to classify them broadly into the following four main categories: subjective; statistical extrapolation; O.R. and econometric models; and technological. Some of these are applicable to any timescale, but the role of technological forecasting, frequently extrapolative but ideally normative in character, is essentially of a long-term nature.

A second type of classification framework (Makridakis and Wheelwright, 1977) involved four main classification areas by relating the type of pattern experienced (repetitive historical as opposed to external factor-determined) to the type of information available (quantitative as opposed to subjective or qualitative). By way of illustration, 'time-series methods' would fall into the category in which 'history repeats itself' *and* the available information is quantitative. In contrast 'normative methods' (e.g. cross-impact matrices and the Delphi technique) would be classified by reference to the dual criteria that events are determined by external factors and also that the information available is qualitative or subjective.

A more extensive framework (Makridakis and Wheelwright, 1978; Wheelwright and Makridakis, 1977) used several different criteria for evaluating forecasting methodologies. The criteria used were: forecasting time horizon; type of data pattern (e.g. trend, seasonal, cyclical); cost; complexity; data requirements; and accuracy. The importance of the 'accuracy' criterion is recognised, but it is conceded that lack of available knowledge permits no conclusive statements regarding relative accuracy of competing methodologies.

McLaughlin (1979) advocated a three-step process to the development of a total forecasting system for the organisation. The first step is to build an objective (quantitative) model; this is then tested by reference to eclectic systems (both quantitative and qualitative) and finally it is subjected to judgemental consensus, which is, of course, essentially qualitative. This approach involved various levels of development embracing the medium and long term as well as the short term. McLaughlin's work is also of interest in that it traces developments in organizational forecasting.

It would seem that a convenient classification on which to base further discussion is that proposed by Higgins (1976) referred to previously. Using such a framework the starting point is therefore the category described as subjective forecasting. This is based on forward projection or extrapolation but is in essence largely intuitive. It may frequently constitute the initial approach to building up the sales forecast, although it is subject to the psychological limitations previously discussed.

Statistical extrapolation is linked with time series analysis, which is basically non-causal in character in that no relationship is specified between the dependent variable and the independent variable(s). The application of time series analysis to forecasting involves a process of curve-fitting whereby the series is smoothed by removing seasonal and random factors. The resulting trend line is then extrapolated. A linear or straight-line trend projection might be appropriate to the short term, as, for example, to a sales budget, but growth curves such as the logistic curve would be more realistic in the long term. It should be borne in mind, however, that the secular trend reflects only a smooth, continuous and gradual change; and knowledge of fluctuations around the trend would therefore be necessary to forecast the position at a precise point of time in the future.

The 'smoothing' process referred to above is generally effected through the use of moving averages. 'Exponential smoothing', which really covers a class of methods, does, however, attach greater weight to the present than to the past in assuming that the future is a weighted average of past and present periods. Basically, the effect of applying the exponential smoothing formula is to adjust the previous smoothed statistics by the forecast error. By its adaptiveness, or responsiveness through the use of the error term in the formula, exponential smoothing is classified as an 'adaptive' forecasting technique. It is particularly appropriate for short- and medium-term planning, usually at the operational level, e.g. sales and production forecasts.

The 'Box–Jenkins' technique is apparently often preferred by academics to other time-series approaches by virtue of its completeness and statistical features. Other factors, such as cost, accuracy, and complexity, might well induce practitioners to favour exponential smoothing or other simpler approaches to forecasting. However, it has been claimed that the Box–Jenkins approach performs better than exponential smoothing methods (Reid, 1969; Newbold and Granger, 1974).

The presence in a time series of cyclical, seasonal and irregular elements imposes obvious limitations on the usefulness of trend projections in short-term forecasting, where one is faced with the difficult problem of predicting the point at which cyclical changes will arise. Their overall usefulness is also very limited if changes are likely to arise in major independent variables which have influenced the series in the past. This point reinforces the need for isolation and measurement of relationships between variables, or in other words the need for a causal model specifying the causal relationship between a dependent variable and a set of independent variables. A causal model of this type can be estimated by applying regression techniques. Such a model can then be used for generating forecasts, subject to the limitation that their adequacy will be dependent on the forecast period having similar characteristics to those applicable to the period in respect of which the model was built.

Compared with simple time series models, the functional form of causal models is typically based on a more rigorous theoretical underpinning. Theobald (1980, p. 100–101), however, points out that the usefulness of some causal models will be limited 'because they show the variable to be forecast as depending on the *future* value of some other variable'. This limitation does not apply to time series models, which may also be favoured on cost considerations.

Reverting to the four-fold classification of forecasting methods, no specific reference has so far been made in this chapter to operational research and econometric models. Both these may be applicable to any timescale but econometric models are largely strategic by nature, used, for example, in forecasting the general economic environment and the particular industrial sector under consideration. Forecasting at this macro level may thus be regarded as a valuable, or indeed possibly essential, preliminary step in the forecasting of demand for the firm's products and hence in the preparation of sales budgets.

OR models are often special purpose models, usually prescriptive by nature and quite frequently stochastic. It is inappropriate here to delve further into the techniques of operational research; suffice to say that they have planning applications of obvious value – for example, in the fields of inventory management and control, production planning, and transport planning and scheduling.

As indicated previously, the fourth category of forecasting methods, i.e. technological forecasting, is essentially of a long-term nature and is not therefore considered further in this chapter.

It has not been the intention of this chapter to provide a comprehensive listing of forecasting tools and/or procedures, particularly as some of the interesting and useful tools are oriented to the longer term. It is, however, convenient to make some brief reference here to examples of techniques applicable to the longer term. Thus, in the wider planning context, Wilson (1977) has given as examples of the more available methodologies for *systematic* monitoring of the environment not only trend projections but also Delphi forecasting, scenarios and cross-impact analysis. The latter technique represents an attempt to assess the impact of one specific event on numerous other trends/events selected for their high combined rating of probability and importance. The scenario approach recognises that we shall never know what *will* happen, but we can have a fairly good idea of what *could* happen; it accepts that a wide range of possible developments must be considered and attempts to describe a number of possible futures. Wilson also mentions, in his discussion of General Electric's strategic-planning process, three techniques found to be useful in particular cases; techniques to be used with care and which have, as their main purpose, the stimulation of the planner 'to improve on them rather than to use them blindly'. These techniques, all concerned with environmental forecasting, are:

— Probability–Diffusion Matrix, designed not only to assess the probability of a trend or event but also the extent to which it is uniformly distributed over the relevant population.

— Values Profile (i.e. profile of significant value-system changes).

— Social Pressures Priority Analysis (assignment of corporate priorities to social pressures on the company).

IV. SUMMARY

In this chapter an attempt has been made to deal with the various aspects of planning and forecasting as applied to the short term. It is not entirely possible to view the short term in isolation and there has, therefore, been some overlapping with other chapters.

There are presumably few who would deny the reality of the advantages to be gained by planning business operations in the short term. However, the scope and nature of the planning exercise, and indeed the possibilities of successful outcomes, must vary with a number of factors, some of which are interlinked, e.g. the nature of the business, the extent of uncertainty and the availability of reliable information. To illustrate this point one need only compare an industry such as deep-sea fishing with one for whose product there is a steady demand and in which supply can be controlled within reasonable limits. In this age of uncertainty there are, however, some who would question the validity of longer term planning. Thus, at a recent symposium of the European Management Forum held at Davos, the head of a Dutch company made the rather caustic observations that 'Planning is just a waste of time nowadays – especially so-called strategic planning. In today's world there's no point looking further forward than a one or two-year budget. Anything longer-term is just not worth the paper it's written on.' The validity of this attitude is strongly challenged by the quoted experience of General Electric in facing new challenges much earlier than many of its competitors, a factor described as 'one of the prime purposes of its elaborate planning system' (Lorenz, 1979).

In an uncertain economic environment it is understandable that the horizon of the average businessman has tended to grow much shorter, with the danger that essential long-term decisions may often be deferred. It is important, therefore, not to confuse the respective roles of short-term and long-term planning. Thus, in an earlier part of this chapter, the point was made that short-term budgets set out the company's intentions concerning the exploitation of its existing resources whereas planning for the longer term involves wider strategic issues regarding the company's future. If, then, a company takes only a short-term view, in effect by default, it will, as Emerson (1979) suggests, find itself 'reacting to events and moving from one crisis to another'. As he further states, 'Planning will not always anticipate these events, but properly carried out it will help to position a company so that the effect of shocks is minimised and the chances of surviving are increased.'

REFERENCES

Ackoff, R. L., 1970. *A Concept of Corporate Planning*: Wiley.

Amey, L. R., 1979. *Budget Planning and Control Systems*: Pitman.

Amey, L. R. and Egginton, D. A., 1973. *Management Accounting – A Conceptual Approach*: Longman.

Ansoff, H. I., 1965. *Corporate Strategy*: McGraw-Hill.

Ansoff, H. I. and Brandenburg, R. C., 1967. A program of research in business planning, *Management Science* **XIII**, February, pp. 219–239.

Argenti, J., 1976. Whatever happened to management techniques?, *Management Today*, April, pp. 78–79.

Argenti, J., 1978. Long term budgets can damage your company's health, *Accountancy*, May, pp. 105–107.

Armstrong, J. S., 1978. Forecasting with econometric methods: folklore versus fact, *Journal of Business*, **51** (4), pp. 549–564.

Bunnell, S. H., 1911. Standardizing factory expense and cost, *Iron Age*, 16th November.

Cazaux, L. F. G. de, 1825. *Eléments d'économie privée et publique*, Vol. II, chapter III, pp. 105–108.

Cyert, R. M. and March, J. G., 1963. *A Behavioural Theory of the Firm*. Prentice-Hall.

Dougharty, L. A., 1972. Developing corporate strategy through planning, programming and budgeting, pp. 409–422 in B. Taylor and K. Hawkins (eds), *Handbook of Strategic Planning*: Longman.

Drucker, P. F., 1959. Long-range planning: challenge to management science, *Management Science*, V, April, pp. 238–249.

Edwards, W., Guttentag, M. and Snapper, K., 1975. 'Effective evaluation: a decision theoretic approach', in E. L. Struening and M. Guttentag (eds), *Handbook of Evaluation Research* vol. 1, Beverly Hills, Calif: Sage.

Eilon, S., 1981. 'Z.B.B. – Promise or Illusion?', editorial article, *Omega* **9** (2).

Emerson, R. V., 1979. Corporate strategy in the wilderness, *The Financial Times*, 29th June.

Hicks, J. R., 1946. *Value and Capital*, 2nd edn: Oxford University Press.

Higgins, J. C., 1976. *Information Systems for Planning and Control – Concepts and Cases*, p. 87: Edward Arnold.

Hogarth, R. M., 1975. Cognitive processes and the assessment of subjective probability distributions, *Journal of the American Statistical Association*, **70** (350), pp. 271–289.

Hogarth, R. M. and Makridakis, S., 1981. Forecasting and planning: An evaluation, *Management Science*, **27** (2), February, pp. 115–138.

ICMA, 1974. *Terminology of Management and Financial Accountancy*. London: ICMA.

Janis, I. L. and Mann, L., 1977. *Decision Making: A Psychological Analysis of Conflict, Choice and Commitment*. New York: The Free Press.

Kahneman, D. and Tversky, A., 1979. 'Intuitive prediction: biases and corrective procedures, pp. 313–327 in S. Makridakis and S. C. Wheelwright (eds) *TIMS Studies in the Management Sciences 12 (1979) – Forecasting*: North-Holland Publishing Co.

Keeney, R. L. and Raiffa, H., 1976. *Decisions with Multiple Objectives: Preferences and Value Tradeoffs*. New York: Wiley.

Lichtenstein, S., Fischhoff, B. and Phillips, L. D., 1977. 'Calibration of probabilities: the state of the art', in H. Jungermann, and G. de Zeeuw (eds), *Decision Making and Change in Human Affairs*, The Netherlands: Reidel, Dordrecht.

Lin, W. T., 1979. Corporate planning and budgeting: an integrated approach, *Managerial Planning*, **27**, May–June, pp. 29–33.

Lorenz, C., 1979. General Electric's painful re-think, *The Financial Times*, 27th June.

Makridakis, S. and Hibon, M., 1979. Accuracy of forecasting: an empirical investigation, *Journal of the Royal Statistical Society, Series A*, **142**(2), pp. 97–125.

Makridakis, S. and Wheelwright, S. C., 1977. Forecasting: issues and challenges for marketing management, *Journal of Marketing*, October, pp. 24–38.

Makridakis, S. and Wheelwright, S. C., 1978. *Forecasting: Methods and Applications*: Wiley.

McLaughlin, R. L., 1979. 'Organizational forecasting: its achievements and limitations', in S. Makridakis and S. C. Wheelwright (eds) *TIMS Studies in the Management Sciences 12 (1979) – Forecasting*.

Modigliani, F. and Cohen, K. J., 1961. The role of anticipations and plans in economic behaviour and their use in economic analysis and forecasting, *Studies in Business Expectations and Planning, No. 4*: University of Illinois Bureau of Economic and Business Research.

Newbold, P. and Granger, C. W. J., 1974. Experience and forecasting univariate time series and the combination of forecasts, *Journal of The Royal Statistical Society, Series A*, **137**, pp. 131–165.

Office of Management and Budget, 1977. *Assessment of Zero-Base Budgeting*. Washington, D.C.

Pyhrr, P. A., 1970. Zero-base budgeting, *Harvard Business Review*, November-December, pp. 111–120.

Pyhrr, P. A., 1973. *Zero Base Budgeting: A Practical Management Tool for Evaluating Expenses*: John Wiley & Sons.

Reid, D. J., 1969. A comparative study of time series prediction techniques on economic data. PhD Dissertation, University of Nottingham.

Robinson, C., 1972. 'Forecasting and strategic planning', pp. 396–408 in B. Taylor, and K. Hawkins (eds), *Handbook of Strategic Planning*: Longman.

Sherlekar, V. S. and Dean, B. V., 1980. An evaluation of the initial year of zero-base budgeting in the federal government, *Management Science, 26*, pp. 750–772.

Slovic, P., Fischhoff, B. and Lichtenstein, S., 1977. Behavioural decision theory, *Annual Review of Psychology, 28*, pp. 1–39.

Solomons, D., 1952. 'Historical development of costing', pp. 3–49 in D. Solomons (ed.), *Studies in Cost Analysis*: Sweet and Maxwell.

Sowell, E. M., 1973. *The Evolution of the Theories and Techniques of Standard Costs*: University of Alabama Press.

Spetzler, C. S. and Stael von Holstein, C. A. S., 1975. Probability encoding in decision analysis, *Management Science, 22* (3), pp. 340–358.

Starr, M. K., 1971. *Management: A Modern Approach*: Harcourt Brace Jovanovich.

Stonich, P. J., 1977. *Zero Base Planning and Budgeting*. Homewood, IL: Dow Jones-Irwin.

Theobald, M., 1980. 'Forecasting models', in J. Arnold, B. Carsberg and R. Scapens (eds), *Topics in Management Accounting*: Philip Allan, pp. 84–102.

Thune, S. S. and House, R. J., 1970. Where long-range planning pays off, *Business Horizons, 13* (4), pp. 81–87.

Wetherbe, J. C., 1976. 'A general purpose strategic planning methodology for the computing effort in higher education: development, implementation and evaluation', PhD Dissertation, Texas Tech. University.

Wetherbe, J. C. and Montanari, J. R., 1981. Zero based budgeting in the planning process, *Strategic Management Journal, 2*, pp. 1–14.

Wheelwright, S. C. and Makridakis, S., 1977. *Forecasting Methods for Management*, 2nd edn. New York: Wiley.

Wilson, I. H., 1977. Forecasting social and political trends, pp. 96–117 in B. Taylor and J. R. Sparks (eds), *Corporate Strategy and Planning*: Heinemann.

10

Planning in the Longer Term

by Stephen C. Ward

For any organisation, planning ahead is necessary to ensure increasing or at least continuing, achievement of organisational objectives in the future. Failure to plan ahead may result in an inability to counter problems or threats to the organisation, and inability to take advantage of opportunities to enhance performance. However, reluctance to consider increasing uncertainty means that no organisation plans further ahead than it needs to. Indeed, many are reluctant to plan far enough ahead. In the previous chapter the continuum of planning activity in the firm was divided into strategic and tactical planning. Accepting that these terms are relative rather than absolute, one way of distinguishing strategic planning from tactical planning is the time span of the plans involved (Ackoff, 1970). Thus strategic plans are typically of a long-term nature, whilst tactical plans are focused more on the short-term operational activities of the business.

Many of the decisions taken in organisations require a relatively long-term perspective. These decisions, invariably of a strategic nature, involve actions such as: expansion or contraction of the product range; major expansion or contraction of existing operations; diversification into new product/markets; securing key skills and resources for the long term.

The appropriate planning horizon for a strategic decision depends both on the timescale of perceived strategic problems and opportunities and on the time needed to implement appropriate responses to these problems and opportunities. A noticeable feature of strategic decisions is that they take much longer than operating decisions to implement. Effective action depends on decisions being made far enough ahead to make implementation possible and to maximise the chosen strategy's contribution to organisational performance. Thus the choice of planning horizon will be influenced by such factors as: the expected economic life of plant and machinery; the lifetime of existing sources of raw materials; the market life of products; the time required to develop a new product; and production lead times (Hussey, 1982).

A long-term planning horizon is also desirable because it can increase the choice of options available. For example, requiring goals to be achieved in a relatively short period of time increases the likelihood that choice of strategy is restricted to options such as acquisition or merger. Internal development of either or both new product and new market strategies may take too long to be effective against prevailing competitive forces.

Tilles (1963) has also argued that a long-term planning horizon facilitates consistency of strategy which can be maintained over long periods of time. Consistency in strategy has obvious stabilising advantages for an organisation over frequent discontinuities in strategy brought about by myopic planning. A further possibility is that large organisations need to plan further ahead than small organisations because they require longer periods to change direction. Thus, as a small organisation grows in size it should also plan further and further ahead (Tilles 1963). The argument is an appealing one – but more significant than size is the flexibility that organisations can bring to bear on their operations.

Notwithstanding the above considerations, planning horizons may be restricted because of uncertainty about the future and the need to retain management commitment to plans. As organisations attempt to plan further ahead, initial uncertainty about the future increases. As planning horizons lengthen, plans become increasingly speculative. Rather than formulate broad, robust strategies for a highly uncertain future, organisations may prefer to restrict planning to a near-term future that permits the formulation of more reliable plans. In addition, continued management commitment to a long-term plan may be difficult to sustain in the face of continuous personnel changes at all levels of management. The tendency for corporate strategy to undergo radical changes following the arrival of a new chief executive is an obvious example.

Perhaps for these reasons, many firms adopt a planning horizon of about five years (see for example, Ortman and Blackman, 1981; Boulton et al. 1982). It may be that five years is far enough ahead to provide sufficient perspective yet not so far ahead that management commitment is difficult to obtain and forecasts become excessively inaccurate.

Strategic decisions present a number of difficulties for organisations seeking to make rational choices about strategy. Firstly, the relatively long-term orientation of most issues means that decisions involve high levels of uncertainty. Courses of action adopted are likely to have an enduring effect and may be difficult to reverse. Secondly, strategic decisions relate to organisational goals. These ought to be clarified before strategies are chosen. For example, trade-offs between the short and long term, and between profit and sales growth must be considered. Thirdly, strategic issues frequently require the assessment of situations that an organisation has not encountered before. A methodology for identifying and systematically diagnosing strategic problems or opportunities may be lacking (Lyles 1981). Fourthly, identification of possible courses of action to meet a particular problem or opportunity may be problematic. Courses of action are rarely constrained, obvious responses may be inappropriate and creative thinking may be needed to identify worthwhile actions. Considerable design effort is usually necessary to specify strategic options in operational terms (Mintzberg et al., 1976). Finally, strategic issues are broad in scope, affecting and influenced by many factors both inside and outside the organisation. The impact of such interactions must be assessed. In practice even a partial assessment may prove excessively difficult.

A variety of approaches have been developed to handle these difficulties. These are discussed in varying levels of detail in general texts on corporate planning and strategic management (Thompson and Strickland, 1983; Lorange, 1980; Ansoff, 1984).

This chapter focuses on the manner in which the information necessary to make decisions about strategy is collated and interpreted, and on analytical techniques for processing this information. Section I describes an analytical framework and administrative arrangements for formal strategic planning. Section II discusses the need for operational objectives as a prerequisite for the formulation of strategy. Section III considers the information requirements for strategy formulation and focuses on the problems presented by uncertainty and the subjective interpretation of information. Section IV briefly examines the problem of evaluating strategic options, given that discounted cash flow techniques are of limited value in this context. Section V considers the design and use of financial planning models as decision support systems for strategic planning. The management accountant has an important supporting role to play in all of these areas. Indeed, his potential contribution is such that there is a real danger of overemphasising the financial dimensions of strategic issues at the expense of equally significant, and sometimes more significant, qualitative considerations such as the impact of competition or the availability of non-financial resources. This chapter is intended to provide sufficient insight into the strategic planning process to allow the scope and limits of the management accountant's role to be appreciated.

I. FORMAL PLANNING

Concern for the quality of strategic decision processes has led to widespread advocacy of formalised approaches designed to facilitate more systematic and rigorous decision making. Corporate planning is a useful generic term describing a formalised process in which the totality of strategic issues faced by an organisation is examined in a systematic way. In addition to addressing the difficulties presented by the analysis of individual strategic issues, corporate planning recognises the desirability of considering the interactions between them.

In the past, it has often been suggested that corporate planning involves formulation and implementation of a detailed set of strategic plans for the organisation. A more realistic and less ambitious view is to regard corporate planning as primarily a process for coordinating decisions about individual strategic issues into a consistent set of strategies for the organisation as a whole. Emphasis is on the formulation of a coherent framework within which more detailed strategies and plans can be developed. The installation of formal planning in an organisation does not preclude *ad hoc* strategic decisions, but it does seek to provide a method for coordinating these decisions into more coherent patterns.

The corporate planning literature contains a large number of normative planning frameworks (Gilmore and Brandenburg, 1962; Ansoff, 1965; Hofer and Schendel, 1978; Glueck, 1980; Lorange, 1980; Thompson and Strickland, 1983). All incorporate the following activities:
— establishment of a set of strategic objectives for the organisation.
— an assessment of the organisation's current strategies and capabilities.
— an assessment of the organisation's environment in order to identify opportunities and threats facing the organisation.
— gap analysis. Based on the foregoing, the gap between projected performance with current strategies and the strategic objectives is estimated.
— identification or design of alternative strategies to close the gap between projected performance and objectives.
— evaluation of the strategic options and choice of appropriate strategies for implementation.

Some frameworks also include activities concerned with the implementation of the corporate plan and subsequent monitoring of performance of the implemented strategy.

A considerable part of the planning process involves assessment of the organisation's capabilities, the organisation's environment, and prospects for each area of business activity. Much of this assessment should be part of a continuous

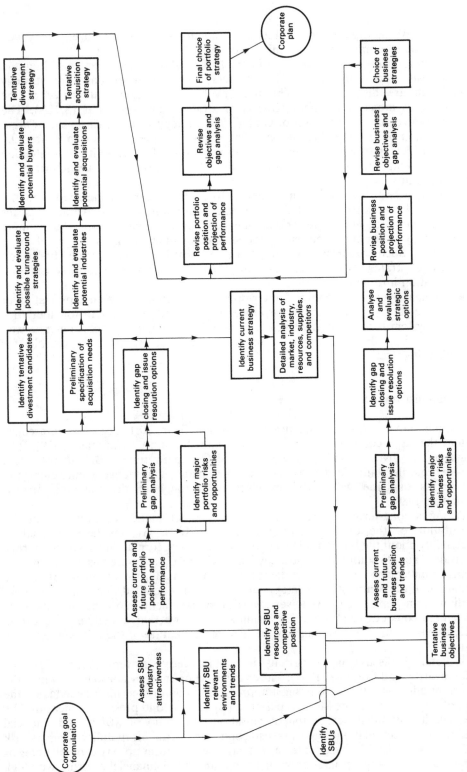

Figure 10.1 *The strategy formulation process*

surveillance of the organisation and its environment. As a consequence, it may well take place outside any regular planning process.

A planning framework is shown in figure 10.1. It shows the objective setting and gap analysis stages of the planning process explicitly. Two stages of strategy formulation are distinguished. The first involves evaluation and choice of the organisation's areas of business activity, or strategic business units (SBUs). The second involves the formulation of competitive strategy within each business area. The exclusion of any reference to operating plans or implementation in figure 10.1 merely reflects a particular concern for the formulation of strategy; it is not intended to suggest that the implementation of the chosen strategy is unimportant or unproblematic.

Planning frameworks like that in figure 10.1 are primarily concerned with the general problem of strategy formulation in an organisation active in several industries or product-markets. For single, or dominant product-line organisations, the planning process can be simplified because of the smaller number of SBUs that need to be considered. Such organisations might be expected to concentrate firstly on appropriate strategies for their existing areas of business before considering diversification into new businesses.

A principal benefit of planning frameworks is that they facilitate an appreciation of the steps required in formulating corporate strategy and how they fit together. If a planning system is to be of any value, the underlying planning process must be well understood by all those involved in corporate planning and responsible for implementing strategy.

The Administrative System

In administrative terms, the analytical framework in figure 10.1 suggests a hierarchical system that is a combination of 'top-down' and 'bottom-up' (Steiner, 1979). Top management gives broad guidelines to SBUs, permitting SBU management considerable flexibility in developing their own plans. Top management remains in continuous dialogue with SBU management throughout the planning process (Lorange, 1980).

Taking a long-term perspective, top management makes decisions about the constitution of the organisation's portfolio of SBUs. At this level of analysis uncertainty about the future is high and plans can only be formulated in general terms. Decisions about competitive strategy in each SBU are circumscribed by top management plans and largely delegated to the managers of each SBU. The formulation of competitive strategy involves more detailed plans and a more medium-term perspective. At lower levels of management, more detailed plans to implement competitive strategy are formulated that warrant a relatively short term perspective. Figure 10.2 summarises the hierarchical nature of the different levels of plan.

A detailed discussion of options in administrative systems is provided by Chakravarthy and Lorange (1984). They suggest a contingency approach in which the choice of administrative system most appropriate to an organisation depends on the portfolio and financial pressures experienced by it. Portfolio pressure is measured by the severity of imbalance in the organisation's portfolio of SBUs, and financial pressure is a function of investor dissatisfaction with overall profitability, financial risk and operating risk. For example, a decentralised 'bottom-up' style of planning is regarded as most appropriate for organisations under low financial pressure with high

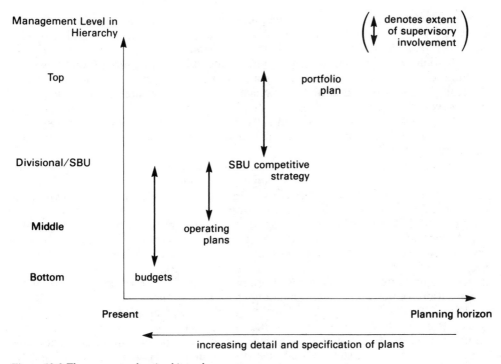

Figure 10.2 *The corporate planning hierarchy*

portfolio imbalance. Conversely, for organisations under high financial pressure with a fairly balanced portfolio of SBUs, a 'portfolio planning' approach involving cooperation between top and divisional management is considered most appropriate.

In respect of the duration of any synoptic, formal planning process, the desire for rigorous analysis using the best possible information would indicate a lengthy period of sustained planning activity. On the other hand, the need to keep the costs of analysis and management time within reasonable limits, minimise the chance of assumptions becoming out of date, and maintain momentum in strategies, all point to formal planning activity confined to short periods of time.

In a study of strategic change processes in a number of large organisations, Quinn (1978) found that formal planning appears to be most successful in bringing about significant changes when carried out as special studies on important strategic issues. Effective strategies tended to emerge from a number of 'strategic sub-systems' in the organisation, each concerned with a major class of strategic issue, such as divestment, major reorganisation, or governmental–external relations. Within each sub-system a class of strategic issues was examined in a systematic way, with the overall corporate strategy emerging by combining the sub-system strategies together into a cohesive pattern over time in an incremental, opportunistic manner. Wide ranging, corporate assessments of strategy were sometimes undertaken, but were always supplemented by special studies focused on particular strategic issues.

In respect of the frequency of synoptic, formal planning activity, it is difficult to see why extensive reappraisal of corporate strategy needs to be undertaken on a particularly frequent basis. Given that strategies may often take several years to reach fruition, wholesale review of corporate strategy may only be appropriate every 3 to 5 years. In the interim, however, some review of key assumptions underlying the organisation's strategy will be desirable, and this may lead to limited, perhaps annual exercises of an essentially incremental nature (Camillus, 1982). Quinn (1978) suggested that synoptic formal planning activity actually institutionalises incrementalism. He identified two reasons for this. Firstly, the utilisation of specialised knowledge requires that planning occur in the organisation from the bottom up in response to general guidelines provided by top management. The knowledge and experience of lower-level managers and the organisation's reward systems cause attention to be biased towards existing products and activities. Secondly, formal plans are regarded only as frameworks for making future incremental decisions in a coherent and consistent way.

In this context, an incremental approach has a number of advantages: it is flexible, options can be kept open, and strategies developed in the light of up-to-date information. A second advantage is that commitment to a strategy can be built up more easily by moving through the organisation's 'corridors of comparative indifference' (Quinn, 1978, 1982). Instead of attempting to implement strategies in a way that creates strong opposition, the successful manager will begin to implement portions of a strategy in areas where there is support or comparative indifference to the new strategy. As more and more parts of the strategy are implemented and increasing pressure for the changes is brought to bear from the altered areas of the organisation, opposition to the remaining changes crumbles.

Quinn (1978; 1982) called this approach 'logical incrementalism', and discussed in some detail the variety of approaches that managers can use to build commitment to strategic changes. For example, managers can seek to (i) develop an awareness and concern for particular issues by studying, questioning, and challenging existing ideas about strategy; (ii) encourage flexibility; (iii) implement pilot projects which can be expanded if successful or (iv) formalise commitment by public pronouncements about strategy or by aligning control and reward systems to reflect intended strategies.

The net benefits of formal planning are difficult, if not impossible, to measure in absolute terms. Once strategies are implemented the organisation and environment change so that it is never possible to compare observed performance with what would have happened without planning. In addition the costs of management participation in planning are not readily differentiated. Several empirical studies support the contention that formal planning leads to improved organisational performance. (For example, Karger and Malik, 1975; Wood and La Forge, 1979; Thune and House, 1970; Ansoff et al., 1970.) However, Armstrong (1982) criticised the weak methodology employed in such studies. In most of the studies examined, Armstrong was unable to find any description of the planning process, and often it was not clear whether planning yielded higher profits or whether firms with more profits invested more in planning. Nevertheless, there can be little doubt that some degree of formalisation can improve the quality of the planning process by encouraging a systematic and comprehensive approach.

Limits on Formal Planning

A question that all organisations embarking on corporate planning must consider is how much planning should be undertaken. An obvious factor is the size and complexity of organisational activities. Small companies, companies with a limited product range and companies operating in stable markets are likely to find a relatively simple corporate planning process most useful. Conversely, large companies active in several industries and companies facing a turbulent environment are likely to need a fairly sophisticated planning process involving extensive analysis of competitors and potential markets (Steiner, 1979).

Whilst the disadvantages of too little planning are usually recognised, the dangers of too much planning are not always appreciated. One potential problem is 'paralysis by analysis'; excessive, detailed planning may reduce an organisation's readiness to respond quickly and flexibly to changes in the environment. A second problem is that emphasis on planning further and further ahead may divert attention away even from recognising the need for flexibility. Rather than trying to make better decisions further ahead, organisations should first consider what they can do to reduce the need to plan ahead by increasing the responsiveness of the organisation to a changing environment (Loasby, 1967).

Bresser and Bishop (1983) argued that under certain circumstances formal planning may have dysfunctional effects. They postulated that the amount of formal planning is greatest in organisations where values, beliefs and know-how are not widely shared between members of the organisation. In such organisations, a high level of direction and coordination will be required to enforce the wishes of the dominant coalition; this will be facilitated by a formalised approach to planning. Bresser and Bishop argued that this behaviour can have dysfunctional consequences for the organisation.

The lack of shared values, beliefs and know-how leads to frequent discrepancies between plans and subsequently implemented actions. There are two reasons for this. Firstly, idiosyncratic interpretations of plans occur as individuals implement plans in terms of their own (preferred) values, beliefs and know-how. Secondly, the more that activity is preplanned, the higher is the chance that parts of plans will be inappropriate. Even contingency plans may fail to achieve flexibility because as Quinn (1980, p.122) found they 'became precapsuled programmes to respond in precise ways to stimuli that never quite occurred as expected '.

Discrepancies between plans and actions may be regarded as failure of the planning process by the dominant coalition, causing it to introduce closer supervision and control systems, to resist suggestions to revise plans, and to adjust and update plans more frequently. Such action results in a shorter-term planning perspective and generates employee dissatisfaction and frustration, which leads to higher rates of employee turnover. Frequent changes in personnel and plans impede the development of widely shared values, beliefs and know-how resulting in further pressures for more formal planning.

In these circumstances, it may be advantageous to *reduce* the amount of formal planning and allow looser specification of strategies. This would allow for more flexible interpretation of plans, thereby reducing both the potential for conflict over strategy specifications and the need for short-term control measures.

Under a different set of circumstances formal planning may become too sophisticated and degenerate into a routine administrative exercise (Lenz and Lyles, 1985). In this event formal planning will cease to be an effective vehicle for considering strategic initiatives. According to Lenz and Lyles, complexity may result from planners pursuing professional interest in sophisticated planning techniques and additional detail being steadily incorporated over time as experience in planning develops. Routinisation of the planning process is facilitated by the extent to which standard quantitative analyses are involved. In this respect a mistaken belief that an ability to quantify implies greater certainty about the future can lead to excessive emphasis on quantitative analysis. Important qualitative issues go unaddressed. Furthermore, to save time and make the planning process less of a chore to manage, planners seek to increase the administrative efficiency of the planning process. Data is requested in fixed formats, executive interactions are formalised with previously set agendas for meetings and the planning process is tied to an annual timetable. The time available for creative reflection about strategy is steadily reduced. As a result of these pressures, top management comes to view corporate strategy as a constrained choice problem for an organisation that is discussed as an abstraction of figures. People, values and commitments seem increasingly irrelevant. Top management gradually withdraws from active participation in the formal planning process and increasingly deals with strategic issues outside of the formal planning process. The corporate planning department becomes an administrator of the planning process instead of a provider of advice on strategic issues. In the absence of active top management involvement, line management view planning as a tiresome administrative exercise. Potentially valuable line management input is reduced to a minimum (Lenz and Lyles 1985).

II. CORPORATE OBJECTIVES

As described in the previous section, all corporate planning frameworks assume that explicit, long-term objectives are a necessary prerequisite for the formulation of a coherent corporate strategy. Corporate planning is, then, concerned with translating specified objectives into operational form, and with devising ways to achieve these operational objectives. It is not concerned with the origins or type of objective formally injected into the planning process. The behavioural and political processes described in chapter 2 that are inherent in the formation of 'organisational' objectives are, in principle, beyond the scope of normative corporate planning activity. Objectives of individuals and various coalitions still have some influence during the design and choice of strategies and throughout the implementation of strategies, but, traditionally, corporate planning techniques have ignored these effects, assuming instead an organisationally rational approach to the analysis.

In considering the variety of possible organisational objectives, Ackoff (1970) makes the useful distinction between stylistic objectives and performance objectives. According to Ackoff, stylistic objectives 'define in qualitative terms the kind of activity in which an organisation wants to be involved'. Such objectives will include statements about how the organisation will conduct business in general terms, and top management's attitude to risk taking. Performance objectives require operational definition and should be quantified so that progress towards them can be measured. These performance objectives might be economic, for example, growth in market share, maintenance of a satisfactory liquidity position, reduction in stock levels; or 'non-economic', such as the improvement of employee relations, or maintenance of the public standing of the company. At first sight non-economic objectives may appear difficult to quantify, but they usually have components that can be quantified: for example, poor employee relations might be evident from high wastage rates and absenteeism.

Where there are a number of equally important objectives, the problem of formulating strategy will be complicated because the relative importance of each objective must be taken into account. In particular, where objectives are inconsistent, choice of strategies may require trade-offs to be made between the conflicting objectives. For example, some degree of trade-off between building efficiency or flexibility is always necessary.

Evidence discussed in chapter 2 (Dent, 1959; Bhaskar and McNamee, 1983), suggested that profit is the most important single objective business organisations pursue, although the importance of other objectives should be recognised. For corporate planning purposes, it would appear appropriate to take return on shareholders' capital (ROSC) as the primary performance objective.

Quinn (1977) found that successful top managers announce only a few corporate objectives at any one time, and those they do announce tend to (i) reflect or help build a developing consensus, (ii) be broad enough in concept to allow opportunism and (iii) be sufficiently distant in time that a variety of options could ensure their achievement. Announcing only a few objectives serves to focus attention and reduce potential conflicts between inconsistent objectives. Broadly stated objectives, like being 'the best' or 'the leader' in a particular product-market, may be more easily adopted by employees than specific numerical goals. This suggests a very superficial level of corporate planning with minimal prespecification of corporate strategies. In a formal planning framework the intention is to be much more specific about future strategies. This implies more operationally meaningful objectives; quantification of key objectives such as ROSC is necessary to provide practical guidance for strategy. Quantification of the ROSC objective does not, however, preclude properties (ii) and (iii) above.

In an uncertain world it is clear that long-term maximisation of return on shareholders' equity (or indeed long-term maximisation of any other objective) has little operational meaning. It is necessary to set specific target levels for ROSC that the organisation will attempt to achieve in future years. Hussey (1982) suggested that the following factors should be taken into consideration when setting such profitability targets:

1. Trends over previous years as they provide a baseline for growth.
2. Progress by other similar companies.
3. Returns available to shareholders from alternative investments.
4. Ambitions and confidence of the chief executive.
5. The level of return required by the company if it is to maintain a healthy position in the market.

In considering the returns required by shareholders, the most important consideration is the rates of return obtainable from alternative forms of investment. In addition, high target rates of return usually imply higher levels of risk than lower rates of return; therefore, in considering returns available elsewhere, due regard must be paid to level of risk associated with alternative investments. In particular, it is important to distinguish between the two components of a share's risk, market risk and specific risk. Specific risk consists of that risk which is related to the organisation's specific factors, whilst market risk reflects factors which affect all shares in the market. The returns required by shareholders need only compensate them for the levels of market risk taken on because the specific risk of individual shares can be virtually eliminated by a diversified holding of shares. A share's market risk is reflected by its beta, or sensitivity to general market movements. The beta of a share is the ratio of the covariance of the share's rate of return with respect to returns on the market portfolio, to the variance of returns on the market portfolio. Beta can be estimated for a particular share by the slope of the regression line of past returns on the share against corresponding past returns on the market portfolio. The rate of return required by shareholders of a share i is then the expected rate of return on share i, ER_i as implied by the capital asset pricing model (see for example, Brealey and Myers, 1984):

$$ER_i = R_F + (ER_m - R_F) \beta_i$$

where R_F is the risk-free rate of return, reflected, for example, by the interest rate on government securities, ER_m is the expected return on the market portfolio and β_i is the beta of the particular share i.

This implies that shareholders require a return over a given investment period equal to the risk-free interest rate plus a premium for the market risk associated with the share. The equation also formalises the notion that a firm should seek a return for shareholders which corresponds with the average return in the firm's industrial sector; that is, with firms that exhibit a similar level of market risk.

This analysis seems to imply that managers should not be concerned with managing specific risk because such behaviour will not be rewarded by the stock market (Bettis, 1983). This conclusion is erroneous. A preoccupation of corporate planning is the identification or creation of opportunities to earn higher returns and/or reduce specific risks facing the organisation. However, there is no contradiction; organisations that can reduce *downside* specific risk will increase expected returns for shareholders. The apparent contradiction arises because the capital asset pricing model assumes a captial market in equilibrium; in reality a constantly changing and uncertain environment gives rise to opportunities for improved risk/return trade-offs.

Projects or strategies should only be undertaken if the expected return from them is sufficiently high to reward the organisation for the level of risk undertaken. In total, the various strategies of the organisation must promise the required rate of return on shareholders' capital. If some activities promise low returns but are relatively risk free, the organisation will need to undertake other activities that promise returns higher than the required ROSC to ensure that the expected return on all operations corresponds to the required return.

In the short term this approach should present little difficulty, as the rate of return required by shareholders will be obtained from estimated values of beta and expected market rates of return. For the longer term, such a procedure will be subject to increasing uncertainty. At the very least, the value of the firm's beta may alter significantly as a result of new strategies or changes in the firm's relationship with other firms. The difficulty in determining appropriate long-term rates of return may help to explain the use of so called surrogate goals, acting as proxies for the main profitability objective, as observed by Bhaskar and McNamee (1983) in their study of UK companies. This difficulty was also noted by Ansoff (1965) who suggested a hierarchy of proxy objectives derived from commonly generated management ratios for which quantitative targets could more readily be set. In particular Ansoff advocated proxies relating to competitive strength and internal efficiency. Under competitive strength a firm could set long-term growth objectives for sales or market share and stability objectives, for example, in respect of future earnings. Internal efficiency objectives could relate to improved profit margins, higher turnover of inventories and the age and condition of plant and machinery. However, it is difficult to see why objectives in these areas, particularly in respect of efficiency, should not be pursued continuously, and long-term future earnings targets set on an approximate basis in addition.

In the private sector, the existence of a primary performance objective, ROSC, greatly simplifies the determination of corporate objectives. In the public sector, specification of objectives is much more problematic. In particular, there is no primary performance objective, but a multitude of potential performance objectives whose relative importance varies with the power of the groups who support them. This has led Lindblom (1959, 1979) to describe public policy making as 'disjointed incrementalism'. Given the difficulty in agreeing a clear priority for objectives or performance criteria, decision making becomes a highly political process where a problem-orientated, incremental approach is the only way of proceeding. Planning–

Programming–Budgeting systems, as outlined in chapter 9, represent an attempt to simplify the objective specification problem by dividing organisational activities into areas with common interests.

III. INFORMATION FOR STRATEGY FORMULATION

A rigorous and systematic approach to strategic planning requires careful assessment of the organisation's capabilities and the relevant business environment. Factors likely to require investigation are shown in table 10.1.

Internally, many resources possessed by the organisation will be difficult to quantify, but the extent of their availability and utility must be assessed. In considering any particular strategy it will be necessary to determine the resources required to implement the strategy, the rate at which they will have to be committed and the likelihood that these resources will be available when required. Choice of strategies will be restricted by the level of resources available. For example, expansion may be restricted by the availability of funds or the availability of suitably skilled managers.

Externally, the business environment for assessment can be identified by considering the scope of existing activities. In chapter 1 the environment was described in terms of levels of stability, complexity, market diversity and hostility. However, for strategy formulation purposes, more precise specification of the environment is appropriate. Thus, table 10.1 includes a wide variety of environmental factors grouped into five areas of concern. In each of the five dimensions of the environment it will be important to identify (i) significant events, (ii) trends, both general and industry specific, and (iii) the expectations of different pressure groups (Neubauer and Solomon, 1977).

A key difficulty for many organisations starting to plan formally is obtaining the information needed for corporate planning. Existing management information systems are likely to be control orientated. Often there is 'budgetary bias' in early plans because of the comparatively large amounts of short-run data provided by accounting and finance departments. Instead of primary concern being with production and marketing factors, financial factors attract the greatest attention. Thus an empirical study by Ringbakk (1971) found that most firms in the study needed greater input in the planning process from sales, marketing and research and development. The introduction of corporate planning generally implies a substantial upgrading of management information systems.

Forecasting the Future

Assessment of all the factors listed in table 10.1 must take in the future position as well as the present. In addition to the complexities of monitoring and analysing many aspects of the present, planners need to take a view of the future in an environment that may be characterised by erratic, and apparently discontinuous, changes.

In a relatively stable environment, uncertainty about the future can be reduced to acceptable levels by identifying trends based on extrapolation of established patterns. However, predicting novel changes in trends during periods of rapid change is very difficult. Forecasting techniques based on statistical extrapolation, such as exponential smoothing or the Box–Jenkins approach, may be of limited use. For example, Ortman and Blackman (1981) reported a considerable decrease in the

Table 10.1 *Dimensions of organisation capability and business environment*

Dimensions of organisation capability	Dimensions of the business environment
Administrative systems Organisational structure Management information systems Investment appraisal procedures Operating and control procedures Service functions (e.g: computing, legal, finance, business development)	*Economic factors* Inflationary or deflationary trends Monetary policies, interest rates, currency exchange rates Fiscal policies Balance of payments Stage of business cycle
Personnel Number, location, type Age, experience, ability Turnover patterns Technical and entrepreneurial skills Organisational requirements Organisational culture Reward systems	*Government/legal factors* Government as customer Subsidies, grants Regulation of industry Trade protection
Production Production facilities: size, location, efficiency, appropriateness Production processes Purchasing function Research and development Breadth of product line Nature of product: quality, capabilities, patents	*Market/competitive factors* Demand: identity of customers nature of needs being satisfied demographic factors Competition: identity of existing and potential competitors entry or exits of major competitors, major initiatives by competitors, possible substitutes or complements for current products
Marketing and sales Market standing: image, brand names, reputation, power Nature and size of sales Distribution channels Customer service Sales force	*Supply factors* Bargaining power of suppliers Raw materials and components: availability, quality, cost Developments in raw materials or components
Finance Capital: availability, cost Earnings: size, stability, growth pattern Liquidity Gearing	*Societal factors* Social values Leisure time Consumer spending patterns Levels of education Expectations of business

accuracy of sales and profits projections between 1968 and 1975 for a sample of 275 USA companies. They suggested that this was due to the increasingly erratic economic climate in the 70s. In these situations, causal models are needed which estimate the causal relationship between a dependent variable and a set of independent variables. Particularly useful may be econometric models of key economic or industry variables. Makridakis (1981) has pointed to the need for planners to be able to distinguish between random deviations from forecasts and the beginnings of systematic changes at as early a stage as possible. This suggests planners should be increasingly vigilant in monitoring and seeking explanations for observed deviations from forecasts. This accords with Ansoff's (1979) analysis of strategic change. Firms are experiencing an increasingly turbulent environment, yet advances in technology and the complexity of the environment mean that organisations require longer to react to changes and prepare appropriate strategies. Ansoff points to a need for firms experiencing highly turbulent environments to move away from an anticipatory attitude to the future, towards a more vigilant posture where the firm seeks out the weak, early signals of impending changes.

In the previous chapter it was suggested that business forecasts should not be based solely on economic and technological factors, but should also take into account social and political factors. The increasing need for chief executives to concern themselves with social and political matters clearly lends support to this view (see, for example, Steiner and Kunin 1981). Firms require forecasting methods that make use of the weak signals of change, whether of a quantitative or qualitative nature, and approaches that encompass areas of social and political development. Such forecasting techniques involve systematic monitoring of the environment and may be considered under the general heading of futures research.

Futures research is based on the premise that a careful analysis of the environment can yield useful insights into likely developments in the future. The aim of systematic futures research is to 'use presently available concrete data to make statements about possible concrete developments in support of long-term policy forming and decision making'; the aim is 'not so much to forecast as to show the possibilities for influencing, by laying bare the causal relationships of mutual influence patterns' (Wissema, 1981, p. 29, 30). Essentially, futures research is concerned with the identification of change processes. Wissema noted that this activity is complicated by four factors in particular:
1. mutual influences between change processes;
2. existence of trends in agglomerated form;
3. some change processes are hidden from perception and
4. casual relationships are complex and not fully understood.

Notwithstanding these problems, the futures researcher is concerned to identify in the area of interest: (i) the nature of current change processes; (ii) factors that may initiate changes; (iii) the phases involved in the different change processes identified and (iv) the nature of interactions between different change processes. In view of the difficulties outlined, and the often unquantifiable nature of changes, it is perhaps not surprising that much futures research is of a somewhat subjective nature. In this context it is as well to recall the systematic psychological biases cited in chapters 5 and 9 which will also influence the research process. Specialist techniques, such as the Delphi process (Stander and Rickards, 1975), morphological analysis (Zwicky, 1962), cross-impact analysis (Helmer, 1981) and scenario building (Lorenz, 1980; Beck, 1982), may be used to provide more objective and less biased analysis, but as yet the problem of subjectivity has not been overcome.

Referring to a number of empirical studies into the practice of strategic planning, Eppink (1981) suggested several reasons for the apparently limited use being made of forecasts derived from futures research. One reason, doubtless related to the subjective nature of forecasts, may be that futures research often fails to show the rationale behind the 'forecasts': cause–effect relationships are not clearly indicated, studies are too speculative and not based on sound information. Eppink also suggested that managers may be reluctant to accept forecasts because they tend to be vague and inconclusive, require drastic changes within the organisation or delineate future developments that management feel to be totally unlikely. Such observations imply that organisations seeking to make use of futures research should be aware of the psychological and organisational factors that may cause a reluctance to use the results of systematic futures research.

Strengths, Weaknesses, Opportunities and Threats Assessment

Assessment of the organisational and environmental factors in table 10.1 should provide a basis from which possible strategic options can be identified and evaluated.

A simple and traditionally advocated preliminary interpretation of this information involves identifying organisational strengths and weaknesses, and the environmental threats and opportunities facing the organisation. Possible strategies for the organisation can then be circumscribed in terms of options that exploit or build on strengths, reduce or eliminate weaknesses, exploit opportunities, and overcome or eliminate threats.

The identification of strengths, weaknesses, opportunities and threats is usually referred to by acronyms such as WOTS UP analysis (Steiner and Miner, 1982; Rowe et al. 1982) or TOWS analysis (Weihrich, 1982). More refined analytical techniques, which serve to narrow down and specify possible strategies more precisely, are beyond the scope of this chapter. A discussion of WOTS UP or TOWS analysis is of interest here because it is such a widely used technique for simplifying the information processing problem facing corporate planners.

Identification of strengths, weaknesses, opportunities and threats requires a knowledge and understanding of both the external environment and the internal operations of the organisation. In certain instances strengths, weaknesses, opportunities or threats may be readily apparent, but often they may be unrecognised without determined efforts to identify them. Sometimes obvious strengths, weaknesses, opportunities or threats may obscure underlying causes. For example, poor market-image may reflect an underlying weakness in lack of marketing or engineering expertise. Alternatively, closer examination of the underlying reasons for apparent strengths or weaknesses may reveal extenuating circumstances which make the identification of persisting strengths or weaknesses less justifiable. In a study of the process of strengths and weaknesses assessment in six firms, Stevenson (1976) found that management evaluations were influenced by company affiliation, areas of responsibility, and level in the organisation. Managers at higher levels tended to be less concerned about production, research and development attributes, but more concerned with personnel and financial attributes than lower level managers. In addition, Stevenson found a general tendency for greater optimism at higher management levels although marketing and financial attributes were usually perceived more positively by lower level management.

A useful way of assessing organisation strengths and weaknesses is to develop a 'Competence Profile' of the organisation's major skills and resources rated with respect to other organisations with the same capabilities (Ansoff 1965). Ideally organisation skills and resources should be rated systematically against both competitors' capabilities and those of other industries in which such capabilities may be found. In this way some 'absolute' notion of organisational capabilities can be developed which does not depend on the peculiarities of individual product-markets. Even so, the assessment will remain highly subjective. Limited data, and the qualitative nature of many of the factors make this unavoidable.

Similar issues arise in the assessment of environmental threats and opportunities. An additional difficulty is that the level of perceived environmental threats or opportunities will depend to some extent on the existence of related organisational strengths and weaknesses. The use of 'Competence Profiles' will serve to avoid perceptions of environmental threats and opportunities influencing assessment of strengths and weaknesses.

Behavioural Aspects of Information Processing

Inevitably, perceptions of organisational activities and the environment will be incomplete and subjective. Judgement has to be exercised in deciding on the quality and quantity of information to be gathered. Subjective interpretation of the information collected will also be necessary, particularly where information is of an uncertain, qualitative, or ambiguous nature. Under such circumstances, planners may exhibit unintentional cognitive biases in interpreting situations, arising from the use of simplifying heuristics (see chapter 5). In the context of strategic planning, possible adverse effects of such biases include underutilised information, inaccurate prediction of consequences of options, inaccurate assessment of risks and premature rejection of options (Barnes, 1984; Schwenk, 1984).

Another consequence of subjective interpretation of the environment is that events and situations are always open to multiple interpretations. Indeed, behaviour of a competitor may be explainable in terms of an alternative perspective of the relevant product-market and the capabilities and objectives of actors in that market. Novel interpretations which run counter to conventional wisdom often occur when firms enter an industry of which they have no specific experience (Smircich and Stubbart, 1985).

Where strategic formulation involves the participation of significant numbers of managers, information may be filtered or used selectively by particular groups. Instead of participation leading to an integration of ideas and a robust corporate strategy, coalitions with opposing viewpoints may interpret information selectively to build their own arguments and refute those of other coalitions. To seek effective representation of their case, each coalition may limit information gathering and analysis to its own perspective, resulting in periodic negotiations and discontinuities in the decision process through delays and rethinking. Moreover, the existence of conflicting interests may lead to the withholding, distortion, and manipulation of information, and the disguising of intentions. Bargaining and negotiation may give rise to an emphasis on the appearance of rationality in the organisational sense, rather than emphasis on organisational rationality *per se*. Thus analytical techniques may be used simply to legitimise a particular viewpoint and disguise the subjective nature of inputs (Narayanan and Fahey, 1982).

Bargaining and negotiating in this manner are an attempt to gain general acceptance for a particular world view. Multiple interpretations are considered irreconcilable and inappropriate. Addressing this problem, Emshoff and Mitroff (1978) suggested that most differences in strategic viewpoint are actually due to differences in fundamental assumptions about the nature of a situation, rather than to disagreement about issues of fact concerning the viability of particular strategies. Accordingly, Emshoff and Mitroff proposed an approach to strategy formulation, called 'Strategic Assumptions Analysis', designed to integrate the different perspectives of participating managers but at the same time encourage wide ranging, creative planning activity. Their approach is based on the following premises.

1. If executives can agree on a set of assumptions they are willing to accept, they are very likely to agree on a strategy based on those assumptions.
2. When strategy options are formulated, most of the critical assumptions upon which they rest are not understood by those who formulate them.
3. Data analysis can be used to facilitate the emergence of implicit assumptions upon which strategy rests.
4. Data analysis can also be used to facilitate executive agreement on assumptions that are not obviously valid or invalid, as well as the relative importance of assumptions that address different aspects of the problems.

In Strategic Assumptions Analysis, management teams identify extreme strategy options, along with the assumption bases implied by each option. At this stage the validity of these assumptions is not questioned. Next a dialectic analysis is undertaken. Different teams create other possible strategy options by considering conditions under which plausible assumptions in the initial assumption bases may be negated. A dialectical debate then takes place between the teams, which highlights the different ways of viewing each situation. Subsequently a process of assumption negotiation leads by synthesis and compromise to a list of key assumptions that all can agree on (Mitroff, Emshoff and Kilmann, 1979). Finally, corporate strategy is deduced from the list of key assumptions. Emshoff and Mitroff argued that this final choice of strategy will usually be straightforward because the number of feasible strategies is restricted by the list of key assumptions, and consensus regarding particular choices of strategy is created during the whole process of analysis.

IV. EVALUATING STRATEGIC OPTIONS

Strategic options invariably involve investment decisions, but discounted cash flow (DCF) techniques are of limited value in their evaluation. The logic of DCF techniques is compelling, but the nature of strategic options makes their rigorous application impractical. The use of DCF techniques requires options to be well defined in terms of scope, relevant cash flows and financial criteria. Strategic options are usually loosely defined, involving many qualitative factors and interdependencies with other options.

As detailed in section I, the problem of formulating corporate strategy can be managed by formulating options in a hierarchical manner (figure 10.2). At the corporate level, strategy is formulated and evaluated in broad terms focusing on the long-term constitution of the organisation's portfolio of strategic business units (SBUs).

At the SBU level, competitive strategies are formulated in the context of the corporate portfolio investment strategy. At this level, shorter planning horizons and more detailed specification of strategies are appropriate. Interactions with strategies of other SBUs are assumed to be minimal. At lower levels, generic competitive strategies must be refined into more operationally meaningful strategies or action plans.

Accordingly, the use of DCF techniques to evaluate options typically becomes more feasible as individual strategies become more precisely delineated. However, this need not confine the use of DCF techniques to middle management levels and below (figure 10.2). Options involving large expenditure on plant such as buildings, power stations, oil rigs or ships, would be the province of top management or SBU-level management. Such options would be amenable to evaluation using DCF techniques and appropriate sensitivity analysis around uncertain future cash flows.

Strategic Portfolio Analysis

Strategic portfolio analysis offers a means of determining a long-term investment programme for the organisation's portfolio of SBUs. The approach identifies investment priorities between SBUs, taking into account the future contribution of each SBU to the organisation as a whole. Conceptually it resembles a crude form of DCF evaluation of each SBU.

Strategic portfolio analysis involves plotting each SBU in the corporate portfolio on a two-dimensional matrix according to SBU profitability or competitive capability and attractiveness of each SBU's area of business. The relative size and location of each SBU on the matrix is then used to determine a corporate investment strategy for the organisation and to identify SBUs where investment should be increased or decreased.

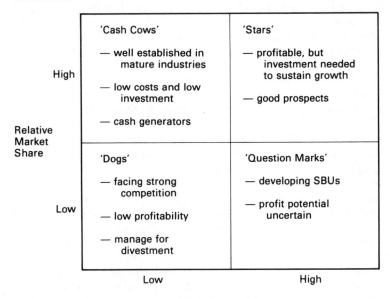

Figure 10.3 *The BCG Growth–share matrix*

Several different matrices are described in the literature (Robinson, Hitchens and Wade, 1978; Ansoff and Leontiades, 1976; Patel and Younger, 1978; Barksdale and Harris, 1982). The most widely known is the growth–share matrix developed by the Boston Consulting Group, often referred to as the BCG matrix. SBUs are plotted on this matrix according to the growth rate of the market in which each competes, and their relative market share. The matrix is shown in figure 10.3.

For long-term profitability a firm should aim to always have a balanced portfolio of developing SBUs ('question marks'), strong, high-growth SBUs ('stars'), and established, profitable SBUs ('cash cows'). Grids like the BCG matrix can be criticised because they make a number of simplistic assumptions about relationships between strategic factors like profitability and market share, or market growth rate and industry attractiveness (Porter, 1982; Coate, 1983).

An implicit assumption of the portfolio approach is that SBUs can be managed effectively as distinct strategic units. It is assumed that broad directives and resource allocations can be determined at a corporate level which require different SBU managers to pursue very different objectives. The SBU concept does not simply mean that each SBU is managed as an independent profit centre. The SBU concept requires each SBU to be managed for the benefit of the organisation as a whole. Thus SBUs identified as 'cash cows' must be managed so as to maximise the generation of cash which is required for investment in other SBUs. Managers of SBUs identified as 'dogs' are expected to manage for divestment and liquidation. Not all SBU managers will be in control of the high growth, promising areas of business which constitute the 'star' SBUs. Ideally, each type of SBU should be managed differently from other types of SBU. This raises the question of whether a firm can develop, and more importantly retain, the diversified managerial talent to achieve this aim (Hall 1978). To facilitate this approach Bettis and Hall (1983) suggested that portfolio planning organisations should vary managerial selection criteria, reward systems and investment criteria according to the strategic role played by each SBU. In practice firms tend not to alter formal administrative systems in accordance with SBU roles because of the administrative complexities that are involved. Not only would the organisation need to set up different systems for the different types of SBU, but it would also require systems responsive enough to switch managers between SBUs when the role played by any SBU was changed. More realistically, corporate management adopt a varied approach in an informal way – for example, by not calling for across the board cuts in manpower, or by the manner in which executives are moved around the organisation (Haspeslagh 1982).

A fundamental problem with the concept of strategic portfolio analysis is the division of the organisation into SBUs that can be regarded as separate business activities for strategic planning purposes. Haspeslagh (1982) noted that SBUs were generally defined as aggregations of existing operating units, but over half the companies in his survey classified at least some SBUs as different from operating units. Larger companies were more likely to define SBUs which did not coincide with operating units. For example, within General Electric nine groups and 48 divisions were reorganised into 43 SBUs crossing traditional group and divisional lines; a housewares SBU resulted from integrating food preparation appliances manufactured in three separate divisions (Hall 1978). In practice the criteria used to define SBUs will depend to a large degree on the nature of the interdependencies between SBUs that are considered acceptable and on the need to avoid creating an excessive number of SBUs. As a guiding principle, Haspeslagh suggests that SBUs be defined to 'incorporate control over those resources that will be the key strategic variables in the future'.

Strategy Design and Evaluation

Throughout the planning process within each SBU, the design and the evaluation of specific strategies frequently take place concurrently. Dispassionate, organisationally rational evaluation of proposals becomes difficult as evaluation is entwined with the creative and political processes involved in devising suitable courses of action. Failure to identify ready-made solutions to novel and complex strategic issues forces management to modify existing options or devise new, custom-made solutions. The design of custom-made solutions is usually a complex, iterative procedure that proceeds in the following manner:

> the designers may begin with a vague image of some ideal solution. They factor their decision into a sequence of nested design and search cycles, essentially working their way through a decision tree, with the decisions at each node more narrow and focussed than the last. Failure at any node can lead to cycling back to an earlier node. Thus a solution crystallises as the designers grope along, building their solution brick by brick without really knowing what it will look like until it is completed.
> (Mintzberg et al., 1976; p. 256.)

A hypothesis strongly supported by Mintzberg et al.'s study is that strategic investment decision processes produce only one custom-made solution (Mazzolini,

1981). One reason for this may be the time and cost involved in designing custom-made solutions. In other circumstances, where the cost of generating alternatives is small, as in the modification of existing solutions, organisations may be prepared to develop a second, alternative choice for consideration. Another reason for design activity terminating with only one custom-made solution is that would-be contenders to a preferred alternative are filtered out during the design process. Thus certain alternatives may not receive full attention and development because they are rejected at an early stage. Early elimination of alternatives may be based on intuitively perceived and non-formalised constraints such as perceptions of management reactions, incongruity with technological capabilities, or uncertainty with respect to the availability of resources (Alexander, 1979; Bower, 1970; Carter, 1971; Fahey, 1981). Bargaining and negotiation between coalitions representing different views may also lead to the development of a single compromise solution, as initial proposals are subjected to mollifying modifications. Thus, difficulty in formulating strategy may be due not only to creative and analytical limitations, but also to difficulty in gaining acceptance for proposals as a result of insufficient power or influence (Narayanan and Fahey, 1982). Strategic decisions in particular depend for successful implementation on the building of acceptance and commitment amongst those who will be expected to carry the strategy through. Acceptance and commitment need to be continually fostered from the earliest stages of strategy formulation.

This requirement led Brunsson (1980) to question the desirability of normative models of investment appraisal that emphasise the selection of desirable projects and rejection of undesirable ones. Brunsson has suggested that a rational approach in which all the pros and cons of a project are considered can have dysfunctional consequences. In particular, perceived uncertainty about projects is increased. This results in fewer projects being accepted and the chances of their succeeding being reduced by a lack of commitment.

Brunsson argued that an impressionist approach that serves to build commitment to a project may be superior. With this approach evaluators concentrate on finding evidence or arguments to support a first impression of the project, rather than trying to find out all the positive and negative characteristics of the project. The tendency to accept projects is relatively high, but since the approach encourages increased commitment, the chances of an accepted project succeeding are also increased.

The preceding discussion highlights the problem of using evaluative DCF techniques which require the estimation of cash flows associated with a strategic option. DCF techniques may be useful during design activity to help filter out partially formulated options. In this role identification and estimation of cash flows associated with individual options is clearly problematic. Emphasis should be on relatively simple models, and rapid, robust evaluations incorporating sensitivity analyses. If a single option is the result of much design activity and impressionist activity to build commitment, subsequent evaluation using DCF techniques would appear to be superfluous (King, 1975).

V. FINANCIAL PLANNING MODELS

It should be evident from the preceding discussion that the strategic planning process can become exceedingly complex. Of course, a sophisticated planning process is not always necessary, and for small companies planning may only need to be in very general terms. However, for larger companies a more detailed approach is essential, and in these cases long-term planning can only be carried out effectively with computer assistance. Most organisations that use computers in the corporate planning process make use of software that models the major financial implications of future strategies. These financial models are usually deterministic, so that all required financial variables are simply calculated directly from data fed into the model. Relationships between variables are specified either by the logic of the model equations or as assumptions or policies input as data (see, for example, Grinyer and Wooller 1978; Naylor and Schauland 1976). The precise nature of the output will clearly depend on the type of financial model constructed, but, for corporate planning purposes, a minimum specification would be estimated balance sheets and profit and loss accounts for each year up to the planning horizon. Additional information is usually helpful in the form of projected flow of funds statements, an estimated capital investment programme and perhaps projected net contributions to profit of existing and proposed new products.

General Advantages of Computerised Planning Models

An obvious advantage of using computerised financial models in the planning process is that large numbers of calculations can be performed very rapidly. This enables planning to be carried out in a more rigorous fashion than would be possible with a manual system. Moreover, planning calculations can be repeated quickly under different sets of assumptions with comparative ease. This is useful in an iterative planning process where adjustments to proposed actions, and perhaps changes in unrealistic objectives, are necessary before a satisfactory plan is produced.

Another advantage of being able to repeat calculations rapidly under differing assumptions is that it is practicable to carry out sensitivity analysis and to answer questions of a 'what if?' nature. Sensitivity analysis involves recalculating all planning variables under varying sets of assumptions in a systematic way. Unfortunately, the number of combinations of possible circumstances to be considered quickly becomes unacceptably high as the number of key variables increases. Nevertheless, if such sensitivity runs are carried out selectively, followed by intelligent examination of the results, a number of important advantages accrue. Firstly, an understanding of the way future performance can be affected by changed circumstances can be obtained. Secondly, the significance and desirability of the various model assumptions can be assessed. Thirdly, proposed plans can be tested for robustness in the light of an uncertain future. Finally, where plans are over-reliant on particular outcomes occurring, sensitivity analyses can indicate the extent to which plans should be more flexible.

Model Construction

A major consideration when constructing and developing a computerised financial planning model is the level of detail that should be incorporated. In a well-known, and still useful, description of the construction of a corporate financial model at the Sun Oil Company, Gershefski (1969) described this decision as the choice between 'forest' and 'tree' designs. The forest approach implies a model of the entire organisation with little attention to detail, whilst the tree approach is to model individual parts of the organisation in fine detail. Initially, the Sun Oil model was developed as a broad scope model which considered the parent company in detail but treated subsidiaries' operations as gross inputs. This served to provide a means of consolidating existing functional plans into an overall corporate picture. Gershefski noted that the model was further designed to conform closely to Sun Oil's existing accounting system and to produce financial reports following existing formats.

Clearly, there is a trade-off between complexity and comprehension. A complex model presents a number of difficulties. Firstly, it takes a long time to construct and test, often much longer than intended. Delays in producing such a model do not inspire management confidence in its potential value because they imply problems with design and errors in the model calculations that are having to be corrected. A second difficulty is the large quantity of data required by a complex model. Such data may be difficult to obtain, time consuming to feed into the model and expensive to maintain. Thirdly, a complex model can be very difficult to alter quickly and correctly when new features are required or assumptions built into the logic need updating (e.g. Schrieber, 1982). Taken together, these difficulties make it less convenient to carry out sensitivity analyses and test the effect of differing assumptions and policies on future organisational performance. Unless such analyses can be carried out rapidly, there will be a tendency to rely exclusively on 'best estimate' projections. This considerably reduces the value of carrying out planning calculations via a computer model.

The disadvantages of complex-integrated models are now well recognised. Thus, Grinyer and Wooller (1980) reported a trend away from this type of model to relatively simple, deterministic, simulation models. This followed an increase in the use of a modular approach to corporate model building in which small, application-specific models are linked together in a hierarchical fashion. Grinyer and Wooller noted a number of advantages of the modular approach over large, integrated models: (i) an earlier payoff is achieved after relatively little expenditure of time and money; (ii) managers can identify more closely with specific models clearly designed to meet their particular decision making needs; (iii) the models are more comprehensible to managers; (iv) individually the models have smaller data requirements; (v) individual models are more easily amended to meet changing circumstances, and more easily integrated into the planning process and (vi) data may be inspected and amended before transfer between models.

The construction and use of computerised planning models has been further simplified by the development of numerous computer modelling packages designed specifically for planning applications (Grinyer and Wooller, 1978). It seems likely, for example, that the development of spread-sheet packages like Lotus 1-2-3 has encouraged greater use of financial planning models. A further consequence of this provision has been the displacement of operational research specialists as the dominant model builders by accountants and planners (Higgins and Finn, 1977). The facility to construct financial planning models rapidly, and with the minimum of mathematical and computing expertise, has made it practicable for accountants and planners to become more active in developing planning models without the assistance of model building specialists. Grinyer and Wooller (1980) suggest that dominance of accountants in the field of financial modelling is likely to continue and may even extend to modelling beyond the financial domain.

The Role of Financial Models in the Planning Process

One effect of constructing a financial planning model is to give the planning process a degree of discipline that might otherwise be lacking. In any computer model, data input and planning assumptions require explicit specification and, in order to construct a model, management must define assumptions and policies precisely and unambiguously. This is frequently a valuable exercise in itself because it is often instrumental in bringing to the fore inconsistencies and controversies in the activities of the organisation. Subsequently, before the model can be run, the necessary data must be collected. The specification of this data must set out precisely the information required, and it follows that this also defines the minimum information that must be obtained for an effective planning exercise.

Once a suitable computer model has been constructed and the necessary data collected, the model can play a key role in charting the progress towards a final corporate plan. Initially, it provides a convenient way of collating information about the current situation and constructing a 'baseline' forecast of the future state of the organisation – assuming current trends and policies continue. This collation and simple projection has two significant benefits. Firstly, it is a useful way of checking the internal consistency of information collected. Secondly, the effects of external factors and the impact of a continuation of existing policies into the future are highlighted. This can lead to the identification of policies which cannot be allowed to continue, or suggest critical external factors which either need to be forecast with more accuracy or else investigated with a view to estimating their likely variability. Usually the construction of this 'base-line' projection is an aggregation process where information is gathered together and collated to produce estimates of future profits, and an indication of the return on shareholders' capital in future years. These latter figures can be compared directly with the desired rate of return on shareholders' capital to arrive at a measure of the planning gap that must be bridged by new strategies.

The need to choose a set of strategies which will fill this gap is another aspect of the planning process in which a computerised planning model can play a significant role. In order to choose appropriate strategies for the corporate plan, it is necessary to determine the net effect of the combined set of strategies in terms of their ability to meet the firm's objectives. A computerised model not only provides a framework for this testing of the joint effect of different strategies, but greatly facilitates such testing where the number of potential strategies and combinations of strategies is large. This is a further reason for adopting a modular approach to the construction of a planning model. The modules or subunits of the planning model can deal with different SBUs of the organisation and different resource areas such as production facilities, manpower and finance (Probert, 1981). Sets of strategies can then be selected and evaluated in the context of each SBU before the modules are merged to show the overall corporate effect of the strategies. This has the advantage of providing a detailed strategy and information on its effect for each SBU, as well as reducing the number of strategy combinations which need to be evaluated at a corporate level.

VI. SUMMARY

Most writers on corporate strategy advocate the use of a formalised approach to strategic planning. The typical analytical framework for formal planning distinguishes two levels of analysis: (i) evaluation and choice of areas of business activity and (ii) formulation of competitive strategy within each business area (figure 10.1). In administrative terms, top management first decides on the organisation's portfolio of strategic business units and then delegates responsibility for formulating more detailed competitive strategy to individual SBU managers. The resultant formal plans serve as a framework for making future incremental decisions in a coherent and consistent manner (figure 10.2).

The management accountant has a significant supporting role to play in the formal planning process. Firstly, there is a need to provide background information about the organisation's capabilities and the relevant business environment. This includes information about past performance, product mix, future sales, cost–volume–profit relationships, profit margins, capital expenditure and so on. As section III shows, even this kind of quantitative information will be highly uncertain and require subjective interpretation. Part of this provision of information may also include the determination of performance objectives, especially the identification of feasible profit targets and proxy objectives for the long term. Secondly, the management accountant can help in the evaluation of alternative strategic options, including assessment of risk as well as return. However, the use of DCF techniques may be restricted because of uncertainty about the nature of options and the number of qualitative factors that are relevant. The management accountant should beware of overselling DCF techniques in this context. Thirdly, the management accountant can help in presenting the effects of both SBU and corporate level plans in financial terms, and in translating the short-term implications of those plans into operating budgets. In respect of this work, financial planning models, which are increasingly the province of the management accountant, are indispensable. However, corporate plans should not be quantified in financial terms alone; the nature of other organisational resources, such as production capacity, raw materials and personnel, should be examined and planned for. The management accountant's role in respect of planning models suggests a natural progression towards involvement in the modelling and planning for these other resources.

Discussion in this chapter has concentrated on the process of formulating strategy. Little has been said about the problems of implementing, and subsequently controlling, strategy. Clearly the management accountant may also be involved in establishing control mechanisms for appraising and reviewing progress towards corporate objectives. The danger here, as discussed in section I, is that of viewing discrepancies between plans and actions as a failure of the planning process. Control must be cautiously exercised in acknowledgement of the need for flexibility in strategic plans.

REFERENCES

Ackoff, R. L., 1970. *Concept of Corporate Planning*. New York: Wiley.

Alexander, E. R., 1979. The design of alternatives in organisational contexts, *Administrative Science Quarterly*, **24**, pp. 382–404.

Ansoff, H. I., 1965. *Corporate Strategy – An Analytical Approach to Business Policy for Growth and Expansion*: McGraw-Hill.

Ansoff, H. I., 1979. *Strategic Management*. London: Macmillan.

Ansoff, H. I., 1984. *Implanting Strategic Management*. Englewood Cliffs, NJ: Prentice-Hall International.

Ansoff, H. I., Avner, J., Brandenburg, R. G., Partner, F. E., and Radosevitch, R., 1970. Does planning pay? The effect of planning on the success of acquisition in American firms, *Long Range Planning*, **3**(6), December, pp. 2–7.

Ansoff, H. I. and Leontiades, J. C., 1976. Strategic portfolio management, *Journal of General Management*, **4**(1).

Armstrong, J. S., 1982. The value of formal planning for strategic decisions: review of empirical research, *Strategic Management Journal*, **3**, pp. 197–211.

Barksdale, H. C. and Harris, C. E. Jr., 1982. Portfolio analysis and the product life cycle, *Long Range Planning*, **15**(6), December, pp. 74–83.

Barnes, J. H., 1984, Cognitive biases and their impact on strategic planning, *Strategic Management Journal*, **5**, pp. 129–137.

Beck, P. W., 1982. Corporate planning for an uncertain future, *Long Range Planning*, **15**(4), August, pp. 12–21.

Bettis, R. A., 1983. Modern financial theory, corporate strategy and public policy: three conundrums, *Academy of Management Review*, **8**(3), pp. 406–415.

Bettis, R. A. and Hall, W. K., 1983. The business portfolio approach – where it falls down in practice. *Long Range Planning*, **16**(2), April, pp. 95–104.

Bhaskar, K. and McNamee, P., 1983. Multiple objectives in accounting and finance, *Journal of Business Finance and Accounting*, **10**(4), pp. 595–621.

Boulton, W. R., Franklin, S. G., Lindsay, W. M. and Rue, L. W., 1982. How are companies planning now?–a survey, *Long Range Planning*, **15**(1), February, pp. 82–86.

Bower, J. L., 1970. *Managing the Resource Allocation Process*. Cambridge, MA: Harvard University Press.

Brealey, R. and Myers, S., 1984. *Principles of Corporate Finance*, 2nd edn. Singapore: McGraw-Hill International.

Bresser, R. K. and Bishop, R. C., 1983. Dysfunctional effects of formal planning: Two theoretical explanations, *Academy of Management Review*, **8** (4) October pp. 588–599.

Brunsson, N., 1980. The functions of project evaluation, *R&D Management*, **10**(2), February, pp. 61–65.

Camillus, J. C., 1982. Reconciling logical incrementalism and synoptic formalism, *Strategic Management Journal*, **3** (3), July-September pp. 277–284.

Carter, E. E., 1971. The behavioural theory of the firm and top level corporate decisions, *Administrative Science Quarterly*, **16** pp. 413–428.

Chakravarthy, B. S. and Lorange, P., 1984. Managing strategic adaptation: options in administrative systems design, *Interfaces*, **14** (1), January-February pp. 34–46.

Coate, M. B., 1983. Pitfalls in portfolio planning, *Long Range Planning* **16** (3) June, pp. 47–56.

Dent, J. K., 1959. Organisational correlates of the goals of business management, *Personnel Psychology* **12** (3), Autumn, pp. 365–394.

Emshoff, J. R. and Mitroff, I. I., 1978. Improving the effectiveness of corporate planning, *Business Horizons*, October, pp. 49–60.

Eppink, D. J., 1981. Futures research: is it used? *Long Range Planning* **14** (2), March-April, pp. 33–36.

Fahey, L., 1981. On strategic management decision processes, *Strategic Management Journal* **2** pp. 43–60.

Gershefski, G. W., 1969. Building a corporate financial model, *Harvard Business Review* **47** (4), July-August, pp. 61–72.

Gilmore, F. F. and Brandenburg, R. G., 1962. Anatomy of corporate planning, *Harvard Business Review* **40** (6) November-December pp. 61–69.

Glueck, W. F., 1980. *Business Policy and Strategic Management*, 3rd edn. New York: McGraw-Hill.

Grinyer, P. H. and Wooller, J., 1978. *Corporate Models Today*, 2nd edn. London: ICAEW.

Grinyer, P. H. and Wooller, J., 1980. An overview of a decade of corporate modelling in the UK, *Accounting and Business Research*, Winter, pp. 41–49.

Hall, W. K., 1978. SBUs: hot, new topic in the management of diversification, *Business Horizons*, February.

Haspeslagh, P., 1982. Portfolio planning – uses and limits, *Harvard Business Review*, January-February, pp. 98–73.

Helmer, O., 1981. Reassessment of cross-impact analysis, *Futures*, **13**(5), October, pp. 389–400.

Higgins, J. C. and Finn, R., 1977. Planning models in the UK: a survey, *Omega*, **5**(2), pp. 133–147.

Hofer, C. W. and Schendel, D., 1978. *Strategy Formulation: Analytical Concepts*. St. Paul, Minn: West Publishing.

Hussey, D. E., 1982. *Corporate Planning: Theory and Practice*, 2nd edn: Oxford: Pergamon Press.

Karger, D. and Malik, Z., 1975. Long range planning and organisational performance, *Long Range Planning*, **8**(6), December.

King, P., 1975. Is the emphasis of capital budgeting theory misplaced? *Journal of Business Finance and Accounting,* **2**(1), Spring, pp. 69–82.

Lenz, R. T. and Lyles, M. A., 1985. Paralysis by analysis: is your planning system becoming too rational?, *Long Range Planning* **18** (4) August, pp. 64–72.

Lindblom, C. E., 1959. The science of muddling through, *Public Administration Review,* **19**, pp. 79–99.

Lindblom, C. E., 1979. Still muddling, not yet through. *Public Administration Review,* **39**, pp. 517–526.

Loasby, B. J., 1967. Long-range formal planning in perspective, *Journal of Management Studies* **4**, pp. 300–308.

Lorange, P., 1980. *Corporate Planning – An Executive Viewpoint*: Prentice-Hall.

Lorenz, C., 1980. Shell strikes a refined way of exploring the future, *The Financial Times*, 4th March.

Lyles, M. A., 1981. Formulating strategic problems: empirical analysis and model development, *Strategic Management Journal*, **2** pp. 61–75.

Makridakis, S., 1981. If we cannot forecast how can we plan? *Long Range Planning* **14** (3), May-June pp. 10–20.

Mazzolini, R., 1981. How strategic decisions are made, *Long Range Planning* **14**, pp. 84–96.

Mintzberg, H., Raisinghani, D. and Theoret, A., 1976. The structure of unstructured decision processes, *Administrative Science Quarterly* **21** pp. 246–275.

Mitroff, I. I., Emshoff, J. R. and Kilmann, R. H., 1979. Assumptional analysis: a methodology for strategic problem solving, *Management Science,* **25**(6), June, pp. 583–593.

Narayanan, V. K. and Fahey, L., 1982. The micro politics of strategy formulation, *Academy of Management Review* **7**(1) pp. 25–34.

Naylor, T. H. and Schauland, H., 1976. A survey of users of corporate simulation models, *Management Science* **22** (9) May, pp. 927–937.

Neubauer, F. F. and Solomon, N. B., 1977. A managerial approach to environmental assessment, *Long Range Planning* **10**(2) April, pp. 13–20.

Ortman, R. F. and Blackman, D. D., 1981. Corporate planning – how successful is it?, *Management Accounting*, July, pp. 16–20.

Patel, P. and Younger, M., 1978. A frame of reference for strategy development, *Long Range Planning* **11** (2) April p. 6–12.

Porter, M. E., 1982. 'Industrial organisation and the evolution of concepts for strategic planning', in Naylor, T. H. (ed) *Corporate Strategy*, Studies in Management Science and Systems 8: North Holland.

Probert, D. E., 1981. The development of a long range planning model for the British Telecommunications Business: from initiation to implementation, *Journal of the Operational Research Society* **32** (8), August, pp. 695–720.

Quinn, J. B., 1977. Strategic goals: process and politics, *Sloan Management Review* **19**(1), Fall, pp. 21–37.

Quinn, J. B., 1978. Strategic change: logical incrementalism, *Sloan Management Review* **20** (1) pp. 7–21.

Quinn, J. B., 1980. *Strategies for Change: Logical Incrementalism.* Homewood, IL: Irwin.

Quinn, J. B., 1982. Managing strategies incrementally, *Omega* **10** (6) pp. 613–628.

Ringbakk, K. A., 1971. Why planning fails, *European Business*, Spring. (Reprinted in Hussey, D. E. (ed.) *The Truth about Corporate Planning.* Oxford: Pergamon Press.)

Robinson, S., Hitchens, R. and Wade, D., 1978. The directional policy matrix tool for strategic planning, *Long Range Planning*, **11**(3), June, pp. 8–15.

Rowe, A. J., Mason, R. O. and Dickel, K., 1982. *Strategic Management and Business Policy: A Methodological Approach*, Reading, MA: Addison-Wesley.

Schrieber, A. N., 1982. 'Some ways to bridge management's confidence gap in corporate planning models', in Naylor, T. H. (ed) *Corporate Strategy: The Integration of Corporate Planning Models and Economics, Studies in Management Science and Systems 8.* Amsterdam: North-Holland.

Schwenk, C. R., 1984. Cognitive simplification processes in strategic decision making, *Strategic Management Journal*, **5**, pp. 111–128.

Smircich, L. and Stubbart, C., 1985. Strategic management in an enacted world, *Academy of Management Review* **10** (4) pp. 724–736.

Stander, A. and Rickards, T., 1975. The oracle that failed, *Long Range Planning* **8** (5) October pp. 13–17.

Steiner, G. A., 1979. *Strategic Planning: What Every Manager Must Know*. New York: The Free Press.

Steiner, G. A. and Kunin, H & E., 1981. The new class of chief executive officer, *Long Range Planning* **14** (4) July–August pp. 10–20.

Steiner, G. A. and Miner, J. B., 1982. *Management Policy and Strategy*, 2nd edn, Macmillan.

Stevenson, H. H., 1976. Analysing corporate strengths and weaknesses, *Sloan Management Review* **17** (3), pp. 51–68.

Thompson, A. A. Jr., and Strickland, A. J., III, 1983. *Strategy Formulation and Implementation: Tasks of the General Manager*, Plano, Tex: Business Publications, Inc.

Thune, S. and House, R., 1970. Where long range planning pays off, *Business Horizons*, August, pp. 81–87.

Tilles, S., 1963. How to evaluate corporate strategy, *Harvard Business Review* **41**(4), July–August pp. 111–121.

Weihrich, H., 1982. The TOWS matrix – a tool for situational analysis, *Long Range Planning* **15** (2) April, pp. 54–66.

Wissema, J. G., 1981. Futures research – is it useful? *Long Range Planning* **14** (2) April, pp. 29–32.

Wood, D. R., Jr. and La Forge, R. L., 1979. The impact of comprehensive planning on financial performance, *Academy of Management Journal* **22** (3) pp. 516–526.

Zwicky, F., 1962. *Monographs on Morphological Research*, Pasadena, Calif: Society for Morphological Research.

PART THREE
Control Models and Techniques

11

Markets, Hierarchies and Agency Theory*

Organisation theorists have long been concerned with the effectiveness of alternative organisation structures. As indicated in chapter 1, classical organisation theory promotes a universalist approach according to which the bureaucratic structure, with its emphasis on centralised decision making and the clear delineation of formal lines of authority and responsibility, is advanced as the best form of organisational design. Although neoclassical organisation theorists did not focus explicitly on formal structures, they devoted much of their work to studying the effects of informal structures on performance, emphasising the importance of greater decentralisation and democratic leadership styles. Through its systems and contingency orientations, modern organisation theory emphasises the self-regulating nature of organisations and their requisite structural designs. No specific structure is universally favoured. Rather, it is suggested that structural design is a function of the relevant situational contingencies.

Similarly, economists have devoted some attention to the formal aspects of structural designs. For example, economies in information handling and transmission have been frequently advanced as a rationale for decentralised decision making (e.g. Marschak, 1959). Furthermore, the case for the superiority of the control mechanisms associated with divisionalised structures for controlling the activities of the large, diverse enterprise has been repeatedly argued (e.g. Chandler, 1962; Arrow, 1964; Zannetos, 1965). More recently Williamson (1970; 1975; 1981) extended and formalised these arguments into the Multidivision-form (M-form) hypothesis which has subsequently been tested by several researchers. This represents an important development of Williamson's early work on managerial discretion, which was discussed in chapter 2. In this later work, he clearly acknowledges the significance of internal organisation.

The M-form structure has been defined by Williamson as one that attains optimal divisionalisation through the allocation of strategic and operating decisions to different managerial levels, and the use of an appropriate control apparatus. Williamson hypothesises that, compared with the centralised form (unitary form), the M-form would result in greater company profitability. The above argument is centred on the 'optimal' M-form, i.e. one in which the requisite internal control has been systematically implemented and strategic and operating decisions have been clearly differentiated. This may imply that the intended benefits will be forgone, or at least mitigated, if 'less optimal' divisionalised forms are employed. Accounting researchers and practitioners have strong interest in these developments because of their potentially important impact on the design of management control systems. This is

*This chapter is based on an article in *Accounting and Business Research* (1985), **61**, pp. 23–34, and the material is used with the permission of the journal.

particularly relevant to choice issues relating to control mechanisms such as divisional profitability indices (e.g. Solomons, 1965; Amey, 1969), transfer pricing methods (e.g. Abdel-khalik and Lusk, 1974; Watson and Baumler, 1975) and the extent of divisional autonomy with respect to various decision-making areas (e.g. Tomkins, 1973; Ezzamel and Hilton, 1980b). Furthermore, these developments have broader implications for the design of accounting information systems, for example, in terms of the number and type of communication channels, the design and frequency of accounting reports, and the nature of information to be reported. There are also important implications with respect to the variety of informal controls that may be developed and the ways in which they support or counteract formal controls. Spicer and Ballew (1983) and Tiessen and Waterhouse (1983) have discussed some of the above points and considered their relevance in the context of designing management accounting control systems.

This chapter investigates further the arguments put forward concerning the M-form hypothesis. Some of the implications for the M-form of recent developments in the literature on agency theory, post-contingency theory and organisational life cycles are discussed. It is argued that these implications need to be considered in the design of future empirical work in order to further our understanding with respect to the nature and magnitude of the effects of the M-form on company performance, if indeed such effects can be quantified.

In section I, the economic analysis of the performance effects of the M-form is discussed. In section II, some of the results of contingency theory with respect to the performance attributes of the M-form are presented. This is followed in section III by an overview of empirical research which attempts to test the M-form hypothesis. In section IV, the implications for the M-form hypothesis of recent developments in the literature on agency theory and post-contingency theory are discussed. Finally, section V contains a summary of the chapter.

I. THE ECONOMIC ANALYSIS OF THE PERFORMANCE POTENTIAL OF THE M-FORM

Although several economists have devoted some considerable attention to the study of the formal aspects of decentralised structures, few have explicitly considered the impact of the M-form on firm performance. Presumably, it could be argued that all that is required is a judicious adaptation of the conclusions reached from the study of decentralised structures to the special case of M-form structures. It should be noted, however, that the two structures are not identical (see, for example, Mintzberg, 1979).

Amongst the few economists who have explicitly considered the performance potential of the M-form, Chandler and Williamson have offered the most notable contributions. In his pioneering study of American enterprise, Chandler (1962) suggested that the M-form was developed in order to deal with increased organisational complexity. He also suggested that complexity is caused not only by growth in firm size, but more so by greater diversification into new lines of business and increased vertical integration across widely separated geographical areas.

Williamson (1970; 1975; 1981) extended and formalised Chandler's work. He developed a theory of the organisation of markets and hierarchies in which the ramifications of internal organisation are explicitly considered.

The notion of transactions costs is central to the markets and hierarchies theory. Indeed, it has been argued that the main contribution of that theory draws from its ability to operationalise transactions costs in a manner which facilitates measurement of the efficiency of alternative modes of mediating transactions (Spicer and Ballew, 1983). According to the theory, hierarchies replace markets when it is more economical to organise transactions through hierarchies.

In the markets and hierarchies theory, transactions are closely linked to changes in markets and technologies which are initiated and sustained by environmental forces. These changes lead to the emergence of new opportunities and constraints related to markets and technologies, which in turn may lead to changes in the characteristics of transactions. As transactions change, the contracts that govern them may also change (see Spicer and Ballew, 1983). Thus, both transactions and contracts are likely to be influenced by the dynamics of the organisation's environmental forces.

The markets and hierarchies theory is based on two sets of factors, human and environmental. The human factors are bounded rationality (Simon, 1961) and opportunism; the environmental factors are uncertainty/complexity and small numbers. Bounded rationality means that economic actors are not hyper-rational but are subject to constraints in receiving, storing, retrieving and processing information, and also in formulating and solving complex problems. Opportunism means that economic actors seek their own self-interest and that their actions could be in conflict with the welfare of the organisation. Thus, individuals may intentionally manipulate and distort information. They may also misrepresent intentions and outcomes in situations where it is too costly for other interested parties to verify them (the moral hazard problem). Uncertainty/complexity refers to incomplete knowledge of future states of the world. Small numbers relate to exchange relations, i.e. the number of parties interested in exchange relations is small. It is further assumed that the combination of opportunism and uncertainty/complexity leads to a derived condition known as information impactedness. This means that information is neither free nor symmetrically distributed.

In situations characterised by uncertainty/complexity and bounded rationality, the cost of writing and enforcing complete long-term contracts will be prohibitive. Although it is possible to write incomplete long-term market contracts and shorter-term market contracts, they are subject to opportunistic behaviour and costly negotiations. Thus, even though initial market contracting may occur in large numbers competition, because of the idiosyncratic nature of the product or service which is subject to exchange the winner of the initial contract either (i) acquires significant first-mover advantages in the form of specialised knowledge and skills or (ii) invests in physical and/or human capital to attain economies in production cost. The specialised knowledge in the first case and the prohibitive cost in the second case are likely to lead to small numbers exchange relationships (see Williamson, Harris and Watcher, 1975). Under these conditions market contracting will be inefficient and will be replaced by contracting through hierarchies (internal organisation).

In the markets and hierarchies literature the concept of the firm is augmented to include its role as a governance structure (i.e. an explicit or implicit contractual framework within which transactions are located). Firms and markets are viewed as alternative governance structures. Williamson (1970, p. 134) proceeded to develop his M-form hypothesis:

> The organisation and operation of the large enterprise along the lines of the M-form favours goal pursuit and least cost behaviour more nearly associated with the neoclassical profit maximisation hypothesis than does the U-form organisational alternative.

The basic tenets of the M-form hypothesis derive from the contention that it is transactions rather than technology which mainly determine the efficacy of one organisational design compared with another. It is held that a transformation from the centralised, or unitary form (U-form), to the M-form contributes to the attenuation of both the control loss experience and sub-goal pursuit usually associated with the U-form. Specifically, it is held that the M-form possesses the requisite control apparatus needed for effective performance in a profit maximising sense. This requisite control apparatus has three parts. Firstly, incentive machinery, employing both pecuniary and non-pecuniary rewards, which can be manipulated to motivate the behaviour of divisional managers towards the goals of central management. Secondly, an internal audit system which reviews and evaluates the performance of divisional managers. Thirdly, an allocation system which assigns cash flows to high-yield uses 'rationally' selected by central management after soliciting and evaluating divisional investment proposals. Johnson (1978) discussed the development of these controls at General Motors, and evaluated their contribution to the success of that giant company.

Williamson articulated his thesis in support of the M-form hypothesis by emphasising the role of the M-form firm as a miniature capital market. Firstly, he argued that the M-form firm is more efficient than the capital market as a means for allocating resources: 'its (the capital market) external relation to the firm places it at a serious information disadvantage; it is restricted to non-managerial adjustments; it experiences non-trivial displacement costs', (Williamson, 1970, p. 139). By contrast, the M-form firm: (i) has an internal control mechanism which facilitates obtaining required information at a low cost; (ii) can make fine-tuning as well as discrete adjustments; (iii) can perform head office monitoring more economically.

Secondly, Williamson pointed out that the M-form firm is more internally efficient than the U-form firm particularly with respect to communication costs (see also Chandler, 1962, p. 311). He argued that the former achieves communication savings in at least two ways: (i) by decoupling richly-interacting from weakly-interacting parts of the firm and thus eliminating redundant information and/or (ii) by introducing relatively high thresholds to suppress sensitivity to connectedness.

Thirdly, Williamson contended that the M-form offers more appropriate forms of strategic decision making and goal pursuit activities compared with the centralised form (see also Chandler, 1962, pp. 309–312). Under the centralised structure, it is argued, operating executives, with their partisan interests, become involved in strategic decision making thus placing more emphasis on creation of slack and non-pecuniary benefits. This tendency is held to be reduced under the divisionalised structures by: (i) assigning strategic decision making to top executives who have no operating responsibilities; and (ii) supporting top executives with an elite staff who are experienced in the rigorous analysis required for strategic decisions. Because of its emphasis on the operating division rather than the functional division as the principal operating unit, it is argued that the divisionalised firm is able to focus on enterprise viability. Thus, according to Williamson (1970, p.125) 'strictly functional issues are therefore resolved intradivisionally with the result that partisan functional input can be greatly reduced, if not eliminated from the strategic decision making process'. Williamson proceeded to argue that pursuit of organisational goals is further improved because the relationship between the elite staff and the operating divisions is usually instrumental with no partisan interest. Hence, divisional performance is assessed in the light of firm goals rather than divisional size or influence.

Clearly, one may be inclined to be sceptical about the force of Williamson's arguments. For example, as Williamson (1975, pp. 10 and 20–21) himself pointed out, when markets are fairly efficient they are not likely to be inferior substitutes for internal organising (see also Johnson, 1983, p. 145, for a similar argument). Neither are M-form firms immune from partisan associations between divisional controllers (elite staff) and divisional managers (e.g. Schiff and Lewin, 1968, 1970), which may be just as costly as similar behaviour in U-form firms. Again, although the M-form innovation can considerably economise certain types of transactions costs, it can also trigger off others that may otherwise be avoided. For example, it has been argued that diversification through the M-form tends to be relatively expensive (e.g. Moyer 1970) and is not defensible as a strategy from a finance theory point of view, given shareholders' wealth maximisation as an objective in efficient capital markets (e.g. Haley and Schall, 1979). Under such conditions it would be cheaper for shareholders to pursue their own diversification strategies. However, Amihud and Lev (1981) offer an appealing argument for managerial preference for diversification on the grounds that it reduces the risks of unemployment which can be associated with their management of highly volatile businesses. Moreover, de-emphasising the importance of technology in favour of information and transactions cost as the rationale for the M-form hypothesis is likely to be questioned by those who consider that technology plays an important role in the selection of appropriate structures (e.g. Rumelt, 1974; Mintzberg, 1979).

Nevertheless, it must be emphasised that Williamson has formalised the case for the M-form in a concise, testable hypothesis that has stimulated some relevant empirical research which is reviewed later. However, it is appropriate to consider first how organisation theorists, and in particular contingency theorists, view the performance potential of the M-form.

II. CONTINGENCY THEORY AND THE M-FORM

In contrast to the above analysis, contingency theorists have attempted to relate structural designs to various contingencies. Their main thesis is that organisational effectiveness requires that a fit is achieved between a firm's structural design and its situational contingencies. In the context of the M-form innovation, these researchers considered the implications of firm environment, age and size, power distribution and technology.

The firm's environment has several dimensions including market diversity, stability, complexity, and competition (see chapter 1). Empirical research suggests that market diversity, and in particular product diversity, is probably the most important single factor contributing to the development and spread of the M-form innovation (e.g. Chandler, 1962; Channon, 1973; Rumelt, 1974). Thus, as firms diversify their products and markets, it becomes increasingly convenient (or even necessary) to divisionalise their structures. Notice, also, that the line of influence runs in both directions; the existence of divisionalised structures tends to encourage further diversification (e.g. Fouraker and Stopford, 1968; Rumelt, 1974). Through divisionalisation, it is held, the organisation can create 'boundary-spanning units', which reduce environmental uncertainties and thus help to insulate and stabilise the organisational core. This also implies that by spreading its risks the organisation can reduce the consequences of partial failure (i.e. 'failure' in one or more division may be compensated for by 'success' in other divisions).

The remaining environmental dimensions interact with divisionalised structures but in a manner less pronounced than in the market and product diversity case. Mintzberg (1979) argued that divisionalisation is the appropriate structure for diversified firms operating in simple and stable environments. If the firm operates in a complex and dynamic environment a hybrid functional divisional structure is likely to emerge; one in which there is more emphasis on the indoctrination of divisional managers and on the surveillance of their divisional activities by the central management. There is also some evidence to suggest that active competition leads to increased divisionalisation (e.g. Scott, 1973; Franko, 1974).

Available 'evidence' on the interaction between age and size of the firm and the adoption of the M-form is rather sparse. Although one of Williamson's (1970, 1975) arguments in favour of the M-form is the increase in firm size, the study by Stopford and Wells (1972) suggested that absolute size by itself does not have a direct relationship with divisionalisation. One problem with attempting to test this relationship empirically is that most large organisations tend to be diversified and thus it is difficult to separate the effects of size from those of diversification. One is almost tempted to accept Mintzberg's (1979) argument that there is 'an important relationship between size and divisionalisation, with diversification the intermediate variable' except that this is not yet conclusively proven. A similar line of argument about the effect of age on structure seems plausible on a priori grounds: as companies age they tend to diversify their activities outside their traditional markets and this leads to more divisionalisation. Thus, because of the lack of sufficient evidence, the interactions between age and size of the firm and the M-form remain ambiguous.

There is also little evidence on the nature of the interaction between various dimensions of power distribution and fashion on the one hand, and the M-form innovation on the other hand. Rumelt (1974) reported that several companies adopted divisionalisation because it was fashionable at the time. It has also been argued (e.g. Mintzberg, 1979) that divisional managers tend to favour growth and diversification, and to support divisionalisation in order to enhance their own power. Moreover, the existence of a divisionalised structure makes it easier for the central management to add new divisions which are economically viable and consequently increase the organisation's overall power.

With respect to the interaction between technology and divisionalisation, at least two technological dimensions have been examined in the literature. The first technological dimension is the scale of operations: the findings (e.g. Rumelt, 1974) suggest that companies with substantial investment in high fixed cost technologies tend to control their supplies by following vertical diversification (integration) strategies in relation to their different products, which could lead to an incomplete form of divisionalisation. The second, but related, technological dimension is the degree of indivisibility of the firm's technological system, which may be summarised by Thompson's (1967) well-known typology of interdependence: pooled; sequential and reciprocal. As has been suggested (e.g. Mintzberg, 1979) divisionalisation is greatly facilitated when the firm's technological system can be appropriately allotted between divisions, thereby reducing the potential of excessive divisional inter-dependencies.

Overall, the results of contingency research are quite useful. In contrast to Williamson's theoretical derivation of the M-form hypothesis the contingency results are predominantly empirically derived. Moreover, the results could be arranged to provide a list of situational contingencies in which the M-form is held as the appropriate structural design. For example, given Thompson's categorisation of divisional interdependence and the perceived influence of product and market diversity on divisionalised structures, one can engage in one-to-one matchings between situational contingencies and structure. Thus, in the context of divisionalised structures Lorsch and Allen (1973) suggested the matchings given in table 11.1.

Of course, not all divisionalised firms can be simply classified into these configurations. Some firms may represent a hybrid structure, e.g. conglomerate/

Table 11.1 *Matching of situational contingencies with organisational structure*

Structure	Extent of product/market diversity	Nature of divisional interdependence
The conglomerate	High	Pooled
Vertically integrated firm	Moderate	Sequential
Large single-product firm	Low	Reciprocal

vertically integrated. Indeed, the measures of diversity and interdependence are in themselves vaguely defined (e.g. Thompson, 1967).

These, as well as similar matchings, can contribute towards a better understanding of the nature of the processes which influence the development and diffusion of the M-form innovation. There are, however, many inherent limitations in the contingency approach. Most of these limitations are well documented in the literature (e.g. chapters 1 and 4 *ante*; Dent and Ezzamel, 1982) and will not be fully reported here, but those of most relevance to the context of this chapter will be referred to in sections III and IV below. Moreover, when assessing the effects of the M-form on performance, contingency studies have rarely included measures of effectiveness. In most cases assertive statements are made about the consequences on firm effectiveness of the fit between structural design and situational contingencies. This supposed link clearly requires rigorous testing, otherwise it will remain unproven. In the following section a summary of the findings of some recent empirical studies on the effects of the adoption of the M-form structure on performance is provided.

III. AN OVERVIEW OF EMPIRICAL RESEARCH

With few exceptions, the empirical studies conducted to date to assess the performance differential of divisionalised structures were stimulated by the development of the M-form hypothesis. These studies employed various approaches to the measurement of performance including return on assets or on shareholders' equity (Armour and Teece, 1978; Steer and Cable, 1978; Teece, 1981; Cable and Dirrheimer, 1983), stock market prices (Ezzamel and Hilton, 1980a; Thompson, 1981), capital structure (Roberts and Viscione, 1981) and simulation (Burton and Obel, 1980).

Armour and Teece (1978) conducted an investigation into the performance of some USA oil firms. Their findings suggest that divisionalised firms in their sample earned superior rates of return on shareholders' equity (an extra two per cent) relative to functional (non-divisionalised) firms during the period in which divisionalised structures were in the process of being diffused (i.e. when inferior structures simultaneously existed). Once divisionalised structures had replaced other structures, differential performance was not observed, which prompted the authors to conclude that this was an indication that the sample firms had become 'appropriately' organised.

More recently, Teece (1981) generalised these findings using matched pairs of firms in major USA industries. The performance of the 'leading principal firm', that is the first firm in an industry to adopt the M-form, was compared with the performance of a matched control firm with which it was paired. The differential performance before and after the M-form was adopted by the control firm was calculated. The results supported the M-form hypothesis and were consistent with the earlier Armour and Teece results.

Steer and Cable (1978) conducted a UK-based study which produced similar conclusions except that the performance differential in favour of the M-form was reported to be greater than in Armour and Teece (1978) and Teece (1981): an extra six per cent in the rate of return on shareholders' equity.

Thompson (1981) used share price returns in an attempt to reconcile the gap between the differential performance of the M-form reported by Armour and Teece and by Steer and Cable. The results again supported the M-form hypothesis, but Thompson was able to attribute the difference in the performance differential of the two studies to an abnormal short-term decline in the performance of the U-form firms in the Steer and Cable sample.

Building on the case made for divisionalised structures in both economic theory and organisation theory, Ezzamel and Hilton (1980a) attempted to assess the effects of divisionalised structures on company performance. Their approach involved comparing the share price behaviour of each divisionalised company in their UK sample, before and after divisionalising, relative to the share price behaviour of the relevant industrial classification. Their results suggest that a significant number of companies in their sample which experienced deterioration in their share price behaviour before divisionalising showed a noticeable improvement after divisionalising. There was no discernible impact, however, on companies that were 'doing well' before divisionalising. These results were further contrasted with qualitative judgements given by the respondents on the effects of divisionalised structures on the performance of their companies. The two sets of results were reported to be fairly consistent.

Roberts and Viscione (1981) tested Williamson's hypothesis that divisionalised structures help to raise finance more efficiently than the capital market. The authors hypothesised that setting up a finance subsidiary, which is one form of divisionalisation, improves the corporation's internal efficiency and eases the task of monitoring by lenders, thereby facilitating further borrowing. They examined the debt ratios of firms in five US industries. In three of these industries, firms forming financing subsidiaries had a significantly higher use of debt. Although the 'evidence' is inconclusive, the authors concluded that it is consistent with the M-form hypothesis. Burton and Obel (1980) performed a computer simulation test using data generated from a perturbed decomposed mathematical programming model coordinated by a Dantzig–Wolfe pricing mechanism. Again, their results were reported to be consistent with the M-form hypothesis.

Cable and Dirrheimer (1983) replicated the Steer and Cable study using 48 West German companies. Their results provide some contrast with those reported above. Thus, M-form firms showed a reduction in profitability for at least several years following reorganisation, with no evidence of an eventual positive gain. Two further studies by Buhner (1984) using 40 West German firms and Cable and Yasuki (1985) using 89 Japanese firms yielded results similar to those obtained by Cable and Dirrheimer. The discrepancies between these results and those of the above studies may be due to institutional and cultural differences across countries (see Cable and Dirrheimer, 1983).

Overall, the results of the studies reviewed above seem to provide strong support for the M-form hypothesis. Yet, these results remain somewhat ambiguous and are, at times, confounded, possibly because, as Kaplan (1984) argued, they have only tested the M-form hypothesis in a limited way on actual organisations. This may be reflected in one or more of the following points.

Firstly, it is possible that other extraneous variables may have influenced the reported differential performance in favour of M-form firms. In ·particular, characteristics of ownership structure and the extent to which effective control systems are employed to monitor agency costs could be important. Two questions of some consequence are thus raised: (i) are effective monitoring systems of agency costs antecedent to M-form structures so that the effects of the latter on performance are incidental? or (ii) are agency monitoring systems subsumed under M-form structures? Only two studies (Steer and Cable, 1978; Bühner, 1984) addressed this issue, albeit in a very limited capacity by incorporating an ownership variable in their multiple regression models, and thus many pertinent questions remain unanswered.

The second point relates to organisational goals and archetypes. Explicit in the M-form hypothesis is the emphasis on greater profitability. Empirical tests of the M-form were conducted in the main on the basis of comparing profitability rates of M-form and U-form firms. This presupposed emphasis on profitability is rather restrictive. M-form firms and U-form firms may assign different priorities to profitability. Even if greater profitability ranks equally high as a long-run objective for all firms considered, in the short run different firms may pursue different strategies in which profitability may be accorded different priorities. Consideration of these important issues is completely lacking in both contingency theory studies and the empirical tests of the M-form hypothesis. In general, these studies: (i) calculated profit differentials over short periods of time (except for Armour and Teece, 1978) and (ii) did not reflect in their models short-run differences in corporate strategies.

Thirdly, the M-form hypothesis assesses the profitability differential when comparing M-form firms directly with U-form firms. It is not clear, however, how profitability should compare for 'intermediate' structures. For example, Williamson and Bhargava (1972) and Williamson (1975) developed the following six-way classification scheme of large corporate structures:

1. Unitary (U-form): a traditional, functionally organised enterprise, including those with measures of diversification which account for less than a third of the firm's value added.
2. Holding Company (H-form): a divisionalised enterprise for which the requisite internal control apparatus has not been provided because of the subsidiary nature of divisions.
3. Multidivisional (M-form): a divisionalised enterprise in which a separation of operating from strategic decision making is attained and for which the requisite internal control apparatus has been provided and is systematically employed.
4. Transitional Multidivisional (M'-form): an M-form enterprise in the process of adjustment and learning.
5. Corrupted Multidivisional ($\overline{\text{M}}$-form): a divisionalised enterprise with the requisite control apparatus but where the central management is extensively involved in operating activities.
6. Mixed (X-form): an enterprise in which H-form structure, M-form divisions, and even centrally supervised divisions, may simultaneously exist.

This classification has been used by several researchers (Armour and Teece, 1978; Steer and Cable, 1978; Teece, 1981) but the results remain somewhat ambiguous. For example, the results obtained by Armour and Teece (1978) indicate that (i) the rate of return differential of the transitional form was similar to that of the M-form, and (ii) the performances of the remaining structural forms were not significantly different from the performance of the U-form. This raises the questions: do the results in (i) imply that a mere change from the U-form towards a divisionalised form will be, at least initially, profitable? Or does the transitional form fully reflect the performance potential of the M-form? Also, with respect to (ii), should we infer that the 'in-between' structures, other than the transitional form, are a mere irrelevance to profitability?

In general, evidence on the implications of the above arguments for the efficacy, or otherwise, of the M-form is not available. As Kaplan (1984) suggests, it is not clear which of the alternative objective functions would suffice to attenuate control loss in divisionalised organisations, or even whether a single objective function would. Further research assessing the performance effects of the above alternatives is needed.

IV. RECENT THEORETICAL DEVELOPMENTS AND THE M-FORM HYPOTHESIS

The last decade has witnessed several developments in the literature of economics and organisation theory which have various implications for the relationship between structure and performance. This section explicitly considers some of these implications and outlines their potential influence on the design of future empirical testing of the M-form hypothesis. In particular, the emphasis here is on recent agency theory formulations, post-contingency theory, and organisational archetypes and life cycles.

Agency Theory and the M-form Hypothesis

As indicated in the introduction to this book, an agency relationship is defined through a set of contractual arrangements, written and unwritten, whereby one party (the principal) hires another party (the agent) to perform some specific function in return for some reward. A classic agency problem exists when the agent can take actions that favour his interests at the expense of those of the principal. The organisation is perceived as a nexus of contracts regulating exchange relationships among interested parties who are the suppliers of different factors of production and the users of the firm's output (Jensen and Meckling, 1976). The purpose of such contractual relationships is to bring the conflicting interests of different parties into equilibrium.

According to agency theory, both the principal and the agent are rational, wealth seeking and utility maximisers. Because of the uncertainty relating to the agent's behaviour, usually only imperfect monitoring of such behaviour is possible at a reasonable cost. The central problem is, thus, how to structure the relationship between the agent and the principal so that the agent is motivated to take actions which maximise the wealth of the principal.

An important feature of agency theory is the explicit treatment of uncertainty. The beliefs of the principal and the agent regarding uncertainty could be the same or could be different. In either case the agent takes action *before* expectations about the future become known (this is *ex ante* uncertainty). Such uncertainty could be reduced by purchasing information (see chapter 6). To both the principal and the agent wealth represents utility, and in addition effort represents disutility to the agent. Outcome is assumed to be determined jointly by the level of uncertainty and the agent's effort; this makes it difficult, if not, impossible, for the principal to verify the agent's reported effort (i.e. moral hazard). Similarly, the skill levels of the agent may not be observable. This would make it possible for the agent to claim the possession of better skills than he actually has without the principal being able to verify the claim (the adverse selection problem). Uncertainty about what determines outcome is *ex post* in nature and can also be reduced by purchasing information. Various models of defining the agent's fees under these conditions and their implications for the principal and the agent are discussed in chapter 12.

The emphasis in this chapter is on the broader control implications of agency theory. These are better understood by reference to some of the more recent literature on agency theory (e.g. Fama, 1980; Fama and Jensen, 1983a, 1983b), which emphasises three functions: residual risk bearing, decision management, and decision control. These functions, it is argued, may be combined in the same agents or separated among different agents depending upon the extent of organisational complexity.

Residual risk is the difference between stochastic inflows of resources and agreed payments to agents as specified by the contract. This risk is borne by the principals who contract for the rights to net cash flows, and are thus called residual risk bearers (or residual claimants). Decision management refers to initiation of decisions (generation of proposals to utilise resources and structure contracts) and implementation of ratified decisions. Decision control denotes ratification and monitoring of decisions.

Depending upon cost conditions, including technology and control of agency problems, the 'optimal' organisation may be non-complex or complex. The extent of complexity is taken to be related to the degree of concentration/diffusion of relevant information. Thus, in non-complex organisations specific information relevant to decisions is concentrated in one or a few agents. Consequently, it is efficient to assign both decision control and decision management to these agents. This, however, leads to an agency problem as the agents can engage in decisions detrimental to residual claimants. To reduce these agency costs, Fama and Jensen (1983a) suggested that the organisation should restrict residual claims to important decision agents, rather than engage in designing costly control devices to monitor agents' activities.

Fama and Jensen acknowledged that this solution to the agency problem has its costs. In particular, by combining the status of residual claimants and management in a few individuals, many of the benefits of risk reduction through diversification and specialisation of decision functions are sacrificed. This could be detrimental to the organisation's chances of survival. However, Fama and Jensen argued that most non-complex organisations are small, that small organisations do not require a wide range of specialised decision agents, and their total risks are generally small. Overall, they argue (1983a, p. 307) that 'the benefits of unrestricted risk sharing and specialisation of decision functions are less than the costs that would be incurred to control the resulting agency problems'.

Complex organisations pose more serious agency problems. In these organisations, knowledge relevant to decision making is widely diffused amongst many agents. Moreover, management and risk bearing are assigned separately to different groups: managers and residual claimants (stockholders) respectively. When residual claimants are few in number, they can control decision management in a relatively simple manner (Alchian and Demsetz, 1972). However, when residual claimants are plentiful, as is usually the case, it would be too costly for them to control decisions because requisite knowledge is widely spread. In such cases residual risk bearing tends to be separate from decision control, thereby leading to a classic agency situation in which the agents may further their interests by taking actions which are detrimental to the interests of the principal. Several researchers (e.g. Ross, 1973; Shavell, 1979; Holmstrom, 1979) have suggested various models to monitor the decisions taken by agents in various settings. However, the work of Fama (1980) and Fama and Jensen (1983a, 1983b) offers a broader control perspective which is summarised here.

In the context of agency theory, control is exercised through decision hierarchies, mutual monitoring systems and boards of directors. Decision hierarchy is a formal control system with a diffused hierarchical structure in which the decision initiatives of lower level agents are ratified and monitored by multiple higher level decision agents. No single individual is thus likely to possess enough power to resemble the classic single entrepreneur. Moreover, decision management and decision control rights tend to be separate (i.e. for any one decision the two functions are not both handled by the same agents) and diffused across agents (i.e. for any one decision each function is handled by *more* than *one* agent). This reduces the potential for decision agents at all levels of the hierarchy to coalesce at the expense of residual claimants. The formal system is complemented by a set of organisational rules, e.g. accounting systems that define the decision rights of each agent as well as the performance criteria that determine rewards (Fama and Jensen, 1983a).

Mutual monitoring is a less formal system which is reflected in the mechanisms of managerial labour markets. Both shareholders and managers are assumed to have markets for their services. The existence of capital markets facilitates shifting and diversifying investments and thus an individual shareholder is not likely to be interested in personally overseeing the detailed activities of any firm. Managers, however, rent their human capital to the firm and the rental rates are likely to depend on the success or failure of the firm. Thus, managers may be seen to have a vested interest in overseeing contractual relationships and in ensuring the viability of the firm in order to maximise the market value of their human capital. Appropriate signals to managerial labour markets indicating favourable developments in human capital are sought by managers. Each manager has a stake in the performance of managers above and below him. Thus, managers in an organisation engage in mutual monitoring, evaluating each other in part on the basis of perceived contributions to their human capital. In this perspective lower level agents become important in constraining the power of higher level agents. The board of directors has the power to hire, fire and reward top level managers and to ratify and monitor important decisions. Equipped with this power, the board of directors can ensure that decision management and decision control are separated even at the top of the organisation.

Control Under Markets and Hierarchies and Agency Theories

Having briefly outlined the notions and mechanisms of control underlying agency theory, it is interesting to contrast them with those implied by markets and hierarchies. The advocates of each theory have cited arguments aimed at illustrating the superiority of their own theory. It is instructive, however, to think of the two theories as complementary rather than competitive. But, before pursuing this idea further, the arguments underlying both theories should first be contrasted. These arguments are summarised here on the bases of: theory orientation; underlying causes of control loss; rationalisation of control; breadth of control; mode of control and mechanisms of control.

The markets and hierarchies theory and agency theory are based on differing methodological orientations. Markets and hierarchies is a positive theory, seeking to explain organisational arrangements that are most economical for mediating transactions in different settings. The theory also shows how opportunistic behaviour by individuals (agents) can be reduced through the use of internal organisation mechanisms. Agency theory is a deductive, analytical theory based on a number of restrictive and abstract assumptions. Its aim is to regulate relationships between the principal and the agent so that their conflicting interests are brought into equilibrium.

Because agency theory is based on subjective utility maximisation, its descriptive validity is open to question (Tiessen and Waterhouse, 1983).

The underlying causes of the potential control loss associated with centralised systems in the respective theories are not identical, but, nevertheless, are closely related. In the markets' and hierarchies' literature, control loss arises because of information impactedness and bounded rationality associated with the increase in firm size and the greater geographic, product and market diversity. In the agency theory literature, control loss is caused by information becoming specific (i.e. detailed and costly to transfer amongst agents) as organisations become more complex. Specific information is closely related to information impactedness and bounded rationality, and complex organisations tend to be characterised by large sizes and greater product and market diversity. The correspondence, however, is not always clear cut.

The two theories appear to advance differing control rationalisations. The markets' and hierarchies' literature emphasises economies in transactions costs whereas agency theory emphasises both cost economies and benefits which, it is held, give an organisation survival value. These include (Fama and Jensen, 1983a): (i) the allocation of risk bearing to residual claimants and the consequent reduction of costs of monitoring contracts; (ii) the potential of human capital development within the organisation and (iii) mutual monitoring by managers at different levels which reduces the potential for collusion against residual claimants. It is worth noting that the economies in transaction costs contribute to organisational survival both by increasing net cash flows available to residual claimants and by making it possible to deliver products at low prices. Despite the similarities, agency theory offers a broader framework within which organisational survival is attained through cost economies and benefits of human capital development. This is an important contribution that is lacking in the markets and hierarchies model.

The concept of control underlying agency theory is also broader than that promoted by markets and hierarchies. In the latter, control appears to be almost exclusively premised on top-down (hierarchical) formal control. Williamson (1970; p. 129) does refer to pressures that can be exercised by lower level participants on deviant divisional managers to bring them into line with corporate policy in order to avert cuts in divisional resources that may be imposed by the centre. The justification given in this respect is that lower level participants are amongst the first to suffer the consequences of cuts in divisional resources; but, in general, top-down control is over-emphasised in the markets and hierarchies model. By contrast, in agency theory less formal control, in the form of mutual monitoring by agents in different hierarchical levels, is advanced explicitly as a complement to hierarchical control. This is an important addition. Notice, however, that even under agency theory, control remains incomplete. The broader notions of informal control and intra-organisational politics are not explicitly considered. Thus, although Fama and Jensen (1983a) recognised that both written and unwritten contracts are used to regulate relationships between principals and agents, their analysis predominantly emphasised the former. This overemphasis on written contracts almost reduces the organisation to a 'bureaucratic flow chart defining the rules of the game regarding who gets paid what as a function of what measure' (Klein, 1983, p. 374).

Moreover, different modes of control are promoted under the two theories. Thus, even though both theories emphasise control through some notion of 'decision separation', markets and hierarchies theory is essentially concerned with separation of decision types, whereas agency theory focuses on separation of decision processes. The markets and hierarchies theory advocates allocating strategic decisions to top-level managers and operating decisions to divisional managers. This allocation of decision types, in addition to the incentive and control systems, is used to mitigate small numbers opportunism. By contrast, agency theory postulates a decision-making arrangement in which no important decision, irrespective of its type, is both managed and controlled by the same agent. At the extreme this may imply, as Williamson (1983, p. 355) suggests, that 'strategic decision making should permeate the organisation' rather than being concentrated in the hands of top managers. If this is an intended tenet of agency theory then we are likely to observe real costs reflecting the dysfunctional consequences of diffused strategic decision making. Even if this interpretation is not strictly correct, Fama and Jensen's notion of separation of decision management from decision control remains problematic. They (1983a, p. 304) suggested that decision systems endowed with such separation properties are the result of the separation of residual risk bearing from decision management. However, Williamson (1983) offers evidence which indicates that management and residual risk bearing were joined in Du Pont and General Motors, the pioneering M-form firms that have been characterised by the separation of strategic and operating decisions.

The two theories emphasise the importance of an array of formal control mechanisms. In the markets and hierarchies approach the control apparatus incorporates such techniques as internal audit, reward structures and resource allocation schemes, in all of which accounting is clearly implicated. In the agency approach the control apparatus regulates contracts and activities through decision hierarchies, mutual monitoring systems and boards of directors. Decision hierarchies are complemented by organisational rules of the game as defined by the accounting and budgeting systems.

The above discussion illuminates and contrasts the underlying tenets of both markets and hierarchies theory and agency theory. The analysis in this section has, thus far, been fully confined within the bounds of theory. Available empirical evidence to date on both theories is not easy to contrast. As indicated in the previous section, the empirical tests of the M-form hypothesis are, on the whole, supportive of that hypothesis. Available empirical evidence on agency theory indicates that owner-controlled firms tend to attain higher profit rates, but lower growth rates, compared with manager-controlled firms (e.g. Florence, 1961; Berle and Means, 1968; Nyman and Silberston, 1978; Cubbin and Leech, 1983; but see Radice, 1971 and Fatemi, Ang and Chua, 1983). Taken at face value, these results indicate that agency costs may be incurred in firms where residual risk bearing is separated from decision management; but this interpretation implies that owners would always prefer higher profits and lower growth rates to lower profits and higher growth rates. Rather than make such value judgements the present authors prefer to emphasise the needs for more refined empirical testing of the implications of agency theory.

Integration

Given the differences outlined above, an interesting question arises as to whether the two theories can be integrated. It is argued here that agency theory provides a framework within which M-form firms can be formally analysed. Viewed in the context of agency theory, a divisionalised organisation is a nexus of multi-level contracts, written and unwritten, covering 'the way inputs are joined to create outputs and the way receipts from outputs are shared among inputs' (Fama, 1980, p. 290). Moreover, a divisionalised organisation may be treated as a 'legal fiction which serves as a focus for a complex process in which the conflicting objectives of individuals ... are brought into equilibrium within a framework of contractual relations' (Jensen and Meckling, 1976, p. 311). Such ideas can enrich the arguments implied in markets and hierarchies by augmenting the concept of the organisation as a governance structure.

The two theories also seek to control exchange relationships and to monitor human performance in organisations. Indeed, it has been suggested (Tiessen and Waterhouse, 1983) that the two theories combined offer a more complete control framework than either theory alone. Thus, agency theory deals with control issues in situations where the relationship between the principal and the agent is highly structured, as applies when technology is routine and the environment is predictable. In contrast, the markets and hierarchies theory analyses control issues in situations where information relevant for decision making is highly localised, as is the case when technology is non-routine and the environment is uncertain.

Uncertainty and its implications for the design and flow of information are considered in both theories. Agency theory emphasises the distinction between *ex ante* uncertainty (the agent taking actions before knowing their actual consequences) and *ex post* uncertainty (insufficient knowledge of what determines outcome). Markets and hierarchies theory emphasises the importance of *ex ante* uncertainty. Both types of uncertainty can be reduced by developing or purchasing and using information. It may thus be desirable for *ex ante* information to be predictable, and for *ex post* information to be identifiable, verifiable and acceptable by the affected parties (Tiessen and Waterhouse, 1983). The specification of these information characteristics does not rule out those situations in which information is manipulated by actors in order to gain strategic advantages (power), or in which it has purely symbolic value (Feldman and March, 1981).

Moreover, it would be beneficial to complement the control apparatus of the M-form with some of the formal and less formal controls advocated by the agency approach. Mutual monitoring would be useful in divisionalised organisations, but more so when significant interdependencies exist between sub-units. Mutual monitoring by agents directly influenced by interdependencies may even be more effective than the fully formalised and centralised controls of the M-form, and is likely to enhance the survival value of the organisation. Indeed, just as the intracompany transfer of goods and services is regulated by internal markets, so can the development of human capital be monitored by internal labour markets. Thus, in designing the M-form control apparatus more emphasis should be given to internal human capital development.

A further important implication for the design of M-form controls is the notion of diffused decision rights. By designing control systems so that responsibility for a particular decision process is not concentrated in the hands of one or few agents, the efficiency of M-form structure is likely to improve by reducing the potential for collusion. Greater diffusion of decision management and decision control could thus be a feature of both strategic and operating decisions.

Finally, the efficiency of M-form structures is likely to be enhanced if the role of the board of directors as a means of control is explicitly emphasised. The composition of the board of directors (the ratio of inside to outside members) could provide a useful insight into the extent of agency costs in U-form and M-form organisations. Williamson (1983) and Ezzamel (1985) have suggested a number of testable propositions relating to board composition, and other characteristics of M-form firms. Together, these propositions and hypotheses provide illustrative examples of how agency research may be fruitfully integrated with markets and hierarchies research.

Post-Contingency Theory and Organisational Archetypes

More recent developments in organisation theory, and in particular post-contingency theory, literature offer some useful insights of potential relevance to the M-form

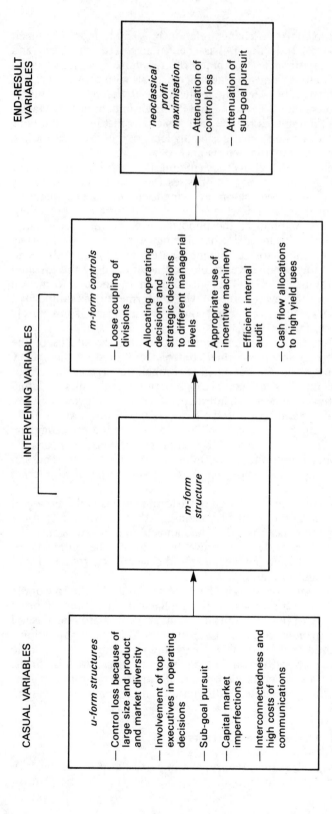

Figure 11.1 *A diagrammatic representation of the M-form hypothesis (Source: M. Ezzamel (1985) On the assessment of the performance effects of multidivisional structures: a synthesis, Accounting and Business Research, **61** (Winter), pp. 23–34. Used with permission).*

hypothesis. Illustration of this point will be facilitated by referring back to the basic argument underlying the M-form hypothesis. Briefly, this may be presented by a straightforward set of unidirectional linkages as shown in figure 11.1. In this figure it can be seen that a set of causal variables (information imperative) lead to the development/adoption of the M-form structure with the latter guiding the activities of the firm towards a behaviour pattern akin to neoclassical profit maximisation. The links and directions of causation in this model are similar to those implied by contingency theory. Thus, situational contingencies (information imperative) determine the most optimal structure (M-form) which in turn leads to the most desirable company performance (profit maximisation).

The familiar limitations of contingency theory (see chapters 1 and 4 of this book; Dent and Ezzamel, 1982) are clearly applicable to this formulation of the M-form hypothesis. In particular, such a model imposes a mechanistic relationship in which the information impactedness imperative is seen to determine structural form. The role of managerial preferences in influencing structure is suppressed. Moreover, the model is static in the sense that it portrays firms as if they have a predetermined form of existence. The evolutionary and dynamic nature of organisation life cycles is ignored.

Post-contingency theorists developed arguments with respect to these two issues (see chapters 1 and 4). For example, Pfeffer (1978); Weick (1979); and Galbraith (1977) amongst others, emphasised the multidirectional relationships between the firm and its situational contingencies. Organisational performance is not seen as simply a dependent variable, but rather as an input in the complex network of managerial decision making (Child, 1974, 1975). Moreover, managerial choice is seen to play an important role in shaping the situational contingencies facing the organisation and in designing structure (Child, 1972; 1973; 1977). Taken in the present context, this argument implies that the M-form structure should not be considered as a universal solution for the problems of information handling in large organisations. Large and diversified firms may attain high profitability even though they employ structures other than the M-form.

Similarly, a growing body of literature in organisation theory has recently emphasised the evolutionary and multifaceted nature of organisational life cycles. Miles and Snow (1978) distinguished between four organisational archetypes: the defender; the prospector; the analyser; and the reactor. The defender is an organisation with a narrow product line and highly expert management. As a result of its narrow focus it seldom fundamentally changes its technology, structure, or methods of operation. Instead it concentrates on improving the efficiency of existing operations. The prospector, on the other hand, continually searches for market opportunities and regularly experiments with methods of production. It often creates change and uncertainty in its environment which triggers off responses from its competitors. Because its primary emphasis is on product and market innovation, it is usually not completely efficient. The analyser is characterised by operations in both stable and dynamic product domains. Top managers watch their competitors carefully and rapidly adapt promising new ideas to fit their existing technology. The reactor, on the other hand, frequently perceives environmental change and uncertainty but seldom makes any adjustment until forced to do so by the environment. It appears, therefore, that different organisations pursue different strategies and that the *same* organisation is likely to follow different strategies as its perceptions of the role it seeks to play change over time.

Many more interesting aspects of organisational life cycles and archetypes can be discussed (e.g. Kimberly and Miles, 1980; Cameron and Whetten, 1981; Quinn and

Cameron, 1983). The most relevant point in the context of this chapter, however, is that models which confine the measurement of organisational performance within a partial and pre-supposed configuration of organisational life cycles, as is the case with the M-form hypothesis, can only lead to partial understanding of organisational performance.

V. SUMMARY

Research into the effects of alternative organisational structures on firm performance is still at a fairly early stage of development. Numerous problems, some of which may be insurmountable, face researchers in this field. For a start, terms like 'structure' and 'performance' are typically multidimensional. To single out any one dimension for research purposes is likely to impair the generality of the results obtained. Furthermore, several extraneous variables, which may operate simultaneously, can have significant effects on performance. To gain a true perspective on the effects of a particular structural form on performance, the influence of these extraneous variables needs to be carefully considered. Moreover, much of the data required for this research lie within firms. All the problems associated with obtaining internal data are therefore present, e.g. the extent of cooperation of firms and the effects of the researcher's perceptions on the quality of the data.

In this chapter, an attempt has been made to investigate the potential impact of divisionalised structures on firm performance. The review of the literature indicates that, in the context of research into the M-form, the problems alluded to above are quite real. The models so far developed to assess the effects of the M-form on performance have provided some interesting and promising insights. But more research is needed to improve the perspective in this area. Such research should explicitly take into account many of the recent developments in agency theory, post-contingency theory and organisational life cycles.

It has been indicated in this chapter that the control apparatus of the M-form operates through: (i) incentive machinery, e.g. monetary and non-monetary rewards, which aims to motivate the behaviour of divisional managers towards the goals of central management; (ii) an internal audit system, which evaluates the performance of divisional managers and (iii) an allocation system, which assigns cash flows to the most profitable investments. It has also been suggested that M-form controls are essentially formal, hierarchical, top-down systems. These controls can be complemented by agency theory controls. The latter include separation of decision initiative and implementation from decision authorisation and monitoring, diffusion of decision rights across many organisational participants, mutual monitoring by organisational participants (less formal controls), and the formal power of the board of directors. It should be noted, however, that even such a wide range of controls is far from complete (see chapter 14).

REFERENCES

Abdel-khalik, A. R. and Lusk, E. J., 1974. Transfer pricing – a synthesis, *Accounting Review*, January, pp. 8–23.
Alchian, A. A., and Demsetz H. 1972. Production, information costs, and economic organisation, *American Economic Review*, **62**, December.
Amey, L. R., 1969. *The Efficiency of Business Enterprises*: George Allen and Unwin.

Amihud, Y. and Lev, B., 1981. Risk reduction as a managerial motive for conglomerate mergers, *The Bell Journal of Economics*, **12** (2), Autumn, pp. 605–617.

Armour, H. O. and Teece, D. J., 1978. Organisational structure and economic performance: a test of the multidivisional hypothesis, *The Bell Journal of Economics*, **9** (1), Spring, pp. 106–122.

Arrow, K. J., 1964. Control in large organizations, *Management Science*, **10** (3), April, pp. 397–408.

Berle, A. A. and Means, G. C., 1968. *The Modern Corporation and Private Property*, revised edition, New York: Harcourt, Brace and World.

Bühner, R., 1984. Internal organisations and returns: an empirical analysis of large diversified German corporations, working paper.

Burton, R. M. and Obel, B., 1980. A computer simulation test for the M-form hypothesis, *Administrative Science Quarterly*, pp. 457–466.

Cable, J. and Dirrheimer, M. J., 1983. Hierarchies and markets: an empirical test of the multidivisional hypothesis in West Germany, *International Journal of Industrial Organization*, **1** pp. 43–62.

Cable, J. and Yasuki, H., 1985. Internal organisation, business groups and corporate performance: an empirical test of the multidivision hypothesis in Japan, *International Journal of Industrial Organization*, **3** pp. 401–420.

Cameron, K. and Whetten, D. A., 1981. Perceptions of organisation effectiveness across organizational life cycles, *Administrative Science Quarterly* **26** pp. 525–544.

Chandler, A. D., 1962. *Strategy and Structure: Chapters in the History of the American Industrial Enterprise*, Cambridge: MIT Press.

Channon, D. F., 1973. *The Strategy and Structure of British Enterprise*. New York: The Macmillan Press.

Child, J., 1972. Organizational structure, environment and performance: the role of strategic choice, *Sociology*, pp. 2–22.

Child, J., 1973. 'Organisations: a choice for man' in J. Child (ed.) *Man and Organisation*: George Allen and Unwin.

Child, J., 1974. Managerial and organisational factors associated with company performance – part I, *The Journal of Management Studies*, October, pp. 175–189.

Child, J., 1975. Managerial and organisational factors associated with company performance – part II. A contingency analysis, *The Journal of Management Studies*, February, pp. 12–27.

Child, J., 1977. *Organisations: A Guide to Problems and Practices*. London: Harper and Row.

Cubbin, J. and Leech, D., 1983. The effect of shareholding dispersion on the degree of control in British companies: theory and measurement, *The Economic Journal* **93** June, pp. 351–369.

Dent, J. F. and Ezzamel, M. A., 1982. Organisational control and management accounting, paper presented to the American Accounting Association Annual Conference, San Diego, USA, August.

Ezzamel, M., 1985. On the assessment of the performance effects of multidivisional structures: a synthesis, *Accounting and Business Research* **61**, Winter, pp. 23–34.

Ezzamel, M. A. and Hilton, K., 1980a. Divisionalisation in British industry: a preliminary study, *Accounting and Business Research*, **10**, (38), Spring, pp. 197–214.

Ezzamel, M. A. and Hilton, K., 1980b. Can divisional discretion be measured? *Journal of Business Finance and Accounting*, Summer, pp. 311–329.

Fama, E. F., 1980. Agency problems and the theory of the firm, *Journal of Political Economy*, pp. 28–307.

Fama, E. F. and Jensen, M. C., 1983a. Separation of ownership and control, *Journal of Law and Economics*, June, pp. 301–325.

Fama, E. F. and Jensen, M. C., 1983b. Agency problems and residual claims, *Journal of Law and Economics*, June, pp. 327–349.

Fatemi, A. T., Ang, J. S. and Chua, J. H., 1983. Evidence supporting shareholder wealth maximisation in management controlled firms, *Applied Economics* **15** (1) February, pp. 49–60.

Feldman, M. S. and March, J. G., 1981. Information in organizations as signal and symbol, *Administrative Science Quarterly*, June, pp. 171–185.

Florence, P. S., 1961. *Ownership, Control and Success of Large Companies*. London: Sweet and Maxwell.

Fouraker, L. E. and Stopford, J. M., 1968. Organisational structure and the multinational strategy. *Administrative Science Quarterly*, pp. 7–64.

Franko, L. G., 1974. The move toward a multidivisional structure in European organisations, *Administrative Science Quarterly*, pp. 493–506.

Galbraith, J. E., 1977. *Organisation Design*:Addison Wesley.

Haley, C. W. and Schall, L. D., 1979. *The Theory of Financial Decisions*, 2nd edn: McGraw-Hill.

Holmstrom, B., 1979. Moral hazard and observability, *Bell Journal of Economics* **10** (1) Spring, pp. 74–91.

Jensen, M. C. and Meckling, W. H., 1976. Theory of the firm: managerial behaviour, agency costs and ownership structure, *Journal of Financial Economics*, **3** October, pp. 305–360.

Johnson, H. T., 1978. Management accounting in the early multidivisional organisation: General Motors in the 1920s, *Business History Review* **L.11** (4) Winter, pp. 490–517.

Johnson, H. T., 1983. The search for gain in markets and firms, *Accounting, Organizations and Society*, pp. 139–146.

Kaplan, R. S., 1984. The evolution of management accounting, *Accounting Review* **LIX** (3) July, pp. 390–418.

Kimberly, J. R. and Miles, R. H., 1980. *The Organizational Life Cycle*. San Francisco, CA: Jossey-Bass.

Klein, B., 1983. Contracting costs and residual claims: the separation of ownership and control, *Journal of Law and Economics*, **XXVI** June, pp. 367–374.

Lorsch, J. W. and Allen, S. A. III, 1973. *Managing Diversity and Interdependence*: Division of Research, Graduate School of Business Administration, Harvard University.

Marschak, J., 1959. Efficient and viable organisational forms, in M. Haire (ed.) *Modern Organization Theory*: John Wiley and Sons.

Miles, R. E. and Snow, C. C., 1978. *Organizational Strategy, Structure and Process*: McGraw-Hill.

Mintzberg, H., 1979. *The Structuring of Organizations*: Prentice Hall.

Moyer, R. C., 1970. Berle and Means revisited: the conglomerate merger, *Business and Society*, Spring, pp. 20–29.

Nyman, S. and Silberston, A., 1978. The ownership and control of industry, *Oxford Economics Papers*, pp. 74–101.

Pfeffer, J., 1978. *Organizational Design*. Arlington Heights, IL: AHM Publishing.

Quinn, R. E. and Cameron, K., 1983. Organizational life cycles and shifting criteria of effectiveness: some preliminary evidence, *Management Science* **29** (1), January, pp. 33–51.

Radice, H. K., 1971. Control type, profitability and growth in large firms: an empirical study, *The Economic Journal*, September, pp. 547–562.

Roberts, G. S. and Viscione, J. A., 1981. Captive finance subsidiaries and the M-form hypothesis, *The Bell Journal of Economics*, **12**, (1), Spring, pp. 285–295.

Ross, S. A., 1973. The economic theory of agency: the principal's problem, *The American Economic Review*, **63**, (2), May 1973, pp. 134–139.

Rumelt, R. P., 1974. *Strategy, Structure, and Economic Performance*: Division of Research, Graduate School of Business Administration, Harvard University.

Schiff, M. and Lewin, A. Y., 1968. Where traditional budgeting fails, *Financial Executive*, May, pp. 50–62.

Schiff, M. and Lewin, A. Y., 1970. The impact of people on budgets, *Accounting Review*, April, pp. 259–268.

Scott, B. R., 1973. The industrial state: old myths and new realities, *Harvard Business Review*, March-April, pp. 133–143.

Shavell, S., 1979. Risk sharing and incentives in the principal and agent relationships, *The Bell Journal of Economics*, **10**, (1), Spring, pp. 55–73.

Simon, H. A., 1961. *Administrative Behaviour*, 2nd edn, New York: The Macmillan Company.

Solomons, D., 1965. *Divisional Performance: Measurement and Control*: Financial Executives Research Foundation.

Spicer, B. H. and Ballew, V., 1983. Management accounting systems and the economics of internal organization, *Accounting, Organizations and Society*, **8**, (1), 1983, pp. 73–96.

Steer, P. and Cable, J., 1978. Internal organisation and profit: an empirical analysis of large UK companies, *The Journal of Industrial Economics*, **XXVII** (1), September, pp. 13–30.

Stopford, J. M. and Wells, L. T. JR., 1972. *Managing the Multinational Enterprise: Organization of the Firm and Ownership of the Subsidiaries*: Basic Books.

Teece, D. J., 1981. Internal organisation and economic performance: an empirical analysis of the profitability of principal firms, *The Journal of Industrial Economics*, December, pp. 173–199.

Thompson, J. D., 1967. *Organizations in Action*: McGraw-Hill.

Thompson, R. S., 1981. Internal organisation and profit: a note. *The Journal of Industrial Economics*, December, pp. 201–211.

Tiessen, P. and Waterhouse, J. H., 1983. Towards a descriptive theory of management accounting, *Accounting, Organisations and Society*, pp. 251–268.

Tomkins, C., 1973. *Financial Planning in Divisionalised Companies*: Haymarket Publishing.

Watson, D. J. H. and Baumler, J. V., 1975. Transfer pricing: a behavioural context, *Accounting Review*, July, pp. 466–474.

Weick, K. E., 1979. *The Social Psychology of Organizing*: Addison-Wesley.

Williamson, O. E., 1970. *Corporate Control and Business Behaviour*. Englewood Cliffs, NJ: Prentice-Hall.

Williamson, O. E., 1975. *Markets and Hierarchies: Analysis and Antitrust Implications*. New York: Free Press.

Williamson, O. E., 1981. The modern corporation: origins, evolution, attributes, *Journal of Economic Literature* **XIX** December, pp. 1537–1568.

Williamson, O. E., 1983. Organization form, residual claimants, and corporate control, *Journal of Law and Economics*, June, pp. 351–366.

Williamson, O. E. and Bhargava, N., 1972. Assessing and classifying the internal structure and control apparatus of the modern corporation, in K. Cowling, (ed.) *Market Structure and Corporate Behaviour: Theory and Empirical Analysis of the Firm*. London: Gray-Mills Publishing.

Williamson, O. E., Harris, J. and Watcher, M., 1975. Understanding the employment relation: the analysis of idiosyncratic exchange, *Bell Journal of Economics*, Spring, pp. 250–278.

Zannetos, Z. S., 1965. On the theory of divisional structures: some aspects of centralisation and decentralisation of control and decision making, *Management Science*, December, pp. 49–68.

12

Divisional Control and Performance Evaluation

In chapter 4 it was suggested that organisational control is a dynamic and a broad concept embedded in a set of multidirectional interrelationships between several control elements. These may include situational contingencies; managerial choice; structural configurations; information system and organisational activity. In chapter 11 two formal models of control were contrasted: markets and hierarchies and agency theory. The discussion there pin-pointed the contributions made by each theory to the notion of organisational control. That discussion, however, concentrated on broad issues of control associated with divisionalised structures.

This chapter is devoted to a more detailed discussion of control systems and performance evaluation techniques related to divisionalised organisations. Here, divisional control is taken not only to include the means by which central management monitors and evaluates the performance of company divisions, but also the influence which divisional managers may exert upon the organisation. Moreover, divisional control as discussed here is taken to be a subset of the much broader organisational control system developed in chapter 4.

The procedures for effective implementation of divisionalised structures may be summarised as follows (see for example, Williamson, 1975): (i) the identification of divisional boundaries (which in turn relates to defining divisional environment and technology, determining divisional size, and defining divisional interdependencies); (ii) the assignment of a quasi-autonomous status to each division (determining the extent of divisional autonomy); (iii) the allocation of company resources to divisions; (iv) the use of performance measures and rewarding schemes to monitor divisional activities and (v) the performing of strategic planning whenever applicable.

In the accounting literature, little attention has been given to (i), (ii) and (v). With few exceptions, consideration of issues like identification of divisional boundaries and extent of divisional discretion has not progressed much beyond elementary statements of methods used in practice, e.g. how much autonomy divisional managers have over pricing decisions. Otherwise, it has traditionally been assumed that such questions are not the concern of accounting researchers. Yet, as indicated below, these issues are extremely important to the broad notion of divisional control which is adopted here.

The control apparatus available to divisionalised organisations is perceived here in a much wider sense than is typically assumed in the accounting literature. Thus, rather than exclusively addressing financial measures of performance, such measures are considered to represent only a part of the total control apparatus. A more comprehensive control apparatus that is consistent with effective implementation of divisionalised structures would incorporate not only financial controls but also structural and other organisational controls. Indeed, the latter can frequently turn out to be more crucial than the former. Financial controls typically involve using performance evaluation techniques (item (iv) above) in addition to stipulated limits on delegated decisions, for example, limits on capital expenditures made by divisional managers beyond which higher authorisation would be sought. Structural controls incorporate such control means as those covered by items (i) and (ii) above and in addition internal audit and reward systems.

This chapter is divided into four sections. Section I contains a discussion of structural controls. Section II reviews financial measures of divisional performance. These include traditional accounting profit, return on investment (ROI), residual income, and discounted cash flow (DCF). Section III reviews some of the literature on risk sharing schemes and principal–agent relationships in the context of divisionalised organisations. Section IV provides a summary of the previous sections, and some concluding remarks.

I. STRUCTURAL CONTROLS IN DIVISIONALISED ORGANISATIONS

Almost exclusively, the accounting literature on divisional control has been concerned with the development of *financial* measures of performance. In the few cases where structural controls have been addressed the analysis has neither been comprehensive nor rigorous. This deficiency is one of the most serious drawbacks in the divisional accounting literature. By contrast, divisional control as defined here emphasises *both* financial and structural control devices. These different control devices interact with and, to a certain extent, constrain each other.

In the context of divisionalised organisations the overall control apparatus can encompass a variety of controls. These may relate to: (i) defining divisional environment; (ii) determining divisional size; (iii) defining and coordinating divisional interdependencies; (iv) determining the extent of divisional decision-making autonomy; (v) characteristics of information and information flow; (vi) designing an internal audit system and (vii) designing an appropriate reward system. Such characteristics may be viewed by organisational participants as a set of interacting decision variables which constrain their actions as well as being the subject of their manipulations. Each of these means of control has an important role to play in harmonising the activities of various company divisions and in achieving some form of overall organisational coherence.

In order to achieve the required or 'permissible' degree of control over some of these variables, the central management would typically make use of some set of administrative rules as well as various informal measures. Formal administrative rules have been the focus of some considerable attention in the management science, economics and organisation theory literature. Bonini (1964), for example, advocated the notions of 'control-in-the-large' and 'control-in-the-small'. The former comprises rules and procedures which concentrate on the totality of the firm and lead to greater measures of decentralisation, whilst the latter deals with segments of the firm and prescribes detailed standards of performance. Similarly, Arrow (1964) advocated the notions of 'operating rules' and 'enforcement rules' to deal with the specification of decision criteria and the monitoring and evaluation of performance.

In the organisation theory literature divisional control is seen by some (Lorsch and Allen, 1973) as being attainable through the judicious use of differentiation and integration. It will be recalled from chapter 1 that according to Lawrence and Lorsch (1967), differentiation refers to differences in goal, time and interpersonal orientations and in formality of practices amongst managers in different organisational units. Integration refers to the quality of collaboration existing amongst organisational units required to achieve unity of effort. By contrast, informal control measures have rarely been explicitly considered particularly in the accounting and economics literatures. In this section the control implications of the structural characteristics outlined above are discussed, emphasising some of the formal and informal control measures suggested in the literature.

Divisional Environment

Consider first the control implications of divisional environment. Lawrence and Lorsch (1967) have reported that: (i) the degree of differentiation required in the firm depends on the extent of diversity of its environment: the more diverse the environment, the more differentiated the sub-units are likely to be, (ii) the difficulty of attaining integration is a function of the extent of differentiation: the more differentiated any two units are, the more difficult it is to achieve integration between them.

What the above argument amounts to is this: the more sub-units (e.g. divisions) operate in diverse environments, the more difficult it is to integrate their activities because of their greater requisite degrees of differentiation. It is desirable, at least from the point of view of the central management, that the divisional control system facilitates the attainment of the requisite degrees of differentiation and integration.

Lorsch and Allen (1973) have considered the influence of the environment on organisational practices, human relations and performance evaluation systems. They reported that within each division, functional (operating) units tended to develop organisational practices which were consistent with the state of the environment, thus: (i) greater certainty in the environment resulted in more formalised organisational practices, and (ii) greater diversity, complexity, and competitiveness of divisional sub-environments resulted in higher differentiation within the division. Similarly, the extent of differentiation amongst divisions seems to be influenced by the diversity of divisional environments in a manner analogous to that of functional units. The degree of central–divisional differentiation has been reported by Lorsch and Allen to be positively related to the extent of diversity of the firm's total environment. Furthermore, cognitive limits at both headquarters and divisional levels, and greater environmental diversity seem to restrict the degree of central–divisional differentiation.

It is worth noting that differentiation can only reduce, and not eliminate, the consequences of interdependence. To manage interdependence more successfully, the organisation needs to achieve some degree of integration between its units. Here again, the findings of Lorsch and Allen (1973) provide some useful insights in the context of divisionalised organisations. Their results point to three major sets of factors which are reported to be related to the effective management of differentiation and integration, namely: integrative devices; integrative effort and decision-making processes. They reported that both within divisions and at corporate-divisional levels, more complex patterns of interdependence among the relevant units result in the development of more complex integrative devices.* Their findings also suggest that at corporate-divisional level greater interdependence associated with lower diversity calls for greater integrative effort in order to manage inter-unit relationships appropriately.

---

*Following the authors, integrating devices may be classified in terms of increasing complexity into paper systems (e.g. budgets); integrative positions (e.g. divisional specialists at headquarters); committees, task forces, and form meetings and direct managerial contact.

Lorsch and Allen also indicated (in consistency with Lawrence and Lorsch, 1967) that some of the characteristics of effective decision making are independent of the particular environmental requirements whilst others are contingent upon prevailing environmental forces. In organisations characterised by patterns of differentiation and integration which are consistent with their environmental settings, persons performing inter-divisional and corporate-divisional integration were reported to have cognitive and interpersonal orientations that were balanced amongst units they were expected to integrate. They also tended to have greater influence compared with members of these units irrespective of environmental contingencies. Further, the researchers reported that such organisations were characterised by flow of high quality information and that they resort to confrontation as a means of resolving inter-unit conflict.

Decision-making characteristics that were contingent upon the environment included speed of headquarters' response to divisional requests; distribution of influence over decision making; and divisional performance evaluation systems. The results indicated that the lower the interdependence required by the environment, the smaller the corporate headquarters units, and the less complex the integration devices and information transmission, the more rapid the headquarters response to divisional requests.

Lorsch and Allen further considered some of the characteristics of divisional performance measurement systems. They reported that conglomerates employed performance evaluation systems that were characterised by explicitly defined criteria, a direct linkage between performance and monetary rewards and greater emphasis on financial/end result criteria. Vertically integrated firms, faced with lower diversity and uncertainty but higher interdependence, developed performance evaluation systems that were more informally administered without a direct linkage between performance and monetary rewards and with emphasis on both financial/end result and operating/intermediate criteria.

Divisional Size

Implications for the optimal sub-unit (divisional) size, from the perspectives of economic efficiency of production, information transmission, and control, have been extensively discussed in the economics and management science literature (see for example, Lioukas and Xerokostas, 1982). This literature, in general, suggests that economic units with similar technological and structural characteristics have comparable optimal economic size.

Yet, this may not always be the case in reality. Economic efficiency may not be the only consideration guiding the decisions of the central management: e.g. cultural, political, and societal considerations may have significant influences. Moreover, even if the central management aims at attaining optimal economic size in pursuit of economic efficiency, divisional managers may have a vested interest in managing larger divisions in order to maximise their non-pecuniary benefits, or in order to increase the extent of formal and informal control they exert upon the organisation. Conversely, the central management (and other divisional managers) may oppose expansion in the size of a particular division in order to restrict the power that can be wielded by its manager. Divisional size is, then, an important control variable which may be subject to frequent manipulations both by the central management and by divisional managers. The resulting size may be as much a reflection of compromise as of economic and administrative efficiency.

Divisional Interdependence

In the context of divisionalised organisations, it may be expedient to consider levels and types of interdependence. Levels of interdependence refer to positions in the organisation's hierarchy at which interdependence may occur. A convenient way of depicting this is to collapse the hierarchy of a divisionalised organisation into a small number of essential organisational levels. Although there are several alternatives, Ruefli (1971a) provides a useful scheme in which he distinguishes between three levels: (i) central management; (ii) divisional management and (iii) operating units within each division. Therefore, there are at least four sets of relationships which would reflect interdependencies:

— The relationships between central management and each divisional manager.
— The relationships between managers of different divisions.
— The relationships between every pair of operating units within a division.
— The relationships between divisional management and each of its operating units.

Other relationships could be considered, e.g. between the operating units of different divisions, but these are assumed away for simplicity. At each of the three specified levels several forms of interdependence may occur:

1. Demand interdependence: complementary; competitive (see, for example, Hirshleifer, 1957).
2. Technological interdependence: pooled; sequential; reciprocal (see, for example, Thompson, 1967).
3. Behavioural interdependence: uni-directional; bi-directional; multi-directional (see, for example, Ruefli, 1971b).

Without 'appropriate' coordination of such interdependencies, inefficient, and even adverse, decisions may be taken. For example, when the demand for the products of company divisions is competitive, some divisional managers may engage in practices (e.g. significant price reductions) which further their own interests at the expense of those of other divisions and of the company as a whole. Similarly, when the technologies of some divisions are sequentially or reciprocally interdependent the flow of activities between these divisions has to be carefully coordinated.

Lorsch and Allen (1973) provided some useful insights relating to managing interdependence. They considered divisional differentiation at three levels: within each division; between divisions; and between each division and the central management. Their results indicate that interdependence is higher among functional (operating) units within a division, than amongst divisions or between divisions and the headquarters. This observation has important implications for the design of divisionalised organisation. Thus, in the face of complex and uncertain environments the organisation may be able to confine complex interdependencies within divisional units whilst permitting less complex interdependencies to exist either between the divisions and the headquarters or amongst the divisions. This leaves managers at each level with the relatively easy task of managing a limited portion of the firm's total environment. It is worth noting, however, that containing complex interdependencies within divisions has implications for other divisional control variables. For example, this may lead to changes in divisional size, the definition of divisional tasks, the identification of lines of authority and responsibility and so on.

In their historical analysis of administrative practices, Chandler and Daems (1979) found that as task interdependence increased there was less reliance on market mechanisms to coordinate activities. Instead, administrative coordination mechanisms were developed.

Divisional Autonomy

Divisional autonomy underlies a number of important control issues. For instance, it can play a crucial role in the evaluation of alternative performance measures (see for example, the Solomons/Amey debate regarding whether or not a cost of capital figure should be levied against divisional revenues). Moreover, it may be closely associated with company overall effectiveness and other organisational characteristics. There are a number of key questions that may be asked in this connection. For example, how much autonomy should divisional managers have in a given decision-making area? What considerations should be taken into account in deciding upon that degree of automony? Should the degree of autonomy in the *same* decision area differ for *different* managers? And so on.

Unfortunately, the literature in this area is sparse. Some of the relevant conceptual problems have been alluded to. Examples include problems of quantifying discretion and assigning appropriate weights to different decision areas (e.g. Leibenstein, 1965, but see Ezzamel and Hilton, 1980b). Moreover, Williamson (1970; 1975) considered the question of how decision-making responsibility should be divided between the headquarters and divisional managers. He stipulated that responsibility for decision making should be split between divisional managers and central managers so that the former handle operating decisions whereas the latter take strategic decisions. Any confounding of such split, he contends, will result in sub-optimal divisionalisation which will, in turn, have detrimental effects on company performance. This argument is supported by the historical analysis of the practices of pioneering divisionalised organisations such as General Motors and du Pont (see Chandler and Daems, 1979).

Thus, if central managers become directly involved in operating decisions, a corrupted divisionalised structure emerges in which at least four types of decision-making inefficiency may occur. Firstly, inferior operating decisions are likely to be made because central managers are not as well informed as divisional managers in operating matters. Secondly, operating decisions may be untimely if, as would be expected, central managers have to wait for local information to be collected and submitted to them. Thirdly, communication channels will be overloaded by information transfers from divisional managers to central managers and vice versa leading to greater system noise and cost. Fourthly, strategic decisions will be of poorer quality because central managers, being immersed in operating matters, would be unable to devote the requisite time and attention to such decisions. Similarly, if divisional managers become directly involved in strategic decisions overall company survival could be endangered because these managers (i) lack the corporate view required for making such decisions and (ii) may pursue personal interests that are detrimental to the company.

A decision-making area of prime importance is the one relating to the allocation of resources amongst divisions. This, Williamson argued, is the prerogative of central management who can effectively replace and even outperform the external capital market by regulating the divisionalised firm as a miniature capital market. Rather than allowing newly generated cash flows to simply revert back to the divisions where they have been realised, they are exposed to internal competition and are ultimately allocated to divisions with the most potentially profitable investment proposals. Thus, resource allocation is made responsive to differential performance.

The implications of such a resource allocation system for divisional control are significant. Resource commitments are clearly essential for divisional continuity and growth. Financially successful divisions are likely to command greater resources which, in turn, could lead to greater size and importance. Moreover, divisions with tendencies to conform less with central policies could be brought into greater conformity with such policies through the resource allocation system. Less conformity could imply less resources being allocated to the division. This may lead to pressure being exerted on divisional managers by lower-level participants, who would possibly suffer most of the consequences of resource cuts, so that the former may conform better with central policies.

How do these theoretical arguments compare with empirical results? In general, available empirical evidence is neither comprehensive nor conclusive. Several studies (e.g. NICB 1961; Mauriel and Anthony 1966; Tomkins 1973; Ezzamel and Hilton, 1980a; 1980b; Scapens and Sale, 1981; 1985) have attempted to provide some assessment of the extent of divisional autonomy in several decision-making areas, but few related their findings to other organisational characteristics. This body of evidence suggests that the extent of divisional autonomy varied greatly from one decision-making area to another. Thus, it appears that divisional managers enjoy greater discretion with respect to operating policy decisions and less discretion in the areas of financing policy, investment policy and accounting and internal control systems (e.g. Ezzamel and Hilton, 1980b; Tomkins, 1973). The results of Scapens and Sale (1981), however, suggest that divisional managers may be able to influence capital investment decisions, even though such decisions are typically subject to formal authorisation by higher managers.

Although this descriptive evidence is useful, it clearly fails to provide answers to questions such as: why should the extent of discretion vary between decision-making areas? Is there an optimal level of divisional discretion and if so, how can it be defined? A common sense approach would presumably imply that divisional discretion should be limited in decision areas characterised by excessive inter-dependencies as well as in areas of crucial importance to the organisation as a whole. This may be particularly true if the performance evaluation system employed by the organisation does not sufficiently reflect the consequences of decisions taken by divisional managers. Is there much evidence in support of such common sense argument?

Here again, available evidence is limited and inconclusive. A useful contribution in this context is the work of Lorsch and Allen (1973). They reported that in organisations characterised by appropriate patterns of differentiation and integration the distribution of decision-making power, both lateral and hierarchical, tended to coincide with the location of relevant information. Thus, at corporate-divisional interface influence tended to be concentrated at divisional management level in conglomerates which were faced with higher uncertainty and diversity and lower interdependence. By contrast, in vertically integrated organisations senior vice presidents exercised greater influence on decision making.

In a study undertaken by Ezzamel and Hilton (1980a) the authors attempted to investigate: (i) the association between divisional discretion (autonomy) and other company characteristics, and (ii) the question of optimal divisional discretion. Their results suggest that there is little difference in the extent of overall divisional discretion across different industrial classifications. They noted, however, that companies in their sample with outside markets for *all* their products seem to operate with greater measures of divisional autonomy compared with companies with outside markets for only some of their products. This may be rationalised on the grounds that in the absence of an outside yardstick, greater central control may be required to motivate divisions to act in accordance with overall company interest. Scapens and Sale (1985), however, tested for the possibility that differences in divisional autonomy contribute to the variety in accounting methods used to control divisionalised operations. Such expected association was not observed in their results. The results of Ezzamel and Hilton also suggest that their sample of companies seem to be operating with sub-optimally high degrees of divisional discretion: the estimated probability of company success was reported to rise as the autonomy score falls.

Characteristics of Information and Information Flow

As discussed in chapter 11, one of the important implications of agency theory and the markets and hierarchies theory for the design of accounting systems is their focus on the characteristics and flow of information. Information has been advanced by these theories as an effective means for the reduction of uncertainty. *Ex ante* information reduces *ex ante* uncertainty (arising from the agent taking actions before their consequences reveal themselves) by helping the divisional manager to predict future states of the world. *Ex post* information reduces *ex post* uncertainty (arising from inability to identify determinants of outcome) by facilitating the writing and enforcement of contracts between headquarters and divisional managers: 'the knowledge that such information will be available, *ex-post*, enables *ex-ante* agreements to be reached by the contracting parties' (Tiessen and Waterhouse, 1983, p. 258).

As suggested earlier, certain information characteristics facilitate the reduction of uncertainty. *Ex ante* information should be predictable, and thus it should be possible to obtain and harness it to reduce uncertainty. *Ex post* information should be verifiable, unequivocal and acceptable to relevant economic users. These characteristics minimise disputes in performance evaluations which may arise in the context of a division in relation to measurement of outcomes, causes of outcomes and other dimensions of performance (Tiessen and Waterhouse, 1983).

The nature of information may also vary depending on prevailing conditions. Thus, in situations where it is possible to write and enforce complete employment contracts between headquarters and divisional managers, the focus of the accounting system would be on providing the detailed information necessary for complete contracting. However, in situations where the writing and enforcement of complete contracts is not possible, information about output becomes more important. When output is difficult to observe and verify, owing to high technological and environmental uncertainty, the focus of information is likely to shift towards 'soft' information about divisional technology and environment, corporate ethos, managerial seniority and so on (Spicer and Ballew, 1983).

Internal Audit and Reward Systems

Consider first the role of internal audit in controlling divisional activities. Internal audit can involve performance evaluation at three levels; advance, contemporaneous and *ex post*. Advance evaluation involves reviewing divisional proposed alternative courses of action and forming judgements as to their merits, cost and overall desirability. Contemporaneous evaluation entails continuous monitoring of current divisional performance against some previously stated target. *Ex post* evaluation involves comparing divisional actual performance against targets at the end of a given period.

Williamson (1970; 1975) argued that internal audit systems in divisionalised organisations are more effective than the external capital market in controlling divisional activities for two reasons. Firstly, the relationships between divisional managers and central managers are regulated through employment contracts. As a consequence, the records and files of divisional managers, as subordinates, are directly available for review by central management. Much of this information is not disclosed to outsiders and thus capital markets cannot engage in comparable evaluations. Secondly, internal disclosure of information is usually assumed to be essential for maintaining organisational integrity and is thus expected to foster greater cooperation between organisational participants. By contrast, disclosure of internal information to outsiders (unless authorised) is not treated favourably by the organisation.

The reward system is another means through which the management of the divisionalised company can regulate and motivate divisional activities towards desired ends. Rewards may be pecuniary or nonpecuniary; both types can be adjusted by the headquarters to reflect differences in performance and to bring divisional activities in line with corporate policy. The reward system can be structured in such a way that persistently deviant (uncooperative) divisional managers are penalised through job transfers, or even dismissal. Moreover, as Williamson (1975) noted, managerial changes at divisional level are frequently undertaken because they can lead to better motivation of lower-level participants. Employment policies, including employment contracts, can be specified and organised in a way that maximises the chances of divisional activities being in line with corporate interest.

The preceding discussion illustrates the wide repertoire of controls available to divisionalised organisations. It is clear from the discussion that financial control, which has long been cherished in the accounting literature as the most important form of control, is only a subset of that repertoire. Moreover, the controls discussed above are not mutually exclusive: rather, they complement each other. Thus, instead of endorsing the contingency view of deterministic matchings between situational contingencies and control devices, the above discussion emphasises the considerable choice of controls available to divisionalised organisations. In the following section divisional financial controls are examined.

II. FINANCIAL MEASURES OF DIVISIONAL PERFORMANCE

As suggested earlier, divisional accounting literature has been predominantly concerned with financial measures of performance. Non-financial measures have received relatively little attention. An implicit assumption underlying these financial measures is profit-maximisation, which has its roots in the economics literature. Williamson (1970, 1975) has developed a model for multidivision organisations which he calls the 'M-form hypothesis' (see chapter 11). According to this hypothesis a change from the centralised, or unitary form (U-form) to the M-form contributes to the reduction of both the control loss and sub-goal pursuit usually associated with the U-form.

It has been suggested in chapter 11 that empirical studies by Armour and Teece (1978); Steer and Cable (1978); Teece (1981) and Thompson (1981) support the M-form hypothesis but that more recent studies (e.g. Cable and Dirrheimer, 1983; Bühner, 1984) provided no support for that hypothesis. Clearly, much more evidence is needed before the empirical credibility of the M-form hypothesis can be established. More fundamental for the purposes of this chapter, however, is the argument that compared with the U-form the M-form is more consistent with neoclassical profit maximisation. This is particularly relevant because, as is shown later, the notion of profit maximisation underlies much of the literature in the area of divisional accounting.

In pursuing the notion of profit maximisation, the divisional accounting literature has focused on the development of effective resource allocation and performance evaluation techniques. For convenience, in much of the subsequent discussion the former topic will be subsumed under the latter. However, before considering performance evaluation measures, it is convenient first to briefly outline the objectives of divisional financial performance measurement.

Objectives of Divisional Financial Performance Measurement

Divisional accounting literature typically suggests three main reasons for which an index of divisional profitability would be desired (e.g. Solomons, 1965). Firstly, to help the central management in assessing the efficiency with which divisional managers run the activities of their divisions. Secondly, to guide divisional managers in making decisions with respect to their own divisional activities. Thirdly, to guide the central management in making divisional viability decisions (e.g. whether to expand, contract, or even close down a division).

The categorisation of the objectives of divisional performance measurement along these lines reflects the narrow view of control underlying the accounting literature. Control is taken to be exclusively a central management problem. The much wider organisational aspects of control are not fully addressed. The interests of members of the organisational coalition other than those of the central managers are typically ignored. Yet, other organisational participants (both insiders and outsiders) may have considerable interest in obtaining information on sub-unit performance. Ortman (1975), for example, has reported that financial analysts use disclosed segmental (divisional) data when estimating the per-share value of the firm's capital. With the use of segmental data, it was reported, the value of each firm's capital was in accordance with the present value of its expected returns as reflected by industry average P/E ratios whilst without such segmental data there was no such consistency.

There is also an increasing tendency towards companies' disclosure of financial information by major segments (divisions) in the USA, the UK, and many EEC countries. However, there is some evidence of the presence of statistically significant differences between these countries with respect to both the overall level of disclosure of a particular type of analysis (e.g. sales, profit) and the extent of disclosure with regard to the dimensions of both business (product or industry) and geographical activity (Gray, 1978).

Clearly, more empirical evidence is needed before firm conclusions can be drawn about the relevance of the disclosure of segmental data to various decision makers. Nevertheless, it seems plausible to suggest that segmental data are likely to be useful to various external user groups. Below is a discussion of the relevance of some traditional profitability measures to divisional performance measurement.

Traditional Profitability Measures

The search for a unique index of profitability which best serves the objectives of divisional performance measurement stimulated an interesting debate in the accounting literature of the last three decades. Guided either by practical expedience or economic rationality different writers advocated different profitability measures.

These measures include accounting profit; return on investment (ROI); residual income (RI) and discounted cash flow (DCF).

Shillinglaw (1957) and Amey (1969a; 1969b; 1975) are amongst the most prominent advocates of profit as a measure of divisional performance. Arguing from the position of macro economic efficiency rather than the efficiency of a single enterprise, Amey contended that firms should simultaneously maximise profits and minimise total costs. By more careful specification of required data, it is held, it would be possible to produce profit figures which would be a good proxy for economic efficiency. Briefly, this would involve setting profit targets, measured *ex ante* in economic terms, against which actual profits may be compared. Decision making and performance evaluation are thus kept, as far as possible, in line with economic efficiency.

Shillinglaw discussed the usefulness of four variants of accounting profit for divisional accounting purposes: net profit; contribution margin; controllable profit and sales margin. Net profit seems to be the least useful of these variants. The arbitrary allocation of extra-divisional overheads distorts divisional profitability and can induce sub-optimal decisions, for example, if divisions attempt to recover these overheads in their product prices. However, sometimes such allocations are desirable at least as proxies for relevant but unobservable costs, and for facilitating the centre's control over divisional perquisites (e.g. Zimmerman, 1979; Ezzamel and Bourn, 1987). Contribution margin (sales revenue less divisional variable costs and divisional separable, controllable and non-controllable fixed costs) is useful in indicating the extent of divisional contribution towards the recovery of extra-divisional overheads. However, it is not particularly helpful for current operating decisions nor for control purposes because it takes account of divisional separable non-controllable fixed costs. Such costs are clearly 'sunk-costs' and are usually initiated and changed by decisions made by headquarters. Controllable profit (sales revenue less divisional variable costs and divisional separable controllable fixed costs) seems more useful for evaluating the performance of divisional managers because it emphasises traceability and controllability, the two conventional pillars of responsibility accounting. Sales margin (sales revenue less variable costs) is useful in showing the effects of current decisions on divisional performance, for instance, changing the selling price by a given amount (see Shillinglaw, 1957; Henderson and Dearden, 1966).

Accounting profit does, then, have its advocates. However, it has been suggested that, compared with accounting profit, ROI is a more useful measure of profitability. Gabor and Pearce (1952), for example, have argued that equilibrium for an economic entity is attained when ROI is maximised. Assuming perfect competition, when the industry is in equilibrium, each firm maximises its return (i.e. earns the normal rate of return on capital) at that level of output which corresponds to minimum average cost. When the industry is in disequilibrium, it is held, extra units of the same size should be established to absorb abnormal profits. Gabor and Pearce have also extended their conclusions to the conditions of imperfect markets.

As is already well known, if divisional managers have discretion over the allocation of central resources, then maximising ROI need not be consistent with maximising absolute profit; only if divisional capital is a constant will the two be consistent. Yet, as Amey (1969a; 1969b) has argued, it is difficult to think of many cases in which capital is constant. Even if divisional capital is determined by the headquarters decisions concerning its use, e.g. changes in activity level, will frequently change its value.

Both measures, however, have some crucial limitations. One basic limitation of ROI is that it could lead divisional managers into making sub-optimal decisions. Thus, in non-capital-rationing situations it may be in the best interest of the firm for all its capital resources to be invested as long as they earn a return greater than the opportunity cost of capital. Yet, under ROI, divisional managers will have an incentive to restrict their investments to those projects which are expected to yield the highest ROI even though the return on rejected projects may be above the firm's opportunity cost of capital.

Further, problems in addition to those usually associated with accounting profit are likely to be encountered when using ROI. For example, the use of either gross book value or net book value to calculate the investment base under ROI can lead to sub-optimal decisions. If gross book value is used to define the divisional investment base there is an incentive for divisional managers (provided they have the power) to scrap any equipment which may be temporarily idle in the short-run in order to increase their ROI. The use of net book value tends to exaggerate divisional ROI particularly if the divisional asset portfolio contains a large number of old but serviceable assets whose original costs are significantly below their replacement costs. This can lead to misallocation of company resources if the exaggerated ROI is instrumental in influencing the amount of resources committed to each division. It may also make the divisional manager reluctant to invest in projects that are profitable but have a lower ROI, because this would result in a lower overall ROI (see Dearden, 1960). Moreover, to calculate the divisional investment base the central management will usually have to engage in arbitrary allocations of those resources such as receivables, payables and cash which are not directly attributable to individual divisions but which are clearly related to divisional activities (see Vatter, 1959; Dearden, 1961).

Because of these and other limitations Horngren (1962) has suggested that the change in the rate of return is often more significant than its absolute size. Amey (1969a; 1969b) has also suggested that it may be expedient to set profit maximisation as the objective and merely express the result as a rate of return. Absolute ROI as an optimal profitability index seems to have been rejected by most writers.

Similarly, accounting profit has not been widely blessed in the literature. In addition to the well-known shortcomings of its measurement conventions, it has been criticised, particularly by Solomons (1965) for its failure to account for the cost of capital resources entrusted to divisions in those cases where divisional managers have considerable control over the determination of their investment bases. This, Solomons argued, can induce sub-optimal decisions by encouraging divisional managers to invest extra capital as long as it can generate a greater than zero return, even though that return may be lower than the company's cost of capital. Moreover, divisions may be encouraged to produce apparent, rather than real, improvements in their efficiency by substituting capital services for labour services. A problem similar to this can arise in firms subject to public control when regulatory agencies specify a 'fair' rate of return target for these firms. Averch and Johnson (1962) have shown that, in this situation, the firm has an incentive to substitute production factors in an uneconomic fashion that is difficult for the regulatory agency to detect.

Solomons (1965) contended that residual income (the excess of net earnings over the cost of capital) would overcome these limitations. He pointed out that charging cost of capital to divisions would fulfil the dual role of guiding decisions and evaluating performance. Thus, divisional managers would have an incentive to invest in all projects that promise internal rates of return higher than, or at least equal to, the cost of capital. No profitable projects would be avoided, as under ROI, and no inefficient investments (in the sense of having expected returns below the cost of capital) would be encouraged, as might be the case under accounting profit. It is also held that residual income facilitates comparisons of performance of company divisions because they all have to cover the cost of capital on their resources. Shwayder (1970) also made the point that under residual income the actions of divisional managers are made sensitive to changes in the capital market by manipulating the division's required rate of return as the company's cost of capital changes. Solomons (1965) further contended that residual income is the short-run analogue of maximising the long-run discounted cash flow (DCF) value of the firm. This would imply that the use of residual income is consistent with the maximisation of long-run shareholders' wealth as reflected in the DCF model.

The Cost of Capital Debate

The case for residual income, as argued by Solomons in particular, has stimulated some considerable debate in the accounting literature. The debate effectively centres around examining the justifications for, and the consequences of, levying a cost of capital charge against divisions.

It has been pointed out that if the goal of the firm is profit maximisation, and if the cost of capital charges does not affect divisional prices, then the level of activity at which residual income is maximised will in general be smaller than the level at which profit is maximised (because of the higher total costs under residual income). Only in the unlikely case of the cost curve shifting iso-elastically, i.e. the cost curves under both residual income and profit having the same slope in the region of profit maximising output, will the two activity levels coincide. Thus, charging cost of capital can lead to sub-optimal use of company resources.

This argument may be taken to imply that under profit maximisation the cost of capital should not be treated as part of the total cost. Indeed, Gabor and Pearce (1952) have argued, in respect of individual firms, that the inclusion of the cost of capital in the total cost curve is incorrect for theoretical and practical reasons. Firstly, they argued, traditional economic theory does not distinguish between the two fundamental functions of the entrepreneur: provision of money capital and management. In seeking to draw this distinction they defined costs as payments to contracting factors, including payments (salaries and compensation) to management, who offer their services at an agreed price. Profit is defined as what remains from the revenues after meeting such costs and therefore represents a residue to be distributed to controlling factors (providers of capital). The opportunity cost of capital (normal profit under some restrictive assumptions) is a part of that residue. Secondly, Gabor and Pearce pointed out that according to accounting practice, the cost of equity capital is not treated as a cost element but rather as a profit to be distributed amongst ordinary shareholders.

Further criticisms of charging divisions for the cost of capital they utilise have been made by Amey (1969a; 1969b). Firstly, he argued that charging cost of capital, as suggested by Solomons, does, in fact, confuse investment considerations with production considerations. In evaluating investment proposals, the cost of funds available for investment should be considered. However, the determination of the efficient production set, he argued, does not depend on levying a cost of capital charge but rather on relevant technological possibilities, e.g. scale of production. Once this is solved, economic factors (e.g. relative input prices) rather than *ex post* imputed cost of capital are the relevant variables to consider before deciding upon which techniques to employ. Secondly, Amey was critical of Solomons' assertion that the cost of capital can fulfil the dual role of guiding decisions and appraising performance. He argued that, in considering how funds should be allocated amongst divisions, it is the opportunity cost of uncommitted money capital that is relevant. Once investment has occurred, however, decisions will not be concerned with evaluating performance but rather with the best use to which assets should be put, in which case the opportunity cost of capital goods will be relevant.

Amey's argument in connection with capital cost charges has caused much confusion and debate in the accounting literature. Some writers (e.g. Tomkins, 1975a) have attempted to reconcile the arguments of Amey and Solomons by suggesting that each is concerned with different problems: Solomons with motivational aspects of project selection decisions and Amey with appraising divisional performance given that the investment decision has already been taken. Bromwich (1973) has also suggested Amey's argument implies that charging an imputed cost of capital is irrelevant for marginal decisions since marginal cost, as it is normally defined, already includes all costs associated with additional output. Amey (1975), however, has rejected both these two attempts to reconcile his views with those of Solomons.

Amey's argument was made somewhat clearer in his 1975 paper. In defining costs associated with capital inputs he distinguished between cash outlay costs (explicit costs) and opportunity costs (implicit costs). Cash outlay costs represent interest payment on debt for working capital and maintenance expenditure for fixed capital. Opportunity costs reflect economic depreciation (including obsolescence) for fixed capital. Interest payment on working capital is treated by Amey as part of his cost function. It represents a variable cost paid to contracting factors (money lenders). In the case of new investments, the cost of funds available for investment should be taken into consideration because it represents the opportunity cost of investing. Once investment decisions have been taken, divisions should be charged with the cost of holding and using the assets, in this case maintenance expenditure and economic depreciation.

One issue that is relevant to the above debate is the extent of autonomy granted to divisions with regard to investment decisions. Solomons addressed cases in which divisional managers have some considerable influence on resource allocation. Amey, however, argued that in the interest of corporate optimality divisional autonomy with respect to determining divisional investment levels should be limited. Available empirical evidence seems to be consistent with this contention (e.g. NICB, 1961; Tomkins, 1973; Ezzamel and Hilton, 1980a; 1980b, but see Scapens and Sales, 1981, for evidence of greater divisional autonomy in this area). In such situations, it may be argued that charging cost of capital to divisions is not justified.

Another related issue is whether maximising residual income is compatible with maximising the net present value of the firm. Although Solomons contended that the two concepts are consistent Amey argued that they are not, essentially because the *imputed* cost of capital suggested by Solomons is not always the correct cost of capital to consider, as argued above. Flower (1971) suggested a reconciliation between residual income and DCF. Under Flower's scheme, residual income figures are calculated using DCF principles for valuing assets, depreciation and interest charges. Given that annual net cash flow is made up of depreciation and interest on capital (normal profit), the target residual income for divisional managers under Flower's scheme will always be zero. To instruct a divisional manager to meet a zero residual income target may not induce the desired motivational consequences (see Bromwich, 1973, for a discussion of the adverse motivational consequences of such a measure). Tomkins (1975a; 1975b) showed that Solomons' argument holds when multi-period effects are absent: i.e. each period begins and ends without working capital balances and current output decisions have no effect on future cash flows. Adjustments for multi-period effects, Tomkins argued, can simply be introduced into the non-multi-period effects model by allowing for the carrying forward of working capital balances. Amey (1975) criticises Tomkins' argument on the grounds that once we consider multi-period effects it is not helpful to concentrate on any one period in isolation because of likely interactions between different periods. Moreover, as Amey points out, it is not only the past which may interact with the present, as Tomkins appears to imply; the future may interact with the present and the present with the future.

The above discussion indicates the nature of the debate on the cost of capital in the context of divisional accounting. The debate is far from resolved and is likely to continue as long as discussion is constrained within the confines of the three traditional performance indices so far discussed.

It is worth noting that, even if the cost of capital debate is resolved, traditional profitability indices are inadequate for the purposes of divisional profitability measurement. Traditional accounting measurement techniques are typically employed in the measurement of accounting profit, ROI, and residual income. Consequently, these indices share two common limitations which greatly restrict their usefulness. Firstly, all three indices concentrate on short-run performance at the expense of long-run performance. For example, divisional managers will be induced to make sub-optimal decisions so long as they result in higher short-run profits. This may be achieved, for instance, by cutting down expenditures with potential services extending over more than one period, by transferring profits from one period to another, e.g. over-stating assets, or by choosing projects with higher expected short-run returns but which are non-optimal in terms of their net present values. Secondly, all three indices generate *ex post* information that is clearly inadequate for the purposes of decisions relating to divisional viability and operating activities (see Ezzamel, 1973).

Several writers have suggested that instead of the traditional profitability measures discussed above, a DCF-based divisional profitability index should be used to monitor divisional performance (see, for example, Bodenhorn, 1964; Lawson, 1971; Lee, 1972; Rappaport, 1975; Ezzamel, 1979). Such a position renders irrelevant the debate on whether or not a cost of capital should be charged. Rather, the relevant question then becomes what cost of capital (discount rate) should be used.

Discounted Cash Flow Income

To evaluate the case for and against the use of DCF in assessing divisional profitability it will be convenient to consider this model in some detail here. In a world of complete certainty and perfect markets, the income of division j in period t may be expressed as:

(1)

$$\pi_t^j = PV_{t+1}^j - PV_t^j$$

$$= \sum_t^\infty \frac{C_t^j}{(1 + R_f)^{t-1}} - \sum_t^\infty \frac{C_t^j}{(1 + R_f)^t}$$

where π_t^j = the DCF income of the jth division in period t: t=1,2 ... ∞; PV_t^j = the present value of the jth division in period t; C_t^j = the cash flow of the jth division in period t; R_f = the risk-free interest rate (assumed constant over all periods for simplicity).

But given that

(2)

$$PV_{t+1}^j = PV_t^j (1 + R_f)$$

it follows that

(3)

$$\pi^j_t = PV^j_t (R_f)$$

Equation (3) shows that divisional income in period t is the product of the present value of the division at the start of the period and the interest rate.

However, once the assumptions of certainty are relaxed, the model presented above becomes more complicated. Divisional future cash flows will be stochastic and their probability distributions will need to be estimated. Appropriate adjustments taking account of risk will have to be introduced. Writing $E(C^j_t)$ to denote the expected cash flow of division j in period t, Y^j_t as some appropriate certainty equivalent, λ as the price of risk in the market, and $Cov[C^j_t, \tilde{r}_m]$ as the covariance of the random returns of division j with those of the market portfolio, the present value of division j in period t can be re-written as:

(4)

$$PV^j_t = \overset{\infty}{\underset{t}{\Sigma}} \frac{Y^j_t \, E(C^j_t)}{(1 + R_f)^t} = \overset{\infty}{\underset{t}{\Sigma}} \frac{E(C^j_t) - \lambda Cov|\tilde{C}^j_t, \tilde{r}_m|}{(1 + R_f)^t}$$

with $\lambda = [E(r_m) - R_f]/\sigma^2_{rm}$, where σ^2_{rm} is the variance of the market returns.

Alternatively, a risk-adjusted discount rate K^j_t may be used in which case (4) can be rewritten as:

(5)

$$PV^j_t = \overset{\infty}{\underset{t}{\Sigma}} \frac{E(C^j_t)}{(1 + k^j_t)^t}$$

The DCF models under uncertainty expressed in (4) and (5) raise several interesting questions. One question is how can divisional performance be assessed in DCF terms? A possible approach would be to compare the expected end of period present values as calculated at the beginning and at the end of the period. Let Z^j_t represent the *ex ante* present value target for division j at the end of period (t=1) as calculated at the beginning of that period. Hence, we have:

(6)

$$\text{Maximise } Z^j_{t=1} = \overset{\infty}{\underset{t=1}{\Sigma}} \frac{E(C^j_t)}{(1 + k^j_t)^{t-1}}$$

Now let $Z'^j_{t=1}$ be the present value of division j at the end of period (t=1) as calculated *ex post* at the end of that period. Hence, we have:

(7)

$$Z'^j_{t=1} = C^j_1 + \overset{\infty}{\underset{t=2}{\Sigma}} \frac{E(C'^j_t)}{(1 + k^j_t)^{t-1}}$$

Equation (7) differs from equation (6) in at least two respects. Firstly, the actual net cash flow achieved at the end of period (t=1), C^j_1 could be different from the expected cash flow $E(C^j_1)$. Secondly, new expectations of future net cash flows, $E(C'^j_t)$, may now be different from the original expectations $E(C^j_t)$. Such differences in expectations could be due to changes in economic conditions, changes in forecasting ability, or actions taken by the divisional manager, or other managers, during the current period. The assessment of managerial performance would therefore require careful stipulation of the causes of the difference between (6) and (7). Clearly, alternative DCF approaches to the assessment of divisional performance are viable, e.g. maximising period cash flows subject to a minimum constraint on expected end-of-period value.

A second question relates to how divisional cost of capital should be determined. More specifically, should a unique rate for all divisions be used or should use be made of different discount rates that reflect differing divisional risk classes? Solomons (1965) and Flower (1971) suggest using the company cost of capital as a unique discount rate for all divisions. This argument implies that the risk class of each division and of the parent company is the same. Solomons acknowledged the variations in the riskiness of individual divisions, but justified his argument for a unique discount rate by claiming that divisional effects on the riskiness of the parent company cannot be assessed by looking at each division separately.

Whilst admitting the difficulties involved in attempting to assess the effects of each division on overall company riskiness, Solomons' argument for the use of a unique discount rate is not convincing. The typical multi-division firm combines divisions with different risk classes. If a unique discount rate is used for all divisions in this case, the expansion of the divisionalised firm may tend to be in favour of divisions with higher risk classes; such divisions are assumed to generate higher returns compared with divisions with lower risk classes. Furthermore, divisions with 'high' risk classes are likely to accept investment projects which would be deemed non-optimal if a differential divisional cost of capital were used to evaluate them.

Shwayder (1970) proposed using an imputed default-free (riskless) interest rate whilst letting the users of divisional financial statements apply their own subjective risk premiums to obtain risk-adjusted present values. Whilst this proposal may seem to add some flexibility to the DCF model it does little to resolve the discount rate problem. On the one hand, some uniformity in the ways of handling risk would be convenient for internal decision-making purposes. On the other hand, it may be desirable to provide outside users with advice with respect to how risk can be taken into consideration in the context of various financial decisions.

Given that divisions typically have no shares traded on the stock market some writers have suggested using the capital asset pricing model and some accounting instrumental variables, e.g. periodic earnings, as a proxy for market returns to derive estimates of divisional cost of capital. These estimates would be based on the covariance of some chosen divisional variable and a similar market portfolio variable (see, for example, Gordon and Halpern, 1974; Ezzamel, 1979; Fuller and Kerr, 1981). Such attempts provide encouraging improvements, but further theoretical and empirical research is needed before they can gain wider recognition.

A third important question concerns the reliability of cash flow forecasts under uncertainty. It has often been argued that forecasting techniques have improved in the last few decades (see Chambers, Mullick and Smith, 1971), but clearly they remain uncertain. It may be argued that the unreliability of cash flow forecasts are most pertinent when DCF is used to assess the efficiency of divisional managers. If the net cash flow expectations of a divisional manager are different from those of the central management it is usually difficult to know whose expectations are realistic.

A fourth point relates to the treatment of depreciation under DCF. Jaedicke (1967) made the point that DCF does not distinguish between return *on* capital and return *of* capital; it does not treat depreciation explicitly. Although the depreciation equivalent is included in the annual net cash flow, it has no necessary relationship with the physical depreciation of the assets involved. The implicit depreciation allowance follows the pattern of annual net cash flows – it increases with them and decreases with them.

Clearly, these and other arguments against the use of DCF need to be carefully assessed and contrasted with arguments for DCF. In so far as some profitability index is needed in the context of divisional reporting, the following points are worth noting:

— If profit is defined in terms of economic income (as suggested by, for example, Amey), then maximising profit as defined above will generate decisions that will maximise net present value of wealth as measured by DCF (see Scapens, 1979 for a detailed discussion of this).

— It is generally acknowledged that rational investment, operating and sub-unit viability decisions should be guided by some form of DCF analysis.

— The subjectivity associated with the estimation of expected future cash flows and divisional discount rates may not be greater than the subjectivity inherent in the traditional indices.

III. RISK-SHARING SCHEMES AND PRINCIPAL–AGENT RELATIONSHIPS

One major drawback in the previous analysis is that it structures the problem in a restrictive setting. The implications of uncertainty and its potential impact on the incentives and the behaviour of various decision makers is not explicitly considered. Gaming (for example, submitting untruthful information) amongst divisional managers, and between divisional managers on the one hand and the central management on the other hand, is hardly addressed. Moreover, the possibilities of coalition between divisional managers against the centre are not adequately treated. Clearly, the analysis in section II is incomplete.

Essentially, the problem addressed in this section is a typical agency problem: the central management (the principal) entrusts resources and decisions with respect to the use of these resources to the divisional manager (the agent) at an agreed price (the fee). Both the principal and the agent have goals and such goals are likely to be conflicting. To achieve his goals, the principal may engage in judicious choice of policies to monitor the behaviour of the agent and these may include designing incentive schemes and sanctions, observing the agent's efforts and using other monitoring devices. But typically the cost of these monitoring devices is non-trivial and even if the principal is prepared to incur such cost it is unlikely, owing to uncertainty and information asymmetry, that these monitoring devices will be completely effective.

Structuring the agency problem in this manner is clearly problematic. Firstly, it gives the impression of reducing the organisation to simply two individuals (the principal and the agent) locked into an agency relationship. Secondly, the nature of the relationship between the principal and the agent appears to be adversarial. In relation to the first problem, it should be noted that much of the recent analysis using the information economics approach, which forms the basis for agency theory research, focuses on multi-period, multi-person settings. This section focuses on two-person models to make the analysis tractable. In relation to the second problem, it should be noted that despite the differences in their interests and tactics, the principal and agent may share broad strategic concerns, for example, towards growth, corporate survival, and so on. However, from the perspective of the present analysis, the important issue is to show if, and by what mechanisms, the conflicting interests of the principal and the agent are brought into equilibrium. As indicated in chapter 11, this is precisely the problem that both the agency theory and the markets and hierarchies theory purport to be addressing.

Several writers have investigated the relationship between the agent's fee and the outcome of his organisational role, the characteristics of risk-sharing schemes in general (e.g. Ross, 1973; Stiglitz, 1974 and 1975; Mirrlees, 1976; Shavell, 1979; Holmstrom, 1979) as well as risk-sharing characteristics in the context of divisionalised firms in particular (e.g. Groves and Loeb, 1975, 1976, 1979; Loeb and Magat, 1978; Kanodia, 1979). Shavell (1979), for example, pointed out that for the agent's fee schedule to be Pareto optimal, it must provide a satisfactory allocation of the risk attaching to the outcome of the agent's activity and appropriate incentives for the agent in his activity. The formal analysis by Shavell shows that, irrespective of whether the principal has knowledge only of the outcome of the agent's activity or whether, in addition, he has information (most likely imperfect) of the agent's activity itself, characteristics of the Pareto-optimal fee schedules are related to the attitudes of both the agent and the principal towards risk.

This argument can be illustrated by considering various agency relationship settings in which the optimal rewards, and their associated risks, for both the principal and the agent are determined. Two main settings are considered in the analysis: (i) situations in which the principal and the agent have the same beliefs about the state variable (which affects the agent's productivity), and (ii) situations in which they have differing beliefs about the state variable.

Assume first that the principal and the agent have the same beliefs about the state variable which affects the agent's productivity, e.g. the weather. The principal may, or may not, have information about the agent's efforts. Further, it is frequently assumed that the principal is risk neutral whereas the agent could be risk neutral or risk averse. If the principal has no information about the agent's effort and the agent is risk neutral, the agent's fee could be set equal to the outcome minus a constant representing the principal's share. In such a contract total risk will be entirely allocated to the agent, given that outcome is stochastic which implies that the agent's fee is a non-constant. If the agent is risk-averse, such a fee, and the total risk associated with it, will be undesirable. To protect the agent against this by offering a constant fee would, however, provide little incentive for him to expend effort. An appropriate fee in this case, particularly where no information on the agent's effort is available, would be one which would always depend to some extent on outcome. The principal's share will be a constant plus a fraction of the outcome so that risk is shared by both the agent and the principal. If the principal has information about the agent's effort, it will be advantageous to provide the agent with an incentive by making his fee dependent, at least in part, on his effort rather than solely on the risky outcome. Indeed, if effort is accurately observable, the fee could be set very low *unless* the agent selects the effort level that best suits the principal.

If effort is observable but not with complete accuracy or not at zero cost, imperfect information about effort may lead to a fee being set which is based on inaccurate, or incomplete, measures of the agent's effort. If imperfect information is costless, Holmstrom (1979) has shown that such additional information, even though it is imperfect, can improve the welfare of the principal and the agent. If effort is observable but at a non-trivial cost, a contract can be written based on indirect measures of effort, as long as it is possible to measure the outcome and the state variable and to specify the functional relationship between the state variable, effort and outcome. This means that the applicability of such contracts will be restricted only to divisions which are highly structured (Tiessen and Waterhouse, 1983).

But typically, as Holmstrom (1979) has shown, if imperfect information is costly and the principal–agent relationship is subject to moral hazard, i.e. lack of knowledge by the principal of the effort level chosen by the agent, only a second-best solution is possible. In such cases, Pareto-optimal risk sharing is generally precluded because it will not provide appropriate incentives for taking correct actions. The written contract will have to trade off some of the risk-sharing benefits for provision of incentives, and thus the agent will have to assume greater levels of risk.

Consider now the situation where the principal and the agent have different beliefs about the state variable. Holmstrom (1979) suggests that, after the contract is fixed, the agent will frequently obtain new information about the task or the environment in which he operates. Thus, information will be asymmetrically distributed between the principal and the agent. Harris and Raviv (1978) and Shavell (1979) argue that the contract written in this case will be similar to the one used when information distribution is symmetric. However, Holmstrom (1979) shows that information asymmetry may lead to a renegotiation of the contract. After observing the difficulty of the contract, the principal may agree to new contractual terms, within some limits, which will benefit him as well as the agent.

Agency Theory in a Divisionalised Context

Other writers have investigated the development of incentives and bonus/penalty schemes which would encourage divisional managers to transmit 'truthful' information about their activities to the centre. Groves (1973) suggested a divisional performance measure based on divisional *actual* realised profits plus the *forecast* profits of the other company divisions given the actual resources allocated to them. Formally, this can be expressed as:

(8)
$$G_i = \pi_i^a (x_i^*) + \sum_{\substack{j=i \\ j \neq 1}}^{n} \pi_j^f (x_j^*) - A_i$$

where G_i is the Groves measure for division i; $\pi_i^a (x_i^*)$ is the *actual* profit for division i with resource allocation x_i; $\pi_j^f (x_j^*)$ is the *reported* profit function for division j based on the actual resource allocation level of x_j^* for division j, and A_i is a constant for division i, independent of its forecast or actual profit.

The Groves measure as expressed in **(8)** has a number of desirable properties. Firstly, since the measure is an increasing function of divisional actual profit the divisional manager will be motivated to maximise that figure.

Secondly, the model fosters the submission of truthful information. Irrespective of how a divisional manager perceives the way other divisional managers generate their forecast profit he is better off sending an accurate forecast function $\pi_i^f(x_i)$; see Groves (1973). Notice that the measure is not solely based on the actual profit of the particular division. If that were the case the divisional manager could be motivated to distort the information submitted to the centre relating to issues of corporate resource allocation. Instead, the Groves measure uses a combination of actual divisional profits and a profit-sharing scheme represented by forecast profit for other company divisions. This, it is held, induces divisional honesty in communicating information about its own opportunity set. The reason is that, for the manager of division i, the problem of choosing a profit forecast π_i^f and an actual profit level π_i^a to maximise his profit measure G_i is equivalent to the problem of choosing

$$\pi_i^f \text{ to maximise } \pi_i^a (x_i^*) + \sum_{\substack{j=1 \\ j \neq 1}}^{n} {}_j^f \pi_j^f (x_j^*),$$

since A_i is independent of π_i^f and π_i^a by definition (for a proof of this see Loeb and Magat, 1978).

Thirdly, each division's performance measure is independent of the actual profits or operating efficiency of other company divisions. Performance variances relating to other divisions are traced back to the appropriate divisions through the term $\pi_i^a(x_i^*)$.

Fourthly, the Groves measure is flexible in the sense that it can be varied, by adopting varying levels of A_i, to reflect different interpretations of the performance measure (see Groves and Loeb, 1979). For example, the central management can set

$$A_i = \sum_{\substack{j=1 \\ j \neq 1}}^{n} \pi_j^f(x_j^*)$$

in which case the Groves measure for division i represents the opportunity cost of closing down division i (that is overall company profit *less* maximum company profit obtainable without division i). Similarly, A_i can be manipulated to reflect other notions of divisional performance.

The Groves measure, however, has a number of limitations. Some of these limitations are of a general nature, in the sense of being relevant not only to the Groves measure but also to other measures, and are therefore discussed later in this section. Others are specific to the Groves measure and are discussed below. Firstly, the divisional performance measure is dependent upon forecasts submitted by other divisions. As Kaplan (1982) argued this is inevitable because of divisional interdependencies, for example, through sharing common resources. It could be argued that this is a desirable property of the measure because it emphasises the need for divisional cooperation. None the less, it introduces an element of uncontrollable forecasting performance, but *not* uncontrollable operating performance, into the manager's performance measure. Secondly, the measure compensates the manager for maximising the divisional performances index, G_i, but offers no reward for achieving the optimal plan (profit maximising plan). Thus, there is no incentive for optimal resource allocation by division managers (e.g. Kaplan, 1982). Thirdly, the central management will have to determine the value of A_i before the individual divisions submit their forecast profits. It is thus difficult for the central management to assess *ex ante* the adequacy of the measure as a rewarding scheme from a motivational point of view.

Thus far, the Groves measure has been discussed in some detail because it underlies much of the subsequent research in this area. Loeb and Magat (1978) analysed divisional incentives in a setting of asymmetric information. Divisional managers are assumed to possess knowledge of their divisions' technologies and market conditions. The centre is assumed to rely, at least partially, on information submitted from divisions to make coordinating decisions. The Loeb and Magat scheme uses the Groves measure, and thus the evaluation of a manager's performance is independent of the realised profits of other divisions.

One of the implicit assumptions of the Groves-based measures is that divisional managers seek to maximise their performance measures. They do not consider managerial effort to be a decision variable. As indicated earlier, when effort is recognised as a decision variable the problem of moral hazard, i.e. providing incentives that induce truthful reporting of information, comes to the fore. These measures also assume that divisional managers face no uncertainty when dealing with the activities of their divisions. Both assumptions have been relaxed by other researchers.

Demski (1972) and Itami (1975) developed models that specifically deal with the relationship between the performance evaluation measure and the degree of risk sharing between owners (the principal; the centre) and managers (the agents) under uncertainty. In Demski's model, uncertainty is reflected in the design of the performance evaluation systems by the principal, and in the behaviour of agents (divisional managers). Itami's model considers a manager's actions, his performance and its evaluation under conditions of uncertainty. It emphasises goal congruence in the operating behaviour of managers.

Cohen and Loeb (1984), amongst others, extended the Groves measure to situations of moral hazard. Specifically, their analysis assumed both information asymmetry and divergence of preferences for the level of managerial effort supplied. They assumed that the centre seeks to maximise a measure of total gross profits, not profits minus payments to divisions. Thus, the centre is not assumed to be concerned in its decision making with the cost of managerial rewards. They also explicitly considered the problem of intrafirm resources allocation. Symbolically, Cohen and Loeb developed the Groves measure expressed in (8) into:

(9)
$$G_i = \pi_i^a (x_i^*), (e_i) + \sum_{\substack{j=1 \\ j \neq 1}}^{n} \pi_j^f (x_j^*) - \alpha(\sum_{j=1}^{n} K_j) - A_i - g_i(e_i)$$

where e_i is the divisional manager's effort level; $\alpha(\sum_{j=1} k_j)$ is the cost of capital, which is assumed to be known by the centre and the individual divisions; $g_i (e_i)$ measures the disutility of expending effort by the divisional manager, and the remaining terms in (9) are as in (8) above.

In (9), the function $\pi_i^a(x_i^*)(e_i)$ is assumed to be known only to the manager of division i, although the centre is assumed to be able to observe the realised value of profits. For any capital allocation to division i, the divisional manager will choose an effort level that maximises the difference between $\pi_i^a(x_i^*)(e_i)$ and $g_i(e_i)$. This implies that the divisional manager can make decisions with the knowledge that he can optimally adjust his effort *after* the headquarters allocate capital.

General Assessment of the Models

The above models are useful in so far as they explicitly address some of the characteristics of incentive schedules in a principal–agent setting under different conditions of information availability and risk attitudes. Subsequent models introduced some desirable improvements into the basic Groves measure which clearly enhance its overall usefulness. Yet, these models have several limitations. Some of these limitations are model specific and have been raised already. Others are more general and are discussed briefly here.

Essentially, what these models attempt to achieve is to encourage the agent to take actions that are consistent with the interests of the principal and to discourage actions that are in conflict with those interests through the use of a schedule of rewards and penalties. In a world of uncertainty, asymmetric information and costly information the effectiveness of such models is seriously called into question.

Consider first the level of the reward/penalty. To discourage actions by the agents that are not consistent with the interests of the principal, a penalty equal to the agency cost of deviant behaviour needs to be incorporated into the reward function. But even if this penalty can be appropriately quantified there is no guarantee that deviant behaviour by the agent will be avoided. This is because the welfare gain (wealth change) of such actions as calculated by the agent might be greater than the welfare loss inflicted upon the principal (Fama, 1980).

Next, consider the definition of the reward/penalty. As pointed out, the agency models define an optimal reward as one that is stochastic, i.e. one which is dependent on the firm's profit rather than being a fixed amount. Given that the agent cannot diversify the risks associated with his rewards and human capital, in the same sense as a shareholder can, he will have an incentive to engage in risk reduction strategies, e.g. slack-building or income-smoothing, which may be in conflict with the interests of the principal (see Amihud and Lev, 1981).

Now consider the implementation of the reward/penalty system. If the system is characterised by noise, in the sense that deviations of observed performance from expected performance cannot be unambiguously detected, one cannot expect the agent to refrain from deviant behaviour. Moreover, as Amihud and Lev (1981) pointed out, given imperfect monitoring the expected cost of deviant behaviour will tend to be *ex ante* reflected in the agent's reward. Once the employment contract is drawn up, the agent is likely to take actions which will compensate for the agency cost imposed upon his contract.

It has already been argued that the cost of monitoring devices and bonus schemes is likely to be non-trivial. Moreover, as Loeb and Magat (1978) pointed out, it is almost impossible to design performance measures which simultaneously result in: (i) equating divisional allocated profits with firm-wide profits and (ii) motivating divisions to send truthful forecasts, irrespective of the accuracy of the forecasts of other divisions. Some trade-off between these two desirable properties of performance measures will have to be undertaken, if the measures themselves are to prove acceptable in the context under discussion.

IV. SUMMARY

This chapter addressed the topic of divisional control and performance evaluation from a perspective consistent with the broad notion of organisational control advocated in chapter 4. Divisional control has been interpreted not only to include the means by which the centre monitors and evaluates the performance of divisions, but also the influence which may be exerted by divisional managers upon the organisation. Divisional control is also perceived here as a subset of the much broader organisational control concept developed in chapter 4. This perspective made it possible to consider a fairly comprehensive divisional control apparatus. Rather than exclusively concentrate on financial measures the roles of structural and other organisational controls have also been considered.

Structural and organisational controls covered issues concerned with defining divisional environment and technology, determining divisional size, defining and coordinating divisional interdependencies, determining the extent of divisional decision-making autonomy, designing internal audit systems and designing appropriate reward systems. It has been argued that each of these controls has a role to play in attaining organisational coherence.

The role of financial performance indices in controlling and monitoring divisional activities has also been considered. In an ideal world, a DCF-based profit measure would be the most optimal index. However, real-world imperfections make such a measure undesirable to practitioners. Several proxies for this ideal measure have been advocated by many researchers. These include, in particular, traditional accounting profit, ROI and residual income. Two main conclusions emerged from the evaluation of these proxies. Firstly, there is no *one* single proxy that fulfils all the objectives of divisional performance measurement. Secondly, all these proxies fall clearly short of the ideal income concept contained in DCF. Each of the proxies has been shown to induce sub-optimal decisions in many situations. These deficiencies may be offset, to some extent, through the judicious use of structural and organisational controls.

Finally, some of the formal aspects of divisional reward functions have been examined in a setting where agency problems were explicitly addressed. Models assuming perfect knowledge by the agent (the divisional manager) but not the principal (the centre) were examined. This was followed by a discussion of models which incorporated uncertainty for the agent as well as the principal, and which reflected disutility to the agent to expend effort. The overall aim of these models has been to induce truthful reporting by the agent and to minimise the chances of the agent engaging in practices detrimental to the interests of the principal. Some explanations relating to why these models may be less effective in practice have been suggested. None the less, employment contracts and reward structures remain an indispensable part of the divisional control apparatus. One important aspect of the reward structure that has not been considered here is the possibility of divisional managers entering into joint risk-sharing arrangements as a form of collusion against the centre, or indeed the possibility of risk sharing between divisional managers and the centre. For convenience of presentation, the discussion of this topic is deferred to chapter 13.

REFERENCES

Amey, L.R., 1969a. *The Efficiency of Business Enterprise*. London: George Allen and Unwin.
Amey, L. R., 1969b. Divisional performance measurement and interest on capital, *Journal of Business Finance* **1** Spring, pp. 1–7.
Amey, L. R., 1975. Tomkins on residual income, *Journal of Business Finance and Accounting* **2** Spring, pp. 55–68.
Amihud, Y. and Lev, B., 1981. Risk reduction as a managerial motive for conglomerate mergers, *The Bell Journal of Economics*, **12** (2) Autumn, pp. 605–617.
Armour, H. O. and Teece, D. J., 1978. Organizational structure and economic performance: a test of the multidivisional hypothesis, *The Bell Journal of Economics* **9** (1) Spring, pp. 106–122.
Arrow, K. J., 1964. Control in large organizations, *Management Science*, **10** (3) April, pp. 397–408.
Averch, H. and Johnson, L., 1962. Behaviour of the firm under regulatory constraints, *American Economic Review*, December, pp. 1052–1059.
Bodenhorn, D., 1964. A cash flow concept of profit, *Journal of Finance*, March, pp. 16–31.
Bonini, C. P, 1964. Simulation of organizational behaviour, in C. P. Bonini, R. K. Jaedicke, and H. M. Wagner (eds) *Management Control – New Directions in Basic Research*: McGraw-Hill
Bromwich, M., 1973. Measurement of divisional performance – a comment and an extension, *Accounting and Business Research*, Spring, pp. 123–132.
Bühner, R., 1984. Internal organisation and returns: an empirical analysis of large diversified German corporations, working paper.
Cable, J. and Dirrheimer, M. J., 1983. Hierarchies and markets: an empirical test of the multidivisional hypothesis in West Germany, *International Journal of Industrial Organization* **1**, pp. 43–62.
Chambers, J. C., Mullick, S. and Smith, D., 1971. How to choose the right forecasting technique?, *Harvard Business Review*, July-August, pp. 45–74.
Chandler, A. D. and Daems, H., 1979. Administrative coordination, allocation and monitoring: a comparative analysis of the emergence of accounting and organization in the U.S.A. and Europe, *Accounting, Organizations and Society*, **4**(1/2), pp. 3–20.

Cohen, S. I. and Loeb, M., 1984. The Groves Scheme, profit sharing and moral hazard, *Management Science* **30** (1) January, pp. 20–24.

Dearden, J., 1960. Problems in decentralized profit responsibility, *Harvard Business Review*, May-June, pp. 79–86.

Dearden, J., 1961. Problems in decentralized financial control, *Harvard Business Review*, May-June, pp. 72–80.

Demski, J. S., 1972. Optimal performance measurement, *Journal of Accounting Research*, Autumn, 243–258.

Ezzamel, M., 1973. Divisional performance measurement: a critical review and some possible solutions, *AUTA News Review*, Autumn, pp. 3–21.

Ezzamel, M., 1979. Divisional cost of capital and the measurement of divisional performance, *Journal of Business Finance and Accounting* **6** (3) Autumn, pp. 307–319.

Ezzamel, M. and Bourn, A. M., 1987. Why do firms allocate costs? in J. Arnold, D. Cooper and R. W. Scappens (eds) *Case Study Research in Management Accounting*: ICMA.

Ezzamel, M. and Hilton, K., 1980a. Divisionalisation in British industry: a preliminary study, *Accounting and Business Research*, Spring, pp. 197–211.

Ezzamel, M. and Hilton, K., 1980b. Can divisional discretion be measured?, *Journal of Business Finance and Accounting* **7** (2) Summer, pp. 311–329.

Fama, E. F., 1980. Agency problems and the theory of the firm, *Journal of Political Economy*, **88** (2), April, pp. 288–307.

Flower, J. F., 1971. Measurement of divisional performance, *Accounting and Business Research,* **1**(3), Summer, pp. 205–214.

Fuller, R. J. and Kerr, H. S., 1981. Estimating the divisional cost of capital: an analysis of the pure-play technique, *Journal of Finance*, December, pp. 997–1009.

Gabor, A. and Pearce, I. F., 1952. A new approach to the theory of the firm, *Oxford Economic Papers*, October, pp. 252–265.

Gordon, M. J. and Halpern, P. J., 1974. Cost of capital for a division of a firm, *Journal of Finance*, September, pp. 1153–1163.

Gray, S. J., 1978. Segmental reporting and the EEC multinationals, *Journal of Accounting Research* **16** (2) Autumn, pp. 242–253.

Groves, T., 1973. Incentives in teams, *Econometrica* **XLI** July, pp. 617–631.

Groves, T. and Loeb, M., 1975. Incentives and public inputs, *Journal of Public Economics*, August, pp. 211–226.

Groves, T. and Loeb, M., 1976. Information, incentives, and internalisation of production externalities, in S. Lin (ed.) *Theory and Measurement of Economic Externalities*: Academic Press, pp. 65–83.

Groves, T. and Loeb, M., 1979. Incentives in a divisionalized firm, *Management Science*, March, pp. 221–230.

Harris, M. and Raviv, A., 1978. Some results on incentive contracts with application to education and employment, health insurance, and law enforcement, *American Economic Review*, March, pp. 20–30.

Henderson, B. and Dearden, J., 1966. New system for divisional control, *Harvard Business Review*, September-October, pp. 144–160.

Hirshleifer, J., 1957. Economics of the divisionalized firm, *The Journal of Business*, April, pp. 96–108.

Holmstrom, B., 1979. Moral hazard and observability, *The Bell Journal of Economics*, **10** (1) Spring, pp. 74–91.

Horngren, C. T., 1962. *Cost Accounting: A Managerial Emphasis*, Prentice-Hall.

Itami, H., 1975. Evaluation measures and goal congruence under uncertainty, *Journal of Accounting Research*, Spring, pp. 73–96.

Jaedicke, R. K., 1967. A Critique, in *The Use of Accounting Data in Decision Making*, T. J. Burns (ed.). Columbus, Ohio: Ohio State University.

Kanodia, C., 1979. Risk sharing and transfer price systems under uncertainty, *Journal of Accounting Research* **17** (1) Spring, pp. 74–98.

Kaplan, R. S., 1982. *Advanced Management Accounting*: Prentice-Hall.

Lawrence, P. R. and Lorsch, J. W., 1967. *Organization and Environment – Managing*

Differentiation and Integration: Harvard: Division of Research, Graduate School of Business Administration, Harvard University.

Lawson, G. H., 1971. Measuring divisional performance, *Management Accounting*, May, pp. 147–152.

Lee, T. A., 1972. A case for cash flow reporting, *Journal of Business Finance* **4** (2) Summer, pp. 27–36.

Leibenstein, H., 1965. *Economic Theory and Organizational Analysis*: Harper and Row and John Weatherhill.

Lioukas, S. K. and Xerokostas, D. A., 1982. Size and administrative intensity in organisational divisions, *Management Science* **28** (8) August, pp. 854–868.

Loeb, M. and Magat, W. A., 1978. Soviet success indicators and the evaluation of divisional management; *Journal of Accounting Research* **16** (1) Spring, pp. 103–121.

Lorsch, J. W. and Allen, S. A. III, 1973. *Managing Diversity and Interdependence*: Harvard: Division of Research, Graduate School of Business Administration, Harvard University.

Mauriel, J. and Anthony, R. N., 1966. Misevaluation of investment center performance, *Harvard Business Review*, March-April, pp. 98–105.

Mirrlees, J. A., 1976. The optimal structure of incentives and authority within an organisation, *The Bell Journal of Economics* **7** (1) Spring, pp. 105–131.

NICB, 1961. *Divisional Financial Executives*, Studies in Business Policy 101, by C. G. Baumes, National Industrial Conference Board.

Ortman, R. F., 1975. The effects on investment analysis of alternative reporting procedure for diversified firms, *The Accounting Review* April, pp. 298–304.

Rappaport, A., 1975. A capital budgeting approach to divisional planning and control, in *Information for Decision Making: Quantitative and Behavioural Dimensions* 2nd edn. A. Rappaport, L. (ed.): Prentice-Hall.

Ross, S. A., 1973. The economic theory of agency: the principal's problem, *American Economic Review* **63** (2) May, pp. 134–139.

Ruefli, T. W., 1971a. A generalised goal decomposition model, *Management Science* **17** (8) April, pp. B/505–B/517.

Ruefli, T. W., 1971b. Behavioural externalities in decentralised organisations, *Management Science* **9** (5) June, pp. B/649–B/657.

Scapens, R. W., 1979. Profit measurement in divisionalised companies, *Journal of Business Finance and Accounting* **6** (3) Autumn, pp. 281–305.

Scapens, R. W. and Sale, J. T., 1981. Performance measurement and formal capital expenditure controls in divisionalised companies, *Journal of Business Finance and Accounting*, Autumn, pp. 389–419.

Scapens, R. W. and Sale, J. T., 1985. An international study of accounting practices in divisionalised companies and their associations with organisational variables, *The Accounting Review* **LX** (2) April, pp. 231–247.

Shavell, S., 1979. Risk sharing and incentives in the principal and agent relationship, *The Bell Journal of Economics* **10** (1) Spring, pp. 55–73.

Shillinglaw, G., 1957. Guides to internal profit measurement, *Harvard Business Review*, March-April, pp. 82–94.

Shwayder, K., 1970. A proposed modification to residual income – interest adjusted income, *Accounting Review* April, pp. 299–307.

Solomons, D., 1965. *Divisional Performances: Measurement and Control*: Irwin.

Spicer, B. H. and Ballew, V., 1983. Management accounting systems and the economics of internal organization, *Accounting, Organizations and Society*, **8**(1), pp. 73–96.

Steer, P. and Cable, J., 1978. Internal organisation and profit: an empirical analysis of large UK companies, *The Journal of Industrial Economics* September, pp. 13–30.

Stiglitz, J., 1974. Risk sharing and incentives in sharecropping, *Review of Economic Studies* **61** (2) April, pp. 219–256.

Stiglitz, J., 1975. Incentives, risk and information: notes towards a theory of hierarchy, *The Bell Journal of Economics*, **6** (2) Autumn, pp. 552–579.

Teece, D. J., 1981. Internal organisation and economic performance: an empirical analysis of the profitability of principal firms, *The Journal of Industrial Economics*, December, pp. 173–199.

Thompson, J. D., 1967. *Organizations in Action*: McGraw-Hill.

Thompson, R. S., 1981. Internal organisation and profit: a note, *The Journal of Industrial Economics*, December, pp. 201–211.

Tiessen, P. and Waterhouse, J. H., 1983. Towards a descriptive theory of management accounting, *Accounting, Organizations and Society*, **8**(2/3), pp. 251–267.

Tomkins, C., 1973. *Financial Planning in Divisionalised Companies*: Haymarket Publishing.

Tomkins, C., 1975a. Another look at residual income, *Journal of Business Finance and Accounting* **2** (1) Spring, pp. 39–53.

Tomkins, C., 1975b. Residual income – a rebuttal of Professor Amey's arguments, *Journal of Business Finance and Accounting*, **2** (2) Summer, pp. 161–168.

Vatter, W. J., 1959. Does the rate of return measure business efficiency?, *NAA*, January.

Williamson, O. E., 1970. *Corporate Control and Business Behaviour*: Prentice-Hall.

Williamson, O. E., 1975. *Markets and Hierarchies: Analysis and Antitrust Implications*: Free Press.

Zimmerman, J. L., 1979. The costs and benefits of cost allocation, *Accounting Review*, July, pp. 504–521.

13

Transfer Pricing

Economists have long been concerned with developing price mechanisms that are assumed to operate through a market system to attain rational allocation of economic resources. The literature on divisionalisation followed the same path; in that literature it has generally been assumed that to attain economic rationality, transfer prices should be developed to facilitate the allocation of intracompany resources. Typically, a transfer price is defined as the intracompany charge at which goods or services exchange hands within a company (see Goetz, 1967). Where there is a relevant external market the transfer price is usually determined by reference to the market price. In the absence of relevant external markets the transfer price would be internally derived.

Transfer prices play a crucial role in the allocation of company resources between divisions and in the assessment of the performance of these divisions and their managers. Thus, a 'lower' transfer price could, other things being equal, result in the buying division expanding its activity level and the selling division reducing its activity level thereby causing shifts in the resources utilised by these divisions. Further, the transfer price affects divisional profitability by influencing the cost function of the buying division and the revenue function of the selling division.

The success of the price mechanism, in optimally coordinating and guiding the activities of the divisionalised company, depends largely on its ability to capture the relevant economic and organisational characteristics of that company. The organisational characteristics are typically complex, and may be summarised as follows (see Bailey and Boe, 1976):

— The measure of decentralisation adopted by the organisation, e.g. substantial *v.* limited.
— The degree of interdependence between divisions of the same organisation. Thompson (1967) suggests a scale of divisional interdependence increasing in complexity from pooled through sequential to reciprocal; these are discussed later in this chapter.
— The degree of cooperation existing within the organisation, e.g. more cooperative *v.* less cooperative.
— Integration mechanisms adopted by the organisation ranging from standardised rules and routines to more liberal integrating mechanisms, e.g. matrix organisation (see Galbraith, 1970).

A major deficiency of the transfer pricing literature is that these important organisational characteristics are typically ignored in the design of transfer pricing mechanisms. As will be argued later in the chapter, overemphasising the technical aspects of transfer pricing at the expense of the organisational and behavioural aspects is fundamentally unhelpful.

This chapter provides a review of the literature on transfer pricing. The first three sections contain discussions and evaluations of the traditional economic model, the linear programming approach and the decomposition approach respectively, in the context of transfer pricing. Section IV briefly reviews some of the behavioural implications of transfer pricing. Finally, section V contains a summary of the chapter.

I. TRADITIONAL ECONOMIC THEORY OF THE FIRM

The Model

As stated in chapter 2, on organisation goals, traditional economic theory assumes that firms seek to maximise their profits. Implicit in this assumption is the notion that the rational use of the price mechanism guides the firm in determining the optimal product mix that maximises its profit. Typically, the theory posits some restrictive assumptions to facilitate the analysis.

The early work on transfer pricing was modelled on the traditional economic theory of the firm. Despite the important contributions offered by such pioneering work, the analysis was not sufficiently rigorous. Cook (1955) advocated a transfer pricing system based on market prices, at least as an ideal, whereas Dean (1955) recommended using negotiated competitive prices. However, it was not until the work of Hirshleifer (1956, 1957), Arrow (1959), Arrow and Hurwicz (1960) and Gould (1964) that a systematic framework for the analysis of the economics of transfer pricing was established.

In order to evaluate the traditional transfer pricing model it is crucial to specify the assumptions on which it is based. The following is a typical statement of these assumptions.
1. The divisionalised firm under consideration has two divisions; one is the intermediate division (D_I), which manufactures and sells the intermediate product, and the other is the final division (D_F), which buys the intermediate product. Each division handles only one product, and the market for the intermediate product (intermediate market) could assume different structures.
2. Both technological independence and demand independence characterise the activities of the two divisions.
3. Each division is 'autonomous' with respect to running its activities, but the overriding criterion is the maximisation of overall company profit.

Given this initial set of assumptions, optimal transfer prices were derived under different intermediate market settings, ranging from perfect competition through imperfect competition to complete absence of an intermediate market.

The Perfect Intermediate Market Case

Given the familiar assumptions of perfect competition, it is easy to show that the optimal transfer price is the market price. Furthermore, in attempting to maximise their own profits, divisions will automatically maximise overall company profit: company divisions will behave as if they all constitute one entity whose purpose is to maximise a given objective function (Arrow, 1959; Gale, 1960). Thus, it will be in the best interest of the parent company that each division be granted full autonomy in determining its activity level. Setting a joint level of activity for two or more divisions will usually lead to sub-optimal results for the parent company. This is because such a procedure results in one division subsidising the other, but the net benefit to the subsidised division will be less than the loss incurred by the subsidising division.

Finally, there are no benefits to be gained from vertical integration between divisions: internal organisation is no more efficient than the market.

Despite the unrealistic assumptions of the perfect market case, at least two formal results emerge. Firstly, under the assumed set of conditions optimal transfer prices can be derived in the sense that absolute divisional autonomy and optimisation of company goal(s) are simultaneously attained. Thus, complete decentralisation is not only possible but also desirable in order to economise the costs of information transmission which would be required under a centralised system (see Arrow, 1959). Secondly, optimal allocation of company resources is attained through the price mechanism. The optimal level of activity for each division is determined independently of other divisions, such that $P^* = MC = MR$, where P^* is the transfer price, MC is marginal cost and MR is marginal revenue. Vertical integration is not advantageous and the buying and selling divisions will be indifferent as to trading internally or in the external market.

The Imperfect Intermediate Market Case

The case of perfect markets is not typical – markets are usually far from perfect. A convenient way to proceed from the perfect market case is to assume a slight imperfection in market conditions. One example is the case where the intermediate market is perfect in every sense except in so far as there are additional costs involved in entering the market, e.g. transportation cost. In considering this situation, Cook (1955) concluded that the optimal transfer price is indeterminate and that the relevant divisions should negotiate the price.

However, Gould (1964) has shown that, under the above conditions, the optimal transfer price can be determined. To clarify this, define P_b as the price for the buying division (equals the market price *plus* transportation cost), P_s as the price for the selling division (equals the market price *less* transportation cost), such that $P_b > P_s$, and $\bar{P}$ as the point at which MC_I intersects NMR_F (NMR_F is the marginal revenue of division F less its marginal cost except the price for the intermediate product). Gould shows that the optimal price depends on which of the following relationships obtains: $P_b > P_s > \bar{P}$, $\bar{P} > P_b > P_s$, and $P_b > \bar{P} > P_s$. The last case refers to a situation in which the outside intermediate market is either absent or irrelevant; this will be considered later. Gould shows that when $P_b > P_s > \bar{P}$, setting $P^* = P_s$ results in maximising overall company profit. Figure 13.1 illustrates this case.

In figure 13.1, the effective marginal cost curve for the firm becomes ABC and the effective net marginal revenue curve becomes JKL. The intersection of ABC and JKL determines $P^* = P_s$ and the optimal level of activity for division I at OQ_I. At $P^* = P_s$, division F handles the quantity OQ_F. Compared with outside trading, internal trading increases the profit of division F and of the overall company by the amount P_sP_bSK. The quantity $Q_I - Q_F$ should be sold on the outside market at P_s. It is straightforward to establish that when $\bar{P} > P_b > P_s$, the transfer price should be set equal to the purchasing price ($P^* = P_b$).

Several important observations emerge from Gould's analysis. Firstly, once some form of intermediate market imperfections are assumed, the benefits to the parent company of internal trading become obvious. Secondly, if the overall goal of the parent company is profit maximisation, divisions can no longer be permitted to act indifferently with respect to internal trading. When $P_b > P_s > \bar{P}$, enforcement rules must be designed to ensure that division I sells the quantity OQ_F to division F at $P^* = P_s$. If division I exercises its monopolistic power over division F and charges $P^* > P_s$,

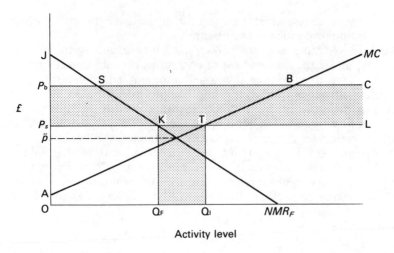

Figure 13.1 $P_b > P_s > \bar{P}$

the company will operate below its optimal activity level. A similar argument applies to division F when $\bar{P} > P_b > P_s$. Hence, under Gould's analysis, divisional discretion is sacrificed in favour of overall company optimality. Thirdly, under Gould's analysis there are incentives for only *one* division to trade internally – only *one* division reaps all the benefits of internal trading. Either the selling price, P_s, or the buying price, P_b, is taken as the optimal price, whereas the ruling market price is completely ignored. Fourthly, unless the central management has knowledge of divisional costs and revenue functions, a highly unlikely assumption, divisions are likely to engage in manipulations of these functions to their advantage but with suboptimal consequences for the company. Fifthly, divisional profit cannot be used to rationally assess divisional viability. For example, in figure 13.1 if division I is to be discontinued, the loss to the company as a whole will be more than the apparent divisional profit (A P_s T less divisional fixed costs) by the amount $P_s P_b SK$.

The Discriminating Monopoly Case

Assuming that interdivisional externalities are absent, Hirshleifer (1956) has shown that when the intermediate division acts as a discriminating monopolist the optimal transfer price, P^*, should be set equal to the marginal cost of the intermediate division at the output level which maximises company profits ($P^* = MC_I$).

In figure 13.2 the output of division (I) is established by the intersection of MC_I and mr_t ($MR_I + NMR_F$) at point H (i.e. OQ_1). The quantity to be sold to division (F) is OQ_2 at $P^* = OA = MC_I$. The quantity OQ_3 is to be sold in the outside market at OB $> P^*$.

The above solution may be derived by the central agency assuming that it has knowledge of the divisional demand and supply functions. Alternatively, the same solution can be derived by the divisions if either provides the other with its demand or supply function, whichever is appropriate. Thus, if division (F) were to determine the optimal solution, it would need to obtain d, MR_I and MC_I from division (I). If division (I) were to derive the optimal solution, it would need to obtain NMR_F. In figure 13.2 it is assumed that division (I) plays the dominant role in determining the transfer price after securing the demand function of division (F), NMR_F. However, enforcement

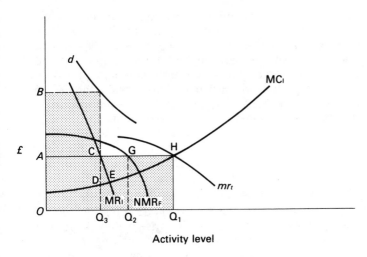

Figure 13.2 *The optimal transfer price for a discriminating monopolist*

rules are needed to ensure that division (I) does not exercise its monopolistic power and charge division (F) a higher transfer price which would be against overall company interest.

Once more, most of the limitations associated with imperfect competition are present here, albeit in a stronger form. Thus (i) apparent divisional profit does not reflect 'real' divisional contribution to company profit; (ii) interference by central management greatly restricts divisional autonomy; and (iii) because of information asymmetry, even with central management interference, there is no guarantee that divisional managers will not manipulate cost and revenue functions to their advantage.

The No-Intermediate Market Case

Given the initial assumption of only one intermediate division and only one final division, the transfer pricing setting here lends itself directly to the case of bilateral monopoly. Under such conditions, the supplier estimates the cross-elasticity of demand in relation to the price of products offered by others to be zero. Moreover, the demander is a monopsonistic buyer of the product under consideration.

The micro-economic analysis of bilateral monopoly as developed by Bowley (1928), Fellner (1947), Foldes (1964) and Schneider (1969) amongst others shows that there are some 'modes of behaviour' according to which the quantity and the price of an exchanged commodity can be determined:

— One division acts as a quantity adjuster and the other as a monopolist.
— One division fixes an option for the other, with the latter division having the right to take or leave that option.
— Both divisions engage in successive negotiations.
— Both divisions act as quantity adjusters. (See Ezzamel, 1975, for an investigation of transfer pricing policies under these modes of behaviour.)

The last mode of behaviour was the one contemplated by Hirshleifer (1956) and Gould (1964) when they analysed the case of no intermediate market. Hirshleifer (1956) showed that, assuming a competitive market for the final product, the best solution for the firm is to produce that level of output at which its overall marginal cost equals the price in the final market. Again, this optimal solution can either be achieved by a central agency or by any division possessing the relevant information. The optimal transfer price is deemed to be equal to the marginal cost of the intermediate division at the activity level which maximises company profits ($P^* = MC_I$). The benefits of vertical integration are particularly important in this case. Here again, all the limitations of the Hirshleifer/Gould transfer pricing system under imperfect and monopolistic market conditions are most prominent.

An Evaluation of the Traditional Transfer Pricing Model

As indicated above, the traditional micro economic transfer pricing model provides a valuable contribution to the literature. However, the model does not provide a complete analysis of transfer pricing. The reasons for this arise mainly because of the simplifying and restrictive nature of the assumptions used in deriving the model: in reality transfer pricing situations are much more complex than is assumed in the model. The limitations of the model are considered below.

Overall Company Optimality and Divisional Autonomy

Although divisional autonomy is frequently discussed under the traditional model, overall company optimality is typically considered the overriding criterion. This has a number of important implications.

Firstly, the traditional model assumes that, given some enforcement rules stipulated by the central management for divisional managers, marginal cost pricing will automatically lead to optimal company behaviour. This is based on the unwarranted assumption that central management has knowledge of divisional cost and revenue functions. But, as Naert and Janssen (1971) have shown, divisional managers are likely to engage in sub-optimal strategies that are not likely to be detected, at least in full, by the central management. Pondy (1970) has pointed out that to the extent that information is not costless, individuals with knowledge superior to that of the central management could change the resource allocation pattern to their own advantage. Further, the firm should carefully compare the benefits and costs of coordination; in some cases it could be more economical for the firm to incur the loss caused by externalities.

Secondly, factors other than prices tend to affect the resource allocation process. One example is the compliance parameter (i.e. the proportion of a subordinate's activities which contribute to his immediate superior's objectives). Thus, under certain assumptions, a division with a higher compliance parameter will tend to grow bigger, and hence secure more resources, than a division with lower compliance (Pondy, 1970). A second example is the effect of uncertainty on divisional motivation. Kanodia (1979) has shown that under uncertainty coordination of divisional activities becomes too complicated because of differences in risk aversion amongst divisional managers, and also between divisional managers and the central management. Thus, the more risk averse the manager of division F, (i) the lower will be his activity level, and hence his demand for the intermediate product, (ii) the lower will be the equilibrium transfer price P^*, (iii) the lower will be the profits of division I. Such behaviour is not Pareto optimal. To attain better results, risk-sharing schemes may be subscribed to by divisional managers and possibly by central management.

Thirdly, according higher priority to company optimality compared with divisional autonomy leads to adverse behavioural implications which may curtail overall company interests in the long run (for a similar argument see Abdel-khalik and Lusk 1974, and Watson and Baumler 1975). Ronen and McKinney (1970) alluded to this problem and suggested an extension of the traditional model which, they claimed, would generate transfer prices that promote greater measures of divisional autonomy. They first pointed out that divisional managers can never be fully autonomous; the criterion for measuring the extent of divisional autonomy should be the degree with which it compares with the conditions under which independent buyers and sellers operate. For example, an independent supplier enjoys neither perfect autonomy nor full control over the variables which determine his profits; his profitability is partially a function of the variables controlled by his buyers and his suppliers.

Given the above definition of divisional autonomy, Ronen and McKinney suggested a dual transfer pricing system. This, they argued, would preserve the measure of divisional autonomy whilst maintaining overall company interest. Thus, the intermediate division would continue to handle the optimal level of activity which is determined by the intersection between its marginal cost curve and the company's net marginal revenue, i.e. $MC_I = NMR_F$ ($NMR_F = MR_F - MC_F$). However, the intermediate division receives a transfer price determined along its average revenue curve, i.e. $AR_I = P_I^*$. To the final division, the supply curve of the intermediate division is represented by the latter's average cost curve, AC_I. Hence, the transfer price charged to the final division is derived along the supply curve of the intermediate division, i.e. $AC_I = P_F^*$. Given that AR_I and AC_I are not likely to be the same, $P_I^* \neq P_F^*$. The two divisions submit this information, P_I^* and P_F^*, to the central management which credits division I by $P_I^* - P_F^*$, if $P_I^* > P_F^*$, or taxes (debits) it in the reverse case. By using this dual pricing system Ronen and McKinney argued that divisions reap the benefits of any monopolistic power they enjoy whilst ensuring that they handle the optimal level of activity for the company.

The dual transfer pricing system suggested by Ronen and McKinney has at least two advantages over the traditional model: (i) divisional apparent profits reflect divisional 'real' contribution to company profits, hence more rational continuation/abandonment decisions are likely to be made, (ii) unlike the Gould system, the Ronen and McKinney system is not situation specific: no knowledge of the exact relationship between P_b, P_s, and $\bar{P}$ is required before the transfer price is derived. However, the authors' claim that their dual system fosters greater divisional autonomy is doubtful. Firstly, the dual system is administered by the central management and this could result in restrained divisional behaviour. Secondly, cost inefficiencies could be passed on from the final division to the intermediate division, since the average revenue curve of the intermediate division is derived under this system by deducting the average cost curve of the final division from the average revenue curve in the final market. This could result in a lower AR_I and a lower P_I^*, and the apparent divisional profit may, therefore, be inadequate for continuation/abandonment decisions. Hence, it may be necessary under this system for either the intermediate division or the central management to audit the cost records of the final division thereby reducing the latter's autonomy (see Abdel-khalik and Lusk, 1974).

Theoretical and Practical Implications of Marginal Cost Pricing

There are several implications here. Firstly, the traditional model typically considers one class of marginal cost and marginal revenue function: that of a rising marginal cost and a declining net marginal revenue. Other classes of function are rarely, if ever, considered (for different types of cost and revenue functions see Gould, 1960). Secondly, divisional apparent profit under marginal cost pricing is inadequate for continuation/abandonment decisions as suggested previously. Thirdly, marginal cost is equal to opportunity cost only in a limited sense. Dopuch and Drake (1964) pointed out that when the intermediate market is either perfectly competitive or highly competitive, the market price, and hence the marginal cost of the intermediate division at the optimal activity level, is either equal to or very close to the opportunity cost. When the intermediate market is either irrelevant or non-existent, marginal cost is close to opportunity cost only if there exists a single demanding division. In the case of more than one demanding division for the same intermediate product, the opportunity cost will be the highest of the marginal cost and the revenue forgone by diverting resources from alternative uses. Fourthly, from a realistic point of view, marginal cost as defined by the economist cannot be directly observed. As a proxy, the accountant uses variable cost, which is assumed constant for each unit within the relevant range of output. To set the transfer price equal to variable cost would only generate enough revenues to cover variable cost, leaving the intermediate division with a net loss equal to its total fixed costs. Finally, as under the Ronen and McKinney system, marginal cost pricing could result in passing on inefficiencies and/or efficiencies from one division to another. This could lead to obscuring true divisional contributions. Some form of cost audit by the central management or the affected divisions would be needed but this would reduce divisional autonomy.

Cost and Demand Independence

The assumptions that divisions enjoy technological independence as well as demand independence are hard to justify. Hence, the alleged 'optimal' transfer prices derived under the traditional model can only be optimal in a very limited sense. Friedman (1962) has shown that a derived demand, like the demand for the intermediate product, has two important implications. Firstly, solutions based on derived demand are consistent *only* at the point of equilibrium. Secondly, the elasticity of derived demand becomes crucial when the market for the intermediate product is not perfectly competitive. In these cases, such elasticity is a function of several variables: the extent of vertical integration of production processes, the elasticity of demand for the final product and the elasticity of supply of the intermediate product. The greater the significance of these variables the more difficult it will be to justify demand independence (see Abdel-khalik and Lusk, 1974).

To make amends for this, the proponents of the traditional model extended the model somewhat to deal with certain aspects of divisional interdependence. The best known examples of this are the extensions suggested by Hirshleifer (1957) and Arrow (1959) which will be reviewed later.

Temporal Stability

Under the traditional model the time dimension is not considered as a dynamic variable. Thus, pricing strategies are usually developed with reference only to one point in time. Furthermore, the model assumes that cost relationships continue over a period of time long enough to be covered by pricing policies. Pricing strategies, e.g. price discrimination, may take place in the same market but over different time periods (see Abdel-khalik and Lusk, 1974).

II. THE LINEAR PROGRAMMING APPROACH

Because of the limitations of the traditional micro economic model outlined above, many researchers attempted to introduce further refinements into the analysis of transfer pricing. Thus, opportunity cost has been advanced as a general rule for pricing intracompany transactions (see, for example, Samuels, 1969; Onsi, 1970). As indicated earlier, marginal cost approximates opportunity cost as long as there is only *one* demanding division for the intermediate product. When there is only one intermediate division and more than one demanding division the intermediate division resembles a monopolist, and the demanding divisions can no longer control their input levels. Here, the opportunity cost is the greater of the marginal cost of producing the intermediate product and the revenue forgone by diverting the resources from alternative uses. Moreover, where the activities of the firm involve the use of fixed facilities shared by a wide range of possible outputs, no single intermediate division can attain optimal allocation without affecting the activity levels of similar intermediate divisions within the firm. In this case a formal and more centralised programming solution, which takes these interdependencies into consideration, may be required (see Dopuch and Drake, 1964).

The characteristics of linear programming imply that the optimal solution of the primal is equivalent to the optimal solution of the dual. The optimal values of the dual are known in the literature as 'shadow prices'.

Shadow prices show the opportunity cost of a unit of scarce resources in terms of the amount of contribution that could be added if the intermediate division increases its productive capacity by adding one more unit of the scarce resource. The transfer price is typically determined as follows:

(1)

$$P^* = VC_I + W_I$$

where VC_I = variable cost of the intermediate division, and W_I = the shadow price of the scarce resources used in producing the intermediate product.

The advantages of linear programming for allocating scarce resources amongst alternative outputs are well known. Assuming that the problem under consideration can be properly formulated, *optimal* allocation of resources can be obtained through the use of shadow prices which approximate opportunity cost. There are, however, several other implications that should be noted.

Firstly, under linear programming divisional autonomy is restricted. The optimal solution for the company is typically derived by the central management, and divisions are sent detailed instructions with respect to levels of output and transfer prices. It is also implicit in the model that the central management has detailed knowledge of divisional cost and revenue functions. Under such, unrealistic, assumptions it is hard to justify having a divisionalised structure.

Secondly, apart from the familiar limitations of assuming linear cost and revenue functions, the existence of shadow prices alone is not sufficient to guide divisional managers in implementing the optimal solution. Thus, shadow prices can guide divisional managers only in selecting the optimal *combination* of products but not in deciding on the optimal *level* of activity: alternative means will be required to determine the latter (Dopuch and Drake, 1964). Various modifications of the basic linear programming model have been advanced to overcome some of the limitations of the linearity assumptions. Samuels (1969) suggested that the transfer price should equal an arbitrarily determined basic price plus a bonus per unit which increases with each unit produced up to the optimal level, but decreases (and could be negative, i.e. incurring a penalty) after the optimal level has been reached. Jennergren (1972) advocated a system according to which the central management announces a set of 'perturbated' prices which would cause the transfer price to increase by a fluctuating margin for increased demand of the intermediate product. However, the above modifications do not add 'genuine' advantages to the basic linear programming model because: (i) they still assume that divisional revenue and cost functions are known to central management, and (ii) divisional autonomy remains restricted as the transfer price is set by central management.

Thirdly, the economic implications of shadow prices are dependent upon the bases underlying the solution to the original problem; if the bases change, the shadow prices change. Thus, Bernhard (1968) points out that shadow prices are accurate measures of opportunity cost only if: (i) the product mix does not change, and (ii) resources are utilised efficiently. Changes in either of these bases could lead to a change in shadow prices (e.g. when a previously non-binding constraint becomes binding after the change) and, thus, render previously derived shadow prices irrelevant for transfer pricing.

Fourthly, transfer prices based on shadow price are likely to have several adverse behavioural and motivational consequences. Thus, if the resources used in producing the intermediate product are non-binding constraints in the optimal solution for the company, the shadow price of the intermediate product will be zero and its transfer price will only equal its variable cost. Similar arguments could apply to the final division. Furthermore, using shadow prices to derive transfer prices could curtail rational capital budgeting decisions because of possible short-run effects on shadow prices. Manes (1970) pointed out that divisional managers would be unwilling to acquire excess plant capacity for future expansion since this would reduce their shadow prices and, hence, their transfer prices if plant capacity becomes non-binding. Another example is when the shadow price is so high that it discourages internal trading to the detriment of overall company interest. Consider the case of an intermediate division producing two products: I_M, which has an outside market, and I_N with no outside market. The opportunity cost of I_N is its shadow price which is based on the value of the scarce resources used by the intermediate division to produce I_M. A higher contribution margin for I_M would lead to a higher shadow price and, hence, a higher transfer price for I_N, which may discourage demanding divisions to buy I_N. This could force the intermediate division to abandon producing I_N and concentrate on producing I_M, which is clearly suboptimal, assuming that the optimal plan for the company indicates that a given quantity of I_N should be produced. A problem at issue here is how the intermediate division can be motivated to produce the optimal quantity of I_N. Onsi (1970) suggested an algorithm that would generate a dual transfer pricing system with the aim of motivating the intermediate division to produce the optimal quantity of I_N. Thus, an optimal solution for the company is first derived (presumably by central management). The transfer price charged to the buying division would be the variable cost of I_N. The selling division would be credited by the difference between its maximum profit derived under the divisional optimal solution (which is suboptimal for the company) and divisional profit derived under the company optimal solution; Onsi calls this difference 'motivational costs'. Here again, the refinement suggested by Onsi is centrally administered and assumes knowledge of cost and revenue functions.

Fifthly, under the linear programming model economies in information transmission usually associated with decentralisation may be lost. The calculation of the optimal solution is typically performed by central management. However, to calculate the solution, information on the objective functions and the constraints will be required. Two alternative ways for the collection, processing and channelling of this information can be sought. The first is to allow divisional managers to collect and process information and then submit it to central management. This alternative has the attraction of retaining some (albeit limited) measure of decentralisation: divisional managers would be made responsible for the accuracy of the information they submitted (Dopuch and Drake, 1964). But, in this case, communication channels will be overloaded thereby causing information diseconomies. The second alternative is for the central management to collect and process the information and then derive the optimal solution. Even if this alternative is feasible, it generates too centralised a structure to make sense of using divisional accounting systems. Furthermore, it is not clear if genuine information economies can be realised.

Sixthly, although the linear programming model does take account of divisional interdependencies to some extent, this is only done in a rather restricted sense. Thus, different types of externality, like those discussed in the following section, are not explicitly entertained by the model.

The limitations of linear programming in the context of transfer prices prompted researchers to look for a new model which would overcome these problems. This has led to the development of the decomposition model.

III. THE DECOMPOSITION APPROACH

The Basic Decomposition Model

Assume there is a divisionalised organisation made up of m divisions, where $m > 1$. In the absence of externalities, as assumed under the traditional economic approach, it has been shown earlier that the independent profit maximising behaviour of divisions will, under certain conditions, be consistent with maximising the global objective function of the company. In the presence of externalities, the maximisation of the global objective function of the parent company is not guaranteed through the independent behaviour of divisions; central interference is necessary in order to keep divisional behaviour in line with company interest. The crux of the problem is how to devise a system which leads to the maximisation of the global objective function and yet allows a 'reasonable' measure of autonomy for divisional managers. Three notable studies based on the traditional economic model attempted to deal with externalities in the context of transfer pricing.

In his model, Hirshleifer (1957) treated demand and cost dependence through a process of trial and error until the optimal solution was achieved. A bonus or penalty was used to account for demand dependence and, hence, to derive the effective divisional marginal revenue of the company. The intermediate division set a *provisional* transfer price, P^*, equal to its marginal costs, MC_I, at a provisional output level and the demanding divisions placed their demands accordingly. If supply was not compatible with demand, a new provisional P^* would be suggested at a different output level. This process would continue until demand equals supply. Since the final $P^* = MC_I$ at the optimal level, the demanding divisions would operate optimally by producing until $MR' = MSC_F + P^* (= MC_I) = MC'$, where MSC_F denotes the marginal separable cost of division F. This is subject to the condition that the market should be cleared.

Arrow (1959) advocated another model which was based on successive approximations until the optimal solution was reached. Unlike the Hirshleifer model, where the approximation process is conducted by the divisions, the central agency in the Arrow model controls the flow of information between divisions and sets the provisional transfer prices. Arrow and Hurwicz (1960) used a gradient adjustment mechanism to derive efficient prices for resource allocation. These efficient prices would, typically, be adjusted to account for externalities so that efficient allocation of central resources is attained.

These three 'traditional' models share some common limitations. Firstly, not *all* types of externalities are explicitly considered by any *one* model. Secondly, the extent of divisional discretion promoted by the models, especially the last two, is *very* limited. Thirdly, convergence to an optimal solution can require an infinite number of iterations.

Dantzig and Wolfe (1960) developed a computational model based on linear relations called the decomposition model, where convergence to an optimal solution takes a finite number of iterations. The model is also assumed to lead to greater decentralisation, compared with linear programming, through the concept of division of information. Each decision unit (e.g. division) uses only its technological coefficients and imputed prices to solve its local problem, whilst the control unit uses only the overall linking information and the results of computations of individual decision units to solve its global problem. Baumol and Fabian (1964) extended the decomposition model to deal explicitly with transfer prices and divisional externalities as illustrated in equation (2).

(2)

$$\text{Maximise } Z = C_1Q_1 + C_2Q_2 + \ldots + C_mQ_m = \sum_{j=1}^{m} C_jQ_j$$

$$\text{Subject to} \quad a_{11}Q_1 + a_{12}Q_2 + \ldots + a_{1m}Q_m \leq A$$

$$a_{21}Q_1 \qquad\qquad\qquad\qquad \leq B_1$$

$$a_{32}Q_2 \text{-------} \qquad\qquad \leq B_2$$

$$a_{mn}Q_m \leq B_m$$

where all $Q_j \geq 0$, and,
Z = total profit for the company,
C_j = the contribution margin, or profit, per unit of product j of division j,
Q_j = the quantity produced of product j of division j,
a_{ij} = the amount of input i required to produce a unit of product j,
A = the maximum amount of the central resource available,
B_j = the maximum amount of resource i available for division j.

Instead of centrally solving (2), it is divided into a central programme and m divisional programmes. The central programme would be solved by the central management and would be of the form:

(2a)

$$\text{Maximise } Z = \sum_{j=1}^{m} C_jQ_j$$

$$\text{Subject to} \quad \sum_{j=1}^{m} a_{ij}Q_j \leq A$$

The divisional programme would be solved independently by each division, and for the jth division would be:

(2b)

Maximise $Z_j = C_j Q_j$

Subject to $\quad a_{ij} Q_j \leqslant Bj$

The decomposition approach operates in the following manner. The central management announces a set of *provisional* transfer prices for the jointly demanded resources. Given the provisional prices, each division solves a problem similar to **(2b)** and submits its plans to central management. Initially, except by chance, the demand for the jointly required resources will not be equal to their supply. Thus, central management announces a new provisional vector of prices with the objective of attempting to equate supply of and demand for these resources. Divisions, again, solve problem **(2b)** with the new set of prices. This process continues until central management announces that an optimal solution has been reached. Divisional final plans would be a weighted average of the plans submitted earlier by the division, and the weight is determined by central management. It is also clear from **(2a)** and **(2b)** that central management need not know the internal technological arrangements of the individual divisions, since central constraints are the only constraints which appear in the central programme.

The Baumol and Fabian model presented above is strictly linear; in many real-life situations at least some constraints are non-linear. Jennergren (1972) has pointed out that transfer prices derived from a strictly linear model only exist in some degenerate cases. To overcome this criticism, at least in part, Whinston (1964) developed a model of a decomposition algorithm based on quadratic programming. The model uses a linear objective function and linear central constraints, but divisional constraints are non-linear representing the existence of diminishing returns. Consequently, **(2)** may be rewritten as follows:

(3)

$$\text{Maximise } Z = \sum_{j=1}^{m} C_j Q_j$$

$$\text{Subject to } \quad \sum_{j=1}^{m} a_{ij} Q_j \leqslant A,$$

$$f_j(Q_1, \ldots, Q_w) \leqslant B_{ij}$$

$$g_m(Q_1, \ldots, Q_r, Q_{jk}) \leqslant B_{im}$$

Where any $f_j(Q_1, \ldots, Q_w)$ is a convex non-linear divisional constraint, and the existence of Q_{jk} in division (m) constraints means that the activities of division (k) produce a shift in one of division (m)'s technological relationships. The decomposition algorithm in **(3)** remains the same as in **(2)** except that each of the (m) divisions would solve a non-linear problem in each iteration. Each division is asked to state in each iteration the production level at which it wishes other divisions on whom it is dependent to produce in order to maximise its own profits. This would be considered by the central agency in calculating new divisional profit coefficients. Whinston showed in his model that when 'externalities are separable, the price mechanism generates "efficient" prices which lead to economically correct decisions'. When inseparable externalities exist, Whinston argued, the price mechanism no longer gives reliable signals to guide divisional managers towards optimal divisional behaviour, let alone corporate optimal behaviour. It is worth noting that under the Whinston model a divisional manager may be forced to make non-boundary, i.e. non-optimal, divisional decisions in order to preserve overall company interest. Thus, the autonomy of divisional managers can be severely curtailed.

An Evaluation of the Decomposition Approach

Model Sophistication

One of the attractive features of decomposition models is that they utilise an internal market mechanism to derive 'optimal' values for scarce resources. Typically, these models handle transfer pricing problems for multi-products in multi-division firms. To this extent, the decomposition approach is more realistic than the traditional economic approach which typically considers a *two*-division firm with only *one* intermediate product. Furthermore, as shown above, externalities are *explicitly* treated under the decomposition approach whilst they are typically assumed away under the traditional economic model.

Economies of Information Transmission

One of the main advantages claimed for the decomposition approach is that it economises the costs of information transmission through division of information. Each division uses only its own technological coefficients and imputed prices, whilst the central management uses only the overall linking information; i.e. central or common constraints, and the results of divisional solutions – see (2a) and (2b). Furthermore, compared with the trial-and-error approaches, e.g. Arrow (1959), the properties of the decomposition approach ensure that the algorithm converges to an optimal solution after a finite number of iterations. Although the number of iterations required for convergence could be very large if arbitrary prices or functions are initially selected, the number can be greatly reduced if iterations start with a 'guesstimate' by the central management of the final solution (Hass, 1968). In this sense, the central management operates the organisation as a learning system; the experiences obtained from past activities are used to economise future solutions. However, given that the organisation is a dynamic system the decomposition approach should be considered as an on-going process. Thus, changes in contingency factors, e.g., environmental conditions or the prevailing technology, will change the underlying problem, thereby somewhat reducing the benefits of organisational learning.

Divisional Autonomy

The above analysis shows that the extent of divisional autonomy under the decomposition approach is rather limited. More specifically, the mechanism of the decomposition approach leads to two interrelated behavioural problems. Firstly, final output decisions are made and enforced on divisions by the central management. Secondly, the decomposition mechanism does not lead divisional managers to arrive at the optimal combination of outputs of their own volition; they *must* be told by the central management what these optimal combinations are (see Baumol and Fabian, 1964).

The motivational shortcomings of the decomposition approach arise mainly because *prices alone* are not adequate to ensure optimal decentralisation of decision making. Whether linear or non-linear decomposition is used, it is possible for the corporate optimal solution to be a non-boundary divisional solution, i.e. to be a subset of the divisional feasible region. This could arise because of the scarcity of corporate resources. In this case, the corporate optimal solution will not correspond to divisional optimal solutions. There is no fixed set of prices which will induce the divisional manager to select independently the corporate optimal solution (see Baumol and Fabian, 1964).

To overcome some of the above problems several refinements of the decomposition approach have been suggested in the literature. Hass (1968) developed a quadratic decomposition algorithm under which corporate optimal behaviour is effected through the manipulation of divisional demand and supply curves rather than the manipulation of pure prices (as is the case with Whinston's model). For example, if the original demand curve of division (j) is $P + \phi_j Q_j$, where P, ϕ_j, and Q_j represent the parameters of division (j) demand curve, the following adjustment would be effected on that demand curve: $- \alpha'_j \bar{\omega} + 2\phi_3 \hat{Q}_m$ where α'_j represents the corporate technological coefficient for division (j), $\bar{\omega}$ is the shadow price for the central programme, ϕ_3 represents the matrix of externalities, and $\hat{Q}_m$ represents the previous solution for division m. Therefore, $\alpha'_j \bar{\omega}$ is a functional adjustment which indicates prices for central resources shared by divisions at $\bar{\omega}$ per unit. The functional adjustment $2\phi_3 \hat{Q}_m$ reflects a tax or a subsidy for producing or using an additional unit of $\hat{Q}_m$ given the last feasible solution. This adjusted demand/supply curve is sent to the division to derive a new solution. The adjustment process continues until a corporate optimal solution is reached.

The model credits each division with the full benefit of its power in the market and the externalities it generates. Thus, if all relevant inputs and outputs are bought and sold in *imperfect markets*, the model derives final divisional demand and supply curves which independently lead each division to joint profit maximisation, i.e. corporate optimal solutions correspond to divisional optimal solutions. However, if goods are traded in *perfect markets* and if the final solution is an interior point, divisional managers will be indifferent with respect to the volume of activity, because they achieve a net profitability of zero. Hence, the optimal level of activity must be specified by the central management.

Again, under the Hass model the basic shortcomings of the decomposition approach are still present: (i) central interference is required when products are traded in perfect markets, (ii) optimal weights and final demand/supply functions are derived by central management and (iii) possibilities of divisional manipulation are present. Furthermore, the model credits the full benefit of an externality to *each* division associated with the generation of that externality, i.e. it results in multiple counting of externality effects. This has direct bearing on which index to use in making divisional continuation/abandonment decisions.

Jennergren (1972) developed another quadratic decomposition algorithm for decentralised organisations. The central agency derives a price schedule from the final iteration of the executive (central) programme and sends it to its divisions. Accordingly, each division determines the level of company resources it needs. The price schedule, S, has the shape of a linear upward sloping supply curve and its equation is: $S = P + \lambda \alpha_j \hat{Q}_j$, where P is the supply curve intercept, λ is any arbitrary constant, α_j is the corporate technological coefficient for division (j). Jennergren showed that the appropriate derivation of P is $P = \bar{\omega} - 2\lambda\alpha_j\hat{Q}_j$ where $\bar{\omega}$ is the shadow price of central resources as determined by the final executive programme, and $\hat{Q}_j$ is the optimal production for division (j). Again, this model shares most of the limitations raised above with respect to decomposition models.

Charnes, Clower, and Kortanek (1967) suggested a concept of 'coherent decentralisation' which is based on a set of 'pre-emptive goals'. Goals are pre-emptive if: (i) they are well ordered, or (ii) they are assigned priorities according to the relative importance of individual goal fulfilment. Pre-emptive goals may be incorporated into the constraint set or the objective function set. They relate activity levels within the division to specific goals not considered previously by the division. Penalty costs are assigned to handle deviations from stated goals. Thus, the central agency transmits to each division prices coupled with pre-emptive goals. One characteristic of this model is that, with trivial exceptions, uniqueness of divisional optimal solutions is not required and this permits divisions more flexibility without violating company goals. Furthermore, approximate fulfilment of the pre-emptive goals, i.e. non-optimal but close to optimal fulfilment, usually results in only small deviations from optimal profit. In particular, pre-emptive goals represent the motivation mechanism of this model in the case of non-binding divisional constraints. They induce the divisions concerned to handle the optimal activity levels by assigning to each division a set of 'ordered' goals coupled with penalty costs whenever deviations from those goals arise.

Ruefli (1971a and 1971b) developed a 'Generalised Goal Decomposition', or GGD, model based on goal programming which was subsequently utilised by Bailey and Boe (1976). As indicated in chapter 12, under the GGD model three organisational levels interact in arriving at the final solution for the algorithm: Corporate Management (CM), Division Management (DM) and Operating Management (OM). The GGD model operates as follows:

1. The CM determines the goals of the organisation and uses a linear programming model to determine the initial role of each division in meeting the corporate goals.
2. Each DM uses its set of goals to generate a set of shadow prices which minimise deviations around goal levels. These prices are then transmitted to the CM and to the OM belonging to each division. The DM can have goals other than those specified by the CM.
3. Given these prices, the OM is responsible for determining the optimal resources to be used in its products or projects as well as the optimal lot size which will minimise costs.
4. The CM uses the shadow prices to generate new sets of goal levels which maximise overall company contribution. Steps (2), (3), and (4) are repeated until the deviations from divisional goals are at minimum and no adjustments of goal levels by the central agency or modifications by sub-divisions would result in a decrease in the deviations from the goal levels of the company. The algorithm terminates in a finite number of iterations if goal levels, alternatives and shadow prices are all generated through the use of the simplex rules.

The GGD model is different from the basic decomposition model in three respects. Firstly, it is organisation dependent in the sense that the organisation structure of the firm under study partially determines the structure and final solution of the model. Secondly, it is a multiple goal model in which uni-directional, bi-directional and multi-directional technological and behavioural externalities are explicitly considered. Technological externalities refer to those situations where interdependencies exist among projects within the same sub-unit, or across sub-units, and where the goal levels of one sub-unit are dependent on those of other sub-units. Behavioural externalities occur when the goal-seeking behaviour of one sub-unit is affected by the goal-seeking behaviour of another sub-unit. Thus, one sub-unit may seek to reduce deviations from a specific goal to a level below the corresponding deviations of another sub-unit. Thirdly, goal consensus is not expected, i.e. divisional managers can be non-cooperative.

However, the GGD model has several limitations. Firstly, sub-optimisation is permitted because of the absence of a single objective function for the organisation. Secondly, the weights of the negative and positive goal deviations are determined by individual divisions independently of the central management; this makes it difficult for the central management to assess divisional bid prices for corporate resources. Thirdly, corporate balancing constraints are required to avoid the problem of only one division receiving company resources (a consequence of the linearity of the CM problem). Fourthly, divisional gaming is still possible, e.g. to acquire more of a particular resource, the division need only assign a very high priority to the goal relating to that resource.

Godfrey (1971) suggested a decentralised model promoting a substantial measure of divisional autonomy (using a general coordination mechanism between divisions) which need not lead to an optimal solution for the company. Divisions are asked to submit full information to the central agency which in turn solves the overall company programme and provides each division with (i) central resources allocated to that division, (ii) a statement of minimum expected profit contribution from the division, and (iii) a suggested production plan. Given its share of central resources each division could modify its marketing and production policies without being forced to follow the suggested production plan. However, deviations from the minimum expected profit contribution should be reported to the central agency. Although Godfrey's model has some desirable behavioural incentives, it is amenable to criticism on the grounds that it may result in significant sub-optimal behaviour. This would depend, in any event, on the particular structure and circumstances of each company.

The above refinements clearly enhance the usefulness of the basic decomposition model, but, as yet, they only represent a partial solution to some 'crucial' organisational and behavioural issues. The reason for this limited improvement can be traced back to the original Hirshleifer analysis. Thus, even in the simplest 'real world' cases, where certainty and divisional-pooled or sequential interrelationships could be expected to hold, Hirshleifer's analysis has demonstrated the deficiencies of approaching the transfer pricing problem from a strictly mathematical modelling point of view. These deficiencies become more severe when uncertainty is introduced (as is shown by Kanodia, 1979) and when reciprocal intra-divisional relationships exist. Following Watson and Baumler (1975), Bailey and Boe (1976) made the point that the transfer pricing problem is as much a behavioural issue as it is a solution algorithm issue. An algorithm which ignores the behavioural issues can only provide limited insight into the transfer pricing problem.

Corporate Optimality

As the above discussion indicates, the decomposition approach overemphasises corporate optimality. Thus, just as under the traditional economic and the linear programming approaches, whenever divisional discretion conflicts with corporate optimality the former is typically sacrificed in favour of the latter. Under the decomposition approach, unlike the traditional economic approach, no interdivisional exchange of marginal cost information is sought. Given this, it is generally assumed that sub-optimal behaviour is avoided. However, Naert and Janssen (1971) have shown that even in the absence of interdivisional exchange of marginal cost information, the decomposition approach will not necessarily yield a solution which is optimal for the company as a whole. The way to induce this sub-optimal behaviour is for the final division to treat its own marginal cost, MC_F, as its average cost and the transfer price, MC_I, as its marginal cost. The final division would then derive a quasi-average revenue curve, $ar_F = P_F - MC_F$, the corresponding marginal revenue curve mr_F which intersects MC_I at a lower transfer price and a sub-optimal level of activity for the firm. The authors showed that the condition for a division's profit at the sub-optimal output level exceeding its profit at the optimal output level is: $b_1 (1 + \sqrt{3})$ b_2, assuming non-negative values for b_1 and b_2, where b_1 and b_2 denote the slopes of MC_F and MC_I respectively. Thus, if the slope of MC_FQ is less than approximately 2.7 times the slope of MC_IQ, then division F can increase its profits at the expense of overall company profit by limiting its demand below the optimal level for the company. Although division F needs to know b_2, the slope of MC_I, an exact knowledge of it is not required as long as it can be estimated reasonably. To ensure that the decomposition approach yields a transfer price which maximises the profit of division F, even at the expense of the company, the manager of division F need only realise that iterations will continue until the demand and supply curves intersect. Thus, by moving along mr_F, division F can ensure maximising its profit.

IV. THE ORGANISATIONAL AND BEHAVIOURAL CONTEXTS OF TRANSFER PRICING

As the analysis offered in this chapter so far will have illustrated, the literature on transfer pricing is replete with models based on the axioms of rational choice. In seeking to attain corporate optimality, these models (with the exception of Godfrey's, 1971) allow divisional managers limited measures of autonomy. Further, the specifications of these models ignore much of the relevant organisational and behavioural contexts of transfer pricing. Nowhere in the literature reviewed so far is there a systematic exposition of a coherent theory of divisionalisation within a behavioural context. This is a serious limitation, given that in many cases 'the problems associated with transfer pricing and related decision performance questions are as much issues of organizational design as they are choices of accounting alternatives' (Spicer and Ballew, 1983, p. 92). For example, forming divisions through replication reduces significantly the degree of interconnectedness, and hence the flow of products and services, between divisions. In such situations, the problems of designing transfer price mechanisms can be significantly minimised.

More recently, a few researchers have attempted to redress the imbalance in favour of rationalistic economic models by focusing explicitly on the organisational and behavioural contexts of transfer pricing. The main contributions of those researchers are discussed below.

Drawing on contingency theory, Watson and Baumler (1975) view decentralisation as a response to environmental and technological uncertainties. Thus, in the terminology of Lawrence and Lorsch (1969), the success of the divisionalised structure is measured in terms of the extent to which it simultaneously achieves the requisite degrees of differentiation and integration of company divisions. The authors defined differentiation as encompassing: (i) the segmentation of the company into specialised sub-units, *and* (ii) the differences in the attitude and behaviour of organisational members arising from this segmentation. The incorporation of point (ii) in the definition of differentiation allows for the possibility that different organisational members may have different interpretations of the same organisational problem.

On this basis, Watson and Baumler argued that, when designing a management accounting system, the requisite degree of differentiation should be taken as given. Thus, whenever differentiation necessitates a particular segmentation which conflicts with the one desired by the accountant, differentiation segmentation should prevail, i.e. the accountant should not attempt to impose artificial profit centres on the organisational structure. The management accounting system plays a vital role in facilitating both differentiation and integration. Thus, the transfer pricing mechanism enhances differentiation in so far as it helps separate and illuminate responsibility for different stages of production. Furthermore, if the transfer pricing mechanism is routine, as is the case when it is based on a well-defined formula such as cost-plus, it helps to achieve the required integration in situations of low to moderate complexity.

Having pointed out the dual role of transfer pricing as a differentiation and an integration mechanism, Watson and Baumler argued the case for negotiated transfer prices. They suggested that the transfer price question is one facet of a multidimensional conflict-resolution process. There is sufficient evidence to suggest that negotiation is an appropriate conflict-resolution process (e.g. Lawrence and Lorsch, 1969; Cyert and March, 1963). Also, transfer pricing can be seen as part of the organisation's integrating mechanism. Hence, a strong case can be made for negotiated transfer prices as a means for effective integration by helping to resolve inter-divisional conflicts.

It is worth noting, however, that in the absence of a relevant outside market, the transfer price may reflect the divisional manager's ability to 'negotiate rather than his ability to control economic variables'. Moreover, negotiations between divisional managers may degenerate into personal conflicts. Watson and Baumler made light of the personal conflict problem by the use of three explanations. Firstly, although organisational members could have different perceptions, working styles and so on, they have many common attributes by virtue of being members of the same organisation, and hence agreement amongst them can always be attained. Secondly, the use of skilful mediators would help to maintain the rational flow of negotiations. Thirdly, guidelines can be provided for conducting negotiations. Empirical evidence, however, does not seem to support these contentions conclusively. Dearden (1964) and Whinston (1964), for example, cite evidence which indicates that in several cases agreement between negotiators is not automatically secured without central directives. Furthermore, negotiations can lead to the rise of personal conflict between divisional managers (see also Abdel-khalik and Lusk, for an exposition of some of the limitations of negotiated transfer prices).

Bailey and Boe (1976) combined some of the behavioural analysis of Watson and Baumler (1975) and the characteristics of the GGD model (Ruefli, 1971a; 1971b) to develop a more behaviourally orientated transfer pricing model. As indicated earlier, three important characteristics of the GGD model are that (i) it is dependent upon the organisational structure of the firm, (ii) it uses multiple goals, and (iii) divisional managers are not expected to subscribe to organisational goals (i.e., they can be non-cooperative). The Bailey and Boe model retains these characteristics.

As in the GGD model, the Bailey and Boe (1976) model is based on a tri-level structure: Corporate Management (CM), Division Management (DM) and Operating Management (OM). While remaining deterministic, the model specifically allows for the possible existence of alternative production characteristics at the operating level. The optimal solution to the problem is guided by derived shadow prices and is organisationally dependent; it is a satisficing rather than a global solution.

The model explicitly accounts for pooled, sequential and reciprocal interdependencies (Thompson, 1967). Pooled interdependence means that two or more tasks can be performed independently of one another. Sequential interdependence refers to situations where tasks have to be performed according to strict ordering, say task 1 before task 2, task 2 before task 3 and so on. Reciprocal interdependence occurs when a constant input/output interrelationship has to be observed among several tasks, so that individuals involved in these tasks coordinate their efforts through frequent interactions.

In the Bailey and Boe model, pooled interdependence is represented at any of the three levels, CM, DM and OM. Sequential interdependence is represented along the lines: CM→DM→OM; this establishes the order of the tasks associated with the three organisational levels. This means that each higher organisational level is responsible for integrating the activities of lower sub-units. Direct contact between sub-units not sequentially linked is not permitted. Reciprocal interdependence is reflected in the formulations at the next higher organisationa level. Thus, if OM_1 and OM_2 were reciprocally dependent, this would be reflected in the formulations of the relevant DM (the one to which OM_1 and OM_2 belong).

The model also allows for the existence of gaming, given the possibility that multiple and conflicting goals exist at each organisational level. Gaming is also likely to be problematic in the case of reciprocal interdependence, particularly when it is not uniquely known to the higher management level.

The Bailey and Boe model offers a good illustration of how some important organisational concepts can be combined with formal modelling to generate a plausible transfer pricing scheme. However, the model has many of the limitations associated with mathematical programming techniques alluded to earlier (see also Bailey and Boe, 1976).

The above discussion indicates, to some extent, that underlying any transfer pricing system developed is a theory of the organisation. This particular notion has been elaborated by Swieringa and Waterhouse (1982). They argued that, in relation to issues like transfer pricing, different models of the organisation offer different explanations of the same events. At a different level, different models emphasise different events, lead to different definitions of the problem, raise different diagnostic questions and provide different answers to the questions. To illustrate their argument, they contrasted five models of the organisation: (i) the traditional model (used predominantly in the literature on transfer pricing), (ii) the Cyert and March behavioural model, (iii) the Cohen and March garbage-can model, (iv) the Weick organising model, and (v) the markets and hierarchies model. In contrasting these models they use four 'paradoxes': goals versus determinants; process versus outputs; adaptability versus stability; and simplicity versus complexity. They are discussed very briefly below.

Goals Versus Determinants

The traditional model is premissed on the notion of well-defined, pre-existent organisational goals. Goals are assumed to be antecedent to actions. The analysis typically focuses on determining what goals account for the choice of a specific action. Thus, from this perspective actions relating to transfer pricing are analysed in terms of their contributions to well-specified organisational goals. Optimal actions are assumed to be consistent with organisational goals. The central management reserves the right to interfere and modify actions should they threaten the supremacy of such goals.

The remaining four models of the organisation do not view goals and actions as following a specific order. Their main focus is on understanding factors that determine outcome. The Cyert and March behavioural theory views goals as fluid, being influenced by the nature of bargaining that takes place between organisational members, the composition of the coalition and the definition of organisational problems. Goals are viewed as emerging through experience (see chapter 2). In this model, transfer pricing activities can be seen as reflecting long-term bargaining between divisional managers with the aim of arriving at an acceptable-level rule. Such a rule can then be used to negotiate the internal environment and to contribute to the avoidance of uncertainty.

In the garbage-can model, goals are decoupled from actions; actions result from a context-dependent set of problems, solutions, participants and choice opportunities. Outcomes are not likely to appear closely related to goals. Choices are made when the combination of these elements makes action possible (see chapter 2). The transfer pricing situation would thus be viewed as a choice opportunity. The problems brought to the choice opportunity could include, for example, the inability of divisions to exploit their external environments, and the manoeuvering by divisions to exploit each other. The solutions may include divisional bids, dual pricing schemes, and so on. The participants will be the relevant divisional managers and the headquarters.

According to Weick's organising model, actions are not goal directed, but goal interpreted. Past histories are used to endow actions with plausibility and legitimacy. Actions are related to the reduction of uncertainty rather than to pre-specified goals (see chapters 1 and 2). Thus, the choice of a specific transfer pricing system can be seen as a means of explaining, or legitimising, past actions and making them appear consistent with highly valued organisational goals.

Markets and hierarchies rely on the mechanisms of internal organisation and the norms of socialisation to curb the tendency towards opportunism in situations of small numbers bargaining and asymmetric information. The argument that there exist various economies in mediating transactions does not have to be based on the existence of well-specified goals (see chapter 11). This theory is likely to focus on using transfer pricing mechanisms to settle disputes, developing incentive schemes which foster cooperative internal trading, economising and regulating the flow of transfer pricing information, determining which goods (or services) transfers should be regulated through markets and which should be the subject of internal trading, and so on.

Process Versus Outputs

The traditional model focuses on the development of transfer pricing systems and procedures which motivate divisional managers to act in a manner consistent with the interest of the company as a whole. Divisional interests are assumed to be subordinated to company interests. The remaining four models focus on the *process* of determining transfer pricing rules, procedures and prices. The Cyert and March behavioural model views this process as an episode of ongoing, long-term bargaining between divisional managers. The garbage-can model treats it as a choice opportunity into which problems and solutions are dumped by divisional managers and the headquarters. Weick's organising model views this process in terms of enactment and legitimisation of past actions. According to the markets and hierarchies theory the process is viewed in terms of mediating transactions through markets or hierarchies and curbing tendencies towards opportunistic behaviour.

The analysis of Swieringa and Waterhouse (1982) suggests that, by emphasising transfer pricing processes, shared beliefs and cooperative behaviour may emerge and thus different expectations held by various organisational factions may converge. Shared understandings of situations, and agreements on future actions can be attained by exchanging information, interactions and retrospective enactment.

Adaptability Versus Stability

This 'paradox' is used by Swieringa and Waterhouse (1982) to illustrate the differences between and within the four non-traditional models of organisation. Viewing transfer pricing as a process through which structure and control evolve, they note that this process can be subject to pressure for organisational adaptation and learning which may conflict with pressures for organisational stability and predictability.

As indicated in earlier chapters (1, 2 and 11), all four non-traditional models (the behavioural, the garbage-can, the organising, and the markets and hierarchies) emphasise organisational learning and adaptation to cope with information asymmetry and uncertainty. They also show awareness of the presence of stabilising elements in organisations as reflected in programmed activities, rules, standard procedures and incremental changes in behaviour.

Swieringa and Waterhouse suggest that transfer pricing could contribute to both organisational stability and change. Thus, the transfer pricing system can act as a stabilising force if the pricing rules become part of the organisation's enacted reality. Such rules can also help to stabilise the organisational coalition by determining the basis for the distribution of rewards and by legitimising authority. To contribute to organisational learning and adaptation, transfer pricing rules can be coded with expiry dates; this is likely to introduce greater uncertainty and stimulate search behaviour.

Simplicity Versus Complexity

Under the traditional model, the transfer pricing situation is greatly simplified because of the assumptions of economic rationality, existence of well-defined goals and antecedence of goals to actions. This also allows for the abstraction of the transfer pricing process from its organisational context. Swieringa and Waterhouse note that such a situation requires little information. The locus of emphasis is simply on evaluating the degree of consistency of transfer pricing methods and procedures with the goals of the organisation.

The remaining models offer more complex views, in which the dimensions and the process of the transfer pricing choice situation are intertwined with many dynamic organisational features, so that it is not sensible to abstract them from their organisational context.

The insightful analysis of Swieringa and Waterhouse demonstrates the richness and complexity of transfer pricing in an organisational context. Their work also warns of the serious limitations of analysing transfer pricing through the lens of any one model of the organisation to the exclusion of others. Considered in combination, these models *together* offer a more comprehensive view of transfer pricing.

V. SUMMARY

The main problem which has occupied attention in this chapter has been that of controlling what is essentially a relatively decentralised, non-cooperative and interdependent organisation to ensure the attainment of some goal(s). Stated in general system theory terms, the organisation is a multigoal, multilevel, dynamic, and adaptive structure. To this extent, the interactions and interdependencies between organisation subunits, e.g. divisions, represent basic issues which should be explicitly considered by the control system. Further, the existence of heterogeneous knowledge amongst organisation members implies that the transmission and assimilation of information is costly. These two conditions (interrelated activities and diffused knowledge) constitute the central problem of organisational control in Arrow's terms (Arrow, 1964). Knowledge is disseminated within the organisation by virtue of an active and rather complex information system. Thus, each individual transmits, at a cost, a signal compatible with his knowledge. Upon receiving this signal, other members of the organisation modify their original conditional distributions of the states of the world and then make decisions. New signals arise from these decisions as well as from the outside world leading to new decisions.

Economists have long established that the price mechanism is one such important information signal which can be used to control and coordinate the complex interrelated activities of the divisionalised firm. The price mechanism developed by the economist for regulating the divisionalised firm ranges from the less sophisticated traditional economic model of a two-division firm with no externalities to the more sophisticated decomposition models of multiproduct, multidivision firms with differing externalities.

The development of the more sophisticated transfer pricing models has, undoubtedly, added considerably to the extent of realism of the transfer pricing problem setting. Nevertheless, the review undertaken in this chapter reveals that these models share some underlying assumptions which reduce their validity.

Firstly, these models assume goal consensus. The possibility of goal conflict, which is considered inevitable under modern organisation theory, is not explicitly entertained in these models (with the exception of the models developed by Ruefli and by Bailey and Boe). Further, participants are assumed to submit complete and honest information either to each other, as under the traditional economic model, or to the central management, as under mathematical programming models. Thus, information manipulation by divisional managers is not assumed to occur. To the extent that both goal conflict and gaming occur in reality, control over the allocation of resources within the divisionalised organisation may be dictated by forces other than the pricing mechanism, e.g. personal power and specialised knowledge.

Secondly, underlying the above transfer pricing models is the common belief that the price mechanism is a theoretically sound tool for regulating economic activities. However, the price system may not always be useful. One example is if returns are non-convex, i.e. increasing. A second is the presence of externalities. Under these conditions, prices do not lead to an optimal solution. The price mechanism can be appropriately modified in order to handle these conditions, but typically this increases the extent of centralised control.

Thirdly, the problem of uncertainty is hardly, if ever, considered by transfer pricing models. Thus, under the traditional transfer pricing model uncertainty is generally assumed away, whilst under decomposition models uncertainty is introduced but only in a very rudimentary way. Uncertainty is likely to affect greatly the determination of appropriate transfer prices. Arrow (1964) viewed the divisionalised organisation as an economic entity facing different sets of transfer prices with each set corresponding to a particular state of the world. Hence, each divisional manager will be faced with a probability distribution of transfer prices. Under such conditions it may be appropriate to replace profit maximisation with maximising the utility of profits.

Kanodia (1979) has also shown that differences in risk aversion amongst divisional managers, and between divisional and central managers, greatly complicates the regulation of organisation activities. In these situations, the development of risk-sharing schemes between managers becomes a real possibility.

Fourthly, the use of the price mechanism greatly complicates the development of operating and enforcement rules. Arrow (1964) alluded to these problems and pointed out some of the difficulties involved. Thus, ideally speaking, one could conceive of the existence of a separate price for each commodity for each separate date of delivery (operating rules). Further, the ways in which a manager's compensation can be related to his division's profits would need to be determined (enforcement rules). It is not clear how both rules can be established in an optimal manner.

Fifthly, the existing transfer pricing models do not capture fully all the relevant organisational and behavioural issues. The pricing mechanism does not yet completely penetrate all organisational levels and does not appropriately take account of reciprocal or even sequential divisional interactions. Furthermore, the trade-off between corporate optimality and divisional autonomy is an issue of major importance; it is not entirely clear, when in conflict, which of the two should be sacrificed in favour of the other.

The above argument does not imply that the price mechanism should be discarded altogether. All that it implies is that it is necessary for the price mechanism to be buttressed by 'non-market' mechanisms to ensure that resource allocation within the divisionalised organisation fully reflects the relevant economic, organisational, and behavioural characteristics.

REFERENCES

Abdel-khalik, A. R. and Lusk, E. J., 1974. Transfer pricing – a synthesis, *Accounting Review*, January, pp. 8–23.

Arrow, K. J., 1959. Optimization, decentralization, and internal pricing in business firms, pp. 9–17 in *Contributions to Scientific Research in Management*: Western Data Processing Centre, University of California, January.

Arrow, K. J., 1964. Control in large organisations, *Management Science*, April, pp. 397–408.

Arrow, K. J. and Hurwicz, L., 1960. Decentralization and computation of resource allocation, in R. W. Pfouts (ed.) *Essays in Economics and Econometrics*: Chapel Hill: The University of North Carolina Press, pp. 34–104.

Bailey, A. D. Jr., and Boe, W. J., 1976. Goal and resource transfers in the multigoal organisation, *Accounting Review*, July, pp. 559–573.

Baumol, W. J. and Fabian, T., 1964. Decomposition pricing for decentralization and external economies, *Management Science*, September, pp. 1–32.

Bernhard, R. I., 1968. Some problems in applying mathematical programming to opportunity costing, *Journal of Accounting Research*, Spring, pp. 143–148.

Bowley, A. L., 1928. Bilateral monopoly, *The Economic Journal*, December.

Charnes, A., Clower, R. and Kortanek, K., 1967. Effective control through coherent decentralization with pre-emptive goals, *Econometrica*, April, pp. 294–320.

Cook, P. W., Jr., 1955. Decentralization and the transfer price problem, *The Journal of Business*, April, pp. 87–94.

Cyert, R. M. and March, J. G., 1963. *A Behavioural Theory of the Firm*: Prentice-Hall.

Dantzig, G. B. and Wolfe, P., 1960. Decomposition principle for linear programs, *Operations Research*, January-February, pp. 101–111.

Dean J., 1955. Decentralisation and intra-company pricing, *Harvard Business Review*, July-August, pp. 65–74.

Dearden, J., 1964. The case of disputing divisions, *Harvard Business Review*, July-August.

Dopuch, N. and Drake, D. F., 1964. Accounting implications of a mathematical programming approach to the transfer price problem, *Journal of Accounting Research*: Spring, pp. 10–24.

Ezzamel, M. A., 1975. *A study in the theory and practice of divisional accounting.* PhD Thesis, University of Southampton.

Fellner, W., 1947. Prices and wages under bilateral monopoly, *The Quarterly Journal of Economics*, August.

Foldes, L. A., 1964. A determinate model of bilateral monopoly, *Economica*, May.

Friedman, M., 1962. *Price Theory: A Provisional Text*: Aldine Publishing.

Galbraith, J. R., 1970. Environmental and technological determinants of organisation design, pp. 113–139 in J. Lorsch and P. Lawrence (eds) *Studies in Organisation Design*: Irwin.

Gale, D., 1960. *The Theory of Linear Economic Models*: McGraw-Hill.

Godfrey, J. T., 1971. Short-run planning in a decentralized firm, *Accounting Review*, April, pp. 282–297.

Goetz, B. F., 1967. Transfer prices: an exercise in relevancy and goal congruence, *Accounting Review*, July.

Gould, J. R., 1960. The firm's demand for intermediate products, *Economica*, February, pp. 32–41.

Gould, J. R., 1964. Internal pricing in firms when there are costs of using an outside market, *The Journal of Business*, July, pp. 61–67.

Hass, J. E., 1968. Transfer pricing in a decentralized firm, *Management Science*, February, pp. B/310–B/331.

Hirshleifer, J., 1956. On the economics of transfer pricing, *The Journal of Business*, July, pp. 172–184.

Hirshleifer, J., 1957. Economics of the divisionalized firm, *The Journal of Business*, April, pp. 96–108.

Jennergren, P., 1972. Decentralization on the basis of price schedules in linear decomposable resources-allocation problems, *Journal of Financial and Quantitative Analysis*, January, pp. 1407–1417.

Kanodia, C., 1979. Risk sharing and transfer price systems under uncertainty, *Journal of Accounting Research*, pp. 74–98.

Lawrence, P. R. and Lorsch, J. W., 1969. *Organisation and Environment*: Irwin.

Manes, R. P., 1970. Birch Paper Company revisited: an exercise in transfer pricing, *Accounting Review*, July.

Naert, P. A. and Janssen, C. T. L., 1971, On sub-optimization in decomposition approaches to transfer pricing, *Journal of Industrial Economics*, July, pp. 220–230.

Onsi, M., 1970. A transfer pricing system based on opportunity cost, *Accounting Review*, July, pp. 535–543.

Pondy, L. R., 1970. Towards a theory of internal resource-allocation, pp. 270–311 in N. Z. Mayer (ed.) *Power in Organisations*. Nashville: Vanderbilt University Press.

Ronen, J. and McKinney, G. III, 1970. Transfer pricing for divisional autonomy, *Journal of Accounting Research*, Spring, pp. 99–112.

Ruefli, T. W., 1971a. A generalised goal decomposition model, *Management Science*, April, pp. B/505–B/517.

Ruefli, T. W., 1971b. Behavioural externalities in decentralized organisations, *Management Science*, June, pp. B/649–B/657.

Samuels, J. M., 1969. Penalties and subsidies in internal pricing policies, *Journal of Business Finance* 1 (2).

Schneider, E., 1969. *Pricing and Equilibrium*: Unwin.

Spicer, B. H. and Ballew, V., 1983. Management accounting systems and the economies of internal organization, *Accounting, Organizations and Society*, 8(1), pp. 73–96.

Swieringa, R. J. and Waterhouse, J. H., 1982. Organizational views of transfer pricing, *Accounting, Organizations and Society*, 7(2), pp. 149–165.

Thompson, J. D., 1967. *Organizations in Action*: McGraw-Hill.

Watson, D. J., and Baumler, J. V., 1975. Transfer pricing: a behavioural context, *Accounting Review*, July, pp. 466–474.

Whinston, A., 1964. Price guides in decentralized organizations, in W. W. Cooper, H. J. Leavitt, and M. W. Shelly II (eds) *New Perspectives in Organization Research*: Wiley.

14

The Conventional Management Accounting Control Model

Before any attempt is made to evaluate conventional management accounting control systems it is necessary to make two observations. Firstly, in this chapter no attempt is made to deal with conceptual issues underlying control theory and the nature of control as such. These issues formed the subject of discussion in chapter 4. It does, therefore, suffice to say here that accounting controls in the narrower sense constitute only a sub-set of a wider spectrum of quantitative controls and, in a practical context, tend to be basically coercive and authoritarian.

Secondly, there is no uniformity of opinion as to what precisely is the conventional management accounting control system or model. Thus, several writers would regard budgetary control as a technique which could be placed quite firmly within the framework of the 'conventional' model or system; yet, as Argenti (1976) points out 'You do not have to travel far to find quite large firms which still have no budgetary control.' Nevertheless, it is suggested that the conventional management accounting control system may be conceived, in broad terms, as one based on budgetary control and standard costing, to which, when viewed in unison, the label 'variance accounting' has been applied (ICMA, 1974). Marginal (Direct) costing, as an instrument of income reporting, does not qualify particularly well for inclusion in this framework unless combined with standard costing to form a unified 'standard/direct' costing system.

If, then, it is accepted that the conventional management accounting control model is built substantially on the technique of 'variance accounting', what are its limitations? The present chapter aims to address this question. Section I outlines the main criticism of the conventional management accounting control model. Section II contains a description and an evaluation of cost variance investigation models. In section III the importance of variances (for costs and revenues) as conventionally analysed is considered. Section IV contains some extensions of traditional variance analysis using the open systems approach. Finally, in section V a summary of the chapter is provided.

I. CRITICISMS OF THE CONVENTIONAL SYSTEM

In the context of this chapter it is not unreasonable to equate control with performance evaluation. Baiman and Demski (1980) describe the requirements of performance evaluation as follows:

326

In standard cost performance evaluation systems (sic) standards are set; budgets are constructed; actual and budgeted outcomes are compared and factored into individual variances; and 'significant' variances are investigated. Such systems are typically rationalized in terms of bookkeeping economy, decision-making usefulness, and motivational effects.

Despite its undoubted importance, the former aspect calls for no further comment in a book of this nature; the two latter aspects are given separate treatment in later sections of this chapter.

Without expanding unnecessarily the foregoing description, a few brief comments on 'standards' and 'variances' seem to be appropriate. Standards are related to expectations, but do not necessarily reflect optimal performance: indeed it is usually considered that standards should be reasonably attainable in the circumstances envisaged. Tight standards may be expected to have a disincentive effect, whereas standards which are set too loosely are likely to instil a sense of complacency; the importance of the behavioural implications of standards and budgets is, therefore, obvious, but considerable.

The setting of standards is of course not confined to costs, but has equal relevance to such areas as, for example, production volume, and sales volume/value. The main advantage of standard costing is, however, in the area of cost control, although a standard which is reasonably representative of a future cost may be used for planning purposes.

The degree of disaggregation of a total cost variance (i.e. deviation of actual total cost from the pre-determined 'standard') beyond the conventional basic variances depends on the needs of management, bearing in mind the probable benefits of further detailed analysis in relation to the disaggregation costs involved. In essence, such basic variances, in the case of both materials and direct labour, are associated respectively with price and usage (efficiency). As regards the breakdown of the total *overhead* variance the position is not so clear cut, and the form of analysis depends on the availability of an appropriate measure of effort assessment (e.g. standard hours) and also on the underlying assumption regarding overhead variability. Thus, if there is no effective means of assessing effort, and variable overheads are assumed to be a function of output, a 'two-variance' approach to overhead variance analysis is appropriate, and indeed the only one possible, showing respective figures for a 'controllable' (or spending) variance and a 'non-controllable' (or volume) variance. On the other hand, if effort can be measured and variable overheads are assumed to be a function of an input measure (e.g. labour hours) the 'conventional' three-way analysis into 'spending', 'volume', and 'efficiency' variances is feasible.

There have been criticisms from various writers of this conventional approach to variance analysis. These have included suggestions that the analysis is insufficiently rigorous and refined (Solomons, 1968; Demski, 1967), measurements are inappropriate (Demski, 1968), certain variances are redundant (Bromwich, 1980) and attention is not appropriately directed to the truly relevant control areas including motivational aspects (Drucker, 1964). These and other criticisms of the conventional model are considered further below.

In chapter 9 attention was drawn to criticisms directed at the efficacy of budgets in a planning context. In this section the alleged defects of the overall conventional systems are examined, with the main thrust directed at the defects and limitations of standard costing and, to some extent, budgetary control. Initially, however, the extent to which a budget may also serve as a control device is considered here.

As indicated in chapter 9 a 'fixed' or 'static' budget is of limited value for purposes of control in the sense of performance evaluation. The flexible budget is a much more effective* control instrument in that due allowance is made for changes in costs and/or revenues in accordance with the level of activity actually attained.

Opinion is divided on the extent to which budgets can serve the dual purpose of planning and control. Amey (1979) recognised the relationship between the two activities but argued that, to be effective, the two functions should be represented by different and distinct models. In this respect he differed from Anthony (1965) and would also assign a much more positive planning role to the annual budgeting process. Argenti (1978) took the view that *both* functions could be served by the short-term budget but, as mentioned previously, he argued that for longer periods, e.g. five years, the budget is a planning tool only on the grounds that it is meaningless to use the word 'control' in the context of the future. Corlett (1977), whilst subscribing to the view that budgets are used for both purposes, suggested that the control aspect is predominant.

By definition the budgetary control technique serves a dual purpose, and in a business context most writers and practitioners would presumably view the use of budgets in such a framework. It is, therefore, of some importance to consider the grounds on which Amey based his contention that the two functions should be represented by separate models. The grounds are threefold. Firstly, they serve entirely different ends, planning is essentially concerned with resource allocation and claims to resources whereas control does not have this economic orientation. Secondly, to be fully effective, control budgets require consideration of behavioural issues. Thirdly, it is generally observed that in accounting and business practice the control system is viewed as a mirror image (or identity mapping) of the planning system; this, Amey (1979, p. 5) maintained is untenable, as 'the sets and systems are not even approximately the same'. Despite these arguments for separation of the functions of planning and control, the most widely held view seems to support dual-purpose budgets.

Considering specifically the alleged limitations and defects of standard costing, these may be related conveniently to three main areas: (i) standard-setting; (ii) establishing criteria for variance investigation and (iii) the significance and value to management of the variances actually disclosed.

Within these main areas some specific aspects which invite criticism can be identified. Thus, in the standard-setting context and ignoring for the time being the motivational issues associated with unrealistic performance standards, one can point to the defects of a conventional system where standards are viewed as point estimates and not as a range of values. The result is that the subsequent variance investigation takes no account of what may, in fact, be purely random fluctuations. An improved cost control model designed to remedy this defect might involve the application of statistical quality control to the examination of variances, and the standard would thus be regarded not as a point estimate but as a band or range of possible acceptable values. The model would then be concerned basically with maintaining, in a statistical sense, a chosen state of control, a distinction being drawn between chance variances and those variances requiring investigation.

As regards investigation of cost variances, conventional criteria can be criticised on the grounds of arbitrariness and the failure to provide adequate guidance regarding the costs/benefits of variance investigation and correction of errors.

---

*Various writers, notably Demski, have criticised the effectiveness of the conventional management accounting control model in that no allowance is made for optimal adjustment to changed circumstances or, in other words, no attempt is made to measure the significance of a change in the firm's environment (see later, page 342).

When considering the significance and value of the variances themselves, the following specific defects can be pin-pointed.
— Variance analysis should be more sufficiently refined if it is to provide information which will be adequate and will not mislead. Moreover, some of the information provided by conventional analysis is redundant in that it is obtainable elsewhere.
— The measurements are inappropriate in that performance is monitored by reference to the original plan as laid down in the budget. Shifts in the original plan are therefore ignored except insofar as the budget is adjusted, and by failing to measure profit forgone the conventional standard cost system does not act as an opportunity cost system.
— Attention is not adequately directed to some of the truly relevant control areas, for example qualitative factors.

Much of the criticism directed at the setting of standards is associated with such behavioural issues as the disincentive effects of inappropriate standards and the deleterious impact on performance of non-participation or pseudo-participation in the budgetary or standard-setting process. These behavioural issues are discussed in the following chapter.

The concept of a 'standard', discussed above, has implications for determining the criteria for the investigation of cost variances. This is the subject of discussion in the following section.

II. COST VARIANCE INVESTIGATION MODELS

The question of whether or not a variance is significant is the point at issue when developing criteria for variance investigation. Significance in this context has variously been associated with the size of the deviation, its randomness and the net benefits expected to be derived from its investigation/correction. Investigation criteria can therefore be classified as:
1. arbitrary criteria based on 'materiality', as determined by reference to the relative, or possibly absolute, magnitude of the variance.
2. arbitrary criteria based on statistical significance, and thus involving the application of statistical quality control.
3. criteria associated with the aim of maximisation of net pay-off, thus involving quantitative assessments of (i) cost savings over the planning horizon arising from the correction of an out-of-control process, and (ii) the relative costs of investigation/correction. This assessment process usually implies a Bayesian approach to the assignment of probabilities to the respective states of control.

The arbitrary element in 1 above is associated with the substantial reliance placed on managerial experience, judgement, and intuition in selecting 'cut-off' values. Similarly, in 2 above, although a model based on such criteria 'uses a mathematically derived long-range frequency distribution as a basis for setting control limits' (Onsi 1967) the 'cut-off' values (e.g. two standard deviations, 2σ, or three standard deviations, 3σ) are arbitrarily chosen.

The essential feature of the 'classical statistical theory' model, based on the criteria referred to in 2 above, is the isolation of chance variances from those requiring investigation. It could be argued that the presence of random causes is implicitly recognised by the setting of 'cut-off' values as in 1 above, but no conscious effort is made to allow for such factors.

From time to time various writers have commented on the apparent lack of sophistication in practical approaches to variance investigation. In an enquiry from some prominent USA corporations, Koehler (1968) reported that no single use of statistical procedures was made for variance control. Kaplan (1975) also claimed that 'despite the widespread use of quality control techniques in industry – the application of these ideas in actual standard cost accounting settings can generously be characterised as minimal'.

General support for these views can be found in Awadallah (1975). His results, based on the practices of 64 leading UK manufacturing companies, indicate that only 23 per cent of them calculated the probability of cost variances resulting from random causes. Furthermore, although only 27 per cent reported the use of control charts in their respective organisations less than one quarter of the applications of such charts were related to control of costs.

Where reasons are sought for the paucity of practical applications of statistical procedures in this field, there is certainly no unanimity of opinion. Koehler's (1968) explanation was that accountants generally lacked the necessary statistical training to recognise the conceptual distinction between significant and insignificant variances. Anthony (1971) took the view that statistical procedures were not appropriate in this particular context. Magee (1976) concluded from his simulation analysis that other possibilities exist, and that motivational factors are relevant in that the basis on which the decision maker is evaluated and rewarded will affect the choice of model. Thus, a rational manager who is evaluated on the basis of his operating results or on the number of times he 'makes the budget' may prefer a 'naive' cost investigation rule. A further possible explanation is the difficulty associated with the determination of the part played by random causes in relation to deviations in specific items of cost when viewed in strict isolation.

Anthony (1971) argued that it must be left to empirical studies to determine the extent to which formal statistical and mathematical models can be considered appropriate in cost variance analysis. He suggested that some form of screening model would be helpful to managers in eliminating the need for them to engage in detailed examination of variance reports in order to detect a significant variance.

Several cost variance investigation models have been developed in the literature. These models vary considerably in terms of degree of sophistication. Kaplan (1975) offered a useful taxonomy in which he classified these models along two dimensions. The first is the period of analysis according to which a model can be single-period, that is the decision to investigate is based on a single observation, or multi-period, where the decision to investigate is based on some past sequence of observations. The second dimension relates to whether or not the model takes cognisance of costs and benefits of investigation. This taxonomy produces four broad classifications: models which *do not* take cognisance of costs and benefits of investigation, which may be single-period or multi-period, and models which take costs and benefits of investigation into consideration, and these likewise could be single-period or multi-period.

Models Which Ignore the Costs and Benefits of Investigation

The simplest form of these models is based on single-period analysis which aims to test whether a shift has occurred in the probability distribution of the process generating outputs. A shift may be represented by a change in one of the distribution location parameters such as the mean. An example of these models is the Shewhart $\bar{X}$ chart. This model operates by specifying a target mean and a standard deviation for the process when it is in-control. Moreover, upper and lower control limits are defined so that the probability of an in-control process with normally distributed outcomes producing a deviation beyond these limits is minimised. The system would signal the need for an investigation when the probability that an observation could have come from the in-control distribution falls below a given level. The analysis used is only single-period and only relates to a process in control. It does not explicitly consider costs and benefits of investigation nor the costs of failing to correct for an out-of-control process. Examples of models of this kind include Zannetos (1964), Koehler (1968), Probst (1971) and Buzby (1974).

An important refinement of the Shewhart $\bar{X}$ model involved the use of prior observations in order to facilitate the detection of shifts in the location parameters of the distribution being studied. The early developments occurred outside the accounting literature (see Kaplan, 1975). Examples include Page (1954), Barnard (1959) and Chernoff and Zacks (1964). An illustration of these models is the one developed by Barnard (1959). In his model, he assumed that shifts in the mean are governed by a Poisson process. If a shift occurs, its amount is assumed to be a normally distributed random variable with a zero mean and a known variance. A mean likelihood estimator is derived which is simply a weighted mean of recent observations. The mean estimate would correspond to the current level of average cost for the process under consideration. If the estimate is sufficiently different from the standard level, an investigation would be required.

Such models are an improvement over the simple Shewhart $\bar{X}$ chart. Instead of successive observations being treated as independent they are combined in the analysis (i.e. stochastic dependence is formally modelled). Thus, potentially useful information contained in prior observations is not lost as in the case of the Shewhart $\bar{X}$ chart. Notice, however, that such models are incomplete because they do not explicitly account for the costs and benefits of variance investigation.

Models Which Account for the Costs and Benefits of Investigation

These models also divide into those which are single-period and those which are multi-period. In the accounting literature, the best known single-period model which considers the costs and benefits of investigation is the one developed by Bierman, Fouraker and Jaedicke (1961). Invoking the normal distribution, they assumed that for any cost items a budget mean is established so that unfavourable and favourable random variances from the mean are approximately equally likely. Various ranges for cost variances can then be defined, and the probability that a given variance was the result of random causes can be derived.

Bierman, Fouraker and Jaedicke suggested that the decision of whether or not to investigate a variance depends on two factors: (i) the size of the variance and (ii) the probability that the variance results from random, non-controllable causes. The decision maker is expected to choose the act (investigate or do not investigate) that minimises the expected cost. A variance may be caused by factors either beyond (state 1) or within (state 2) the control of management. If state 1 is true, the cost of investigation (C) is wasted. If state 2 is true investigation may be worth while, i.e. it could result in future cost savings. If no investigation is undertaken in state 2, the company incurs the cost of not investigating a variance which could be controlled (L, where L is assumed to be greater than C). This analysis is summarised in table 14.1. The decision rules may be specified as follows:

1. Investigate if $C < (1 - P)L$
2. Do not investigate if $C > (1 - P)L$

Table 14.1 *Conditional cost table*

States	Acts		Conditional probabilities of states given an unfavourable variance has occurred
	(1) Investigate	(2) Do not investigate	
(1) The unfavourable variance resulted from non-controllable causes	C	O	P
(2) The unfavourable variance resulted from controllable causes	C	L	$(1-P)$
Expected cost of act	C	$L(1-P)$	1.00

Source: H. Bierman, L.E. Fouraker and R.K. Jaedicke (1961). A use of probability and statistics in performance evaluation. *Accounting Review*, July, pp. 409–417. Reproduced with the permission of the American Accounting Association.

By explicitly accounting for the costs and benefits of investigation, the Bierman et al. model offers a significant improvement over the previous models. However, the model has, at least, two serious limitations. Firstly, the model bases the investigation decision on only the most recent observation and, hence, prior information is ignored. Secondly, some of the model parameters, particularly L, are difficult to estimate because of the single-period nature of the model. Kaplan (1975) pointed out that future cost savings (L) depend upon future actions. For example, Bierman et al. defined (L), in situations where inefficiency will be repeated, as the present value of cost that will be incurred in the future if an investigation is not made now. But in such situations there will be opportunities in the future to correct the process and, hence, the discounted future costs assuming no future investigation will be an overestimate of (L).

These limitations led to the development of various multi-period models which explicitly consider the costs and benefits of investigation (e.g. Kaplan, 1969; Dyckman, 1969; Ozan and Dyckman, 1971; Dittman and Prakash, 1978; 1979).

Kaplan (1969) developed a two-state Markov model; an in-control state (Don't investigate) and an out-of-control state (Investigate) with the actual costs associated with each state. Thus, if investigation is delayed for one period there is a risk of operating one more period out of control, which means that higher costs will be incurred by operating away from standard. If investigation is undertaken, however, a cost is incurred which none the less might find the system still in control. Both costs are balanced against each other using dynamic programming to derive optimal policies which minimise discounted future costs. Relevant information from prior observations are summarised in a single state variable – the probability that the system is in control, the variable being updated after each observation via Bayes' theorem.

Formally, the model may be represented by a two-state, discrete-time Markov process with the following transition matrix:

(1)

$$
\begin{array}{c}
\text{At start of} \\
\text{the period}
\end{array}
\left\{
\begin{array}{l}
\text{state 1} \\
\text{(in-control)} \\
\text{state 2} \\
\text{(out-of-control)}
\end{array}
\right.
\quad
\begin{array}{cc}
& \text{During the reporting period} \\
& \begin{array}{cc} \text{state 1} & \text{state 2} \\ \text{(in-control)} & \text{(out-of-control)} \end{array} \\
\begin{bmatrix} q & 1-q \\ 0 & 1 \end{bmatrix}
\end{array}
$$

where q is the probability that the system will remain in state 1 during the reporting period, and $1 - q$ is the probability that the system will go to state 2 sometimes within the reporting period.
Define:

(2)

$$\tau_X q = g[1 + \lambda(X)(1 - q)/q]^{-1}$$

as the operator which updates the posterior probability, q_i, after receiving an observation X, where $\lambda(X) = f_2(X)/f_1(X)$ is the likelihood ratio of the out-of-control distribution to the in-control distribution. In this sense, q_i summarises all previous observations. There will be a critical value, $q^*(0 < q^* < 1)$ such that if $q_i < q^*$, an investigation is signalled and if $q_i > q^*$, no investigation is required. In Kaplan's model, the optimal decision is to choose the alternative which results in minimum expected costs, $C_n(q)$, so that:

(3)

$$C_n(q) = \min\{\underbrace{k + \int[X + \alpha C_{n-1}(\tau_X g)]f_g(X)\,dX}_{a}; \underbrace{\int[X + \alpha C_{n-1}(\tau_X q)]\,f_q(X)\,dX}_{b}\}$$

where k is the cost of investigation, α is the discount rate and $f_q(X) = qf_1(X) + (1 - q)f_2(X)$ is the weighted sum of the in-control and out-of-control density functions. In expression (3), the terms grouped under (a) represent the current and future costs if an investigation is made now. The terms denoted (b) represent the expected costs if no investigation is made now. After an investigation is performed, it is assumed that there is a probability g that the process will remain in control for one full period.

Despite its greater sophistication, Kaplan's model has a number of limitations. Firstly, the model dichotomises the process into a discrete two-state system, in-control and out-of-control. It suppresses the evolutionary nature of the process in the sense of moving gradually away from standards. This limitation can be overcome by expanding the number of states, but such procedure will not be practical because it will be difficult to derive the optimal policy. Secondly, the model assumes that an out-of-control process can always be returned to the in-control state. But, as Kaplan (1975) later acknowledged, irreversible shifts in the process may occur (e.g. changes in operating procedures) and thus expected benefits from restoration to the in-control state may not be realised. Thirdly, the model does not handle problems relating to below-average cost (Kaplan, 1975). Thus, permanent cost savings, through greater efficiency, are ignored because the model assumes that the process reverts back to its original cost standard. Moreover, the model assumes that lower costs are always better than higher costs even if the former are attained through inferior quality. Finally, the model does not allow for the possibility that an investigation may fail to detect an existing out-of-control situation.

Dyckman (1969) developed a variance investigation model which is similar in many respects to Kaplan's model. However, as in the Bierman et al. model Dyckman assumed that the savings from investigating an out-of-control situation (L) are constant. Such savings are assumed to extend over a time horizon which represents the minimum of the average time after which the process goes out of control *and* the time needed for standards to require revision. An interesting feature of Dyckman's model is that it extends Kaplan's investigate/do not investigate dichotomy by introducing an exploratory investigation which is less costly than a complete investigation but has a probability h; $h < 1$, for detecting an existing out-of-control situation. If k' is the cost of the exploratory investigation, the expected future cost from performing such investigation is:

(4)

$$k' + (1 - q)h \int [X + \alpha C_{n-1}(\tau_X g)]f_g(X)dX + [1 - (1 - q)h] \int \int [X + \alpha C_{n-1} \atop (\tau_X q')]f_q'(X)dX$$

where $(1 - q)h$ is the probability of finding the system out of control following an exploratory investigation,

(5)

$$q' = q/[1 - h(1 - q)].$$

The probabilities of being in control or out of control can be revised to reflect the results of the exploratory investigation.

Despite the useful extensions introduced by Dyckman, his model is essentially based on a two-state process and is thus subject to the limitations of such a process as described above. Kaplan (1975) further pointed out other limitations of Dyckman's model. Firstly, the non-sequential nature of the model causes problems with respect to the definition of cost savings, L. Thus, discounting L over the relevant planning horizon, its value is affected by the number of periods since the process started, n. As n increases, fewer periods remain in the planning horizon and the value of L decreases. Secondly, Dyckman assumed that the process is stationary and used the sample mean of consecutive observations to summarise them. Using the mean as such is valid as long as the process remains in the same state for all observations. However, when dealing with a non-stationary process the mean may shift over time, and the sample mean may not adequately summarise all the information contained in a given number of observations.

Duvall (1967) developed a model which treats the level of controllable cost as a continuous variable. According to the model, a deviation away from standard consists of a controllable component and a non-controllable component with each component assumed to be normally distributed and independent of the other. Reward from investigation is derived as a function of the controllable component be it favourable or unfavourable. However, the model assumed that investigations are undertaken only in the present period but *not* in future periods. Moreover, the model lacks a sequential strategy according to which the value of obtaining additional information after each observation is compared with the cost of operating another period at high, but controllable cost level. Kaplan (1975) documented further limitations which arise from the internal inconsistency of Duvall's model.

In commenting on the literature reviewed above, Kaplan (1975) suggested a three-tier variance investigation strategy. Firstly, to implement a procedure that systematically processes the current data with all prior observations (i.e. the Cusum chart). Secondly, to develop models that are closer to being 'right' from a cost–benefit analysis. Thirdly, given the additional experience and data derived from this procedure, to directly model the underlying stochastic process and implement procedures which are optimal for that particular stochastic process.

A brief reference has already been made to Magee's (1976) simulation analysis. This empirical work was also concerned with evaluating the effectiveness of several existing models and, additionally, suggesting possible reasons for their rather limited acceptance in practice. Assuming that a rational manager will seek to maximise expected utility of the outcomes associated with the model in the light of the relevant costs, Magee examined the performance of seven cost variance investigation rules over a twelve-month time horizon. His aim was to explore possible explanations why managers apparently prefer not to accept the more 'sophisticated' approaches.

In summary these seven rules are as follows:

1. Investigate all unfavourable cost variances. This conforms to the behaviour pattern of a manager who fails to distinguish between a significant and an insignificant variance.

2, 3 and 4. In combination, these produce the single rule: investigate all variances which exceed the standard by a designated margin, namely: 10 per cent, 1 standard deviation, or 2 standard deviations. All, thus, correspond to a simple control chart approach.

5. On the basis of cost observation and Bayesian revision, find the probability that the cost process is in control at the end of the period. Investigate if this probability is less than the 'trigger' value.

6. This rule is similar to rule 5 above, except that the 'trigger' values which initiate an investigation are found by using the dynamic programming approach suggested by Kaplan (1969).

7. This is based on the assumption that the manager has perfect knowledge regarding the state of the cost process. Fundamentally it uses the dynamic programming framework referred to in rule 6, with the probability of either 'zero' or 'one' that the process will be in control at the end of a period.

For practical reasons Magee used simulation procedures in preference to analytical methods, and each cost variance investigation rule was used for 200 simulated 12-month periods. In his conclusion he did not maintain that sophisticated cost variance investigation models are never useful, and he pointed out that there may well be situations in which dynamic programming could be the optimal model choice. However, he argued that it is just as easy to conceive of situations in which this is not so, and that 'even in the stochastic setting assumed by the dynamic programming method of cost variance investigation, there is no overwhelming evidence that a manager who uses a "naive" method is making a poor model choice decision'. He suggested that the opposite may be true, and that the added cost of re-estimating the parameters of an unstable process and resolving a dynamic programme each period could exceed any potential benefits.

Magee's conclusion that a rational manager may prefer a simple investigation rule led Capettini and Collins (1978) to suggest that one potentially fruitful area of research would be the refinement and further development of existing simplified models of variance investigation. To follow up this point Dyckman's (1969) statistical decision theory approach was selected for examination, but the assumption of equal variances for 'in-control' and 'out-of-control' states was relaxed, leaving, however, the simplistic nature of the model undisturbed. They reported that, for this simplified one-period variance investigation model, the introduction of the additional information involving unequal state variances results in decision rules with lower expected costs. They then suggested that the determination of the best model should be based on cost–benefit analysis.

Using a field experiment Jacobs (1978) evaluated six specific models to assess the significance of cost variances in a manufacturing firm. The six models were:

— Shewhart $\bar{X}$ control chart.
— Cusum chart.
— Economic $\bar{X}$ chart.
— Economic Cusum chart.

— Single-period Bayesian model.
— Multi-period Bayesian model.
Two techniques were used to evaluate the relative effectiveness of the models:
1. analysis of relative frequencies of Type I and II errors.
2. a sensitivity analysis ranking technique to provide further evidence of relative cost effectiveness.

His results indicated that multi-observation models were consistently more effective for all variables; the cumulative sum chart was consistently the most effective for variables with low loss/investigation cost ratios; and economic models were consistently more effective than non-economic models for variables with high loss/investigation cost ratios.

Dittman and Prakash (1978) addressed the problem of determining the optimal cost control limit for those policies which use a fixed critical cost to signal the need for investigation. They developed a simple solution technique which avoids the possible complexities of dynamic programming and does not require Bayesian updating of probabilities after each observation to obtain an explicit cost function for these policies. They developed the following rule:

If $g \Delta \mu \leq (1 - g)(N + K)$; Never investigate
     $g \Delta \mu > (1 - g)(N + K)$; Decision to investigate depends upon whether 'always investigate' is more costly, same as or less costly than 'never investigate'.

where

$\Delta \mu$ is the difference between the expected cost per period of operating out-of-control and operating in-control;

N   is the constant cost of correction;

K   is, as before, the constant cost of investigation;

$(1 - g)$ is, as before, the constant probability that the process moves to the out-of-control state in the next period.

In a subsequent paper, Dittman and Prakash (1979) tested their model against a Bayesian control model, i.e. one in which the probability of the process being out of control is updated after each observation. The results indicate that their model performs almost as well as the best Bayesian model except in situations where the in-control cost has a moderately large coefficient of intrusion* and a substantially greater dispersion than the out-of-control cost.

The main thrust of the discussion in this section has been to trace the general sequence of developments from the simple and purely arbitrary investigation rules to some of the more sophisticated approaches found in the research literature. A fully comprehensive review of such literature has not been attempted; for example, no specific reference has been made to multi-step investigation processes. Even so, it is felt that the discussion has been sufficiently wide-ranging to compel agreement with Bhaskar's (1981, p. 251) conclusion that 'The practitioner is almost bound to dismiss most of the literature as far too complex with excessively high information demands.' He argued that control charts, used in conjunction with some of the simpler decision rules, have the strongest appeal to the practitioner. On the investigation cost side he points out (p. 252) that

> It is not clear that the cost of investigation is anything other than a fixed cost, since in most organizations it would represent a body of accountants who would be retained on the staff of a company, irrespective of whether they investigated a variance or not.

*For each of the two cost distributions, in-control and out-of-control, the coefficient of intrusion is defined as the ratio of the statistical variance of the cost to their mean difference.

This is an important point to be observed when considering the cost factors pertaining to any variance investigation decision rule.

A concluding point, and one worthy of comment, concerns an examination by Baiman and Demski (1980) of traditional (sic) standard cost variance analysis procedures as motivational devices in a 'principal–agent model'. This is obviously related to the problem of the firm's organisational design structure in that the aim is to determine the manner in which the agent is to be evaluated and rewarded in terms of expected utilities, i.e. in non-pecuniary as well as pecuniary returns. In the context of variance investigation policy, and assuming the objective of maximisation of the principal's expected return, Baiman and Demski derived a solution based on a 'cost benefit' interpretation of the investigation decision. However, as they pointed out, formulation of the problem on game theory lines indicates that the precise economic content of the 'benefit' term is far more complex than its counterpart in the quality control literature.

III. IMPORTANCE OF VARIANCES AS CONVENTIONALLY ANALYSED

The Need for Further Refinement in Variance Analysis

The question posed in this section is whether variances as conventionally analysed do in fact convey to management the meaning which they purport to convey or which their designation, e.g. 'efficiency' variance, does actually imply. This question has given rise to suggestions that further expansion of the more widely recognised variances is required, and that more meaningful and relevant variances should be produced.

To deal effectively with these criticisms of conventional variance analysis it is necessary to consider separately the respective elements of the *total* cost variance, i.e. direct cost variances and overhead variances, and to give some thought to 'sales' variances as well as 'cost' variances.

Direct Cost Variances

On the direct cost side Solomons (1968) selected for particular criticism the conventional price variance in respect of raw materials and other purchased resources. Stressing the inadequacy of a single price variance, he made the point that a price variance could result from at least five different causes. These are price fluctuations arising since standards were set, inefficient buying, quality substitutions differing from standard, inflationary pressures on prices in general and the effect on buying price of purchasing in more or less than the budgeted quantities. It is not suggested that it is economically justifiable, or indeed in every case possible, to quantify the variances ascribable to all these various causes. However, recognition of their existence shows clearly the inadequacy as an explanatory device of a single 'price variance'.

Bromwich (1980) recognised the potential value of the conventional materials price variance in the planning field. It acts as a check on forecasts and standards, as a possible means of assessing forecasting ability and as an indicator to show whether price trends call for changes in existing plans. He did, however, question the value of this variance for appraising the performance of the purchasing officer, and advocated that such price variance be broken down into two separate variances, namely 'control of planning' variance and 'appraisal' variance. The former pin-points the difference between the actual market price and that previously assumed in the standard; whereas the latter measures the performance of the purchasing officer in the conditions which actually prevailed.

In general the materials usage variance has apparently invited less criticism. However, its value as an appraisal device has also been criticised where, for example, an adverse variance is the result of the employment of poorer quality labour than that prescribed in the standard. In such circumstances the suggestion is that the standard be adjusted for comparison with actual consumption.

The problem of a 'joint' or 'common' materials variance is well known, but should perhaps be examined nevertheless. Thus, using Q to denote quantity, P to denote price and subscripts a and s for actual and standard respectively, the variances for materials, *excluding* the joint element, are derived as under:

Total variance: $(Q_s \cdot P_s) - (Q_a \cdot P_a)$
Price variance: $Q_s(P_s - P_a)$
Usage variance: $P_s(Q_s - Q_a)$

The arguments for assigning responsibility for the 'joint' variance are not particularly convincing, and it can therefore be argued that the most appropriate course is to report it as a separate variance. Despite this it is common practice to include the joint variance as part of the quantity or price variance, usually the latter, with the result that the materials price variance is then denoted $Q_a(P_s - P_a)$. Assuming that both actual quantities and actual prices exceed their respective standards, the position can be shown diagrammatically as under:

P_a			
	Price variance	Δp	Joint variance $\Delta p.\Delta q$
P_s			
			Δq
Prices			Usage variance
	Quantities per unit	Q_s	Q_a

Bromwich made a similar point to Solomons in suggesting that the variances, even when modified on the lines indicated, do not reflect in full the responsibility of the buyer. Thus, purchasing in bulk to secure a favourable price variance may result in an inventory build-up with its associated additional holding cost, so indicating the desirability of establishing inventory standards. Or, again, the need to deal with rush orders could lead to increased transport costs; which might suggest the need for a 'transport cost variance'.

The price (i.e. labour rate) variance and quantity (i.e. efficiency) variance, as applied to direct labour, came in for equal criticism from Bromwich. He accepted the possible validity of the conventional labour rate variance for control of planning, but questions its use as a satisfactory appraisal variance.

The conventional labour efficiency variance, if adjusted to take account of currently attainable standards, may serve as an appraisal variance but the true cost is the opportunity cost of production lost due to inefficiency. Such cost should include not only wages payments but also any lost contribution, unless it is expected that there will be idle capacity in the future and unsatisfied demand of this period can be carried forward to next period. For control of planning Bromwich made the point that there are two aspects of the efficiency variance which, taken together, are relevant. These are the efficiency (appraisal) variance based on current attainable standards, and the uncontrollable efficiency variance, which represents labour inefficiency due to environmental conditions.

Interpretation of the variances requires that appropriate attention be paid to mutual dependencies. Thus, it may be that labour efficiency is improved at the expense of higher material consumption through increased wastage.

Overhead Variances

Discussion of suggested refinements in variance analysis has, up to this point, been concentrated on direct cost variances. In the area of overhead variance analysis there is even greater scope for criticism, focused mainly on the extent to which certain of the variances as conventionally isolated are truly meaningful.

There are a number of methodological approaches to the break down of a total overhead variance into its constituent elements. Basically however, assuming the possibility of effort assessment, these elements will be composed of a budget (or expenditure) variance, a volume variance and an efficiency variance.

Both the 'two-variance' and 'three-variance' methods of analysis are based on the assumption that variable overheads are a function of a single variable. As indicated earlier in this chapter, the two-variance approach assumes variability with output, whereas the three-way form of analysis assumes variability with some input measure, for example direct hours. Thus, quite apart from the availability of some appropriate means of assessing effort, it is not possible with the two-way approach to isolate an efficiency variance in the true sense. This is because a 'true' variance of this nature is associated with the degree of efficiency of *utilisation of inputs*, and consideration of this is precluded by the basic assumption that overheads vary only with output (see Table 14.2).

It is now well recognised that the variability assumption referred to above is quite unrealistic in that overheads may vary with both input and output measures. The four-way approach to overhead variance analysis, as suggested by Amerman (1953) and Solomons (1968), takes cognisance of this fact. It introduces a 'true' efficiency variance and divides the volume variance into two separate components, namely a 'volume (capacity) variance' and a 'volume (efficiency) variance'. The remaining variance would be the budget (or expenditure) variance. The 'true' efficiency variance then reflects excess costs or savings resulting from the use of additional or reduced man hours than the standard prescribed for actual production. In other words, it reflects true excesses or savings in terms of those expenses linked directly to man hours. The division of the volume variance into two recognised, separate elements indicates not only the extent of capacity usage but also the effectiveness of such usage (see Table 14.2).

The meaningfulness of a volume variance as such can be called into question. It is originated by the mechanics of the system and is not in any real sense a 'cost' or 'saving', but is a reflection rather of a difference in the amount of overhead absorbed. Thus, it arises because a standard rate for the absorption of fixed overhead, as calculated by reference to a planned activity level, is applied to production at some different (i.e. actual) activity level. In effect, this amounts to a recognition of the fact that if actual performance in terms of activity had been known in advance the fixed overhead recovery rate would have been based on such an actual figure, so ascribing to fixed overhead the fictitious quality of variability with production.

Overhead capacity (or volume) variances do not measure the cost of idle capacity, since this should reflect profits forgone and should therefore be evaluated in opportunity cost terms. Idle capacity would be costless if no alternative use were available. A volume variance, as such, would be obviated by the standard/marginal (direct) costing approach in which fixed costs are deducted in total from the net 'contribution' (i.e. standard contribution as adjusted by variances) irrespective of the scale of production. This approach retains the control features of standard costing in conjunction with flexible budgets. It also removes a possible source of misunderstanding regarding the apparent profits created in the short term by a build-up of inventories.

As regards the conventional overhead efficiency variance, Bromwich (1980) argued that this can be 'both misleading and redundant'. It is potentially misleading in that it does not reflect the real loss arising from lost opportunities, and redundant insofar as the causes will be reported in some other form, notably as direct cost variances.

In the context of sales variances Bromwich emphasised the need to consider interdependencies of sales volume variances and sales price variances. He questioned the value of the sales volume variance and stressed that the really important issue is to determine how well the sales manager has exploited the opportunities available to him during the period in question.

Miscellaneous Variances

Readers will have noted the omission of any reference to certain miscellaneous variances, such as the mix variance and the yield variance in the context of material usage. It seems inappropriate to discuss here all of the variances which can be isolated. In practice, the extent to which detailed analysis of variances may be undertaken depends on cost–benefit considerations. Conventional mix and yield variances have little practical value (see, for example, Bromwich). It may also be noted that a calendar variance should not arise if the budget for a period covers the actual number of working days in that period. These points call for no further discussion here, but it seems appropriate in the present context to make some reference to the ideas embodied in the work of Dopuch, Birnberg and Demski (1967). They argued that variance analysis should extend to an evaluation of performance of formal decision models. They observed that such a procedure would require 'changes in both the types of variances the accountant should calculate and in his methods for assessing the significance of these variances'.

Variance analysis under the two-, three- and four-way approaches

Suppose that the basic data for a manufacturing concern for a specific budget period is:

	Budget	Actual
Activity (working hours)	3200	2800
Production (standard hours)	3200	2880
Overheads: fixed	£1600	£1620
variable directly with output	£ 800	£ 880
variable directly with time	£2400	£2320

Under the two-way approach and the 'conventional' three-way approach, the budget allowance for variable overheads is regarded as a function of a single variable, i.e. output and working hours respectively; hence the additional information about variability is not required for these two approaches, i.e. one total variability figure suffices.

Table 14.2

	Standard hourly rate	Original budget (hours)	Revised budget (hours)		
			Actual hours worked (3-variance analysis)	Standard hours produced (2-variance analysis)	Actual/standard as appropriate
		3200	2800	2880	2800/2880
Overheads	(1)	(2)	(3)	(4)	(5)
	£	£	£	£	£
Fixed	0.50	1600	1600	1600	1600
Variable with output	0.25	800	2800	2880	720
Variable with time	0.75	2400			2100
	1.50	4800	4400	4480	4420

Actual overheads incurred   (1620 + 880 + 2320) = £4820
Absorbed overheads   2880 × 1.50 = 4320
Total overhead variance   (F = favourable; A = adverse) (500)A
2-Variance analysis
  1. 'Controllable' variance (budget variance)
      £4480 − 4820 (340)A
  2. Non-controllable variance (volume variance)
      £4320 − 4480 (160)A
      or (2880 − 3200)0.50 = 160
  This could be further analysed into:
  (i) use of capacity, i.e. (2800 − 3200)0.50 = (200)A
  (ii) efficiency   (2880 − 2800)0.50 = 40F
3-Variance analysis
  1. Budget variance   £4400 − 4820 (420)A
  2. Capacity (or volume) variance   (2800 × 1.50) − 4400 (200)A
    or (2800 − 3200)0.50
  3. Efficiency variance   (2880 − 2800)1.50 120F
4-Variance analysis
  1. Budget variance: £4420 − 4820 (400)A
  2. Volume (capacity) variance   (2800 − 3200)0.50 (200)A
  3. Volume (efficiency) variance   (2880 − 2800)0.50 40F
  4. 'True' efficiency variance   (2880 − 2800)0.75 60F

Flexible budgets prepared according to each method are shown in table 14.2. It can be seen from table 14.2 that the so-called 'true' efficiency variance of the four-variance approach is hidden in the 'controllable' variance of the two-way method. However, it could be argued that such 'controllable' variance of £340 could also be broken down into two separate elements, i.e. a 'spending' (or 'budget') variance and an 'efficiency' variance, the respective figures for which would be £420 adverse and £80 favourable. The spending variance can be further analysed into an element applicable to fixed overheads, i.e. £20 adverse, and the figure applicable to variable overheads, namely, £400 adverse.

The 'controllable' variance of the two-variance method is thus made up of the algebraic sum of the budget variance of the three-way approach (£420 adverse) and that part of the efficiency variance of such an approach (i.e. £80 favourable) attributable to the variable overheads, and reflected in the flexible budget as the difference between the budget allowance for actual hours worked and the budget allowance for standard hours produced. The remaining part of the 'efficiency' variance of the three-way approach (i.e. £40) is included in the 'non-controllable' (or 'volume') variance of the two-variance method.

Inappropriate Measurements

Criticisms have been directed at the failure of the conventional standard cost system to act as an opportunity cost system, in that performance is monitored solely by reference to the original plan (e.g. Demski, 1968; Bromwich, 1980). Demski's criticism relates to the *ceteris paribus* approach inherent in the conventional management accounting control model, whereby a variance is measured by a simple comparison between actual and standard results for the output produced. In contrast the *mutatis mutandis* approach, the one advocated by Demski, would seek to measure the significance of a change in the firm's environment. In other words the model would set up a standard of comparison which would allow for optimal adjustment to the changed circumstances, thus comparing actual with revised optimal results.

Decomposition of this total variance on the lines advocated would produce a 'forecasting' variance and an 'opportunity loss' variance which represents income forgone. The former variance, 'a rough indicator of the efficiency of the planning process', is measured by the difference between the planned outcome (in this case *ex ante* optimum income) and the *ex post* optimum. The 'opportunity loss' variance is measured by the difference between the *ex post* optimum and the outcome as actually observed. It reflects the difference between what the firm could have accomplished given the additional information acquired up to the time of analysis and what it actually did accomplish.

The approach advocated by Demski has strong conceptual appeal. It may indeed be operationally feasible when applied to processes such as oil refining, where inputs and outputs have approximately linear relationships and proportions can be varied. Its operational viability as a generally applicable model must, however, be open to some doubt, and here again the question of costs in relation to resultant benefits is an important consideration.

In conclusion, although perhaps not strictly relevant to the present discussion, it is worthy of note that the obvious need to take explicit cognisance of changes in output volume and mix presupposes a decision model; in Demski's analysis this took the form of a linear programming model. In an earlier work Samuels (1965) proposed an integrated planning and control system using the control features of standard costing and a decision model based on linear programming. As Bhaskar (1981) has suggested, Samuels was probably the first to recognise such a possibility.

Failure to Direct Attention to Relevant Control Areas

Recognition of the need to lay greater emphasis on qualitative factors is in line with the increasing attention devoted in recent years to behavioural issues in the accounting field. Drucker (1964) maintained that the fundamental question in relation to any control system is not 'How do we control' but rather 'What do we measure?' A business entity is a social institution and in this respect the 'controls' which are imposed are not only 'goal-setting' but also 'value-setting'. Thus the mere act of selecting some event for measurement endows that event with value in the eyes of the observer, and is, therefore, subjective and biased.

In business there are both quantifiable events and also events which, despite their importance, are not easily quantifiable in any meaningful way. As an example of a highly important non-quantifiable event Drucker cited the ability or otherwise of a business to attract and hold capable employees. Quantifiability does not imply relevance as a control area, whereas an event which is not quantifiable in any accepted sense may nevertheless call for the maximum control effort which is available. Further, Drucker pointed out that, apart from selecting the right control areas, the measurement must also be appropriate in that it presents the events that are measured in structurally true form. Thus, a statement that has formal validity may nevertheless be quite misleading unless it is placed in perspective.

The requirement of structural validity in business reports, including statements of variances from a standard or budget, may be exemplified by the phenomenon which has given rise to the 80/20 rule as based on observation but derived from the Pareto distribution*. For example, in the areas of quality control and inventory holding, application of the 'rule' would indicate that in the former case approximately 80 per cent of defects would occur in 20 per cent of the products, and in the case of mixed inventories 80 per cent of total inventory value could be expected to be accounted for by only 20 per cent of the items held in stock. The 'rule' would thus suggest that attention be focused on the 20 per cent minority group in these situations. In the specific field of variance analysis, however, it could have relevance in determining the 'significance' in value terms of certain variances, particularly in relation to product groups.

Management control will be further facilitated by reporting dynamic variances, or variances 'showing the *rate of change of a rate of change* variance' (Bromwich, 1980 p. 195). Such a variance, ideally produced on a continuous basis, would serve the purpose of monitoring trends in performance variations, so acting as a useful indicator of the need to revise targets in those instances where a trend persists.

The areas of criticism examined up to this point have, in general, ignored those deficiencies associated with behavioural implications of the conventional management accounting control model. These are examined in the following chapter.

IV. BEYOND TRADITIONAL VARIANCE ANALYSIS

The discussion of the limitations of conventional variance analysis in the preceding section focused almost exclusively on the technical aspects of variance analysis without questioning the underlying design of the control system. One of the main themes of this book has been the call for studying accounting in its organisational context. It is, therefore, relevant to identify and evaluate the organisational model underlying traditional variance analysis.

As indicated in chapter 4, several researchers have commented on the limitations of the organisational model underlying traditional accounting control. Ansari (1977, 1979) characterised traditional accounting control as a highly mechanistic, closed system. Flamholtz (1983) also hinted at the similarity of traditional accounting control to closed systems by suggesting that, according to the former, budgeting is viewed as an independent control mechanism instead of being a *component* of a control system

---

*So named after the 19th century economist who applied it to describe the distribution of income, the bulk of which was, not surprisingly, distributed over a very small proportion of the population.

that interacts with various other components. Further, Collins (1982) argued that traditional management accounting systems are not related to intra-organisational control.

Given the orientation of this chapter, it is worth considering some of the characteristics of traditional management control which liken it to a closed system. The discussion of variance investigation models revealed that two types of variance exist: those which need not be investigated and those which should be investigated. Reports explaining the latter variances are usually submitted to higher level managers as a form of feedback in order to facilitate control. Ansari (1979) pointed out that both types of variance are errors which make the accounting control system analogous to the closed cybernetic model known as the 'error-controlled regulator'.

Further, the traditional control system relies on cost traceability and the principles of responsibility accounting. Managers are held responsible only for those costs which are deemed controllable by them. The organisation is typically segmented into a number of cost centres which are designated responsibility centres, reflecting the vertical 'chain of command'. Thus, artificial boundaries are drawn between the various centres in order to emphasise responsibility, but at the same time this leads to ignoring interdependencies between different centres, as is the case in closed systems.

Ansari (1979) outlined three problems which emanate from the tendency of the traditional accounting control system to ignore interdependence between responsibility centres. Firstly, the traditional control system encourages competition and not cooperation. Secondly, traditional variance analysis defines controllability in terms of outcomes rather than causes and thus ignores the possibility that a variance which occurs in one centre could have been initiated in another centre. Thirdly, classifying variances into those which should be investigated and those which should not leads to a greater emphasis on performance evaluation but ignores the learning aspects of variances. Focusing on the responsibility centre as the independent unit of analysis means that information about the causes of system-wide variances, and thus about system-wide learning, is ignored.

These limitations led several writers to suggest structuring management accounting control systems using the open systems approach (e.g. Ansari, 1977, 1979; Collins, 1982; Flamholtz, 1983; Flamholtz, Das and Tsui, 1985). As indicated in chapter 4, an open systems view of accounting control would explicitly recognise the dynamic interactions which are critical to the survival and the success of the system. According to that view, accounting control is viewed as a part of the total organisational control process.

Ansari (1979) has pointed out that using an open systems approach to the design of accounting control systems has two important implications. Firstly, because of the difficulty of engaging in clear-cut allocations of tasks and resources within a given responsibility centre, there is a need to develop shared systems of responsibility. Secondly, because no manager can exercise full control over all resources the system should emphasise cooperation instead of competition.

Ansari (1979) developed a budget variance model based on the open systems approach which purports to address these implications. His model provides a causal classification of variances so that emphasis is not only on whether a variance is significant but also on the sources of the disturbances which cause the variance. Thus, Ansari's variance classification scheme has two dimensions. The first, relating to the significance of the variance, distinguishes between 'expected' and 'unexpected' variances. This distinction is consistent with situations where management includes controllable variances within a standard, either because it is costly to remove them or because it is desirable to include them for motivational purposes (building budgetary slack).

The second dimension relates to the source of variances and classifies the environment of a responsibility centre into internal, external and exogenous. Internal refers to disturbances originating within a responsibility centre, external relates to disturbances which originate in other centres, and exogenous ones are disturbances which originate outside the organisation but represent part of the organisational environment. Combining the two dimensions means that each of these three variances (disturbances) can be either expected or unexpected.

Ansari's variance classification scheme is useful in focusing the attention of the responsibility centre's manager on the sources of disturbances that he should manage. For example, if significant variances arise from exogenous forces, the manager would need to focus on managing relationships with the environment. Similarly, the reporting of external variances helps in managing organisational interdependencies. This scheme shows that total reliance on the traditional variance analysis scheme and the failure to go beyond outcomes and unravel causes of variances can lead to serious dysfunctional consequences for the organisation.

V. SUMMARY

This chapter has been concerned with evaluating the conventional management accounting control model. This included examining some of the broad criticisms of the conventional model as a performance evaluation tool. A description and an evaluation of various models of cost variance investigation followed and, finally, the importance of variances as conventionally analysed was considered.

The broad criticisms of the conventional model are mainly directed at the limitations of standard costing and budgetary control. These criticisms related to:
1. using point estimates rather than a range of values in setting standards;
2. using arbitrary criteria and failing to use cost–benefit analysis in variance investigation;
3. using crude variance classifications, inappropriate measurements and calculation of redundant variances whilst failing to consider other important control areas.
4. being primarily based on the closed systems approach, thereby ignoring interdependence between different responsibility centres.

Attempts to address these three main criticisms were then described and evaluated. Thus, various cost variance investigation models were considered. These ranged from the simple single-period models which ignore the costs and benefits of investigation, at one end of the continuum, to the multi-period models which explicitly account for the costs and benefits of investigation at the other end of the continuum. Suggested improvements to variances as traditionally analysed were then considered. These included refinements in variance analysis, suggestions to improve measurements, suggestions of relevant control areas which deserve examination, and suggestions to extend variance analysis to account for interdependencies and exogenous environmental forces using the open systems approach.

The main tenor of analysis in the chapter related primarily to the *technical* limitations of the conventional control model. The behavioural implications and deficiencies of the model were not considered. This is the subject of the following chapter.

REFERENCES

Amerman, G., 1953. The mathematics of variance analysis–11, *Accounting Research*.

Amey, L. R., 1979. *Budget Planning and Control Systems*: Pitman.

Ansari, S. L., 1977. An integrated approach to control system design, *Accounting, Organizations and Society*, **2**(2), pp. 101–102.

Ansari, S. L., 1979. Towards an open systems approach to budgeting, *Accounting, Organizations and Society*, **4**(3), pp. 149–161.

Anthony, R. N., 1965. *Planning and Control Systems: a Framework for Analysis*. Cambridge, Mass.: Harvard University Press.

Anthony, R. N., 1971. 'Some fruitful directions for research in management accounting', in Dopuch, N. and L. Revsine (eds), *Accounting Research 1960–1970: A Critical Evaluation* : Center for International Education and Research in Accounting, University of Illinois.

Argenti, J., 1976. Whatever happened to management techniques?, *Management Today*, April, pp. 78–79.

Argenti, J., 1978. Long term budgets can damage your company's health, *Accountancy*, May, pp. 105–107.

Awadallah, A. A., 1975. 'Impact of modern management accounting techniques upon the development of cost control models: an inquiry into the adequacy of managerial accounting analysis of cost control signals and a feasibility appraisal of a discriminant analysis model constructed for serving cost control objectives'. PhD Thesis, University of Southampton.

Baiman, S. and Demski, J. S., 1980. Variance analysis procedures as motivational devices, *Management Science* **26** (8) August, pp. 840–848.

Barnard, G. A., 1959. Control charts and stochastic processes, *Journal of the Royal Statistical Society*, Series B, pp. 239–257.

Bather, G. A., 1963. Control charts and the minimization of costs, *Journal of the Royal Statistical Society*, Series B, pp. 49–70.

Bhaskar, K. N., 1981. 'Quantitative aspects of management accounting', pp. 229–273 in M. Bromwich and A. Hopwood (eds) *Essays in British Accounting Research*: Pitman.

Bierman, H., Fouraker, L. E. and Jaedicke, R. K., 1961. A use of probability and statistics in performance evaluation, *Accounting Review*, July, pp. 409–417.

Bromwich, M., 1980. 'Standard costing for planning and control', in *Topics in Management Accounting*, J. Arnold, B. Carsberg, and R. Scapens (eds): Philip Allan Publishers.

Buzby, S. L., 1974. Extending the applicability of probabilistic management planning and control models, *Accounting Review*, January, pp. 42–49.

Capettini, R. and Collins, D., 1978. The investigation of deviations from standard costs in the presence of unequal state variances, *Journal of Business Finance and Accounting*, Winter, pp. 335–351.

Chernoff, H. and Zacks, S., 1964. Estimating the current mean of a normal distribution which is subjected to changes in time, *Annals of Mathematical Statistics*, December, pp. 999–1018.

Collins, F., 1982. Managerial accounting systems and organizational control: a role perspective, *Accounting, Organizations and Society*, **7**(2), pp. 107–122.

Corlett, S., 1977. 'Financial aspects of corporate planning', pp. 130–154 in Taylor, B. and J. R. Sparkes (eds) *Corporate Strategy and Planning*. London: Heinemann.

Demski, J. S., 1967. Analysing the effectiveness of the traditional standard cost variance model, *Management Accounting* (USA), October, pp. 9–19.

Demski, J. S., 1968. 'Variance analysis using a constrained linear model', pp. 526–540 in D. Solomons (ed) *Studies in Cost Analysis*, 2nd edn. London: Sweet and Maxwell.

Dittman, D. A. and Prakash, P., 1978. Cost variance investigation: Markovian control of Markov processes, *Journal of Accounting Research* **16** (1) Spring, pp. 14–25.

Dittman, D. A. and Prakash, P., 1979. Cost variance investigation: Markovian control versus optimal control, *Accounting Review* **LIV** (2) April, pp. 358–373.

Dopuch, N., Birnberg, J. E. and Demski, J. S., 1967. An extension of standard cost variance analysis, *Accounting Review*, July, pp. 526–536.

Drucker, P. F., 1964. 'Controls, control and management', in Bonini, C. P., R. K. Jaedicke, and H. M. Wagner (eds) *Management Controls – New Directions in Basic Research*. New York: McGraw-Hill.

Duvall, R. M., 1967. Rules for investigating cost variances, *Management Science*, June, pp. 631–641.

Dyckman, T. R., 1969. The investigation of cost variances, *Journal of Accounting Research*, Spring, pp. 215–244.

Flamholtz, E. G., 1983. Accounting, budgeting and control systems in their organizational context: theoretical and empirical perspectives, *Accounting, Organizations and Society*, **8**(2/3), pp. 153–169.

Flamholtz, E. G., Das, T. K. and Tsui, A. S., 1985. Toward an integrative framework of organizational control, *Accounting, Organizations and Society*, **10**(1), pp. 35–50.

ICMA, 1974. *Terminology of Management and Financial Accountancy*. London: ICMA.

Jacobs, F. H., 1978. An evaluation of the effectiveness of some cost variance investigation models, *Journal of Accounting Research*, Spring, pp. 190–203.

Kaplan, R. S., 1969. Optimal investigation strategies with imperfect information, *Journal of Accounting Research*, Spring, pp. 32–43.

Kaplan, R. S., 1975. The significance and investigation of cost variances: survey and extensions, *Journal of Accounting Research*, Autumn, pp. 311–337.

Koehler, R. W., 1968. The relevance of probability statistics to accounting variance control, *Management Accounting* (USA), October, pp. 35–41.

Magee, R. P., 1976. A simulation analysis of alternative cost variance investigation models, *Accounting Review*, July, pp. 529–544.

Onsi, M., 1967. Quantitative models for accounting control, *Accounting Review*, April, pp. 321–330.

Ozan, T. and Dyckman, T. R., 1971. A normative model for investigation decisions involving multi-origin cost variances. *Journal of Accounting Research*, **9**(1), Spring, pp. 88–115.

Page, E. S., 1954. Continuous inspection schemes, *Biometrika*, pp. 100–115.

Probst, F. R., 1971. Probabilistic cost controls: a behavioural dimension, *Accounting Review*, January, pp. 113–118.

Samuels, J. M., 1965. Opportunity costing: an application of mathematical programming, *Journal of Accounting Research*, Autumn, pp. 182–191.

Solomons, D., 1968. 'The analysis of standard cost variances', pp. 426–493 in D. Solomons (ed.), *Studies in Cost Analysis*, 2nd edn. London: Sweet and Maxwell.

Zannetos, Z. S., 1964. Standard costs as a first step to probabilistic control: a theoretical justification, an extension and implications, *Accounting Review*, April, pp. 296–304.

15

Behavioural Implications of Accounting Controls

Accounting controls generally, and budgets in particular, are assumed to serve as devices for coordination, communication, performance evaluation and motivation. Accordingly, budgets are used for the purposes of performance evaluation by providing lower-level managers with well-specified targets (feed forward), and by providing higher-level managers with information about the extent to which those targets have been met (feedback).Comparisons of actual achievements with prespecified targets, and investigation of the main causes of deviations, reveal ways of improving efficiency. Through the preparation and use of budgets various organisational functions and activities can be coordinated and harmonised. This is particularly crucial where tasks are highly interdependent.The budget also operates as an important formal communication tool. Organisational goals are decomposed and communicated via the budget to managers at lower levels in the hierarchy. In turn, achievements of lower-level managers and the problems they encounter are communicated upwards to senior managers through the reporting system usually used with budgets. Budgets also play an important role in employee motivation.The reward systems typically associated with budget use define the criteria for rewarding high performance and for imposing sanctions for non-atttainment of target in the light of results shown by comparisons between budget and actual performance.

These roles reflect the traditional rationalistic philosophy of budgets, or what Argyris (1977) calls the theories of control that practitioners espouse. They do not fully reflect the theories that practitioners use. For instance, they do not explicitly refer to the political-negotiation mode through which budgets are 'negotiated' between budgeters and budgetees given the asymmetric power distribution of those groups (Wildavsky, 1975), nor do they necessarily reflect the fundamental views of reality held by individual practitioners. Argyris (1976 and 1977) has called for broadening our understanding of control by examining both the theories espoused *and* the theories used by practitioners: this he refers to as 'double-loop learning' (see Bourn and Ezzamel, 1987).

Both sets of roles have been discussed in the accounting literature, and some of the relevant arguments can be traced in various parts of this book, particularly chapters 7, 9 and 14. Because, *inter alia*, accounting controls are, at least in part, designed to regulate and monitor human behaviour in organisations, they have important and inescapable behavioural implications.

This chapter is devoted to a review of some of the important behavioural implications of management accounting controls. The chapter is divided into four sections. Section 1 contains a discussion of the impact of accounting controls, particularly traditional controls, on employee (i.e. both managers and non-managers) behaviour. Section II is devoted to the various implications of participation in the budgetary control process. Section III contains a review of the literature on the effects of leadership styles and various personal characteristics of subordinates on their attitude towards jobs, budgets, human relations and performance. Finally, a summary of the chapter is presented in section IV.

I. THE IMPACT OF TRADITIONAL ACCOUNTING CONTROLS ON EMPLOYEE BEHAVIOUR

Styles of Accounting Information Use

Evidence concerning the impact of accounting controls on managerial behaviour abounds in the literature. Although predominantly concentrating on budgets, the behavioural implications of other accounting controls have also been examined. Hopwood (1973) offered a classification of different styles of using accounting information; a classification which can be utilised to synthesise much of the existing literature on the behavioural implications of accounting controls. According to Hopwood, three styles may be distinguished: a budget constrained style; a profit conscious style and a non-accounting style.

The budget constrained style is primarily concerned with a short-term based evaluation of performance. It uses accounting information as a comprehensive measure of managerial performance. It concentrates on performance that can be measured, even if at times it is unimportant from an organisational point of view, and it ignores other dimensions of performance which are not susceptible to precise measurement. The profit conscious style emphasises aspects of performance that are of a longer-term nature and are desirable to the organisation. Limitations of accounting imformation are acknowledged in the sense that such information is used in a flexible manner. Moreover, accounting information tends to be buttressed by non-financial information. The non-accounting style is treated in Hopwood's classification as a residual category in which a low priority is accorded to accounting information in the context of performance evaluation. Ronen and Livingstone (1975) suggested that, in the context of expectancy theory, subordinates can be motivated to accomplish non-monetary objectives, which are traditionally viewed as non-accounting if these are incorporated into the control system. This may be achieved by: (i) making extrinsic rewards dependent upon achievement of non-monetary objectives; (ii) improving task clarification to facilitate attainment of non-monetary objectives and (iii) making the attainment of non-monetary objectives intrinsically valent (i.e. giving personal utility or satisfaction) to the subordinates.

Each style of information use has specific behavioural implications. Thus, if the profit conscious style is adopted the problems associated with the use of accounting information in performance evaluation are attenuated. This is likely to be the case even though: (i) the superior and the subordinate will typically have different perceptions of not only the dimensions that are relevant to performance evaluation, but also of the appropriate level of each dimension and (ii) the subset of accounting information that is relevant to performance evaluation may be difficult to identify. The main reason is that with this style it is held that the superior is aware of the limitations of accounting information and of the need to consider wider and more long-term aspects of performance (Hopwood, 1973).

By contrast, the budget constrained style is conducive to various dysfunctional behavioural consequences. Thus, because the superior typically views accounting information as a complete and unbiased indicator of managerial competence, disagreements between manager and subordinate are likely to be strong. This may be because the subordinate perceives accounting information to be biased and/or incomplete. Non-accounting information may be espoused by the subordinate as being significantly relevant to his performance. Moreover, given a budget constrained style the imperfections in accounting information are likely to cause greater uncertainty in the subordinate's task environment. The presence of task and behavioural interdependencies would mask the causal link between effort and performance. Thus, the subordinate can never be sure of the consequences of increased effort on performance; accounting measures typically fail to reflect in full the effects of interdependencies.

Most traditional accounting controls appear to fall within the category of budget constrained style, as indicated by a voluminous body of research. Caplan (1966; 1968) traced the origins of the management accounting model of the firm to both the classical economic theory of the firm and the classical organisation theory. These two theories underlie the behavioural assumptions of traditional management accounting thinking which cover such areas as organisational goals, participants' behaviour, management behaviour and the role of management accounting.

Thus, in traditional management accounting, it is assumed that the principal goal of the firm is profit maximisation and that this goal can be subdivided between organisational subunits. It is further assumed that goals are additive in the sense that maximising subunit goals leads to maximising corporate goals. With respect to organisational participants, it is assumed that they are naturally inefficient and wasteful, that they avoid work and responsibility whenever possible and that they are solely motivated by economic rewards and sanctions. The role of management is assumed to be one of maximising profits. This is assumed to be done through manipulating the reward structure of the subordinates and exerting pressure on them so that inefficient and wasteful behaviour is kept to a minimum. As a planning and control device, the management accounting system is perceived as assisting management in maximising profits. It is further assumed that the accounting system is objective and that it is sufficiently comprehensive, rational and accurate for the purposes of performance evaluation. In summary, the accounting controls advocated in traditional management accounting correspond well to Hopwood's budget constrained style. Frequently, the system involves the use of an imperfect single criterion for the purposes of decision making – a practice which Ridgway (1956) has characterised as conducive to dysfunctional behaviour.

Traditional Accounting Controls and Employee Behaviour

Evidence on the adverse effects of accounting controls on employee tension is plentiful. Argyris (1952; 1953) documented cases in which budgets were used, or at least perceived to have been used, as a pressure device. Not only was pressure experienced by shop-floor workers but also by supervisors, particularly front-line supervisors. Hofstede (1967) described cases where departmental budget reports led to feelings of excessive pressure by employees. Becker and Green (1962) reviewed the history of the use of budgets in local government institutions and businesses in the United States of America. They observed that in early practices 'imposed' budgets were used as an instrument of control over employees and that these resulted in some dissatisfaction. Many subsequent studies document various cases of budget-induced pressure (e.g. De Coster and Fertakis, 1968; Schiff and Lewin, 1970; Hopwood, 1972, 1973; Onsi, 1973).

Some of the literature cited above explicitly considered various consequences of pressure on employees induced by accounting controls. Argyris (1953) documented some useful insights relating to the ways in which employees handle budget pressure. Initially, the use of imposed budgets as a pressure device leads to greater employee tension, resentment, suspicion and mistrust. After a given level of budget pressure is reached any further pressure becomes intolerable to employees who then actively seek ways of reducing or absorbing pressure. One apparently effective way of reacting to pressure is through cohesive group formation which not only reduces pressure and tension on employees but also offers a feeling of security and group-belonging which itself helps to relieve pressure. Once these groups are created they remain in existence even when pressure is reduced, possibly in anticipation of future pressures being exerted or simply because group members become used to a pattern of relationships which they find fulfilling.

However, whilst group formation is a viable strategy for shop-floor workers to combat management pressure, it may not be an advisable strategy for supervisors to relieve their own pressure. The supervisor is typically trapped in a difficult situation; unlikely to pass all the pressure down the line to his subordinates and likely to avoid joining groups which may be identified by superiors as anti-management. Argyris, however, identified at least three strategies through which the supervisor might relieve pressure: blaming other supervisors for problems that exist; blaming budget staff, production staff and sales staff; and internalising pressure.

The results of several pieces of empirical research also indicate that incomplete and ambiguous accounting controls lead to increased task uncertainty. Whilst the final outcome may in many cases be measurable in a relatively clear manner, standards may be inappropriately set, and the effects of an employee's actions on his own performance index can be extremely difficult to trace if other people's actions can influence such performance. The results of the studies of Deutsch (1949) and Thomas (1957) indicated that in situations of task interdependence, whether of a facilitative or hindering nature, uncontrollability over performance is positively correlated with work related tension. A study by Cohen (1959) has shown that employees who were unclear as to how to improve their performance found it difficult to adjust to their jobs which subsequently resulted in greater insecurity. Similarly, Kahn, Wolfe, Quinn, Snoek and Rosenthal (1964) reported that performance ambiguity led to a loss of self confidence and ultimately to tension and reduced job satisfaction.

Moreover, the use of imposed, rigid, and autocratic accounting controls can lead to employee alienation, resentment of other organisational participants perceived to be associated with these controls and ultimately to detrimental dysfunctional consequences for the organisation as a whole. Thus, Argyris (1953) spoke of the 'wall' which may isolate factory employees from budget staff. This may be created not only as a result of the imposition of rigid budgets and the emphasis on budget attainment but may also be the result of the ignorance of factory employees concerning budgets. Such a wall can play a dual role; it can be a major source of insecurity for employees but, at the same time, a prime screen of security for budget staff behind which they can operate 'unmolested'.

Argyris (1952; 1953) further documented situations in which imposed budgets and management attitudes towards employees were observed to lead to dysfunctional consequences. Thus, budget staff perceived themselves as 'watchdogs' whose main responsibility was to look for and report on deviations from budgets. Budgets were perceived by budget staff as legitimate means of exerting pressure on employees by providing a challenge for them. Evidence of antagonistic attitudes between employees and budget staff were plentiful. The budget staff viewed employees as essentially lazy and reluctant to take on responsibility and challenge. Employees perceived budget staff as inflexible, insatiable and as continually seeking to exert more pressure. They were also criticised for making targets unrealistically high, for being reluctant to change targets when conditions altered and for failing to explain whether the causes of variances were avoidable or unavoidable. All in all, budgets and other accounting controls were viewed by employees with considerable distrust. Hostility between budget staff and employees was much in evidence.

Furthermore, Argyris noted that emphasis on budget attainment resulted in many employees being task-centred and many supervisors being department-centred. Thus, by overemphasising individual departments, relationships *between* departments were disregarded. The detrimental consequences of such behaviour for the organisation as a whole are likely to be reflected not only in high levels of conflict, but also in the frustration of the organisational mission.

Similarly, Hughes (1965) described the endless cycle of the conventional budgetary control process which is characterised by continuous unresolved conflict between top management and lower management. In his analysis, such endless cycle is primarily caused by the failure of each side to appreciate fully the needs of the other. Top management, he argued, needs control whereas lower management needs flexibility. When there is little support from lower management, top management pursues its need for control by placing greater emphasis on the use of budgets and rules, and on the communication of more detailed budget rules to lower management. Lower management pursues its quest for flexibility by general avoidance of controls and rules, particularly budgets, and by a continual search for loopholes in the system. The more lower management avoids controls, the more top management seeks ways of strengthening these controls, with the result that lower management searches for new loopholes, and so the cycle repeats itself.

Stedry (1960) conducted a major investigation into the budget as a formal statement of organisational goals, its relationship with individual goals (aspirations) and the effects of budgetary reports on performance. His research methodology involved three main steps: (i) developing a mathematical model of individual behaviour in a goal-striving situation; (ii) conducting an empirical investigation of human performance under different budget conditions and (iii) developing a linear programming model to handle the planning and coordinating aspects of budgets.

Stedry's mathematical behavioural model postulates that in attempting to attain a cost budget an employee has to deal with three interrelated levels of cost: the budgeted level; his own aspired level and the actual level. The effect of the budget on employee behaviour is assumed to vary depending upon factors such as individual differences, personal traits and state of mind, and the structure of rewards obtainable and penalties imposed. The typical budgetary control system involves comparing the actual level of performance against the budgeted level and reporting the variance between the two levels. Stedry argued that this at times leads to undesirable results, because such a reporting system in usual budgetary practices ignores the motivational variables pertaining to the individuals concerned. As the unfavourable deviations between actual performance and aspired performance levels exceed some threshold, the individual becomes discouraged and no longer seeks to improve his performance. Such threshold is a function, amongst other things, of the individual's personality traits which tend to differ between individuals. Traditional budgetary systems overlook these differences by implying that subordinates are treated impartially and equally.

In his empirical investigation, Stedry used a laboratory experiment to measure the relationship between performance, aspiration levels, and budget levels. Participants in the experiment were divided into four budget-level groups : low budget; medium budget; high budget and implicit budget (that is, no specific budget standard was defined). The results indicated that budget level influences performance. The implicit budget group performed best, followed by the medium, high, and low budget groups respectively. The results further indicated that there is a significant relationship between budget levels, aspiration levels, and performance. This was tested by dividing members of each group into those who set their aspiration levels after receiving their budget and those who were not asked to set an aspiration level. It was found that the best performance occurred in the high budget group which set its aspiration levels *after* receiving the budget, and the poorest performance occurred in the high budget group which set its aspiration levels *before* receiving the budget. One possible rationalisation of these latter results is that when participants set their aspiration levels after receiving the budget they modified their aspiration levels in line with the budget levels, i.e. budget targets became internalised. However, when the aspiration levels were set before the budget was received, budget targets were treated as separate and perceived to be in conflict with already defined aspiration levels.

Stedry also suggested that departmental suboptimisation is the outcome of traditional budgetary control practices. He developed a linear programming model to explore the effects of such suboptimisation activities on overall organisational performance. His model illustrates the, by now obvious, point that if each subunit concentrates exclusively on its own goals overall company interest may be endangered.

The Stedry study is interesting not only because it is one of the earliest accounting studies using a laboratory-based experiment, but more importantly because it shows that a relationship may exist between budgets, budgetary practices and human motivation. Its results, however, should be interpreted with caution for at least two reasons. Firstly, like all experimental studies it may not reasonably approximate to real-life settings. Secondly, there are some technical failings in Stedry's research design which Becker and Green (1962) have pointed out. In particular, he appears to have used an inaccurate measure of aspiration level by defining it as the performance level that an individual 'hopes' to attain rather than 'expects' to attain. Aspiration level reflects what an individual expects to attain.

Notwithstanding these limitations, Stedry's work remains important. Ronen and Livingstone (1975) used the expectancy theory approach to reconcile and explain some of Stedry's results. They suggested that attaining higher performance under non-participation conditions is possible because, in comparison with other levels of attainment, the expectancies that work-goal attainment 'will lead to extrinsic valences will be higher the nearer the performance level is to the imposed standard'. Thus, an individual will select the aspiration level that maximises his motivation to work. However, if imposed targets are set too high, aspiration level will lag behind because the expectancy that goal-directed behaviour will lead to work-goal attainment is likely to be negatively correlated with the perceived difficulty of attaining targets.

In this section discussion was mainly concentrated on illustrating some of the counter-productive consequences of traditional accounting controls; but the way in which the accounting system is used reflects the leadership style of the particular management team. A discussion of this topic is given in section III of this chapter. It has, however, been repeatedly argued that the counter-productive consequences of traditional accounting controls can be attenuated if participation of lower-level management in the budgeting process is allowed. This is considered in more detail below.

II. PARTICIPATION IN THE BUDGETARY PROCESS

Several researchers have long argued that participation by lower-level managers in selecting controls, e.g. preparing budgets, would help in alleviating, or at least reducing, many of the dysfunctional consequences associated with traditional control models (e.g. Argyris, 1952, 1953; Becker and Green, 1962; Hughes 1965). Emphasis in such arguments has been on true participation rather than pseudo-participation. Argyris (1953) and Sord and Welsch (1958) documented several cases in which it was only possible to secure pseudo-participation from employees. This may have occurred because the budget setting process lacked the genuine characteristics which encourage true participation, or because the supervisors and employees themselves were unwilling to cooperate or be bothered with budgets. In such cases employees tend to accept budgets only half-heartedly. This form of participation is inevitably dysfunctional. By contrast, true participation implies spontaneous and free discussions amongst all those involved in controls, and appreciation of each other's needs and points of view.

Some Consequences of Participation

The literature on the consequences of participation abounds. In their investigations, some writers relied almost exclusively on a priori theoretical reasoning (e.g. Hughes, 1965); others used carefully controlled experiments (e.g. Schachter, Ellerton, McBride and Gregory, 1951; Foran and De Coster, 1974); and still others used actual firms as a means of capturing real-life situations (Coch and French, 1948; French, Israel and As, 1960; Milani, 1975). Although there is much commonality in the results of these and many other studies, there is also much ambiguity and, at times, conflict as is indicated below.

Some writers have expressed an almost unqualified support for participation by perceiving it as a fully successful means of attaining mutual recognition of the limitations of controls, avoiding conflict and achieving harmony in attending to organisational goals (e.g. Hughes 1965). Others have been quick to acknowledge that participation is not a panacea and that it could be inappropriate in particular circumstances (e.g. Becker and Green, 1962).

One of the main themes of the studies on participation is the relationship between participation and productivity. Coch and French (1948) conducted an empirical investigation with the aim of clarifying the effects of participation on production after work changes were introduced. Their results indicated that those who participated in initiating the change were more productive and better disposed towards their work than those who did not participate. Moreover, unlike the participating group, the non-participating group expressed grievances and several of them quit their jobs. An experimental study by Schachter at al. (1951) indicated that, with participation held constant, high-cohesive groups more frequently accepted instructions which induced changes in production (both increases and decreases) than did the low-cohesive groups.

Becker and Green (1962) used the above two sets of findings to suggest that participation affects productivity through cohesiveness. Thus, they argued, since cohesiveness without participation affects productivity (Schachter et al.) and since participation affects morale, or cohesiveness (Coch and French), it is likely that cohesiveness is dependent on participation and that productivity is more directly related to cohesiveness.

Morse and Reimer (1956) conducted an investigation which indicated that the non-participation group outperformed the participation group in terms of productivity. This significant differential in productivity in favour of the non-participation group was not accounted for by a general rise in productivity of other groups in the company. Rather, it appeared to be related to the non-participation style of decision making. These findings were subsequently supported by the results of a laboratory investigation carried out by Bryan and Locke (1967).

Participation in budgets, then, is perceived by various writers to be conducive, either directly or indirectly, to high morale, greater initiative and greater desire to attain, or even improve upon, targets. Thus, even though Becker and Green (1962, p. 401) suggested that participation is not a panacea, they went on to argue that:

> A successful participation budget does two things:
> (1) it induces proper motivation and acceptance of specific goals, and (2) it provides information to associate reward or punishment with performance. These lead to new aspirations and motivations that set the stage for the next participation budget.

Implicit in the above quotation is that true participation is beneficial. This appears to be a commonly held view (Sales, 1966).

Moreover, there are further arguments based on the theory of cognitive dissonance which are supportive of the notion that participation is beneficial. Foran and De Coster (1974) summarised the findings of a number of studies which provide some revealing explanations of these benefits. Cognitive dissonance may be defined as 'a negative drive state which occurs whenever an individual simultaneously holds two cognitions (ideas, beliefs, opinions) which are psychologically inconsistent' (Aronson, 1968, pp. 5–6).

According to the theory, if a person exercises a free choice amongst decision alternatives, that person is voluntarily committed to the selected alternative. In other terms, such a decision maker will experience dissonance because he cannot enjoy the positive attributes of the alternatives which were not selected (Brehm, 1956). The decision maker engages in various subjective changes of attitude to reduce dissonance. This may be attained by overemphasising the positive aspects and de-emphasising the negative aspects of the selected alternative, and vice versa for the discarded alternatives. Hence, in order to secure the commitment of employees to targets and goals, these employees should not only have a choice but should also exercise that choice. True participation may thus be interpreted as combining both the availability and exercise of free choice.

Similar arguments supportive of participation can be found in the expectancy approach. Participation can create and enhance both extrinsic and intrinsic valences (Ronen and Livingstone, 1975). Thus, if group norms are conducive to higher levels of performance, participation can lead to better performance through increasing group cohesiveness. A cohesive group enhances the extrinsic valence associated with work-goal attainment for each member as each reflects the group's norms (determined by group consensus) and thus maintains his acceptability by the group. Moreover, intrinsic valences may be created in a participative environment through an individual's tendency to become 'ego-involved' in a decision he or she helped to make.

Brownell and McInnes (1986) used expectancy theory to assess the relationship of budgetary participation to motivation and performance. They collected questionnaire data from 108 middle-level managers in three manufacturing firms. The authors hypothesised that motivation mediates the effect of budgetary participation on performance. The results, however, did not support that hypothesis. The relationship between participation and the intrinsic valences associated with work-goal accomplishment and goal-directed behaviour was negative. This is inconsistent with the above discussion (see also Ronen and Livingstone, 1975). The authors attempted to explain their surprising results by invoking the concept of budgetary slack (this concept is discussed more fully later in this section). They argued that participation strengthens the expectations of formal reward based on budget attainment, thereby providing a motive for managers to submit easy budgets, and thus trade off expectations of intrinsic for extrinsic rewards. This may be a plausible, but not a complete, explanation of their surprising results.

A growing body of research on budget participation draws attention to two important considerations. Firstly, that the effects of participation may be strongly influenced by personality and environmental factors. Secondly, that participation may be associated with the creation of budgetary slack.

Personality and Environmental Factors

Consider first the evidence relating to the extent to which the effects of participation are influenced by personality and environmental factors. The results of the studies subsequent to those of Coch and French (1948); Schachter et al. (1951) and Morse and Reimer (1956) appear to be less supportive of the universality of beneficial effects of participation. Thus, in attempting to corroborate the findings of Coch and French in a different cultural setting, French et al. (1960) reported that participation had no effect on productivity even though it apparently improved morale. As Stedry (1964) pointed out, it is not clear from their results whether the reduction of beneficial participation effects is due to differences in organisational cultures or in national cultures.

The results of a study by Vroom (1960) indicated that personality factors and leadership styles tend to condition the effects of participation. The study reveals that employees who viewed participation as legitimate were more productive under participative supervision, whereas those who perceived it as illegitimate were less productive.

Moreover, the study by French et al. (1960) suggested that there were no significant differences in goal accomplishment in the case of goals derived on the basis of participation and those derived with no participation (i.e. imposed goals). Not only were the differences insignificant, but they were not in the hypothesised direction (i.e. of greater participation being associated with better goal accomplishment).

The accounting literature contains some useful contributions to the debate on the nature of the consequences of budget participation. An example is the study by Foran and De Coster (1974) which tested a number of hypotheses related to the effects of participation, authoritarianism and feedback on cognitive dissonance. The model used had the following characteristics:
— Employees had choices and freedom to make choices (i.e. valid participation).
— Once an alternative was selected the decision maker was assumed to suffer dissonance.
— Feedback about the acceptability of the selected alternative was assumed to activate dissonance reduction through commitment to that alternative.

The model was tested through an experiment based on the participation of a number of undergraduate students. Specifically, four hypotheses were tested:
1. Subjects in channelled networks (i.e. hierarchical networks) will experience significantly different dissonance to subjects in non-channelled networks; the implication is that in non-channelled networks employees can transfer their felt

responsibility to others during the participation process by remaining silent or by allowing others to take the initiative. By contrast, in the channelled network employees cannot transfer responsibility for performance standards which they set for themselves because they have few communication alternatives.

2. The amount of dissonance experienced by authoritarian subjects will be significantly greater than that experienced by non-authoritarian subjects.
3. Reduction in cognitive dissonance will start only after feedback about the acceptability of targets.
4. Favourable feedback concerning acceptability of targets will lead to greater commitment to these targets, whilst unfavourable feedback will lead to reduced commitment.

The results were not supportive of either of the first two hypotheses. Thus, there were no significant differences in cognitive dissonance between the two respective participative modes of channelled and non-channelled networks. Similarly, there were no significant differences in cognitive dissonance experienced by authoritarian and non-authoritarian subjects. Foran and De Coster suggested that the failure to support the first hypothesis may have been caused by an element of pseudo-participation for channelled network groups in their experiment as distinct from no participation at all. They also suggested that the failure to support the second hypothesis may have been the result of authoritarian subjects managing to transfer their perceived responsibility to the group leader, or because they were unaffected by the opportunity to participate in decision making. The results, however, supported both hypotheses 3 and 4. Reduction in dissonance did not start until feedback about the desirability of targets occurred. Moreover, commitment to targets was significantly greater when feedback was favourable.

The above study has been discussed in some detail here because it is one of the most complete studies on this subject in the accounting literature up to the mid 1970s. Its theoretical framework draws on a number of important contributions from the organisational and psychological literature. This, however, should not overshadow the limitations associated with the methodology of that study. Like all experimentally based studies, it is impossible to judge whether or not the conditions under which the experiments were conducted genuinely approximate to real-world settings. For example, the subjects in the experiments did not know each other, and their leaders had no real power. Similarly, favourable feedback was synonymous with reward and negative feedback was synonymous with lack of reward. Such a relationship may not strictly hold in reality.

Milani (1975) investigated the relationship of budget participation by foremen to performance and attitudes towards the job and the company. Instead of the typical dichotomy used by researchers in classifying the extent of participation into participative and non-participative, Milani used a participation continuum. The continuum:

> reflects the foreman's *perceptions* of (1) the portion of the budget he is involved in setting, (2) the kind of reasoning provided him by a superior when the budget is revised, (3) the frequency of budget-related discussions held with his superior, (4) the amount of influence he has on the final budget, and (5) the importance of his contribution to the budget.
> (Milani, 1975, p. 277).

The model used in the study hypothesised that the extent of foreman participation in budgets influences his performance directly, and also indirectly, through influencing his attitude towards the job and his attitude towards the company. Greater perception of participation was hypothesised to lead to better attitude towards both the job and the company and ultimately to better performance.

On the whole, the results of the study indicated the presence of statistically significant correlations between the degree of participation and performance. Even when the correlations were not significant, they all had the expected algebraic sign. However, the reported coefficients (whether significant or not) do not provide strong evidence because they were fairly small and had low explanatory values. In this sense they offer only limited support to the contention that performance is an increasing function of participation. Furthermore, the results indicated the presence of a significant positive relationship between attitude towards the job and the company on the one hand and participation on the other hand. But the results revealed no significant relationship between both attitude variables and performance. This appears to corroborate the previous literature which indicates that performance and job satisfaction are not correlated.

The results of the studies reviewed above offer no universal set of relationships between the variables considered, in particular between the extent of participation and the level of morale (attitude) on the one hand and the level of performance on the other hand. Without careful consideration of personality factors and environmental factors it may be impossible for a clear relationship to emerge. Moreover, it is well known that supervisors use budgets and other controls as a means of expressing their leadership styles. The above studies either do not control satisfactorily, or totally ignore, these important factors. In the following section empirical research investigating leadership styles, employee characteristics and organisational character-istics in the context of budgetary controls is discussed in some detail. So far, however, it appears that Stedry's (1960) contention that in some cases participative budgets may not be as beneficial as imposed budgets is not yet discredited.

Budgetary Slack

Another issue worthy of consideration here is the notion of budgetary slack, which is part of total organisational slack. Cyert and March (1963, pp. 36–38) defined slack as the difference between 'the total resources available to the firm and the total necessary to maintain the organisation coalition'. A similar view was expressed by Leibenstein (1979) who defined X-efficiency as the difference between actual costs and minimum costs possible. Total organisational slack incorporates external payments, e.g. more dividends than necessary, and internal payments to coalition members. The latter is what is usually known as budgetary slack.

Budgetary slack can be the outcome of deliberate organisational policies or a manifestation of the invisible power of some organisational members. Whichever is the cause of slack there is sufficient evidence to indicate that it is a frequent and significant phenomenon in many organisations. Thus, Williamson (1964) and Schiff and Lewin (1968; 1970) provide evidence to suggest that slack may account for as much as 20–25 per cent of the division's budgeted operating expenses. Leibenstein (1979) suggested that slack may even be as high as 30–40 per cent of necessary costs. Onsi (1973) reported that 80 per cent of the managers he interviewed in five large companies admitted that they engaged in the creation of slack.

Not only is the notion of budgetary slack an empirical phenomenon; it has also been stressed conceptually in various models of managerial and organisational behaviour. Thus, in modelling the utility function of managers, Cyert and March (1963) included slack as an essential part of that function and perceived it as one means by which managers attain their individual goals. Similarly, Williamson (1964) suggested that managers can best attain both their personal goals and corporate goals in a slack environment. Also, agency theory models emphasise managerial shirking on the job as the main agency problem faced by the principal (see for example Holmstrom, 1979). Given uncertainty, asymmetric distribution of information, bounded rationality and propensity towards opportunism on the part of organisational actors, it is not surprising that creation of slack permeates many organisations.

Budgetary slack is typically created by understating revenues and/or overstating costs. Thus, Dalton (1959) documented a number of cases in which department managers allocated resources to what they perceived to be justifiable purposes but which were not authorised in the budget.

In a longitudinal investigation of budgetary slack in three organisations, Williamson (1964) showed that there is a close correlation between the type of cost reduction undertaken by management and the category of expense in which slack is built. The cost reduction programmes resulted in decreases in overheads, corporate staff, R&D and so on. Schiff and Lewin (1968) showed how slack was incorporated into divisional budgets in a company they investigated over a period of two years. Slack was created in 'good years' so that it can be converted into profits in 'bad years'. Methods of creating slack included:

— Understating gross revenue both by understating potential unit sales and average expected unit prices.

— Including discretionary increases in budgeted personnel positions, advertising budgets, promotional programmes, training programmes and allocations to special projects.

It appears from the Schiff and Lewin investigation that standard manufacturing costs were overstated in the sense of not allowing for available process improvements. The introduction of these improvements was a discretionary managerial decision. Such discretion was exercised only under adverse conditions, otherwise process improvements were kept 'on the shelf'.

Lowe and Shaw (1968) have pointed out that slack has multiple determinants and effects (positive and negative) which are not likely to be detected and corrected by superiors. In their study of the sales budgeting process of a chain of retail shops they observed the following three causes of slack. Firstly, the reward system of the company was based on performance in relation to the budget. In this case slack was built into the budget to make it easier to attain. Secondly, the influence of past company history fostered the perception of continually growing sales. In this case, optimistic budgets were submitted in order to get them approved even though the risk of attaining them was high. Thirdly, there was the insecurity of some managers whose recent performance was poor. Again, optimistic budgets were submitted by these managers.

Some researchers attempted to relate the creation of slack to the characteristics of the organisational structure and the control system employed. For example, it may be that there is a strong need to create slack in centralised organisations as these tend to use highly formalised hierarchic control systems. In these systems employees tend to be held directly responsible for their targets and, because their communication networks are channelled, it may not be easy for them to shift part of their responsibility to other employees. A divisionalised structure may involve greater participation in budget setting, at least at the level of divisional management. Thus, because employees have more say in setting targets through participation, it may be argued that there is less need to incorporate slack into budgets. Moreover, if the communication networks are less well channelled, as is usually the case in decentralised structures, employees can shift part of their responsibilities to other employees. This further reduces the need for slack.

However, Schiff and Lewin (1968; 1970) provided some revealing observations which indicated that slack is created both in non-divisionalised as well as divisionalised companies; the only difference being that the *location* and *form* of slack appear to be dependent on the type of organisational structure employed. In a centralised company, slack was diffused through all management levels. At subunit level, slack was not fully disguised, presumably because the central controller was removed from daily subunit problems and was not personally involved in creating slack. In the divisionalised organisation, slack was concentrated at the divisional management level. Further, the divisional controller tended to be involved both in the creation and management of slack. Schiff and Lewin rationalised this last point by suggesting that the divisional controller and the divisional manager were spatially removed from corporate headquarters. This, they maintained, led to infrequent interactions between the divisional controller and the corporate controller whilst increasing interaction between the divisional controller and divisional management. The divisional controller became more involved in divisional activities, so becoming identified with the goals of divisional management. In short, partisan interests developed between the divisional controller and divisional management.

Although very useful, the 'evidence' provided by Schiff and Lewis should be interpreted with care. They freely treated divisionalisation as synonymous with decentralisation. Given that some divisionalised companies may be highly centralised below divisional level, the extent of employee participation may be smaller than initially suspected. If the divisional controller is so involved in divisional activities then it may be that Schiff and Lewin have been observing corrupted multidivisional structures rather than pure multidivisional structures (see chapter 11). What is implied here is that it is difficult to draw sensible conclusions unless the extent of participation is explicitly addressed in the context of slack building instead of being deduced from the observed organisational structure.

Some later studies addressed this specific issue. Onsi (1973) reported a positive relationship between an authoritarian control system and budgetary slack. Such a control system emphasises the attainment of subunit budgets through the exercise of pressure and the use of heavy sanctions. Onsi's results also indicated that where managers participated actively in setting the budgets, they had less motive to build slack.

Similarly, Cammann (1976) studied the effects of different control systems on a number of factors including the creation of budgetary slack. His results indicated that when rewards were dependent on budgetary information, subordinates engaged in slack building. When subordinates participated in budget setting, slack building was reduced.

The results of the above two studies indicate that the inclination to create slack can be manipulated through the appropriate design and use of accounting control systems. By reducing emphasis on meeting subunit budgets, avoiding exerting unnecessary pressure on subordinates, buttressing performance evaluation indices by non-financial measures and increasing subordinates' genuine participation in budget setting, so the propensity for slack creation can be reduced. The two studies, however, used samples from across functional areas and thus the effects of different organisational contexts on the propensity to create slack cannot be identified in the results.

Merchant (1985) made some advances in that direction by studying slack creation by subordinates in only one functional area – manufacturing. His results indicate that the propensity to create slack is not increased simply through the use of a formal budgetary system. Rather, it appears to increase if a tight budget requires the managers to make 'frequent tactical responses' to ensure meeting the budget. The results also suggest that the extent of technological predictability has only a minor negative effect on the tendencies towards creation of slack. It does, however, appear that technology may interact with the way budgets are used. Greater participation may reduce managers' inclination to create slack only when the technology is relatively predictable.

Another useful set of results which were originally obtained by Onsi (1973) and then corroborated by Merchant (1985) relate to the superiors' ability to detect slack. These indicate that if such ability was strong the following results were observed:
— greater emphasis was attached to meeting targets;
— greater budget participation by subordinates was allowed; and
— propensity to create slack was reduced.

Thus far, the discussion has focused on the creation of slack through deliberate managerial actions. It is also important to note that slack might be built into budgets unintentionally, particularly in periods of high uncertainty where forecasting may turn out to be highly inaccurate. Furthermore, there is evidence to suggest that in preparing budgets, managers tend to use the most likely outcome rather than the mean, since in many cases the former is more well defined than the latter (Otley, 1978). If outputs, revenues, and costs have non-normal distributions, unintentional slack could be built into aggregated budgets (Otley and Berry, 1979). Overall, however, the mechanisms through which unintentional slack is created are little understood. Moreover, the implications of this type of slack for planning and control purposes and the methods by which it may be eliminated, or even attenuated, are little known. Clearly, this is one area which deserves further investigation.

III. LEADERSHIP STYLES, SUBORDINATE CHARACTERISTICS AND ORGANISATIONAL CHARACTERISTICS

The discussion in the preceding section predominantly emphasised the relationship between the design of control systems (e.g. budgets) and participation. The implications of the ways in which the control systems are used were not explicitly considered. Yet, it is well known that superiors tend to use budgets as a way of expressing their own styles of leadership. Moreover, as has been indicated earlier, the results of a study by Vroom (1960) suggested that leadership styles and personality factors tend to condition the effects of participation. This section contains a more detailed discussion of the effects of leadership styles and subordinate characteristics on budgetary practices and employee performance.

Patterns of Leadership Behaviour and Budget Practices

Consider first the patterns of leadership behaviour and budget practices. The discussion in chapter 3 of this book indicates that leadership styles may be classified along two dimensions: 'initiating structure' and 'consideration'. It will be recalled that the 'initiating structure' dimension refers to task-oriented leaders who emphasise formal, and clearly defined relationships with subordinates. The 'consideration' dimension refers to employee-oriented leaders who emphasise mutual trust and friendship with their subordinates. As indicated in chapter 3, the results of some studies suggest that employee-oriented managers achieve better performance than task-oriented managers (see Likert 1958; White and Lippitt, 1960; Kahn and Katz, 1960, but see also the rest of the discussion in that chapter for some contradictory results).

In the context of budgetary control, the above findings yield several testable hypotheses. These would relate to the effects of different budgetary leadership styles on the extent of budget pressure felt by subordinates and on subordinates' performance. Based on these findings one would expect that in using budgets, a considerate leadership style would lead to less pressure on subordinates and also higher performance compared with an initiating structure style.

De Coster and Fertakis (1968) conducted an investigation aimed at testing the relationship between budget-induced pressure and dimensions of leadership behaviour. Their results show a significant positive correlation between budget-induced pressure and the initiating structure of leadership. The results also suggest that pressure is induced by lack of participation in the budgetary process. Surprisingly, however, budget-induced pressure was found to be significantly positively correlated with the consideration dimension of leadership. This result runs counter to the a priori expectation of a negative correlation.

One possible explanation of this unexpected result may relate to the methodology used by De Coster and Fertakis. They used an aggregate index to measure budget-induced pressure; this included not only the pressure felt by those in subordinate positions but also the budget-induced pressure experienced by the supervisor *vis-à-vis* his own immediate superior. The latter was significantly positively correlated with the consideration style of leadership, and this substantially explains the relationship between the aggregate index of budget-induced pressure and the consideration style. De Coster and Fertakis suggested that when the supervisor is subjected to pressure from his superiors he tends to direct his behaviour in both the initiating structure dimension and the consideration dimension. Although plausible, this is not a conclusive argument. More empirical work is needed to corroborate their results.

One further difficulty in interpreting the results of the De Coster and Fertakis investigation relates to their explicit linking of leadership styles with budget pressure and productivity. As already indicated in chapter 3, there is little evidence to suggest that there is only one 'best' leadership style. Much of the evidence suggests that leadership effectiveness is strongly influenced by the situational and personality characteristics of the leader *and* the subordinates.

Hopwood (1972; 1973) investigated the effects of budgetary styles, level of participation, and accuracy of the accounting system, on an employee's job-related tension, relationships both with peers and supervisors and the extent to which he or she manipulates accounting information. He chose for his analysis a number of cost centres in an integrated (interdependent) manufacturing plant.

Hopwood's results can be summarised as follows. Firstly, employees (cost centre heads) who were evaluated on the basis of a budget-constrained style were subject to significantly greater job-related tension compared with employees evaluated on the basis of a profit-conscious style or the non-accounting style. Moreover, the level of financial tension associated with the non-accounting style was significantly lower than with either budget-constrained or profit-conscious styles. Profit-conscious and non-accounting styles were associated with significantly better job satisfaction and feelings of justness of evaluation. Secondly, profit-conscious and non-accounting styles were associated with significantly better relations with supervisors compared with the budget-constrained style. This was reflected in greater trust in and respect for supervisors, greater satisfaction with supervisors' administrative, technical and human relations skills along with greater appreciation of the reasonableness of supervisors' expectations. Thirdly, profit-conscious and non-accounting styles were generally associated with significantly better relations with peers compared with the budget-constrained style. This was reflected in better peer-supportiveness achievement and affiliation; better peer agreement, helpfulness and friendship; and better respect for peers. Fourthly, employees evaluated on the basis of a budget-constrained style engaged in greater manipulation of accounting information compared with profit conscious and non-accounting styles. Fifthly, the profit-conscious style was associated with higher levels of budgetary participation compared with the budget constrained style.

In interpreting the above set of results, Hopwood suggested that managers may be able to attenuate undesirable consequences by merely changing the way in which the existing information system is used, rather than necessarily changing the system or reducing their reliance on it for the purposes of performance evaluation. This contention is partly based on the fact that in most cases accounting systems are imperfect means of reflecting the underlying economic cost structure.

Hopwood (1973, 1974) also investigated the relationship between leadership climate and the use of accounting data in performance evaluation. His results suggest that supervisors with budget-constrained styles were perceived by their subordinates to show significantly less consideration towards them compared with either profit-conscious or non-accounting style supervisors. There was also evidence to suggest that managers perceived to be using a budget-constrained style were themselves being evaluated on the same basis.

Ansari (1976) conducted a laboratory experiment to test the combined influence of variance reports and leadership styles on employee satisfaction and productivity. He postulated that the results generated by the information included in variance reports will depend on leadership style. More specifically, he assumed that a less informative variance report leads to better results with an autocratic leadership style because, with less information, subordinates will find it difficult to evaluate the behaviour of their supervisor. Similarly, he assumed that more informative variance reports will be more suitable to democratic leadership styles. In the latter case, the availability of more information makes it easier for subordinates to form better evaluations of the behaviour of their supervisors and also of their own performance. With democratic leadership styles, this is assumed to lead to minimal cognitive dissonance, greater employee satisfaction, and better performance.

The results of Ansari's experiment were supportive of his main hypothesis: productivity was higher for the task-oriented group with limited information in variance reports and for the employee-oriented group with detailed variance reports (compared with the task-oriented group with detailed information and the employee-oriented group with little information). Also, in general, the productivity of the two employee-oriented groups was higher than the productivity of the task-oriented groups.

As indicated previously, dysfunctional behaviour may occur because of the inadequacy of the accounting system in responding to the complexities of organisational reality. It is worth noting, however, that careful design of accounting systems will not necessarily ensure eliminating or even attenuating dysfunctional behaviour. Organisational participants may have a vested interest in manipulating information because of the divergence between their individual goals and organisational goals (e.g. Schiff and Lewin, 1970). Previous researchers, with the exception of Ansari (1976), have not allowed for this latter possibility in their research designs. Hence, their results may have been confounded by mixing the effects of the technical inadequacies of the accounting system with those relating to the way in which the system is used.

Otley (1978) sought to refine and replicate Hopwood's (1972) earlier study by investigating the procedures of a well-designed budgetary control system within an organisation with substantially independent subunits. Such an organisation is considered well suited to the application of budgetary control. This was thought to mitigate sufficiently the technical inadequacies of the accounting system so that attention could be focused on the effects of differential use of accounting information. Otley tested a number of hypotheses which related to two dimensions. Firstly, the effects of a manager's perceptions that he is primarily evaluated on the basis of meeting his budget on his task-related and budget-related tension, distrust in his supervisor, clarity about how his performance is evaluated and the extent to which he perceives his evaluation to be fair. Secondly, his responses to the above feelings in terms of building budgetary slack, overemphasising short-term results and performing poorly, particularly in relation to performance aspects which generate only long-term benefits.

Otley's results indicate that managers' perceptions of the ways their performance is evaluated by their superiors had little effect on their feelings about their jobs. Specifically, unlike Hopwood's results, the use of budget-oriented style of evaluation was not associated with high job-related or budget-related tension. Job-related tension was found to be associated with the extent to which a manager agreed with the way in which his performance was evaluated; tension increased as the manager increasingly disagreed with his perceptions of his performance evaluation criteria. Similarly, the use of a budget-oriented style of evaluation did not lead to reduced job ambiguity. Rather, it appears that the degree of job ambiguity was associated with how bad or good the manager's performance was. Surprisingly, when performance was poor, the manager apparently had a clearer idea about what his job entailed, whereas when his performance was relatively good he was less sure about what his job involved. Again, in contrast with Hopwood's results, Otley's results suggested that the budget-oriented style of evaluation was associated with meeting performance targets.

An important question here is how the contradictions in the results obtained by Hopwood and Otley can be explained. One plausible explanation is that the results are conditional on the precise organisational context. The units of analysis used by Hopwood were cost centres in an integrated manufacturing plant, whereas those used by Otley were substantially independent profit centres. The use of budgetary control procedures is likely to be much less appropriate in the case of the former compared with the latter. When subunits are highly interdependent, emphasis on the use of budgets is likely to be dysfunctional(e.g.Bruns and Waterhouse, 1975).

In addition to the possible explanation outlined above, Otley suggested that the results could be conditional on the extent of environmental toughness. Thus, instead of treating budgetary style as an independent variable to explain differences in performance, budgetary style *and* performance are both dependent on the prevailing environment (i.e. the contingency view). Otley (1978, p. 146) observed in relation to his field study that:

> A situation had evolved where profitable units produced accurate budgets which were subsequently used as a basis for evaluation, whereas unprofitable units produced optimistic budgets which gave the impression of profitability, but which were not then used in evaluating unit and managerial performance.

The prevailing environments facing Otley's organisation appeared to be different from those facing Hopwood's organisation. Otley's organisation appeared to have operated in a stable, closed environment, whereas Hopwood's were faced with higher environmental instability.

Hirst (1981) argued that the subunits studied by Hopwood were highly interdependent. Given that task interdependence is an important source of task uncertainty, those tasks are likely to have been characterised by either medium or high uncertainty. Hirst proceeded to infer that, because the subunits studied by Otley were highly independent and operated in stable environments, they faced relatively low task uncertainty. One of the problems with the latter rationalisation is that it is not possible to verify the degrees of task uncertainty inferred by Hirst since neither Hopwood nor Otley offered any explicit measures of task uncertainty. Indeed, in a private communication cited in Hirst (1981), Otley pointed out that the units he studied faced medium task uncertainty, rather than the low task uncertainty inferred by Hirst.

Govindarajan (1984) empirically linked environmental uncertainty to the style of performance evaluation. He reported that environmental uncertainty had a significant moderating effect on the relationship between performance evaluation style and measures of organisational effectiveness. Specifically, his results indicated that: (i) business units subject to high levels of environmental uncertainty (like Hopwood's sub-units) use greater subjective judgement in performance evaluation, and (ii) business units subject to low levels of uncertainty (like those of Otley) rely heavily on financial data in performance evaluation.

A further explanation has been offered by Brownell (1982a) who invoked 'budget participation' as an intervening variable. His results suggest that a budget-constrained leadership style is most effective when 'budget participation' is perceived to be high, but is ineffective when participation is perceived to be low.

Clearly, these are all plausible explanations of the conflicting results obtained by Hopwood and Otley. However, these reconciliation attempts are *ad hoc*; they do not have a comprehensive theoretical underpinning. The results of Hopwood and Otley are yet to be comprehensively explained. A much broader organisational framework needs to be developed for future investigations.

Personal and Organisational Characteristics

Some attempts to use a broader behavioural and organisational framework for analysis are reflected in the works of Collins (1978), Kenis (1979), Merchant (1981; 1984) and Brownell (1981; 1982b). In the model developed by Collins, budgetary response attitude (whether positive or negative) was assumed to be dependent on three independent variables: personal flexibility; perceived budget characteristics (accuracy, estimate certainty, controllability and participation) which are moderated by attitudes towards such budget characteristics and, lastly, demographic variables of employees (age, tenure and status). He tested for the interactions between the independent and moderating variables in this model using seven industrial firms engaged in diverse activities and with different characteristics. His results indicate the following. Firstly, personal flexibility alone is unimportant in predicting response attitude to the budget. Secondly, perceived budget characteristics are important in forming attitudes towards the budget, particularly for new members of the organisation. Thirdly, the demographic variables of employees are not significantly correlated with budgetary response attitude. Finally, the interaction effect of flexibility, perceived budget characteristics and attitudes, was significantly better correlated with budget response attitude than any one alone.

One of the important features of the study by Collins in the present context is its emphasis on the relationship between employee personality and demographic characteristics on the one hand and budgetary response on the other hand. However, his results are surprising, particularly in the case of personality. Earlier evidence suggests that individual personality is useful in explaining human behaviour in organisations. More specifically, a flexible person appears to be more concerned with peer relationships whereas an inflexible person emphasises superior–subordinate relationship (e.g. Kahn et al., 1964). The results relating employee demographic characteristics to budget response may be easier to explain, given the reported importance of perceptions of budget characteristics to new organisational members. Collins used socialisation theory to suggest that since new organisational members will be particularly attuned to organisational culture, after a given period members will either adopt that culture or reject it and leave the organisation: 'thus, little correlation should exist between increased age, tenure, and status and greater accession' (p. 330). In situations of high job mobility this could be a plausible argument. However, in situations where job mobility is rather low, it may be possible to observe the existence of organisational members with cultures in conflict with those of the organisation. This may be particularly significant in the cases of older employees with long employment and high status. These characteristics naturally reduce job mobility even in labour markets characterised by high mobility.

Kenis (1979) developed a model in which job-related attitudes, budget-related attitudes and performance were assumed to be dependent on budgetary goal characteristics, which in turn were assumed to be dependent upon internal environmental variables. Job-related attitudes incorporated variables such as job satisfaction, job involvement and job tension. Performance included budgetary performance, cost efficiency, and job performance. Budgetary goal characteristics incorporated variables such as participation, goal clarity, feedback, evaluation, and goal difficulty. Internal independent variables included leadership style, managerial philosophy, organisational structure, organisational level, and organisational size. Relying on the results of previous research, Kenis hypothesised that budgetary participation, budget goal clarity and budgetary feedback will lead to better job-related and budget-related attitudes and to better performance. By contrast, budgetary evaluation and budget goal difficulty were hypothesised to lead to unfavourable job-related and budget-related attitudes and to worse performance.

Kenis tested his model using 19 plants in 16 manufacturing companies. His results offered mixed support for the predicted effects of budgetary goal characteristics on job-related attitudes, budget-related attitudes and performance. Thus, the predicted effects on job tension were strongly supported, those related to job satisfaction were supported only in relation to the hypothesised positive, but not negative, effects, and those related to job involvement were generally not supported. Similarly, the results were supportive of the predicted positive effects of budgetary goal characteristics on budget-related attitudes, but were not supportive of the predicted negative effects. Finally, overall the results were supportive of the predicted effects of budgetary goal characteristics on budgetary performance, but largely unsupportive of the predicted effects on cost efficiency and job performance.

Brownell (1983) investigated the effects of leadership style and budgetary participation on performance and job satisfaction. An important feature of his analysis was that he focused on the *interactional* effects of leadership style and budgetary participation, instead of simply examining them separately as did previous researchers. His data was collected by soliciting questionnaire responses from 48 middle-level cost centre managers involved in manufacturing and distribution activities in a large manufacturing company.

Brownell's results suggest the presence of important interactions between leadership style variables and budgetary participation. Considerate leadership behaviour appeared to have no effect on subordinate performance unless budgetary participation was high, in which case the effect was strongly positive. This offers support to the Path-Goal model of leadership developed by House (1971), discussed in chapter 3, in which budgetary participation was treated as an important contingency variable.

Brownell reported that a leadership style high on consideration and low on structure had strong favourable effects on job satisfaction *irrespective* of the level of budgetary participation. By contrast, in the case of a leadership style that is high on the structure dimension and low on the consideration dimension, participation was reported to be negatively related to both performance and job satisfaction. Also, such leadership style was reported to have a favourable effect on satisfaction under low participation but not under high participation. This may imply that structure is important only when subordinates perceive themselves as having little influence in budget setting.

Brownell also examined the effect of the 'locus of control' on the relationship between budgetary participation and performance, using a laboratory experiment (Brownell, 1981) and a field study using 48 middle-level cost centre managers in a large company (Brownell, 1982b). The term 'locus of control' relates to the congruence between an individual's personality and the characteristics of his task situation. In the context of locus of control, an individual is either an 'internal' or 'external'. 'Internals' generally believe that they are in control of their own destiny and are assumed to perform better in situations perceived to be under their control, as in the case of high budgetary participation. 'Externals' typically attribute outcomes to forces beyond their control. They are assumed to perform better when their task situation is controlled by others, as in the case of low budgetary participation.

In both studies, Brownell reported that the relationship between budgetary participation and performance was moderated by the locus of control. Internals were reported to have higher job satisfaction and better levels of performance under conditions of high budgetary participation. By contrast, externals were reported to have higher job satisfaction and better levels of performance when budget participation was perceived to be low.

One of the important findings of the studies conducted by Collins (1978), Kenis (1979), and Brownell (1981; 1982b; 1983) is that personality characteristics, whether those of the superior or the subordinate, are important variables in studying budgetary participation. These studies, however, have concentrated on the personality characteristics of *either* the superior *or* the subordinate. Thus, the effects of the various configurations of the dyadic relationship between the superior and the subordinate on participation were not considered.

Chenhall (1986) conducted a field study to investigate the effects of dyadic relationships on participation. Data were collected via questionnaires from 39 departmental managers and supervisors from nine manufacturing organisations within a single industry. The results indicated that participation alone had a significant effect on job satisfaction and satisfaction with budgets. This is consistent with the results of some previous research (e.g. Hofstede, 1967; Kenis, 1979). More importantly, the results suggested that the dyadic configurations between the subordinate and superior were related to subordinate job satisfaction and budget satisfaction. Homogeneous dyads (where both superior and subordinate are high or low on authoritarianism) were associated with higher subordinate job and budget satisfaction compared with heterogeneous dyads (where the superior is high on authoritarianism and the subordinate is low or vice versa). Moreover, the results suggested that participation is more strongly associated with subordinate job and budget satisfaction in the homogeneous dyad compared with the heterogeneous dyad.

These results can be rationalised by considering the nature of the two dyad classifications discussed above. In a heterogeneous dyad, where the superior is high on authoritarianism, the superior is likely to be autocratic, conducting relationships with subordinates on the basis of formal authority and power. To the subordinates, who are low on authoritarianism, budgetary participation would be perceived as being imposed and possibly superficial. This may breed antagonism and dissastifaction with budgets and jobs. In the converse heterogeneous dyad, the subordinate who is highly authoritarian would expect, but would probably not get, guidance from his superior who is a low authoritarian. Again, this may breed discontent and may result in less satisfaction with budgets and work. Such conflicts are not likely to arise in homogeneous dyads. If both superior and subordinate are low authoritarians, participation is likely to result in better cooperation and possibly higher subordinate satisfaction. If both superior and subordinate are high authoritarians, the subordinate is likely to respond favourably to the superior's tendency to use his authority (Chenhall, 1986).

Merchant (1981) developed a budgetary framework which, unlike previous models, focuses on higher-level organisational characteristics, e.g. organisational size or diversity, rather than lower-level characteristics, e.g. those at an individual level. In his framework, outcome is perceived to be dependent on budgeting variables which are in turn dependent on the organisational context. Outcomes include managerial motivation and attitude and organisational performance. The design variables relating to a corporate-level budgeting system refer to administrative versus interpersonal orientation as reflected in information detail, frequency of plan revisions and budgeting behaviour. The organisational context includes such things as size, diversity and extent of decentralisation.

Merchant developed a number of hypotheses from the above framework and tested them using 19 organisations in the electronics industry. The results indicate that budgetary practices are contingent upon the organisational context. Thus, managers in the larger, more diversified and more decentralised organisations were reported to engage in greater formal budget participation, with few direct interactions with superiors or subordinates. Moreover, those managers reported that meeting the budget targets is important to their careers. There was also partial support for the hypothesis that middle managers in organisations using an administrative-oriented budgeting system are characterised by higher motivation and attitude towards budgeting. The results further indicate the presence of some form of contingency linkage between organisational performance and the quality of fit between the budgetary system and the organisational contingencies. Thus, high budget participation and greater emphasis on meeting the budget were more strongly related to good performance in the larger firms compared with the smaller firms.

In a subsequent study, Merchant (1984) reported the existence of significant relationships between the extent of formality in budget use and departmental contextual variables. Departmental size, functional differentiation and degree of automation of production processes were all positively related to the formality of budget use which included placing greater emphasis on meeting the budget, more formal budget communication patterns and greater manager participation in budgeting activities. However, the degree of product standardisation, the products' stage in the product life cycle, and the strength of company's market position all seem to have little or no effect on budgeting.

IV. SUMMARY

This chapter has been devoted to an examination of some of the behavioural implications of accounting controls in general and budgets in particular. For convenience of presentation, the chapter was divided into three main sections dealing respectively with the impact of traditional accounting controls on employee behaviour, participation in the budgetary process, and the impact of leadership styles and subordinate characteristics on budgeting practices. As in most chapters in this book, the above distinction between the sections is somewhat artificial because of the considerable overlap between their contents. Hence, this section contains a summary of the chapter as a whole without clear reference to the specific sections.

Generally speaking, the studies reviewed here attempted to investigate the relationships between accounting controls and human behaviour in organisations. These studies employed methodologies with different focus and wide-ranging levels of sophistication in terms of the underlying models used, the nature of model testing undertaken and the type of analysis performed.

Thus, behavioural studies in accounting mainly divide into a majority which focused on lower levels of analysis and a minority which focused on higher levels of analysis. Those studies which primarily focused on lower-level analysis generally concentrated on the behaviour of the individual, albeit at different hierarchical levels ranging from shopfloor workers (e.g. Argyris, 1952) through foremen (e.g. Argyris, 1952; Milani, 1975) to subunit managers, like profit centre managers (e.g. Schiff and Lewin, 1968). Only a few studies, however, explicitly focused on higher-level characteristics such as the organisational context in terms of, for example, its size, diversity, degree of decentralisation, culture and so on (see in particular Bruns and Waterhouse, 1975; Collins, 1978; Kenis, 1979; and Merchant, 1981 and 1985). Both levels of analysis interact with budgetary practices and with performance. Hence, concentration on only one level to the exclusion of others is likely to lead to incomplete conclusions.

The models used in these studies draw heavily on the organisational theory literature. Because that literature is rather diffuse and, in many cases, inconclusive (see chapter 1) the models developed for studying the behavioural implications of accounting controls appear to be somewhat *ad hoc* and incomplete, at least in terms of the variables examined and of their hypothesised functional form. For example, some studies treated budgetary characteristics as independent (or moderating) variables influencing managerial behaviour, attitude and performance. Budgetary characteristics studied included variables such as budget pressure (De Coster and Fertakis, 1968), participation (Milani, 1975), accuracy and controllability (Collins, 1978) and goal difficulty (Kenis, 1979). In other studies budgetary characteristics were treated as dependent variables where some other variables were considered independent, like superior leadership style (Hopwood, 1974) and the personality traits of the manager (Foran and De Coster, 1974). Almost without exception, research published until the mid seventies failed to relate the budgetary models developed to wider organisational contexts. Later models, particularly those developed by Kenis (1979) and Merchant (1981), incorporated some variables relating to the organisational context, invoking a contingency theory-type model. To this extent, these latter studies considerably extended the organisational settings in which budgeting practices can be considered, but the limitations of the contingency approach (see chapters 1, 3 and 4) restrict the validity of their conclusions.

The models developed were tested either through laboratory experiments (e.g. Stedry, 1960; Foran and De Coster, 1974; Ansari, 1976; Brownell, 1981) or field investigation (most other studies). It is well known that the researcher can exercise greater discretion over the subjects and the environment of a laboratory experiment so that the effects of extraneous factors can be attenuated. However, the experiments need to be simplified by invoking assumptions which in most cases have little resemblance to the real world. Empirically-based investigations may use real-world observations but they have two main drawbacks. Firstly, the choice of the research site, the subjects of investigation and the methods of extracting information are strongly influenced by the researcher's own perceptions. Secondly, exogenous variables are likely to affect the results obtained. Together, these two sets of factors may partly explain some of the inconsistent results reported. More importantly, they cast doubt on the general applicability of the results.

The extent of analysis undertaken also varied in terms of levels of sophistication, ranging from largely relying on examination of the sign and significance of correlation coefficients to the use of other multivariate techniques such as factor analysis. More importantly, however, although the models developed hypothesise *causal* relationships the analysis performed tested for *associations* between variables. A more careful interpretation of the results reviewed above should thus emphasise association rather than causation between variables studied. To this extent, our knowledge of the causation linkages between budgeting practices and other variables is rather limited.

REFERENCES

Ansari, S. L., 1976. Behavioural factors in variance control: report on a laboratory experiment, *Journal of Accounting Research* **14**(2), Autumn, pp. 189–211.

Argyris, C., 1952. *The Impact of Budgets on People*. New York; Ithaca.

Argyris, C., 1953. Human problems with budgets, *Harvard Business Review*, **31** January-February, pp. 97–110.

Argyris, C., 1976. Single-loop and double-loop models in research on decision making, *Administrative Science Quarterly*, **21**, September, pp. 363–375.

Argyris, C., 1977. Organizational learning and management information systems, *Accounting, Organizations and Society*, **2**(2), pp. 113–123.

Aronson, E., 1968. Dissonance theory: progress and problems, in R. P. Abelson, E. Aronson, W. J. McGuire, T. M. Newcomb, M. J. Rosenberg, and P. H. Tannenbaum (eds), *Theories of Cognitive Consistency: A Sourcebook*: Rand-McNally.

Becker, S. and Green, D., Jnr., 1962. Budgeting and employee behaviour, *The Journal of Business*, **35**(4), October, pp. 392–402.

Bourn, M. and Ezzamel, M., 1987. Budgetary devolution in the National Health Service and universities in the United Kingdom, *Financial Accountability and Management*, **3**(1), Spring, pp. 29–45.

Brehm, J. W., 1956. Post-decision changes in the desirability of alternatives, *The Journal of Abnormal and Social Psychology*, pp. 384–389.

Brownell, P., 1981. Participation in budgeting, locus of control and organisational effectiveness, *Accounting Review*, October, pp. 844–860.

Brownell, P., 1982a. The role of accounting data in performance evaluation, budgetary participation, and organizational effectiveness, *Journal of Accounting Research*, Spring, pp. 12–27.

Brownell, P., 1982b. A field study examination of budgetary participation and locus of control, *Accounting Review*, October, pp. 766–777.

Brownell, P., 1983. Leadership style, budgetary participation and managerial behavior, *Accounting, Organizations and Society*, **8**(4), pp. 307–321.

Brownell, P. and McInnes, M., 1986. Budgetary participation, motivation, and managerial performance, *Accounting Review*, October, pp. 587–600.

Bruns, W. J. and Waterhouse, J. H., 1975. Budgetary control and organisation structure, *Journal of Accounting Research*, Autumn, pp. 177–203.

Bryan, J. F. and Locke, E. A., 1967. Goal setting as a means of increasing motivation, *Journal of Applied Psychology*, **LI**, pp. 274–277.

Cammann, C., 1976. Effects of the use of control systems, *Accounting, Organizations and Society*, pp. 301–314.

Caplan, E. H., 1966. Behavioural assumptions of management accounting, *Accounting Review*, July, pp. 496–509.

Caplan, E. H., 1968. Behavioural assumptions of management accounting – report of a field study, *Accounting Review*, April, pp. 342–362.

Chenhall, R. H., 1986. Authoritarianism and participative budgeting: a dyadic analysis, *Accounting Review*, April, pp. 263–272.

Coch, L. and French, J. R. P. Jnr., 1948. Overcoming resistance to change, *Human Relations*, **I**, pp. 512–532.

Cohen, A. R., 1959. Situational structure, self esteem and threat oriented reactions to power, pp. 35–52, in D. Cartwright (ed.), *Studies in Social Power*. Ann Arbor, MI: Institute for Social Research, University of Michigan.

Collins, F., 1978. The interaction of budget characteristics and personality variables with budgetary response attitudes, *Accounting Review*, April, pp. 324–335.

Cyert, R. M. and March, J. G., 1963. *A Behavioural Theory of the Firm*: Prentice-Hall.

Dalton, M., 1959. *Men Who Manage*: Wiley.

De Coster, D. T. and Fertakis, J. P., 1968. Budget-induced pressure and its relationship to supervisory behaviour, *Journal of Accounting Research*, Autumn, pp. 237–246.

Deutsch, M., 1949. An experimental study of the effects of cooperation and competition upon group process, *Human Relations* **II** pp. 199–231.

Foran, M. F. and De Coster, D. T., 1974. An experimental study of the effects of participation, authoritarianism, and feedback on cognitive dissonance in a standard setting situation, *Accounting Review*, October, pp. 751–763.

French, J.R.P., Jnr., Israel, J. and As, D., 1960. An experiment on participation in a Norwegian factory, *Human Relations*, **XIII** pp. 3–9.

Govindarajan, V., 1984. Appropriateness of accounting data in performance evaluation: an empirical evaluation of environmental uncertainty as an intervening variable, *Accounting, Organizations and Society*, **9**(2), pp. 125–135.

Hirst, M. K., 1981. Accounting information and the evaluation of subordinate performance: a situational approach, *Accounting Review*, October, pp. 771–784.

Hofstede, G. H., 1967, *The Game of Budget Control*. Assen, The Netherlands: Van Corcum.

Holmstrom, B., 1979. Moral hazard and observability, *Bell Journal of Economics* **10**(1), Spring, pp. 74–91.

Hopwood, A. G., 1972. An empirical study of the role of accounting data in performance evaluation, *Empirical Research in Accounting: Selected Studies*. Supplement to *Journal of Accounting Research*, pp. 156–182.

Hopwood, A. G., 1973. *An Accounting System and Managerial Behaviour*: Saxon House.

Hopwood, A. G., 1974. Leadership climate and the use of accounting data in performance evaluation, *Accounting Review*, July, pp. 485–495.

Hughes, C. L., 1965. Why budgets go wrong, *Personnel*, **42**(3), May-June, pp. 19–26.

Kahn, R. L. and Katz, D., 1960. Leadership practices in relation to productivity and morale, in D. Cartwright and A. Zinder (eds), *Group Dynamics*. New York: Harper & Row, pp. 554–570.

Kahn, R. L., Wolfe, D. M., Quinn, R. P., Snoek, J. D., and Rosenthal, R. A., 1964. *Organisational Stress: Studies in Role Conflict and Ambiguity*. New York: Wiley.

Kenis, I., 1979. Effects of budgetary goal characteristics on managerial attitudes and performance, *Accounting Review*, October, pp. 707–721.

Leibenstein, H., 1979. X-efficiency: from concept to theory, *Challenge*, September-October, pp. 13–22.

Likert, R., 1958. Measuring organizational performance, *Harvard Business Review*, March-April, pp. 41–50.

Lowe, E. A. and Shaw, R. W., 1968. An analysis of managerial biasing: evidence from a company's budgeting process, *The Journal of Management Studies*, **5**(3), October, pp. 304–315.

Merchant, K. A., 1981. The design of the corporate budgeting system: influence on managerial behaviour and performance, *Accounting Review*, October, pp. 813–829.

Merchant, K. A., 1984. Influences on departmental budgeting: an empirical examination of a contingency model, *Accounting, Organisations and Society* **9** (3/4) pp. 291–307.

Merchant, K. A., 1985. Budgeting and the propensity to create budgetary slack, *Accounting Organizations and Society* **10**(2), pp.201–210.

Milani, K., 1975. The relationship of participation in budget-setting to industrial supervisor performance and attitudes: a field study, *Accounting Review*, April, pp. 274–284.

Morse, N. C. and Reimer, E., 1956. The experimental change of a major organisational variable, *Journal of Abnormal and Social Psychology* **52** pp. 120–129.

Onsi, M., 1973. Factor analysis of behavioural variables affecting budgetary slack, *Accounting Review* , July, pp. 535–548.

Otley, D. T., 1978. Budget use and managerial performance, *Journal of Accounting Research* **16**(1), Spring, pp. 122–149.

Otley, D. T. and Berry, J., 1979. Risk distribution in the budgetary process, *Accounting and Business Research,* **9**, pp. 325–337.

Ridgway, V. F., 1956. Dysfunctional consequences of performance measurements, *Administrative Science Quarterly*, September, pp. 240–247.

Ronen, J. and Livingstone, J. L., 1975. An expectancy theory approach to the motivational impacts of budgets, *Accounting Review*, October, pp. 671–685.

Sales, S. M., 1966. Supervisory style and productivity: review and theory, *Personnel Psychology* **XXIV** Autumn, pp. 275–286.

Schachter, S., Ellerton, N., McBride, D. and Gregory, D., 1951. An experimental study of cohesiveness and productivity, *Human Relations* **IV** pp. 229–238.

Schiff, M. and Lewin, A. Y., 1968. Where traditional budgeting fails. *Financial Executive*, May, pp. 50–62.

Schiff, M. and Lewin, A. Y., 1970. The impact of people on budgets, *Accounting Review*, April, pp. 259–268.

Sord, B. H. and Welsch, G. A., 1958. *Business Budgeting*. New York: Controllership Foundation.

Stedry, A. C., 1960. *Budget Control and Cost Behaviour*, Englewood Cliffs, NJ: Prentice-Hall.

Stedry, A. C., 1964. Budgeting and employee behaviour: a reply. *The Journal of Business*, **37**(2), April pp. 195–202.

Thomas, E. J., 1957. Effects of facilitative role interdependence on group functioning, *Human Relations* **X** pp. 347–366.

Vroom, V. H., 1960 *Some Personality Determinants of the Effects of Participation*. Englewood Cliffs, NJ: Prentice-Hall.

White, R. and Lippitt, R., 1960. Leader behaviour and member reaction in three 'Social Climates', pp. 527–553, in D. Cartwright and A. Zander (eds) *Group Dynamics*. New York: Harper & Row.

Wildavsky, A., 1975. *Budgeting: A Comparative Theory of Budgeting Process*: Little Brown.

Williamson, O. E., 1964. *The Economics of Discretionary Behaviour: Managerial Objectives in a Theory of the Firm*: Prentice-Hall.

PART FOUR
Retrospect and Prospect

16
Epilogue

The main aim of this book has been to present an overview of the substance of those areas of accounting which have been developed to assist management in implementing the decision-making process. To achieve this aim the authors have attempted to offer an up-to-date synthesis of management accounting literature particularly as it relates to the concept of organisational control. The role of management control in regulating and monitoring organisational functioning and the role of accounting in facilitating such functioning have been the dominant themes of most of the currently available management accounting textbooks. Although in this book the importance of management control is acknowledged, it is perceived as part of the much wider concept of organisational control. Support for this emphasis can be found in much of the recent literature on management accounting. It has been argued that a better understanding of management accounting and its diverse roles can be gained by studying accounting in its organisational context, and by examining its roles within a framework of organisational control (e.g. Hopwood, 1983).

The book has been divided into three main parts, excluding the present chapter. The first part dealt with the subject in an organisational context. It elaborated on theories of organisational design and alluded to the problematic concept of organisational goals. Theories of work motivation were then discussed in their broadest organisational sense, and some indication was given of their relevance in the management accounting context. This was followed by a discussion of organisational control, and an evaluation of the extent to which much of the recent management accounting research has achieved success in its application to the many parts and dimensions of that concept. Finally, some issues of human information processing and expert system design were considered.

The second part dealt with the role of management accounting in facilitating planning and decision making. This part opened with some detailed discussion of decision theory and information economics. This was followed by a discussion of cost concepts in the context of decision making, and of various important issues relating to Cost–Volume–Profit analysis under uncertainty (Stochastic C–V–P analysis). Attention was subsequently directed to planning problems both in the short-term and in the longer-term.

The third part concentrated on various issues of control and on how management accounting controls integrate with other controls to provide together a more complete repertoire of organisational controls. Part three started with a chapter explicating the roles of the Multi-divisional structure (M-Form) and the agency theory framework in monitoring organisational activities. This was followed by two chapters devoted to various control issues in divisionalised organisations; specifically, control of divisional performance and transfer pricing. A more general discussion of the traditional cost control (performance appraisal) model was presented. Finally, the behavioural implications of management accounting controls and of various leadership styles were discussed.

One of the aims of this present chapter is to provide a brief overview of the research results so far discussed, as well as other results which have not been considered explicitly in the book. Hopefully, the reader may thus gain some insight into the research achievements to date. Another aim is to offer some speculations regarding possible directions of future management accounting research. The chapter is in four sections. In section I a framework relating different modes of organisational control to specific levels of ambiguity in performance measurement and extent of knowledge of the transformation process is developed from the literature. Two perspectives on research, the conventional and the naturalistic perspectives, are briefly referred to. Section II contains a classification of much of the available management accounting research using the framework and ideas developed in section I. Section III considers more critically the virtues of the naturalistic perspective, describes a new perspective borrowed from labour processes, and offers some speculative comments on likely directions of future management accounting research. Finally, section IV provides a summary of the chapter.

I. ALTERNATIVE MODES OF ORGANISATIONAL CONTROL

A main theme developed in this book is that management accounting is both directly and indirectly interconnected with organisational control. As modes of control for a particular organisation evolve over time, accounting controls themselves evolve and shifts in their relative importance occur. But, irrespective of the nature and magnitude of these shifts, accounting control in general remains an important part of organisational control.

In order to facilitate the brief overview of research on management accounting controls to be attempted in this chapter, it is useful first to describe alternative modes of organisational control. Modes of control, or mechanisms of corporate governance, can be classified on the basis of various dimensions, for example, the extent of technological complexity or environmental uncertainty. The classification used here is the one developed by Ouchi (1979; 1980), on the grounds that it offers a broad framework for analysis.

Ouchi's Framework of Organisational Control

Ouchi (1979; 1980) classified modes of organisational control along two dimensions: (i) the extent of ambiguity in output measurement and (ii) the extent of knowledge of the transformation process; i.e., the means–ends relationship involved in the production or service activities. He invoked a transactions-costs perspective, according to which the attributes of different control modes with respect to the above two dimensions determine their relative efficiency. Efficiency is measured in terms of minimisation of transactions costs.

In the transactions-costs approach, the organisation is treated as a network of exchanges or transactions which should be regulated by control modes in the most economic manner. Different control modes have different characteristics which are associated with costs arising from the structure of property rights in organisations. Equity, or reciprocity, in the terms of exchange between the parties involved is a fundamental notion. Transactions costs are intertwined with reciprocity. These costs arise when the goods or services to be exchanged do not lend themselves to easy and precise valuation. To preserve equity in such cases, experts (third parties) tend to be called upon to value the services or goods subject to exchange. This leads to greater transactions costs.

When the ability to measure output is high but knowledge of the transformation process is imperfect, output control mechanisms are most appropriate. This role can be performed by hierarchies, but quite likely markets will offer a more economical control mechanism. The reason is that, given clarity of output measurement, there will be little need for writing detailed, and thus costly, contracts, and there will also be little need for extensive internal monitoring and the mediation of third parties.

When the ability to measure output is low but knowledge of the transformation process is perfect, emphasis would need to shift from output measurement to behaviour measurement. In this case, control through markets becomes associated with high transactions costs, since third parties would be hired to offer assessments of output. They would face relatively high uncertainty in their assessments and in the guarantees which they may have to offer. They will typically insure against such uncertainty by commanding high fees.

In such circumstances, hierarchies offer a more economical mode of organisational control. They rely on employment relations which represent incomplete contracts and are thus an economical means of regulating transactions. Employment relations give legitimate rights to the organisation to direct, regulate and monitor employees' work activities. Moreover, compared with markets there is usually a higher commonality of purpose and trust and a greater sense of affiliation amongst exchange parties within a hierarchy. These feelings are fostered by the sense of belonging to the same organisation, and by the emphasis of hierarchies on technical expertise which is emphasised through skill training and socialisation into professional standards. It is argued that these properties reduce the potential for opportunistic behaviour and the need for elaborate and expensive monitoring systems. In summary, as Williamson (1970) has pointed out, whereas markets have a serious disadvantage in obtaining internal information, hierarchies can obtain it at a low cost, and whilst markets are typically restricted to non-managerial adjustments, hierarchies can engage in both fine tuning and discrete adjustments.

When the ability to measure output is high and knowledge of the transformation process is perfect it would be possible to measure both behaviour and output. In this case, there is a choice of either behaviour control or of output control. These functions can be performed either by markets or hierarchies, the ultimate choice being dependent on the cost of each alternative.

Finally, when the ability to measure outputs is low and knowledge of the transformation process is imperfect neither markets nor hierarchies offer economically efficient means of corporate governance. Control through markets becomes inefficient because there will be a greater need for writing more detailed contracts, extensive use of internal monitoring systems and increased involvement of third parties. Control through hierarchies becomes inefficient because as tasks become unique or highly ambiguous it becomes difficult to monitor performance through formal hierarchical mechanisms. Ouchi argued that, under these conditions, control through clans or corporate cultures is the most economically efficient mode of control. The essence of clan control is the high degree of employee discipline attained through the dedication of each individual to the interests of the whole. The overlap between individual and organisational interests minimises the chances for opportunistic behaviour, and equity in exchange can be attained at relatively low transactions costs.

The behaviour of clan members is regulated through mutual monitoring using symbols and norms not readily susceptible to precise translation into performance measures. Clan control promotes high discipline and aversion to opportunism because members recognise the impossibility of establishing unambiguous performance measures.

In summary, the above framework suggests that the extent of performance ambiguity and the extent of knowledge of the transformation process should both be matched to the appropriate mode of corporate control (markets *v.* hierarchies *v.* clans). The framework emphasises the efficiency of economic exchange, through the minimisation of transactions costs, as the ultimate objective of organisations.

Ouchi (1980) further developed the above framework by discriminating markets, hierarchies and clans, along two dimensions: their underlying normative and informational requirements. These are summarised in table 16.1.

Table 16.1 *An organisational failure framework*

Mode of control	Normative requirements	Informational requirements
Market	Reciprocity	Prices
Bureaucracy (hierarchy)	Reciprocity Legitimate authority	Rules
Clan	Reciprocity Legitimate authority Common values and beliefs	Traditions

Source: Reprinted from 'Markets, bureaucracies, and clans', by W.G. Ouchi, published in *Administrative Science Quarterly*, **25**, March 1980, p.137, by permission of *Administrative Science Quarterly*.

In the table, 'normative requirements' refer to the basic social agreements shared by the exchange parties in order to minimise transactions costs. As has already been indicated, reciprocity engenders equity and fairness in exchange, and if widely held would result in minimising transactions costs. Legitimate authority facilitates the use of hierarchical control not only to assign tasks to employees but also to regulate and monitor their performance. Common values and beliefs promote greater congruence between individual and organisational interests. Ouchi contended that reciprocity is a universal norm, and that legitimate authority is accepted by employees in formal organisations, albeit in varying degrees. By contrast, it is held that common values and beliefs are relatively rare in formal organisations (see Wilkins and Ouchi, 1983, for further evidence concerning the latter point). As can be seen in table 16.1, the repertoire of normative requirements expands as one moves from markets through hierarchies to clans.

Informational requirements are those postulated to match the normative requirements of the particular mode of control. Prices are a highly sophisticated form of information, but frequently it is difficult to derive correct prices particularly in situations of high task interdependence. By comparison with prices, rules are a less sophisticated form of information. Rules tend to be problem-specific and they tend to be formalised for routine decisions. When exceptional situations are encountered they are typically referred to policy makers at the top of the hierarchy who frequently have to invent new rules as required. Traditions are implicit, that is to say not formally specified rules, and are thus not readily accessible particularly to new organisational members. By comparison with prices and rules, traditions are the crudest informational devices. They gain organisation-wide acceptability through the process of organisational socialisation, and if accorded sufficient acceptability could form the basis of an overall organisational philosophy (Ouchi, 1980).

Of the three modes of control suggested in the above framework, this book has thus far addressed the first two – markets and hierarchies. Control through clans (corporate culture) has not been explicitly addressed in the previous chapters. Certainly, the development of clan culture in addition to markets and hierarchies offers a broader framework of control. In consistency with the essence of markets and hierarchies, clan control emphasises the efficiency of economic exchange, through the minimisation of transactions costs, as the ultimate goal for organisations.

An Evaluation of Ouchi's Framework

Although the above framework is employed in this chapter to facilitate providing a synthesis of the existing accounting literature, there are a number of important anomalies which should be noted. Bourn and Ezzamel (1986b) document the following limitations:

—Firstly, the transactions-cost approach has a strong deterministic orientation, postulating one best way of corporate governance under a given set of conditions. Not only may such matching be unnecessary but multiple governance mechanisms may possibly operate simultaneously in a given period within the same organisation.

—Secondly, the transactions-costs approach appears to advocate a monolithic concept of culture in the clan form of organisation. Clan, or organisational, culture is assumed to drive individual behaviour relentlessly towards the objective of the whole. Organisational subcultures are either assumed away, or, if their existence is acknowledged, it is implicit that they cannot seriously contradict the clan. Such characterisation is not always consistent with the realities of organisational life. Organisational members tend to belong to differing religious, occupational, social, political and ethnic groups. These and other characteristics may lead to values and world views which vary from one group to another; that is, they could lead to the rise of multiple cultures and subcultures. Moreover, as individuals change their organisational membership they take with them to their new work settings values and world views developed in previous work settings. This is what Becker and Geer (1960) call latent culture. Empirical evidence on the existence of multiple cultures and subcultures abounds (see Bourn and Ezzamel, 1986b).

— Thirdly, by concentrating exclusively on cultural artefacts that can be linked to economic efficiency, other symbolic cultural expressions without such a link are likely to be ignored. Concentration on economic considerations may suppress unduly those considerations based on other values, such as equity or need. Thus, culture is worthy of study even if it is not conducive to economic efficiency.

Moreover, in the above framework, culture is seen as the outcome of economic exchange networks, rather than being simultaneously their outcome and precondition (Jelinek, Smircich and Hirsch, 1983). Culture as a root metaphor is not explicitly addressed – yet, many researchers would contend that culture can only be sensibly studied as a root metaphor for conceptualising organisation. Under that approach culture is not an organisational attribute. Rather, organisations are viewed as social phenomena portrayed as (i) systems of cognition and beliefs, (ii) patterns of symbolic discourse or (iii) manifestations of unconscious processes. These constitute its culture. Culture is inseparable from organisation which, itself, is seen as a particular form of human expression (Smircich, 1983). The social world is viewed as having a subjective status. Such status only exists as a pattern of symbolic relationships and meanings which are sustained through continuous human interactions.

Whether culture is viewed as an organisational variable or as a root metaphor, researchers may focus on the *same* issues, e.g., language, symbols, rites, images, rituals, stories, myths, and so on. There is one crucial difference. The root metaphor approach treats an organisation as a social phenomenon rather than a purposeful, adaptive mechanism. Organisations are analysed and understood, not by invoking the economic axioms of rational choice, but by focusing on their expressive and symbolic aspects:

> When culture is a root metaphor, the researcher's attention shifts from concerns about what do organizations accomplish and how may they accomplish it more efficiently, to how is organization accomplished and what does it mean to be organized? (Smircich, 1983, p. 353).

To the extent that the above framework ignores the role of culture as a root metaphor in conceptualising organisation, the control modes mentioned above are incomplete. Nevertheless, the framework is useful in reviewing much of the available research in accounting.

The Conventional Perspective Versus the Naturalistic Perspective

For the purposes of this chapter, it is also convenient to refer to a scheme which classifies accounting research into the conventional perspective and the naturalistic perspective. The conventional perspective is essentially based on the main premises underlying both traditional economic theory and classical organisation theory. Organisational members are thus assumed to be rational and cooperative, and organisations themselves are assumed to be purposeful. Organisational goals are assumed to be clearly defined and well ordered. Congruence between the goals of the organisation and those of its members is postulated as both desirable and attainable. Management accounting is assumed to be a neutral mechanism for the collection, processing and dissemination of information to various decision makers (see Hopper, Storey and Willmott, 1985).

This perspective has, however, been criticised on three main grounds. Firstly, attention has been directed to many of its inherent methodological shortcomings (e.g., Tomkins and Groves, 1983). These shortcomings relate in particular to its rationalistic axioms and narrow and partial focus (see chapter 4). Secondly, because the conventional perspective is based on deductive logic it assumes that 'meanings attached to variables are independent of the situation in which they are used'. This may be the case when one is concerned with practical techniques. When one is concerned with the study of social action, as is frequently the case in management accounting research, it should be recognised that variable meanings tend to be situation dependent. Thirdly, several researchers (e.g., Swieringa, 1980; Dent, Ezzamel and Bourn, 1984; Kaplan, 1984; Hopper et al, 1985) have noted that much of the accounting knowledge documented in textbooks and academic journals is not used in practice, and that when it is used it is sometimes counterproductive.

The naturalistic approach refers to interpretative research which in essence focuses on the subjective perceptions of social actors (e.g., organisational members) in constructing reality, rather than the scientific and objective approach implied in the conventional perspective. Specifically, it emphasises studying the relevant human behaviour 'in its natural setting' (Tomkins and Groves, 1983). Thus, according to the naturalistic perspective, meanings are imparted to actions and events through individual perceptions and interactions. Reality is not objective; it is subjective, and different individuals are likely to construct their own perceptions of reality. Subjectivity in individual perceptions creates uncertainty. Social reality is fluid and is created, shaped and objectified through interactions between social actors (Chua, 1986). By interpreting one's own actions as well as those of other social actors with whom one interacts, meanings and norms become intersubjectively real; they become endowed with social reality.

In summary, the naturalistic approach assumes that organisational goals are highly problematic and conflict-laden. They are typically subject to frequent negotiations by social actors. The social interactions between these actors are the focus of analysis rather than individuals, sub-systems or systems *per se*. A typical problem a social actor faces is the uncertainty created by the subjectivity of the perceptions of other actors. Individual actions can only be understood by reference to the context of the actors' subjective meaning system; they are grounded in social and historical practices. Retrospectively, they are endowed with meaning and intention (Chua, 1986). Management accounting is called upon to facilitate negotiations over shared meanings between different actors. In response to these demands, management accounting develops a subjective language, which is created and developed to cope with changing demands (see Hopper et al, 1985, for a good discussion of these points).

Using the naturalistic perspective, it is possible to explore 'how accountants and users of accounting information construct and interpret the reality of organisational life'. Further, the naturalistic perspective will likely contribute to narrowing the current gap between accounting theory and accounting practice, because in studying practice it emphasises the perceptions of practitioners rather than those of 'detached' academic observers (Tomkins and Groves, 1983; Morgan, 1983).

In the following section both the framework of organisational control and the classification scheme of accounting research developed above are used together to review some of the research already reported in this book. Section III contains a summary of some of the objections raised against the naturalistic approach.

II. A CLASSIFICATION OF PAST AND CURRENT MANAGEMENT ACCOUNTING RESEARCH

Most of the existing management accounting literature focuses on the use of the markets and hierarchies modes of control for the purposes of regulating transactions and monitoring performance. The accounting literature relating to markets draws heavily on the traditional economic analysis of markets and firms. Invoking the usual rationalistic assumptions about the behaviour of economic actors (be they firms, other institutions, or individuals), and a number of restrictive assumptions about the prevailing conditions of the market, various cases are specified in which market prices are postulated to offer the most efficient means of regulating transactions.

When appropriately derived, market prices tend to be perceived as objective and they also tend to be widely accepted by economic actors. This is because they are typically rationalised on the basis of at least two appealing arguments. Firstly, market prices are assumed to be determined through the active and free interaction of supply and demand forces. In this sense they are assumed to be objectively determined. But even when markets are fairly imperfect and prices are determined by the powerful few, market prices can still command economic importance because they are taken as the ruling prices in the market-place. Secondly, legitimacy and rationality are typically accorded to market-derived prices on the basis of their proximity to opportunity cost, one of the main pillars of traditional economic and management accounting analysis.

Such is the essence of much of the management accounting research advocating the use of the market mechanism. Examples include the use of market prices in the context of intracompany transfers (chapter 13), other product pricing decisions (chapter 7), the valuation of human resources and capital budgeting decisions. As indicated elsewhere in this book, the models developed in the above contexts are typically based on a set of restrictive assumptions. These include the maximisation of a single goal, or at the very least the optimisation of an unambiguous and well-ordered set of goals, the rational and calculated behaviour by market actors and the ability to quantify the consequences of most decisions. Almost exclusively, the above research is based on the conventional perspective of management accounting referred to in the previous section. It is, therefore, subject to the main criticisms raised against such perspective which have been indicated earlier.

The management accounting research related to control through hierarchies is voluminous. Such research was fostered by the availability of various models of hierarchical control, albeit with varying degrees of sophistication, particularly in the fields of organisation behaviour and economics. Thus, in the literature on organisational design, emphasis gradually shifted from bureaucratic and centralised controls advocated by the classical organisation theory, through decentralised and more informal controls under neoclassical organisation theory, to the systems and contingency views which emphasise appropriate matchings of organisational structure and situational contingencies. Moreover, recent post-contingency views advocate more dynamic interactions between the organisation and its situational contingencies (see chapter 1). Similarly, some economists, particularly Williamson (1970) and to some extent Fama and Jensen (1983a, 1983b), probed further into the characteristics of internal organisation of firms, emphasising in particular the relative virtues of centralised, decentralised and divisionalised structures (see chapter 11).

These theories stimulated much research relating to the design characteristics of accounting information and management accounting information systems, as well as to their roles in furthering control through hierarchies. Thus, a traditional accounting theory of the firm emphasising the main tenets of traditional economic and organisation theories emerged. That theory is based on the rational axioms of choice, on the notion of a single, well-defined goal, and on the use of formal, top-down control mechanisms to monitor the performance of employees who are generally perceived as lazy and wasteful. These main notions are reflected in many traditional management accounting research areas such as budgeting, short-run planning, variance analysis, overhead allocation, variance investigation models, transfer pricing, divisional performance evaluation, capital budgeting decisions, principal–agent models, stochastic C–V–P analysis, and the costs of information acquisition and implementation (for a further discussion see Dent, Ezzamel and Bourn, 1984). The main thrust of these studies is to devise means by which top management can engage in the efficient planning of activities, coordination and monitoring of the behaviour of its employees, mediation of exchanges between organisational subunits and selection and implementation of capital assets in a manner conducive to the maximisation of a given objective function.

The increased awareness of the limitations of the traditional theory of the firm, particularly with respect to its underlying concepts of human behaviour and motivation, has led accounting researchers to incorporate into their research designs many of the ideas promoted by the neoclassical organisation theory. Evidence of that influence can be readily traced in much of the work relating to the behavioural implications of budgets, budgetary participation and the creation of slack, leadership styles and the use of accounting controls to improve human motivation and human information processing. Even though these studies emphasise the informal and behavioural elements in organisation, their ultimate aim is to facilitate management control through appropriate attention to behavioural issues which impinge upon performance. In this sense, such research has been predominantly directed at improving hierarchical control.

The above-mentioned research was followed by another major development based upon the ideas promoted by systems theory and the contingency approach. Thus, various studies emerged which attempted to outline the important characteristics of information and of management accounting systems in the face of differing organisation-specific contingencies, like environment or technology. Similarly, some researchers have attempted to model intra-organisational dependencies by viewing organisational subunits as closed or open systems. Various important notions emerged such as the immediacy and centrality of the work flows of the accounting system to organisational activities and its ability to absorb uncertainty on behalf of the organisation. Naturally, these issues relate directly to the concept of power in terms of its definition, the ways in which it is distributed, the ways in which its locus shifts, and to both the direct and indirect consequences of the acquisition of power (see Bourn and Ezzamel, 1985; Ezzamel and Bourn, 1985). Again, that research is directed at improving the fit between these subunits and the organisational situational contingencies so that hierarchical controls can be more effective.

The influence of post-contingency theory on management accounting research is also in evidence even though that research is rather sparse. Most of it focuses on the use of accounting information and accounting systems as vehicles for destabilising the organisation. It is aimed at helping the organisation to develop fluid, self-organising properties so that future changes can be implemented with minimum noise or cost. Emphasis in this line of research is on the design for tomorrow rather than on the design for today; it is concerned with instability rather than stability. Examples include Hedberg and Jonsson (1978); Bariff and Galbraith (1978); Burchell et al. (1980); Feldman and March (1981); and Cooper, Hayes and Wolf (1981). In this approach, management control is still perceived as important, but it is assumed to be part of the much wider organisational control. The power, particularly informal power, of organisational participants in manipulating and shaping organisational processes and outcomes is more explicitly acknowledged.

Most of that latter research is theoretical, being in essence strongly critical of the underlying assumptions of previous research based on markets or hierarchies as modes of organisational control. More recently, some studies were specifically aimed at documenting organisational work settings and practices and then attempting to derive empirically-based models of the organisation (naturalistic research), instead of starting with an *a priori* developed theory that is then subjected to empirical testing. Such research typically uses either a single case study or a few case studies. Examination is made in depth through a variety of techniques like structured and semi-structured interviews, but above all through the immersion of the researcher in organisational internal practices as a participant observer (ethnographic technique).

Various examples of that research are available in the literature (e.g. Boland and Pondy, 1983; Dent, Ezzamel and Bourn, 1984; Berry et al., 1985; Bourn and Ezzamel, 1985, 1986a, 1986b). These and similar studies have contributed to our understanding of how accounting operates in its organisational context, and of the evolution of the roles of accounting in action. We now have a better appreciation of how accounting is implicated in organisational functioning. These studies have at least partially addressed the role of accounting in creating and shaping organisational and social realities and meanings, and the ways in which accounting can be used by interested parties to reinterpret and modify existing perceptions of reality. It has also been demonstrated that accounting information can act as signals and symbols which may be used to endow past actions and decisions with legitimacy. Moreover, the role of accounting information in creating rituals and ceremonials and in shaping organisational cultures has been addressed, even if only partially.

III. FUTURE MANAGEMENT ACCOUNTING RESEARCH – NEW DIRECTIONS?

The previous section contained a brief overview of existing management accounting research and how that research particularly relates to markets and hierarchies as alternative modes of organisational control. This section specifically addresses some of the most recent management accounting research. As is noted below recent research broadly divides into two categories: (i) research which is developing along the already established routes of inquiry, be it the conventional perspective or the naturalistic perspective, and focusing on modes of organisational control previously discussed and (ii) research which is seeking to bring to the accounting research arena perspectives borrowed from other social science disciplines.

Despite the various criticisms which have been levelled against the conventional perspective, a vast number of researchers still use that perspective to conduct their research. A larger number of assumptions is gradually being invoked in the analysis. More attempts are also being made to expand existing models by incorporating new variables which are derived from other disciplines, as for example in that area in which the effect of budgeting characteristics and leadership styles on performance are examined. Further, greater attention is now directed at rigorous empirical testing of the theories which have been developed *a priori*. Examples include testing the empirical validity of some of the agency theory assumptions. It is worth noting that these developments do little to avert the criticisms of the conventional approach which have been cited earlier. The developments are also aimed at further elaboration of control predominantly through markets and/or hierarchies.

Also, researchers are increasingly using the naturalistic approach to gain greater understanding of organisational realities and of management accounting in action. Several pieces of research currently in progress are using case study material to gain further insights into, for example, methods of overhead allocation used in practice (e.g. Motteram and Sizer, 1986; Ezzamel and Bourn, 1987), the role of accounting in creating organisational symbolics (Capps et al., 1985) and how accounting systems develop and evolve through time (Hopwood, 1984). As a result, a rich and revealing body of evidence is now slowly, but gradually, accumulating.

In spite of its significant contributions to management accounting research, as indicated in the previous section, the naturalistic perspective is incomplete. Hopper et al. (1985) and Chua (1986) documented a number of reservations about that perspective.

Firstly, because the naturalistic perspective focuses on the processes underlying the creation of meanings and symbols, little attention is given to the structure underlying the asymmetric distribution of power within the organisation. Accounting systems are persistently centralised and there is a strong probability, these researchers argue, that the accounting function is linked to the control functions on behalf of capital. The naturalistic perspective fails to address this important social phenomenon. It does not explore the causes of conflict and contradictions nor does it offer judgements on the legitimacy of bureaucratic ends and means or the emergence and prominence of specific organisational cultures.

Secondly, in common with the conventional approach, the naturalistic approach, they argued, neglects the study of organisational goals as manifestations of the vested interests of social actors. This is so even though organisational goals are considered by the naturalistic approach as problematic.

Thirdly, the study of management accounting and its roles is incomplete in the naturalistic perspective. Accounting is perceived as a process through which shared meanings are negotiated by social actors. Accounting language is perceived as being subjectively created, sustained, and modified through social interactions. Hopper et al. argued that this perspective is incomplete because its underlying theory of power and control is inadequate. Accounting language, they argue, is partial and reflects the class structure for managerial work.

Fourthly, the naturalistic perspective does not offer a means of critically evaluating the social phenomena that the researcher observes. Thus, it is not easy, or it may be even impossible, for the naturalistic researcher to analyse forms of 'false consciousness' and domination which misguide social actors in relation to their true interests.

These criticisms may be more appropriately labelled as errors of omission rather than errors of commission. In other words, the main charge against the naturalistic perspective seems to be related to some relevant issues which are not being attended to. This is a fair criticism, but one which is true of any single research perspective. One limitation, however, which has not been addressed above is that, given the emphasis of the naturalistic approach on the subjective perceptions of reality by social actors, it is not clear how the research results can be aggregated either over time or across organisations. It may be that much of what goes on within organisations is not amenable to generalisation. Nevertheless, this is a question which needs to be explicitly addressed.

These limitations led various writers (e.g. Neimark and Tinker, 1986; Hopper et al., 1985) to suggest an alternative perspective for studying management accounting based on labour processes, which they call a dialectical or a critical perspective. This perspective perceives the world as consisting of the following four main elements (see Neimark and Tinker, 1986):

1. The pervasiveness of social change: all social systems evolve through a continuing process of change.
2. The importance of contradictions as sources of social change: contradictions are neither 'good' nor 'bad'; rather, they are part of the dynamic of the process of social change. In a capitalist society, contradictions are caused by the asymmetric distribution of power and the antagonistic nature of social relations (both within and between classes).
3. The totality of the relationship between the organisation and the environment: the organisation and the environment are not separable but are each the product and the determinant of the other's conditions of existence.
4. The importance of self-awareness in instigating social change: the researcher is located within the phenomena being investigated and is partly responsible for instigating, or obstructing, social change.

In this perspective, the organisation is perceived as an arena for class struggle. Managerial control is not assumed to be neutral; it is perceived to attend to the ways in which control mechanisms evolve and are used in power relations which such mechanisms are assumed to sustain. Management accounting practices are assumed to contribute to the asymmetric distribution of power in the context of class structure, for instance, through their strong influence over the definition and distribution/transfer of wealth. Thus, they can be seen to over-represent the interests of social actors who enjoy positions of relative power by more than proportionately elevating their interests and further enhancing their powers. They can also under-represent the interests of social actors who are relatively dependent on others (e.g. Cooper and Sherer, 1984). Management accounting, it is held, should be analysed and understood within the broader structure of relations of which it is both medium and outcome.

The labour processes perspective assumes that deviances in outcomes are predominantly the manifestation of conflicts of interest amongst social actors. Conflict is assumed endemic, arising from fundamental antagonisms between capital and labour. Moreover, in this perspective accounting language is perceived as an instrument for promoting the interests of one class at the expense of another, for example, capital at the expense of labour.

The labour processes perspective clearly offers a useful means of revealing much of what goes on within and between organisations and their members. It is useful in directing the attention of future research inquiries into areas previously assumed to be either non-problematic or irrelevant. However, it does not offer a complete and comprehensive perspective for studying management accounting and its diverse roles.

As in any single perspective, researchers advocating the labour processes perspective invoke assumptions about organisations and people. To the extent that these assumptions are selective, the perspective offers only a partial explanation of organisational practices. Thus, even though it considers the processes through which accounting is used to achieve consent, and the nature of the interplay between conflict and consensus (Neimark and Tinker, 1986), its main thesis is based on the *endemic* nature of conflict and the *antagonistic* relationship between classes. Organisational functioning may be riddled with conflict, but it is also frequently characterised by agreement. By invoking antagonism between classes, researchers may overlook much of the consensus and harmony which do exist within and between organisations. Moreover, if clear-cut demarcation lines are drawn between classes, the presence of groups which cut across classes, and the influence of their shared values in reducing antagonism and conflict, may be ignored. Finally, even though the critical perspective researchers typically reject the notion of relativism, that is, using different research perspectives eclectically to study social organisations, so far they have not agreed on the philosophical criteria which can be used for theory evaluation (see Chua, 1986).

Irrespective of the merits and demerits of different research perspectives, what appears to be clear is that no consensus on which research perspective is superior to all others has yet emerged. Given the unconcrete nature of the social sciences field, such a consensus may never emerge. The implications of that for future research are at least threefold. Firstly, many individual researchers are likely to remain locked into their own research perspectives, each possibly seeking to establish a stronger case for his or her preferred perspective. Secondly, other researchers who hold a relativist view of research perspectives are likely to continue arguing that, because of the immense complexity of social organisations, different research perspectives should be used in combination to unravel the different facets of organisations and their interactions with management accounting. These two observations imply that we are likely to witness the use of all three research perspectives in future accounting research. Even the conventional perspective is still alive and well today and is likely to remain so in the future. We may see greater use of the naturalistic and critical perspectives in the future as many researchers seek to redress the existing imbalance in favour of the conventional perspective. Thirdly, the problem of choosing from among research perspectives is likely to be made more difficult as future researchers scan other branches of knowledge with the aim of bringing new research perspectives into the management accounting discipline.

IV. SUMMARY

The purpose of this chapter was to provide a brief overview of management accounting research and to offer some indications of the direction of future research as a closure for the book. It should be borne in mind that a comprehensive synthesis is beyond the scope of the chapter. What has been offered is therefore a bare minimum by which the reader may acquire a reasonably adequate appreciation of the nature of management accounting as currently viewed by researchers in the field.

In section I of the chapter, a framework of organisational control was described in which different modes of control were linked to the ability to measure outputs and the degree of knowledge of the transformation process. The suggested modes were markets, hierarchies (bureaucracies) and clans. Taking as an ultimate aim the minimisation of transactions costs, it has been demonstrated when each mode is most efficient. Despite some misgivings, it has been argued that such a framework is useful for synthesising current accounting research. Two perspectives of management accounting research were identified and discussed. The first was the conventional perspective which has its roots in traditional economic theory and classical organisation theory. The second was the naturalistic approach which aims to explain the role of accounting in helping social actors derive shared meanings and values. It also aims to explain how these change and evolve through human interactions.

In section II some of the management accounting research described in earlier chapters was classified using the framework developed in section I. It was suggested that the majority of that research related to the regulation of organisational activities through hierarchic controls; even so, control through markets has attracted the attention of several researchers. What was most obvious, however, was that little attention has been given to researching the ramifications of clan control for management accounting. Equally little attention has been accorded to the implications for accounting of using culture as a root metaphor for conceptualising organisation. It was also suggested that the majority of existing research has been conducted using the conventional perspective. Although researchers are increasingly using the naturalistic perspective, it has to be remembered that, at least in the context of management accounting research, this perspective is still in its embryonic stage. It is not clear yet how such evidence can be used to piece together the history of an organisation. Perhaps even more fundamentally, given its emphasis on the subjective perceptions of 'reality' by social actors, it is not clear if and how the research results can be aggregated across organisations.

Section III contains some reservations about both the conventional perspective and the naturalistic perspective. The thrust of the reservations relates to the alleged failure of the naturalistic perspective to interpret organisational conflict as the manifestation of class structure and to perceive accounting information as a non-neutral mechanism aiming to facilitate the exploitation of labour by capital. A perspective relating to labour processes, which has been offered by some researchers as a means of alleviating the above criticisms, was discussed. It was argued that, although that perspective offers some useful insights relating to the ways in which accounting is implicated in social and political relations, the perspective is not without limitations. At the very least, by explicitly postulating that labour and capital are antagonistic, researchers may fail to attend to some of the subtleties in organisational functioning which can more sensibly be explained through consensus and harmony. Organisational realities reflect both conflict and consensus, even though they may not necessarily be symmetrically distributed across time or organisations.

The main tenet of this chapter, and indeed of the whole book, is that organisations are complex and multi-faceted. No single mode of control seems to fully and effectively regulate the organisation. Similarly, no one research perspective appears to be sufficiently versatile and comprehensive to attend to all dimensions of the organisation. By invoking their own criteria for theory evaluation, different researchers may settle on the use of differing theories or research perspectives. Other researchers may advocate an 'eclectic' approach, according to which each perspective would have a role to play. Rather than make value judgements on either alternative, we have preferred here simply to allude to the case for and against each perspective.

REFERENCES

Bariff, M. L. and Galbraith, J. R. 1978. Intraorganisational power considerations for designing information systems, *Accounting, Organizations and Society*, pp. 15–27.

Becker, S. W. and Geer, B. 1960. Latent culture: a note on the theory of latent social roles, *Administrative Science Quarterly*, September, pp. 304–313.

Berry, T., Capps, T., Cooper, D., Ferguson, P., Hopper, T. and Lowe, E. 1985. Management control in an area of the National Coal Board, *Accounting, Organizations and Society* pp. 3–28.

Boland, R. J. and Pondy, L. R. 1983. Accounting in organizations: a union of natural and rational perspectives, *Accounting, Organizations and Society*, 8(2/3), pp. 222–234.

Bourn, M. and Ezzamel, M. 1985. The accounting department, the accounting information system, and accounting language in an organisation experiencing financial crisis, University of Southampton working paper.

Bourn, M. and Ezzamel, M. 1986a. Costing and budgeting in the National Health Service, *Financial Accountability and Management*, Spring, pp. 53–71.

Bourn, M. and Ezzamel, M. 1986b. Organisational culture in hospitals in the National Health Service, *Financial Accountability and Management*, Autumn, pp. 203–225.

Burchell, S., Club, C., Hopwood, A. G., Hughes, J. and Nahapiet, J., 1980. The roles of accounting in organizations and society, *Accounting, Organizations and Society*, pp. 5–27.

Capps, T., Hopper, T., Mourtisen, J., Cooper, D. and Lowe, E. A. 1985. Semiotics and cultural principles, presented at the Management Accounting Workshop, University of Aston, September.

Chua, W. F., 1986. Radical developments in accounting thought, *Accounting Review*, October, pp. 601–632.

Colville, I. 1981. Reconstructing behavioural accounting, *Accounting, Organizations and Society*, pp. 119–132.

Cooper, D. 1983. Tidiness, muddle and things: commonalities and divergences in two approaches to management accounting systems, *Accounting, Organizations and Society*, pp. 269–286.

Cooper, D. J., Hayes, D. and Wolf, F. 1981. Accounting in organized anarchies: understanding and designing accounting systems in ambiguous situations, *Accounting, Organizations and Society*, pp. 175–192.

Cooper, D. J. and Sherer, M. J. 1984. The value of accounting reports: arguments for a political economy of accounting, *Accounting, Organizations and Society*, pp. 207–232.

Dent, J. F., Ezzamel, M. and Bourn, M. 1984. 'Reflections on research in management accounting and its relationship to practice: an academic view', pp. 223–253, in A. G. Hopwood and H. Schreuder (eds), *European Contributions to Accounting Research: The Achievements of the Last Decade*. Ull Uitigeverij/Free University Press.

Ezzamel, M. and Bourn, M. 1985. 'The determinants of budget allocations in a UK university', University of Southampton Working Paper.

Ezzamel, M. and Bourn, M. 1987. 'Why do firms allocate overheads?' in J. Arnold, D. Cooper, and R. W. Scapens (eds), *Case Study Research in Management Accounting*, ICMA.

Fama, E. F. and Jensen, M. C. 1983a. Separation of ownership and control, *Journal of Law and Economics*, June, pp. 301–325.

Fama, E. F. and Jensen, M. C. 1983b. Agency problems and residual claims, *Journal of Law and Economics*, June, pp. 327–349.

Feldman, M. S. and March, J. G. 1981. Information in organizations as signal and symbol, *Administrative Science Quarterly*, pp. 171–186.

Hedberg, B. and Jonsson, S. 1978. Designing semi-confusing information systems for organizations in changing environments, *Accounting, Organizations and Society*, pp. 47–64.

Hopper, T., Storey, J. and Willmott, H. 1985. Three perspectives on management accounting, paper presented at the Interdisciplinary Perspectives on Accounting Conference, University of Manchester, July.

Hopwood, A. G. 1983. On trying to study accounting in the contexts in which it operates, *Accounting, Organizations and Society*, pp. 287–305.

Hopwood, A. G. 1984. The archaeology of accounting systems, paper presented to the Conference on the Roles of Accounting in Organisations and Society, University of Wisconsin, July.

Jelinek, M., Smircich, L. and Hirsch, P. 1983. Introduction: a code of many colours, *Administrative Science Quarterly*, **28**, pp. 331–338.

Kaplan, R. S. 1984. The evolution of management accounting, *The Accounting Review*, July, pp. 390–418.

Morgan, G. 1983. Social science and accounting research: a commentary on Tomkins and Groves, *Accounting, Organizations and Society*, pp. 385–388.

Motteram, G. and Sizer, J. 1986. Costing of advanced manufacturing technology at Rolls-Royce Derby Manufacturing: a case study, paper presented at the Management Accounting Research Conference, University of Aston, January.

Neimark, M. and Tinker, T., 1986. The social construction of management control systems, *Accounting, Organizations and Society*, **11**(4/5), pp. 369–395.

Ouchi, W. G. 1979. A conceptual framework for the design of organizational control mechanisms, *Management Science*, **25** September, pp. 833–848.

Ouchi, W. G. 1980. Markets, bureaucracies, and clans, *Administrative Science Quarterly*, **25** March, pp. 129–141.

Smircich, L. 1983. Concepts of culture and organisational analysis, *Administrative Science Quarterly*, **28** pp. 339–358.

Swieringa, R. J., 1980. 'Behavioral implications of planning and control systems', in P. Holzer (ed.), *Management Accounting*, Urbana-Champaign, IL: University of Illinois.

Tomkins, C. and Groves, R. 1983. The everyday accountant and researching his reality, *Accounting, Organizations and Society*, pp. 361–374.

Wilkins, A. L. and Ouchi, W. G. 1983. Efficient cultures: exploring the relationship between culture and organizational performance, *Administrative Science Quarterly*, **28** pp. 468–481.

Williamson, O. E. 1970. *Corporate Control and Business Behaviour*. Englewood Cliffs, NJ: Prentice-Hall.

Index

390